# The Economics of EC Competition Law: Concepts, Application and Measurement

CW01034030

# The Economics of EC Competition Law: Concepts, Application and Measurement

**Simon Bishop**
*Founding Partner, RBB Economics* (simon.bishop@rbbecon.com)

and

**Mike Walker**
*Vice President, Charles River Associates* (mwalker@crai.com)
*Visiting Professor, Loughborough University* (m.walker@lboro.ac.uk)

SWEET & MAXWELL  THOMSON REUTERS

First Edition    1999   by Simon Bishop and Mike Walker
Second Edition   2002   by Simon Bishop and Mike Walker
Third Edition    2010   by Simon Bishop and Mike Walker

Published in 2010 by Thomson Reuters (Legal) Limited
(Registered in England & Wales, Company No 1679046.
Registered Office and address for service:
100 Avenue Road, London NW3 3PF)
trading as Sweet & Maxwell

Typeset by YHT Ltd, London
Printed and bound in Great Britain by TJ International, Padstow, Cornwall

For further information on our products and services, visit
www.sweetandmaxwell.co.uk

No natural forests were destroyed to make this product; only farmed timber was
used and re-planted.

A CIP catalogue record for this book is available from the British Library.

ISBN 978-0-421-93190-9

# The Authors*

**Simon Bishop** is a partner and co-founder of RBB Economics, an economic consultancy specialising in applying economics to competition law matters. He has advised clients for nearly 20 years throughout Europe and also in South Africa and Australia. He has been the lead economist on numerous high-profile cases, including approximately 20 Phase II merger cases. His clients include Bertelsmann, GE, FA Premier League, Sony, British Airways, BHP Billiton, Heineken and Cargill. He is co-editor of the *European Competition Journal* and is included in the Top Competition Economists list compiled by Global Competition Review.

**Mike Walker**, a Vice President at Charles River Associates in London, is a leading expert on the economic aspects of competition policy, with more than 16 years of consulting experience. He regularly provides economic testimony as an expert witness in competition law proceedings in front of both the courts and regulatory authorities in Europe and in South Africa. He is the Visiting Professor of Competition Economics at Loughborough University, a Visiting Fellow at King's College, London, and the Course Director for the Masters/Diploma in Economics for Competition Law at King's College, London. He is included in the Top Competition Economists list compiled by Global Competition Review.

---

\* The views expressed in this book are those of the authors and not of their respective organisations.

# Foreword

As I remarked in the Foreword to the second edition of *Bishop and Walker*, this is a book that all practitioners of competition law—competition authorities, legal advisers, judges, policy makers and students—should read. Competition law is about economics, and anyone involved in the subject should endeavour to understand its underlying principles and policy objectives; furthermore it is important to be familiar with the various methodologies used by economists when they work on particular cases. The third edition of *Bishop and Walker* is extremely welcome, as much has happened in the seven years since the second edition was published. What is sometimes referred to as the "more economics" approach has taken deep root in recent times. This can be seen in individual cases, particularly under the EC Merger Regulation, where increasingly sophisticated methodologies are deployed and decisions are adopted containing much more economic analysis than was historically the case. The importance of economics is also evident in the Commission's guidelines, for example on horizontal and on non-horizontal mergers, and in its *Guidance on the Commission's Enforcement Priorities in Applying Article 82 EC to Abusive Exclusionary Conduct by Dominant Undertakings*. It is not surprising that the growing influence of economics is reflected in the growth of *Bishop and Walker* itself—the third edition is considerably longer than the second, with much new material that is very welcome.

The structure of the book remains the same as in previous editions. In Part I the reader is introduced to the underlying concepts of the subject—effective competition, the assessment of market power and the relevant market. In the discussion of market power there is new text on countervailing buyer power, the Lerner Index and—a topic that has become very important in recent years—on two-sided markets. In the chapter on market definition the authors provide guidance on a number of errors that are sometimes made in practice (the "*Cellophane* fallacy" being just one of these).

Part II of the book looks at each of Article 81, Article 82 and the EC Merger Regulation. Much has changed in these chapters to reflect developments over the last seven years. The Commission's determination to eradicate cartels has become even stronger over this period: the level of fines is now enormous, and many of the Commission's decisions lead to follow-on actions for damages. At one time economics did not have a large role in cartel cases. However this has certainly changed in recent years, and economists are increasingly involved in the substantive analysis of cases—for example could an agreement for the exchange of information actually have an impact on prices? If not, should that agreement be regarded as restrictive of competition by object (rather than effect)? Economists are also increasingly called upon for assistance in thinking about the correct level of fines in cases, and in the extremely difficult task of working out what level of damages should be awarded in follow-on actions in domestic courts. The new edition of *Bishop and Walker* contains very helpful discussion of these important topics. It also expands the treatment of Article 82 in the wake of DG COMP's *Discussion Paper* of 2005 and the Commission's more recent *Guidance on Enforcement Priorities*. There are now two chapters on merger control rather than just one, reflecting the Commission's adoption of separate guidelines for horizontal and non-horizontal mergers.

It is important to understand the techniques that economists use when working on actual cases as well as the underlying economic concepts. Part III of the book contains an extremely useful discussion of these techniques, including, for example, the use of elasticities; bidding studies; shock analysis; price concentration studies; merger simulation; shipment and transport cost tests; and the calculation of damages.

I have highlighted some of the important changes that have been made to the third edition; there are, of course, many other additions, too numerous to refer to here. Readers who are eager to understand the contribution that economics makes to competition law and policy will find this book to be invaluable: the authors are to be congratulated for producing a new edition of their very fine text.

Richard Whish
King's College London                                        October 2009

# Preface

The first edition of this book, written primarily during 1998, stated that economic reasoning and analysis was assuming greater prominence in EC competition law. That trend has not only continued but accelerated since writing the second edition in 2002. Obvious indicators of this trend are the number and type of cases in which economists are engaged as well as the growing number of economists working at the various competition authorities across Europe. Further confirmation of the importance of economic analysis is provided by the creation in 2003 of the post of the Chief Economist within DG COMP of the European Commission and a specialist team of economists to support that position.[1] Since then that team has grown rapidly in size. But the most important indicator continues to be, in our view, the increasingly economic approach that DG COMP and certain national competition authorities are taking to policy and to policy guidelines. Within the context of EC competition policy, examples of this include the notice on the definition of the relevant market, the vertical restraints guidelines, the horizontal merger guidelines, the non-horizontal merger guidelines and the guidance on the Commission's enforcement priorities in applying Article 82 to exclusionary abuses.[2] All of these documents adopt an explicit economic approach to the relevant policy areas.

These developments have naturally led to more interest in the subject on the part of competition lawyers and officials. But while several excellent textbooks on economics exist at varying levels of complexity, their focus is

---

[1] See Röller and Buigues (2005) for an insider's overiew of the role of the Chief Economist's Team in particular and the role of economists inside DG Competition more generally.

[2] European Commission (1997) "Notice on the Definition of the Relevant Market for the Purposes of Community Competition Law" OJ C372/5; European Commission (2000) "Commission Notice: Guidelines on Vertical Restraints" (2000/C29/01); European Commission (2004) "Guidelines on the assessment of horizontal mergers under the Council Regulation on the control of concentrations between undertakings" (2004/C 31/04); European Commission (2008) "Guidelines on the assessment of non-horizontal mergers under the Council Regulation on the control of concentrations between undertakings" (2008/C 265/07); and European Commission (2008) "Guidance on the Commission's Enforcement Priorities in Applying Article 82 EC Treaty to Abusive Exclusionary Conduct by Dominant Undertakings".

with the techniques of economic analysis, *per se*, and much less with the policy issues to which such analysis is or might be applied in practice. As such, few books have been directly concerned wth the practical application of economics and in particular, even fewer seek to address the needs of competition lawyers and other non-economists.[3] For this reason, the treatment of economic principles in this book focuses squarely on policy issues, how economic reasoning relates to the practical application of the law and the implications the legal approach has for commercial and business practices. The aim of this book is to provide an introduction to the key economic issues that arise in EC competition law cases and to provide examples of practical relevance.

While the book is specifically about the economic issues raised in EC competition law, it should be noted that with the increasing adoption of EC competition law into the domestic law of the Member States, this makes it increasingly relevant for domestic competition law as well.[4] In addition, the techniques of economic analysis described in the book are frequently applicable even in jurisdictions that have not explicitly modelled their competition law on EC competition law.

The book is aimed at competition lawyers, competition authority officials and economists working in the area (both as academics and consultants). Part I of the book will be of interest to all three groups. In this Part we discuss, in an explicitly practical manner, the nature of "effective competition", market power and issues relating to market definition: these are three key concepts of competition policy analysis. Part II is primarily aimed at lawyers and competition authority officials, although doubtless economists may also find the discussion of the practical application of economic principles of interest. It discusses the economic theory lying behind Articles 81 and 82 and the Merger Regulation. The discussion of the economic issues arising in each of these areas has been greatly expanded since the second edition, reflecting the general growth in the number of cases in which economics has featured heavily, as well as the introduction of the two sets of guidelines on mergers and the guidance on Article 82 issued by DG COMP. The discussion of the economic concepts relevant to assessing mergers has been split into two chapters; the first addressing horizontal mergers and the second non-horizontal mergers. Part III is again aimed at all three groups. It discusses various empirical techniques that can be used to distinguish between competing hypothesis in competition inquiries. This Part is more technical than Parts I and II. We appreciate that some of this material will be difficult for non-economists (this is particularly true of parts of chapters 10 and 15). However, it is hoped that Part III will provide the underlying intuition of the various

---

[3]   Notable exceptions to this include Mehta and Peeperkorn (2007), Motto (2004) and Lyons (2009).

[4]   All Member States have merger control and, apart from Germany, all have national laws modelled on Articles 81 and 82.

empirical techniques and thereby allow for a more refined assessment of any empirical analyses that might be encountered.

The list of people who have contributed to the book, either directly or indirectly, is a long one. It includes the many competition lawyers we have worked with and against over the last eighteen or so years. They have forced us on many occasions to re-examine and refine our understanding of applying economic principles to real world markets and of what economics can usefully say about policy issues. This is an ongoing process. Similar comments apply to officials working in DG COMP and various national competition authorities, in particular the Office of Fair Trading, the UK Competition Commission, the South African Competition Commission and Tribunal, the Australian Competition and Consumer Commission and the German Federal Cartel Office. We would also like to acknowledge the contribution of our respective economic colleagues to our continued economic education. Thank you all.

We would like to express our immense gratitude to those individuals who were coerced into reading and commenting, sometimes at length, on earlier drafts of the book. In addition to those who helped on the first and second editions of this book, we would like to thank the following for their help on this edition: Luisa Affuso, Markus Baldauf, Paul Dobson, Pablo Florian, Bojana Ignjatovic, Miguel de la Mano, Richard Murgatroyd, Daria Prigioni, Vitaly Pruzhansky, Franceso Rosati, Tania van den Brande, Matthijs Visser, Chris Walters, Greg Werden, and Richard Whish. Richard Whish deserves special mention for agreeing to write, once again, the Foreword.

# Table of Contents

# Table of Contents

Part III—Measurement

Table of Contents

# List of Tables

## List of Tables

# List of Figures

## List of Figures

# Table of Cases

References are to para. number

## European Cases

# Table of Cases

# Table of Cases

# Table of Cases

# Table of Cases

## National Cases

### Netherlands

### South Africa

### United Kingdom

# Table of Guidelines and Notices

References are to para. number

# Table of Guidelines and Notices

# Table of Legislation

# Table of European Treaties and Agreements

References are to para. number

# 1. Introduction

One of the primary motivating drivers of the programme to create a Eur- **1–001**
opean common market is the economic advantages that are expected to
flow from its completion. The objectives of the European Union are set out
in Article 2 of the EC Treaty. They include an accelerated raising of living
standards and a continuous and balanced expansion of economic activity
to be achieved through the establishment of a common market, unimpeded
by national boundaries. Free movement of goods, services, workers and
capital and the right to establish a business in other Member States are
therefore central to the aims of the Treaty. But the abolition of national
governmental restrictions such as customs barriers and quotas between
Member States would deliver few benefits if these restrictions on competition were to be replaced by cartels and other anti-competitive practices.[1]

The need for European competition rules was recognised by the framers
of the EC Treaty. These are set out in a number of articles. The most
important of these are Article 81 of the EC Treaty and Article 82 of the EC
Treaty.[2] Article 81 prohibits agreements or concerted practices between
firms which restrict, distort or prevent competition between firms unless
such agreements or practices can be shown to provide overriding benefits
to the Community. Article 81 applies to collusive behaviour between firms,
horizontal cooperation, joint ventures and vertical restraints. Article 82

---

[1]  The battle against governmental restrictions is ongoing. In a number of high-profile cases,
    governments have sought to protect or create national "champions" either by supporting
    anti-competitive mergers or by preventing foreign acquisitions. See for example, the issues
    arising from the acquisition of *Endesa*, the Spanish electricity and gas supplier. The
    Spanish government initially supported an acquisition by another Spanish supplier, *Gas
    Natural*, and then after this transaction was prohibited by the Spanish competition
    authorities sought to impose restrictions on an acquisition by the German supplier, E.ON.
    For further details, see Tribunal de Defensa de la Competencia Report on C-94/05, Gas
    Natural/Endesa (January 5, 2006) and Commission Press Release of December 20, 2006
    ("Mergers: Commission decides that Spanish measures proposed in E.ON/Endesa take-
    over violate EC law") IP/06/1853. The financial crisis of 2008–09 led to a large number of
    state aid requests by various governments, many of which are likely to turn out to be
    without merit.
[2]  Article 81 and Article 82 of the Treaty of Amsterdam correspond to Article 85 and Article
    86, respectively, of the Treaty of Rome.

seeks to prevent dominant firms acting in ways detrimental to the interests of the common market, for example through the charging of excessive prices. These rules governing the behaviour of firms were augmented in 1989 by the introduction of the Merger Regulation.[3] The Merger Regulation gave the Commission rights to prohibit anti-competitive mergers, acquisitions and joint ventures which have a substantial Community dimension. The Merger Regulation was amended in 2004.[4]

The EC Treaty also seeks to prevent governments from overly interfering in the competitive process. For this purpose, the Treaty contains rules governing the granting of state aid (Articles 86–89 of the EC Treaty). In principle, economic reasoning has as large a role to play in the application of these articles as in Article 81, Article 82 and the Merger Regulation.[5] In belated recognition of that fact, the Commission began a five-year programme of state aid reform in June 2005. As a result a number of discussion papers have been written and conferences held which outline the role economic analyses can play.[6] An important, and welcome, result of this has been a better focus on the economic justification for any state aid, i.e. what is the market failure that the aid is required to address. Economic analysis also potentially has a role to play in the assessment of anti-dumping duties under the Anti-dumping Regulation. However, the application of the provisions governing state aid and anti-dumping differ from the core area of EC competition law and since both are large fields in their own right, they are treated as being outside the scope of this book.[7]

**1–002** European competition policy lies at the heart of the Single European Market programme. It is clear, and increasingly accepted, that economics has a central role to play in competition law inquiries. The importance of economics is obvious once one recognises that many of the key concepts of competition law—for example, the concepts of "competition", "monopoly", "oligopoly" and "barriers to entry"—are concepts derived not from law, nor from sociology or political science, but from economics. The application of competition law cannot therefore properly take place without regard to economic considerations. To quote Schmalensee:

> "Unless economic efficiency is held to be of no importance, one can no more avoid the use of economic models in this context than one can avoid speaking prose."[8]

---

[3] Regulation 4064/89 [1989] OJ L3951.
[4] Council Regulation (EC) No 139/2004 of January 20, 2004 on the control of concentrations between undertakings. See Chapter 7 for a discussion of the main changes.
[5] For an early proponent of the role of economics in state aid cases, see Bishop (1997).
[6] See, for instance: Office of Fair Trading (2005); Nitsche and Heidhues (2006); and Friederiszick, Röller and Verouden (2008).
[7] The reader is referred to Quigley (2009) and Mueller, Khan and Scharf (2009) for extended treatments of state aid and anti-dumping law respectively.
[8] Schmalensee (1979).

It is therefore unsurprising that the application of economic principles in both submissions to the Commission and in the Commission's own decisions has increasingly played an important role in the decision-making process.[9, 10] In the 1970s and 1980s, the decisions of the Commission and European Court of Justice, to the extent that they gave due regard to economic reasoning, tended to apply economic principles in an imprecise and ad hoc manner. However, particularly following the introduction of the Merger Regulation, the explicit use of economic arguments in both submissions to the Commission and the Commission's subsequent decisions has been increasing. The increasing reliance on economic reasoning can also be seen in the number of guidelines and notices that have been issued in the last decade. These include the notice on defining the relevant market (1997), guidelines on the application of Article 81 to vertical restraints (2000), the horizontal merger guidelines (2004), the discussion paper on the reform of Article 82 which discusses the increasing need for an economic approach (2005), the guidelines on non-horizontal mergers (2008) and the guidance notice on the application of Article 82 (2009).[11]

The importance of economics in EC competition law was further confirmed by the appointment of a Chief Economist in 2003. The Chief Economist reports directly to the Director General of DG Competition and is supported by a team of economists. Initially the Chief Economist's Team (CET) consisted of 10 members, but in recognition of the growing importance of economics in the Commission's decision-making process, this has been expanded to 20, with an intention for further expansion.[12]

The increasing prominence given to economics in the Commission's **1–003** decisions can be attributed in large part to the increase in the use of empirical evidence to support economic arguments.[13] The use of empirical evidence enables competition authorities to help resolve the problem that in many cases a plausible economic argument can be constructed to support either a pro- or anti-competitive view of the market under investigation. At a theoretical level these differences are often not resolvable. Those

---

[9]   In the following text, "Commission" refers to the EC Commission unless otherwise stated.

[10]  Arguably similar comments apply increasingly to the judgments of the Court of First Instance and the European Court of Justice.

[11]  European Commission (1997) Notice on the Relevant Market for the Purposes of Community Competition Law 97/C 372/03; European Commission (2000) Notice: Guidelines on Vertical Restraints 2000C291/01; European Commission (2004) Guidelines on the assessment of horizontal mergers OJ C31, 5–2–4; DG Competition Discussion Paper on the application of Article 82 of the Treaty to exclusionary abuses (December 2005); European Commission (2008) Guidelines on the assessment of non-horizontal mergers; and European Commission (2009) Communication from the Commission: Guidance on the Commission's enforcement priorities in applying Article 82 of the EC Treaty to abusive exclusionary conduct by dominant undertakings.

[12]  In theory, the CET was established to provide an additional check and balance on the investigating case team. In practice, the CET forms an integral part of that team.

[13]  It is a common fallacy to equate the use of empirical evidence with the use of econometric analysis. As Part III of this book demonstrates, econometric anlaysis represents only one method for analysing observed data.

familiar with economic theory will know that a large number of results can often be reversed by making an alternative assumption. This is particularly true of modern economic analysis which employs game theoretic methodology. Empirical analysis offers the chance to test conflicting hypotheses. While recourse to empirical evidence is not always conclusive, it is usually more supportive of one hypothesis than another. Put simply, looking at what is actually happening in the industry under consideration is essential to determining whether the conduct under investigation represents effective competitive behaviour or anti-competitive behaviour.

An understanding of the economic issues that arise in competition law investigations, the underlying basic theory of those issues and the type of empirical evidence that can be used to address those issues is becoming increasingly important to lawyers, economists and officials practising in this area. This book is concerned with economic theory that offers sound policy prescriptions and with measuring the outcomes implied by theoretical arguments against actual market outcomes.[14] For this reason, we do not seek to provide an exhaustive description of the numerous theoretical models that pertain to the issues of interest to competition law practitioners.[15] Instead, we focus on well-established economic models that give rise to propositions that can be tested empirically.

This book examines first the key economic issues raised by the application of EC competition law and how those issues are addressed in practice with reference to the case law,[16] and then discusses how available market evidence can be used to distinguish competitive from anti-competitive behaviour. It should be stressed that empirical techniques are an aid to the legal process of evaluating competitive effects, not an end in themselves; empirical evidence can be used to support an argument but does not constitute the argument itself.

# THE GOALS OF EC COMPETITION POLICY

**1–004** Economic theory and the empirical techniques employed to test that theory should be seen as providing practitioners of competition law with a set of tools with which to assess the relative merits of competing hypotheses. But this immediately raises the question of what hypotheses one should be seeking to test. To answer this question one must have regard to the goals of EC competition law. From a consideration of those goals follows the

---

[14]  Vickers (2002) advocates this approach.

[15]  An excellent overview of the economic theory of industrial economics is provide by Tirole (1988) and a theoretical treatment of competition law economics is provided by Motta (2004).

[16]  The same principles will also apply in other jurisdictions, for example the national competition law of Member States. However, due regard needs to be given to differences that exist across Member States.

economic issues of concern and therefore what type of questions economics should seek to answer. In particular, answering this question will show the weight, if any, that competition authorities and the courts should give to economics in their decision-making processes as well as providing a framework for deciding between competing values.

EC competition law has broadly speaking two goals: the promotion of integration between the Member States and the promotion of effective and undistorted competition.[17] These might be termed the "integration goal" and the "economic goal".

## Integration goal

Community competition policy, unlike competition policies in other jur- **1–005** isdictions, has to take account of the market integration objective as well as the need for a system of undistorted competition.[18] Article 2 of the EC Treaty makes it clear that market integration is seen as an important goal of EC competition law:

> "The Community shall have as its task, by establishing a common market and progressively approximating the economic policies of Member States, to promote throughout the Community a harmonious development of economic activities, a continuous and balanced expansion, an increase in stability, an accelerated raising of the standard of living and closer relations between the States belonging to it."

The integration motivation of EC competition law has an important impact on the Commission's decisions. The existence of the market integration goal explains much of the Commission's hostility towards agreements or business practices which prevent or hinder cross-border trade.

## Economic goal

The wording of the main competition rules of the European Community **1–006** shows that the maintenance of effective competition lies at the heart of EC competition law:

- Article 81 prohibits as being incompatible with the single market agreements that may affect trade between Member States and

---

[17] While EC competition law has other objectives, the economic objective and the furtherance of integration are, in practice, the most important. The reader is referred to Whish (2009) and Neven et al. (1998) for a good overview of these other objectives.

[18] However, European competition law is not unique in having objectives beyond just undistorted competition. For instance, the South African competition law contains provisions relating to employment and minority empowerment. However, European competition law is unique in having market integration as one of its objectives.

"which have as their object or effect the prevention, restriction or distortion of competition within the common market".

- Article 82 prohibits behaviour of individual firms that may give rise to anti-competitive outcomes; "[a]ny abuse by one or more undertakings of a dominant position ... shall be prohibited as incompatible with the common market" where an abuse entails inter alia charging excessive prices or limiting production to the prejudice of consumers.

- The European Merger Regulation states that "[a] concentration which would significantly impede effective competition, in the common market or in a substantial part of it, in particular as a result of the creation or strengthening of a dominant position, shall be declared incompatible with the common market".

But what is meant by effective competition? Standard economic theory tells us that unless firms possess and exercise market power, then they are unable to affect competition adversely. Effective competition can therefore be equated as the absence of market power. Standard economic theory defines market power as the ability to raise prices above the competitive price level.

However, this raises the question of the definition of "the competitive price". In many textbooks "the competitive price" is defined as equal to short-run marginal cost. However, as numerous commentators have noted, virtually all firms possess some market power under this definition. This leads one either to argue that all such industries require regulatory intervention (surely not a tenable position) or that one must distinguish between "significant" market power and "not so significant" market power. Most commentators who have considered this issue resort to this second position. This implies that a market is subject to effective competition when there is not a significant amount of market power being exercised. But when does market power become significant? Ultimately the addition of the adjective "significant" provides no additional practical guidance for determining whether a firm is able to engage in anti-competitive conduct.

In this book, we explicitly recognise that effective competitive can, and indeed usually will, lead to prices above short-run marginal cost. Put simply, prices in excess of unit production costs should not necessarily be seen as indicative of market power.[19] The assessment of whether a market is subject to effective competition must therefore go beyond simply observing price-cost margins. Chapters 2 and 3 provide an overview of the main constituent elements of that competitive assessment.

[19] Support for this position is provided by Tirole (1988) and Katz and Shapiro (1998).

## Conflicting goals

The two goals of EC competition law are potentially at odds with one **1–007**
another. For example, some manufacturers seek to confine the activities of
retailers to certain territories. In some circumstances such practices can be
shown to be pro-competitive in the sense of improving economic efficiency.
However, such practices may be contrary to the goal of European market
integration and are therefore viewed with suspicion by the Commission.
This helps to explain why certain agreements are deemed incompatible
with the objective of the common market while others that have the same
impact on economic welfare are not.

Many commentators have drawn attention to these dual goals to argue
that there is a fundamental difference between the application of EC
competition law and competition law as practised in other jurisdictions,
particularly the United States. In one sense, this is true. EC competition
law has two objectives and US antitrust law only one. But this need not
affect the assessment of the impact of commercial practices, agreements or
mergers on economic welfare. As argued above, a coherent competition
assessment requires explicit consideration of economic principles. Economic reasoning provides the necessary tools to assess the effectiveness of
competition in all industries regardless of the jurisdiction. This implies that
the same economic principles are as valid in the application of EC competition law as in the application of competition law in other jurisdictions,
including the United States.[20]

While the market integration goal of EC competition law might in
practice take precedent over the economic goal, this does not imply that no
attention to economic efficiency should be given even where an agreement
clearly seeks to restrict cross-border trade. By ignoring the impact on
economic welfare, decisions taken solely with regard to the market integration objective can have perverse outcomes.

A good example is provided by the Commission's cases against Glaxo **1–008**
SmithKline's attempts to prevent parallel trade in its pharmaceuticals out
of Spain and Greece.[21] Pharmaceutical prices throughout Europe are set by
the governments of the Member States. These government-set prices are
low in Spain and Greece compared to the rest of Europe. The result is that
it is profitable for wholesalers in Spain and Greece to import pharmaceuticals into Spain and Greece and then re-export them to higher priced

---

[20] The stated alignment between the objectives of EU and US antitrust law has a long history.
Former Commissioner for Competition, Karel Van Miert, stated in the *Financial Times* in
1998 that the European Union and the United States were able to co-operate closely on
antitrust issues because they had competition policies which were "very similar, if not
identical".

[21] See *GlaxoSmithKline Services v Commission* [2006] E.C.R. II-2969, [2006] 5 C.M.L.R. 29;
Opinion of Advocate Jacobs in *Syfait and Others v GlaxoSmithKline and Others* (C-53/03)
[2005] E.C.R. I-4609, [2005] 5 C.M.L.R. 1; appeals to CFI by the Commission and
GlxoSmithKline (C-501/06 P and C-513/06 P); and *http://ec.europa.eu/competition/sectors/
pharmaceuticals/overview_en.html* [Accessed September 9, 2009].

countries, such as France and the United Kingdom. GlaxoSmithKline has attempted to stop this trade by refusing to fulfil all the demand from wholesalers in Spain and by bypassing the use of wholesalers at all in Greece. The Commission has argued that this is contrary to the single market objective and is anti-competitive. At the time of writing, the cases are still under appeal, but were the Commission to win, it is clear that one potential result would be that GlaxoSmithKline could simply stop selling its pharmaceuticals in Spain and Greece. This would be to the detriment of consumers in those countries and would provide no corresponding benefit to consumers elsewhere.[22]

Another good, but old, example of this conflict is provided by the Commission's *United Distillers* decision.[23] In that case, the Commission condemned a deterrent to exporting created by a dual pricing scheme under which British dealers were required to forego discounts of up to £5 per case of whisky that was exported. The Commission did not accept the argument that this was needed to protect Distillers' exclusive distributors on the Continent, who spent considerable sums on promotion from which parallel importers would benefit. The result of this decision was an increase in the price of some brands in the United Kingdom and the withdrawal from sale of Johnny Walker Red Label in the United Kingdom—a clear reduction in the welfare of consumers (at least British consumers) with no clear offsetting benefits. Further, other Distillers' brands ceased to be promoted on the Continent. The net result was therefore one in which the brands sold by Distillers in the United Kingdom differed from those sold on the Continent. Hence, far from promoting the integration of the single market, the Commission's decision may actually have retarded it.

The explicit application of economic principles does not therefore mean that the integration and other goals of EC competition law are to be disregarded or their importance diminished. Rather, it simply states that assessing the impact of commercial practices against the objectives of the EC Treaty can be made both more transparent and more coherent by considering each goal separately.[24] It should also be noted that conflicts between the two goals ought not to arise at the national level.

---

[22]  See also *Silhouette* (C-355/96) (1998), E.C.R. 676 for the interaction between competition and integration objectives. This case also involved restrictions on parallel imports, in this case concerning high-quality fashion spectacles and sunglasses.

[23]  *Distillers Company Plc (Red Label)* [1983] C.M.L.R. 173; [1983] OJ C245/3.

[24]  Whish (2009) states the following: "The important issue therefore is to determine the effect which competition can have on economic performance. To understand this one must first turn to economic theory" (p.4).

# THE IMPACT OF "A MORE ECONOMICS APPROACH"

It is important to stress that "a more economics approach" represents an **1–009** evolutionary development of competition law enforcement in the European Union rather than a radical departure. Contrary to what many observers maintain, many of the previous decisions contain economic reasoning, albeit in an implicit rather than explicit manner. However, the developments described above clearly have had an effect on the application of competition law at the European level. In particular, the focus has been to shift the emphasis of the competitive assessment away from consideration of whether competitors are harmed (which reflected the legacy of the influence that German competition law had on the early development of EC competition law) towards a focus on whether competition is harmed to the detriment of consumers.

As noted above, the economic objective of EC competition law is to prevent harm to competition. This need not always, or even often, involve the protection of competitors. As the Commission's Article 82 guidance paper states, "the Commission is mindful that what really matters is protecting an effective competitive process and not simply protecting competitors."[25] Distinguishing between harm to competitors and harm to competition is particularly important in cases where the potential theory of harm involves the exclusion of competitors; the anti-competitive effects which have adverse consequences for consumers arise through the harm to competitors.[26] The impact of a more economics approach has been to recognise that the former does not necessarily follow from the latter and that a more detailed analysis is required. Indeed, the whole process of competition involves the struggle by firms to achieve positions of superiority over rivals and this almost by definition involves harm to competitors. But this is not necessarily—or even usually—indicative that markets are not subject to effective competition. The fact that a given business practice, e.g. the signing of an exclusive supply contract, makes it more difficult for a firm's rivals to compete with it, does not therefore imply that the competitive process is being harmed.

In summary, the major consequence that has arisen from making economic reasoning more explicit in the Commission's decision-making process has been to move the focus of the competitive assessment away from protecting competitors towards protecting competition and hence towards an analysis of the effects of the conduct under investigation rather than the

---

[25] See para.6, Guidance on Article 82, op. cit.
[26] This issue is considered at length in Chapter 6 which discusses Article 82 and also in Chapter 8 in the discussion of potential competition concerns arising from vertical and conglomerate mergers.

form of that conduct. It is perhaps therefore more appropriate to talk of "a more effects based approach" than simply "a more economics approach".

## THE USE OF EMPIRICAL TECHNIQUES

**1–010** A central element of a more effects-based approach to EC competition law is the increasing importance given to observed market evidence; how else can one assess the likely effects of business conduct? However, the use of empirical evidence in EC competition law has been subject to a number of objections, which fall into three broad categories.

The first category recognises in principle the merits of using empirical techniques as an aid in the competitive assessment. However, concerns are expressed about the applicability of such tests in practice. In particular, a concern that is often voiced is that the necessary data for the tests is not available. While it is certainly true that the amount and type of data often do not match the ideal, this should not be taken to mean that there is no useful data available. Indeed, in many instances, available market evidence can be incorporated into the competitive assessment without the need for apparently sophisticated econometric analysis and it is almost always the case that some appropriate empirical analysis can be undertaken. Arguments incorporating the results of even limited empirical analysis are generally to be preferred to those based purely on theory.

The second category of criticism is more fundamental and concerns whether empirical techniques have any usefulness in aiding the competitive assessment. This strand of criticism can be summarised in the statement: "garbage in, garbage out". There is a degree of merit in that statement. The results of techniques using inappropriate data cannot be relied upon. Similarly, inferences from poor or incorrect analysis can not be relied upon. For example, using list prices when it is known that most transactions take place at varying discounts from the list price would be unlikely to yield useful insights into the competitive process. However, this merely emphasises that there is a distinction between good analysis and bad analysis. One should therefore guard against this type of argument being used to dismiss the results of all empirical studies. This is particularly true where one party is attempting to discredit the evidence of an opposing party. At a minimum, that party should demonstrate why the data are faulty *and* explain the ways in which correcting the faulty data would alter the findings of the original study. Since its investigation of the *GE/Instrumentarium* merger, the Commission has often facilitated such an exchange by providing the parties' economists with access to confidential information provided by third parties, particularly that used by complainants in preparing their own economic submissions. In this way, the parties are able to comment directly on and test the robustness of the analysis prepared both by third-party complainants and that conducted by the Commission.[27]

A third category of criticism argues that such empirical analysis is too **1–011** time consuming and that there are insufficient resources or expertise for competition authorities to either conduct or assess the validity of such analyses. This criticism is often heard from those national competition authorities that object to the introduction of a more effects-based approach to competition law. However, as explained above, empirical analysis does not always require a significant amount of data and can therefore be readily and quickly undertaken. In addition, much of the "heavy lifting" involved in empirical analysis is conducted by the parties under investigation and by complainants. A lack of internal resources does not therefore prevent the use of such analysis as an input into the competitive assessment; it affects only who does that analysis. However, increasingly competition authorities do have the requisite internal economic resources. As noted above, the Commission's Chief Economist Team now has a significant number of staff and this is true of a number of other competition authorities. Fundamentally, this criticism appears to deny that an examination of actual market evidence can have any value in the competitive assessment. That is manifestly incorrect. Effectively, this category of criticism represents an ostrich approach; one simply buries one's head in the sand and hopes the problem goes away!

## THE PLAN OF THE BOOK

Part I of this book examines the central economic concepts applied in EC **1–012** competition law. Chapter 2 assesses in some detail possible definitions of "effective competition". It is argued that useful definitions of "effective competition" for the purposes of competition law must focus on market outcomes rather than just on descriptions of market characteristics. Definitions based on market outcomes provide both a benchmark against which to assess the level of competition in a given industry and moreover provide a benchmark against which competing claims can be assessed.

Chapter 3 introduces the concept of market power, focusing on the ways in which outcomes in markets where significant market power is being

---

[27] The US courts test the reliability of expert evidence by applying the Daubert rules. These provide four questions to be used in deciding whether an expert's evidence is reliable enough to be used in court. The questions are:

- Is the evidence based on a testable theory or technique?
- Has the theory or technique been peer reviewed?
- Does the technique have a known error rate and standards controlling its operation?
- Is the underlying science generally accepted?

This is a good set of questions to be addressed when evaluating any empirical evidence in a competition law case.

exercised differ from markets subject to effective competition. A discussion of the welfare implications of the exercise of market power is provided. Basic factors important for the competitive assessment of market power are briefly discussed.

Chapter 4 discusses the definition of the "relevant market". The relevant market is a key concept in the application of EC competition law.[28] We discuss its role in aiding the competitive assessment and the implications this role has for the basis on which a relevant market should be defined. We provide an extended discussion of the Hypothetical Monopolist Test and how it is to be applied in practice. We also highlight several types of error that commonly arise in defining the "relevant market".

**1–013**  Part II of the book considers the economic principles which apply to assessing competition under Article 81, Article 82 and the Merger Regulation. A chapter is devoted to each of Articles 81 and 82, whilst two chapters are devoted to the Merger Regulation. These chapters provide an introduction to what the respective area of EC competition law says, the relationship between economics and the law in that area and the main economic issues are that are pertinent to the practical application of the law.

Part III discusses the use of formal empirical techniques as an aid to the competitive assessment. As noted above, recourse to the particular facts of the industry under investigation offers competition practitioners the possibility of discriminating between competing theories. In some investigations, empirical analysis is tailored to the particular requirements of the industry and the focus of the inquiry. However, there also exist a number of empirical techniques routinely employed in competition law inquiries. Part III provides an overview of the standard techniques and discusses the role that each test can potentially play in the competitive assessment. Examples of their use in the Commission's reasoning are provided where appropriate. The strengths and weaknesses of each test from a practical perspective are examined.

A concluding remark is in order. The influence of economic reasoning on the application of EC competition law has increased significantly in recent years. This has led to improvements in the Commission's competitive assessment and has also improved the transparency of the decision process. The Second Edition of this book stated that the adoption of the Notice on the Definition of Relevant Market (1997) and the guidelines issued on the Article 81 block exemptions for vertical (2000) and horizontal (2001) agreements strongly suggested that this process would continue. Recent evidence with respect to the developments in the application of Article 81, Article 82 and merger control demonstrates that, for once, economists have been proved correct in their forecast!

---

[28]  The same is true of national competition law in virtually all jurisdictions where competition law is applied.

# Part I. Concepts

"A lawyer who has not studied economics ... is very apt to become a public enemy."

Justice Brandeis (1916)

# 2. Effective Competition

## INTRODUCTION

It is a generally accepted principle that competition is desirable. Competition tends to lead to cost efficiency, low prices and innovation. Markets that are competitive tend to lead to a higher level of consumer welfare in both the short-run and the long-run than markets that are not competitive. Where markets are competitive, regulatory intervention is neither required nor warranted, and could even be detrimental. Conversely, it is generally believed that monopolies are bad for consumer welfare and should therefore be regulated in order to protect the interests of consumers. **2–001**

But while the benefits of competition, or in the words of the law, *effective competition*, are now widely accepted, this raises the issue of how "effective competition" is to be defined in a manner that is useful for policy purposes. This chapter assesses a number of possible definitions of "effective competition". While a number of intuitively appealing definitions are available, they are shown not to provide useful benchmarks for the application of competition law. Instead, we argue that whether observed levels of competition can be deemed effective depends not on the form that competition takes, nor on its description, but rather on the outcomes it produces.

Those market outcomes can then be used as a benchmark against which competing claims over the effectiveness of competition in particular industries can be assessed. In particular, a clear understanding of what is meant by effective competition enables one to give a consistent and logical interpretation to phrases such as "distortion of competition", "restriction of competition" and "excessive pricing". Such phrases necessarily involve the notion of comparing one market outcome with another. For example, "distortion of competition" clearly suggests that the "distorted" outcome is being compared to some other outcome, namely, the "non-distorted" outcome, whilst a claim that prices are excessive must involve a comparison with prices that are held not to be excessive.

In order to understand what outcomes effective competition can be expected to produce, a number of economic models of competition are examined. Economic models of competition can be divided into three **2–002** broad categories. These are "perfect competition", "monopoly" and "oligopoly". While few markets can be characterised as being perfectly competitive or as monopolies (in the economic sense[1]), an understanding of these two models is important because they illustrate the ways in which a lack of effective competition affects market outcomes. The purpose of the discussion of these models is to provide the basic set of analytical tools with which to evaluate whether a market is subject to effective competition and, if not, how the outcomes in that market differ from the competitive outcomes.

While both the models of perfect competition and monopoly provide a useful starting point for analysing the effectiveness of competition, neither of them provides a sound basis for policy decisions. First, most markets are not characterised by either perfect competition or true monopoly. Secondly, and crucially, neither model provides an analysis of the most common situation in reality: the interaction between a limited number of firms in the market. Taking account of that interaction is a critical consideration in the assessment of the effectiveness of competition. It is the third category of models—oligopoly models—that deals explicitly with how the interaction between firms affects the outcomes of the competitive process. The discussion of oligopoly models also helps address what outcomes one can reasonably expect effective competition to achieve.[2] It is argued that the outcomes generated by many oligopolies are likely to be consistent with effective competition.

## SOME POTENTIAL DEFINITIONS OF "EFFECTIVE COMPETITION"

**2–003** The maintenance of "effective competition" lies at the heart of EC competition law.[3] But what is meant by effective competition? For example, what is the benchmark under Article 81 against which agreements can be said to prevent, restrict, distort or hinder effective competition? Similarly, against what benchmark under Article 82 can certain business activities be said to be abusive? Despite the importance of the concept for EC

---

[1] The economic meaning of "monopoly" is that there is only one firm in the market. The legal meaning of "monopoly" is less rigorous in the sense that it refers to a firm that, although not the only firm in the market, is the largest firm in the market and accounts for the majority of sales in the market.

[2] It should be noted that even these models do not describe how firms actually compete. In particular, oligopoly models of the type discussed in this chapter tend to be static.

[3] For instance, the Merger Regulation states that "[a] concentration which would significantly impede *effective competition*, in the common market or in a substantial part of it, in particular as a result of the creation or strengthening of a dominant position, shall be declared incompatible with the common market" (emphasis added). The European Court of Justice, in *United Brands* defined "dominance" with reference to the ability of a firm to "prevent effective competition being maintained on the relevant market".

competition law, the answer to these questions is not clear, either in theory or on the basis of practice[4] and the term "effective competition" is not precisely defined anywhere in EC law. However, there are a number of apparently plausible definitions of "effective competition". Three possible definitions are examined below.

## Effective competition as the process of rivalry

On an intuitive level, effective competition might be equated with the **2–004** process of rivalry. Such a definition is intuitively appealing since rivalry is the means by which a competitively structured industry creates and confers its benefits. Moreover, competition law investigations often arise in those situations in which rivalry is eliminated, e.g. by merger or through a cartel agreement. But this definition of "effective competition" provides no benchmarks for how much rivalry is required for competition to be effective and invites the erroneous conclusion that the elimination of rivalry must always be deemed to be anti-competitive or restrictive of competition. That is clearly not the case. For example, an agreement signed between a manufacturer and a retailer which meant that the retailer sold only the products of that manufacturer would eliminate rivalry between manufacturers to supply that retailer. But does such elimination of rivalry result in a reduction in the effectiveness of competition? Not necessarily. The retailer might be a small retailer with a tiny market share. In that case the agreement has no effect on competition in any substantive sense. Further, as the case law and the various Commission papers regarding the application of competition law to vertical restraints have shown, such arrangements between manufacturers and retailers can actually be beneficial both from the perspective of the parties involved and from that of consumers.[5] Rather than always being anti-competitive, reductions in rivalry may be pro-competitive in the sense that they increase consumer welfare. An example of this is the case of two firms pooling their R&D and as a result of sharing their intellectual property being able to bring a new product to market that neither of them could have introduced unilaterally.[6] Another example is that of shipping pools, whereby a number of vessels owned by different firms are operated under single management. The Competition

---

[4] See Bork (1978) and Phlips (1995). Phlips discusses the concept of "normal" competition and what it might mean.

[5] For further details, see the section on vertical issues in Chapter 5 and the European Commission's Guidelines on vertical restraints [2000] OJ C291/01, included as Appendix B to this book.

[6] *European Night Services* (T-374, 375, 384 and 388/94) [1998] E.C.R. II-3141, is an example of where firms jointly might be able to bring to the market a product or service that they could not bring to the market unilaterally. This case involved four train companies creating a joint venture to run night-time services through the Channel Tunnel. The Commission exempted the agreement under Article 81(3), but the CFI concluded it should be cleared under Article 81(1). As it happens, no such services have yet begun.

has accepted that such arrangements may improve consumer welfare as a result of better utilisation rates and the ability to take advantage of economies of scale.[7]

Hence, such a definition of "effective competition" is not adequate for the purposes of competition law. It would make rivalry an end in itself, regardless of whether the elimination of some rivalry had any substantive negative effect on consumer welfare. One must recognise that all market economies require there to be some elimination of rivalry, since this is necessary to every integration or co-ordination of productive economic efforts and to the specialisation of effort. As Bork notes[8]:

> "No firm, no partnership, no corporation, no economic unit containing more than a single person could exist without the elimination of some kinds of rivalry between persons."

In distinguishing between legitimate and illegitimate reasons for the elimination of rivalry, one must recognise that there is a distinction between harm to competitors and harm to competition. As discussed in Chapter 1, the economic objective of EC competition law is to prevent harm to competition. This need not always, or even often, involve the protection of competitors. As Advocate General Jacobs put it:

> "[I]t is important not to lose sight of the fact that the primary purpose of Article 8[2] is to prevent distortion of competition—and in particular to safeguard the interests of consumers—rather than to protect the position of particular competitors."[9]

This sentiment was echoed by Neelie Kroes, Competition Commissioner:

> "First, it is competition, and not competitors, that is to be protected. Second, ultimately the aim is to avoid consumers harm. I like aggressive competition—including by dominant companies – and I don't care if it may hurt competitors—as long as it ultimately benefits consumers. That is because the main and ultimate objective of Article 82 is to protect consumers, and this does, of course, require the protection of an undistorted competitive process on the market."[10]

**2–005** The whole process of competition involves the struggle by firms to achieve positions of superiority over rivals and this almost by definition involves

---

[7] For more details, see paras 60 to 77 of the European Commission's "Guidelines on the application of Article 81 of the EC treaty to maritime transport service" (July 1, 2008).
[8] Bork (1978).
[9] Opinion of Advocate General Jacobs, *Oscar Bronner GmbH & Co KG v Mediaprint Zeitungs-und Zeitschriftenverlag GmbH & Co KG* (C7/97), at [58].
[10] Kroes (2005).

harm to competitors. But this does not in general indicate that markets are not subject to effective competition. The fact that a given business practice, e.g. the signing of an exclusive supply contract, makes it more difficult for a firm's rivals to compete with it, does not therefore imply that the competitive process is being harmed. If effective competition is equated solely with rivalry, how are competition authorities to decide between exclusive supply agreements which are anti-competitive from those which are efficiency enhancing or have at worst no harmful effects (since both involve reductions in rivalry)? It is evident that a definition of "effective competition" based solely on rivalry is too restrictive.

## Effective competition as the absence of restraints

An alternative, again superficially attractive, definition of "effective competition" is that there is effective competition when there is an absence of restraints on a firm's economic activities by any other firm.[11] But again this definition of "effective competition" ignores the realities of commercial behaviour in market economies. Under this view all commercial contracts are held to restrict competition since every agreement concerning trade involves one firm imposing restraints on the behaviour of another (e.g. that the other firm must deliver a given amount of a product on a given day). In one sense, this is the interpretation of effective competition which is traditionally applied by the Commission in deciding whether agreements are subject to Article 81, though not whether they ultimately fall foul of it.[12] However, equating effective competition with the absence of commercial restraints is far too wide a definition of "effective competition", as is highlighted by the use of block exemptions and de minimis provisions to reduce the number of cases otherwise caught by Article 81.[13] Both block exemptions and de minimis provisions indicate that there are other criteria for defining "effective competition" beyond just an absence of restraints (respectively, to do with the nature of particular industries or practices and with the likely impact of the practice in the marketplace). **2–006**

---

[11]  See, for instance, Hoppmann (1966, 1968).
[12]  The decisions of the European Courts often offer a more reasonable approach to the application of Article 81 (for instance, *European Night Services* [1998] E.C.R. II-3141).
[13]  See Chapter 5 below for a more detailed discussion of Article 81.

### Effective competition is where no firm can influence the market price

2–007 "Effective competition" might also be defined as those circumstances in which no firm is able to influence the market price.[14] This view of effective competition stems from the economic model of perfect competition in which the competitive price is equal to the marginal cost of production.[15] While this model provides a useful model for discussing some basic economic principles, it does not provide a good basis for policy. The model of perfect competition assumes that there is a large number of firms and a large number of buyers, that firms all produce the same product (i.e. products are not differentiated), that there is complete and perfect information, that markets exist for all goods both present and future and that various other restrictive assumptions also hold. This is not a good description of most markets, the majority of which are normally considered to be competitive, and so this paradigm should not be used as the basis for a definition of "effective competition". It is not a realistic nor a sensible goal to attempt to replicate the assumed conditions and its adoption would lead to the perverse conclusion that many firms that operate in competitive markets and so earn only a reasonable level of profit are not, in fact, subject to effective competition. For these reasons, this definition does not provide a useful definition of "effective competition" for EC competition law. As we discuss further below, some price setting power, in both the short-run and the longer-run, is entirely consistent with effective competition.

### Towards a practical definition of "effective competition"

2–008 None of the above "definitions" provides an adequate definition of "effective competition". The last is inadequate because it implies that nearly all industries warrant intervention. The other "definitions" are inadequate for two main reasons. First, neither of them provides a benchmark which would allow competing claims to be tested: how much rivalry is needed, how few restraints can be imposed, before competition ceases to be effective? Secondly, these definitions focus on descriptions of market characteristics rather than focusing on the outcomes that effective competition delivers. The economic goal of EC competition law is the protection and promotion of effective competition. But this is a goal only because of the benefits that it delivers to European consumers. What matters therefore are the outcomes for consumers that competition in a particular market delivers—not the particular form that the competitive

[14] Alternatively stated, effective competition would be said to exist where the elasticity of supply facing any buyer is infinite (i.e. if a buyer offered to pay slightly less than the market price, then he would find no sellers willing to supply him) and the elasticity of demand facing any seller is infinite (i.e. if a seller raised its price slightly above the market price, then it would lose all its sales). See Chapter 3 for a further discussion of elasticities.

[15] See *The perfect competition paradigm*, below.

process takes. Whether a market is characterised by effective competition or not therefore depends on the outcomes it produces.

This raises the question of what outcomes are produced by effective competition and how they can be distinguished from those produced by less than effective competition. The practical application of competition law ought to be interested less in outcomes that are desirable in some theoretical, abstract sense and more in outcomes that are feasible for regulatory intervention to achieve.[16] To draw this distinction requires consideration of the various economic models of competition and the implications each type of model has for consumer welfare.

# THE TWO EXTREMES: PERFECT COMPETITION AND MONOPOLY[17]

The application of competition law should be concerned with those market **2–009** situations in which intervention on the part of competition authorities can improve consumer welfare.[18] The scope for such intervention is illustrated in this section through a discussion of two extreme economic models: perfect competition and monopoly. These models provide two very different market outcomes. In one—perfect competition—consumer welfare is maximised and could not be improved upon even by an omniscient regulator. In the other—monopoly—consumer welfare is not maximised and could, in principle at least, be improved upon by regulatory intervention. While neither of these models provides a good description of the competitive process in most industries, they can be used to illustrate some of the basic economic concepts that enable one to judge whether

---

[16] Kühn et al. (1992).

[17] It will be assumed throughout this book that firms aim to maximise profits. The notion of profit maximisation, in common with the assumptions of all economic models, should not be taken too literally. There are many ways in which business decision-makers may deviate from profit-maximising behaviour and many mechanisms that, in turn, limit managerial discretion. However, despite research on the effects of the separation of ownership and control, the profit maximisation hypothesis remains at the centre of economics. As Scherer and Ross (1995) note:

> "When forced into the trenches on the question of whether firms maximise profits, economists resort to the ultimate weapon in their arsenal: a variant of Darwin's natural selection theory. Over the long haul, there is one simple criterion for the survival of a business enterprise: profits must be nonnegative. No matter how strongly managers prefer to pursue other objectives and no matter how difficult it is to find profit-maximising strategies in a world of uncertainty and high information costs, failure to satisfy this criterion means ultimately that a firm will disappear from the economic science." (p.48)

[18] This statement assumes that the aim of competition policy is to maximise consumer welfare. This is not uncontroversial, particularly amongst economists who are taught to believe that it is social welfare (i.e. consumer welfare plus profits earned by firms) that should be maximised. We return to this issue at para.2.17 below.

intervention by competition law authorities is likely to improve consumer welfare.

## The perfect competition paradigm

The model of perfect competition is the first economic model that most economists learn, but perversely it bears little relation to reality. In the perfect competition paradigm there are many buyers and sellers of the product, the quantity of products bought by any buyer or sold by any seller is so small relative to the total quantity traded that changes in these quantities leave market prices unchanged, the product is homogeneous, all firms are identical, all buyers and sellers have perfect information and there is both free entry into and exit out of the market.

These assumptions have a number of implications. The most important is that the market price of the product will be equal to the marginal cost of producing the product,[19] and in equilibrium this will be the same for all producers.[20] The intuition behind this result is simple. If the market price of the product is above the marginal cost of production for a seller, that seller can make more profit by selling one more unit of production. Since the price obtained for the good exceeds the costs incurred in producing it, a positive margin is made on the sale. Similarly, if the marginal cost were greater than the market price, profits could be increased by reducing output. Since the product is (by assumption) homogeneous and no seller can affect the market price, the market price is the same for all sellers. This implies that each seller will expand output to the point at which marginal cost is equal to the market price. In equilibrium, all sellers have the same marginal cost and this marginal cost is equal to the market price.

Another important implication of this model is that no firm makes positive economic profits.[21] If the price was high enough for firms in the market to make positive profits, other firms that were not in the market would enter in order to earn some of these positive profits. The assumption of free entry into the market means that entry would continue until the

[19] The marginal cost of a product is the cost of producing the next unit of the product. So if it costs a car producer £45,000 to produce nine cars but only £47,500 to produce 10 cars, then the marginal cost of the 10th car for that producer is £2,500. Notice that in this example average cost falls from £5,000 to £4,750 as output is expanded from nine to 10.

[20] In this discussion we abstract from issues to do with which marginal cost (short-run? long-run?) we are concerned with.

[21] This does *not* imply zero accounting profits. Zero profits in economics are taken to indicate that all factors used in production including capital receive their opportunity cost and no more. The opportunity cost of an asset is the value of the asset if put to the best alternative use. In particular, assets earn their cost of capital. The resulting level of profit is also known as *normal* profit. To be more precise, firms earn the rate of return that makes them exactly indifferent to being in the market or not. If this rate of return is factored into the costs of the firms, they make no profit. Economic profits are not the same as accounting profits. Economic profits are defined as revenues minus opportunity cost. For a more detailed discussion of profits and their role in competition policy investigations, see Chapter 3 below.

incumbent firms were no longer making positive profits. The assumption of free exit means that firms would not remain in the market if they were making losses. So in perfect competition firms make zero economic profits. This implies that in addition to being equal to marginal cost, the market price must be equal to the average cost of the firms.

To summarise, markets characterised by the assumptions of perfect **2–010** competition have the following properties:

- price is equal to marginal cost;

- price is equal to average cost (thus implying that marginal cost is equal to average cost); and

- no firm makes positive economic profits.

These properties are shown in Figure 2.1 below.

## Figure 2.1 Perfect competition in an industry

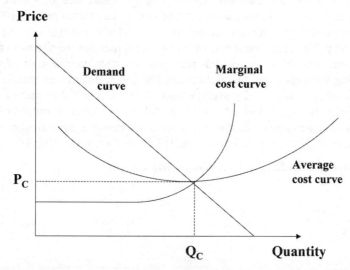

The straight downward sloping line depicts the industry *demand curve*. This indicates how much of the product consumers demand (want to buy) at different prices. As price falls, consumers will wish to buy more of the product, so the demand curve slopes downward (as do the demand curves of virtually all products). $P_c$ denotes the perfectly competitive price in this case and $Q_c$ is the perfectly competitive level of output. As the figure shows, at $P_c$ marginal cost is equal to price (i.e. the marginal cost curve cuts the demand curve) and average cost is also equal to price (so total profits are zero).[22]

---

[22] Note that the average cost curve in this example initially slopes down. This indicates the presence of some fixed costs of production (e.g. the fixed costs of a factory).

**2–011**

> **BOX 2.1: INDUSTRY CURVES AND FIRM-SPECIFIC CURVES**
>
> It is important to note that the curves on Figure 2.1 are for the industry as a whole. They differ from the curves facing an individual firm. The downward sloping demand curve is for the market as a whole. The demand curve facing any single seller under perfect competition will be flat, showing that if they price above the competitive level they will face zero demand. Equally, the average cost curve and marginal cost curve in Figure 2.1 are also for the industry as a whole. The average cost curve and marginal cost curve for an individual seller will differ from the market ones. The industry marginal cost and average cost curves are derived from those of the individual firms so as to minimise total costs. An example should make this clear.
>
> Suppose there are 100 firms in a perfectly competitive industry, that the market price is 10 and that each firm produces 10 units. Total industry sales are therefore 1,000. The left-hand side of Figure 2.2 illustrates this. It shows that at sales of 1,000, the market price is 10 and this is equal to both the marginal cost and the average cost of the industry. The right-hand side of Figure 2.2 illustrates the situation for a specific firm. This shows that for each firm the average cost of producing 10 units is 10. Since there are 100 firms, this means that for the industry as a whole, the average cost of producing 1,000 units is 10. Equally, the right-hand side of Figure 2.2 shows that at an output of 10, each firm's marginal cost is 10. This translates into an industry marginal cost of 10 for 1,000 units (i.e. 100 firms each producing 10 units).
>
> **Figure 2.2 Industry v firm-specific curves**
>
>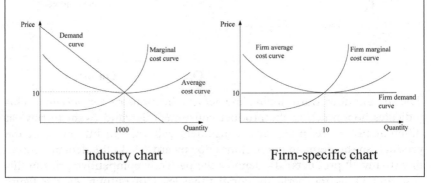
>
> Industry chart      Firm-specific chart

**2–012** If an industry were characterised by perfect competition, then it would not be possible for even an omniscient regulator to increase consumer welfare in this industry.[23] To understand why requires an understanding of the two

---

[23] As we discuss in some detail below, this is true as long as the omniscient regulator is not able to insist that firms continue to operate even though they make losses.

types of benefits that perfect competition delivers. Perfect competition delivers both *productive efficiency* and *allocative efficiency*.

*Productive efficiency* occurs when a given set of products are being produced at the lowest possible cost (given current technology, input prices and so on). This occurs in industries characterised by perfect competition because any firm that does not produce at the lowest possible cost will lose money and exit the market. In perfect competition, economic profits for efficient firms are zero and so inefficient firms must lose money. Perfect competition leads to firms being productively efficient because the pursuit of the maximum possible profits gives firms an incentive to reduce costs as far as possible and, unlike in many other models of competition, firms that do not have costs as low as their rivals will exit the market due to losses. These considerations reveal a possible detrimental effect in those markets not characterised by effective competition. Costs as well as prices may differ between competitive and less competitive markets. If a lack of competition in an industry gives rise to slack and inefficiency in production, then welfare losses will occur. This issue of slack or inefficiency associated with a lack of competition is known as X-inefficiency.[24, 25]

*Allocative efficiency* relates to the difference between the cost of producing the marginal product and the valuation of that product by consumers. If the marginal cost of producing one more unit is different from the amount that consumers are willing to pay for that extra unit, then there is allocative inefficiency. If the marginal cost of producing an extra unit were below the price that consumers are willing to pay for that unit, then both the seller and consumers could be made better off if the seller produced one more unit. He could sell it for fractionally more than it cost him to produce but fractionally less than the price that consumers are willing to pay for it. There is allocative inefficiency because a reallocation of resources towards producing one more unit would improve social welfare (i.e. would improve the sum of consumer welfare and producer welfare). Equally, if the marginal cost were greater than the price that consumers are willing to pay for the unit, there would again be allocative inefficiency. In this case consumers value the product less than it costs to produce and so social welfare would be increased by a reduction in output. Only if price equals marginal cost is there allocative efficiency. Thus, perfect

---

[24] Leibenstein (1966).

[25] Where firms are not subject to effective competitive constraints, the scope for productive inefficiency implies that the lack of effective competition need not necessarily be revealed through observed high profit rates. This was the view that the telecommunications regulator in the UK, Oftel, took in late 2001 in relation to some of the mobile phone companies. Oftel argued that the high profitability of Vodafone indicated a lack of effective competition, whilst the negative profitability of BT Cellnet indicated that it was productively inefficient. Oftel noted that "a firm with low efficiency and low profits may set prices as high as an efficient firm with high profits. Hence, whether or not an operator is making a loss is not a test of market power", Oftel, *Effective competition review: mobile*, September 26, 2001, para.3.4.

competition delivers allocative efficiency because perfect competition ensures that price and marginal cost are equal.

## The monopoly paradigm

**2–013** At the opposite extreme to perfect competition is monopoly. Here the assumption of many sellers is replaced by the assumption of just one seller. Figure 2.3 shows that a monopolist will price above the level that would occur in the presence of perfect competition. Under perfect competition, price equals marginal cost and is determined by the intersection of the demand curve and the marginal cost curve. This price is denoted by $P_c$ in Figure 2.3. Under monopoly, price is at level $P_m$ (also shown in Figure 2.3), which lies above $P_c$.

### Figure 2.3 Monopoly

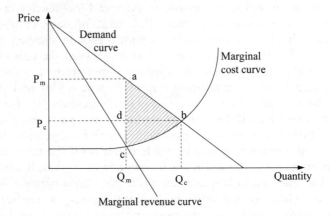

**2–014** The demand and marginal cost curves in Figure 2.3 are the same as those in the Figure 2.1 illustrating perfect competition. However, an additional curve has been added.[26] This is the *marginal revenue* curve. This curve shows the amount of extra revenue that the monopolist earns when he sells one more unit of product. If the monopolist decides to sell x + 1 units rather than x, he will receive additional revenue from selling that additional unit, but because the demand curve slopes down he will have to charge a lower price not only on that extra unit but also on all the other units sold.[27] Thus, the marginal revenue curve always lies below the demand curve because the marginal revenue that the monopolist makes is less than the price at which he sells. The monopolist will expand output to the point

---

[26] To prevent Figure 2.3 from becoming too cluttered, the average cost curve has been omitted.

[27] This assumes that the monopolist is unable to price discriminate between consumers and so has to charge the same price to all consumers. We return to the issue of price discrimination in Chapter 6.

where marginal revenue is equal to marginal cost.[28] The intuition is clear. The cost of producing one more unit is the marginal cost. The benefit to the monopolist of selling that extra unit is the marginal revenue. In equilibrium, these will be equal. Hence in Figure 2.3 the monopolist will sell $Q_m$ units at $P_m$.

Table 2.1 contains a numerical example to illustrate the relationship between marginal revenue, marginal cost and the maximum level of profits. In this example we assume that a monopolist is deciding whether to increase his sales above the current level of 20, each of which is sold at a price of 60 per unit. His constant per unit cost (and hence marginal cost) is 30. His current revenue is 1,200 (20 units at a price of 60 each) and his profit is 600 (revenue of 1,200 less costs of 600 from selling 20 units each costing 30 to produce). Should he increase his sales? Under Scenario A (see table) the answer is yes. In this scenario price falls to 59 when he increases his sales by one unit to 21. Revenue rises to 1,239 and profits to 609. Note that revenue increased by 39 (from 1,200 to 1,239) and so since marginal cost is only 30, it is profitable to increase sales. Now consider Scenario B. Here price falls to 58 when he increases sales to 21. Revenue rises from 1,200 to 1,218, but profits fall from 600 to 588, so it is not a profitable sales increase. Note that in this scenario revenue rises by less than costs (marginal revenue of 18 versus marginal cost of 30) and so the sales increase is not profitable.

## Table 2.1 Numerical example of the monopolist's output decision

|  | Sales | Price | Revenue | Marginal revenue | Marginal cost | Profit |
|---|---|---|---|---|---|---|
|  | 20 | 60 | 1,200 |  | 30 | 600 |
| Scenario A | 21 | 59 | 1,239 | 39 | 30 | 609 |
| Scenario B | 21 | 58 | 1,218 | 18 | 30 | 588 |

Figure 2.3 shows that the monopolist will sell less than would be sold **2–015** under perfect competition, and the price will be higher. It is for this reason that economists talk about a lack of effective competition being associated with a restriction in output. The increase in price and reduction in output mean that the pricing and output decisions of a monopolist fail to maximise social welfare and thus allow scope for a regulator to improve matters. The shaded area in Figure 2.3 (abcd) represents the *deadweight social welfare loss* from monopoly. This is the cost to society of a market not operating

---

[28] This is actually true of virtually all firms, whether the firm operates in a perfectly competitive market, is a monopolist or forms part of an oligopolistic market (as long as they are not colluding). For a firm in perfect competition, the price is the same as its marginal revenue because the market price does not vary as the firm varies its output (in stark contrast to the situation facing a monopolist).

efficiently. It is the area under the demand curve, but above the marginal cost curve, between $Q_m$ and $Q_c$. Between $Q_m$ and $Q_c$ the marginal cost of production is less than the value that consumers put on that production (as shown by the demand curve). There would therefore be a social gain from more production since the costs involved in producing that additional output would be less than consumers' valuation of that production. Hence, social welfare can be improved by lowering the price and raising the output of the monopolised good. Monopoly leads to allocative inefficiency because there is a difference between the marginal cost of production and the valuation of the marginal consumer.[29]

Social welfare is traditionally measured as being made up of two parts: consumer surplus and producer surplus. Consumer surplus is the area under the demand curve but above the price. It represents the sum of how much each unit sold is valued by consumers above its price. The area $P_m$abd$P_c$ in Figure 2.3 is the consumer surplus loss due to the exercise of monopoly. Of this, the area $P_m$ad$P_c$ is a transfer from consumers to the monopolist, whilst the area adb is the part of the deadweight social welfare loss that is lost by consumers. The remainder of the shaded area is made up of producer surplus. This is defined as the area above the marginal cost curve but below the price (i.e. the excess of what the extra goods could be sold for above the cost of producing them).

### *Summary of discussion to date*

**2-016** We have argued at para.2–008 that any sensible definition of "effective competition" must be related to market outcomes rather than just the particular form that competition takes. In order to examine the welfare implications associated with the outcomes of different models of competition, the concepts of allocative and productive efficiency, consumer welfare, producer welfare and the deadweight welfare loss from monopoly have been introduced. We explained why perfect competition leads to allocative and productive efficiency and why monopoly leads to allocative inefficiency. Monopoly may also encourage productive inefficiency. Under perfect competition firms must be productively efficient because otherwise they will make losses. Under monopoly a firm can still make profits even if it is somewhat productively inefficient. As Hicks famously wrote, "[t]he best of all monopoly profits is a quiet life". Note that to the extent that marginal costs are inefficiently high, prices will be even higher under a productively inefficient monopolist than with a productively efficient monopolist. The implication of this discussion is that regulatory

---

[29] There are a number of old studies that attempted to measure the size of the deadweight loss caused by monopolies. The estimates varied between 0.1 per cent of gross national product (Harberger, 1954) and 4 per cent to 13 per cent of gross national product (Cowling and Mueller, 1978) although Littlechild (1981) argued persuasively that methodological mistakes make the Cowling and Mueller estimates too high.

interference can potentially improve social welfare in the presence of a monopoly by lowering price and raising output.

## WHAT IS THE WELFARE STANDARD FOR EC COMPETITION LAW?[30]

In order to have a good understanding of what effective competition **2–017** entails, it is necessary to have some understanding of why it matters. That is, it is necessary to have some idea of what we are trying to maximise by the application of competition law. For an economist, this comes down to the question: what is the welfare standard that we are seeking to maximise? So far we have referred to consumer surplus, producer surplus and social welfare (the sum of consumer and producer surplus) without discussing which of these is the most important.[31]

Economists have traditionally focused on social welfare.[32] They do not make a value judgement between consumers and producers and so treat €1 of gain to either group as being of equal value. If pushed, many economists will point out that when companies are owned by shareholders, many of whom are pension funds, then the distinction between consumer surplus and producer surplus is much less clear cut than it at first seems. However, it is clear that EC competition law does not treat consumer welfare and producer welfare as being of equal importance. Consumer welfare is valued above producer welfare, although this is nowhere made explicit in EC law. For instance, Article 81(3) specifically requires that consumers receive a "fair share" of any efficiency benefits. This implies that mere producer surplus as a result of increases in efficiency is not enough. Neelie Kroes, the European Commissioner for Competition Policy, has made clear that it is consumer welfare that is at the heart of the European Commission's competition policy. For instance, in a speech at the European Competition Day in Paris in November 2008, she said that:

> "Competition works and competition policy makes it work better. That is what it is all about—making markets work better for consumers."

And:

---

[30] Those readers that already accept that the appropriate welfare standard used in European competition law is that of consumer welfare can skip this section.
[31] Note that economists use the words "surplus" and "welfare" synonymously in this context.
[32] Bork (1978) is a strong advocate of the social welfare criterion.

> "One of the best things about being Competition Commissioner is knowing that each and every day the competition rules do something for consumers in Europe."[33, 34]

Referring back to Figure 2.3, this concern with consumer welfare rather than producer welfare means that EC competition law is principally concerned not with the deadweight social welfare cost of monopoly (the shaded area abcd), but instead with the reduction in consumer surplus represented by $P_m abd P_c$. This area can be broken down into two parts: the area $P_m ad P_c$ and the area abd. The area $P_m ad P_c$ represents the additional profits that the monopolist makes from selling $Q_m$ units at the monopoly price $P_m$ rather than at the perfectly competitive price $P_c$. It also represents the additional sum that consumers pay to buy $Q_m$ units at $P_m$ rather than $P_c$. As such it is a pure transfer from consumers to the monopolist. The area abd is part of the deadweight cost of monopoly.

## Does it matter what the standard is?

**2–018** It is reasonable to wonder when the exact welfare standard adopted matters and when it does not matter. We discuss this below.

The first point to note from Figure 2.3 is that maximising consumer welfare and maximising social welfare give the same result.[35] As already discussed, social welfare is maximised when price is equal to marginal cost. At this point (point b in Figure 2.3) the deadweight loss is zero. However, this is also the point at which consumer welfare (i.e. the area below the demand curve but above price) is maximised. At first sight, this is not obvious. One might be tempted to ask, if consumer surplus is all that matters, why could a regulator not improve matters even more by insisting on price below marginal cost since this would involve even more consumer surplus? On the basis of Figure 2.3 this seems a reasonable point to make. However, taking a wider perspective shows that this is not so. If a regulator insisted on a price below marginal cost then, since price and marginal cost

---

[33] Keynote speech at the European Competition Day in Paris, November 18, 2008.

[34] It is interesting to note that US policy is broadly similar to that under EC competition law. Under the 1997 Merger Guidelines, efficiencies must be great enough to entirely reverse any potential harm to consumers from a loss of competition. The Department of Justice states that the antitrust laws "prohibit business practices that unreasonably deprive consumers of the benefits of competition" and that "[a]ntitrust laws protect competition. Free and open competition benefits consumers" ("Antitrust enforcement and the consumer", US Department of Justice). The US Federal Trade Commission states that "[t]he FTC's competition mission is to enforce the rules of the competitive marketplace—the antitrust laws. These laws promote vigorous competition and protect consumers". Furthermore, in its publication "The FTC at 100: into our second century" (January 2009), the FTC states that "[t]here appears to be widespread understanding that the FTC's current mission focuses on consumers and that the improvement of consumer welfare is the proper objective of the agency's competition and consumer protection work."

[35] Technically, this statement requires that there be no price discrimination between different consumers.

would again have diverged, this would involve allocative inefficiency: the marginal cost of production would be above the valuation of the marginal consumer. In this case consumer welfare would be reduced because the resources used to produce the extra output would be valued more than the extra output itself. The extra resources would create more consumer welfare by being put to use elsewhere in producing goods that consumers value more highly than the resources themselves.

In addition to this allocative efficiency argument, there are two more reasons why consumer welfare, as well as social welfare, is maximised when price is equal to marginal cost. First, if the industry is highly competitive with firms making no excess profits, then insisting on firms producing more goods even though they can only sell them for less than the marginal cost of production will cause firms to make losses and potentially exit the market with consequent long-term detrimental effects for consumers. Secondly, we do not believe that a regulator should be able to insist that a firm sells goods at less than the marginal cost of production. Indeed, as we discuss in Chapter 6, persistent pricing below marginal cost is often thought of as representing predatory behaviour.

This discussion has so far taken place within a static environment in **2–019** which demand and cost conditions are assumed to be fixed. One place where policy prescriptions may differ depending on the welfare standard adopted is the area of mergers. Many mergers lead to cost reductions and so potentially may increase productive efficiency. However, such mergers may also lead to price increases to consumers if the merger reduces the degree of competition in the market. If only consumer welfare matters, then a merger that raises prices to consumers will not be allowed by regulators even if it also has cost efficiency benefits. If producer welfare matters as well (i.e. the standard is social welfare), then such a merger might be allowed depending on the size of the productive efficiency benefits. We discuss the role of efficiencies in assessing mergers in Chapter 7 and Chapter 8, but note here that in general the so-called *efficiency defence* for mergers has generally not found favour in EC competition law.[36]

There is a potential danger with the consumer welfare standard if it is not understood properly. If regulators treat the pursuit of consumer welfare in an entirely static framework, then this can lead to significantly sub-optimal outcomes. In particular, problems can arise when the pursuit of consumer welfare leads to an attitude or belief that any profits earned by firms must be at the cost of consumer welfare. Such an attitude might be reasonable in a static framework such as that outlined above, but is not reasonable in a dynamic framework in which firms invest and innovate to the ultimate

---

[36] It should be noted that the term "efficiency defence" is often used loosely. Formally, it refers to the idea that even though a merger might allow prices to rise, the harm to consumers would be outweighed by efficiency benefits enjoyed by producers. In Europe the term is usually used to refer to the argument that efficiencies arising from the merger will lead to prices falling post-merger.

benefit of consumers. A regulatory focus on short-run consumer welfare can be damaging to the incentives that firms face to invest. Firms invest and innovate because they expect to be able to earn profits from doing so. When investments are risky, the return to successful investments must compensate firms for the risk taken. If regulators treat the profitability of firms with too much suspicion, they may be tempted to remove the rewards to risky investment by forcing firms that have successfully taken risks to lower prices. If regulators do this consistently, firms will be deterred from investing or innovating. In short, consumer welfare needs to be maximised within a dynamic, not static, framework.

A different issue to the relative importance of consumer and producer welfare is the relative importance of allocative efficiency and productive efficiency. Allocative efficiency more directly benefits consumers (since it implies that prices are at marginal costs, not higher), but we would expect productive efficiency to also benefit consumers. Reductions in marginal cost feed through into reductions in price even under monopoly.[37] However, despite the fact that the welfare losses arising from productive inefficiency are potentially of equal magnitude to those resulting from allocative inefficiency, most competition inquiries are more concerned with allocative efficiency.[38] The economic goal of EC competition law appears to be concerned with improving allocative efficiency in ways that do not impair productive efficiency so greatly as to produce no increase (or even a net reduction) in total consumer welfare. Given that competition law enforcement should not, in general, be concerned with detailed micro-regulation of industries, this is a reasonable policy objective. Direct regulation of a firm's efficiency is likely to be fraught with difficulty and, given the informational constraints under which regulators usually work, is likely to be prone to substantial errors.

So the conclusion of this section is that the welfare standard for EC competition law is consumer welfare, not social welfare, but that in most cases the distinction is not important because maximising consumer welfare and maximising social welfare require the same outcomes. However, there are times when it does matter (for instance, in some mergers), and on these occasions the focus is on consumer welfare.

---

[37] Those who are unconvinced by this statement should look at Figure 2.3 and consider what would happen if the marginal cost curve shifted down. It would intersect the marginal revenue curve lower down, which implies that output would be greater, which implies that price would be lower.

[38] Where the market demand curve is inelastic (i.e. changes in price have little effect on demand), small movements in price away from marginal cost have relatively little effect on allocative efficiency. In this case, productive efficiency losses could easily outweigh allocative efficiency losses.

# OLIGOPOLY MODELS

Neither the paradigm of perfect competition nor that of monopoly provide **2–020**
adequate descriptions of competition in most industries. While the models
of perfect competition and monopoly provide a good basis for understanding the basic economic principles, particularly in illustrating the
detrimental welfare consequences of monopoly, neither model provides a
solid framework on which to base policy prescriptions. These models
ignore the interaction between firms and how this interaction may affect
the outcomes of the competitive process. In the model of perfect competition, each firm is so small that it can put as much or as little for sale on the
market without affecting the market price. For this reason, a firm in a
perfectly competitive market has no reason to worry about what other firms
will do when it makes its own plans. For example, a farmer selling his
product in an international market does not consider whether his output
will affect the market price but instead takes the market price as a given
that he cannot affect. At the other extreme, the monopolist can directly set
the market price as it has no rivals to worry about.

But in most markets, firms do need to take into account the commercial
decisions of rivals when formulating their own commercial strategy. In
most markets, firms recognise that changes in their own plans—e.g. prices,
planned production and additions to capacity—may affect the decisions of
other firms in the industry and will take this into account when making
commercial decisions.[39] When addressing what constitutes effective competition, these interactions between firms must be taken into account. This
requires one to examine more realistic models of competition: models of
oligopolistic behaviour. It is the outcomes produced by these models which
should underpin our understanding of effective competition.

With advances in game theory, economic models of competition have
become much more sophisticated and have started to take explicit account
of the interactions between competing firms. Until the 1970s, the examination of oligopoly received little attention, reflecting the lack of analytical
tools available in this area. But since that time, a new branch of economics—
non-co-operative game theory—has grown up which directly addresses the
strategic interactions between firms.[40] Non-co-operative game theory sees
competition between firms as each firm trying to do the best it can subject
to the actions of its competitors. A key concept in this analysis is that of the
Nash non-co-operative equilibrium.[41] An equilibrium is a Nash non-co-
operative equilibrium when, given the behaviour of all other firms in the

---

[39] As the discussion below makes clear, the fact that a firm recognises that its actions may also
affect the behaviour of other firms in the industry does not imply that all firms will
therefore co-ordinate their behaviour.
[40] The use of the word "new" is not strictly correct since a seminal book on game theory was
written in the 1940s (von Neumann and Morgenstern, 1944).
[41] Nash (1951).

market, no firm wishes to change its behaviour (i.e. each firm maximises profit given the behaviour of all the other firms).

**2–021**    The concept of a non-co-operative Nash equilibrium can be illustrated by reference to the following game, commonly known as the Prisoners' Dilemma.[42] There are two firms, A and B, who must each decide whether to charge a high price or to charge a low price. There are therefore four possible outcomes: they could both charge high prices, both charge low prices, or one or other could charge a low price whilst the other charges a high price. The numbers in each box in Figure 2.4 denote the profits resulting from the outcome of the decisions of the two firms. The first number in each box shows the profits firm A makes whilst the second number shows the profits firm B makes. For example, if both firms choose a low price, each firm makes profits of 4 (see bottom right quadrant).

**Figure 2.4 Illustrating a Nash equilibrium**[43]

|  |  | **Firm B** | |
|  |  | **High** | **Low** |
| **Firm A** | **High** | 10, 10 | 0, 30 |
|  | **Low** | 30, 0 | 4, 4 |

**2–022** Considering the various outcomes, both firms would prefer an outcome in which both charged a high price to that in which they both charged a low price. In this case, both firms would earn profits of 10 (top left quadrant). But if firm A chooses a high price, what is the best action that firm B can take? With firm A choosing a high price, if firm B also chooses a high price it earns profits of 10 (top left). But if firm B chooses a low price, it earns profits of 30 as a result of undercutting firm A (top right). Hence, given that firm A chooses a high price, firm B's best strategy is to charge a low price.

But if firm B charges a low price, what is the best course of action for firm A? With firm B charging a low price, if firm A charges a high price, it earns zero profits (top right) but if it charges a low price, firm A earns

---

[42]    This game was first told in the context of two prisoners who need to make choices as to whether to confess to a crime or to remain silent. Here, the game is told in the context of two rival firms.

[43]    The numbers in this example are illustrative only and do not reflect any real-world examples.

profits of 4 (bottom right quadrant). Hence, firm A will charge a low price if firm B charges a low price. This outcome (the shaded area) represents a Nash equilibrium: the best firm A can do if firm B charges a low price is also to choose a low price and vice versa. In this example, it is also the only Nash equilibrium. In each of the other three quadrants, at least one of the firms wishes to change its behaviour given the behaviour of the other firm. So in the top left quadrant both firms wish to change their behaviour, in the bottom left Firm B wants to change and in the top right Firm A wants to change.

This simple model shows that while both firms prefer a situation in which both firms charge a high price, the incentive to charge a low price while the rival firm charges a high price results in both firms charging a low price.[44]

Modelling the behaviour of firms in markets where the firms recognise that their commercial actions affect the decisions taken by rival firms requires the identification of plausible views of the way in which firms compete. The following provides a discussion of five economic models of oligopoly. These are the Cournot model, the Bertrand model, monopolistic competition, leader-follower models and cartels.[45]

## Cournot model of oligopoly

Consider an industry with just two firms.[46] The Cournot model of oligo- **2–023** poly assumes that each firm competes by setting their output so as to maximise profits given the output of the other firm. It is assumed that there is only one period (i.e. firms set their quantities only once) and that the competitive outcome is a non-co-operative Nash equilibrium. This model is named after the French mathematician Augustin Cournot.[47] What does the outcome of Cournot competition look like?

Consider the decision-making process of firm 1. For each amount of output produced by firm 2, there is a unique (by assumption) output that maximises firm 1's profits. This is shown by the line $R_1$ (called a reaction function) in Figure 2.5. For each level of output of firm 1, the reaction function for firm 2 indicates the level of output which will maximise firm 2's profits. This is shown by line $R_2$ in Figure 2.5. Along $R_1$, firm 1 is choosing its level of output to maximise profits given the output of firm 2. Similarly, all along $R_2$, firm 2 is doing the same given the output of firm 1. Where $R_1$ and $R_2$ meet is the non-co-operative Nash equilibrium: both

---

[44] This result should by itself be enough to dispel the assumption that the only conceivable outcome in oligopolistic markets is a collusive one.

[45] This discussion can only seek to provide an introduction to oligopoly models. For a more complete analysis, the interested reader is referred to Tirole (1988) or Carlton and Perloff (2004) and the references contained therein.

[46] The following discussion applies equally if there were N firms in the industry.

[47] Cournot (1838).

firms are maximising profit given the output of the other firm. This is the Cournot equilibrium (marked E in the figure).

### Figure 2.5 The outcome of Cournot competition

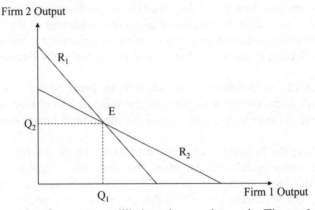

**2–024** The price at the Cournot equilibrium is not shown in Figure 2.5, but is determined by the industry demand curve given the combined output of the two firms (i.e. $Q_1 + Q_2$). From our earlier discussion, it should be clear that the greater is the combined output of the firms, the lower is the price and so the higher is consumer welfare. Price at the Cournot equilibrium will be lower than the monopoly price, but higher than the price under perfect competition, thus indicating that consumer welfare will be higher than under monopoly but less than under perfect competition. As the number of firms increases in the Cournot model, the market price decreases, total output increases and total industry profits fall. Thus, for instance, in the Cournot model price in a given market will be lower and output higher when there are 10 firms rather than five. As the number of firms becomes very large, the Cournot equilibrium comes close to the perfect competition equilibrium.

However, a key aspect of the Cournot equilibrium is that there is neither allocative efficiency nor productive efficiency. There is not allocative efficiency because price is higher than marginal cost (i.e. higher than the perfect competition price). There is not productive efficiency because total industry costs for the given total output are not minimised.[48] As the number of firms increases and the equilibrium moves closer to the perfect competition equilibrium, the deviations away from allocative and productive efficiency decline.

An issue that we have not so far covered is what determines the number of firms in the industry in the Cournot model? The standard Cournot

---

[48] This is true except in the unlikely case that all firms have exactly the same cost structure and sell exactly the same amount. Where cost structures differ, firms with lower marginal costs sell more than firms with higher marginal costs. However, in equilibrium marginal costs are not equal across firms and so there is productive inefficiency.

model treats the number of firms as being exogenously given. However, this is unsatisfactory for practical purposes. In reality, there are two main possibilities. One is that there are barriers to entry that stop other firms entering the market, even if the incumbent firms are making excess profits. The other is that there is free entry into the market, in which case the number of firms will be determined by how many firms can compete in the market before profits become negative. Since price exceeds marginal cost in the Cournot model, profits will only be driven down to zero if there are fixed costs.[49] The number of firms is correspondingly determined by the level of fixed costs. The higher fixed costs are, the further above marginal costs price must be in order to allow firms to recover their total costs and so the number of firms in the market must be lower.

---

## BOX 2.2: NUMERICAL EXAMPLE OF THE IMPORTANCE OF FIXED COSTS IN DETERMINING THE NUMBER OF FIRMS UNDER FREE ENTRY IN THE COURNOT MODEL

Assume the demand curve facing an industry is $Q = 50 - P/2$ where $Q$ is industry sales and $P$ is price. Further, assume that each firm in the industry has a constant marginal cost of 10 and a fixed cost of F. Further, assume that there is free entry into the industry and that firms will enter if they expect to earn positive profits after entering. Table 2.2 shows how the number of firms in the industry varies depending on the size of F. If the fixed cost per firm of entry is 450, then the market can sustain only two firms. If another firm enters, it will lead to each firm making losses of 197. If the fixed cost per firm is only 112, then the market can sustain five firms but not six. If the fixed cost is 33, the market can sustain 10 firms, but not 11.

**Table 2.2 Relation between fixed costs and number of firms**

| Fixed Cost | Number of Firms | Sales per firm | Industry Sales | Price | Profit per Firm |
|---|---|---|---|---|---|
| 450 | 2 | 15.0 | 30.0 | 40.0 | 0 |
| 450 | 3 | 11.3 | 33.8 | 32.5 | −197 |
| 112 | 5 | 7.5 | 37.5 | 25.0 | 0 |
| 112 | 6 | 6.4 | 38.6 | 22.9 | −29 |
| 33 | 10 | 4.1 | 40.9 | 18.2 | 0 |
| 33 | 11 | 3.8 | 41.3 | 17.5 | −5 |

---

[49] More properly, it is *sunk* costs that are required, not just *fixed* costs. Sunk costs are costs that are not recoverable when a firm exits the market, such as advertising expenditure. Fixed costs are costs that are recoverable, such as the costs of buying a truck which can be sold when a firm exits. We return to this issue in Chapter 3 in our discussion of barriers to entry.

**2–026**

> Table 2.2 also illustrates a number of other characteristics of the Cournot equilibrium. It shows that as the number of firms rises, sales per firm fall but total industry sales rise and hence price falls.

An important implication that arises from this discussion has to do with the relationship between allocative efficiency and effective competition. Although we have not so far proposed a definition of "effective competition", an industry in which all firms are efficient and yet make zero profits ought to be considered subject to effective competition.[50] In this case, it is possible for an industry to be effectively competitive, and yet to have prices above marginal cost and hence to have allocative inefficiency. This has two further, very important, corollaries. First, the definition of "effective competition" cannot be that prices are at short-run marginal cost. Secondly, oligopolies can be subject to effective competition.

## Bertrand model of oligopoly

**2–027** The Cournot model assumes that each firm competes by choosing its output to maximise its profits given the output of all other firms in the market. An alternative assumption is to assume that firms compete by setting their prices, not their quantities.[51] Suppose that there are just two firms in an industry and that they compete by each setting their price so as to maximise their profits given the price set by the other firm. Further, assume that the products are homogeneous, that there is only one period (i.e. firms set their prices only once), that marginal costs are the same for both firms and are constant, that there are no fixed costs and that the outcome of competition is a non-co-operative Nash equilibrium. This model is called the Bertrand model after the French economist Joseph Bertrand.[52]

Surprisingly, it turns out that the outcome of competition under Bertrand competition is similar to that under perfect competition. The intuition is straightforward. For any price set by firm 2, firm 1 can maximise profits by setting a price slightly lower and supplying the whole market (leaving firm 2 with zero demand). The situation is the same for firm 2: it has an incentive to just undercut the price set by firm 1. This will only not be true when one firm sets price at marginal cost, since then it does not pay to undercut this price (and make losses). So both firms set price at marginal cost and there is allocative efficiency. This result holds true whether there are two firms or 100 firms.

One must be suspicious of a model that leads to such hugely different outcomes between monopoly and duopoly, but no further differences in

---

[50] After all, what grounds would there be for intervention in such an industry?
[51] The underlying difference between these two assumptions is discussed below.
[52] Bertrand (1883).

outcome thereafter. This result appears to be clearly at odds with reality and so suggests that the model is omitting some important elements of competition. Surely more firms in a market will make the market more competitive, particularly when there are small numbers of players? There are two important problems with the simple Bertrand model.

First, it does not consider the implications of capacity constraints. The   **2–028** assumption is that every firm in the market is able to supply the whole market. However, this is unlikely to be true in most cases, particularly in situations where there are more than two firms. If one firm undercuts the other, it probably will not be able to supply the whole market, so the other firm will continue to make some sales. This can radically alter the outcome of competition. The Cournot model assumes that firms set quantities, not prices. Although this seems a slightly odd assumption (surely firms set prices?), it looks more sensible if Cournot competition is interpreted as firms first choosing capacity and then setting prices subject to their capacity constraints.[53] Suppose there are two firms, two time periods and each chooses its capacity in Period 1 based on its expectations about the other's capacity level. This is essentially the Cournot quantity-setting model that was discussed earlier. In Period 2 the firms simultaneously and independently determine their prices so as to be able to sell all of their respective production. Given the capacity constraints created in Period 1, the equilibrium in Period 2 will not be at the price that would be the result of the homogeneous Bertrand model without capacity constraints.[54] Instead, prices will be higher.[55]

Secondly, the simple Bertrand model assumes that products are homogeneous. However, products in most industries are differentiated from one another in some way (e.g. cars, clothes, houses, etc.). This differentiation may be due to physical differences in products, or due to differences in brand perception due to advertising, differences in location or due to any number of other reasons. Introducing product differentiation changes the model substantially, giving rise to what is known as *monopolistic competition*.

---

[53]   It is worth noting that whether competition is better described as quantity competition or price competition depends largely on which variable (output or price) is most flexible. When prices are fixed, firms will clear the market by changing the amount they supply until supply and demand are in equilibrium. When quantities are fixed, firms will change prices until supply and demand are in equilibrium.

[54]   Kreps and Scheinkman (1983) and Davidson and Deneckere (1986) show that under some conditions the Bertrand solution with capacity constraints is the same as the Cournot solution. However, they will not always be the same. Edgeworth (1897) showed that it is possible that there is no stable solution.

[55]   This is not to deny that there may be times when real-world markets do approximate quite closely to the Bertrand model. Telecommunications firms discovered that the market for bandwidth was one such market. Many European telecommunications firms installed very high capacity cables in the late 1990s in the expectation that the demand for bandwidth would increase substantially. Unfortunately for them, the anticipated increased demand did not transpire, there was widespread excess capacity and prices fell close to marginal cost. Given that marginal costs are very low relative to sunk cost in this business, this was a commercial disaster for the telecommunications firms.

## Monopolistic competition

2-029 Firms in monopolistic competition sell differentiated products and so each firm has a "monopoly" over the particular type of product that it sells. If products are differentiated, then if one firm undercuts the other firms in the market, the higher priced firms do not lose all of their sales because some consumers will continue to prefer their products to the lower priced product despite the now higher relative price. For instance, if one jeans manufacturer lowered its prices, then some consumers would switch from other brands of jeans to the lower priced brand, but many consumers would continue to buy the other brands. The result is that in oligopolies characterised by monopolistic competition, prices are not driven down to marginal cost (unlike in the standard Bertrand model). The monopolistic competition model is a good description of many real world markets in which relatively few firms sell differentiated products.

As argued above when discussing the Cournot model, the fact that prices are above marginal cost does not necessarily mean that there is not effective competition. If there are no barriers to entry, each firm in monopolistic competition makes zero economic profits because positive economic profits would lead to new entry, thus driving profits back towards zero. Figure 2.6 illustrates the equilibrium for a firm in a market characterised by monopolistic competition in which it makes zero economic profits.

### Figure 2.6 Monopolistic competition

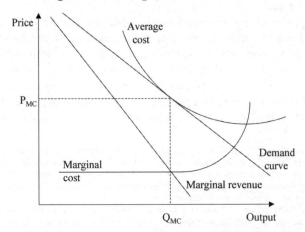

2-030 $Q_{MC}$ and $P_{MC}$ in Figure 2.6 are the sales and price respectively of a firm in monopolistic competition. The demand curve facing the firm is downward sloping, unlike in perfect competition, because the firm sells a differentiated product. As a result, the marginal revenue curve of the firm is downward sloping. The firm maximises profits at the point at which the marginal cost curve cuts the marginal revenue curve ($Q_{MC}$). The assumption of free entry implies that profits are zero and so at this point the average cost curve just touches the demand curve, so price is equal to average cost and the firm makes zero profits.

It is worth considering why the Cournot model and the monopolistic competition model both lead to prices above marginal cost. In perfect competition price is equal to marginal cost because a firm's output decision has no effect on the price that it sells its product for. This is not true in oligopoly models. In the Cournot model the output of each firm directly affects the market price because there are only a few firms in the market. This means that each firm's marginal revenue is less than the price. Since firms equate marginal revenue and marginal cost, this means that marginal cost is also less than the price. In monopolistic competition, each firm faces a downward sloping demand curve because its product is differentiated from the other products. This again implies that each firm's output directly affects the price at which it sells, so again marginal revenue is less than price and so price is above marginal cost. An important implication of this is that competition can be effective even when firms have some control over the price at which they sell their goods. Here, as noted at para.2–007, a definition of "effective competition" based on all firms being price-takers (i.e. having no control over price), rather than price-setters (i.e. having some control over the price they set), is not adequate for policy purposes.

## Leader-follower models

In this section we briefly discuss two models of competition in which one **2–031** firm acts as a leader and the other firms follow. These are the dominant firm model and the Stackelberg model.[56] We start with the dominant firm model.[57] This model assumes that there is one large firm and a large number of small "price-taking" firms. A firm that is a price-taker accepts the market price as given and sets its output accordingly. The small firms are usually referred to as the competitive fringe. In the dominant firm model the dominant firm sets the price and then the competitive fringe chooses its output level. The higher the price set by the dominant firm, the more the competitive fringe is willing to produce because the supply curve for the competitive fringe is assumed to be upward sloping. This is shown in Figure 2.7. Unlike for the monopolist, the dominant firm's demand curve is not the same as the market demand curve. Instead it is the market demand curve less the supply from the competitive fringe. This is referred to as the residual demand curve as it is the residual of the market demand curve after the fringe firms have supplied what they want to supply. The dominant firm will set its price in the same way as a monopolist does, but based on its residual demand curve and not the market demand curve. The residual demand curve has a kink at the lowest price at which the fringe will

---

[56]   The term "dominant firm" here is used in the economic sense and not the legal sense.
[57]   The origin of this model is attributed to Forchheimer (1908).

supply any output. If the price is below the level at which the fringe will supply, then the residual demand curve is the same as the market demand curve. An assumption of the model is that the fringe firms are less cost efficient than the dominant firm and so there is a price below which the fringe firms will not supply any output but the dominant firm will.

Figure 2.7 shows that the dominant firm will price at $P^D$ and sell $Q^D$. This is where the marginal revenue curve derived from the residual demand curve (MR(R) in Figure 2.7) crosses the marginal cost curve of the dominant firm. This is at $Q^D$. The price on the residual demand curve at $Q^D$ is $P^D$. The competitive fringe will supply the difference between total demand at $P^D$, which is $Q^T$, and $Q^D$. Under the dominant firm model the market price is lower than under monopoly and output is correspondingly higher. However, it should be noted that the market price is still above marginal cost and so the dominant firm still has some power over price.

## Figure 2.7 Dominant firm model

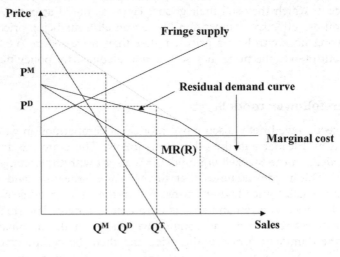

**2–032**  It is important to note the role played by the supply of the competitive fringe. If the supply curve of the competitive fringe was steeper (i.e. the amount the fringe was prepared to supply at each price was lower), then the dominant firm would price above the level shown in Figure 2.7. Equally, if the fringe supply curve was flatter, it would price lower as a flatter fringe supply curve indicates that the fringe is willing to supply more output at each price. So the greater the amount that the fringe is willing to supply at a given price, the less power the dominant firm has over price.

An alternative leader-follower model is the Stackelberg leadership model.[58] This is similar to the dominant firm model in having a leader, but different in that the competitive fringe is replaced by one, or a few, firms. In

---

[58]  Stackelberg (1934).

the Stackelberg leadership model the leader sets its output and then the other firm (firms) chooses how much to sell (i.e. the fringe competes in quantities). The equilibrium with only two firms (i.e. the leader and one follower) is shown in Figure 2.8. This is very similar to Figure 2.5 above illustrating the Cournot solution. Indeed point E in this figure is the Cournot solution. In the Stackelberg model the leader knows that the followers will set their quantity so as to maximise their profits given the output of the leader. The leader therefore knows that the followers will set their output on the basis of their reaction curves. So the leader's problem is to maximise his profits subject to the reaction curves of the followers. In the two-firm case the solution is illustrated below. This shows that in the Stackelberg model the followers will sell less output than in the Cournot solution whilst the leader will sell more.

## Figure 2.8 Stackelberg solution

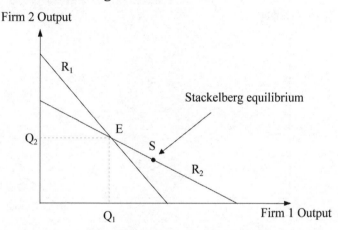

There is an important difference here between the Stackelberg model and **2–033** the dominant firm model. In the dominant firm model the competitive fringe act as price takers and so set marginal cost equal to price. In the Stackelberg leadership model the followers choose their output so as to maximise their profits given the output of the leader. They face a downward sloping residual demand curve and so they do not set price equal to marginal cost. The result is that price will be higher and output lower in the Stackelberg leadership model than in the dominant firm model. However, as the number of followers increases in the Stackelberg leadership model, price moves down towards the price in the dominant firm model and becomes equal to it as the number of followers becomes very large.[59] For both models, as the number of firms becomes large, the solution converges to the perfect competition outcome.

---

[59] Formally, as the number of followers, n, tends to infinity, the price tends to the dominant firm model price.

**Cartel behaviour**

**2–034** Two of the three models of oligopolistic competition discussed above illustrate that prices above marginal cost are not necessarily inconsistent with firms competing vigorously with one another. However, this is not to suggest that all outcomes in oligopolistic markets are the result of effective competition. For example, consider a case in which market outcomes clearly do not reflect effective competition: a cartel.

Cartels are anti-competitive. Assuming they are successful, they raise prices and reduce output to anti-competitive levels. Suppose that the two Cournot duopolists depicted in Figure 2.5 decided to collude. What would the result be? The answer is that the new equilibrium would be at some point such as C in Figure 2.9.

**Figure 2.9 The cartel solution**

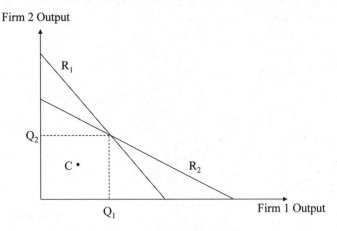

**2–035** At C both firms are selling fewer units than in the Cournot equilibrium ($Q_1$, $Q_2$), but because the price is correspondingly higher, both are making more profits than at the Cournot equilibrium. Since output has fallen, consumers must be worse off at C than at the Cournot equilibrium. Unlike the Cournot equilibrium, the cartel solution is not determinate. There is a wide range of output levels that allow the firms to earn more profits than at the Cournot equilibrium. The ultimate aim of a cartel is to mimic the monopoly solution as this maximises the combined profits of the firms, but most cartels are not this successful. So beyond knowing that price will be higher and output lower than under Cournot, we cannot predict precisely what the market price and output will be under the cartel.

The Cournot solution is determinate because it is defined by the inter-action of the two firms' reaction functions. However, point C does not lie on the reaction function of either firm and hence does not represent the (short-run) best outcome for either firm. Given the output of each firm, the other firm could raise their profits by moving onto their reaction curve.

Hence, point C does not represent a short-run Nash equilibrium[60] since in the short run, both firms have an incentive to change their output. This has an important implication for the stability of a cartel as each firm participating in the cartel has an incentive to deviate.

The reason the firms choose not to increase their output (or to "cheat") is that they will earn higher profits at point C as long as other firms also do not increase their output (or also do not "cheat"). However, each faces an incentive to cheat because, if the other firms do not cheat, they earn more profits by cheating. Also, if other firms do cheat, then each firm earns more profits by cheating. This "Prisoners' Dilemma" is the reason why cartels can often be unstable and short-lived. Numerous other factors are relevant to how stable a cartel is likely to be, such as how likely it is that the other firms would notice a firm deviating from the cartel agreement, how long it would take them to notice, how they would then "punish" the deviating firm and so on. We discuss the economics of cartels in more detail in Chapter 5.

# DYNAMIC CONSIDERATIONS

The models of competition discussed above are essentially static in the sense that the range of products available and the methods of producing those products are taken as given. In consequence, these models omit a number of dynamic issues relating to innovation and ignore the possibility that the range of available products and production processes may well change. Such changes have important consequences for the nature of competition. **2–036**

Static models focus on prices and quantities and in particular tend to focus on price competition between firms *given* current costs and current product offerings. This may be inappropriate in a dynamic environment. In many dynamic competitive environments firms compete not only on prices, but also on innovation. This innovation can take the form of product innovation or cost innovation. For instance, firms can compete not by pricing a given product lower than their rivals, but by carrying out research and development and so being able to sell a product that no other firm supplies (for instance, because it is patented). Alternatively, firms may not take costs as given but may instead compete through cost innovations to be the lowest cost provider of a product. Furthermore, firms may react to the commercial actions of rivals by expanding capacity and/or introducing new products. These important competitive dynamics therefore need to be incorporated into the competitive assessment.

---

[60] Recall that a Nash equilibrium exists when, given the behaviour of all other firms in the market, no firm wants to change its behaviour. In a profit maximising setting, this means that each firm is maximising its profits given the sales of all the other firms in the market.

## 2–036  Effective competition

In particular, account often needs to be given to the fact that in many dynamic markets rather than competing *in* the market, firms compete *for* the market. For instance, firms might compete to be the first to patent a drug that cures a particular disease. Whoever patents a drug first then gets legal protection to be the sole seller of that drug for the life of the patent. The "winner" of the patent race faces no competition *in* the market as he has a legal monopoly and is the sole supplier in the market for the period of the patent. However, he may have faced very strong competition in the patent race, when different firms were competing *for* the market.[61]

2–037    A number of implications flow from this. First, firms spend considerable amounts of money in the research and development stage in order to be the first to innovate and hence win the right to earn monopoly profits thereafter. But firms only invest in research and development because of the expectation of earning profits if such investments are successful in bringing products to market. The lower the expected profits from bringing a new product to market, the less a firm is likely to choose to invest in research and development in the first place. Permitting successful innovators to recoup the benefits of their investments is therefore essential to the operation of the market.[62] Rather than representing an inefficient market structure that harms consumers, monopoly is a necessary market structure that ensures that consumers benefit from firms undertaking risky innovative activities. This is the form of competition that the Austrian School of economists focused on. Schumpeter described dynamic competition as a process of "creative destruction" in which innovative activities led to new markets, new industries and the death of old markets and industries.[63] In this world, current market leaders always face the risk that their market positions will be undermined by a new innovator with a new and better product.

Secondly, markets such as this are often characterised by high fixed costs (of research and development) and low marginal costs of production. Indeed, in some industries the marginal costs of production are close to zero (for example pharmaceuticals or software). When fixed costs are large and marginal costs are low, firms must price substantially above marginal cost in order to cover total costs.[64] Any benchmark for effective competition based on marginal cost pricing is not appropriate for markets of this type.[65] Also, winning firms are likely to enjoy substantial pricing power and so any definition of "effective competition" based on the absence of price-

---

[61] Competition for the market may also take place in less dynamic circumstances. See Chapter 12 for a discussion.

[62] It is the recognition of this that has led to the protection of intellectual property rights via instruments such as patents.

[63] Schumpeter (1950).

[64] The idea that prices may need to be above marginal cost in order to cover fixed costs was discussed in paras 2–024—2–026 in relation to the Cournot model.

[65] This accords with our conclusions from the static models: price equal to marginal cost is not a good definition of "effective competition".

setters is not adequate. Further, since firms incur significant risks when they invest in research and development in the hope of winning the race, we should expect prices to be high enough to generate revenue significantly in excess of total costs.[66] The expected returns to winning must be high enough that even once they are discounted due to the risk of losing, firms expect *ex ante* to make a positive return. For instance, three firms will only engage in a patent race if the expected returns are more than three times the R&D costs.[67]

Thirdly, dynamic industries sometimes exhibit *network effects*. Some products are more valuable to a user the more other people are using the same product. For instance, subscribing to a telecommunications network becomes more valuable when there are already many subscribers on the network who you can call and who can call you. Equally, consumers value using the same software platform as other consumers as this makes it easier to swap files, leads to more software being written for that platform, leads to more self-help manuals being written for that platform and so on. In the presence of network effects customers may choose the product that already has the largest group of users, regardless of whether this is technically the best product on the market. In such cases, it is possible that the market will tend to "tip" towards a monopoly or near monopoly.

---

**BOX 2.3: A DURABLE GOOD MONOPOLIST: ITS OWN WORST ENEMY**   2–038

We explained above that a monopolist will set price above the marginal cost of production and that this will lead to the monopolist earning excess profits and to allocative inefficiency. However, the analysis leading to this result was carried out in a static environment. As Coase (1972) noted, this analysis may not carry over to the case of a monopolist who sells a durable good and has to determine how to price the product over a number of time periods. In its most extreme form, the Coase *conjecture* states that a monopolist of a durable good will sell at marginal cost.[68]

The intuition behind the Coase conjecture is as follows. Suppose a durable good monopolist sells his product at price $P_1$ in the first period and that consumers who value the product at more than $P_1$ buy the product in the first period. What should the monopolist do in the second period? Since customers who purchase a durable good in the

---

[66] This highlights the fact that rejecting marginal cost as an indicator of effective competition is not just a question of rejecting *short-run* marginal cost. Using *long-run* marginal cost does not solve the "problem" that when firms undertake highly risky projects, they will do so only if the potential returns are substantially above total costs.

[67] This assumes that each firm believes it has a one-third chance of winning the patent race.

[68] Although still referred to as the Coase *conjecture*, it has been proven under a number of circumstances.

first period are unlikely to purchase it in the second period as well, the sales by a monopolist in the first period reduce the demand for his product in the future. So he clearly needs to lower the price below $P_1$ in the second period. Thus he sells it at $P_2$, which is less than $P_1$, in the second period. As long as the price remains above the marginal cost of production, the monopolist will reduce it each period in order to serve the remaining consumers and make additional profits. In theory, this process continues until the price equals the marginal cost.

However, the above analysis does not consider consumer expectations. If consumers understand that the monopolist will reduce prices in the next period, many are likely to delay their purchase until that period (depending how long the delay between periods is). This means that even in the first period the monopolist of a durable good may be unable to set the static monopoly price. The Coase conjecture predicts that a durable goods monopolist will continuously lower his price until he starts selling at marginal cost and that consumers, expecting future price cuts, will choose to delay their purchases until price is equal to marginal cost.

**2-039**   Formally, the Coase conjecture states that a monopolist of an infinitely durable good loses all his monopoly power as the period between price adjustments becomes shorter. For this to hold, two additional conditions must hold. First, consumers must be able to delay their purchases without incurring significant costs of delay. Secondly, the monopolist must be unable to commit convincingly to maintaining the high price in the future. However, the monopolist may be able to commit itself to not lowering prices in future in one of the following ways:

- offering a money back guarantee to early purchasers if it subsequently lowers the price of the good;

- leasing the durable good instead of selling it;

- making the life of the good shorter by planned obsolescence or by the introduction of new models; or

- establishing a reputation for never lowering prices.

The point of this discussion is not to argue that the Coase conjecture is likely to hold in practice. Instead, it is to highlight how a durable good monopolist provides his own competition, in the sense that competitive constraints are imposed on the monopolist's current pricing by past sales of his product and by consumer expectations of his future pricing behaviour. It is another example how the outcomes of static models may not be appropriate once dynamic considerations are taken into account.

# SUMMARY

In this chapter we have discussed a number of possible definitions of **2-040**
"effective competition" and have introduced some simple economic
models of competition in order to aid the discussion. We have also introduced the concepts of allocative and productive efficiency, and producer
and consumer welfare. We concluded that the aim of competition policy
was to maximise consumer welfare and not social welfare (i.e. not the sum
of consumer plus producer welfare).

The first possible definition of "effective competition" that we discussed
was based on rivalry: effective competition existed when there was significant rivalry between firms. We rejected this as being an inadequate
definition of "effective competition" for two reasons. First, it does not in
itself provide an answer to the question of how much rivalry is needed.
Secondly, it focuses on the process of competition rather than the outcome.

The second possible definition that we discussed was based on firms
operating without restrictions on their behaviour. We rejected this definition because it is far too prescriptive. Firms voluntarily accept restrictions
on their behaviour on a regular basis (e.g. contracts between firms) and
would not be able to operate efficiently without such restrictions.

The third possible definition revolved around the ability of firms to **2-041**
influence the market price. This definition suggested that effective competition existed when no firm could individually affect the market price and
did not exist where a firm could so influence the market price. However,
our discussion of various economic models has shown that this definition is
not adequate. Although no firm can individually affect the market price in
the standard economic model of perfect competition, this is not a model
that is widely applicable to the real world. We showed that there are a
number of models of competition (e.g. monopolistic competition, Cournot
competition with free entry and Bertrand competition) in which firms did
have influence over the market price and yet competition drove the market
price down to a level at which no firms made positive economic profits. It
would be far too prescriptive to argue that in these models there was not
effective competition even though efficient firms were unable to make
positive economic profits.

Another approach that economists sometimes use is to equate effective
competition with prices being equal to specific cost concepts, usually but
not always marginal costs. For instance, Mehta and Peeperkorn state that[69]:

> "The answer given by economists on the first question—what is
> market power?—concentrates on the power to raise price above the
> competitive level. In the short run this means the power to raise price
> above marginal cost and in the long run above average total cost."

[69] Mehta and Peeperkorn (2007).

49

In their "Guidelines on Vertical Restraints"[70] the Commission defines the competitive price as minimum average total cost: "the extent to which incumbent companies can increase their price above the competitive level, usually above minimum average total cost".

Our discussion of various economic models and of the process of dynamic competition showed that this approach to defining "effective competition" is seriously flawed. Prices can be above marginal costs in situations in which a market should be said to be effectively competitive (e.g. monopolistic competition and Cournot competition with free entry). We also noted that when fixed costs are high and marginal costs are low, prices equal to marginal cost will cause firms to lose money and exit the market.[71] Further, we noted that when competition is *for* the market rather than *in* the market, prices will need to be substantially above the average total cost of the winning firm.[72]

**2–042**     Although this chapter has not provided a formal definition of "effective competition", we have highlighted that when regulators intervene in a market because they think it is not subject to effective competition, there is a belief that intervention will increase consumer welfare. This provides a benchmark for measuring the effectiveness of competition.

With this benchmark in mind, we find that rivalry in the market is generally important, but rivalry for rivalry's sake will not necessarily maximise consumer welfare. We find that many restrictions on the behaviour of firms are entirely consistent with the maximisation of consumer welfare. And we find that firms having some power over price (or, equivalently, having some ability to restrict their output on the market) is also consistent with the maximisation of consumer welfare. We also find that oligopolies can be effectively competitive and that pricing in oligopolies can be consistent with effective competition.[73] Above all, assessing whether a market is effectively competitive or not requires an analysis of the current structure of the market and behaviour of the firms within the market and whether intervention is unlikely to increase consumer welfare taking into account both static and dynamic considerations.

---

[70]  Commission Notice: Guidelines on Vertical Restraints [2000] OJ C291/01, para.126.
[71]  The problem is particularly stark when fixed costs are large and marginal costs are low, but in fact marginal cost pricing will lead to losses whenever there are fixed costs and constant marginal costs.
[72]  There is a tendency to believe that effective competition implies that firms make no economic profit. We deal with this issue in detail in Chapter 3, but re-emphasise here that this is unlikely to be the case in dynamic markets characterised by high investment risk. In markets of this type, the expectation of profits is essential to the successful working of the competitive process. In Chapter 3 we consider various other circumstances under which effective competition does not imply zero economic profits and argue that these circumstances tend to be the rule, rather than the exception.
[73]  We hope that this makes clear the failings of the common knee-jerk reaction that condemns "oligopoly pricing" as a sin almost per se.

# 3. The Assessment of Market Power

## INTRODUCTION

The previous chapter discussed the concept of "effective competition". **3–001** This chapter discusses how to identify in practice whether the degree of competition in a particular market can be characterised as being effective. A characteristic of markets subject to effective competition is the absence of *market power*. The economic concept of market power therefore lies at the centre of the economic assessment of competition policy issues. This is true whether the investigation is made under Article 81, Article 82, or the Merger Regulation.[1]

"Market power" is defined as the ability of firms to increase prices profitably above the competitive price for a sustained period. However, since the competitive price is extremely difficult to identify in practice, determining whether firms enjoy market power in practice usually requires an indirect assessment.[2] This raises the question of how to identify whether a firm or group of firms are able to exercise market power. This chapter therefore provides a discussion of what is meant by market power and how it affects prices and output decisions.

This is not to imply that economic considerations and the identification of market power are the only relevant considerations in the assessment of competition under EC competition law, as discussed in Chapter 1. EC competition law also has as one of its objectives the aim of creating a single European market. However, the competitive analysis should not confuse these objectives (i.e. the "single market" objective and the "effective competition" objective). The analysis of whether a market is currently subject to effective competition, or is likely to be in the future, should be carried out independently of a consideration of whether the conduct of a

---

[1]   Indeed, market power is a key concept in virtually all jurisdictions with a competition law regime.

[2]   The academic economics literature often equates short-run marginal cost with the competitive price; although see Tirole (1988) for a notable exception. As discussed in Chapter 2, many economic models of effective competition give rise to competitive prices above short-run marginal cost.

firm or firms is likely to hinder the development of the single market. Further, when it comes to balancing the two objectives against each other in a particular case, the decision that the conduct of a firm or firms should be found contrary to the objectives of the single market should be based, at least partially, on some explicit or implicit economic analysis showing the effect of the decision on competitive outcomes.

It is not the purpose of this book to comment on the relative importance of the various criteria of EC competition law. However, it is desirable to make explicit the terms of the trade-off between them. For instance, it is important to understand the circumstances under which the pursuit of market integration may involve a significant sacrifice of economic efficiency. For this reason, this chapter focuses solely on assessing competition against the economic goal of EC competition law.

# WHAT IS MARKET POWER?

**3–002** There is a tendency in the academic economic literature to define "market power" as the ability to price above short-run marginal cost.[3] But as the discussion in Chapter 2 shows, this does not provide a useful definition for policy purposes. In Chapter 2 we discussed a number of theoretical models of competition, a number of which imply that effective competition results in prices above short-run marginal cost. Further, we noted that the focus on marginal cost pricing arises from the inappropriate application of the idealised economic model of perfect competition. If "market power" is defined as the ability to price above short-run marginal cost, then virtually all firms have at least a degree of market power. But if virtually all firms have market power, then the existence of market power is not a useful guide to whether or not there is effective competition and whether or not intervention is required.

"Market power" is defined as the ability of a firm or group of firms to raise price, through the restriction of output, above the level that would prevail under competitive conditions and thereby to enjoy increased profits from the action.[4] This definition has been adopted explicitly by several competition authorities. For example, the UK Office of Fair Trading states that "this guideline usually refers to market power as the ability to raise prices consistently and profitably above competitive levels"[5]; the Commission states that "[a]n undertaking that is capable of substantially

---

[3] The *marginal cost* of a product is the cost of producing one more unit of the product.

[4] The standard for assessing mergers is somewhat different as the issue is whether the merger will create or increase market power and so permit prices to increase relative to the pre-vailing price.

[5] Para.1.2 of *Assessment of Market Power*, OFT415, 1999.

increasing prices above the competitive level for a significant period of time holds substantial market power"[6] whilst Mehta and Peeperkorn state that "[t]he answer given by economists on the first question—what is market power?—concentrates on the power to raise price above the competitive level."[7]

The definition of "market power" contains three important elements:

(1)  the exercise of market power leads to lower output;

(2)  the increase in price must lead to an increase in profitability; and

(3)  market power is exercised relative to the benchmark of the outcome under conditions of effective competition.[8]

These three elements are examined in more detail below.

## The exercise of market power leads to lower output

If a firm (or firms) wishes to increase price, it must be prepared to sell fewer  **3–003** units. The higher the price that the firm charges, the lower the quantity demanded and vice versa. Since most demand curves slope downwards, an increase in price is accompanied by a reduction in the level of sales.[9] Figure 3.1 provides an illustration of this effect. An increase in the price of the product, from $p_1$ to $p_2$, causes quantity demanded to fall from $q_1$ to $q_2$. For example, if the price of DVDs increases, some people will buy fewer DVDs. What is true for an individual consumer is true of the market as a whole; the market demand curve is the aggregation of individual demand curves.[10]

---

[6]  Para.24 of "DG Competition Discussion Paper on the application of Article 82 of the Treaty to exclusionary abuses" (December 2005).
[7]  Para.1.18 of Mehta and Peeperkorn (2007).
[8]  This is not correct in all circumstances. We discuss this further at para.3–053. However, for our purposes at this point of the chapter it is an adequate approximation.
[9]  This reduction in the level of sales is often referred to as a *restriction of output*.
[10]  Gorman (1959).

## Figure 3.1 The relationship between price and quantity demanded

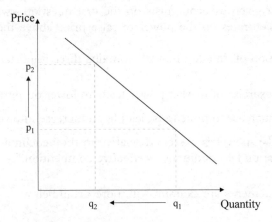

### The increase in price must lead to an increase in profitability

**3–004** The assumption of profit maximisation implies that the exercise of market power must involve an increase in the profitability of the firm. Any firm can choose to raise price at any time,[11] but this does not mean that every firm has market power. As discussed above, the action of raising price will cause demand to fall. If demand were to fall sufficiently so that an increase in price above the competitive level were to lead to lower profits, then the firm would not possess market power. However, if the reduction in quantity sold is sufficiently small that it is outweighed by the higher price (and lower costs since less needs to be produced), restricting output below the competitive level will cause profits to rise and the firm does have market power.

So the key question is how much demand the firm loses when it raises price. This is measured by the *price elasticity of demand* facing the firm. The price elasticity of demand is defined as the ratio of the percentage decrease in sales resulting from a given percentage increase in price. It is often written as $\varepsilon$.

**(1)** *Price Elasticity of Demand* $= \dfrac{Percentage\ change\ in\ sales}{Percentage\ change\ in\ price}$

Formally, equation (1) is the *own-price elasticity of demand*, meaning that it refers to the change in sales when the price of that particular product is changed.[12] Since demand falls as prices rise, the own-price elasticity of demand is always negative. However, it is usual to talk about the absolute value of the own price elasticity (i.e. it is usual to ignore the minus sign and to say that an elasticity of $-2$ is larger than an elasticity of $-1$).

---

[11] Unless it is price regulated.
[12] As opposed to a *cross-price elasticity of demand*, which refers to the change in sales of one product when the price of another product is changed.

The larger the own-price elasticity of demand, the greater the percentage reduction in sales in response to a given percentage increase in price. Thus, an elasticity of $-1$ means that a 1 per cent increase in prices will lead to a 1 per cent fall in sales. An elasticity of $-5$ would mean that a 1 per cent increase in price leads to a 5 per cent fall in sales whereas an elasticity of $-0.5$ would mean that a 1 per cent increase in price leads to only a 0.5 per cent fall in sales. If the elasticity of demand is greater than 1, then an increase in price leads to a reduction in revenue. An elasticity of less than 1 implies that a price increase leads to an increase in revenue. Economists refer to demand curves with an elasticity of more than 1 as being "elastic" and those with an elasticity of less than 1 as being "inelastic". These terms are also used in a relative sense: the demand curve for one product is said to be "more elastic" than that for another (even if both are actually inelastic in terms of having an elasticity of less than 1). For example, Figure 3.2 shows that a rise in price from $p_1$ to $p_2$ has a larger effect on quantity demanded in (a) than in (b). The elasticity of demand in (a) can be said to be more elastic than that in (b).[13]

**Figure 3.2 Two demand curves with different elasticities**

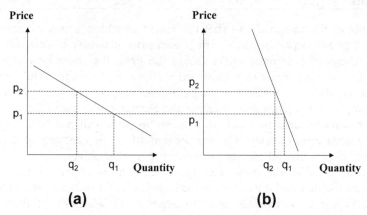

To illustrate the relationship between the own-price elasticity and profit-  **3–005** ability consider the following numerical example. Suppose the price of a product is currently €10. At this price level the firm sells 1,000 units, so revenue is €10,000. Assume that the constant marginal cost is €9 and there are no fixed costs, so total costs are €9,000 and profits are €1,000. Now consider the impact of increasing the price to €11, a 10 per cent price increase. Table 3.1 illustrates how it is the elasticity of demand that determines the impact of the price rise on profits.

---

[13]  In fact, when demand curves are linear, the elasticity of demand varies as price varies (it rises as price rises). So it is not the case that the elasticity of demand at any given price in (a) is larger than the elasticity of demand at all prices in (b). However, what is true is that at any given price, the elasticity in (a) is larger than the elasticity at the same price in (b).

If the elasticity of the demand curve is −6, then the price increase can be seen to lead to a reduction in profits. With an elasticity of −6, the 10 per cent increase in price leads to a 60 per cent fall in sales. Profits fall from €1,000 to €800. On the other hand, if the demand curve is −3 (i.e. less elastic) then the price increase results in an increase in profits. The elasticity of −3 means that sales only fall by 30 per cent in response to the 10 per cent price rise. Profits rise from €1,000 to €1,400.

**Table 3.1 Numerical example of the implication of different elasticities**

|  | Original outcome with price of €10 | Outcome following price rise to €11 | |
|---|---|---|---|
|  |  | Elasticity | |
|  |  | −6 | −3 |
| **Units sold** | 1,000 | 400 | 700 |
| **Revenue** | 10,000 | 4,400 | 7,700 |
| **Costs** | 9,000 | 3,600 | 6,300 |
| **Profits** | 1,000 | 800 | 1,400 |

The above discussion shows that the extent to which a firm can exercise market power depends on the firm's own-price elasticity of demand. The more elastic the demand curve facing the firm, the more limited is the extent to which a firm can increase price above the level that would prevail under conditions of effective competition. Conversely, the exercise of market power becomes more likely as the elasticity of demand facing a firm becomes more inelastic since an increase in price will not be associated with a large drop in sales. The factors that affect the elasticity of demand are therefore a central element in assessing market power.

**3–006**  Before considering these factors, a distinction needs to be drawn between the demand curve facing the industry as a whole and the demand curve facing an individual firm. In general, the elasticity of these two demand curves will be different, with the industry demand curve being less elastic than the demand curve facing any individual firm. It is quite possible for the industry demand curve to be relatively inelastic, but for the demand curve facing each firm to be relatively elastic. To see this, consider a firm's *residual* demand curve. The residual demand facing an individual firm is defined as the demand that is not met by the other firms in the industry, i.e. the residual demand curve for a firm is the industry demand curve minus the supply of other firms.

## BOX 3.1: THE DERIVATION OF THE RESIDUAL DEMAND CURVE

Figure 3.3 shows how the residual demand curve of a particular firm is derived from the industry demand curve and the supply curve of the other firms in the market.

**Figure 3.3 Derivation of the residual demand curve for a homogeneous good**

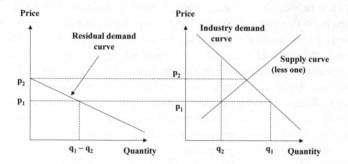

The right hand side of Figure 3.3 shows the industry demand curve and the supply curve for all the firms except one (i.e. the total amount of product that the other firms are willing to supply at a given price). The horizontal difference between the market demand curve and the supply of all other firms is the residual demand facing the remaining firm. The intuition for this is clear. The amount of product demanded from a firm at each price will be the total industry demand at that price, less the quantity of product other firms are willing to supply. For example, at a price $p_1$, the quantity demanded by consumers is $q_1$ but the amount supplied by the other firms is $q_2$. Hence, the residual demand facing the remaining firm at a price of $p_1$ is $q_1$—$q_2$. At a price of $p_2$, the other firms are willing to supply all the demand of consumers (i.e. the supply curve less one cuts the industry demand curve). Hence, at this price and at all prices above $p_2$, the residual demand facing the remaining firm is zero. Note that the residual demand curve is flatter (more elastic) than the market demand curve. Again, the intuition for this is clear: there are more substitutes available for the product of a particular firm than there are for the industry as a whole.

There is an important distinction to be made between the own-price **3–007** elasticity of demand (which has been discussed so far) and the cross-price elasticity of demand. The own-price elasticity of demand measures the extent to which demand for a product changes in response to a change in the price of the product itself. The cross-price elasticity of demand measures the extent to which the quantity of the product demanded changes in response to a change in the price of some other product. If two goods or services are substitutes, a relative increase in the price of one product should cause consumers to shift some of their purchases to the other product, and thus the cross-price elasticities between the two products will be positive.[14]

While there is often a great deal of discussion by competition authorities as to the importance of the cross-price elasticity, especially when defining relevant markets, it is the own-price elasticity that determines the extent of market power. If the own-price elasticity is low, then it would be possible to raise price profitably because the decline in volume would be small. Conversely, if the own-price elasticity of a product is high then a price rise is unlikely to be profitable because the decline in sales will be large. The own-price elasticity of demand for a product is the sum of all the cross-price elasticities of demand for that product. So it is possible for all the relevant cross-price elasticities to be low but for the own-price elasticity still to be high. Where a given product is constrained by the presence of a large number of substitutes, it is possible that the substitutes collectively impose a strong competitive constraint even though individually each provides only a weak competitive constraint.

---

**BOX 3.2: WHICH CROSS-PRICE ELASTICITY?**

An issue that is often not addressed in the discussion of cross-price elasticities is which cross-price elasticity is appropriate for the purposes of analysing the competitive constraint faced by a firm. To discuss a cross-price elasticity intelligently, one must specify whether it is the cross-price elasticity of demand for product X with respect to the price of product Y or vice versa. These two cross-price elasticities are in general not equal and it is therefore important that the correct one be used. For instance, people who drink vodka might have only a weak preference for it compared with gin, whereas people who drink gin may have a strong preference for it compared with vodka. If that were so, then an increase in the price of vodka relative to that of gin might lead to significant numbers of vodka drinkers switching to gin, whilst an increase in the price of gin would lead to only a few gin drinkers switching to vodka.[15]

---

[14] Where the cross-price elasticity between two products is negative—a rise in the price of one product leads to a fall in the demand for the other product—the two products are said to be complements for one another.

[15] Other reasons why the cross-price elasticity of X with respect to the price of Y is not generally the same as the cross-price elasticity of Y with respect to the price of X are dealt with in Chapter 10.

Suppose we are concerned with the competitive constraints faced by **3–008** a manufacturer of widgets. As noted above, what we are really concerned with is the own-price elasticity of widgets. However, suppose a question has arisen as to whether gadgets impose a constraint on widgets. Are we interested in the cross-price elasticity of demand for widgets with respect to the price of gadgets or the cross-price elasticity of demand for gadgets with respect to the price of widgets? What we are *not* interested in is what is the effect of a change in the price of widgets on the demand for gadgets (i.e. the cross-price elasticity of demand for gadgets with respect to the price of widgets). Instead, we are interested in the effect of a change in the price of gadgets on the demand for widgets (i.e. the cross-price elasticity of demand for widgets with respect to the price of gadgets). This is because we want to know whether, if the price of gadgets fell, it would have a significant effect on the demand for widgets. If the answer is that it would, then gadgets impose a competitive constraint on widgets. So the relevant cross-price elasticity of demand when the question is whether the market for product X should include product Y is the cross-elasticity of demand for product X with respect to the price of product Y.[16]

As we noted above, the issue of which is the correct cross-price elasticity to use is often not discussed.[17] It is very rare, even in the various guidance documents issued by competition authorities, to find the correct cross-price elasticity specified. In general, references are just to "the cross-price elasticity", rather than specifying which cross-price elasticity is meant.

## Market power is exercised relative to the benchmark of the outcome under conditions of effective competition

The third element of the definition of "market power" provides a bench- **3–009** mark against which claims that prices are too high or profits are excessive

---

[16]   See Carlton and Perloff (2004).

[17]   The European Commission used the wrong cross-price elasticity in the *Procter & Gamble/ Schickedanz (II)* decision (IV/M.430 (1994)). At [54] of the decision the Commission discusses the issue of whether sales of towels are influenced by the price of tampons. Specifically they focused on the interaction between the towel brands *Always* and the tampon brand *ob*. The Commission stated that:

> "[A] ... reduction in the price of *Always* produced on average a ... increase in *Always* sales (own price elasticity of ...) and a decrease in sales of *ob* tampons of ... (cross-elasticity of ...), while a ... increase in *Always'* price resulted in a ... drop in *Always* sales (own price elasticity of ...) and an ... increase in sales of *ob* (cross-price elasticity of ...). These data therefore seem to indicate a rather high own price as well as cross price elasticity to *ob*."

Looking at the cross-price elasticity of *ob* with respect to the price of *Always* was the wrong cross-price elasticity to consider as it does not provide an estimate of the constraining effect of *ob* tampons on *Always*.

can be assessed. The exercise of market power involves increasing price above the level that would prevail under conditions of effective competition—and therefore also restricting output to below the effective competition level.

As noted above, there is a tendency in the academic economics literature to equate the competitive price level with short-run marginal cost. The adoption of such a view implies that the existence of market power is the rule rather than the exception since in most industries prices do indeed exceed short-run marginal costs.[18] There are two possible responses to this. First, one could advocate the position that most markets require intervention on the part of competition authorities. Alternatively, one can recognise that in many instances prices above short-run marginal cost are entirely consistent with effective competition, as argued in Chapter 2. This may not make the analysis straightforward but at least it focuses attention on those markets where regulatory intervention is likely to be welfare-enhancing in practice, rather than just in theory.[19]

In practice, the direct identification of the competitive price level plays a minimal role in competition investigations. If the competitive price level could be identified, then the application of competition law would be straightforward. One would simply compare the observed price level with the competitive price level. If the observed price level were above the competitive price level, then this would indicate that there was a competition problem that needed to be solved. Competition policy would then just be a question of choosing a remedy that led to prices falling to the competitive level and price regulation would become widespread. However, this is not the approach taken in practice for the good reason that identifying the competitive price level is almost always impossible.[20] This means that the economic analysis of industries is usually far more complex than just a comparison of price levels.

**3–010**     Therefore, for the purposes of examining whether a firm is currently exercising market power, the current price level also does not provide the appropriate benchmark. It is not useful to ask whether a firm can profitably raise price above the current price level. This is because if it was profitable to do so, a well-run profit maximising firm would have already done so.[21] This holds true for all firms, from perfectly competitive firms to monopolists. Thus, in assessing whether market power exists, the issue is not whether the firm could profitably raise price from the current level (to which, if the firm is well managed, the answer should always be no) but

---

[18]   Werden (1998).
[19]   This view is also held by Kühn, Seabright and Smith (1992).
[20]   It should be noted that the implication of this is that regulation implicitly tries to identify the competitive price. Given the difficulty of identifying the competitive price level, industry regulation should be very much the exception rather than the norm.
[21]   We should slightly moderate this statement by accepting that a well-run firm might not profit maximise if this would involve it potentially being found guilty of excessive pricing under Article 82.

whether the firm is able persistently to price at a level above that which would prevail under conditions of effective competition. Since the direct identification of the competitive price level is not usually possible, this means that the existence of market power usually has to be inferred indirectly from the characteristics of the industry and the nature of competition within the market.

## Illustration of the elements of market power

The three components of market power can be illustrated by the following **3–011** example. Suppose there are 100 suppliers of widgets, each selling 10 widgets at 1 each and that 1 is the effectively competitive price for widgets (i.e. this is an industry that is currently characterised by effective competition). Assume that there are constant unit costs of 1, so each firm makes zero economic profits at a price of 1. In this scenario, industry sales of widgets are 1,000 (10 × 100) and total revenues are 1,000. Further, assume that none of the firms faces capacity constraints, so if any firm attempts to increase price by restricting output, the attempt will be thwarted by other suppliers increasing their output and so it will not be profitable for one firm to increase its price.

Now suppose the Government decides that widget producers should be licensed and that there will be only five licences, thus leading to a five firm industry rather than a 100 firm industry. Does the fact that the market is more concentrated imply that the remaining firms have market power? The answer depends on the facts. If competition is such that each of the five firms produces 200 widgets, then total industry sales will remain at 1,000 and price will remain at 1. In this case, the increase in concentration has not allowed the firms to increase price above the effectively competitive price level and so the firms do not have market power.[22]

If, however, competition is such that each of the five firms produces only 190 widgets, leading to industry sales of only 950 and a higher price per widget, then the firms do have market power: they have restricted output, hence raised price and it will have increased their profits. This might come about, for instance, because the five firms collectively recognise that by each reducing their output they can increase prices, or because the five licences were for five distinct geographic areas such that the five firms did not compete with each other.

---

[22] This simple example shows that counting the number of firms or calculating market shares often offers only a very imperfect proxy for market power.

# INDICATORS OF MARKET POWER

**3–012** Assessing whether a market is subject to effective competition or is subject to the exercise of market power is often not a straightforward task. In particular, due to the difficulties of even defining in theory what the price level is under conditions of effective competition, determining whether market behaviour involves the exercise of market power is difficult. However, while direct measures of market power are difficult to find,[23] inferences can be drawn from the various characteristics of competition in the particular industry under investigation. These characteristics provide an indication of the nature of interactions between firms and they can be used to assess the likelihood that current outcomes do or do not represent the outcome of effective competition. Some of these characteristics, such as industry concentration, the number of firms, barriers to entry and expansion and the nature of interaction between firms, are examined below.

Whether firms price at the level that would prevail under conditions of effective competition or not depends on the elasticity of their residual demand curve measured at the effective competition level. If this is high, then firms will price at, or close to, the effective competition level. This implies that much of the economic analysis in non-merger cases should focus primarily on an assessment of the likely elasticity of demand at the effectively competitive price level. In merger cases, however, the focus of the competitive assessment is not so much on whether current prices are those that would prevail under conditions of effective competition, but whether the merger will lead to price increases. So for merger cases it is appropriate to consider the elasticity of demand at the current price level. But what determines the elasticity of demand? The elasticity of demand depends on numerous factors, which are therefore relevant for the assessment of market power. These include, inter alia:

- the number of competing suppliers of the same products, market shares and concentration;

- barriers to entry and potential competition;

- barriers to expansion;

- countervailing buyer power;

- product differentiation; and

- the nature of the oligopolistic interaction between firms.

---

[23] Though not impossible in some circumstances, as we discuss at paras 3.53–3.54 below.

## Number of competing suppliers, market shares and concentration

It is intuitively appealing to proxy the level of competition a particular firm   **3–013** faces with the number of competitors it has. In general, as the number of firms in an industry increases, the demand curve facing any one of them becomes more elastic because consumers have more alternative suppliers to turn to if a firm raises its price.[24] For most market demand curves, there do not have to be very many firms in an industry for the elasticity of demand facing a single firm to be relatively large.

---

**BOX 3.3: THE ELASTICITY OF INDUSTRY AND FIRM DEMAND CURVES**[25]

The general relationship between the own-price elasticity of demand facing a firm and the elasticity of demand facing the industry is given by:

$$\textbf{(2)} \quad \varepsilon_i = \varepsilon \frac{Q}{q_i} - \sum_{j \neq i}^{n} \frac{q_j}{q_i} \eta_j$$

where  $\varepsilon$ is the market elasticity;

$\varepsilon_i$ is the own-price elasticity of firm i;

Q is total industry sales;

$q_i$ is sales by firm i;

$q_j$ is sales by firm j;

$\eta_j$ is the elasticity of supply of firm j and there are n firms in the industry.

If the n firms are identical, this simplifies to:

**(3)** $\varepsilon_i = \varepsilon\, n - \eta\,(n - 1)$

where  $\eta$ is the elasticity of supply of all firms except firm i.

Equation (3) states that the greater the elasticity of supply of the other firms, the greater is the firm elasticity of firm i.[26] The intuition for this is that the greater the elasticity of supply of other firms, the more they increase their sales in response to a price rise, and so the less is the unsatisfied demand available for firm i to supply. Equation (3) also states that the larger the number of firms in the industry, the greater is the firm elasticity. The intuition for this is that the larger the number of firms in the market, the smaller are the sales of any one firm and so a given change in demand for firm i represents a larger relative change in demand.

---

[24]  In terms of Figure 3.3, as the number of firms increases, the supply curve tends to become "flatter" (more elastic) and so the residual demand curve of a firm becomes "flatter" (more elastic).

[25]  This analysis relies heavily on Carlton and Perloff (2004).

[26]  By greater, we mean greater in absolute terms. So since own price elasticities are negative, we mean "more negative".

Table 3.2 shows how the elasticity of demand facing a single firm varies with the number of firms in the industry, the market elasticity and the elasticity of supply of other firms.

**Table 3.2 The relationship between the elasticity facing a firm and the market elasticity**

| | MARKET ELASTICITY | | | | | |
| | Inelastic (−0.5) | | Unitary (−1) | | Elastic(−5) | |
| | ELASTICITY OF SUPPLY | | | | | |
| Number of firms | 1 | 2 | 1 | 2 | 1 | 2 |
|---|---|---|---|---|---|---|
| 3 | −3.5 | −5.5 | −5 | −7 | −17 | −19 |
| 5 | −6.5 | −10.5 | −9 | −13 | −29 | −33 |
| 10 | −14 | −23 | −19 | −28 | −59 | −68 |
| 25 | −36.5 | −60.5 | −49 | −73 | −149 | −173 |
| 50 | −74 | −123 | −99 | −148 | −299 | −348 |
| 100 | −149 | −248 | −199 | −298 | −599 | −698 |

As the table shows, even where the market demand curve is inelastic, the residual demand facing a single firm is still likely to be elastic. For example, if $\epsilon$ equals −0.5, n is equal to 5 and $\eta$ is equal to 1, the firm elasticity is −6.5.

Finally, it is worth noting that the above analysis relies on firms responding to a price increase by supplying more product (i.e. a normal competitive response). In this case, if one firm raises its price, all other firms increase their sales and so increase their profits, whilst the firm that originally raised prices suffers a significant volume decline. In this scenario we are unlikely to see unilateral firm price increases. However, if the firms in a relatively tight oligopoly recognise this, they may respond to a price increase by one firm by also raising their prices, thus *reducing* their output, all sharing in the volume decline, but hoping to earn higher profits due to the higher price. In this scenario, the price elasticity facing each firm is actually the same as the industry price elasticity.[27]

However, the number of competitors in a market does not always provide a good indication of the level of competition in a market. For instance, prices can diverge markedly from the competitive level even in the presence of other firms if conditions are such that it is relatively easy to set up and maintain a cartel (e.g. in very transparent markets where the price set by all firms is very clear). In contrast, if price competition is very vigorous (e.g. as characterised by the Bertrand model of oligopoly discussed in Chapter 2) then it can be enough for there to be two competitors for there to be

---

[27] This is easily seen. If price rises by 10%, industry demand falls by 10% and all firms share equally in the demand decline, then each firm will face a 10% decline in their own sales. In this case, firm elasticity is equal to the market elasticity: −1.

effective competition. Further, if entry and exit were costless and very easy, then even a monopolist might not be able to raise prices above the competitive level because the mere threat of entry would keep prices low.[28] The number of firms can be a particularly poor indicator of market power in markets that are properly characterised as bidding markets. Where firms bid for contracts that are large relative to the size of the market and that are only offered infrequently, competition is likely to be fierce even if there are only a very few firms competing. Furthermore, market shares in such markets can be poor indicators of market power as the competitive constraint provided by an individual firm depends not on its current market share but on its ability to submit a credible bid. Even a firm with a very low market share may still have a major effect on the bidding behaviour of other firms in the market as long as they bid credibly and aggressively. Accordingly, current market shares can provide a very misleading picture as to the level of current competition.[29] Similarly, where barriers to expansion by existing players are low, current market shares are not a good proxy for market power.[30] Finally, highly variable market shares indicate that a high current market share may only be transient and suggest the existence of significant competition between firms, thus implying relatively little market power.

Nonetheless, the most commonly used proxy for the existence of market **3–014** power in an industry is some measure of concentration within the market.[31] This view of competition has its roots in the Structure-Conduct-Performance (SCP) model of competition, formulated in the 1960s. The SCP model holds that the structure of the industry (e.g. number of firms, concentration and so on) determines the way in which firms compete (their conduct) and this in turn determines their performance (i.e. profitability) (see Figure 3.4). The model holds that the more concentrated the market structure, the less competitively firms behave, which in turn leads to both higher prices and higher profits than under more competitive conditions. This is in line with the implications of the Cournot model that were discussed in Chapter 2. As concentration increases, the Cournot equilibrium results in higher prices. Also, the more concentrated the market, the easier it is for firms to co-ordinate their activities, leading to prices above the competitive level. As such, the SCP model suggests that competition law should focus on the structure of markets. The more concentrated markets are, the more likely it is that competition is not effective. Furthermore, in this model the market power that any single firm possesses can be

---

[28] See Box 3.5 below for further explanation of this argument.
[29] The *Boeing/McDonnell Douglas* merger cases provides a good example of this phenomenon. This case is discussed in some detail in Chapter 12.
[30] For a more detailed discussion, see para.3.30 below on barriers to expansion.
[31] Logically, calculating concentration within a market requires the prior definition of that market. The issue of the definition of the relevant market is considered in detail in Chapter 4.

(imperfectly) proxied by its market share. Also, an implication of the approach is that remedies to competition problems should be structural rather than behavioural.

## Figure 3.4 Structure-Conduct-Performance Paradigm

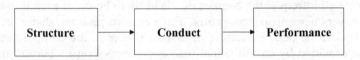

Although the SCP paradigm is the starting point for much competition policy analysis, it is not without its flaws. First, it is too simplistic to think of the flow of causation being entirely in one direction from structure to conduct to performance.[32] In particular, we should expect performance to have an effect on structure. Firms that are successful (perhaps because they are very cost efficient) are likely to grow whilst those that are not successful are likely to shrink. This will lead to increasing concentration. A large firm may be successful not because of the exercise of market power, but because it has used its cost efficiency to price very competitively and hence win market share.

Secondly, the SCP paradigm in its simplest form is silent on the question of what drives structure. The most important drivers of structure are likely to be the cost structure of the industry and the nature of consumer demand. The cost structure of the industry determines the minimum efficient scale of production, whilst consumer demand determines how many firms can operate in the industry at minimum efficient scale. If there are large economies of scale relative to demand, then the market will be naturally concentrated. These "basic conditions" of the industry will be partly exogenously determined, but will also be affected by conduct variables such as the level of investment in advertising or research and development. For instance, R&D can change the cost structure of the industry (e.g. by inventing a process that lowers costs and changes the minimum efficient scale of production) and this will likely change the structure of the industry.

**3–015**   So a better model, though one that provides less clear-cut policy prescriptions, is likely to be one along the lines of Figure 3.5.[33] Here we have also added feedback links from conduct to market structure (e.g. advertising campaigns might raise barriers to entry by increasing consumer loyalty) and from performance to conduct (e.g. profitability affecting investment and R&D expenditure). The key point is that the various aspects of the industry are likely to be interlinked.

[32]   Demsetz (1973) and Sutton (1991).
[33]   This figure is based on Figure 2 of Mehta and Peeperkorn (2007).

## Figure 3.5 A more developed Structure-Conduct-Performance model

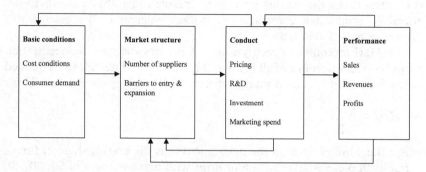

An important implication in this discussion is that conduct is not just a result of the structure of the industry but is itself a choice variable that affects the basic conditions of the industry and the structure of the industry. This conclusion accords with intuition and experience far more than does the conclusion arising out of the simple SCP paradigm (in which only structure matters).

### *Measures of market concentration*

The two most common measures of market concentration are concentra- **3–016** tion ratios and the Herfindahl-Hirschman Index (HHI). The concentration ratio provides a simple summary statistic of the level of concentration in a market. A number of concentration ratios for a given market can be calculated. For example, one can talk of the two firm concentration ratio (commonly written as $C_2$) or the four firm concentration ratio (written as $C_4$). "$C_2$" is defined as the sum of the market shares of the leading two firms in the market and "$C_4$" is defined as the sum of the market shares of the leading four firms in the market.

Concentration ratios have two significant deficiencies as proxies for the effectiveness of competition in an industry. First, they do not take account of the relative sizes of the leading companies. For example, a market which has four firms each with a 20 per cent market share will have the same $C_4$ ratio as a market in which the leading four firms have market shares of 55 per cent, 20 per cent, 4 per cent and 1 per cent. But it is probable that the competitiveness of the two markets will differ. For instance, in the latter case there is a clear potential "leader" for the other firms to follow, whereas in the former case there might be fierce competition to become the largest firm (particularly if there are significant economies of scale in production). The second problem stems from taking into account neither the total number of firms in the market nor the market shares of smaller companies. In many industries, the ability of existing firms to expand capacity can provide a more important competitive constraint than the potential for entry. If smaller firms have the capacity to increase output in response to a price increase by the leading firms in the market, then they can provide an effective competitive constraint on market behaviour. We discuss this further at para.3–030 below.

The HHI attempts to rectify some of the drawbacks of concentration ratios by taking account of all firms in the industry.[34] The "HHI" is defined as the sum of the squared market shares of all firms in the market. Thus:

$$(4) \ HHI = \sum_{i=1}^{N} S_i^2$$

where there are N firms in the market and $S_i$ is the market share of firm i.

**3–017** For example, a market with four firms with market shares of 50, 20, 20, and 10 per cent will have an HHI of 3,400.[35] The HHI must lie between zero (an infinite number of firms in the market, each with essentially zero market share) and 10,000 (a monopolist).

---

**BOX 3.4: CALCULATING HHIS**

If you know the market shares of all the firms in a market, then it is simple to calculate the HHI. However, a question that often arises is how to calculate the HHI of a market when you do not know the market shares of all the players in the market, but instead know the market shares only of the major players. In this case, the best that can be done is to calculate upper and lower bounds for the HHI.

Suppose that we know that there are eight firms in the market, but we know the market shares of only the three largest firms. The lower bound estimate is calculated by assuming that the remaining market share is accounted for equally between the remaining firms. For instance, if there was 15 per cent of the market not accounted for by the top three players, the lower bound is calculated by assuming that each of the other five has three per cent of the market. The upper bound can potentially be calculated in two ways. The crudest way is to assume that all of the unaccounted market share belongs to just one firm. So in the example above we could assume that the fourth largest firm had 15 per cent of the market and the other four firms had essentially zero market share. However, there are times when this is clearly not the correct way to calculate the upper bound. If the three largest firms had market shares of 20 per cent each, leaving 40 per cent of the market unaccounted for, it would not be sensible to attribute the

---

[34] As a theoretical nicety, it can be shown that the HHI is a perfect measure of the competitiveness of the industry if firms behave according to the Cournot quantity-setting model with absolute barriers to entry.

[35] HHI = $(50^2 + 20^2 + 20^2 + 10^2) = (2,500 + 400 + 400 + 100) = 3,400$.

remainder to just one firm. If we know that the three largest firms have 20 per cent each, then the fourth largest player must have less than a 20 per cent market share. In this case, the plausible upper bound would be calculated by assuming that the fourth and fifth largest firms had just under 20 per cent each, and the other three firms had essentially zero market share.

An example should make this clear (see Table 3.3). Suppose there are eight firms in the market and we know the market shares of four of them. These firms have market shares of 35 per cent, 24 per cent, 15 per cent and 10 per cent. While the $C_4$ ratio can be calculated (84 per cent), the precise HHI cannot since the market shares of the remaining four firms are not known. The precise level of the HHI will depend on the exact distribution of the remaining 16 per cent. The lower bound estimate of the HHI would be calculated by assuming that this 16 per cent was distributed evenly between the remaining four firms (i.e. 4 per cent). One possible upper bound estimate would be calculated by assuming that one of the remaining four firms accounted for all of the 16 per cent, but since one of the four firms whose market share we know has only 10 per cent, it seems unlikely that there would be a firm with a 16 per cent share that we do not know of. So the more plausible upper bound would be calculated by assuming that there is a fifth firm with just under 10 per cent (i.e. just under the level of the firm with the lowest market share that we know), a sixth firm with the remaining 6 per cent and a seventh and eighth firm with essentially zero market share.

**3-018**

**Table 3.3 Calculating upper and lower bounds for HHIs: a worked example**

|  | Market share | Market share squared |
|---|---|---|
| Firm 1 | 35 | 1,225 |
| Firm 2 | 24 | 576 |
| Firm 3 | 15 | 225 |
| Firm 4 | 10 | 100 |
| **Total** | **84** | **2,126** |

| | | |
|---|---|---|
| **Upper bound:** | **One firm has 16%, others zero** | **HHI = 2,126 + 16² = 2,382** |
| | **One firm has 10%, one has 6%, others zero** | **HHI = 2,126 + 10² + 6² = 2,262** |
| **Lower bound:** | **Each firm has 4%** | **HHI = 2,126 + 4 (4²) = 2,190** |

So in this example the HHI potentially lies between 2,190 and 2,382, although a much more plausible upper bound is 2,262 rather than 2,382.

**3–018** The assessment of market power

Although concentration ratios and HHIs are relatively easy to calculate and have some intuitive appeal, the use of market shares, concentration ratios and HHIs to assess the competitiveness of an industry raises a number of potentially serious issues. First, the level of observed concentration in a market is affected by many factors. In particular, as noted above, if one firm in a market becomes more efficient than the others (possibly due to a technological advance) or develops a better product, it should be expected that this firm will earn high profits and gain market share, thus increasing market concentration. But it would be a mistake to equate increasing concentration with lessening competition in this case. The problem here is that market structure cannot just be taken as a given that is unaffected by the conduct or performance of the firms in the market (i.e. structure is not exogenously determined but endogenously determined). The structure of the market is likely to be at least partially endogenously determined.

**3–019**    Secondly, the use of market shares logically requires the definition of some market. Serious problems arise with using market shares to make inferences about competition when the definition of the market from which market shares are calculated is inappropriate. Since market shares are often used as an important indicator of market power, the definition of the market should reflect the competitive constraints between products. The question of how the relevant market should be defined is discussed at length in Chapter 4.[36]

Thirdly, as noted above, concentration and the number of competitors in a market does not always provide a good indication of the level of competition in that market. Markets with many players and low concentration can sometimes be cartelised, whilst highly concentrated markets can be characterised by fierce competition when, for instance, entry into and exit from the market are very easy.

## Barriers to entry and potential competition

**3–020** Competition analysis has long understood that a firm's attempt to exercise market power could be defeated by a new supplier entering the market. The possibility that price increases will encourage new firms to enter the market can provide a powerful constraint on the competitive behaviour of incumbent firms. Indeed, the constraint posed by entry, or just the potential for entry, can in certain circumstances prevent even firms which enjoy very high market shares from exercising market power.

The importance placed on barriers to entry in the competitive

---

[36] If market definition is accurately carried out, market shares are useful as a screening device. A firm with a low market share is unlikely to possess market power. However, it does not follow that a firm with a high market share necessarily therefore has market power. A reasonable rule of thumb is that a high market share of a correctly defined relevant market can be taken as a necessary condition for the exercise of market power, but it is not a sufficient condition.

assessment can be seen with reference to the SCP paradigm discussed above. The SCP model posits a one-way chain of causation running from structure to conduct to performance. However, if firms in the market are earning excess profits, then one would expect entry to rectify that situation in the long run. The SCP model therefore sees persistent excess profits as an indication that there are barriers to entry, the nature (height) of which is taken as exogenously given. But the SCP model ignores the possibility (discussed above) of important interactions between the factors that determine market structure and market outcomes, including the possibility that barriers to entry are endogenously determined. In particular, expected market outcomes play a significant role in the entry decisions of firms. If a potential entrant believes that a market is currently characterised by excess profits and that these profits will persist even if it enters the market, then it is likely to have a strong incentive to enter.

It is not only within the recent game theoretical treatment that one finds criticism of the SCP. Various empirical studies in the 1970s drew attention to the need to consider a possible reverse link from conduct or performance to structure.[37] Two factors affect the entry decision of a firm: the level of unrecoverable costs of entry, so-called *sunk costs*, and the expected profitability of entry. For a given level of expected post-entry competition (including, inter alia, the expected level of prices), the greater the unrecoverable costs associated with entry, the less likely entry is to occur. Where sunk costs are large given the size of the market, only a few players will co-exist in the market. However, even if the costs associated with entry are low, no firm would consider entering the market if post-entry competition was expected to result in margins so low that the costs of entry would not be recovered. Vigorous competition in the market place or the expectation of it can therefore deter entry.[38] Thus, there is an interplay between the costs of entry and the degree of price competition expected post-entry which determines market structure.[39]

Hence the observed market structure will reflect a tension between the **3–021** level of sunk set-up costs that must be recovered to justify entry and the intensity of price competition following entry: more entrants usually means lower prices; but lower prices make entry less attractive. This implies that where price competition is extremely vigorous, further entry may not occur even if entry barriers are low. Why would any firm wish to enter a market in which the profit margins implied by prevailing prices are too low to allow it to recover its investment costs? It also implies that an increase in sunk set-up costs will make entry less attractive for a given level of expected post-

---

[37] See Schmalensee (1987) for a review.
[38] This raises the question of whether it is current competition that deters entry or whether it is the level of expected post-entry competition that is the critical factor. In theory, it is the latter; in practice the former often provides an important indicator of likely post-entry competition.
[39] See Sutton (1991).

entry competition. As we discuss below, this gives scope for incumbent firms to engage in strategic entry-deterring behaviour by increasing the level of sunk costs that potential entrants need to incur if they wish to enter.

---

**BOX 3.5: CONTESTABLE MARKETS**

Perhaps the most powerful expression of the competitive constraint posed by potential entry is expounded in the theory of *contestable markets*.[40] In a perfectly contestable market, entry and exit are costless and immediate, but incumbent firms cannot themselves respond to entry immediately. Competition in perfectly contestable markets will always result in competitive outcomes even if there is only one firm in the market. The reason is that if prices are raised above the competitive level, thus potentially leading to excess profits, the opportunity to undercut this supra-competitive price and still make excess profits will immediately attract new entry. This will continue until prices are once more at the competitive level. A contestable market is said to be subject to "hit-and-run" entry. It is important to note the implication here of high exit costs: the higher the costs of exit, the less likely entry is.

The conditions under which a market can be said to be perfectly contestable are very stringent: immediate costless entry and exit so that "hit-and-run" entry is possible, but an inability for incumbents to respond immediately. This implies that firms can enter and begin producing before incumbents have time to adjust their prices. The assumption that incumbents cannot respond immediately is a particularly strong one. If incumbents can respond immediately to new entry, then they do not need to price at the competitive level pre-entry (and hence the pre-entry price is not a good guide to the post-entry price). Instead, they can price above the competitive level pre-entry, knowing that they can lower price post-entry. This may have the effect of deterring entry, as entrants know that the profit opportunity that they see pre-entry can be removed by the incumbents post-entry. Since the most obvious dimension of competition, pricing, can usually be changed at short notice, it is doubtful that the pure theory of contestable markets is widely applicable.[41]

**3–022**   However, the word "contestable" has now entered the legal vocabulary and is used in a looser fashion than that proposed in the economic literature. Broadly speaking, the legal use of the term "contestable" applies to those markets in which potential competition is said to exert a significant competitive constraint on the behaviour of incumbent firms, i.e. where entry is relatively easy and does not

---

[40]   Baumol, Panzer and Willig (1982).
[41]   See Vickers and Yarrow (1988) for a good discussion of these issues.

> require large sunk costs. Although economists may grumble at what they consider to be the misuse of terms, the key point has been well taken by the legal profession: the more difficult it is to enter a market, the less the weight that should be placed on potential entry as a constraining factor on competitive behaviour in that market.

A useful distinction can be made between *exogenous* and *endogenous* sunk costs. Exogenous sunk costs are those which any firm must incur if it is to enter the market. For example, exogenous sunk costs are set-up costs such as the acquisition of a plant with minimum efficient scale. In contrast, endogenous sunk costs are not predetermined in the same way. Rather, the level of endogenous sunk costs incurred is determined by the firms themselves. For example, the amounts that a firm is prepared to spend on research and development or on advertising are not usually pre-determined but are commercial decisions for the particular firm to make. The level of expenditure a firm will undertake in incurring endogenous sunk costs will typically depend on the effect that such spending has on consumer demand for its products. Where sunk costs are endogenous, there arises the possibility that competition between firms will lead to a competitive escalation in such expenditures. Under these circumstances, such escalation can imply that some industries become strategically concentrated.[42] Whether such behaviour is considered anti-competitive requires a view to be taken as to the impact of such spending on consumer welfare.

The 1997 US Horizontal Merger Guidelines make a distinction between *uncommitted* and *committed* entry.[43] The concept of uncommitted entry effectively incorporates the idea of *supply-side substitution* (i.e. of entry from a neighbouring market in which firms already have the assets needed to manufacture products for another market). Uncommitted entry can take place quickly without the need for substantial investment in new plant or equipment. This allows such firms to take advantage on a short-term basis of any profit opportunities that should arise and also to exit once those profit opportunities have disappeared. Committed entrants in contrast need to invest significant amounts before they are able to compete. This means that committed entrants expect to be in the market for more than the duration of short-run profit opportunities. Entry is more risky for committed entrants than for uncommitted entrants. Accordingly, expectations of the level of post-entry competition are more important for committed entrants than for uncommitted entrants.

While entry can provide an important competitive constraint on the **3–023** behaviour of incumbent firms, entry should not be thought of as some abstract characteristic of the market under investigation. One is not

---

[42]　See Sutton (1991) for a discussion and examples of this phenomenon.
[43]　A more detailed discussion of the Guidelines approach towards the analysis of entry is provided in Chapter 7.

interested in whether barriers to entry are "high" or "low", but in whether the potential for entry is able to deter or counteract potential anti-competitive behaviour.

It is important when assessing the scope for new entry to conduct the analysis in the appropriate order. The analysis of the competitive constraint provided by the potential for new firms to enter the market should follow the assessment of the competitive constraints that exist between firms already active in the market. In many cases, there is a tendency to assert that barriers to entry are high because no entry has occurred and from this to conclude that the firms already active in the market are not subject to effective competitive constraint. But such an approach fails to identify those situations in which the reason entry has not taken place is because competition in the market is already vigorous. If there is fierce price competition within a market leading to low prices, it would hardly be surprising if other firms did not choose to enter the market. To conclude from the lack of entry that barriers to entry were high and so the market is not competitive would be precisely the wrong conclusion to draw.

The assessment of entry possibilities is complicated by the need to engage in a counterfactual analysis. The fact that no new significant entry has occurred in recent years does not necessarily imply that the market under investigation is not subject to effective potential competitive constraints. For example, the assessment of the significance of the competitive constraint provided by potential competition in the context of an Article 82 excessive pricing investigation depends to some extent on whether one believes a firm has been abusing a dominant position or not. The fact that no significant entry has occurred in recent years can be explained in two ways. On the one hand, if one believes that the firm under investigation is abusing a dominant position and charging prices above the level that would prevail under conditions of effective competition, this can be explained by postulating the existence of high barriers to entry or abusive exclusionary behaviour. On the other, if one believes that the firm is subject to effective competitive constraints, then the lack of entry in recent years can be explained by the fact that the returns to entry into an effectively competitive market tend to be low. Discriminating between these two possibilities can be difficult.

## BOX 3.6: ACADEMIC DEFINITIONS OF "BARRIERS TO ENTRY"

The academic literature on the structure of markets contains a number of definitions of "barriers to entry". Bain[44] defined this as:

> "[T]he extent to which, in the long run, established firms can elevate their selling prices above the minimal average costs of production and distribution (those costs associated with operation at optimal scales) without inducing potential entrants to enter the industry".

This definition therefore focuses on the ability of incumbent firms to earn excess profits.

Stigler,[45] on the other hand, defined a barrier to entry as:

**3–024**

> "[A] cost of producing ... which must be borne by a firm that seeks to enter an industry but is not borne by firms already in the industry".

Carlton and Perloff,[46] following Stigler, argue that:

> "[A] long-run barrier to entry is a cost that must be incurred by a new entrant that incumbents do not (or have not had to) bear."

Under this definition, the fact that new entrants must incur a set-up cost does not confer an advantage on the incumbent if the incumbent also had to bear the same cost.

Gilbert[47] defined the presence of barriers to entry as "the additional profit that a firm can earn as a sole consequence of being established in an industry". Like the Bain definition, this one focuses on the ability of the incumbent to earn excess profits. There are also further definitions of entry barriers that address issues of economic efficiency.[48] But as Gilbert notes, none of these definitions focuses on the central issue: what factors enable an incumbent or incumbents to earn profits in excess of normal profit levels while other equally or more efficient firms are excluded?

---

[44] Bain (1956).
[45] Stigler (1968).
[46] Carlton and Perloff (2004).
[47] Gilbert (1989).
[48] See Gilbert (1989) for a discussion of these definitions.

## *Absolute and Strategic Barriers to Entry*[49]

**3–025**  Barriers to entry can be categorised as either *absolute barriers to entry* or *strategic incumbent advantages.*[50] Absolute barriers to entry include barriers such as exclusive or superior access to necessary inputs.

Absolute barriers to entry relate to whether it is either not possible to or too costly to enter the market. Entry simply might not be possible due to an inability to obtain access to essential inputs. For example, products covered by a patent could represent an absolute barrier to entry since the patent owner could refuse to provide the products covered by the patent to a new entrant.[51] Equally, new entry by an airline might be deterred at an airport if there were no take-off and landing slots available. Furthermore, if an incumbent controls an essential facility, this can act as an absolute barrier to entry if the incumbent refuses to allow third parties to gain access to the essential facility.[52]

Entry might also not represent an effective competitive constraint on incumbent firms if entry is too costly, i.e. although entry is possible in the sense that new entrants could obtain access to the required inputs, it would not be commerically attractive to do so. Where this is the case, barriers to entry are said to be high. However, it should be understood that the size of investment required to enter a new market needs to be put into the context of the industry under investigation. It is much more costly to build a steel mill than to open a shop selling pizzas, but the revenues that can be expected to flow from a steel mill greatly exceed those to be expected from the pizza shop. Hence, knowing that it would cost a new entrant €10 million to enter a market provides little or no information as to whether this represents a high or a low barrier to entry. This will depend on the turnover of the market under investigation: entry is less likely to be feasible if market turnover is €100 million than if it is €10 billion. It is therefore only by comparing the expected revenues with the expected investments that it is possible to talk of high or low barriers to entry. In assessing whether barriers to entry are low or high, the concepts of *minimum efficient scale* (MES) and *minimum viable scale* (MVS) can be useful. The MES is the lowest output at which average costs are minimised, whilst the MVS is the lowest output at which an entrant can earn positive profits. If the MES or MVS is

---

[49]  Various definitions of a "barrier to entry" have been proposed in the academic literature. See Bork (1978), Bain (1956), Stigler (1968), Carlton and Perloff (2004) and Gilbert (1989) and Box 3.6.

[50]  See London Economics (1991) for an excellent survey of the literature on barriers to entry. See also Gilbert (1989).

[51]  It is, of course, less clear that this is a competition policy problem. The high returns that a firm makes from a patented good may well be merely reasonable returns to research and development, particularly when the cost of failed research projects is included in the calculation. Indeed the apparent high returns may be necessary in order to ensure the correct incentives to make risky investments.

[52]  We discuss essential facilities in detail in Chapter 6.

large relative to the total size of the market, then entry is likely to be difficult.

Strategic incumbent advantages relate to asymmetries between the incumbent and the entrant due to timing (i.e. the incumbent "entered" first) and are generally rather harder to analyse than absolute barriers to entry. In many cases the incumbent is able to "change the rules of the game" to its advantage.[53] By changing the rules, the incumbent is able to change the competitive dynamics of the industry and this may have the effect of deterring entry. Sunk costs are central to such a strategy. Many strategies to deter entry are based on ensuring that the best response of the incumbent to entry is such that entry is not profitable. If we assume that an incumbent can respond to entry either by aggressively "fighting" the entrant or by "accommodating" the entrant, then entry is more likely to be deterred if potential entrants expect the incumbent to fight. This means that the incumbent wants to be able credibly to threaten to fight entry. If accommodation is the best strategy for the incumbent given that entry has occurred, it is not usually credible for the incumbent in advance of entry to threaten to fight in the event of entry. However, if the incumbent is able to incur some sunk costs which ensure that his best strategy post-entry is to fight, then the threat to fight is credible and entry may be deterred.[54]

Consider Figure 3.6 and Figure 3.7. These figures show the potential profits of two firms: the incumbent and a potential entrant. These potential profits are shown in brackets. In Figure 3.6, if the potential entrant chooses not to enter, the incumbent firm will earn profits of 4 whilst the potential entrant will earn profits of zero. If the potential entrant chooses to enter, the incumbent has the choice of either "fighting" or "accommodating" the entry. If the incumbent fights, then both it and the entrant make losses of −1. If the incumbent accommodates, both make profits of 1. In this circumstance, it is not credible that the incumbent will fight entry, and so we should expect the potential entrant to enter.[55]

**3–026**

---

[53] These benefits to being an incumbent are often referred to as "first mover advantages".

[54] Sutton (1991) argues that where sunk costs are endogenous (i.e. the incumbent chooses to incur them, rather than them being a necessary cost of production), industries are likely to be relatively highly concentrated as the incumbents use endogenous sunk costs to deter entry. High levels of advertising are one example that Sutton quotes.

[55] This conclusion may not be correct in a dynamic competitive environment. In particular, when the incumbent faces potential entry from a number of entrants, then fighting the first entrant may make sense if it discourages other entrants, even when the pay-offs are as in Figure 3.6. This is discussed in more detail in Chapter 6 when we discuss predatory behaviour by a dominant firm.

**Figure 3.6 Pay-offs leading to entry**

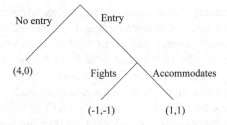

Now consider Figure 3.7. The pay-offs are different in Figure 3.7 to Figure 3.6. Specifically, the incumbent has done something (e.g. made some investment), which means that although it makes less money in the absence of entry (3 rather than 4), it now makes more money fighting entry ($-0.5$), rather than accommodating entry ($-1$). This makes the threat of fighting entry credible, which means that the potential entrant is likely to stay out of the market and earn zero profits rather than make losses of $-1$.

**Figure 3.7 Pay-offs leading to no entry**

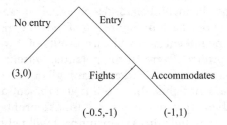

**3–027** An example of this type of strategic entry barrier is investing in excess capacity.[56] If the incumbent can lower his marginal costs of increasing output through investing in excess capacity, this may make it more credible that the incumbent will respond aggressively to entry. This is particularly relevant if the incumbent is currently capacity constrained. Excess investment in research and development may have the same effect if it allows the incumbent to keep a stock of new products that he can launch in response to new entry (thus reducing the entrant's potential demand below the break-even level).

Another way to deter entry strategically is to alter directly the demand or cost curves facing a potential entrant. The incumbent can reduce the demand that a potential entrant faces in a number of ways. It could advertise heavily in order to increase the demand for its product at the expense of any potential substitute products (e.g. increasing consumer

---

[56]   See, for instance, Spence (1977) and Dixit (1980).

loyalty or increasing the attractiveness of the brand to consumers). When the product requires consumers to buy inputs (e.g. refills, game cartridges, etc.), the incumbent can deter entry into the input market by creating costs to consumers of switching to potential substitutes.[57] For instance, the incumbent might ensure that potential substitute inputs do not work so well with the product as its own inputs do. The incumbent might engage in a product proliferation strategy in order to reduce the amount of product space available to an entrant in which to position its product.[58] A more benign barrier to entry may be the reputation of the incumbent. If the incumbent invests in a good reputation (e.g. by consistently selling high quality products relative to their price), this may well act as a barrier to new entry. However, this is not a barrier to entry that we should expect a competition authority to be concerned about. It is based on the firm satisfying consumer preferences and so is to the benefit of consumer welfare.[59] The incumbent might directly alter the costs of the potential entrant by signing exclusive contracts with the suppliers of necessary inputs. The entrant would then have to use other, less well suited, inputs, thus raising his costs. Note that it is key to all of the strategies outlined in this paragraph that the incumbent incurs costs before entry occurs, rather than threatening to incur costs after entry (e.g. by fighting even when accommodation is the more profitable strategy). All these strategies reduce the entrant's expectations of the profitability of entry and so make entry less likely.

Vertical restraints (or vertical integration/vertical mergers) can be used to foreclose a market to entry.[60] Exclusive distribution contracts may foreclose the market to new retail entry by making it impossible for new retailers to get access to products that they require. Exclusive dealership contracts may foreclose the market to new manufacturers by making it impossible for new manufacturers to find retail outlets for their products. This issue is dealt with in much more depth in Chapter 5.

Tirole (1988) argues that capital market imperfections can also act as **3–028** barriers to entry. Specifically, he argues that by engaging in predatory behaviour, firms can reduce the expected short-term profitability of entry, which can increase the level of funds that an entrant needs to raise in order to enter, and capital market imperfections can make it impossible for the entrant to raise the necessary funds even though entry would be profitable

---

[57] Klemperer (1987).

[58] See Schmalensee (1978). However, as Judd (1985) points out, this strategy requires products to be relatively fixed in product space. Otherwise, products could move within the product space post-entry in order to accommodate entry. This possibility would reduce the credibility of the entry deterring strategy. For more details of this entry deterring strategy, see Chapter 6.

[59] If the incumbent is making excess returns through this strategy and still not inducing entry, this implies that he is earning rents on some input that he has. This might, for instance, be a return to innovation.

[60] Ordover, Saloner and Salop (1990).

in the long run. Bolton and Scharfstein (1990) also argue that capital market imperfections may lead to barriers to entry. As we note in Chapter 6, we are not in general convinced by arguments that rely on capital market imperfections. However, we accept that the economic argument that capital constraints are not a barrier to entry is not widely accepted by business people. As such, Schmalensee (1987) is probably right to argue for a "common sense" approach: if business people think capital constraints are a barrier to entry, then their perceptions of such constraints are likely to affect entry decisions, regardless of what economists think of it all.[61]

There is a large literature on predatory behaviour and how it can be used to deter entry. This issue is fully explored in Chapter 6. Rather than repeat the discussion here, the interested reader is referred to Chapter 6.

---

**BOX 3.7: LIMIT PRICING TO DETER ENTRY**

Limit pricing refers to the idea that an incumbent might set its price below the profit maximising level in order to deter entry. Suppose that a potential entrant believes that the incumbent will continue to produce the same amount of product if the potential entrant enters as it is producing before entry. The incumbent can set its output so that there is no level of output that the entrant can produce that leads to a price above the entrant's average cost curve. If the incumbent does this, then the entrant will not enter. In effect the incumbent is setting its output so that there is not enough demand left for an entrant to be profitable.

**3–029** However, there is a serious problem with this argument. It relies on the assumption that the entrant believes that the incumbent will not change its output if the entrant enters. But if the entrant were to enter, then the incumbent would make more profit by accommodating entry and lowering its output. Knowing this, the entrant will enter and the incumbent will rationally accommodate.

One way to make the limit-pricing strategy credible is for the incumbent to engage in some form of commitment investment that means that it is optimal for it to maintain its output even after entry. This might be some sort of investment in capacity, in which case this is essentially the situation illustrated in Figure 3.7 above. Another way to make this strategy credible is to interpret the low pre-entry prices as generating a loyal customer base that reduces the demand for the entrant's product. This strategy requires that there are some switching

---

[61] It is, however, worth remembering Bork's (1978) comment that:

> "Capital requirements exist and certainly inhibit entry—just as talent requirements for playing professional football exist and inhibit entry. Neither barrier is in any sense artificial or the proper subject of special concern for antitrust policy."

costs between products that mean that the demand for the incumbent's product does not decline significantly even when an alternative product becomes available.

Another rationalisation of limit pricing is based on the idea that the behaviour of the incumbent pre-entry can convey information to the entrant. For instance, the behaviour of an incumbent firm can signal to the potential entrant that it will not make profits if it enters, and hence can be used to deter entry. Consider the situation where the incumbent firm can be one of two types, high cost or low cost, but that only the incumbent knows which it is. Further, suppose that the entrant will make positive profits if it enters and the incumbent is high cost, but will make losses if it enters and the incumbent is low cost. In this situation the incumbent may find that mimicking the behaviour of a low cost firm is its best commercial strategy even if its costs are actually high since this may deter entry. For this to be a profitable strategy, it is necessary that the high cost incumbent makes a greater level of profits from acting like a monopoly low cost firm than from acting like a high cost firm and sharing the market.

## Barriers to expansion

Barriers to entry and the potential effect of new entry relate to the ability of **3–030** firms *outside* a particular market nonetheless to impose a constraint on the potential for exercising market power *within* the market. But in most markets, it is competition between existing firms that has the most influence on competitive outcomes. An important source of competitive constraint in most industries is therefore provided by the ability of firms already within the market to respond to any attempts by a firm to increase its price (or equivalently reduce the quantity of its offering) by expanding sales. Where firms can quickly and cheaply increase their output, they are likely to provide an effective competitive constraint.

A barrier to expansion is therefore something that prevents a firm already in a market from being able quickly and cheaply to increase its output. A firm that is capacity constrained and would have to incur significant sunk costs to expand its output faces a barrier to expansion, whereas one that currently has spare capacity does not face such a barrier to expansion (up to the point at which it is using all its capacity). Equally, a firm that is currently producing at full capacity may not face significant barriers to expansion if it can increase its capacity quickly and relatively cheaply (in particular, without incurring significant sunk costs). If rival firms in a market do not face barriers to expansion, then they are likely to be able to respond to a price rise imposed by another firm by undercutting the price rise and selling more output than previously, thereby undermining the attempt by the original firm to raise prices profitably.

Barriers to expansion are important in competition policy analysis because they can be low even though barriers to entry are high. A failure to take account of barriers to expansion might lead to the erroneous conclusion that a firm with a high market share has market power because there are high barriers to entry into the market, when in fact low barriers to expansion by firms already in the market mean that that firm does not possess market power. In the same way that sunk costs are key to the analysis of barriers to entry, they are key to the analysis of barriers to expansion. If a firm would need to incur significant sunk costs to expand its output, then it probably faces significant barriers to expansion. However, it is quite possible that there could be significant sunk costs to entering a market, but low sunk costs to expanding output once in a market. Two examples should make this clear. When branding matters, barriers to entry can be high but barriers to expansion low. Firms often need to incur significant sunk costs (usually of advertising) to create a brand and this may be a pre-requisite for entering a market. However, once the firm has established its brand and is in the market, expanding sales may not require significant sunk costs. A second example is that when investment is very "lumpy",[62] it may be necessary to incur large sunk costs to enter a market, but then the costs of expanding output to full capacity may be very low. Of course, once such a firm reaches full capacity, the lumpiness of investment might mean that it then faces high barriers to further expansion.[63]

The simple conclusion from this analysis is that a large market share and high barriers to entry do not necessarily translate into significant market power. The ability of other firms already in the market to expand their output quickly and cheaply can undermine this apparently simple relationship.

### Countervailing buyer power

**3–031** Sometimes the exercise of market power can be thwarted by buyers. When this occurs it is referred to as "countervailing buyer power".[64] Countervailing buyer power is often thought of as just being about the size of the

---

[62] Investment is said to be "lumpy" when the investment necessary to produce one unit of a good is very similar to the investment needed to produce many more units. For instance, if a firm needs to buy a piece of machinery that is very expensive before it can start producing any units, but this machine will then be able to produce, say, a million units, then investment is lumpy. If the size of the "lumps" is large relative to the size of the total market, then we should expect to see relatively concentrated markets.

[63] The ability to incrementally expand capacity provides an example of where barriers to further expansion can be low.

[64] We are distinguishing countervailing buyer power from the standard economic concern of monopsony. Monopsony is the buying equivalent of monopoly: just one buyer facing a number of sellers. Like monopoly power, monopsony power can lead to anti-competitive outcomes. Whereas a monopolist restricts output in order to raise prices, a monopsonist restricts its purchases in order to reduce the price at which it buys. For more details, see Carlton and Perloff (2004).

buyers, with the idea being that large buyers can exercise buyer power. A supplier will be much more concerned about the potential loss of a large buyer than a small buyer and so will be more inclined to offer large buyers discounts. However, countervailing buyer power is really about the *outside options* of buyers. If a seller wants to raise its price to a buyer and that buyer has no alternative options except that seller, then the seller may well be able to raise prices or exercise market power. However, if the buyer has alternatives to that seller that he can switch to, then the seller will not be able to exercise market power.

The most obvious outside option is other sellers. So if the buyer can switch to alternative sellers, then this will stop the seller being able to exercise market power. This requires that there are alternative sellers, that the costs of switching between sellers are not high and that those suppliers are able to meet the buyer's requirements for increased volumes. If switching costs are high for buyers, then this will reduce the scope for switching to alternative sellers. Where there are switching costs, or where buyers are concerned about the danger of relying too heavily on a particular seller, buyers will often dual-source their supply if this will make it easier for them to switch their purchases away from a seller that tries to raise prices.

Large buyers can sometimes sponsor new entry or help existing small sellers to expand. In many markets uncertainty over demand is a reason why new firms do not enter the market or why existing firms do not invest in extra capacity in order to expand their sales. However, a large buyer can remove this demand uncertainty from a potential entrant or an existing small player. Alternatively, the large buyer can vertical integrate upstream and effectively become a new entrant itself in the selling market. The European Commission concluded that Tetra Pak could sponsor new entry or the expansion of existing small players and this was one reason why the Commission allowed the *Enso/Stora* merger, despite high post-merger market shares in some markets.[65] Large buyers can also undermine seller cartels. A firm operating in a cartel is more likely to "cheat" and offer a price below the cartel level in order to win a new customer when that customer is a large player rather than a small player.

The fact that large buyers may be able to protect themselves against the **3–032** exercise of market power does not mean that small buyers are in the same position. Competition authorities are often concerned that whilst large buyers may be able to resist a price rise, small buyers are not able to do this. Thus the Article 82 Guidance states:[66]

---

[65] IV/M.1225 *Enso/Stora* (1998). For more details of the buyer power argument in this case, see Chapter 7.
[66] Article 82 Guidance, para.18.

"Buyer power may not, however, be considered a sufficiently effective constraint if it only ensures that a particular or limited segment of customers is shielded from the market power of the dominant undertaking."

So when assessing buyer power, it is important to confirm that it will protect small buyers as well as larger buyers. Indeed, there is an argument that the buyer power of large buyers can actually harm smaller buyers. This is referred to as the "waterbed effect". The idea is that if sellers have to offer concessions to large buyers in order to keep their business, then they will seek to increase the revenues that they earn from smaller players. A reduction in prices to large buyers would therefore be mirrored by an increase in prices to smaller players. This would harm consumers because these smaller players would have to raise their prices as a result of their input prices. This might also lead to larger players raising their prices to consumers as a result of the reduction in competitive constraint from smaller players.[67, 68] In general, we are suspicious of this argument, principally because if a seller was able to raise prices to smaller buyers, it is not clear to us why it would not do this regardless of the prices it was charging to larger buyers.[69]

## Product differentiation

**3–033** Although it is the elasticity of demand facing an individual firm that is of interest for the application of competition law, competition law inquiries often begin by determining those products that provide an effective competitive constraint on the price and other terms of supply of the products of the parties under investigation (i.e. they focus on cross-price elasticities). This is a sensible approach since the elasticity of demand depends partly on the degree to which consumers are willing to switch to alternative suppliers following a relative price increase. In markets where all goods are

[67] The "waterbed effect" argument has been used by complainants in a number of inquiries into supermarkets in the UK. For instance, in the 2006–2008 supermarket inquiry the Association of Convenience Stores (ACS) submitted an economic model of the waterbed effect to the Competition Commission. After considerable analysis, the Competition Commission rejected the analysis on the grounds that the empirical evidence did not support it and there was no likely harm to consumers in any case. See Appendix 5.4 ("The waterbed effect in supplier pricing") of "The supply of groceries in the UK market investigation", Competition Commission, April 30, 2008.

[68] This "waterbed effect" should be distinguished from the waterbed effect often discussed in mobile telephony. This latter waterbed effect has to do with the structure of pricing by firms operating in two interlinked markets (e.g. call origination and call termination). This is essentially a two-sided market issue, not a buyer power issue. For further details, see Genakos and Valletti (2008), Muysert, Reynolds and Walker (2006) and Armstrong and Wright (2007).

[69] There is however a literature that seeks to provide a theoretial basis for the waterbed effect. See, for instance, Inderst and Valletti (2008), Dobson and Inderst (2007) and Majumdar (2005).

identical—firms produce homogeneous products—an increase in the price of one firm's products relative to the price of other firms' products will result in consumers switching to other suppliers since all suppliers offer identical products. In these circumstances, the elasticity of demand facing a particular firm will be high.[70]

But in most industries, products are not homogeneous. Instead, they are differentiated from one another in one or more ways. For example, there are a number of different makes of cars, a range of brands of washing powder and different makes of jeans. Product differentiation exists where different consumers have different preferences for the various product offerings. While some consumers prefer to buy a pair of Levi jeans, others prefer to make do with secondary brands whilst yet others prefer to spend more on designer jeans. Products can be differentiated either on grounds of intrinsic quality differences or on grounds of perceived quality differences (such as those created by investments in advertising).[71]

The overall economic effect of product differentiation is to "soften" the degree of price competition between firms. It is no longer necessarily the case that a firm setting price slightly above the price set by other firms means that its sales fall to zero. In effect, product differentiation makes the residual demand curve of each firm less elastic. Clearly, the extent to which consumers will switch away from a product following a relative price increase depends on how close substitutes other products are (i.e. it depends on the degree of differentiation).

Economists draw a distinction between horizontal product differentia- **3–034** tion and vertical product differentiation. Horizontal product differentiation relates to differences in the preferences of consumers, whilst vertical differentiation relates to differences in quality. An example of horizontal product differentiation is that, *ceteris paribus*, buyers of cement will prefer to take supplies from a nearby cement manufacturer rather than from one far away. Similarly, some people prefer red cars, others blue. But the existence of horizontal product differentiation does not mean that there is no competition between the various suppliers. If prices charged by cement manufacturers far away are low enough to offset the increase in transport costs, then consumers will consider buying from these suppliers. Or if red cars are priced higher than blue cars, then some people will switch to buying blue cars even though at equal prices, they prefer red cars.

---

[70] With perfectly homogeneous products and in the absence of capacity constraints on the other firms, the elasticity facing each firm is infinite.
[71] Products can also be differntiated by geographical lcoation and by time.

---

**BOX 3.8: ILLUSTRATING HORIZONTAL DIFFERENTIATION**

Figure 3.8 shows three firms each producing a different brand of, say, breakfast cereal. These brands are distributed along a line that represents the preferences of different consumers. Each consumer prefers, *ceteris paribus*, the product "closest" to him on the line. For example, those consumers with preferences to the left prefer brand A to the other products, assuming equal prices. The price of each brand is represented by the height of the vertical segment. The higher the price, the higher the vertical segment. The market shares depend on how close a substitute each product is to its neighbour. In Figure 3.8 this is represented by the slope of the "umbrella". The gentler the slope, the more substitutable each product is for one another. Where the umbrella of two products cross, consumers are indifferent between the two products. So consumers to the left of ab choose product A, those to the right choose product B up to point bc, whilst consumers to the right of bc choose product C. Note that as the slope of the umbrella gets closer to zero, neighbouring products are increasingly viewed as being more alike. As the slope becomes zero (i.e. the umbrella becomes a flat line), all consumers choose the cheapest product.

**Figure 3.8 Competition between differentiated products**

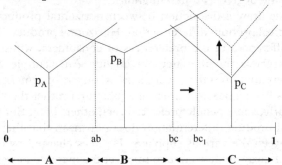

Figure 3.8 shows that each brand has a positive market share even though the price of each brand is different. The volume market shares are represented by how much of the line representing consumer preferences is accounted for by each product. Figure 3.8 also depicts the impact of an increase in the price of product C. The increase in price means that the vertical segment $p_c$ becomes taller, thus pushing the intersection of the "umbrellas" of products B and C to the right (from bc to $bc_1$). This means that the increase in the price of product C has led to a loss of market share for product C as consumers switch to product B and this loss is represented by the horizontal gap between point bc and point $bc_1$ in Figure 3.8.

Whereas horizontal product differentiation examines the effect on com-   **3–035** petition from differences in consumer preferences, vertical product differentiation considers how competition is affected by differences in the quality of products on offer. In many markets, products can be ranked in terms of their quality, whether perceived—as in many fashion industries— or actual. For example, most people would acknowledge that a custom made suit is superior to an off-the-peg suit. At equal prices, all consumers would buy the higher quality product. This is not to say, of course, that all consumers buy the higher quality product in reality as prices will not be equal (i.e. the higher quality product will be more expensive than the lower quality product). Although consumers recognise the differences in quality, which product individual consumers buy will depend on their willingness to trade-off between price and quality.

Where there is considerable scope for vertical differentiation of products, there may be a tendency for markets to become relatively concentrated. If firms can alter consumers' willingness to pay by incurring endogenous expenditures such as advertising or R&D (i.e. where vertical differentiation is possible), then they may choose to incur large sunk costs. If the sunk costs of competing in a market are large relative to the size of the market, this will lead to the market being concentrated as it can only sustain a few firms.[72]

Of course, in many cases, products will exhibit both horizontal and vertical attributes. For example, in the car industry there is horizontal differentiation between different types of car (e.g. small car, MPV, sports car or saloon car), but also vertical differentiation within each type (e.g. between a Mazda MX5, a Porsche Boxster and an Audi R8 in the sports car segment).

## The nature of the oligopolistic interaction between firms

The elasticity of the residual demand curve facing a particular firm   **3–036** depends in part on the decisions of competing firms. If a firm's competitors raise their prices, that shifts the demand curve of the firm outward and so changes the residual elasticity of demand that the firm faces at its current price. Equally, if the competitors lower their prices, this shifts the firm's demand curve inwards. In most industries, firms recognise that their competitive stance—e.g. pricing and marketing decisions—affects the competitive stance of rival firms and is in turn affected by the competitive stance of these firms. Recognition of this competitive interdependence raises the question of whether firms will seek to reduce the vigour with which they compete with one another. This can be illustrated in the Prisoners' Dilemma.[73] Acting in a non-co-operative manner, each firm

[72]   For further details of this argument and empirical support, see Sutton (1991).
[73]   See Box 2.2 in Chapter 2.

adopts a low price strategy even though both firms would prefer to adopt a high price strategy. In this example, the low price strategy earns profits of 4, whilst the high price strategy earns profits of 10. However, a different outcome is possible if the game is played not once but several times, as then firms can earn reputations for acting in a co-operative manner. In this way a high price equilibrium can be reached. The critical issue from a practical perspective is that an assessment of competition requires an examination of whether market mechanisms prevent or alternatively facilitate co-operative behaviour which results in "high price" equilibria rather than competitive "low price" equilibria.

Co-operation between firms can take place either through explicit means—via the formation of a cartel agreement—or through tacit recognition that vigorous competition is not in the best interests of each firm.[74] However, whether co-operative behaviour of either form is sustainable depends to a large degree on the characteristics of particular markets. Those market characteristics which affect the ability of firms to engage in explicit or tacit collusion are examined in more detail in Chapter 5.[75] However, two points should be stressed. First, there is no basis for the often-stated view that the only conceivable outcome in oligopolistic markets is a collusive one.[76] Secondly, distinguishing between competitive and co-operative behaviour is difficult. For example, if one firm increases price and other firms follow, is this evidence of intelligent competitive responses or co-operation? Moreover, the term "oligopoly pricing" does not necessarily indicate a lack of effective competition. In particular, the fact that firms act intelligently in response to the pricing of their competitors should not be automatically condemned. Our view is that, in the absence of a "smoking gun", distinguishing between competitive and co-operative behaviour usually requires careful analysis of the data, which even then may not be dispositive. We are sympathetic to the argument that when the evidence does not point reasonably clearly one way or the other, then there ought to be a general inference that market outcomes are the result of competition rather than co-operation.

---

[74] The possibility of tacit co-operation between firms is recognised in European competition law and gives rise to the notions of collective dominance, coordinated effects and conscious parallelism.

[75] See also Chapter 7.

[76] Philips (1995) expresses a similar view.

# THE LERNER INDEX: A MEASURE OF MARKET POWER?

A measure of market power that is sometimes used is the Lerner Index.[77]   **3-037**
The Lerner Index is the price-marginal cost margin and is defined as:

(5)   $L = \frac{P-MC}{P}$

The Lerner Index is often equated to the inverse of the own-price elasticity of demand. Thus for Firm i:

(6)   $L_i = \frac{P_i - MC_i}{P_i} = \frac{-1}{\varepsilon_i}$

The derivation of this equation is shown in Box 3.9.

The Lerner Index appears to provide an intuitively appealing measure of market power. First, it is directly related to the ability of a firm to raise its price above short-run marginal cost which, as discussed in Chapter 2, is often equated in the academic literature with the competitive price. Secondly, it implies that market power is inversely related to the elasticity of demand facing a firm, which is consistent with what we discussed in paras 3.02–3.11 above. If the elasticity of demand is very high, then the price-marginal cost margin will be low. Equally, a low elasticity is associated with a high price-marginal cost margin. If the elasticity of demand for a firm is −20, then its price will be only 5 per cent above its marginal cost.[78] If instead the elasticity of demand is −2, then its price will be double its marginal cost.

However, great care needs to be taken when using the Lerner Index as a measure of market power. As we argued in Chapter 2, the short-run marginal cost of a firm will only rarely provide a good approximation to the competitive price. Where firms incur fixed costs, the competitive price will necessarily exceed the short-run marginal cost of production. In some industries, the competitive price will exceed the short-run marginal cost of production by a significant amount in order to recoup substantial upfront investments in sunk costs. Industries characterised by intellectual property, such as software or music, provide good examples of where the competitive price must exceed the short-run cost of production.

Furthermore, the Lerner Index is often used to infer the own price   **3-038**
elasticity facing a firm on the basis that the own-price elasticity is the inverse of the Lerner Index. This suggests that estimates of a firm's own-price elasticity can be obtained by knowing only the gross margin (i.e. the difference between price and short-run marginal cost) that the firm earns. Unfortunately, such estimates are often likely to be flawed. First, it requires

---

[77]   Lerner (1934).
[78]   More precisely, it will be 5/95 or 5.3% above marginal cost.

the investigator to have a good estimate of marginal cost, which is often not the case.[79] Secondly, as noted above, even if precise estimates of short-run marginal costs can be obtained, gross margins will not necessarily provide a good indicator of the level of competition that a firm faces where firms also incur sunk costs.

Thirdly, the simple Lerner equation only holds for a single product firm and most firms produce multiple products. This will affect the optimal pricing decisions of the firm. Firms may often sell products that are complements to one another, i.e. by offering one product at a lower price, it may be possible to stimulate demand for other products. It is standard that when a firm sells two complementary products, it has an incentive to price each one lower (in order to stimulate demand for the other one) than if it sold only one product. For instance, product complementarities reduce the incentive for retailers to increase prices, since raising the price of one product risks causing consumers to switch to rival retailers, meaning that the firm will lose out on sales of other products that consumers would have ordinarily purchased. Thus product complementarity gives rise to pricing behaviour that differs significantly from that embodied in the Lerner Index.[80]

The same is true when a multi-product firm sells substitute products. In this case the firm will tend to price its product higher than if it was a single-product firm. This is because it will take account of the fact that some of the sales that it loses by pricing one of its products higher will be captured by sales of another product that it sells. So again using the Lerner Index to derive an own-price elasticity would be inappropriate.

**3–039**    Fourthly, the Lerner Index assumes that the firm is choosing prices to maximise short-run profits, i.e. competing according to a static short-run non-co-operative Nash equilibrium. But this will often not be the case and where it is not the case, the Lerner Index cannot provide a good estimate of a firm's own-price elasticity of demand.[81]

---

[79]    Slade (2004) found examples of actual price-marginal cost margins that were below the level predicted by the Lerner equation. This may have been because of mis-estimated elasticities (i.e. estimated elasticities below the actual elasticities), but Kühn argues that it may also have been because of mis-measured marginal cost (Kühn (2008)).

[80]    See Appendix A for a mathematical exposition of this position.

[81]    Slade (2004) and Nevo (2001) have both used the Lerner equation to estimate the extent of the departure of an industry from the short-run Nash equilibrium. Using estimates of the elasticities and marginal costs for firms, they compute the price predicted by the Lerner equation. They then compare this price to the actual price in the market and use the difference between the two as a measure of how far away the industry is from the Nash equilibrium.

---

**BOX 3.9: DERIVATION OF THE LERNER INDEX EQUATION**

A profit-maximising firm will set marginal cost equal to marginal revenue. If revenue is equal to PQ, then:

(7) $\quad MR = \frac{d(PQ)}{dQ} = P + Q\frac{dP}{dQ} = P(1 + \frac{QdP}{PdQ}) = P(1 + \frac{1}{\varepsilon})$

Setting MR equal to MC then yields the expression:

(8) $\quad \frac{P-MC}{P} = \frac{-1}{\varepsilon}$

---

# POWER TO EXCLUDE[82]

So far in this chapter we have discussed market power in terms of *pricing* **3–040** *power* and the ability of a firm (or firms) to raise prices profitably above the level that would exist under conditions of effective competition (i.e. the effectively competitive price). There is a sense in which discussing market power purely in terms of pricing power runs the risk of omitting an important alternative type of market power: the power to exclude or *exclusionary power*.

The concept of exclusionary market power has found its place in both the literature and judicial interpretation of market power. For example, in *Du Pont*[83] the US Supreme Court defined "monopoly power" as "the power to control prices or exclude competition". The OFT states that[84]:

> "An undertaking may be dominant if it possesses a substantial level of market power. The essence of dominance is the power to behave independently of competitive pressures. This can allow a dominant undertaking to charge higher prices profitably (or, if it is a dominant buyer, extract lower prices) than if it faced effective competition. It can also use its market power to engage in anti-competitive conduct and *exclude or deter competitors* from the market" [emphasis added].

Krattenmaker, Lande and Salop (1987) argue for the need to:

> "Recognis[e] explicitly that anticompetitive power can be exercised by either of two methods: raising one's own prices or raising competitors' costs. These two methods of exercising market power correspond, respectively, to the 'power to control price' and 'power to exclude competitors' distinction expressed in the *du Pont* formulation."

---

[82] This section relies heavily on the OFT Economic Discussion Paper 3 (2002) "Innovation and competition policy" by Charles River Associates.

[83] *United States v E.I. du Pont de Nemours Co* (1956) 351 US 377.

[84] "The Chapter II Prohibition", OFT 402, 1999, para.3.9.

## 3–040  The assessment of market power

Krattenmaker *et al.* distinguish between "the power to control price profitably, directly by restraining one's own output" (classical or "Stiglerian" market power) and "exclusionary or 'Bainian' market power". The latter occurs where a firm can raise its rivals' costs and thereby reduce their ability to compete or exclude them from the market altogether.

**3–041**  The question arises as to whether there is a genuine distinction between pricing power and exclusionary power. It might be argued that exercising exclusionary power is a way of reducing the degree of competition and thereby allowing firms to raise prices. In general this is true. However, it has been argued that there are occasions where there are genuine differences between the two types of market power and that there are (more) occasions when the analysis is simplified by thinking primarily in terms of exclusionary power. This argument holds that consumers can be harmed in more ways than just by being required to pay higher prices than they would under conditions of effective competition. For instance, they might be harmed by behaviour that limits the ability of competitors to introduce new, innovative products that, as a result of anti-competitive behaviour by an incumbent, never make it to the market. Behaviour of this type by an incumbent can harm consumers and increase the incumbent's profits relative to what they would be absent the anti-competitive behaviour, without necessarily raising the prices of any products in the market.[85]

Certainly, it is noteworthy that most allegations of an abuse of a dominant position under EU law focus on what are referred to as *exclusionary abuses* rather than directly on what are referred to as *exploitative abuses*. The former include abuses such as refusing to supply, some vertical restraints and predation, whilst the latter refer to abuses such as excessive pricing and price discrimination. Further, the concept of exclusionary power is also consistent with the legal definition of "dominance" which holds that dominance involves, inter alia, the power to act independently of competitors. This is consistent with the notion of being able to exclude competitors.

The most important reason, however, for taking account of exclusionary power as well as pricing power is that a failure to do so can lead to inappropriate conclusions being drawn. For example, there may be occasions when a firm does not appear to have any pricing power, but does have the ability to exclude new entry that might lead to lower prices, or better products, in future and hence benefit consumers. It is notable that most of the cases brought against Microsoft have focused not on an alleged ability to raise prices, but instead on its ability to exclude rivals.

---

[85]  Strictly speaking, excluding a firm is equivalent to forcing it to price its product at such a high level that there is zero demand for the product.

# TWO-SIDED MARKETS[86]

Two-sided markets occur where there are two distinct customer groups **3–042** that have inter-related demand and so one or both groups impose a positive externality on the other group. A much-analysed example is the credit card market. The groups in this case are retailers and consumers. The more consumers have credit cards, the more retailers benefit from accepting them. The more retailers accept credit cards, the more consumers benefit from having them. Thus, each group imposes a positive externality on the other through the platform provided by the credit card companies (i.e. Visa, Mastercard, Amex, etc.). Another example is that of heterosexual nightclubs, which are more attractive to men the more women go to them, and vice versa. In this case the nightclub is the platform for the two sides of the market meeting. eBay is another platform that links two customer groups: those wanting to sell things and those wanting to buy them.[87]

The standard approaches to efficient pricing are sometimes not appropriate to two-sided markets. Before explaining why, we should stress that most of the time two-sided markets do not require a different approach to standard markets from the perspective of the assessment of market power. There has been a tendency in recent years for practitioners to argue that just because a market is two-sided, the old rules do not apply to it. We hope that it will be plain by the end of this section that this is not in general correct.

Consider the nightclub example mentioned above. What price should the nightclub charge to each side of the market (i.e. to men and to women)? The first point to note is that it is probably not optimal to charge both sides the same amount. Suppose that women create a larger positive externality for men than vice versa, i.e. the effect on the demand from men from the addition of one extra woman attending the nightclub is greater than the effect on the demand of women from the addition of one extra man. The implication of this is that women should be charged less than men because of the greater positive externality that they impose. So one element of the pricing decision is: which side of the market imposes the greater positive externality on the other side?

The second point is a more standard one: the more price sensitive one **3–043** side of the market is compared to the other, the less the price should be to that side of the market. This is intuitive. Suppose one customer group is more price sensitive than another but the platform charges the same price to both. Then by slightly cutting the price to the more price sensitive

---

[86]  This section is necessarily a very brief survey of the area. For further details, see Rochet and Tirole (2008), Evans and Schmalensee (2008) and Armstrong (2006).

[87]  Two-sided markets should be distinguished from markets where there is an aftermarket (e.g. razors and razor blades, printers and toner cartridges, etc.). In these markets the demand for two products is interlinked, but the demand for both products comes from the same consumer. Two-sided markets involve two separate groups of customers.

group, but slightly increasing the price to the less price sensitive group, the platform could increase total numbers using the platform without losing revenue.[88]

Where the value of the platform to each customer increases as the number of customers on the other side of the platform increases, pricing should take this positive externality into account and this may well mean different prices charged to the two customer groups. A number of implications flow from this. First, price discrimination may well be optimal.[89] If one side is more price sensitive than the other side and is more valuable to the other side than vice versa, then we should expect that side to pay lower prices. At the limit, zero (or negative) prices on one side of the market might be optimal. Even if the platform is a monopoly, this structure of prices should not be taken to imply either exploitative price discrimination or exclusionary predation.

An important distinction is between single-homing and multi-homing. Single-homing occurs when customers on one side of the market choose just one of several competing platforms. Multi-homing occurs when customers choose to be on more than one platform. Global distribution systems (GDS), such as Galileo or Amadeus, provide an example of where one side of the market multi-homes and the other single-homes. A GDS acts as a platform on which travel agents and airlines meet. A travel agent subscribes to a GDS and uses this to book flights for their customers. It is expensive for travel agents to subscribe to more than one GDS and so they typically do not. This means that airlines need to subscribe to all the GDS if they want access to all the travel agents.[90] So travel agents single-home and airlines multi-home. Since all the airlines are on all the GDS, the GDS platforms compete to win travel agent customers, since this makes them more valuable to the airlines and so gives them more bargaining power with respect to the airlines. The result is that prices to travel agents are low. Indeed, travel agents tend to be paid by GDS to use their system. Conversely, the airlines are charged to use a GDS. Competition between the various GDS platforms means that these revenues earned from the airlines are largely transferred to travel agents.[91]

**3–044**     This example illustrates a number of important aspects of two-sided markets. First, it illustrates how the price structure can be unbalanced between the two sides. Secondly, it illustrates that this is not necessarily a competition policy problem as competition between platforms can lead to

---

[88]   This logic is similar to that underlying the theory of Ramsey pricing (see Chapter 6 for further details).

[89]   This is not unique to two-sided markets. Price discrimination is often optimal. For more details, see Chapter 6.

[90]   In general, we should not expect to see both sides multi-homing. If one side multi-homes, the other side can access all suppliers via single-homing.

[91]   For further discussion of this market in the context of a merger, see the European Commission's decision in the *Travelport/Worldspan* merger (COMP/M.4523 (August 21, 2007)).

any apparent excess rents earned on one side of the market being competed away on the other side of the market. So in a two-sided market of this type it is necessary to look at price levels rather than just price structure. This issue may on rare occasions be important when defining relevant markets.

We noted above that there is a tendency to suggest that the standard approach to market power analysis does not hold in two-sided markets. This is not correct. First, there are many two-sided markets in which competition authorities routinely use a standard approach to the analysis. For instance, supermarkets can be considered as being two-sided markets. A supermarket is more valuable to a supplier the more customers it has (i.e. greater footfall), whilst a supermarket is more valuable to a customer the more different products it stocks. However, this has not prevented the UK competition authorities, correctly, taking a standard approach to the ana-lysis of market power in this market. Employment agencies are another two-sided market. An agency is more valuable to a worker the more employers it has contracts with, whilst an agency is more valuable to firms the more workers it has on its books. But in the European Commission's investigation of the *Randstad/Vedior*[92] merger there was no suggestion that this "two-sidedness" meant that the Commission should take a non-standard approach to the assessment of market power.

The reason for this is that the same factors that are relevant to the assessment of market power in "standard" markets are also relevant to the assessment of market power in two-sided markets. For instance, barriers to entry remain important: if barriers to entry into the platform market are low, then platforms cannot exercise market power. If barriers to expansion by existing platforms are low, then we should expect competition between platforms to be vigorous in the absence of collusion. Buyer power also remains important, particularly as it may be key to understanding the structure of prices in the market (i.e. lower prices to the side with buyer power).

Another characteristic of two-sided markets is that they can sometimes **3–045** exhibit "tipping", primarily if multi-homing is expensive for both sides of the market. This means that one platform will become dominant. This may lead to market power at the platform level, although not necessarily. Three examples should illustrate this. First, Microsoft has market power in the operating system market as a result of the network externalities associated with this market. An operating system is more attractive to customers the more software is written for that operating system and an operating system is more attractive to software writers the more users it has. There are significant costs to both sides of the market to multi-homing and so both sides tend to single-home. The result is that the market has tipped to Windows and Microsoft has market power. Secondly, consider video cassettes. Studios will prefer to release film on the video format that most

---

[92]  COMP/M.5009 (2008).

consumers use and consumers will want to own a video player that plays the format that most films are available in. The result is that this market tipped to the VHS format rather than the Betamax format. However, there is no market power in the video cassette player market as in this market there are multiple firms. Competition occurs *in* the market, whereas competition in operating systems is competition *for* the market. Thirdly, market power in the games console market is at most fleeting. There are potentially similar network effects as in the operating system market. Consumers will want to own the console with the most games written for it, whilst software writers will want to write for the console with the most users. But what appears to distinguish this from the operating system market is that the level of innovation in the games console market is very high and so new consoles can "leap-frog" the existing consoles via higher quality. The current most successful platform is unlikely to still be the most successful platform in a few years' time.

It should be noted that tipping is not necessarily sub-optimal, although it can lead to market power. Where there are positive externalities between the two sides of the market that mean that customers on each side of the market want to use the most popular platform, then markets are likely to tip. Where there is competition in the platform market, this is not a competition policy concern. Where there is only competition for the market, then there may be market power concerns if the winning platform cannot be challenged over time.

# THE RELATIONSHIP BETWEEN PROFITABILITY AND MARKET POWER[93]

**3–046** The economic model of perfect competition involves firms earning zero economic profits, whilst the economic model of monopoly involves a firm potentially earning very large profits. These two models are at opposite ends of the "competition spectrum". It would therefore appear intuitive that the level of profits that a firm is earning could be used as a proxy for the degree of competition in the market in which it operates. The UK OFT states that:

> "Depending on other available evidence, it might, for example, be reasonable to infer that an undertaking possesses market power from evidence that it has ... persistently earned an excessive rate of profit."[94]

---

[93] For a good analysis of many of the issues covered in this section, see Oxera (2003).
[94] *Assessment of Market Power* (2004) OFT 415, para.6.5.

In this section we argue that this apparently simple and obvious relationship holds only rarely and should not be used generally as the basis for assessing the competitiveness of particular markets or industries.

The logic that is used to defend the use of profits as a measure of the degree of competition in a market is broadly as follows: the role of competition policy is to maximise consumer welfare; profits are a transfer from consumers to producers; producers need to earn only their cost of capital to stay in the market and any profits above this level should be dissipated by new entry; so any profits above the cost of capital are excessive and indicate the lack of effective competition. It is worth noting that profitability analysis is much more a feature of the UK competition law regime than it is of the EU or US regimes.[95]

Before using profitability as a measure of market power for competition **3–047** law investigations it is necessary to consider the possible sources of economic profits. Potential sources of profits include:

- rewards for taking risks and innovating (Schumpeterian rents);

- rewards to a competitive advantage such as superior efficiency or better management (Ricardian rents); and

- the result of having and exercising market power.

Only the last of these three categories of possible sources of profits should concern regulators.

Entrepreneurs who take large risks in investing in projects with highly uncertain returns do not do so in the expectation that if the project turns out to be a success, they will earn a return equal to their cost of capital. Instead, they invest in the expectation that they might well lose all their investment, but that if the investment turns out to be successful, they will earn substantially in excess of their initial investment. An example of the former is the Iridium satellite telephone system, which cost billions of dollars to start and was a commercial disaster, leading to the investors losing virtually all of their initial investment. An example of the latter is the iPod, which has earned Apple many times its initial investment. High profits that are the result of taking a large risk are not indicative of a failure of competition. What may look like excessive profits once the investment has turned out to be a success might represent only a modest "risk-adjusted" return based on the ex ante risk of the project. If a particular investment has only a 10 per cent chance of success, a firm will only make that investment if it expects to earn returns of more than 10 times its original investment if the project is a success. This is necessary to

---

[95] Although in *United Brands* (*United Brands v Commission* [1978] E.C.R. 207; [1978] 1 C.M.L.R. 429) the Court did imply that there was a potential role for profitability analysis in excessive pricing cases. For further details, see Chapter 6 below.

compensate the firm for accepting the 90 per cent risk that it will earn nothing from the investment.

Another legitimate source of high profitability is competitive advantage such as superior efficiency relative to competitors or better management. It should be noted that economics predicts that even in a competitive market, it is only the marginal firm that makes zero economic profits. Those firms that are more efficient than the marginal firm will make positive economic profits, whilst those that are less efficient will either exit the market or never enter it. Consequently, there will be many industries which are subject to effective competition, but where firms earn more than their cost of capital without therefore concluding that there are competition policy problems.[96]

**3–048** We explained in Chapter 2 that a monopolist raises prices above the competitive level, and earns excess profits, by restricting output below the competitive level. Those who invest in risky projects do not do this. They seek to create products that would not otherwise exist, i.e. they seek to expand output. Equally, profits earned from being more efficient than one's rivals are also not typically earned by restricting output. So the profits earned from these two sources are not profits that should concern policy makers.

It is also important to note that economic theory only holds that firms operating in competitive conditions make zero economic profits *in equilibrium*. When markets are not in equilibrium, then firms may make economic profits or losses during the period of disequilibrium. For instance, a new lower cost production technique available to some participants in a market will likely lead to those participants earning positive profits in the short run, until the market settles down in a new equilibrium. In many dynamic markets (e.g. software and video games), equilibrium may never be reached as each product is soon superceded by a new, better product. In such markets it is not to be expected that firms consistently earn zero economic profits. Instead, there will be periods when they make losses and periods when they make positive economic profits.

This is not to deny that there may be excess profits that are earned as a result of the exercise of market power. However, the measurement of economic profits (i.e. revenues minus opportunity cost over the lifetime of the project) is fraught with difficulty. Economic profits are substantially different to accounting profits. Accounts are designed for financial reporting to external parties, and have a focus on producing information that is objective and reliable and are based on the principle of "prudence". They are not intended to record potentially more economically relevant, but subjective, information and do not measure economic costs. For instance, capital assets such as the value of a firm's brand or intellectual

---

[96] For instance, Professor John Kay noted in the *Financial Times* of April 5, 2000 that 41 of the 45 FT 500 sectors earned returns above their cost of capital.

property do not usually appear on the balance sheet.[97] However, these may be a key part of a firm's competitive advantage and should be included in any calculation of the economic return that a firm is earning on its assets. Intangible items such as R&D and advertising are often expensed in the current period rather than capitalised and then depreciated over time. From an economic perspective, this is not the correct approach since such expenditures constitute investments undertaken to generate revenues over time.[98] Competition law cases deal with the nature of competition within relevant antitrust markets, whereas accounts are typically put together at the firm level and are rarely disaggregated on the basis of antitrust markets.

This means that using accounting profits as a direct measure of eco-   **3–049** nomic profit is unlikely to be reasonable. Indeed Bain (1941) argued that:

> "[U]nadjusted accounting rate of profit, as computed by the usual methods from balance sheets and income statements, is prima facie an absolutely unreliable indicator of the presence or absence of either monopoly power or excess profits".

Fisher and McGowan (1983) echoed this comment:

> "There is no way in which one can look at accounting rates of return and infer anything about relative economic profitability or, a fortiori, about the presence or absence of monopoly profits."

This does not mean that accounting data is entirely useless for calculating economic profits, but it does mean that accounting profits cannot be used unthinkingly as a proxy for economic profits. The correct measurement of the economic profitability of an investment involves measuring the costs[99] and revenues associated with that investment throughout its entire lifetime. This can only be measured by modelling the activity, over the project lifetime, using discounted cash-flow techniques. In stylised form, most projects involve an initial investment period, when accounting profits are low or negative, a mature phase when accounting profits are high, and a sunset phase when accounting profits fall to zero and the activity is discontinued. Observing high accounting profits in the mature phase of a product's life conveys no useful information on whether excess profits are being earned over the lifetime of the project. Economists refer to such profits as *quasi*-profits. They appear as if they are real (excess) profits, but

---

[97] An exception is if the firm has been recently traded, in which case the valuation of these factors will be captured in "goodwill".

[98] Oxera (2003) argues that asset values tend to be understated in accounts.

[99] Note that some of these costs will be difficult to measure. For instance, calculating a firm's cost of capital can be fraught with difficulty.

in fact are only an artefact of taking a snapshot at a particular stage of the product lifecycle.[100]

A good example of the dangers of looking only at a snapshot is provided by the UK Monopoly and Mergers Commission report into Video Games in 1995.[101] The MMC concluded that:

> "It is reasonable to conclude that Nintendo is an exceptionally profitable enterprise and, at least until 1993/94, Sega was also very profitable."

The MMC treated this as evidence that the industry was not subject to effective competition. However, this was an incorrect conclusion to draw. It took no account of the level of risk that Sega and Nintendo had incurred when they entered the market in 1987 or of the fact that there was ample evidence that the firms did not have any lasting market power. History showed that even very large players had failed in this market (Atari, Commodore and Philips) and it was public knowledge that Sony was about to enter. As we subsequently know, Sony became the worldwide market leader by the late 1990s, Sega exited the market in 2001 and Microsoft entered the market to challenge Sony's position. The high levels of profitability generated by Sega and Nintendo in the mid-1990s conveyed no useful information about the state of competition. Rather than relying on measures of profitability the MMC ought to have considered direct evidence of competitive behaviour and barriers to entry to assess whether the market was competitive.[102]

**3–050**     Most firms produce more than one product line. When there are shared costs (common costs) across different product lines, measuring the profitability of any particular product line becomes difficult. A firm will earn positive profits as long as the overall revenues that it earns exceed its overall costs. In the presence of common costs, the firm will need to ensure that in aggregate its products earn an amount exceeding variable costs sufficient to cover the common costs. Assessing the profitability of a particular product in such circumstances therefore requires that a proportion of the common costs should be allocated to each product. This allocation procedure may be highly controversial and from an economic perspective there is no single "right" way to allocate common costs.

---

[100] The conceptual and practical problems of inferring monopoly rents from accounting rates of return are well understood and a full recounting of the arguments is beyond the scope of this book. For a full discussion of the issues, see Fisher and McGowan (1983).

[101] Report of the Monopolies and Mergers Commission, *Video Games, A report on the supply of video games in the UK*, MMC, March 1995, para.2.55.

[102] A more detailed analysis of this case can be found in the OFT publication 377, "Innovation and competition policy" (2002).

## BOX 3.10: AN EXAMPLE OF ALLOCATING COMMON COSTS

Figure 3.9 provides an example to show how different allocations of common costs alter the apparent profitability of a product line. In this example there are common costs of 400 between products A and B, variable costs of 50 for product A and variable costs of 150 for product B. Product A earns revenues of 400, whilst product B earns revenues of 200, so both products cover their variable costs. Total costs and total revenues are both 600, so the firm makes zero profits on these products. However, depending on how the common costs are allocated, product A might appear excessively profitable. Figure 3.9 shows three possible allocations.

1.  Common costs are allocated in the same proportion as variable costs are incurred (i.e. 25 per cent to product A, 75 per cent to product B).

2.  Commons costs are allocated in the same proportion as revenues are earned (i.e. 67 per cent to product A, 33 per cent to product B).

3.  Common costs are allocated so as to make the implied return on both products the same (i.e. 350 to product A, 50 to product B).

**Figure 3.9 Alternative allocations of common costs**

|  |  | Product A | Product B |
|---|---|---|---|
| **Common cost** |  | 400 | |
| **Revenues** |  | 400 | 200 |
| **Variable costs** |  | 50 | 150 |
| **Contribution** |  | 350 | 50 |
| **Possible allocations** | Allocation | 100 | 300 |
|  | Implied return | 167% | −56% |
|  | Allocation | 267 | 133 |
|  | Implied return | 26% | −29% |
|  | Allocation | 350 | 50 |
|  | Implied return | 0% | 0% |

When the common costs are allocated on the basis of variable costs, product A looks to be excessively profitable as it has a total cost of 150, but earns revenues of 400. When the common costs are allocated on the basis of revenues, product A's return is much less. When the common costs are allocated to lead to equivalent implied returns on

**3–051**

the two products, then both earn zero return. So the way in which common costs are allocated has important implications for calculations of profitability.

As we noted above, there is no single economically correct way to allocate common costs. If a regulator wishes to look at profitability, then we would strongly advocate looking at profitability at a high enough level within the firm so that common cost allocation issues do not drive the results. In our example above, that would imply looking at the summation of products A and B, not just at product A alone.

A further issue that needs to be considered before deriving conclusions from profitability analysis is the issue of the reliability of the profits figures. For example, suppose it is claimed that a firm is making supra-normal profits that are, say, 20 per cent above its cost of capital. An important question to ask is what are the confidence intervals for that figure? Since any measure of profitability represents only an *estimate*, it is only possible to be sure that the estimate of profitability lies within a certain range, rather than that it is exactly equal to a particular number. The interpretation of the estimated 20 per cent supra-normal profits will be somewhat different depending on whether the confidence interval for that figure is 18–22 per cent or −10–50 per cent.

We would not go so far as to say that analysing the profitability of a firm under investigation will never yield information that is useful for assessing the effectiveness of competition in a market. For instance, it would be surprising to find long-run high returns in a mature capital intensive commodity business in which brand names and advertising were not important. However, as we move away from industries of this type towards dynamic industries, that involve significant ex ante risk and where knowledge and other intangible assets are important, profitability analysis will be less useful in discriminating between markets subject to effective competition and those that are not. Once the other difficulties with measuring profitability are recognised, such as cost allocation problems, it can be seen that the exercise can quickly become virtually meaningless.

**BOX 3.11: THE TRUNCATED INTERNAL RATE OF RETURN**

**3–052**

If it is necessary to estimate economic profitability over a relatively short period, then the most reasonable approach is to use the truncated internal rate of return (IRR) approach. The IRR of a project is the discount rate that makes the NPV of the project zero. The truncated IRR approach looks at the change in the profitability of a firm (or project) over only part of the total life of the firm (or project). The change in the value of the firm between time zero and time T is the total value of the cash flows during that period plus the change in the value of the assets owned by the firm, all discounted by the relevant discount rate. Thus the IRR is given by the formula:

$$(9) \quad A_0 = \sum_{t=1}^{T} \frac{CF_t}{(1+r)^t} + \frac{A_T}{(1+r)^T}$$

where   $A_0$ and $A_T$ are the value of the assets at time zero and time T;
        $CF_t$ are the cash flows at time t; and
        r is the IRR.

Suppose we have a project that has the pattern of accounting profits we discussed above: initial losses during investment, followed by large cash flows, followed by a decline in cash flows during the sunset period of the project. Suppose the formula above is used to estimate the IRR during the period of large cash flows. We should expect the value of the assets at the end of the period ($A_T$) to be less than the value at the beginning of the period ($A_0$) since, by assumption, the future cash flows that can be generated by the asset are substantially less at time T than at time zero.[103] Thus the IRR will be less than would be given by a naïve use of accounting profits.

The IRR calculated in this way will not be the same as the IRR of the project as a whole. However, Edwards et al. (1987) argue that it does yield information about profitability that is useful for competition policy purposes and that reduces the risk of identifying quasi-rents as genuine rents.

# ANALYSING MARKET POWER IN THE LIGHT OF THE ALLEGED ANTI-COMPETITIVE BEHAVIOUR[104]

The standard procedure to assessing competitive behaviour is conducted in **3–053** two stages: first define the relevant market,[105] and assess whether a firm has market power within this market; secondly if a firm is found to possess market power, consider the competitive effect of the alleged anti-competitive conduct. It has been argued that this approach treats market definition and the analysis of market power as threshold issues: if you do not find market power within a relevant market, you stop the analysis.[106] In general, this is a reasonable way to approach competition policy issues. However, it is important not to lose sight of the fact that the core of competition policy is the effect on consumer welfare of allegedly anti-

---

[103] It should be noted that when using the truncated IRR formula to estimate whether profits are excessively high, the assets should be valued on the basis of their modern equivalent asset value (or replacement cost).

[104] See particularly Salop (2000).

[105] See Chapter 4 for the motivation for this two-stage approach as well as a detailed discussion of how to define the relevant market in a particular case.

[106] This is the approach advocated by Easterbrook (1984).

competitive behaviour. Market definition and market power are only analysed to the extent that they aid the assessment of whether behaviour has had anti-competitive effects. An interesting question to ask is whether the "standard" approach is likely to lead to errors in the analysis of competitive effects in practice. The answer is that if the market definition and market power analysis is completely divorced from the analysis of competitive effects, then mistakes will sometimes be made.

Market power should be analysed as the power to maintain price above the level that would prevail in the absence of the alleged anti-competitive conduct. If the market power analysis is carried out without regard to the alleged anti-competitive conduct and the implied counterfactual, then errors in the competitive assessment can be made. Two examples illustrate this point.

Suppose the allegation is that a firm has excluded a rival firm through anti-competitive conduct and that this has harmed competition. In this case the theory of anti-competitive behaviour would be that in the absence of the excluding conduct, price would be lower than the current price. The benchmark for the exercise of market power in this instance should be whether the current price is higher than it would have been in the absence of the conduct.

**3–054** Alternatively, suppose the allegation is that a joint venture by two firms will lead to a reduction in competition in the future. Here the theory of anti-competitive behaviour is that the joint venture will lead to prices increasing relative to the current price level. So the benchmark for the exercise of market power in this instance should be the current price level.

However, it is worth noting that on rare occasions a proper focus on competitive effects can mean that the relevant market and market power analysis is not needed at all. Where there is direct evidence of anti-competitive effect, the market power analysis is likely to be redundant. In *Kodak*,[107] the US courts stated that:

> "[I]t is clearly reasonable to infer that Kodak has market power to raise prices and drive out competition in the aftermarkets, since respondents offer direct evidence that Kodak did so."[108]

Of course, this is not the end of the analysis: it is still necessary to show anti-competitive harm to consumers, but this will not likely require a market definition or market power analysis. Instead, it requires direct analysis of the effect of the behaviour on consumers. Salop (2000) notes, quoting *Indiana Federation of Dentists*[109]:

---

[107] *Eastman Kodak Co v Image Technical Serv. Inc* (1992) 504 US 451.
[108] *Eastman Kodak Co*, 477.
[109] *FTC v Indiana Federation of Dentists* (1986) 476 US 477.

"Since the purpose of the inquiries into market definition and market power is to determine whether an arrangement has the potential for genuine adverse effects on competition, proof of actual detrimental effects, such as a reduction of output, can obviate the need for an inquiry into market power, which is but a surrogate for detrimental effects."

However, it should be noted that even in such cases, it should still be possible to define a relevant market within which the firm in question has market power that it is able to exercise anti-competitively. The point is just that relatively little extra analysis will be required to define the market and find market power when a careful direct analysis has conclusively shown the existence of anti-competitive behaviour causing harm to consumers. Before leaving this issue, we should stress that this approach to the assessment of market power is likely to be applicable only relatively rarely.

## SUMMARY

This chapter has discussed the key economic concept of competition law: **3–055** market power. The exercise of market power by a firm requires that the firm can restrict output in a relevant market, that this restriction is profitable for the firm and that price is raised above the level implied by effective competition. We then discussed various basic indicators that assist in the assessment of whether a firm has (or firms have) market power. These basic indicators are: the number of competing suppliers of the same products, their market shares and market concentration; the existence of barriers to entry and potential competition; the existence of barriers to expansion; the existence of countervailing buyer power; the degree of product differentiation and the nature of the oligopolistic interaction between firms. Of course, consideration of these factors alone does not provide a complete competitive analysis. As Part II of this book illustrates, a complete competitive assessment will depend on the specific facts of the industry under investigation and the specific behaviour in question. We discussed the use of the Lerner Index as a direct measure of market power and argued that its usefulness was limited.

In addition to discussing market power in terms of pricing power, we also noted that market power can also be manifested via the power to exclude rivals and argued that there are occasions when the analysis is simplified by thinking in these terms, rather than in terms of power over price. We discussed two-sided markets and argued that in general such markets do not require a different approach to be taken to the assessment of market power. We argued that measuring the profitability of firms is usually not a very useful guide to measuring whether a firm is exercising market power. Finally, it was noted that, on occasion, anti-competitive effects can be observed directly, without a need to define a market or formally analyse market power.

## Annex A: Multi-Product Firms and the Lerner Index

**3-056** We explained in the main text of this chapter why the Lerner Index is not appropriate for deriving own-price elasticities when firms sell multiple products. In this Annex we provide a mathematical presentation of this point.

For simplicity, consider a multi-product monopolist selling N products (although the implications of this result hold across markets of varying degrees of concentration). The monopolist maximises the following profit function:

$$(1) \quad Profits = \sum_{i=1}^{N} p_i D_i(p) - C_i(D_i(p))$$

where    $p_i$ is the price of product i;

$D_i(p)$ is the demand for product i at price $p_i$ given the price of all the firm's other products; and:

$C_i(D_i(p))$ is the total cost of producing $D_i(p)$.

This profit function is simply the revenue of each product (price multiplied by demand) less the cost of producing each product, which is dependent upon the vector of prices the firm sets across all of the products it produces.

Maximising his profits by optimising this function across all his products and rearranging terms gives us the following first order condition for each product i:

$$(2) \quad \frac{p_i - mc_i}{p_i} = \frac{1}{\varepsilon_{ii}} - \sum_{j \neq i} \frac{(p_j - C'_j) D_j \varepsilon_{ij}}{p_i D_i \varepsilon_{ii}}$$

where    $\varepsilon_{ii}$ and $\varepsilon_{ij}$ are the own price elasticity and cross-price elasticity of demand for j with respect to the price of i respectively; and

$mc_i$ is the marginal cost of producing product i.

**3-057** The second term of the RHS of equation (2) will be positive when $\varepsilon_{ij}$ is negative (i.e. when product i and product j are complements) and positive when $\varepsilon_{ij}$ is positive (i.e. when i and j are substitutes). This means that where products are complements, then for any given gross margin the firm's own-price elasticity of demand inferred from the Lerner Index will overstate the true firm level own-price elasticity of demand. This is intuitive. When products are complements, the firm will "underprice" each one compared to the single product outcome, which implies that the Lerner Index will be lower than in the single product outcome and so the implied own-price elasticity will be higher than the actual own-price elasticty.

When the products are substitutes, the reverse logic applies and the own-price elasticity inferred from the Lerner Index will be an under-estimate of the correct value.

# 4. The Relevant Market

## INTRODUCTION

The concept of the relevant market plays a central and often critical role in **4–001** the application of European competition law. The definition of the relevant market features in all decisions made under Articles 81, 82 and the Merger Regulation and in many competition decisions made by the national authorities of the Member States.[1] The relevant market is an important concept in EC competition law for a number of reasons.

The primary legal reason for the important role that the relevant market plays in European competition law assessments is provided by the decisions of the European Court of Justice and the Court of First Instance. The Courts have stated on a number of occasions that the definition of the relevant market is required.[2] However, while those judgments of the Courts indicate the importance of the relevant market concept, they provide little if any guidance as to how one ought to define a relevant market. In order to understand the basis on which relevant markets should be defined, it is therefore necessary to examine the role that the definition of the relevant market plays in the overall competitive assessment. Once that role is understood, the basis for defining the relevant market becomes clear.

Assessing the nature of competition in a given industry is rarely a straightforward task. As noted in Chapter 3, a proper competitive assessment needs to take into account a wide range of factors specific to the industry under investigation in order to assess whether a firm or group of firms possess market power and if so how much (in the context of Article 81 and Article 82 investigations) or whether as a result of a merger, the merged firm, perhaps together with other competing firms, will enjoy

---

[1] Market definition issues also arise in state aid cases, although in a less formal setting than in other competition issues. For instance, a common question is whether alleged aid distorts competition between undertakings and this analysis requires an understanding of which undertakings compete with each other. This analysis is similar to that underlying relevant market definition. See Bishop (1997).

[2] See, e.g. 6/72 *Europemballage Corp and Continental Can Co Inc v EC Commission* [1973] E.C.R. 215 at 247; [1973] C.M.L.R. 199 at 226; Sixteenth Report on Competition Policy (1986) paras 337 et seq.

enhanced market power. The list of factors that need to be taken into account include inter alia the number of firms supplying competing products; the degree of competition between those products, i.e. the degree of product differentiation; the existence of barriers to expansion; the ability of firms to reposition their product offerings; the existence of barriers to entry and potential competition; the potential responses of customers; and the nature of the oligopolistic interaction between firms. Even if consideration could be limited to only these industry factors, the assessment of competition can be seen to be, in general, a complex task.

**4–002**   Given the complexity involved in assessing the degree of competition in a given industry, the competitive assessment is usually conducted in two stages: first define the relevant market; then assess competition in that relevant market.[3] In the first stage, the relevant market is defined so as to encompass all those products or services which are considered to be effective substitutes for the products or services at the centre of the investigation. The relevant market in effect allows attention to be focused on the "important" or "primary" competitive constraints which exist between products and between regions. The definition of the relevant market allows the second-stage assessment to include, inter alia, an analysis of market shares and market concentration.

The definition of the relevant market is therefore a tool for aiding the competitive assessment by identifying those substitute products or services which provide an effective constraint on the competitive behaviour of the products or services being offered in the market by the parties under investigation. In effect, the relevant market seeks to restrict attention only to those products or services which have a "significant" impact on competition. The Commission made precisely this point in its *Notice on the Definition of Relevant Market for the Purposes of Community Competition Law* (hereafter, "the Relevant Market Notice).[4] The Relevant Market Notice states that:

> "[M]arket definition is a tool whose purpose is to identify in a systematic way the competitive constraints that the undertakings involved face. The objective of defining a market in both its product and geographic dimension is to identify those actual competitors of the undertakings involved that are capable of constraining their behaviour and of preventing them from behaving independently of any effective competitive pressure."[5]

---

[3]   As noted in Chapter 3, the traditional focus on market shares reflects a structural approach to the competitive assessment. However, even in the current mode of competition enforcement in the EC, which has begun to see less emphasis placed on market shares and concentration ratios and more on qualitative competitive effects, the definition of the relevant market still has an important role to play in the competitive assessment.

[4]   European Commission's Notice on the Definition of the Relevant Market for the Purposes of Community Competition Law [1997] OJ C372/5; [1998] 4 C.M.L.R. 177.

[5]   Relevant Market Notice, para.2.

As the Relevant Market Notice states, the concept of the "relevant market" is different from other definitions of market that are often used in other contexts, for example marketing initiatives.[6]

Defining the relevant market as an intermediate step in the competitive assessment has two significant benefits. First, it provides a focus for the competitive assessment. By defining the relevant market so as to encompass all those products or services which are considered to be effective substitutes for the products or services at the centre of the investigation, the relevant market focuses the attention of both the Commission and interested affected parties on the main competitive constraints which exist between products and between regions. Excluding such competitive constraints from the analysis will likely result in a flawed competitive assessment.[7]

Secondly, the definition of the relevant market provides an initial screen **4–003** for the competitive assessment. Defining the relevant market enables market shares and market concentration to be calculated.[8] But market shares can provide meaningful information regarding market power for the purpose of the competitive assessment only if the relevant market is defined in a systematic way that captures the competitive constraints that the firms under investigation face, and hence identifies their effective competitors.[9] In consequence, market shares provide a useful first filter to determine whether a more detailed competitive assessment is required. In most instances, low market shares are not compatible with firms possessing market power. Therefore, only when firms are shown to have relatively high market shares in a properly defined relevant market will a detailed competitive assessment be required.[10]

However, this is not to suggest, as is commonly misunderstood, that high market shares represent a presumption of competitive harm. Rather, a full and complete assessment of competition within the defined relevant market taking into account the other factors that affect competition needs to be taken into account. The competition investigation is typically concerned

---

[6] Relevant Market Notice, para.3.
[7] We discuss at para.4–047 the scope for undue weight to be given to some of the competitive constraints existing between different products and regions that form part of the same relevant market.
[8] The calculation of any market share, or concentration ratio, necessarily requires a definition of the relevant market, whether this is undertaken explicitly or implicitly.
[9] Relevant Market Notice, para.2.
[10] As discussed later in this chapter and in Part II, market shares can in certain circumstances over- or under-state the competitive constraints facing firms. Where that is the case, a more detailed competitive assessment may be justified even where the firms under investigation are shown to have only relatively low market shares.

with whether effective competition *is being* adversely affected in the case of Article 81 or Article 82 investigations or whether it *will be* adversely affected in the case of a merger.[11] It is not concerned per se with the definition of the relevant market. The definition of the relevant market therefore is merely an intermediate step which facilitates the second competitive assessment. That assessment includes an analysis of market shares and concentration, but also includes crucial questions such as the ease of entry, the scope for strategic oligopolistic behaviour, the strength of buyer power and so on. Undue focus on relevant market definition often means that these important questions are given too little consideration.

Having determined the role that the definition of the relevant market plays in the competitive assessment, the basis on which relevant markets should be defined becomes clear. The definition of the relevant market can be a useful intermediate tool to aid the competitive assessment only if it is defined on a basis which permits a useful assessment of market power. From an economic perspective Article 81 and Article 82 inquiries are normally concerned with whether current business activities allow firms to increase prices above competitive levels. Merger inquiries differ somewhat in that they are concerned with whether the merger will lead to a lessening of competition such that prices will increase above prevailing levels.[12]

**4–004**    Whether a firm or firms can exercise market power will depend on the own-price elasticity of demand facing the firm or firms at the price level appropriate for the particular investigation. This in turn depends in part upon the availability of suitable substitutes for the products or services of the firm or firms in question. The definition of the relevant market is therefore directly concerned with the identification of these substitute products or services. In other words, the appropriate basis for defining relevant markets is one that focuses directly on the competitive constraints that products or services impose upon one another. Clearly, any sensible basis for defining relevant markets must be consistent with this basis.

This reasoning explains why the fundamental guiding principle of defining relevant markets can be summarised as follows: *a relevant market is*

[11]   This difference between Articles 81 and 82 cases and merger cases is not always as clear-cut as this. The analysis of joint ventures under Article 81 is typically a forward-looking analysis, whilst some Article 82 allegations also give rise to essentially forward-looking analyses (e.g. what alleged exclusionary behaviour will do to the ability of a firm to compete in the future). Furthermore, many theories of harm in non-horizontal merger cases are predicted on existing market power.

[12]   Where the competitive assessment is concerned with the current level of competition, then the appropriate benchmark is the competitive price. Where the competitive assessment is concerned with the future (e.g. the impact of a merger or of an agreement yet to be put in place) then the appropriate benchmark is the prevailing price. In what follows, unless otherwise stated, references to the elasticity of demand are taken to mean the elasticity of demand at the competitive price level if the investigation is conducted in the context of Articles 81 or 82 and the elasticity of demand at the prevailing price level if the investigation is a merger inquiry.

*something worth monopolising.*[13] A market is worth monopolising if mono-polisation permits prices to be profitably increased. This will be the case if the collection of products contained in this "market" are not subject to significant competitive constraints by products outside the market.

The remainder of this chapter describes that test and how it should be applied in practice. We note at the outset that the Hypothetical Monopolist Test represents the appropriate analytical framework for defining relevant market in *all* cases, even if in practice it is not always possible to apply it empirically. We discuss a number of common errors or fallacies in defining relevant markets that are often encountered in practice. Section 4.2 explains the theoretical principles that underpin the Hypothetical Monopolist Test. Section 4.3 discusses the *Cellophane* fallacy. Section 4.4 discusses a number of other common fallacies encountered in defining relevant markets in practice. Section 4.5 raises some further issues that often arise in the practical application of the Hypothetical Monopolist Test.

# DEFINING RELEVANT MARKETS: THE HYPOTHETICAL MONOPOLIST TEST

The standard approach to defining the relevant market is known as the **4–005** Hypothetical Monopolist Test.[14] The test originated in the US horizontal merger guidelines issued jointly by the Department of Justice and the Federal Trade Commission. The 1992 Guidelines state that[15]:

> "A market is defined as a product or group of products and a geographic area in which it is produced or sold such that a hypothetical profit-maximising firm, not subject to price regulation, that was the only present and future producer or seller of those products in that area likely would impose at least a 'small but significant and non-transitory' increase in price, assuming the terms of sale of all other products are held constant."[16]

---

[13] Bishop and Darcey (1995).

[14] The test is also known as the SSNIP test or 5% test.

[15] The Hypothetical Monopolist Test was first introduced into US merger control in the 1982 US Horizontal Merger Guidelines. The original idea was expressed in an article by Adelman (1959).

[16] The Small but Significant and Non-transitory Increase in Price (SSNIP) is usually taken to be either 5% or 10%.

An equivalent statement of the test is that a market is a collection of products such that a (hypothetical) single supplier of that collection would be able to increase price profitably; in other words, a relevant market is something worth monopolising.[17] Defining the relevant market in this way ensures that all products which pose a significant competitive constraint on the parties under investigation are taken into consideration. A market is worth monopolising if monopolisation permits prices to be profitably increased. This will be the case if the collection of products contained in this "market" (ie products controlled by the hypothetical monopolist) are not subject to significant competitive constraints by products outside the market.

---

**BOX 4.1: A PROFIT-MAXIMISING HYPOTHETICAL MONOPOLIST OR A PROFITABLE PRICE RISE**

**4-006**

There appears to be a subtle difference between the DoJ/FTC approach and the EU approach. The DoJ/FTC version of the hypothetical monopolist test asks whether a hypothetical profit-maximising monopolist would raise prices by more than 5–10 per cent above current levels.[18] The EU version of the hypothetical monopolist test appears to be whether a hypothetical monopolist would make more profits if prices were 5–10 per cent higher than the current level. There is an important difference between these two versions of the test. It might be that a hypothetical monopolist would make higher profits if prices were more than 5 per cent above the current level, but also that the hypothetical monopolist would maximise profits by raising prices by less than 5 per cent above the current level. The DoJ/FTC version of the test is the correct one and is the one that is used in practice.

Figure 4.1 illustrates the issue. The horizontal axis corresponds to increases in price above the current level, whilst the vertical axis corresponds to increases in profits to the hypothetical monopolist. In Figure 4.1, an increase in price above the current level increases the profits of the hypothetical monopolist up to a 4 per cent price rise. Thereafter, profits decline, though they remain above the original profit level. However, above 10 per cent profits actually fall below the original level. In this case, a profit-maximising hypothetical monopolist over the relevant group of products would raise prices by 4 per cent, which is clearly less than the 5–10 per cent required by the

---

[17] More precisely, the test is whether a hypothetical monopolist could profitably increase price above the price benchmark relevant to the particular case under investigation. This will usually be the prevailing price in mergers and the competitive price in other types of investigation. We discuss issues arising from applying the Hypothetical Monopolist Test in practice where the appropriate benchmark is the competitive price in paras 4–017—4–022.

[18] For clarity, we are ignoring here potential issues raised by the *Cellophane* fallacy. We consider them in detail below.

hypothetical monopolist test to define a separate market. So in this instance the relevant market is wider than the group of products currently included.

**Figure 4.1 Relating changes in prices to changes in profits for a hypothetical monopolist**

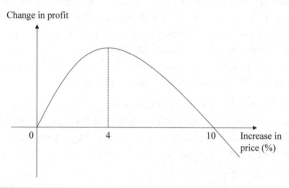

A relevant market has two dimensions: the *product market* and the *geographic market*.[19] The product market dimension considers those products that provide an effective competitive constraint on those products produced by the parties under investigation. For example, if the pricing of steel plate cans provides an effective competitive constraint on the pricing of aluminium cans, then the relevant product will contain both aluminum and steel plate cans. Similarly, the relevant geographic market is defined with reference to the competitive constraints that firms located in one region pose for those firms located in the same region as the firm or firms under investigation. Thus, a relevant market might be the market for apples in Belgium. The product market in this case is "apples" (i.e. it does not include other fruit), whilst the geographic market is Belgium. A relevant market cannot just have a product dimension or just have a geographic dimension: it must be a collection of products in a given area.[20]

The underlying concept of the Hypothetical Monopolist Test is therefore to identify those products and regions that provide the most important competitive constraints on the firms under investigation. The extent to which firms are able to increase prices above the price level appropriate for the particular inquiry depends on, inter alia, the availability of substitute products (demand-side substitution) and the ability of other firms to begin supplying those products (supply-side substitution). The fewer good substitute products available and/or the more difficult it is for other firms to

---

[19] In some instances, the relevant market is also defined with reference to time. For instance, weekday (peak) train travel before 9.30am might be considered to be in a separate market to (off-peak) train travel after 9.30am.

[20] However, in practice either the definition of the relevant product market or the relevant geographic market is often implicit.

begin to supply those products, the less elastic the demand curve facing the hypothetical monopolist and so the more it can raise prices.

4–007   It is important to note the following.

- It should be stressed that defining relevant markets on a basis that does not accord with the conceptual framework of the Hypothetical Monopolist Test will, almost by definition, not take into account the main competitive constraints posed by demand-side and supply-side substitution and, in consequence, any market shares calculated will not provide, except purely by chance, any meaningful indication of market power.

- The Hypothetical Monopolist Test is expressly designed to assess competition between differentiated offerings. In other words, the principles of defining relevant markets apply equally regardless of whether the products in question are homogeneous or differentiated.[21]

- The Hypothetical Monopolist Test does, contrary to what many commentators have suggested, take account of non-price elements of competition and of physical characteristics and intended use. To argue otherwise is to misrepresent the nature of the Hypothetical Monopolist Test. Whether a hypothetical monopolist would be able to impose profitably a relative price increase will depend on how consumers and the producers of other products react to that relative price increase. Non-price elements, for example the quality of the various products on offer, physical characteristics and intended use are all integral to that assessment.

- Finally, as the following discussion will show, and again contrary to what many commentators have suggested, the practical application of the hypothetical monopolist test does not require formal econometric analysis. Rather, the test should be seen as providing a framework for identifying the key questions and for assessing available data. So whilst econometric analysis can often be helpful in carrying out the Hypothetical Monopolist Test, it is not a necessary requirement for the test being useful.

## Applying the Hypothetical Monopolist Test

4–008   The application of the Hypothetical Monopolist Test begins by considering the products or services of the type supplied by the firm or firms under consideration and asking whether a hypothetical monopolist with control

---

[21]   Indeed, the Hypothetical Monopolist Test was specifically designed to address competition between differentiated products.

over all of these products would be able to profitably raise the price of those products permanently by 5–10 per cent, assuming that the prices of all other products remained constant.[22] If the answer to that question is yes, then this set of products defines a relevant market and competition between suppliers of those products provide the main sources of competitive constraint. If the answer is no, then this implies that suppliers of other products also provide important competitive constraints. These products should then be added to the putative market and the test reapplied. This continues until the collection of products is worth monopolising. A market is defined as the smallest set of products that meets the Hypothetical Monopolist Test. In other words, the Hypothetical Monopolist Test defines the relevant market as the smallest set of products worth monopolising.

As noted earlier in this chapter, a relevant market has both a product dimension and a geographic dimension. Both of these dimensions ought in theory to be co-determined. However, in practice, the product market tends to be defined first and then the extent of the geographic market for those products is defined. The following discussion is therefore put in terms of defining the relevant product market. Much the same discussion applies, *mutatis mutandis*, for the definition of the relevant geographic market.

Whether or not a hypothetical monopolist over a given set of products would be able to increase profitably the relative prices of a specified set of products within any given area depends on the sales volume that would be lost following such a price increase. Whenever the prices of a set of products are increased, some sales will be lost.[23] The key issue is whether the loss of those sales would be sufficient to offset the increased profits that would be made from retained sales following the price increase. For example, if a 5 per cent relative price increase would lead to a reduction in sales volumes of less than 5 per cent, that price increase would be profitable since revenue would have increased and production costs reduced. In contrast, if a 5 per cent relative price increase would lead to an 8 per cent fall in volumes, total revenues would fall and unless cost savings resulting from the reduction in production volumes offset such reduction, this price increase would be unprofitable.[24]

---

[22] *Note bene*, that the test applies to all suppliers of those products. If the test were applied to only the products supplied by an individual firm, a 5% relative price increase above prevailing levels would never be profitable. This is because we would expect a firm that could profitably increase its prices to have already done so.

[23] This will be true as long as the demand curve facing a firm is not vertical or upward sloping, both of which are very unlikely.

[24] For details on the empirical application of this logic, see Chapter 11.

---

**BOX 4.2: CRITICAL LOSS: HOW MANY SALES DOES A HYPOTHETICAL MONOPOLIST NEED TO LOSE?**

**4–009**   In assessing how many sales the hypothetical monopolist would need to lose in response to a 5 per cent relative price increase in order for that price increase not to be profitable reference is often made to *critical loss*.[25] The critical loss refers to the (proportional) loss sales that would (just) make it unprofitable for the hypothetical monopolist to impose a small but significant increase in price. This critical loss can be readily calculated. Assuming constant marginal costs of production, the critical loss is given by[26]:

$$s / (s + m)$$

where s is the hypothesised small but significant increase in price in percentage terms and m is the pre-merger gross margin.[27, 28] As Table 4.1 shows, the critical loss varies according to the gross margins earned on each sale; the higher the margin, the lower the critical loss.

**Table 4.1 Critical loss for a given range of margins and hypothesised price increases**

|  | Small but Significant Increase in Price | |
| --- | --- | --- |
| **Gross Margin (%)** | **5%** | **10%** |
| 100 | 4.8% | 9.1% |
| 90 | 5.3% | 10.0% |
| 80 | 5.9% | 11.1% |
| 70 | 6.7% | 12.5% |
| 60 | 7.7% | 14.3% |
| 50 | 9.1% | 16.7% |
| 40 | 11.1% | 20.0% |
| 30 | 14.3% | 25.0% |
| 20 | 20.0% | 33.3% |
| 10 | 33.3% | 50.0% |

---

[25]   For a more detailed discussion of critical loss analysis, see Chapter 11.

[26]   See Farrell and Shapiro (2008).

[27]   The "gross margin" is defined as the difference in price and the short-run marginal cost of production. The gross margin therefore excludes fixed costs incurred by a firm. As discussed in Chapter 3, the magnitude of the gross margin does not therefore provide a good indicator of the degree of competition that a firm faces.

[28]   *Nota bene*, the critical loss does not depend on the elasticity of demand facing the hypothetical monopolist. However, the actual loss (see below) most certainly does.

For example, a hypothetical monopolist that earned gross margins of 70 per cent would find it profitable to increase prices by 5 per cent provided that relative price increase did not result in a loss of volumes exceeding 6.7 per cent of existing sales; whereas a hypothetical monopolist that earned gross margins of 30 per cent would find it profitable to increase prices by 5 per cent provided that relative price increase did not result in a loss of volumes exceeding 14.3 per cent of existing sales.

The critical loss is therefore just arithmetic. However, by itself the critical loss provides little information as to whether the hypothetical monopolist would find the relative price increase profitable. In order to address that question, one needs to consider the *actual loss*.[29]

Although, as demonstrated in Table 4.1 above, it is certainly true that a firm earning high gross margins has a lower critical loss than a firm earning low gross margins, a firm's gross margin does not convey definitive information on how many sales would actually be lost in response to the hypothesised relative price increase.[30] Before concluding that *actual loss* exceeds the *critical loss* further analysis is therefore required.[31] A standard approach to examining actual loss is to undertake an econometric analysis of the effect of past price changes on demand. Another approach is to use a consumer survey and ask consumers how they would respond to a hypothesised price increase. These responses provide an estimate of the actual loss and can then be compared to the critical loss.

**4–010**

Assessing the likely extent of lost sales requires a case-by-case assessment of the various constraints that firms face. As the Relevant Market Notice notes, firms can face competitive constraints from three potential sources[32]:

- demand-side substitutability, i.e. the extent to which consumers consider other products as effective substitutes;

- supply-side substitutability, i.e. the extent to which productive assets outside the control of the hypothetical monopolist can be rapidly re-directed for the production of directly competing products; and

---

[29] The term "actual loss" means the *predicted* loss that would result from a *hypothetical* monopolist's attempted increase in relative price.

[30] We discussed in Chapter 3 the theoretical link between gross margins and own-price elasticities of demand. We also discussed the serious practical difficulties that arise when trying to use gross margins to derive own-price elasticities.

[31] See Scheffman and Simons (2003), Katz and Shapiro (2003), Farrell and Shapiro (2008), O'Brien and Wickelgren (2003) for a discussion of the appropriate role of critical loss analysis.

[32] Relevant Market Notice, para.13.

- potential competition, i.e. the extent to which new firms are able to enter the market.

The definition of the relevant market focuses on the first two constraints, with the primary focus being on demand-side substitutability.[33] These are discussed in more detail below. The third source of competitive constraint provided by potential competition is not normally taken into account when defining the relevant market. The conditions under which potential competition provides an effective competitive constraint will depend on the analysis of the characteristics of the market including the likely competitiveness of the market should a new entrant enter the market. The assessment of the effect of this competitive constraint is therefore properly undertaken in the second stage of the competitive assessment.[34] For this reason, we do not consider this source of competitive constraint further in this chapter.[35]

## Demand-side substitution

4-011    Demand-side substitution takes place when consumers switch from one product to another in response to a change in the relative prices of the products. A relative increase in the prices of products in the collection under consideration may lead consumers to switch their purchases towards other products. How does this possibility affect a single supplier of that collection? In order for the single supplier to raise price profitably (i.e. for the market to be worth monopolising), the reduction in the level of demand must not be too large. Whether or not this is the case will depend upon how responsive demand is to an increase in price.

The possibility of demand-side substitution provides an immediate and effective disciplinary force on the suppliers of a given product. If consumers are in a position to switch to available substitute products or to begin sourcing their requirements from suppliers located in other areas, then it is unlikely that price increases will be profitable. The easier it is for consumers to meet their requirements through the purchase of other substitute products, the greater the change in the demand for a collection of products for a given relative price increase. In this case, the attempt by a hypothetical supplier to increase price is likely to result in a loss in sales sufficient to render the price increase unprofitable. The products in

---

[33]   The Relevant Market Notice states that "demand substitution constitutes the most immediate and effective disciplinary force on the suppliers of a given product, in particular in relation to their pricing decisions" (para.13).

[34]   See para.13 of the Relevant Market Notice. The US authorities effectively undertake the same approach.

[35]   We discuss the importance of new entry in the competitive assessment in Chapters 3, 6 and 7.

question would not therefore be worth monopolising and so would not define a relevant market. If the relevant market were defined as consisting of those products alone, any assessment of market power based on market shares would be an overstatement, potentially to a significant degree. In order for market shares to provide a reasonable proxy for the extent of market power it is therefore necessary to add progressively the products to which consumers would most likely switch in response to a relative price rise, repeating the test at each stage until a collection of products is reached that is worth monopolising. Note that it is not necessary for all or even most customers to switch, or for those customers that do switch to switch all of their purchases to render the attempted price increase unprofitable. It is sufficient simply that enough switching takes place so that the attempted increase in price is not profitable. As we discuss in more detail below, this implies that what matters is not the behaviour of "average" consumers, but the behaviour of "marginal" consumers (i.e. those most likely to switch in response to relative price changes).

As a hypothetical example, consider whether mineral water constitutes a relevant market. Is mineral water worth monopolising in the sense that a single supplier would find it profitable to raise the price of mineral water by 10 per cent relative to the price of other products? If 90 per cent of mineral water consumers would react to such an increase in the relative price of mineral water by switching to Coca-Cola and other soft drinks, then mineral water does not delineate a relevant market—monopolising the mineral water market would not be worthwhile. But if only 5 per cent of consumers were willing to switch away to other products, then mineral water would define a relevant product market.

## Supply-side substitution

Even if there are no alternative products to which consumers would con- **4–012** sider switching, a collection of products may still not be worth monopolising. Even if consumers are unable to react to an increase in price, producers may be able to do so. If other producers respond to an increase in the relative price of the products supplied by the single supplier by switching some of their production facilities to producing the monopolised collection of products, the increased level of supply may render any attempted price increase unprofitable. In this case the products in question do not define a relevant market because of the potential for supply-side substitution.

Hence, although supply-side substitution is a less obvious form of substitution, under certain circumstances it may represent as effective a competitive constraint as demand-side substitution. In essence two products are supply-side substitutes if the supplier of one of the products already owns all of the important assets needed to produce the other product and has the commercial incentives and capabilities to commence such production.[36] For example, a hypothetical monopoly supplier of plastic knives and forks is unlikely to be constrained from raising prices by the possibility of customers switching their purchases to plastic plates (i.e. plastic plates are not demand-side substitutes for plastic cutlery). Nonetheless, it may be that the assets of the plastic plate maker, such as the injection moulding equipment and distribution systems, could easily be used to make plastic knives and forks at short notice and without the need to make any significant new investments or incur any significant new risks. If that were the case, it is unlikely that a hypothetical monopolist of plastic knives and forks would be able to sustain a profitable price increase.

For a rival firm to provide a genuine source of supply-side substitution it is not sufficient for that firm to have just some of the assets required, if this means that significant additional investments are required in the other productive assets needed. For example, it may be possible for a firm physically to produce the products of another firm using pre-existing production assets, but not for it to replicate the necessary marketing assets (e.g. an established brand) or distribution assets (e.g. depots). In this case, the ability to produce the physical product is insufficient to be able to regard the supplier as an effective source of supply-side substitution since the investments needed to create a brand and a distribution network are likely to be significant and largely sunk.[37] Moreover, for the products of a firm to be regarded as supply-side substitutes it is not only necessary for production of the relevant products to be possible without the need for significant new investments, it must also be possible within a relatively short period of time. This is often taken as a period of up to one year.

**4–013**     In some cases, supply-side substitution is explicitly recognised in the product market definition. However, in many more cases it is implicitly recognised. For example, a strict demand-side analysis would place shoes of different sizes in different markets because no customers seeking size 5 shoes would switch to size 8 shoes in the event of a relative increase in the price of size 5s. However, there is no suggestion that in reality different relevant markets would be defined for separate sizes. Products of different sizes or made of different raw materials can often be grouped together in this way, not because they are substitutes from the customers' perspective, but because it is trivial for the production process to be modified to change the size or raw material composition of the output.

There is considerable debate over whether supply-side substitution should be considered when defining the relevant market, or whether it

---

[36]  The commercial capability to switch production will depend on whether the change in relative margins makes commencing production of the other product profitable. Where a firm enjoys spare capacity, it is likely that this will be the case; since producing the other product will not involve a reduction in the production of existing products.

[37]  A sunk investment is one that is irreversible. For example, assets that can be re-sold on exit from a market, such as offices, vehicles or multiple-use machinery are not sunk. Conversely, assets that cannot be sold on exit, such as industry-specific machinery or industry-specific brands, are sunk.

should be taken into account after the market has been defined. This debate concerns whether it is better to not take supply-side substitution into account at the market definition stage (i.e. define relevant markets narrowly) but to recognise this constraint when interpreting market shares. The US approach to market definition is to define markets only on the basis of demand-side substitutability, but then to take account of supply-side substitutability when calculating market shares. Conversely, the Relevant Market Notice, while placing primacy on demand-side substitution, does acknowledge a role for supply-side substitution and states that supply-side substitution will be taken into account when defining the market when "its effects are equivalent to those of demand substitution in terms of effectiveness and immediacy."[38]

In one sense, the issue of whether to take supply-side considerations into account at the market definition stage or in the second stage of the competitive assessment does not matter. Provided the competitive constraint posed by supply-side substitutability is taken into account at some point of the competitive analysis, the same conclusions on market power ought to be reached. However, excluding supply-side considerations at the market definition stage may lead to higher market shares which will overstate the degree of market power possessed by firms.[39]

The following example illustrates these two points.[40] Owners of boats **4–014** that are kept in seawater need to paint the hull of the boat with anti-fouling paint to stop barnacles sticking to the boat. Assume that there is only one manufacturer of anti-fouling paint, but that there are also many, larger manufacturers of ordinary paint, which can easily begin to manufacture anti-fouling paint by adding some readily available copper compound to their paint. If the relevant market were defined with reference to demand-side substitution only, then the relevant market would be anti-fouling paint and the single supplier of anti-fouling paint would have 100 per cent of that market. However, in assessing the market power of the anti-fouling paint monopolist it is also necessary to take into account the competitive constraints posed by ordinary paint manufacturers, which are able to begin supplying anti-fouling paint if changes in relative prices make it attractive to do so. On that basis, one would conclude that even possessing 100 per cent market share would not be sufficient to exercise market power. Alternatively, by taking supply-side substitution into account when defining the relevant market, one would conclude that the relevant market includes both producers of anti-fouling and ordinary paint. In this case, the anti-fouling paint manufacturer has only a very small share of this market, indicating the absence of market power.

It can be seen that (assuming the analysis is properly undertaken) the

---

[38]  Relevant Market Notice, para.20.
[39]  As noted above, the US horizontal merger guidelines when calculating market shares include the productive assets of firms held to represent effective supply-side substitutes.
[40]  This example was supplied to us by Professor Franklin Fisher.

same conclusion will be reached whichever market definition is used. However, if supply-side substitution is not taken into account when defining the relevant market, the market shares within that market are not informative in terms of analysing market power. In the above example, only if supply-side substitution is taken into account will market shares be informative as to the level of market power possessed by the monopoly supplier of anti-fouling paint.

For this reason, where supply-side substitutability can be shown to take place both quickly and easily, we believe that it should be taken into account in defining the relevant market.

**4–015**  The concept of supply-side substitution has been accepted by the European Court of Justice as relevant. In *Continental Can*, the Commission held that there were three relevant product markets: a market for light metal containers for canned meat products; a market for light metal containers for canned seafood; and a market for metal closures for the food packing industry (other than crown corks).[41] That definition was rejected by the Court on the basis that the Commission had failed to consider substitutes on the supply-side:

> "In order to be regarded as constituting a distinct market, the products in question must be individualised, not only by the mere fact that they are used for packing certain products, but by particular *characteristics of production* which make them specifically suitable for this purpose." [emphasis added]

The ECJ argued that in order to support its market definitions the Commission needed to explain why producers of others types of can would not be able to begin producing cans that competed directly against those of Continental Can.

However, while the concept of supply-side substitution is recognised in practice, experience suggests that the Commission's delineation of the relevant market focuses principally on demand-side considerations—supply-side substitution, if it is considered at all, tends to be more of an afterthought. Indeed Form A/B and Form CO both suggest that supply-side substitutability plays no role in product market definition as they state that:

> "A relevant product market comprises all those products and/or services which are regarded as interchangeable or substitutable *by the consumer*." [emphasis added][42]

---

[41]  6/72 *Europemballage Corp and Continental Can Co Inc v Commission* [1972] E.C.R 215; [1973] C.M.L.R 199; [1972] OJ L7/25.

[42]  Section 6 of Form A/B and Section 6 of Form CO.

Certainly there are few examples of the Commission defining markets primarily on the basis of supply-side considerations and in practice the Commission's view of whether two products or regions should be included in the same relevant market will generally depend on their substitutability from the perspective of the consumer.[43]

## Conclusions on the Hypothetical Monopolist Test

The Hypothetical Monopolist Test has much to commend it. First, the **4–016** Hypothetical Monopolist Test provides a hypothesis which can in principle be tested with reference to available industry data.[44] The Hypothetical Monopolist Test therefore provides a framework that, in principle, permits the settlement of competing claims. Experience indicates that in most cases some relevant data is available which, though not representing a complete or ideal set of data, is nonetheless useful in helping to ground the market definition on "hard, scientific evidence".

It cannot be stressed enough that defining relevant markets on a basis that is not consistent with the principles of the Hypothetical Monopolist Test will, almost by definition, fail to take properly into account demand-side and supply-side substitution possibilities. In consequence, any market shares calculated from such market definitions will not provide, except purely by chance, a good proxy of market power. Although the Hypothetical Monopolist Test is often proposed as one possible way of defining relevant markets, no alternative that is consistent with the principles of assessing demand-side and supply-side substitutability has been proposed.[45]

Secondly, the Hypothetical Monopolist Test provides a coherent framework in which to consider the relevant issues relating to the competitive constraints faced by firms under investigation and consequently assists in moving the analytical debate beyond ad hoc introspection and focuses it explicitly on the key concepts of demand-side and supply-side substitution. Although the Hypothetical Monopolist Test is often seen as necessarily involving quantitative analysis, this misrepresents its true value which lies more in its role as providing a conceptual framework within which to conduct the analytical assessment. The Commission itself implicitly notes

---

[43] This is not to deny that on occasions the Commission does take into account supply-side substitutability. For example, in *Royal Bank Private Equity/Cineven/Chelwood Group*, IV/M.2737 (2002), the Commission accepted that there existed supply-side constraints in the supply of different types of brick.

[44] See Part III for a detailed discussion of the empirical techniques that have been employed.

[45] For example, the Relevant Market Notice states the following. "The assessment of demand substitution entails a determination of the range of products which are viewed as substitutes by the consumer. *One way of making this determination* can be viewed as a speculative experiment, postulating a hypothetical small, lasting change in relative prices and evaluating the likely reactions of customers to that increase." Para.15, emphasis added. But it is totally unclear as to what other ways the determination of demand-side (and the same applies for the assessment of supply-side substitutabilty) could be made.

this possibility when it states in the Notice that the Hypothetical Mono-polist Test can "be viewed as a speculative experiment".[46] This is clearly not the same as requiring a formal econometric test to be undertaken in each and every case, although such analysis is often useful when the data is available.

## THE *CELLOPHANE* FALLACY[47]

**4–017** One of the benefits of the Hypothetical Monopolist Test is the potential to use observed industry data to assess the merits of competing claims as to whether two products or regions should be included in the same relevant market. As noted above and discussed in some detail in Part III, there are a number of empirical techniques that can be used. However, the application of many of these techniques can raise serious concerns when applied in the context of Article 81 and Article 82 investigations.[48] These concerns arise from what is known as the *Cellophane* fallacy.

In order to understand the *Cellophane* fallacy, it is important to note a fundamental difference between the nature of the competitive analysis undertaken in assessing the likely competitive effects of a merger and that generally undertaken in Article 81 and Article 82.[49] In assessing the likely competitive effects of a merger, the main competitive concern is whether the merger will result in an increase in prices above the *prevailing level*.[50] For this reason, the competitive analysis focuses on the competitive constraints on the current commercial behaviour of the merging parties. In this sense, the analysis conducted in merger inquiries is *forward-looking* and is con-cerned with the identification of competitive constraints at *prevailing levels*.

In contrast, the competitive assessment under Articles 81 and 82 is often concerned with whether the firms under investigation are currently subject to effective competition. In other words, do the firms under investigation currently possess market power? In undertaking this assessment, the issue is whether prevailing prices have already been increased above the com-petitive level and not, as is the case with merger, whether those firms are able to increase prices still further.

**4–018** This difference has some important ramifications for the practical application of the Hypothetical Monopolist Test since evidence of sub-stitution at prevailing prices (upon which observed industry empirical

---

[46] Relevant Market Notice, para.15.
[47] This section draws heavily on Baker and Bishop (2001).
[48] Contrary to Crocioni (2002), the *Cellophane* fallacy arises only in extremely rare cases in the context of horizontal merger analysis, even in the presence of pre-existing dominance.
[49] We say generally since in some cases the competitive analysis in Article 81 and Article 82 will also be forward-looking and therefore the analysis will be more akin to that conducted in a merger investigation.
[50] As noted in the introduction to this chapter, references to price increases encompass reductions in quality.

evidence necessarily relies) cannot identify whether current competitive constraints are effective in constraining prices to the competitive level rather than merely constraining them from rising further. In short, the problem arises because in many non-merger investigations the prevailing price level does not provide the appropriate benchmark against which to assess competitive constraints.[51] Profit-maximising firms will always set prices at a level at which further price increases would be unprofitable.[52] This means that the extent to which products exert competitive constraints on one another depends in part on the current relative prices. While products may be substitutes at one price level, at a lower level this may not be the case. As was noted in *US v Kodak*, if the price of the monopolised product is high enough, even inferior substitutes will look attractive to consumers.[53]

This is a standard result of economic theory. However, it has potentially serious implications for market definition and the assessment of market power. It means that noting that at current prices the firm faces binding competitive constraints from other products and firms does not tell us much about whether the firm has market power that it is exercising. Put another way, the fact that a firm has a relatively high own-price elasticity of demand does not mean that it therefore does not possess market power which permits it to raise price above the effectively competitive level. It may be that its own-price elasticity of demand at the effectively competitive price level is actually rather low and that it has thus been able to raise price (possibly substantially) above that price level to the current price level, at which point further price rises are not profitable due to the existence of demand-side substitutes or supply-side substitutability by other firms.

This problem is known in competition policy analysis as the *Cellophane* fallacy after the celebrated *Du Pont* case.[54] In that case, Du Pont argued that cellophane was not a separate relevant market since empirical evidence showed that it competed directly and closely with flexible packaging materials such as aluminium foil, wax paper and polyethylene. But, as many commentators have since noted, Du Pont's argument was not sound. Du Pont was the sole supplier of cellophane and is likely to have already raised its prices to the point at which the competitive constraints imposed on it by other products became binding on it. The mere fact that at the prevailing price level Du Pont was unable to raise prices further does not provide an answer to the question of whether Du Pont had market power and so had already raised prices above the effectively competitive price level. The US Supreme Court in this case failed to recognise that a high own-price elasticity may mean that a firm is already exercising market power.

The key implication of the *Cellophane* fallacy is that the identification of **4–019**

---

[51] The same may also be true in non-horizontal merger investigations.
[52] This is true for all firms, whether or not they possess market power.
[53] *Eastman Kodak Co v Image Technical Serv. Inc* (1992) 504 U.S. 451.
[54] *United States v E.I. du Pont de Nemours & Co* (1956) 351 U.S. 377; 76 S. Ct. 994; L.Ed 1264.

substitutes at existing prices does not necessarily identify those products that are effective substitutes at the competitive price, which is the relevant benchmark for defining markets in most non-mergers cases. Evidence that products are effective substitutes at current prices merely identifies those competitors that constrain the prices of the firm or firms under investigation from increasing prices above the current level. It does not necessarily provide information on whether those products are constraining prices to the competitive level.

---

**BOX 4.3: A HYPOTHETICAL EXAMPLE OF THE *CELLOPHANE* FALLACY**

Suppose there are just two manufacturers of CD players, one manufacturer of tape players and one manufacturer of DVD players. Tape players sell for €50, CD players for €100 and DVD players for €200. Further, assume that €100 for CD players is the effectively competitive price. However, if the two CD player manufacturers merged, they could profitably raise their price to €130. If we carried out a hypothetical monopolist test at prevailing price levels we would find that it would be profitable for a hypothetical monopolist of CD players to raise prices by 5–10 per cent above the prevailing price level and so would conclude that CD players was a relevant market for the purpose of this merger. We would then conclude that the merger would lead to a monopoly of this market and should be blocked. This would be the correct decision.

Now suppose that there is already only one CD player manufacturer and that it prices at €130, which it believes is the profit maximising price level. A potential competitor complains that the CD player manufacturer is abusing a dominant position on the market for CD players. If we carry out a Hypothetical Monopolist Test at the prevailing price level, we will ask whether it is profitable for the CD player manufacturer to raise prices from €130 to €136.50 (5 per cent rise) or €143 (10 per cent price rise). If the CD player monopolist is correct that the monopoly price is €130, the answer to our hypothetical monopolist question will be that it is not profitable to raise prices by 5–10 per cent. Suppose instead that, on the basis of further analysis at prevailing price levels, we concluded that the relevant market included tape players and DVD players as well as CD players, and that the CD player manufacturer had only 30 per cent of this market. We might well conclude that the CD player manufacturer is not dominant. But this would be the wrong result since, by construction, we know that the CD player manufacturer has in fact been able to raise the price of CD players by 30 per cent above the competitive price level, indicating that he is dominant.

---

## Resolving the Cellophane fallacy

Since the *Cellophane* fallacy raises some fundamental issues, it is tempting **4-020** to suggest resolving the problem by merely redefining the benchmark at which competitive constraints are assessed. Since the key issue in defining relevant markets in most non-merger cases is the identification of those products that provide an effective competitive constraint at competitive prices, in principle the Hypothetical Monopolist Test can be modified to take this into account by asking whether the hypothetical monopolist could profitably increase prices above the competitive level. This is the approach advocated in the Commission's Notice[55]:

> "Generally, and in particular for the analysis of merger cases, the price to take into account will be the prevailing market price. This might not be the case where the prevailing price has been determined in the absence of sufficient competition. *In particular for investigation of abuses of dominant positions, the fact that the prevailing price might already have been substantially increased will be taken into account*" [emphasis added].

Unfortunately, the Notice does not provide any suggestions as to how this "fact" "will be taken into account". As noted in Chapter 2, it is rarely possible to identify the competitive price and if we could do so, defining the relevant market, along with all other analysis, would be redundant.[56] In general, the Commission's practice since the Notice came into force gives little indication that the Commission fully appreciates the practical issues thrown up by the *Cellophane* fallacy or knows what to do about them.[57] A marked exception is the discussion contained in the Commission's discussion paper on the application of Article 82 to exclusionary abuses.[58] In short, this attempt to resolve the *Cellophane* fallacy is of little practical relevance since if one could identify the competitive price so as to undertake the necessary analysis, it would not be necessary to undertake the analysis of market definition in any event.[59] Moreover, as noted in Chapters

---

[55]   Relevant Market Notice, para.19.
[56]   The circular nature of the discussion is revealed in the following (actual) cross-examination of a well-known academic economist. After accepting that market definition in dominance cases needs to be examined with reference to the competitive price, he responded to the question: "Do you know what the competitive price of [Product] is?" with "Significantly below what it is [currently]". Clearly, if this statement were true there would be absolutely no need to engage in the exercise of defining the relevant market.
[57]   This criticism can also be levelled at other competition authorities. For example, the UK Office of Fair Trading states in its Market Definition Guidelines (1999): "The Director General must make some judgment on whether or not the current price is likely to be significantly above competitive levels already".
[58]   DG Competition discussion paper on the application of Article 82 of the Treaty to exclusionary abuses (2005). See paras 11 to 19. It is disappointing that this discussion is excluded from the Article 82 Guidance Paper.
[59]   Other than the legal requirement to do so.

2 and 3, identifying the competitive price level is extremely difficult and in most cases impossible to determine.

This raises the question as to how one should take the *Cellophane* fallacy into account. Certainly, it would be incorrect to ignore the implications of the *Cellophane* fallacy when defining markets in non-merger cases since this will tend to lead to markets being defined too widely. However, it would be incorrect to think that the principles of the Hypothetical Monopolist Test no longer apply. As the discussion above has shown, the Hypothetical Monopolist Test provides a conceptual framework in which to assess competitive constraints. The fact that the application of many empirical techniques in many non-merger cases requires careful analysis does not mean that the fundamental underlying principles of the Hypothetical Monopolist Test, as opposed to its practical implementation, no longer apply. To argue otherwise suggests that relevant markets can be defined without reference to competitive constraints between products and regions. Where relevant markets are not defined with reference to competitive constraints that exist between products and regions the resulting market shares will generally provide poor indicators of market power and hence are likely to result in inappropriate conclusions on dominance.

**4–021** Indeed, the Hypothetical Monopolist Test continues to provide the appropriate framework for assessing competitive constraints and provided it is interpreted with reference to the problems raised by the *Cellophane* fallacy, empirical evidence can still be used in non-merger cases.

First, there are some non-merger cases where the correct benchmark price level for implementing the test is the current price level. When the allegation is that a firm is trying to exclude one of its rivals in order to raise prices once they have been excluded, then carrying out the Hypothetical Monopolist Test from the current price level is the correct approach. Suppose that even if the rival firm is excluded, then the alleged excluding firm would have only 5 per cent of the market that it would need to monopolise in order to be able to raise prices by 5–10 per cent above the prevailing price level. In this case, it would be reasonably clear that the allegedly exclusionary behaviour is not going to lead to prices rising.

Secondly, there are occasions when even though the correct benchmark for using the Hypothetical Monopolist Test is not the prevailing price level, it is possible to deduce that the prevailing price level is above the benchmark price level. In these cases, it is not necessary to formally identify a relevant market in order to assess market power.[60] Suppose a firm has 60 per cent of the "market" for cement in a region of the United Kingdom and is being accused of abusing a dominant position. Before we can say whether that 60 per cent share is likely to convey market power, it is necessary to know whether cement in a narrow region represents a relevant

---

[60] We mean here that it is not necessary from an economic perspective to define a relevant market. From a legal perspective, it usually is necessary.

market (or whether the geographic dimension of the relevant market is wider). One way to do this is to look at cement "markets" in other regions of the United Kingdom. If we find that firms systematically charge higher prices when they have a large share of a regional cement market relative to when they have a small share of a regional market, this implies that having a large share of a regional market confers market power. This then provides an answer to our question about whether the firm we are investigating that has 60 per cent of a particular regional cement market has market power.[61] Having concluded that it likely does, we can continue with the analysis of whether it is abusing its market power. Economically, we do not need to define a market as we have directly identified market power, but legally the sensible approach is to conclude that we have defined the relevant market as a regional cement market and that the firm under investigation has 60 per cent of this market.

Thirdly, even when we cannot avoid the problem raised by the *Cello-*   **4–022** *phane* fallacy entirely, we can still use market definition, and the Hypothetical Monopolist Test, to structure our thinking in an economically coherent fashion.[62] We recommend undertaking the analysis using the following three steps.

1. Ensure that all hypothesised market definitions are consistent with principles of demand-side and supply-side substitutability. This means ensuring that there are good demand-side or supply-side reasons for including particular products or areas within the potential market definition. This step should appear obvious, but is nonetheless not always addressed in market definition exercises.

2. Ensure that those products included in hypothesised market definitions are at least substitutes at current prices. We have explained why the fact that two products are substitutes at prevailing prices does not therefore mean that they are substitutes at the effectively competitive price. However, the argument is not symmetric. If two products are not substitutes at prevailing prices, then they will not be substitutes at the (potentially lower) effectively competitive price. If consumers are not willing to switch from Product A to Product B at prevailing prices, it is hard to understand why they might be willing to switch from Product A to Product B if Product A's price fell.[63]

---

[61] What we are loosely describing here is a price-concentration study. We consider these in detail in Chapter 14.

[62] See also para.16 of DG Competition Article 82 Discussion Paper (2005).

[63] No doubt a rationale could be produced to explain behaviour of this type (perhaps Product A is a conspicuous consumption item that is valued less by consumers when it is cheaper), but it will be rare and can be factored into the analysis in the particular case at hand.

It should be noted that where the allegation is that a firm is currently pricing too low (i.e. some sort of predation allegation), then the implication is that the prevailing price is below the effectively competitive price and so it may be that a lack of substitution at prevailing price levels does not imply that the products are not substitutes at the effectively competitive price level.

3. Ensure that all hypothesised market definitions are plausible on the basis of an analysis of the characteristics and uses of the products included. The Commission (along with other competition authorities in the various Member States) has frequently defined markets on the basis of the physical characteristics of the products concerned. This is a reasonable approach to take when direct evidence on substitutability is not available provided that evidence is interpreted correctly. It is important to ensure that any physical characteristics that are used to define a market are relevant to the degree of substitutability between products. Thus, it does not make sense to define a separate market for red cars on the basis that they differ from other cars on the basis of a physical characteristic (i.e. colour). Consumers may have preferences over car colour, but supply-side substitutability for manufacturers between different car colours is clearly very high. On the other hand, it might make sense to define separate markets based on the engine size of the car.

The result of this approach may well be that there is more than one plausible market definition. This may not be as useful as being able to narrow it down to just one market definition, but it is significantly better than narrowing it down to just one market definition if there is a substantial risk that that market definition is wrong. Recall that the purpose of market definition is to aid the competitive assessment. Using a wrong market definition will not aid the competitive assessment, but instead will lead an investigator to focus on the wrong set of competitive constraints and, in all likelihood, therefore to get the competitive effects analysis wrong. Carrying out the competitive effects analysis on the basis of a number of possible market definitions, on the other hand, can be useful. If the market shares of the firms under investigation are low under all plausible market definitions, then this suggests that they do not have market power and so no further analysis is needed. So in this case the market definition exercise still acts as a useful screening device. Where market shares are high under some plausible market definitions, it clearly is necessary to carry out a further competitive effects analysis, but this will be informed by avoiding focusing on market definitions that do not accord with the underlying principles of the Hypothetical Monopolist Test.

# COMMON FALLACIES IN DEFINING RELEVANT MARKETS

This section considers several different types of fallacious reasoning that **4–023** often arise in defining relevant markets in practice. Most of these "fallacies" arise as a result of not properly applying the logical framework of the Hypothetical Monopolist Test.

Common fallacies include the following.

- "The Hypothetical Monopolist Test represents only 'one possible' approach to defining the relevant market."

- "Average consumers matter, not marginal consumers."

- "A relevant market requires products or regions to be effective demand-side substitutes *and* effective supply-side substitutes."

- "Competitive responses need to be 'instantaneous'."

- "Differences in physical characteristics imply separate relevant markets."

- "Different end use/different distribution channels imply separate relevant markets."

- "Differences in price levels imply separate relevant markets."

- "Regional difference including differences in market shares across regions imply separate relevant geographic markets."

- "Absence of imports implies separate relevant geographic markets."

- "The definition of the relevant market is independent of the particular competition concern."

The remainder of this section explains why none of these statements is correct.[64]

## All Relevant Markets should be consistent with the underlying principles of the Hypothetical Monopolist Test

Although most competition authorities have now adopted the Hypothetical **4–024** Monopolist Test or an almost identical variant of it, it is sometimes asked whether there is any alternative methodology that could be used to define markets. The Commission has suggested that the market definition test set

---

[64] Although in some cases, the logic underlying these statements may lead to the correct conclusion as to the extent of the relevant markets, in many others they will lead to erroneous conclusions.

out in the Relevant Market Notice represents only one of the possible tests for defining relevant markets, but not necessarily the only test. For example in *Virgin/British Airways*, the Commission states:

> "The Commission has provided detailed guidance on how it applies this principle in practice in its Notice on market definition. The Notice describes how the Commission uses information about product characteristics, evidence of past substitution and so forth to define a product market. The Notice mentions the idea of a hypothetical price rise but does so to explain the concept of a relevant market".[65]

We cannot agree with this view.[66] It is only possible to describe how one uses information if there exists a framework in which to make the assessment. As discussed above, the Hypothetical Monopolist Test seeks to identify the main competitive constraints and does so with reference to demand-side and supply-side substitutes. If market definition is to have any useful role to play in competition law it must be capable of capturing, as best as is possible in the circumstances, the nature of the competitive constraints that act on the firms within the market. Since competitive constraints can only originate from the behaviour of customers (e.g. demand-side considerations) or the behaviour of other firms (e.g. supply-side considerations) demand-side substitution and supply-side substitution must lie at the heart of any analytically useful market definition test and it is therefore hard to see how any alternative approach could be consistent with the basic requirement to assess competition between products and regions.

Indeed, the Relevant Market Notice provides no indication as to what the alternative to the Hypothetical Monopolist Test might be.[67] Any statement to the effect that the Hypothetical Monopolist Test is just one example of how to define a relevant market without clearly specifying what the alternative to the Hypothetical Monopolist Test might be, clearly runs the risk of a return to a process of market definition by ad hoc reference to product characteristics. Of course, the Hypothetical Monopolist Test does not fully resolve all of the competitive issues raised in a case and may not even fully capture all relevant aspects of demand- and supply-side substitution, notably in cases where products are differentiated. Nonetheless, demand- and supply-side substitution—concepts at the heart of the Hypothetical Monopolist Test—will always be key and the Hypothetical Monopolist Test provides a useful framework on which to build the remainder of the competitive analysis. In short, we do not believe that an

[65] IV/D-2/34.780 *Virgin/British Airways* (1994) at para.70.
[66] If the Commission's view were correct, then its Notice on market definition is largely redundant and cannot fulfil its stated claim of improving the transparency of the process of market definition.
[67] Similar comments apply to the guidance provided by numerous other competition authorities.

alternative sensible methodology for market definition to the Hypothetical Monopolist Test exists.

An alternative suggestion that has been advocated is to abandon market **4–025** definition altogether. Some commentators, often academics, argue that the definition of the relevant market represents an artificial step in the analysis and that one would be better off proceeding directly to the analysis. We disagree with that proposition, believing that advocates of this approach misunderstand the role that market definition plays in the practical assessment of competition cases. In our view, the omission of market definition altogether from the process may be harmful because it leaves all subsequent analysis without any rigorous framework, leaving too much of the analysis resting on subjective judgment, particularly in the case of dominance investigations.

We believe that the exercise of thinking about how the relevant market should be defined provides a focus and scope to the more detailed competitive analysis of the activities of the firms under investigation. In the absence of an explicit market definition stage, subsequent analysis might be undertaken in an arbitrary manner. Without any coherent framework in which to conduct the analysis, there is a real danger that the analysis could degenerate to the level of "I know market power when I see it" without providing any identifiable benchmarks against which to discriminate between "competitive behaviour" and "anticompetitive behaviour"[68].

## The responses of marginal consumers are more important than the responses of average consumers in assessing substitutability

Whether the increase in relative prices hypothesised in applying the **4–026** Hypothetical Monopolist Test is profitable or not depends on how many consumers would switch to alternative products. As should be clear from the above discussion, for a relative price increase to be unprofitable does not require that the majority of consumers would switch, but only that sufficient numbers would do so. In other words, when examining the likely responses of consumers, it is the response of the *marginal consumer* and not the *average consumer* that is important.

As the calculation of critical loss makes clear, it is not necessary for *all* consumers to be willing to switch to render a given collection of productions a market not worth monopolising, only that *enough* would switch in response to a price increase for it to be a profitable price increase. In other words, what is the elasticity of demand for that collection of products?

[68] This is not to deny that, as noted in Chapter 3, there may be occasions when it is possible to infer market power directly from the behaviour of firms in the market. However, even in these rare cases, we believe that it is still good practice to define the relevant market on the basis of the Hypothetical Monopolist Test methodology (informed by the implications of the directly inferred market power).

Determining both the likely extent of demand-side substitution, and the level of substitution which would imply that a given set of products is not worth monopolising, requires an assessment of the price elasticity of demand.

The focus on the likely responses of *marginal* consumers rather than *average* consumers is particularly important when interpreting the results of consumer surveys.[69] It is the behaviour of marginal consumers that matters: as long as a reasonable number of consumers are "marginal" and are willing to switch in response to a relative price change, the existence of other consumers who would not switch (even if these account for the majority of consumers) does not imply a narrow market. The existence of even a large group of consumers who would not switch in response to a relative price increase is not by itself sufficient to conclude that the relevant market should be defined narrowly. This important point is still frequently overlooked by the Commission when interpreting the responses to its Article 11 questionnaires.[70] The following example illustrates this point.

**4–027**  Suppose that 80 per cent of the consumers of a particular product ("widgets") would not consider changing to another product in response to a 10 per cent rise in the price of widgets. Does this make widgets a separate relevant market? If the other 20 per cent would switch to another product in response to a 10 per cent price rise, then raising prices by 10 per cent will lead to a 12 per cent decline in revenue for the widget manufacturer. Depending on what costs the manufacturer saves by making 20 per cent fewer widgets, this may well not be a profitable price increase, even though 80 per cent of customers did not switch.

The mistake of focusing on the behaviour of particular groups of consumers, or on average consumers, when defining a relevant market has been referred to as the "toothless fallacy" after the *United Brands* decision.[71] In this decision, the Commission argued that bananas defined a separate relevant market because the very young and the very old (i.e. those without teeth) did not consider other fruit a suitable substitute for bananas. However, the fact that there is a captive group of consumers for whom there are no substitute products available is not enough to define the relevant market. The important question in *United Brands* was not "will the

---

[69]  The Relevant Market Notice states that surveys undertaken for the purpose of the competition investigation should be treated with "utmost care". The need for "utmost care" applies equally to the Commission's use of consumer surveys, including those that form part of Article 11 requests.

[70]  The same comment applies even more frequently to some national competition authorities.

[71]  27/76 *United Brands Co and United Brands Continental BV v Commission* [1978] E.C.R. 207; [1978] 1 C.M.L.R. 429.

toothless switch to other fruit in response to a rise in the price of bananas?", but "will enough consumers switch to other fruit in response to a rise in the price of bananas to make that price rise unprofitable?".[72]

## Relevant Markets should be defined widely if either demand-side or supply-side substitution provides an effective competitive constraint

A hypothetical monopolist of a set of products would not find it profitable **4–028** to increase prices relative to other products if either a sufficient number of consumers would switch to other products (i.e. demand-side substitution provides an effective competitive constraint) *or* suppliers of other products could easily and quickly begin to supply the products of the hypothetical monopolist (i.e. supply-side substitution provides an effective competitive constraint). Hence, if demand-side substitution represents an effective competitive constraint, then the relevant market needs to be widened: a hypothetical monopolist would not find it profitable to increase prices. Similarly, if supply-side substitution represents an effective competitive constraint, then the relevant market needs to be widened: again a hypothetical monopolist would not find it profitable to increase prices. It ought therefore to be clear that the relevant market should properly be defined more widely even if only one of these potential sources of competitive constraints is effective in constraining the hypothetical monopolist. This simple point has on occasion been forgotten. For example, the relevant market can be erroneously defined narrowly due to a lack of supply-side substitutability even when it is acknowledged that the products are demand-side substitutes. Put another way, it is not necessary for both conditions to be fulfilled; having considered one form of substitution, consideration of the other can only widen the market—it will never imply that the market should be narrowed again.

## In order to represent an effective competitive constraint, demand-side and supply-side responses need to occur within a one- to two-year time period

In considering the competitive constraints posed by both demand-side and **4–029** supply-side substitution, it is necessary to consider the time period over which such substitution takes place. In general, the longer the time period considered, the greater scope there is for substitution to take place. For example, consumers might not be able to switch from Product A to

---

[72] This analysis assumes that sellers of bananas were not able to price discriminate between different groups. If they were able somehow to charge "the toothless" a different amount to what they charged other consumers, then the fact that "the toothless" have no substitutes to bananas might make a price rise directed solely at "the toothless" profitable. We have seen no evidence or suggestion that this was the case in *United Brands*.

Product B immediately, but might be able to do so easily after a period of two months. The time period over which substitution is considered will therefore have a critical impact on the definition of the relevant market.

As a hypothetical example, consider a market in which consumers can make purchases under one-year supply contracts and on the spot market; the products are identical. Prices for purchases made under one-year supply contracts are determined at the beginning of each year, i.e. prices for contract sales are constant throughout the year. The price of purchases on the spot market however varies over the course of the year, reflecting prevailing conditions of demand and supply. Now consider the application of the Hypothetical Monopolist Test to the question of whether contract sales delineate a relevant market separate from spot sales. If the scope for consumers to substitute away from contract sales is limited to a period of less than 12 months then it would appear that there is little demand-side substitution between contract and spot sales, i.e. the relevant market would appear to be contract sales only. However, if the time period over which consumers can switch is extended to 12 months or more, then an increase in the price of contract sales relative to that of spot sales would likely lead to substitution to spot sales, i.e. the relevant market would include both contract and spot sales.

The DoJ/FTC guidelines refer to a two-year period over which substitution responses take place. A period of at least one year would appear to be appropriate since we are interested in the responses of customers and suppliers to a permanent change in relative prices; to adopt a short time frame over which substitution can occur would lead to important competitive constraints that affect competitive outcomes being ignored. Surprisingly, the Relevant Market Notice is silent on this question and this has led in practice to an implicit very short time period being considered, which has led to a bias towards defining relevant markets narrowly.

## Differences in physical characteristics do not preclude products from being part of the same relevant market

**4–030** It is sometimes argued that products that have different physical characteristics cannot form part of the same relevant market. But using differences in physical characteristics to delineate relevant markets raises a real danger of defining overly narrow relevant markets: by simply adding another adjective to the "definition" of the relevant market, more and more products can be excluded.

As an example of the problems that arise when overly relying on physical characteristics to define relevant markets, consider *Nestle/Perrier*.[73] This case involved a merger of two suppliers of mineral water. Two issues arose in the definition of the relevant market: did still and sparkling mineral

---

[73] *Nestle/Perrier* IV/M190 [1993] 4 C.M.L.R. M17; [1992] OJ L356/1.

water form part of the same relevant market? And did mineral water (either narrowly or widely defined) face effective competitive constraints from soft drinks such as Coca-Cola? Applying the physical characteristics approach, it could be argued that still and sparkling water lie in separate relevant markets since one product (still mineral water) is not fizzy while the other (sparkling mineral water) is. Furthermore, applying the "logic" of differences in physical characteristics, it could be argued that Coca-Cola and sparkling mineral water form part of the same relevant market since both are fizzy!

Of course, even if the conclusion on the extent of relevant market were correct, such reasoning is flawed. Applying the principles of the Hypothetical Monopolist Test requires one to focus not on whether different products can be described differently, but rather the extent to which consumers would switch from one product to the other in response to a relative change in the prices of those products. At one level, consideration of differences in the physical characteristics of products would appear to be a relevant factor in defining relevant markets; if products have different physical characteristics doesn't this suggest that consumers would be unlikely to consider those two products as effective demand-side substitutes? The answer is of course that it depends on how many consumers would switch in response to the relative price change hypothesised in the Hypothetical Monopolist Test. Ultimately that is an empirical question. Put simply, the fact that products have different physical characteristics by itself cannot be dispositive that those products lie in separate relevant markets. What matters is the effect of these physical differences on substitution patterns.

There is a similarity between these sorts of arguments and the process of **4–031** narrowing market definitions by simply adding more and more adjectives. The process is arbitrary and any market definition can be advanced simply by selectively appealing to product characteristics. Too much importance is then laid on physical differences since such a focus does not answer the main question—what is the extent of lost sales following a price rise?

This point is demonstrated clearly in the *United Brands* case.[74] In *United Brands* the European Court of Justice found that the banana market had certain special features that were sufficiently distinctive for it to be regarded as representing a distinct relevant product market—year round availability, the ability to satisfy the constant needs of an important part of the population and the limited effect of competition from other fresh fruits at the banana's peak periods. This conclusion appears to have been made on the basis of very limited empirical evidence, and there appears to have been no attempt to determine whether these differences were meaningful in that they imply that bananas are a product worth monopolising. It will always be possible to construct a list of differences. But the real question is

[74] *United Brands* 27/76 [1978] E.C.R. 207; [1978] 1 C.M.L.R. 429.

whether or not these differences are meaningful—an issue that needs to be settled by having recourse to empirical observation of how consumers substitute between products when relative prices change.

## Differences in end use do not preclude products from forming part of the same relevant market

4–032 The Commission has on a number of occasions argued that relevant markets can be defined with reference to differences in end use, particularly in relation to different distribution channels. For example, in *Friesland Foods/Campina*, the Commission argued that cheese products sold to out of home (OOH) wholesalers did not form part of the same relevant market as sales to retailers. This conclusion was based on differences in packaging; the Commission argued that:

> "Cheese sold at the retail level is typically packed in small consumer units of maximum 400g or as whole wheels which are cut at location. Cheese delivered to OOH wholesalers is typically packed in bigger units of 500g to 2kg (or very small units of 1 or 2 slices per pack)."[75]

But such reasoning is clearly not determinative. Although customers served by one distribution channel may not consider products sold through the other distribution channel as an effective substitute, the two different methods of distribution to retailers and to the horeca sector may be linked via the ability of suppliers to switch easily between the two distribution channels. The proper application of the Hypothetical Monopolist Test would ask whether a hypothetical single supplier of cheese, say, to retailers would find it profitable to increase prices to retailers. The answer to that question depends on whether suppliers to the horeca sector could divert volumes (or expand production) from distribution to the horeca sector to distribution to the retail distribution; in other words, could suppliers engage easily in supply-side substitution? The fact that the products have different intended uses within the two distribution systems does not by itself preclude such substitution possibilities providing an effective constraint on a single supplier of cheese to retailers.

## Differences in price levels do not imply separate relevant markets

4–033 It is sometimes argued that two products or two regions cannot form part of the same relevant market if their respective prices are at different levels. The argument appears to be that two products cannot be reasonably substitutable if they have substantially different prices. Price differences

---

[75] COMP/M.5046 *Friesland Foods/Campina* (2008), at para.544.

have therefore been used to distinguish between products which may be "functionally substitutable, but in reality are not interchangeable".[76] Following the "logic" of that argument, one would argue that while a secondary brand perfume and a perfume marketed by a leading couture fashion house are both perfumes which carry out the same function, the difference in price means that the two products cannot be in the same market.[77]

But again, this line of reasoning does not address the fundamental questions that are central to the Hypothetical Monopolist Test. In particular, defining relevant markets on the basis of differences in price will be flawed if price differences reflect (actual or perceived) quality differences. Wherever there are quality differences, consideration of absolute price levels will ignore the possibility of consumers making a trade-off between price and quality. If product A is universally considered to be "twice as good" as product B (perhaps because it lasts twice as long) then both products can co-exist in the market with product A priced twice as high as product B (€10 for product A versus €5 for product B). If the manufacturer of product A tried to raise price to €15, it is clear that customers would switch to product B. If product A is only "twice as good", it is not worth paying three times as much for it. As another example consider price differentials between two perfumes. While the contents of the two bottles may be very similar, the fact that one is sold at a higher price may reflect higher perceived quality from the consumers' perspective. Thus, the price of the higher-priced perfume could still be constrained by the price of the lower-priced perfume. Whether or not this is so is an empirical question.

The use of differences in absolute price levels stems from a confusion between defining a market as an area in which the "law of one price" holds—the so-called "economic" market—and defining the relevant market, which takes into account the competitive constraints between products and regions.[78] The relevant market can coincide with, be wider than or be narrower than the economic market. In the perfumes example, the relevant question to be answered in the context of a competition law inquiry is whether or not a relative increase in the price of a cheap perfume will lead a substantial number of consumers to switch to, inter alia, couture fashion house perfumes to render the price increase unprofitable—in other words, the relevant question is whether cheap perfumes are worth monopolising.

Similar problems arise when the issue is whether heavily branded pro- **4-034** ducts compete with unbranded equivalents. This issue featured in the

---

[76] Jones and González-Díaz (1992), p.112.
[77] The UK Monopolies and Mergers Commission Fine Fragrances references proceeded on the same basis (Fine Fragrances: Report on the Supply in the United Kingdom for Retail Sale of Fine Fragrances (1993) Cm. 2380).
[78] See Stigler and Sherwin (1985).

Commission's investigation of *SCA/P&G (European tissue business)*.[79] A question central to that competitive assessment was whether own-branded tissue products were in the same relevant market as branded tissue products. Branded tissues—not surprisingly—cost more at the retail level than own-branded tissues, despite the fact that there was little to distinguish the two products on a physical basis. Indeed, many own-branded products are produced by manufacturers of branded products. Using differences in absolute prices to delineate relevant markets would place the branded product and own-brand product in separate relevant markets. But it is clear that part of this price differential is due to quality differences, both actual and perceived, to which consumers clearly attribute a value. The real question is the degree to which the pricing behaviour of branded products is constrained by the pricing of own-branded products. If the price of branded products is constrained by the price of own-brands, then branded products do not delineate a market that is worth monopolising. In other words, price differences need not imply that two products necessarily lie in separate relevant markets. In *SCA/P&G (European tissue business)* the Commission concluded that the:

> "[M]arket investigation broadly confirmed that at the retail level, branded products and private labels compete on the shelves and are part of one single market".[80]

That it is the competitive impact of changes in relative prices which matters was recognised in *Nestle/Perrier*.[81] The Commission distinguished between bottled waters and soft drinks on the basis of a number of factors, one of the most important being price. The Commission found that soft drinks cost typically twice as much as bottled water and this was taken as a strong indication that the two products were in separate markets. However, this conclusion was supported by a study of price trends, employing price correlation analysis. The decision states:

> "Manufacturers' prices of source water and soft drinks have had a very different evolution during the last five years. Suppliers of the national mineral waters have been able to substantially increase their prices in both nominal and real terms, in spite of the decreasing trend of soft drink prices during the same period. Manufacturers in both sectors do not seem to take into account in their pricing policies possible substitution by consumers of source waters by soft drinks. This price evolution seems to indicate that even strong and sustained reductions of soft drink prices in real terms would not force source water suppliers

[79] COMP/M.4533 *SCA/P&G (European tissue business)* (2007). See also IV/M623 *Kimberly-Clark/Scott Paper* (1995) OJ L183.
[80] op cit., para.20.
[81] IV/M190 [1993] 4 C.M.L.R. M17; [1992] OJ L356/1.

to also reduce their own prices, nor would it affect their ability to increase them."

The Commission appears to have acknowledged that, for the purposes of defining relevant product markets, what matters is not so much absolute price differences, but whether or not a change in the price of one product is likely to have a competitive impact on the price of another. Thus, for instance, in *Airtours/First Choice* the Commission argued that short-haul package holidays were in a separate market from long-haul package holidays.[82] Among other evidence (such as absolute price differences), the Commission noted that the movement in price of short-haul holidays to Spain was not correlated with the movement in price of long-haul holidays to Florida.[83]

Similar arguments relating to price differences apply to the definition of **4–035** the relevant geographic market. If two regions lie in the same relevant market, then one would expect the prices charged in one region to affect (and be affected by) prices charged in the other region. However, this is not the same as saying that prices in both regions must be at precisely the same level: the degree of demand substitutability is measured by the willingness of consumers at the margin to switch their purchases. The geographic extent of the relevant market should therefore reflect similarity of price *movements* rather than the similarity of price levels.

In *ABF/GBI Business*, the Commission noted that price levels for compressed yeast were different between France, Portugal and Spain.[84] However, as noted above, differences in price levels do not provide a sufficient basis for concluding that two regions lie in different relevant geographic markets. Accordingly, the Commission in this case placed more weight on the dynamic evolution of price levels. Employing price correlation analysis,[85] the Commission found that average prices were not highly correlated across these three countries.[86]

## Regional differences do not imply separate relevant geographic markets

The Commission sometimes cites regional differences as a basis for **4–036** defining a narrow relevant geographic market. For example, national procurement policies, the existence of cross-border import duties, the need to access distribution and marketing infrastructure, and language are all cited as reasons why competitors from outside the region under consideration can be disregarded. But, while in some cases regional differences

---

[82]   IV/M1524 (1999).
[83]   op cit., para.22.
[84]   COMP/M.4980 *ABF/GBI Business* (2008), at para.73.
[85]   See Chapter 10 for details of this test.
[86]   One could however question the appropriateness of using average prices in this analysis.

will mean that the region under consideration is worth monopolising, in other cases they will not. As with most of the other factors considered by the Commission, regional differences, while of some interest, are not necessarily dispositive on the issue of the geographic market.

In particular, the Commission cites differences in market shares between Member States as a determining factor in defining relevant geographic markets. In *ABF/GBI Business*,[87] the fact that suppliers' respective market shares varied widely from Member State to Member State was taken as one factor indicating separate relevant geographic markets. However, there is little theoretical basis for using differences in market shares as a way of defining relevant markets. It is not possible to derive a "similar market shares" condition from the fundamental question of market definition: is this collection of products in a given region worth monopolising? Moreover, there is no relationship between a "similar market shares" condition and the concept of substitution in demand or supply. There is no basis whatsoever for expecting that, within a relevant geographic market, shares in all areas of that market should be the same as for the market as a whole. Indeed, it would be unusual if they were the same throughout. The most that can be said of differences in market shares across regions is that it is often useful to understand why the differences exist, as they may illustrate some aspect of the nature of competition. However, this is a long way from saying that they define separate markets.

## Absence of imports does not imply separate relevant geographic markets

**4–037**  Although it appears intuitive that the absence of trade between two geographic regions is suggestive of a lack of competition between those regions, inferences on the extent of the relevant geographic market drawn from the observation that imports are *currently* low or non-existent need to be made carefully. The fact that imports are currently low does not necessarily imply that imports would continue to be low if relative prices across regions were to change. For a region to be worth monopolising it must be possible to *raise* price above the appropriate benchmark level. The question to be asked is, notwithstanding the fact that imports are currently low, what would happen if a hypothetical sole supplier were to raise price by, say, 10 per cent? In some cases the answer will be that nothing would change, but in other cases a 10 per cent increase, for instance, may be all that is needed to induce a significant increase in the level of imports. As an example, consider two distinct regions, A and B, which are competitively supplied at a price of €100. Transport costs between the two regions are €3, so no firm currently finds it worthwhile to export to the other region.

---

[87]  COMP/M.4980 *ABF/GBI Business* (2008).

However, if price in A were to rise to €105 or €110, it is clear that firms in region B would then have an incentive to export to A.

Similarly, evidence on transport costs should not, however, be used as a definitive arbiter of market definition, since other factors may make it feasible for outside firms to supply to the country in question despite the apparent transport cost handicap. If this possibility is ignored, there is a danger that high transport costs can be used to "prove" that trade is infeasible.

## Market definitions are not unique

A common misconception is that market definitions are independent of the   **4–038** particular competition issue at hand. This is not so.[88] The correct market definition depends on the particular issue in dispute. This is clear with regard to mergers as opposed to Article 82 cases. In the former the market definition question is whether a hypothetical monopolist can raise prices by 5–10 per cent above *prevailing* price levels. In the latter, depending on the exact allegation, the market definition question is likely to be whether a hypothetical monopolist could raise prices above a benchmark price, which is unlikely to be the prevailing price. These two different questions may well give rise to different relevant market definitions. For this reason, it is possible for the relevant market to be defined more widely in a merger investigation than in a non-merger inquiry. This issue was raised in *Tetra Laval/Sidel* in which the Commission's analysis of the merger was apparently constrained by a previous market definition adopted in two Article 82 cases in which the relevant market was defined as the supply of carton packaging.[89] But this market definition is not inconsistent with defining the relevant market in a merger context as wider than carton packaging. Even if it is appropriate to consider competition from PET bottles not to be effective enough to constrain the behaviour of a hypothetical single supplier of carton packaging to competitive levels, it is possible that at the margin, PET bottles provide the competitive constraint that prevents further price increases from being profitable and that the elimination of that constraint would permit carton packing prices to increase. If that were the case, it could be appropriate to define the relevant market for the purposes of assessing the likely competitive impact of the merger as carton packaging and PET bottles.

It is also quite possible to have different market definitions depending on the exact nature of an Article 82 case. If the allegation is that an allegedly dominant firm is charging excessive prices, then the benchmark price for the market definition exercise is the effectively competitive price, not the

---

[88]   This is accepted by the CFI (see *Coca-Cola Company v Commission*, joined cases T-125/97 and T-127/97).
[89]   *Tetra Laval*, COMP/M.2416 [2001].

prevailing price (and in this case the *Cellophane* fallacy is a real problem). On the other hand, if the allegation is that an allegedly dominant firm has just ceased supplying a key input to a competitor, then the concern is likely to be that this will increase the allegedly dominant firm's market power and allow it to raise prices above the prevailing level. In this case, asking whether a hypothetical monopolist could raise price above the prevailing price level is a reasonable question to ask.

Furthermore, in some industries, the strength of competitive constraints will be asymmetric; suppliers of Product A may constrain suppliers of Product B, but not vice versa. For example, Product A and Product B might both be suitable inputs in the production of certain products but only Product A can be used in the production of other higher "quality" products. This might be the case due to the need for Product A to meet certain health and safety standards. In this case, producers of Product A could constrain producers of Product B, but not vice versa. If this were the case, then the definition of the relevant market would depend on the precise competition issue to be examined. For example, a merger between producers of Product A might involve a relevant product market confined to Product A whereas a merger between suppliers of Product B might properly involve a relevant product market that included producers of Product A and Product B.[90]

4–039    Similar reasoning might apply when defining relevant geographic markets. To illustrate this point, consider a situation in which prices in regions A and B are €100 and €120 respectively and where it costs €20 to transport the relevant product between the two regions. If one were to use price differences to delineate the relevant market, then we would conclude that A and B are separate markets. The reality is more subtle: region A might be a separate market but region B probably is not. The reason is that region A does not face a competitive constraint from region B, but the converse is not true. If prices in region A rose by, say, 5 per cent to €105, we would likely not see exports from region B to region A. This is because producers in region B can sell in region B for €120, but can only sell for €105 in region A and would have to incur additional transport costs of €20. However, if prices in region B rose by, say, 5 per cent to €126, then producers in region A could export to region B, incur transport costs of €20, and still be better off selling in region B than in region A. So A is a distinct market, but a market which includes B should also include firms supplying region A.

---

[90]  In *SCA/P&G*, the Commission found that the competitive interaction at the procurement level between producers of branded products and producers of private labels was asymmetric; branded producers constrained producers of private label but not vice versa.

# SOME FURTHER ISSUES IN THE PRACTICE OF MARKET DEFINITION

## Continuous chains of substitution

An argument that is frequently used in market definition exercises is that **4–040** there is a "continuous chain of substitution" between products so that even products that do not directly compete against each other should be considered to be in the same relevant market. The argument often arises in geographic market definition with products that are relatively expensive to transport. The argument goes along the following lines: output from Plant A competes with output from Plant B because they are relatively close to each other; output from Plant B competes with output from Plant C because they are relatively close to each other; therefore Plant A and Plant C are in the same relevant geographic market because the price of output from Plant A constrains the price of output from Plant B, which in turn constrains the price of output from Plant C. Figure 4.2 illustrates this example. Competition in Area AB and in Area BC is enough to ensure that Plant A is price constrained by Plant C and vice versa.

*Pilkington-Techint/SIV* provides an example of this reasoning.[91] This case concerned the acquisition of *Società Italiana Vetro Spa*, an Italian state-owned glass manufacturer, by a joint venture involving Pilkington Glass. The Commission noted that although glass is a bulky, heavy product, a significant volume of glass is transported across national borders. The Commission concluded that, while the "natural area of supply" for a given producer could be represented by a concentric circle with the radius determined by relative transport costs, these circles of supply overlapped one another "so that effects can be transmitted from one circle to another". So while a producer in Spain, say, might not compete directly with a producer in Northern Germany due to transport costs, there might still be a competitive linkage between these two. The Commission therefore defined the relevant geographic market as the whole of the Community.

---

[91]   IV/M358 *Pilkington-Techint/SIV* (1994) OJ L158/24.

## Figure 4.2 A continuous chain of substitution

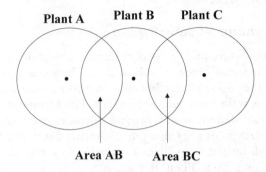

The continuous chain of substitution argument can also be relevant to product markets. Where there is a continuum of different types of a product (e.g. cars) it may be that there is a continuous chain of substitution between them. A small hatchback does not compete directly with a luxury car, but it may compete directly with a mid-sized car, which may compete directly with an estate, which may compete directly with a luxury car, thus potentially putting all cars into a single market.

**4–041** Care needs to be taken with the continuous chain of substitution argument. The mere fact that there is a continuum of types of a product, or a continuous chain of overlapping areas of competitive interaction, does not of itself mean that there is a single product market for all types of the product or a single geographic market containing all the overlapping areas of competitive interaction. Suppose there is a continuum of products from A to X whereby each product competes directly with the two "nearest" it. Thus B competes with A and C, C competes with B and D and so on. Suppose further that each product is constrained by its neighbouring products so that prices are kept at the effectively competitive level. Does that mean the relevant market is the full continuum? Not necessarily. It may be that a merger of products D, E and F would lead to the merged firm being able to raise the prices of D, E and F profitably. The increase in price of E would lead to some consumers of E switching to D and F, but that would not harm the merged firm as it now owns D and F. The increase in the price of D would lead to some consumers of D switching to C, but equally some of them would switch to E, which the merged firm owns. The same logic holds for an increase in F. The result may be that a price rise of more than 5–10 per cent is profitable and that for merger purposes DEF is a separate relevant market.

---

**BOX 4.4: AN EXAMPLE OF A NARROW MARKET WITHIN A CHAIN OF SUBSTITUTION**

Assume that there are five firms, A, B, C, D and E. Each currently sells 100 units at €1. Unit costs are €0.5 and there are no fixed costs, so each firm currently makes a profit of €50. If any firm raises its relative price by 10 per cent, it loses 10 per cent of its sales to each of its neighbours. So if firm C raised its price by 10 per cent, its sales would fall to 80. Since its price would rise to €1.1, its revenue would fall to €88. Costs would fall to €40 and so its profits would fall to €48. Hence the price rise would not be profitable.

Now suppose that firms B, C and D merge and the merged firm raises its prices by 10 per cent. B will lose 10 of its sales to A, but none to C as their relative prices have not changed. C will lose no sales as its price relative to B and D is unchanged.[92] D will lose 10 sales to E, but none to C as its relative price has not changed. The end result is that the merged firm now sells 280 units at €1.1 rather than 300 at €1. Its revenues rise to €308, its costs fall to €140 and so its profits rise from €150 to €168. Hence BCD is a relevant market, despite the continuous chain of substitution from A to E.

---

The continuous chain of substitution argument may also fail because there   **4–042** is a "break" in the chain. Figure 4.3 is similar to Figure 4.2, but now includes six plants, not three. In this case there is no overlap between Plant C and Plant D and hence no competition between them. The result is that there is a break in the chain and so no mechanism for competitive constraints is to be communicated from Plant A to Plant F. The relevant geographic market will be no wider than ABC (and DEF).

**Figure 4.3 A break in the chain of substitution**

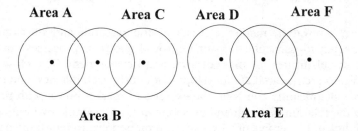

Area A        Area C        Area D        Area F

Area B                    Area E

---

[92]   Note that for illustrative convenience we are implicitly assuming an overall price elasticity for the industry of zero.

The Commission is aware of continuous chain of substitution arguments and, importantly, of their potential weaknesses.[93] At para.57 of the Relevant Market Notice it states that:

"In certain cases, the existence of chains of substitution might lead to the definition of a relevant market where products or areas at the extreme of the market are not directly substitutable."

And then notes at para.58 that:

"From a practical perspective, the concept of chains of substitution has to be corroborated by actual evidence, for instance related to price interdependence at the extremes of the chains of substitution, in order to lead to an extension of the relevant market in an individual case."

## Innovation markets

**4–043** The concept of an "innovation market" has been used in the United States. The idea behind an innovation market is that there may be times when the competitive issue at hand relates to an intermediate "market" for research and development (R&D), rather than to a market for goods or services. For instance, the issue may be a merger that is likely to reduce the intensity of R&D post merger because the parties are currently the only firms researching a particular area. Or the issue may be a licensing arrangement that reduces incentives to engage in R&D, perhaps because a firm with a patent on a production process licences that patent, thus reducing the incentive of other firms to engage in R&D to try and find an alternative, possibly better, production process. In cases such as these, it may make sense to define an innovation market.

The US DoJ and FTC state that[94]:

"An innovation market consists of the research and development directed to particular new or improved goods or processes, and the close substitutes for that research and development. The close substitutes are research and development efforts, technologies, and goods that significantly constrain the exercise of market power with respect to the relevant research and development, for example by limiting the ability and incentive of a hypothetical monopolist to retard the pace of research and development."

---

[93] The same is true of the UK Office of Fair Trading, which considers the continuous chain of substitution argument at paras 3.9 to 3.12 of its guideline "Market Definition" (OFT 403, 1999).

[94] DoJ and FTC, "Antitrust Guidelines for the Licensing of Intellectual Property" (1995).

An innovation market should include those things that constrain the ability of a firm to exercise market power in R&D. The most obvious manifestation of such market power would be to have the ability to slow the rate of innovation in the absence of competing R&D.

There has been considerable disagreement over whether the concept of an innovation market is useful. However, in cases involving competition to produce the next generation product, where it is not clear what that product is likely to be or look like, it is hard to analyse the competitive issues without using the innovation market concept. Thus the FTC used the concept of an innovation market when analysing the merger of Ciba-Geigy and Sandoz to form Novartis in 1996. The competition issue arose in the area of gene therapy research. This involves treating diseases or medical conditions by modifying genes and then inserting the modified genes into a patient's cells. Until the research produced commercial products, it was not clear what the relevant product markets were that might be affected by the merger. However, the FTC believed that Ciba and Sandoz controlled crucial inputs for commercialising gene therapy products and that after the merger no other firm would have an adequate incentive to compete against the parties in trying to commercialise the results of gene therapy research. As a result, the FTC imposed a licensing remedy on the parties in order to safeguard post merger gene therapy research competition.

However, it is important to note that R&D is an *input*, not an *output* and **4–044** the empirical relationship between the level of R&D expenditure and the speed of innovation is weak. This means that reducing the level of R&D undertaken is not equivalent to a monopolist constraining quantities in an output market. Whereas a monopolist restricting output leads to consumer harm in the standard microeconomic model, the welfare effect of restricting R&D is not clear-cut. It may lead to slower innovation and consumer harm, or it may avoid wasteful duplication of R&D effort or even increase the pace of innovation if the reduction in R&D expenditure is coupled with knowledge sharing across firms (such as in a merger).

Our views on innovation markets are as follows. First, where possible it is probably better to define standard product markets than more speculative innovation markets. Secondly, there will be competition issues that are best analysed using the concept of an innovation market. Thirdly, where the issue is best analysed using an innovation market, it is important to interpret market shares with great care. Innovation markets are not likely to be subject to collusion even if concentrated because the incentives to innovate before your rivals is so strong (e.g. you "win" and patent the innovation first). Further, the nature of intellectual property and the patent system is that there is often only one "winner" from R&D expenditure: the firm that innovates first (gets the patent) wins. This means that competition in an innovation market can be very fierce even with only a very few players.

## Aftermarkets[95]

**4–045** Aftermarkets arise where consumers purchase durable goods that require the purchase of some complementary products, at least some of which are purchased at a later date than the purchase of the durable product. The consumer durable is referred to as the "primary product" whilst the complementary product is referred to as the "secondary product" or the "aftermarket". Some examples are given in Figure 4.4.

### Figure 4.4 Industries with aftermarkets

| Industry | Primary Product | Secondary Product |
|---|---|---|
| Video games | Games console | Video game |
| Cars | Car | Spare parts |
| Computers | Hardware | Software and peripherals |
| | | Maintenance services |
| Mobile telephony | Mobile phone/network | Mobile telephony calls |

The peculiar competitive feature of these types of industry lies in the competitive interaction between the primary durable product and the secondary or aftermarket for associated complementary products or services. Technical differences between the various primary products often mean that the choice of complementary products compatible with a primary product is limited. This implies that once the primary product has been purchased, consumer choice is confined to those aftermarket products or services compatible with that primary product. For example, the owner of a Ford motorcar needs to purchase spare parts which are compatible with that type of car. In the case of video games, once a consumer has purchased a particular games platform, this can only be used to play games compatible with that platform. In other words, consumers are to a greater or lesser extent locked in to certain aftermarket suppliers.

The starting point for defining the relevant market when dealing with a secondary market should be the standard hypothetical monopolist test and a focus on demand-side and supply-side substitutability. This may lead to a wide or narrow market definition. The video games for games consoles tend to be proprietary to the particular console, so there is usually no demand-side substitutability (i.e. a Nintendo Wii game will not work on a Microsoft XBox console). The intellectual property rights belonging to the games console manufacturer (e.g. Sony) mean that other suppliers cannot supply games for a console unless the console manufacturer sells them a licence, so there is also usually little or no price constraints on the supply-side. On the other hand, printers that work with a particular brand of PC are not proprietary and so there is considerable demand-side substitutability, leading to a relevant market that includes many brands of printer.

[95] See Chapter 6 for a further discussion of aftermarkets.

Analytical confusion can arise when the nature of the primary product is   **4–046**
such that the producer of that product has 100 per cent of the associated
secondary market. The Commission has investigated a number of industries with this aftermarket feature, such as *Hugin/Liptons*[96] and *AB Volvo v
Veng*.[97] For instance, in *Hugin/Liptons* the Commission found that spare
parts for Hugin cash registers were not interchangeable with those of other
cash registers. Hugin cash registers could not therefore be maintained,
repaired or rebuilt without Hugin parts, thus giving Hugin a 100 per cent
market share of the market for spare parts for Hugin cash registers.

The important question that arises is what do we make of a firm having
100 per cent of a secondary market? The answer depends on their position
in the primary market and the nature of competition in the primary market.
If there is strong competition in the primary market to win consumers, then
it is unlikely that the 100 per cent share of the secondary market confers
market power. In *Hugin/Liptons*, the Commission found that Hugin had a
dominant position in respect of spare parts for its cash registers despite
having only a 12 per cent share of the European cash register market. This
intuitively seems unlikely to have been the right result, since we should
expect competition in the primary market (i.e. European cash registers) to
have competed away any excess profits that might in theory be attached to
the 100 per cent share of the spare part market. On the other hand, if
Hugin had had a 60 per cent share of the European cash register market,
then the Commission's decision would look more reasonable. In *Kyocera/
Pelikan* the Commission rejected a complaint that Kyocera was abusing its
dominant position in the market for secondary products for its printers on
the grounds that Kyocera faced strong competition in the primary market
for printers.[98, 99] So what does this imply about the correct market definition? As we have noted before, since the aim of market definition is to aid
the competitive assessment, the answer to this question should be based on
which definition is likely to aid the competitive assessment the most.

Three possible types of market definition are often put forward as
regards after markets[100]:

1.  a *system* market: a unified market for the primary product and the
    secondary product (e.g. a market for all razors *and* replacement
    heads);

[96]  IV/29.132 *Liptons Cash Registers and Business Equipment Ltd v Hugin Kassaregister AB*
     [1978] 1 C.M.L.R. D19; [1997] OJ L22/23.
[97]  238/87 [1988] E.C.R. 6211; [1989] 4 C.M.L.R. 122.
[98]  See European Commission, XXVth Report on Competition Policy (1995).
[99]  The OFT followed the *Kyocera/Pelikan* decision in its assessment of a complaint that ICL,
     a mainframe supplier, was not providing non-ICL hardware maintenance supported
     customers with certain diagnostic software and that this enabled ICL to prevent third-party
     maintainers from competing for hardware maintenance contracts for ICL mainframes.
     OFT CA98/6/2001, *ICL/Synstar* (2001).
[100]  See OFT Market definition, OFT 403 (2004) for a more detailed discussion.

2. *multiple markets*: a market for primary products and separate markets for the secondary product(s) associated with each primary product (e.g. one market for all razors, individual markets for each type of replacement head); and

3. *dual markets*: a market for the primary product and a separate market for the secondary product (e.g. one market for all razors, a separate market for all replacement heads).

The appropriate definition depends on the facts of the case. A system market may be appropriate either where customers engage in whole life costing or where reputation effects mean that setting a supra competitive price for the secondary product would significantly harm a supplier's profits on future sales of its primary product. Where neither of these conditions applies, a multiple markets or a dual markets definition may be appropriate. The former is likely where, having purchased a primary product, customers are locked in to using only a restricted number of secondary products that are compatible with the primary product. A dual markets definition is appropriate where secondary products are compatible with all primary products (and perceived to be so by customers).

## INTERPRETING MARKET SHARES WHERE PRODUCTS ARE HIGHLY DIFFERENTIATED

**4–047** Although market definition is a useful analytical tool for assessing mergers, particular care must be exercised when defining the relevant market and more importantly in any subsequent interpretation of market shares where products are differentiated. In differentiated products markets a naïve approach to the analysis of market shares can be misleading. Analysis of market shares assumes that the competitive constraint posed by each firm active in the relevant market is in proportion to their market shares: the larger the market share, the greater the competitive constraint. This analysis implies that mergers between large firms are more likely to raise competition issues than between small firms. However, where products are differentiated, such market share analysis may not provide a useful indicator of the competitive constraints that exist between various firms and in some cases can significantly under- or over-state the competitive constraints between firms.[101]

The following example illustrates how the analysis of market shares can yield misleading results. Consider an industry in which there are seven independent suppliers of various brands of soup. The various brands of soup are assumed to fall into various categories. Brands A and B are

---

[101] A more detailed discussion of this point is provided in Chapter 7.

considered to be "deluxe" brands with high quality ingredients and an up-market image; brands C, D and E are considered to be "standard" brands; and brands F and G are unadvertised "economy" brands. The sales of each brand are shown in Table 4.2.

## Table 4.2 Market definition and differentiated products

|  | Sales | Share of Total Market |
|---|---|---|
| Deluxe Brand A | 50 | 5% |
| Deluxe Brand B | 100 | 10% |
| Standard Brand C | 100 | 10% |
| Standard Brand D | 100 | 10% |
| Standard Brand E | 200 | 20% |
| Economy Brand F | 300 | 30% |
| Economy Brand G | 150 | 15% |
| **Total** | **1,000** | **100%** |

In order to illustrate the impact of a pure market-share analysis, consider two mergers. The first merger is between brand A and brand B, both deluxe brands. The second merger is between brand B and brand F, an economy brand. Assuming that the relevant market is all soup, then the first merger would not appear to raise any major competition issues—the post-merger market shares of the merging parties would be only 15 per cent. Conversely, the second merger would appear more likely to raise significant competition issues as the post-merger market share is 40 per cent.

However, the first merger is between two firms that both operate in the **4–048** same market segment ("deluxe") and so could be said to be close competitors. The merger of these two firms may remove the strongest competitive constraint from each firm. The second merger is between two firms that operate in different market segments ("deluxe" and "economy") and so could be said to be less close competitors. It is reasonable to believe that brand F's strongest competitive constraint comes from the other economy brand (brand G) and that the competitive constraint from brand B is relatively weak. So despite the higher post-merger market share in the BF merger, it may be that the reduction in competitive constraints post-merger is actually greater in the AB merger.

The point that we are making here is not that the AB merger necessarily raises competitive concerns, or that the BF merger necessarily does not. We are just illustrating the standard fact that in a differentiated products market not all products will not necessarily be equally close competitors to each other and that fact needs to be borne in mind when interpreting market shares.

## SUMMARY

**4–049** As in most other jurisdictions, the relevant market is a key concept in the application of EC competition law. However, this raises the issue of what role the relevant market plays in the competitive assessment and how it should be defined. While the decisions of the European Court of Justice have underlined *why* relevant markets are defined, less guidance has been given on *how* to define such a concept. This analytical gap can be resolved by both examining the role market definition plays in competition law inquiries and the objectives of those inquiries.

The definition of the relevant market plays only an intermediate step in the competitive assessment. It provides a tool for aiding the competitive assessment by identifying those substitute products or services which provide an effective constraint on the competitive behaviour of the products or services being offered in the market by the parties under investigation. This allows the complex task of assessing competition to be broken down into two steps. First, define the relevant market and, secondly, assess the nature of competition between firms within that market.

The definition of the relevant market can only be a useful intermediate tool to aid the competitive assessment if it is defined on a basis consistent with the goals of competition law. Since the definition of the relevant market is used to assess competition against the economic goal of European competition law, namely the maintenance of effective competition, the basis for defining a relevant market should focus directly on the competitive constraints products or services impose upon one another. This approach can be roughly summarised as follows: "A relevant market is something worth monopolising".

The Relevant Market Notice provides a framework based on economic principles (i.e. the "Hypothetical Monopolist Test") which has led to greater consistency and transparency in the application of European competition law. However, experience indicates that insufficient regard is given to the fundamental principles of the Hypothetical Monopolist Test, namely, the competitive constraints provided by demand-side and supply-side substitution possibilities, when defining relevant markets in practice. We noted some of the common fallacies commonly encountered in the application of the Hypothetical Monopolist Test.

# Part II. Application

"For the rational study of the law, the black letterman may be the man of the present, but the man of the future is the man of statistics and the master of economics."

Justice O.W. Holmes (1897)

# 5. Article 81

## INTRODUCTION

Article 81 of the EC Treaty prohibits a large range of agreements between **5–001**
undertakings. Article 81 states:

"(1) The following shall be prohibited as incompatible with the
common market: all agreements between undertakings, decisions
by associations of undertakings and concerted practices which
may affect trade between Member States and which have as their
object or effect the prevention, restriction or distortion of competition within the common market, and in particular those
which:

(a) directly or indirectly fix purchase or selling prices or any
other trading conditions;

(b) limit or control production, markets, technical development, or investment;

(c) share markets or sources of supply;

(d) apply dissimilar conditions to equivalent transactions with
other trading parties, thereby placing them at a competitive disadvantage;

(e) make the conclusion of contracts subject to the acceptance
by other parties of supplementary obligations which, by
their nature or according to commercial usage, have no
connection with the subject of such contracts.

(2) Any agreements or decisions prohibited pursuant to this Article
shall be automatically void.

(3) The provisions of paragraph 1 may, however, be declared inap-
plicable in the case of:

• any agreement or category of agreements between
undertakings;

- any decision or category of decisions by associations of undertakings;
- any concerted practice or category of concerted practices;

which contributes to improving the production or distribution of goods or to promoting technical or economic progress, while allowing consumers a fair share of the resulting benefit, and which does not:

(a) impose on the undertakings concerned restrictions which are not indispensable to the attainment of these objectives;

(b) afford such undertakings the possibility of eliminating competition in respect of a substantial part of the products in question."

An agreement which is caught by Article 81(1) is therefore automatically void by virtue of Article 81(2) unless it qualifies for an individual or block exemption under Article 81(3).

Article 81 applies to all agreements which entail "the prevention, restriction or distortion of competition". This immediately raises the question of when competition can be said to be prevented, restricted or distorted. Traditionally, the Commission has interpreted Article 81(1) in a wide sense so that nearly all agreements fall within its scope regardless of the market position of the parties involved or of the economic impact of the agreement. The result of such a wide interpretation has little to do with an analysis of competition and if taken literally would be nonsensical (see below). Moreover, it also caused an administrative log-jam. Under the procedures laid down in Regulation 17/62, the Commission was able to adopt only around 20 formal decisions per year. Although the backlog was somewhat eased by the introduction of "comfort letters", the Commission's ability to close a case by informal comfort letter was limited to around 150 per annum. As a result, the Commission has introduced a number of policy solutions to address this problem. The two most important are the use of Block Exemption Regulations (BERs) and the removal of the Commission's exclusive competence to grant exemptions under Article 81(3). The latter initiative is often referred to as the modernisation of EC competition policy.[1]

## Block Exemption Regulations

**5–002**  Faced with such a huge backlog and the unsatisfactory nature of comfort letters, the Commission has adopted an approach of "block exemptions".

---

[1]   See EC Commission, White Paper on the Modernisation of the Rules Implementing Articles 85 and 86 of the EC Treaty, OJ C132 (1999) and the resulting Council Regulation (EC) No 1/2003 of 16 December 2002 on the implementation of the rules on competition laid down in Articles 81 and 82 of the Treaty.

Under Council Regulation 19/65, the Commission is able to adopt "block exemption" Regulations which define certain categories of agreements which generally fulfil the conditions of Article 81(3). Council Regulation 19/65 requires that BERs adopted by the Commission contain lists of conditions which must be fulfilled, the types of agreement covered, restrictive clauses which are exempted and clauses which must not be included.[2] While the use of block exemptions helped to reduce the backlog of cases, they were traditionally subject to the criticism that their form-based, rather inflexible character tended to restrict the type of agreements entered into by undertakings, simply to obtain clearance under the block exemption. The possibility of falling within a block exemption and therefore gaining an automatic exemption from Article 81(3) led in the past to too much emphasis being placed on individual clauses regardless of the economic impact of that clause. Gaining exemption depended not on the impact of the agreement but on whether it was structured to fall within the relevant block exemption.

Such a formalistic approach is at odds with economic reality. Standard economic theory dictates that unless firms possess and exercise market power, they are unable to affect competition adversely. In other words, in the absence of market power, agreements between firms will not give rise to anti-competitive outcomes. This distinction explains why it is perfectly consistent for a given contract clause in one agreement to have benign outcomes whilst the same clause in other agreements is anti-competitive. Whether an agreement adversely affects competition depends not on its form but its impact on the market and that in turn will depend on the firm's position in the market.[3]

To illustrate this point, consider a shoe manufacturer that wishes to restrict the supply of its products only to those retailers who agree not to stock the products of other manufacturers. Is such an exclusivity agreement anti-competitive? The answer to this question depends on the facts of the particular case. For example, if the shoe manufacturer has a relatively small market share of retail sales of shoes—say 10 per cent—then it is unlikely that the exclusivity agreement would adversely affect competition since competing shoe manufacturers can easily gain access to other retail outlets not subject to such restrictions.[4] On the other hand, if the shoe manufacturer was able to sign up 90 per cent of shoe retail outlets the impact on competition might be different.

In recognition of the inadequacies of the form-based approach to block **5–003** exemptions, the Commission has implemented over the last decade a move towards an economics-based approach that focuses on market power and market outcomes. In 1999, the Commission implemented a block

---

[2]  For details of block exemptions that are currently in force, see Whish (2009), Chapter 4.
[3]  This point was recognised in the Commission's Green Paper on Vertical Restraints (1997).
[4]  We are assuming here that the relevant market has been correctly defined.

exemption covering vertical agreements together with Guidelines that set out the principles for their assessment under Article 81.[5] Under this block exemption, vertical agreements entered into by firms with market shares below 30 per cent gain automatic exemption from the Article 81 prohibition. A similar market share threshold approach is used in the guidelines on horizontal agreements.[6] The use of market share thresholds is intended to eliminate the regulatory burden of notifiying agreements from those firms that are unable to act anti-competitively.

## Towards a more economics-based approach

**5–004** Although these policy changes are to be welcomed, we are nonetheless left with a legal structure that appears rather odd to an economist. The Commission's traditional interpretation of Article 81(1) adopts a very formalistic interpretation of when an agreement is said to affect competition, but then the assessment of the compatibility of agreements under Article 81(3) tends to revert to a more economic view of the impact on competition. At one level, these views are inconsistent. Either an agreement is pro-competitive or it restricts competition. Under the current application of Article 81, many of the Commission's decisions appear to imply that both outcomes are possible.[7] In one sense, provided that a complete assessment of the economic impact of a particular agreement is made at some stage, it could be argued that the argument over the scope of Article 81(1) is academic. However, there is a lack of economic coherence in the relationship between Article 81(1) and Article 81(3). Although formally the BER grants those firms with market shares below a particular share threshold an automatic Article 81(3) exemption, the reality is that those agreements are deemed acceptable only because the firms in question do not possess significant market power and therefore are incapable of entering into anti-competitive vertical agreements. Such agreements might therefore be said to fall outside the scope of Article 81(1). Such an approach would also be in line with the decisions of the Courts. For example, in *European Night Services*, the Court states the following:

> "Before any examination of the parties' arguments as to whether the Commission's analysis as regards restrictions of competition was correct, it must be borne in mind that in assessing an agreement under Article 8[1](1) of the Treaty, account should be taken of the actual condition in which it functions, in particular the economic context in

[5] Commission Regulation No 2790/1999 ([1999] OJ L336, pp.0021–0025) and European Commission (2000) "Commission Notice: Guidelines on Vertical Restraints" [2000] OJ C291/01.

[6] Commission Notice: Guidelines on the applicability of Article 81 of the EC Treaty to horizontal cooperation agreements [2001] C3/02.

[7] See Korah (2000) for a legal perspective on this issue.

which the undertakings operate, the products or services covered by the agreement and the actual structure of the market concerned unless it is an agreement containing obvious restrictions of competition such as price-fixing, market-sharing or the control of outlets. In the latter case, such restrictions must be weighed against their claimed pro-competitive effects only in the context of Article 8[1](3) of the Treaty, with a view to granting an exemption from the prohibition in Article 8[1]3)''.[8]

In effect, the CFI stated that it is necessary to adopt a rule of reason in assessing whether an agreement falls within the scope of Article 81(1) except in the case of cartel agreements.[9] In *European Night Services* the CFI held that the absence of such an assessment of the restrictions of competition arising from the agreements under consideration from the Commission's decision meant that that decision was vitiated by an absence or insufficiency of reasoning.[10]

## Article 81(3) conditions

Article 81(3) contains four conditions for allowing an agreement that falls   5–005 within the scope of Article 81(1). These conditions are all necessary conditions, so an agreement that fails any one of them cannot be allowed. The four conditions are as follows.

1.  The agreement must lead to some efficiency benefit ("improving the production or distribution of goods or contribute to promoting technical or economic progress").

2.  Consumers must receive a fair share of these efficiencies.

3.  The anti-competitive restrictions in the agreement must be indispensable to the attainment of the efficiencies.

4.  The agreement must not "eliminate competition in respect of a substantial part of the products in question".

There are a number of comments relating to these conditions that should be noted. First, the efficiencies could be cost savings or they could be

---

[8]  *European Night Services v Commission* (joined cases T-374/94, T-375/94, T-384/94 and T-388/94) [1998], E.C.R. II-3141, at [136].

[9]  "Rule of reason" is used here simply to imply that conclusions cannot be drawn purely on an assessment of the form of the agreement, but rather that an assessment of the effects is required. See Whish (2009) for a discussion of the dangers of importing terminology from US antitrust into EC competition law.

[10]  A similar aproach was adopted by the Dutch NMa in its assessment of exclusive purchasing agreements entered into by Heineken and retail outlets in the Netherlands (see NMa press release "NMa approves Heineken's new beer contracts" of May 29, 2002).

related to the quality of the products available (e.g. a better version of an existing product or a new product). If the efficiencies are cost savings, then they must not just be the result of an exercise of market power. An agreement that leads to prices rising will lead to demand falling and so will lead to total production costs falling. However, a cost saving of this type does not count as an efficiency.[11] The Commission requires that any claimed efficiency must be clearly linked to the agreement, it must be verifiable and it must be quantifiable.[12] These requirements are consistent with those imposed by the Commission in the assessment of efficiencies in horizontal mergers.

Secondly, the Commission has made clear that it considers a "fair share" for consumers as meaning that consumers are no worse off as a result of the agreement that they are without the agreement. So the requirement is that consumer welfare remains the same or is improved. This implies that it is not acceptable for consumers to be harmed but for producers to gain more benefit than the harm caused to consumers. That is, the Commission is clear that it is applying a consumer welfare standard, not a social welfare standard.

**5–006**   Thirdly, consumers can benefit either from lower prices or from a new or improved product. Where the efficiency is a cost efficiency, it is necessary for it to be passed on to consumers in the guise of lower prices. We deal with the conditions under which pass-through will be high or low in Chapter 17 and so here we deal only with two common misconceptions. First, it is not the case that cost savings will not be passed on if competition is weak. Even a monopolist will pass on cost savings to some extent and, depending on the shape of the demand curve, may even pass on 100 per cent of any cost saving. Secondly, it is not the case that cost savings will necessarily be passed on when competition is strong. When competition is strong and all firms are able to cut their costs, then the cost reduction will be passed on. But when competition is strong and only one firm gains the cost reductions (e.g. only one firm has a new production process), then they are unlikely to be fully passed on.[13]

Fourthly, analysing whether competition has been eliminated in a substantial part of the market essentially requires a market power analysis of the type discussed in Chapter 3. If the agreement is unlikely to lead to the creation of market power, then it will not eliminate competition to any significant degree. Of course, if the agreement has already been implemented then it may be possible to observe directly whether it created market power. For instance, did prices increase after the agreement? If so,

---

[11]   This is analogous to the treatment of cost efficiencies arising from horizontal mergers. See Chapter 7 for details.

[12]   "Guidelines on the application of Article 81(3) of the Treaty" (2004/C 101/08) at para.51.

[13]   Röller, Stennek and Verboven (2006) argue that the available empirical literature suggests pass-through rates of 30–70%.

was this increase in prices associated with an improved product or was it just as likely to have been the result of the creation of market power?

The remainder of this chapter is organised as follows. Paragraphs 5–007—5–033 consider the economics of cartels and collusive behaviour. This section is complementary to the discussion of co-ordinated effects in mergers in Chapter 7. Paragraphs 5–034—5–055 consider the economics of vertical issues and discusses the Commission's policy towards and assessment of vertical agreements. Paragraphs 5–056—5–062 consider horizontal agreements. Paragraphs 5–063—5–064 discuss the role of market definition in Article 81 cases. Paragraphs 5–065—5–066 conclude.

# CARTELS AND COLLUSION

In most markets firms recognise that the profitability of a given commercial **5–007** strategy is dependent on the strategies pursued by competing firms. This raises the possibility that by entering into an agreement with other firms to co-ordinate their behaviour with the aim of reducing the effectiveness of competition between them, each firm will be able to increase price above the level that would have otherwise prevailed and consequently to increase profits. Such behaviour is to the obvious detriment of consumers. Such collusive behaviour is prohibited by the EC Treaty. Article 81(1) makes reference to both agreements and to concerted practices. As noted above, in *European Night Services* the CFI stated that agreements between firms that involved price-fixing or market-sharing entailed obvious restrictions on competition and always fall within the scope of Article 81(1). Given the rationale for such behaviour, such agreements are extremely unlikely to benefit from an exemption under Article 81(3).[14]

Under Article 81, a concerted practice relates to a form of co-operation between undertakings which, while it may not have reached the stage where firms enter into written agreements, knowingly substitutes practical co-operation for the risks of competition. The object of the Treaty in creating a separate concept of concerted practice is to prevent the possibility of undertakings evading the application of Article 81(1) by colluding in a manner which does not involve an agreement, per se, but still has an adverse impact on the competitive process.[15] For example, firms may

---

[14] The Commission has stated as far back as 1980 that cartels are a "category of manifest infringements under Article 81(1) which it is almost always impossible to exempt under Article 81(3) because of the total lack of benefit to the consumer" (*10th Report on Competition Policy*, para.115). The Commission's Article 81(3) Guidelines (2004) note that whilst in principle Article 81(3) applies to all agreements caught under Article 81(1), "severe restrictions of competition are unlikely to fulfil the conditions of Article 81(3)" and specifies that price-fixing cartels are an example (see para.46 of the Guidelines).

[15] In fact, the Commission's decisions in cartel cases focus less on the impact of the cartel on competition and more on whether a cartel existed. The former consideration is however relevant to the assessment of fines and third-party damages.

163

collude by reaching an understanding to inform one another of the prices they intend to charge. This means that in general nothing turns in cartel cases on the precise form of the collusive arrangements. Recent examples in which the Commission have found firms to be guilty of operating explicit cartels include, inter alia, *Car Glass, Gas, Elevators and Escalators, Gas Insulated Switchgear, Paraffin Wax* and *Flat Glass*.[16] Less recent cases include *Graphite Electrodes*,[17] *SAS/Maersk*,[18] *Sodium Gluconate*,[19] *Vitamins*[20] and *Zinc Phospate*.[21]

Before considering those market characteristics that make collusion both possible and sustainable, a distinction needs be drawn between explicit collusion and tacit collusion.[22] While firms can collude explicitly by setting up formal cartels, the recognition of their interdependence may lead firms to collude tacitly. Tacit collusion exists where in the absence of any formal attempts to implement a collusive outcome, firms understand that if each firm competes less vigorously they might all be able to enjoy higher prices and higher profits. For example, a firm may realise that cutting prices will lead to rival firms following suit. Hence, the best the firm can do given the likely reactions of its rivals is to maintain prices at the current level. Equally, a firm may believe that if it raises its price, its rivals will also raise their prices, thus making the price rise profitable.

**5–008**    In theory, firms might be able to mimic the monopoly outcome through tacit collusion. Studies by academic commentators have sought to test for tacit collusion.[23] These studies conclude that interaction over time may

---

[16] In *Car Glass* (COMP/39.125 [2008]) four firms were fined a total of just over €1.4 billion for market-sharing and for the sharing of confidential information. St Gobain and Pilkington were given individual fines of €896,000 and €370,000 respectively. In *Gas* (COMP/39.401 [2009]) E.On and GdF Suez were each fined €553,000 for market-sharing in France and Germany. In *Elevators and Escalators* (COMP/38.823 [2007]) four firms were fined just over €990,000 for operating a cartel in the installation and maintenance of elevators and escalators in Belgium, Germany, Luxembourg and the Netherlands. ThyssenKrupp was individually fined nearly €480,000. In *Gas Insulated Switchgear* (COMP/38.899 [2007]) 11 groups of companies were fined €750,000 for bid-rigging, price-fixing, market-sharing and information-sharing in the EEA. Siemens was fined more than half of this amount (almost €400,000). In *Paraffin Wax* (COMP/39.181 [2008]) nine groups of firms were fined €676,000 for price-fixing and for allocating markets and customers. In *Flat Glass* (COMP/39.165 [2007]) four firms were fined nearly €500,000 for co-ordinating price increases and other commercial terms for flat glass in the EEA.

[17] Eight companies were fined a total of €218.8 million for fixing the prices and sharing markets during most of the 1990s for graphite electrodes worldwide (COMP/36.490 [2001]).

[18] SAS and Maersk Air were fined €52.5 million for market-sharing routes to and from Denmark (COMP/D2/37.444 and COMP/D2/37.386; OJ L265).

[19] The Commission fined six companies a total of €57.53 million for operating a worldwide cartel between 1987 and 1995 to fix prices and share the market for sodium gluconate (COMP/36.756).

[20] Eight companies were fined a total of €855.23 for fixing the price of eight different vitamins (COMP/37.512). The simultaneous investigation in the US led to criminal penalties.

[21] The Commission fined six companies €11.95 million for participating in a cartel between 1994 and 1998 that covered the whole of the EEA.

[22] Tacit collusion is also known as *implicit collusion* or *conscious parallelism*.

[23] These include Green (1984), Slade (1987) and Borenstein and Shepard (1996).

enable firms to increase their profits relative to the one shot non-co-operative outcome. Nevertheless, total industry profit falls short of the monopoly or perfect cartel level. It has been argued that this suggests that co-ordination and communication difficulties are probably greater in practice than most theoretical treatments assume.[24]

The factors which imply that tacit collusion is more likely are similar to those which make sustainable cartel behaviour more likely. For this reason, those industries in which firms have formed, or attempted to form, cartels are more often viewed as being prone to tacit collusion.[25] However, it should be noted that in general firms should prefer to collude tacitly rather than explicitly since explicit cartel behaviour lays firms open to more serious legal penalties, such as large fines or, in the case of the United States and some EU Member States such as the United Kingdom and Ireland, criminal penalties.[26] This implies that firms should only engage in explicit collusion where tacit collusion would not be successful. Where conditions are such that it is relatively easy for firms to tacitly collude successfully (i.e. to achieve close to the monopoly equilibrium), we should not expect to see explicit cartels.

The possibility that firms can engage in tacit collusion raises a difficult policy issue.[27] How can one discriminate between anti-competitive tacit behaviour and normal effective competition? It should be recognised that the mere fact that firms recognise their interdependence with other firms is not a sufficient ground for inferring that observed outcomes are not the result of effective competition. The Prisoners' Dilemma demonstrates this.[28] Each firm knows that its profits depend crucially on the behaviour of its rivals, but nonetheless firms have an incentive to choose the "low price" option.

Given the difficulties in discriminating between tacit collusion and **5–009** effective competition, policy should not as a general rule attempt to intervene in a market on suspicion that firms are competing tacitly without there being very good reasons to believe that the market outcome is substantially different to the effectively competitive outcome. It should also be noted that it is not clear what remedy the Commission could impose in the event of a finding of tacit collusion. The Commission dislikes (with good reason) price regulating firms and it does not impose structural remedies in

---

[24] Jacquemin and Slade (1989).

[25] See US DoJ/FTC Merger Guidelines (1992), section 2.1 and the joint UK Competition Commission/Office of Fair Trading Draft Merger Assessment Guidelines (April 2009) at para.4.120.

[26] Criminal sanctions for cartel behaviour also exist in other jurisdictions, such as Australia, Japan, South Africa and South Korea.

[27] See Chapter 6 for further discussion of this issue in the context of applying the concept of joint dominance in Article 82 cases.

[28] See Chapter 2 and paras 5.10–5.16 below of this chapter for further discussion of the Prisoners' Dilemma.

non-merger cases.[29] The implication of this is that the principal policy weapon against tacit collusion is likely to be merger control and is therefore preventive in nature rather than corrective.[30] For these reasons, the remainder of this section is concerned with explicit collusion.

We first outline the underlying rationale for firms to engage in collusion and then discuss the factors that potentially allow firms to successfully establish a cartel. We then discuss the factors that affect the stability of cartels. Although firms have incentives to engage in explicit co-ordination, this does not mean that firms will necessarily do so. Even absent competition laws preventing such behaviour, the characteristics of many industries imply that firms will not be able to engage in sustained explicit co-ordination. We therefore consider in some detail the factors that determine whether such collusion is likely to be sustainable. We then consider the role for economic analysis in cartel investigations.

Before doing this, there is one point that we want to make. It is common to hear cartels described as the worst of antitrust offences and the resulting overcharges being compared to theft. In our view, this characterisation is not correct.[31] When a consumer or customer buys a cartelised product, they are making a voluntary choice and by definition they value the product at more than the price that they are paying, since otherwise they would not buy the product. This is very different to the involuntary deprivation of property that occurs under theft. It also highlights the fact that cartels still give consumers the option to buy the product. This is different to some

---

[29] There is a substantial difference here between EU competition law and UK competition law. In the United Kingdom the Competition Commission can undertake market inquiries under the Enterprise Act (2002) and can impose structural remedies and/or price regulation where it finds an "adverse effect on competition". More formally, the Competition Commission has to decide "whether any feature, or combination of features, of each relevant market prevents, restricts or distorts competition in connection with the supply or acquisition of goods or services in the United Kingdom or a part of the United Kingdom." (s.134(1) of the Enterprise Act). The inquiry into banking services to the small and medium sized firms (Cm 5319 (2002)) is an example of the Competition Commission imposing price regulation on an oligopoly. The BAA airports inquiry (2009) is an example of the Competition Commission requiring a divestment: BAA was required to divest two of its three London airports (in effect, Gatwick and Stansted). The European Commission can also undertake sector inquires under Article 17 of Regulation 1/2003 EC, but these do not lead directly to price regulation or divestments. Instead, they may lead to follow-on Article 81 or 82 (or state aid) investigations or to legislative proposals. The pharmaceuticals inquiry (final report July 2009) has led to follow-on investigations, whilst the energy inquiry (2007) led to legislative proposals. The supply of beer inquiry (Cm 651 (1989)) led to a structural remedy (the "Beer Orders").

[30] For further discussion of tacit collusion in the context of mergers, see Chapter 7 below, Kühn (2008) and Motta (2004).

[31] It should also be noted that not all cartels successfully raise prices in any case.

exclusionary behaviour which is designed to drive firms out of the market, or stop new firms entering, and which may well deprive consumers of potential new products.[32] We consider that such behaviour ultimately causes more consumer harm and so should be considered a worse offence that collusion.

## The incentive to collude

The incentive for firms to collude can be illustrated by the Prisoners' **5–010** Dilemma game presented in Chapter 2. This example showed that even though a high price outcome benefited both firms, competition resulted in a low price outcome. Figure 5.1 (repeated from Chapter 2) shows the outcomes of the pricing behaviour of two firms. For simplicity, each firm can choose to charge either a high price or a low price. The first number in each quadrant shows the profits earned by firm A and the second number shows the profits earned by firm B. For example, if firm A charges a high price and firm B charges a low price (top right quadrant), firm A will earn zero profits and firm B will earn profits of 30.

## Figure 5.1 The incentives for firms to co-ordinate

**Firm B**

|  | | High price | Low price |
|---|---|---|---|
| | High price | Cartel 10, 10 | 0, 30 |
| **Firm A** | | | |
| | Low price | 30, 0 | Competition 4, 4 |

The figure shows that both firms would prefer to co-ordinate their behaviour and both charge a high price. In this case, the profits earned would be 10 each (see top left quadrant which is labelled "Cartel"). Contrast this to the outcome if both firms were to compete with one another by charging a

---

[32] Fershtman and Pakes (2000) go further. They argue that under some circumstances cartels can actually increase consumer welfare by increasing product variety. Essentially, their argument is that where economies of scale are such that competition would lead to only one, or a few, firms in the market, then the higher prices associated with a cartel may lead to more firms and hence more product variety. Although prices are higher than under competition, the consumer detriment of these prices is outweighed by the increased product variety.

low price. In this case, the profits earned by each firm would be 4 (see bottom right quadrant, labelled "Competition").

However, as this game also illustrates, while there is an incentive for firms to collude, there is also an incentive for one firm to cheat on the collusive agreement. Having reached an agreement that both firms will charge a high price, each firm has an incentive to cheat by charging a low price as it will then earn profits of 30. However, if both firms cheat, this will lead back to the competitive outcome of both firms pursuing a low price strategy and earning profits of only 4. This illustrates a key point, which is often forgotten, namely, that: while firms may have an incentive to collude, achieving and then sustaining a collusive equilibrium can be extremely difficult. Indeed, in a one-period oligopoly game, while all firms will earn more if they co-ordinate their pricing and output than if they pursue a non-co-operative strategy, each player can earn more individually by under-cutting the shared monopoly price. That being the case, co-ordination cannot be observed in a single-period game.[33]

**5–011** Co-ordination therefore requires that firms interact over a period of time. Where this is the case, a firm that is tempted to deviate from the co-ordinated agreement by charging a low price today knows that the benefits from pursuing such a strategy may be short-lived if the other firms are able to detect such behaviour and react by also charging a low price (that reaction is often termed "punishment"). On the other hand, if firms coordinate today and this is reciprocated by competitors tomorrow, then firms can successfully tacitly collude.[34]

We now turn to the question of the characteristics of an industry that are likely to allow firms to successfully raise prices and to reach a cartel agreement.

---

[33] The conclusion that there cannot be tacit coordination in the one-shot game is the result of the assumption that agents act as rational profit maximisers. There is some evidence that in experimental settings agents do not always act in this manner. For a general introduction to experimental economics and some of the results that suggest agents are not always rational, see Ariely (2008). For a discussion focused on antitrust, see Stucke (2009) and the references contained therein.

[34] There is an oddity in the theoretical literature around this point. If the "game" is repeated but all participants know when it will end, the theoretical literature argues that co-ordination is not sustainable. This is because participants know that co-ordination is not sustainable in the final period as this is effectively equivalent to a one-shot game. But if co-ordination is not possible in the last period, then there is no point not cheating in the penultimate period since you know your competitors will not reciprocate this in the last period. By a process of backward induction this implies that however long the game, co-ordination is not possible in any period. Common sense and experimental results both suggest that this conclusion is wrong. If there is uncertainty over when the game will end, then even the theorists accept that co-ordination is possible. See Kreps and Wilson (1982) and Milgrom and Roberts (1982).

## *Ability to raise prices*

The purpose of engaging in illegal cartel activities is to increase prices **5–012** above the level that would otherwise have prevailed by restricting output below the level that would otherwise have prevailed. The ability of the cartel to increase price depends on the elasticity of the demand curve facing the cartel members.[35] The more inelastic the demand curve facing the cartel, the higher the price the cartel can set and the greater the profits which will result from the collusive behaviour. In contrast, where the elasticity of demand facing the firms participating in the cartel is relatively high, there is less scope for raising prices profitably. The demand curve facing the cartel members is more likely to be relatively elastic when:

- an increase in price by the cartel members leads existing competitors who are not part of the cartel to increase their output (i.e. low barriers to expansion); and/or

- an increase in price by the cartel members leads rapidly to new entry into the industry (i.e. low barriers to entry).

In both cases, output rises above the cartel equilibrium and so prices fall. It should be noted that these supply-side constraints can be thought of as "trumps" when analysing whether a particular industry could plausibly be successfully cartelised. A cartel will not be sustainable where barriers to entry or barriers to expansion by non-cartel members are low. For instance, it has been argued that it was the expansion of Chinese Vitamin C manufacturing capacity that led to the demise of the Vitamin C cartel.[36]

Furthermore, "maverick" firms can undermine cartels. Maverick firms are firms known to pursue aggressive commercial strategies, e.g. always pursuing a low price policy. Even in concentrated markets, the ability of firms to sustain a collusive outcome can be undermined by maverick firms.[37] Where fringe firms have low barriers to expansion, the cartel members may have to offer these firms considerable inducements to join the cartel, such as a share of the cartel profits that is disproportionately large compared to their size. Thus, a cartel is more likely to be able to raise prices when barriers to expansion by existing non-cartel member competitors are high or when there are high barriers to entry.

Buyer power can also thwart attempts by a cartel to raise prices. Where **5–013**

---

[35] Where all the firms in an industry are part of the cartel, this will be the same as the industry demand curve.

[36] Levenstein and Suslow (2001).

[37] See Baker (2002). For an example of how a maverick firm can upset co-ordinated behaviour (albeit in relation to tacit co-ordination) see the Commission decision on the Pilkington-Techint/SIV merger [1994] OJ L158/24. For an interesting, but ultimately misguided, discussion of the role of a maverick, see COMP/M.3916 *T-Mobile/tele.ring* (2006).

there are strong buyers, they may be able to resist attempts by the cartel to increase prices and/or they may be able to sponsor new entry in response to any increase in prices. Either of these forms of buyer power reduces the benefit to firms of setting up a cartel.

The potential benefit of setting up a cartel is also related to the level of competition in the absence of the cartel. The fiercer the competition, and the lower the prices, in the absence of a cartel, the greater is the likely benefit from setting up a cartel. Four factors that are important in determining the level of competition in the absence of collusion are the number of firms in the market, the level of spare capacity in the industry, the cost structure of the firms and how homogeneous the products are. As discussed in Chapters 2 and 3, competition tends to be fiercer when there are more firms in a market, although this relationship is by no means perfect.[38] The level of spare capacity affects the incentives that firms have to lower prices to win additional sales. If a firm has no spare capacity, then it has no incentive to lower its price as its lack of spare capacity means that it cannot sell more units. The relationship between marginal costs and average costs is also relevant to the likely level of competition in the absence of the cartel. Where marginal costs are low relative to average costs (or, equivalently, fixed costs are high), prices close to marginal cost are likely to be loss-making. This gives firms a strong incentive to avoid such prices by colluding and hence raising prices above average cost. Finally, when products are relatively homogeneous, this tends to increase the intensity of competition because it means the products are close substitutes to each other. Conversely, competition is often less intense when products are differentiated from each other.

Perhaps the biggest cost of setting up a cartel is the danger that the cartel will be discovered by the competition authorities. It is more likely to be profitable to set up a cartel when the likelihood that the competition authorities will discover it is low, and when the punishment that is likely to be imposed in the event of detection is relatively small (e.g. just an order to desist, rather than a large fine). Hence, the toughness of the stance of competition law towards detecting and punishing cartel behaviour can have a significant effect on its existence. We discuss this further at para.5.23 below.

### Ability to reach agreement

**5–014** Even where the benefits of establishing a cartel are clear, these may still be outweighed by the costs and difficulties of setting up a cartel. In particular,

---

[38] For instance, we noted in Chapter 2 that Bertrand competition with homogeneous products can be extremely competitive with just two firms in the market.

a cartel agreement needs to set the cartel price and to divide the benefits from colluding between the various firms.[39] Factors relevant to how costly and difficult it is to set up a cartel include:

- how heterogeneous the products are;
- differences in cost structure or operating efficiency between firms;
- the number of firms in the industry and market concentration;
- high demand growth and/or uncertainty; and
- the number of markets involved.

We consider each of these issues below.

Generally speaking, it is easier for firms to agree on prices when there are few differences between firms, both in terms of the products they sell and in their cost structure or operating efficiency. Firms are more likely to have difficulty in agreeing on relative prices when each firm's product has different qualities or properties, especially where some of the differences cannot be resolved objectively. Conversely, where products are homogeneous, it is easier for firms to agree on the appropriate cartel price. This explains, in part at least, why many of the major cartel decisions taken by the Commission have concerned industries producing such products as steel beams,[40] cement,[41] PVC,[42] vitamins,[43] zinc phospate,[44] flat glass,[45] and hydrogen peroxide and perborate.[46] Products in all of these industries are to a large extent homogeneous. When products are differentiated, the nature of competition becomes multidimensional and is no longer focused solely on price. This means that co-ordination can become much more complex unless it is possible for firms to co-ordinate on another dimension of competition, such as capacity.

Similarly where firms in an industry have different cost structures or operate at different levels of efficiency, the optimal price for one firm will not be the optimal price for another. There are two distinct issues here. First, firms may have essentially the same cost structure, but one may be less efficient than the other and so have higher unit costs. Secondly, the firms may both be efficient, but have different cost structures, with one firm choosing a low fixed cost, high variable cost production process whilst

---

[39] Agreeing on the terms of the co-ordination is clearly easier when firms collude explicitly. This represents an another important difference between explicit and implicit co-ordination.
[40] COMP/38.907 (2006).
[41] COMP/39.520 (2008).
[42] IV/31.865 (1994).
[43] COMP/37.512 (2001).
[44] COMP/37.027 (2001).
[45] COMP/39.165 (2007).
[46] COMP/38.620 (2000).

another chooses a high fixed cost, low variable cost approach. As discussed in Chapter 2, economic theory tells us that the relevant cost for a firm to consider when setting its price is its marginal cost. The lower a firm's marginal cost, the lower *ceteris paribus* is its profit-maximising price. Thus, a firm with a relatively low marginal cost will want to set a relatively lower price (and hence higher output) than a firm with a relatively high marginal cost. This is not to say that when firms have different marginal costs they will not be able to agree on a compromise price, but merely to point out one potential difficulty that arises when trying to agree on a cartel price. It also highlights the fact that the ability of firms to co-ordinate can be affected by changes in the cost structures of firms over time. For example, if one firm introduces a new technology which gives it a marginal cost advantage over its rivals, then this is likely to make continued co-ordination more difficult as the innovating firm will now want lower prices than it wanted before it reduced its marginal cost. It will also, as we discuss further below, potentially make cheating more profitable than previously.

**5–015**    One structural feature which has an influence on the ability of firms to co-ordinate behaviour is the number of firms competing in the market. Generally speaking, the more firms active in a market, the more difficult it is to co-ordinate successfully. The ability to create a cartel also depends on the level of concentration of a market. Even if there are a large number of firms operating in the industry, if a few firms account for a large proportion of industry sales, then these firms may be able to co-ordinate behaviour without taking into account the numerous other smaller firms. Whether or not this is the case depends on the ability of fringe firms to expand their sales through price cutting (i.e. do the fringe firms face barriers to expansion?).[47] It should also be noted that there are examples of collusion involving many firms. For instance, the UK Office of Fair Trading fined 103 construction firms £129.5m for bid rigging in September 2009.[48] The Dutch construction cartel involved price fixing and market sharing within a large number of local areas and led to about 1,400 firms being fined.

It is important to note that co-ordination can take many forms and that the cost of contracting may vary widely across them.[49] Many cartels fix the market shares of the various players. There are two good reasons for doing this. First, it is often easier to observe a competitor's market share than its price (particularly if there is scope for secret price cuts). Secondly, if a cartel sets price but not market shares, then firms have an incentive to engage in non-price competition (e.g. level of service offered) in order to raise their market share and hence profits. If all firms do this, then the likelihood is that consumers benefit but the firms do not. Hence cartels

---

[47]   Scherer and Ross (1990) discuss the issues relevant to assessing the role fringe firms play in restricting the ability of leading firms to collude successfully. See also Carlton and Perloff (2004).

[48]   For further details, see OFT Press Release of September 22, 2009.

[49]   Stigler (1964).

often set market shares in addition to prices in order to reduce the danger of non-price competition.

Cartels may also engage in market or customer allocation, whereby one firm supplies one area or distinct group of customers and another firm supplies another area or group of customers, with neither competing in the area, or for the customers, of the other firm. Such co-ordination is often easier to police than price co-ordination and does not require any explicit agreement on prices. Instead, the reduction in competition as a result of the market or customer allocation allows prices to rise.[50] The wide scope for cheating has led cartels to pursue a number of additional factors of control over and above price. These include dividing up separate relevant geographic markets, fixing market shares, using most-favoured-nation clauses, using meeting-competition clauses and establishing trigger prices whereby all cartel members agree to expand output to the pre-cartel level if the market price falls below an agreed price floor (the "trigger price").

It is often hard to reach an agreement over market shares when demand **5–016** is growing strongly or there is considerable demand uncertainty. When demand is growing unusually strongly firms wish to earn profits from this demand growth while it lasts, and this may make it hard for the firms to reach an agreement over market shares.[51] When demand is uncertain, firms need to agree how to respond to unanticipated increases or decreases in demand. Co-ordination can also be difficult when demand is falling as this increases the relative attraction of cheating now compared to earning cartel profits in a smaller market in future.

The more markets that the various firms compete in, the more complicated it becomes to agree on a cartel solution. This is particularly true if the different markets are served by different divisions of the various firms and if these divisions are run relatively separately from each other. It should be noted, however, that collusion is also potentially more worthwhile when it covers a number of markets.[52]

The costs of establishing and enforcing a cartel can be facilitated if there exists an easy way for firms to meet and co-ordinate their activities without raising the attention of competition authorities. One such mechanism is via the establishment of a trade association.[53] Trade associations can play a particularly important role when the cartel involves a large number of firms. Hay and Kelley (1974) found that trade associations were involved in more than 80 per cent of the cartels they studied that had more than 15

---

[50] Dick (1996) found that cartels that primarily fixed prices, rather than some other dimension of competition such as market sharing, tended to be more unstable than other cartels.

[51] See, for instance, Rotemberg and Saloner (1986).

[52] However, it should not be presumed that such multi-market contracts necessarily facilitate collusion (Bernheim and Whinston (1990)). See Chapter 7 for a further discussion.

[53] See, for instance, *AROW v BNIC* (1982) and *Fenex* (1996). Of course, not all trade associations provide a mechanism for co-ordination. For a general discussion of the issue, see Leibowitz (2005).

members, and in 100 per cent of cartels with more than 25 members. Levenstein and Suslow (2006) found that 29 per cent of the cartels in their sample involved trade associations. In 2003 the Commission found AC-Treuhand AG, a Swiss consultancy, guilty of cartel behaviour because it facilitated a cartel even though it did not itself produce or sell the relevant product. The actual cartel was for organic peroxides and included Akzo Group, Atofina SA and Peroxid Chemie GmbH.[54] The Commission found that AC-Treuhand had actively organised the cartel and provided support to it, such as organising meetings, providing share information and storing contracts.[55]

## The stability of cartels

**5–017** As noted above, firms in a cartel have an incentive to undercut the cartel price. This was illustrated in Figure 5.1, where a firm could earn profits of 30, rather than just 10, by charging a low price and undercutting the high price charged by the other firm. That is, if one firm is charging a high price, the other firm earns higher profits by charging a low price. In Chapter 2, we noted that the cartel solution does not represent the best short-run outcome for each firm. Figure 2.9 showed that, given the output of the other firms in the market, each firm could raise its profits by moving onto its reaction curve (as long as the other firms did not then change their output in response). Hence, the cartel solution does not represent a short-run Nash equilibrium.[56] This has an important implication for the stability of cartels: they are frequently unstable. The firms in a cartel have an incentive to cheat, i.e. to undercut the cartel price or by engaging in other activities that destabilise the collusive agreement. By slightly undercutting the cartel price, firms can potentially dramatically increase their sales and hence profits.

However, before a firm does this it needs to weigh up the potential benefits of deviating from the agreement (i.e. "cheating") against the possibility that the other firms in the cartel will discover that it is cheating and "punish" it. So the stability of a cartel depends on three factors:

1. the benefits to firms of cheating;

---

54 COMP/37.857 (2003).
55 Connor (2001) notes that the Amino Acid Manufacturers International Association was formed by the members of the Lysine cartel whilst Funderburk (1974) noted that the Oklahoma Highway Department started to receive identical bids from suppliers only after the formation of the Asphalt Refiners Association.
56 Recall that a Nash equilibrium exists when, given the behaviour of all other firms in the market, no firm wants to change its behaviour. In a profit-maximising setting, this means that each firm is maximising its profits given the sales of all the other firms in the market.

2.   the likelihood that cheating will be detected; and

3.   the extent of any "punishment" that firms can impose on a "cheater".[57]

We consider these factors in turn. Note that we are ignoring issues to do with how competition authorities can make cartels less stable. We deal with this issue at paras 5–023—5–025 below.

## The benefits of cheating

The benefits of cheating are the extra profits that a firm can earn by selling  **5–018** significantly more units as a result of undercutting the collusive price. However, there are also costs to cheating as the firm will earn lower profits on those sales that it would have made anyway at the higher cartel price. The extra profits from the additional sales as a result of cheating need to be traded off against the cost of earning lower profits on the sales the firm would have been made anyway. The extra profits will depend on the marginal cost of the cheating firm, the price that it sets when it cheats and the increase in sales generated. The lower the marginal costs are relative to price, the greater the benefits are from cheating for any given increase in sales. Equally, for given marginal costs and price, the benefits from cheating are greater the greater is the increase in sales (i.e. the greater is the cheating firm's own-price elasticity). Table 5.1 should make this clear. This describes six scenarios showing how the increase in profits varies with marginal costs and with the firm's own-price elasticity of demand. We assume that the collusive price is 100, that the cheating firm prices at 95 and that its sales at the collusive price (i.e. before cheating) are 1,000. Scenarios 1 to 3 show how the profits from cheating rise as the firm's marginal cost falls, keeping the firm's own-price elasticity of demand constant. Scenarios 4 to 6 show how the profits from cheating rise as the firm's own-price elasticity of demand rises, keeping marginal costs constant.

---

[57]   The breakdown in the cartel agreement may be permanent or temporary. Some authors have suggested that periods of price war are necessary for the long-run sustainability of collusive behaviour. See Green and Porter (1984).

## Table 5.1 The benefits from cheating

| | Marginal Cost | Collusive Price | Cheating Price | Sales of Collusive Price | Elasticity | Extra sales | Increase in profits |
|---|---|---|---|---|---|---|---|
| Scenario 1 | 70 | 100 | 95 | 1,000 | −5.0 | 250 | 1,250 |
| Scenario 2 | 60 | 100 | 95 | 1,000 | −5.0 | 250 | 3,750 |
| Scenario 3 | 50 | 100 | 95 | 1,000 | −5.0 | 250 | 6,250 |
| Scenario 4 | 60 | 100 | 95 | 1,000 | −4.0 | 200 | 2,000 |
| Scenario 5 | 60 | 100 | 95 | 1,000 | −5.0 | 250 | 3,750 |
| Scenario 6 | 60 | 100 | 95 | 1,000 | −6.0 | 300 | 5,500 |

Note that we have assumed in these scenarios that the cheating firm either has spare capacity or that it can add spare capacity at constant marginal cost. In general, marginal costs are likely to increase sharply if firms are operating at close to capacity and adding extra capacity is likely to involve significant fixed costs. So if firms are operating close to their full capacity, this is likely to reduce the benefit to them of cheating.

The above implies that in industries that are characterised by high fixed costs relative to marginal costs, the short-run benefits to cheating are likely to be high. However, as we noted earlier, it is also the case that in such industries competition that drives prices down towards marginal cost is likely to lead to firms making losses and this increases the incentive for firms to find a way to collude. It is not a priori clear which effect will dominate, i.e. whether the incentive to cheat will undermine a cartel or whether firms will manage to create a stable cartel. Scherer and Ross (1990) argue that in industries of this type collusion is likely to be explicit, rather than tacit, and that it is likely to involve highly organised monitoring of the behaviour of each cartel member. Grout and Sonderegger (2005) find evidence that the higher the economies of scale are in an industry (i.e. the higher the fixed costs are relative to variable costs), the more likely there is to have been a cartel prosecuted in that industry.

**5–019**     Other factors that affect the benefit of cheating include the number of other firms in the market. A firm's elasticity of demand usually rises as the number of competitors that it faces increases (because there are more substitutes for its own product), so we should expect the benefit from cheating to be larger the greater the number of firms is in the market. Moreover, the gains from price cutting may increase as the number of firms increases since detecting price cuts becomes more difficult. In general, as the share of industry output supplied by each firm decreases, individual producers are increasingly prone to ignore the impact of their own-price and output decisions on those of rival firms, which makes them more likely to cheat.

The incentives for a firm to cheat on the cartel agreement depend on the relative magnitude of the short-term gains of doing so. If the short-term gains of cheating are large relative to the long-term gains from colluding, this raises the incentive to cheat. One important factor here is the discount rate that firms apply to future profits compared to current profits. The more highly that firms value current profits relative to future profits, the greater the incentive to cheat. Another factor that affects whether the short-term gains to cheating are important depends in part on the size and frequency with which buyers make purchases. The short-run gains to a firm from cheating are greater when the order at stake is large relative to total likely future sales than when it is small (e.g. when an industry is characterised by a few, large orders placed at irregular time intervals). The short-term gain is also partly dependent on the amount of spare capacity the cheater has or on how low barriers to expansion are. A firm that can increase its output significantly in the short-term is more likely to find it profitable to cheat than one that can only increase its output by a small amount. Finally, if a firm has the option of cheating in a number of markets simultaneously, this will yield larger short-term profits than if it can cheat in only one market.

However, this analysis is only a partial analysis of the incentives to cheat since it does not take into account the likelihood of detection or of what might happen if the firm is caught cheating. The more likely it is that cheating will be observed by the other cartel members, and the harsher the resulting punishment, the less likely a firm is to cheat. We now turn to this issue.

### Deterence: likelihood cheating will be detected

The longer a firm can cheat on the cartel agreement without detection, the **5–020** greater the gains from doing so. Hence, the more difficult and/or costly detection is, the less sustainable the cartel agreement is likely to be. There are a number of factors that affect the ease with which firms can monitor the behaviour of the other firms in the industry.

The most obvious of these is the level of price transparency. If the industry price is very transparent, then any cheating will become apparent immediately. Conversely, if prices are non-transparent, perhaps because of secret price setting or because quality differentials across firms make it hard to compare prices directly, it is harder to detect cheating. A common method to forestall the consequences of retaliation is to grant secret rebates. Whenever price exceeds marginal cost there is a temptation to grant secret price cuts. If such practices can be confined to a small proportion of total industry sales, the impact of these rebates will not have a significant impact on prices and may not be detected by other cartel members. But if secret price cutting extends to a larger share of the market, this is likely to have a significant effect on prices and so may undermine the cartel agreement. As a result, cartels have an incentive to find ways to make prices more transparent. As we note below, this is one possible effect of trade associations. If a trade association can collect and verify price and sales data from the various firms, then sharing this information can facilitate collusion. Alternatively firms may do this themselves by making public announcements about the prices they intend to charge. An interesting example of this was the airlines in the United States. It used to be the case that airlines could post prices on the computer reservation systems that did not take effect immediately. For instance, an airline could post a price that would not come into effect for two weeks. If the other airlines adjusted their prices in the light of the posted price, then the original airline would use that price. But if the other airlines did not adjust their prices, then the original airline could remove the price from the reservation system before it came into effect. The Department of Justice argued that this facilitated collusion via an exchange of information on future prices.

The number of firms in the industry is also important. When there are only a few firms in the industry, the members of the cartel can more easily monitor each other's behaviour. In contrast, where there are many firms present in the market, monitoring is more difficult. As the number of firms increases, the number of two-way informational flows increases rapidly.[58] Thus as the number of firms increases, it is harder to know who is cheating even if it is clear that someone is cheating (perhaps because prices have fallen significantly).

**5–021** The nature of the products also affects the ease with which cheating can be detected. When products are homogeneous, not only is it easier for firms to agree on the appropriate cartel price but detection is easier. Changes in market share are more likely to provide an indication of price cutting than when products are heterogeneous. When products are heterogeneous, changes in market shares may reflect changes in consumer preferences across products, rather than cheating.

Where an industry is subject to unpredictable fluctuations in demand, it becomes more difficult for firms to determine whether changes in the demand for their products reflect cheating on the part of one or more cartel members or whether it simply represents a change in the overall level of industry demand.[59]

### Deterrence: the extent of any "punishment" that firms can impose on a "cheater"

**5–022** The incentive to cheat will be affected by the "punishment" that the "cheater" potentially faces. "Punishment" refers to the response of the other firms to the discovery that a firm is cheating on the cartel agreement. This will entail a movement away from the cartel equilibrium towards a more competitive equilibrium, thus reducing the profits of the cheater. The

---

[58] The number of two-way informational exchanges is given by the following formula: N(N–1)/2. Hence, with two firms, the number of exchanges is 1; with three, 3; with six, 15; and with 10 firms, 45.

[59] See Green and Porter (1984).

closer to the competitive outcome the punishment phase is, and the longer it lasts, the lower is a firm's incentive to cheat and risk being punished.

However, there is a clear tension between the wish of the other firms to punish the cheater and their wish to minimise the damage to their own profits. Once they have discovered the cheating, the other firms want to reinstate the cartel equilibrium as quickly as possible. But if they do not impose some punishment (lost profits) on the cheater, then they will encourage other firms to cheat as well. Green and Porter (1984) argue that periods in which a cartel reverts to competitive behaviour are actually necessary for the stability of the cartel as they keep firms "honest" by making the threat of punishment real. Thus it is important for the stability of a cartel that the threat of punishment is credible. One way to increase the credibility of the threat of punishment is for the punishment mechanism to be formalised as part of the cartel agreement. This makes the threat more credible in the sense that it makes clear what firms will do in response to cheating (e.g. lower price by 10 per cent for six months), but does not solve the more fundamental problem that non-cheating firms want the punishment period to be as painless for them as possible, and so have an incentive to revert to the cartel equilibrium as soon as possible. A better way to make the threat credible is to have a punishment mechanism that is targeted solely on the cheating firm. For instance, if part of the cartel agreement is that each firm has its own exclusive territory that other firms do not actively compete in, the punishment mechanism could be for other firms to compete in the territory of the cheater for a given time period. This will allow the other firms to punish the cheater whilst not sacrificing the cartel profits they earn in their own exclusive territories.

Three other factors that affect the extent of any punishment are the existence of spare capacity, the speed with which a cheater can be punished and the number of markets in which punishment can take place. First, a necessary condition for punishing a cheater is that the other firms in the industry have spare capacity that allows them to increase output. If they cannot raise their output and hence lower prices, they cannot punish the cheater. Secondly, the longer that rival firms cannot respond to cheating, the greater are the gains from cheating (since current profits are worth more than future profits, which must be discounted according to the time value of money). So the less quickly firms can punish the cheater, the greater the punishment must be in order to counteract the effects of the delay. Thirdly, if the cheater operates in a number of markets, the cartel members may be able to increase their output in more than one market and hence make the punishment harsher.

## The role of competition authorities in deterring cartels

Competition authorities themselves can have a significant effect on the  **5–023** trade-off that firms face when deciding whether to start, or to continue, cartel behaviour. There are two ways in which competition authorities can discourage cartels. First, by increasing the likelihood of detecting them. Secondly, by increasing the sanctions against them once they have been found. Competition authorities throughout the world have pursued both approaches in recent years.

### Increasing likelihood of detecting cartels

**5–024** Three approaches have been adopted to increasing the likelihood of deterrence. The first is the now widespread use of leniency programmes whereby firms engaged in a cartel are encouraged to confess this activity to the relevant competition authority on the understanding that they will then not face sanctions, or at least substantially reduced sanctions, as a result. This approach has the effect of forcing the cartelists to play a form of "chicken": none of the firms wants any of the firms to confess to the competition authorities, but if any firm is going to confess then each firm wants to be the first to confess. It is widely accepted that leniency programmes have been very effective at increasing the number of cartels that are detected.[60] Secondly, competition authorities have encouraged individuals within firms to report cartel behaviour. The UK OFT, for instance, offers financial rewards of up to £100,000 for "inside information" on cartel behaviour.

Thirdly, competition authorities have begun to look for cartels themselves, based on observations on the structure of industries and behaviour within those industries. Grout and Sonderegger (2005), in a paper commissioned by the UK Office of Fair Trading, concluded that there were three pieces of "fundamental background" that should be considered as "almost basic requirements for cartel formation". Based on empirical research and a review of the theoretical literature, they found that these were:

- product homogeneity;

- a lack of sustained volatility within the industry; and

- stability amongst the leading players (i.e. large and stable market shares).

They also found that an important indicator for the creation of a cartel is either a long-term decline in demand and prices affecting all players in the

---

[60] For instance, Scott Hammond, the Director of Criminal Enforcement at the Antitrust Division of the US Department of Justice, stated in 2000 that "over the last five years, the United States' Corporate Leniency Program ('Amnesty Program') has been responsible for detecting and cracking more international cartels than all of our search warrants, secret audio or videotapes, and FBI interrogations combined. It is, unquestionably, the single greatest investigative tool available to anti-cartel enforcers." (speech at the International Workshop on Cartels, November 21–22, 2000).

market or a sudden negative market shock affecting all players. For instance, it appears that it was the entry in 1991 of Archer Daniels Midland (ADM) that led to the formation of the lysine cartel. ADM's entry increased industry capacity by 65 per cent and led to a dramatic fall in prices from about $1.1 per pound to $0.69. The lysine cartel was set up in June 1992 with the expressed intention of raising prices back above $1 per pound.

It should be noted that these factors should only be considered as screening devices. The presence of the three "fundamental background" factors does not mean that an industry is therefore cartelised, although the absence of these factors makes it very unlikely that it is cartelised.

## Increasing level of sanctions against cartels

Secondly, competition authorities have increased the level of sanctions **5–025** used against cartels. The European Commission has consistently increased the level of fines that it levies against cartels. Total fines imposed by the Commission between 1990 and 1994 and between 1995 and 1999 were €567 million and €297 million respectively. This rose to almost €3.7 billion in the period 2000 to 2004 and has risen again to more than €9 billion in the period 2005 to 2009. As noted above, some Member States, such as the United Kingdom and Ireland, also have the option of criminal sanctions in cartel cases, meaning that employees of the firms involved can potentially go to jail.[61]

---

**BOX 5.1: A MORE FORMAL TREATMENT OF COLLUSION INCENTIVES**[62]

It will only be profitable for a firm to collude if the profits from doing so outweigh the profits from cheating. Denote the profit this period from colluding for firm i as $\Pi_i^C$. Denote future profits from colluding as $\Sigma_i^C$. These profits need to be discounted and we will denote the discount factor as $\delta$. $\delta$ will be less than one since future profits are worth less than current profits, but more than zero, since they have some value. Thus the profits from colluding are:

(1)   $\Pi_i^C + \delta \Sigma_i^C$

Denote the profits from cheating (i.e. deviating from the collusive equilibrium) as $\Pi_i^D$. If a firm cheats, then in the next period and all periods thereafter we assume that they revert to the competitive equilibrium (i.e. the punishment mechanism is a "grim" strategy).

---

[61] For instance, three individuals received jail terms in the United Kingdom in June 2008 as a result of their participation in the Marine Hose cartel. No individuals have so far been jailed in Ireland, although suspended sentences have been imposed (e.g. in the Irish *Ford Dealers Association* case in 2007).

[62] This treatment follows Tirole (1988).

Denote these competitive equilibrium profits as $\Sigma_i^{Comp}$. Profits from cheating are then:

(2) $\quad \Pi_i^D + \delta \, \Sigma_i^{Comp}$

Collusion will only be stable if, for all firms, the following inequality holds:

(3) $\quad \Pi_i^C + \delta \, \Sigma_i^C \geq \Pi_i^D + \delta \, \Sigma_i^{Comp}$

This then implies the standard condition on the discount factor that collusion is only sustainable if:

(4) $\quad \delta \geq \dfrac{\Pi_i^D - \Pi_i^C}{\Sigma_i^C - \Sigma_i^{Comp}}$

We can illustrate a number of simple points with Equations (3) and (4). First, collusion is only sustainable if the discount factor is high enough. This is intuitive. If a firm does not value future profits, then it should cheat and earn the higher profits that are available this period. The less the firm values future profits, the more likely it is to find cheating profitable.

**5-026**     Secondly, we can see that where orders are large and lumpy, this makes collusion harder to sustain. The effect of a large order is to increase the profitability of cheating (in order to win the large order) which implies an increase in $\Pi_i^D$. Equation (3) shows that this increases the likelihood that the inequality does not hold and that cheating is optimal.

    Thirdly, we can see the trivial point that the larger the profits are from cheating, the more likely it is that collusion is not sustainable. So if there is a one-period demand shock that increases the profitability of cheating, this may undermine the cartel (assuming that the demand shock increases the current profitability of cheating by more than it increases the current profitability of colluding, which is intuitive). But note that if the demand shock is persistent, this conclusion changes. If the demand shock is persistent, then a positive shock both increases the current profits from cheating, but also increases the future profits from colluding (i.e. increases $\Sigma_i^C$). So a one-period positive demand shock potentially undermines the cartel, whereas a persistent positive demand shock will likely make it more stable. In contrast, a one-period negative demand shock makes collusion more stable, but a persistent negative demand shock makes it less stable.

    Fourthly, we can deduce the effect of increasing numbers of firms on collusion. If there are no capacity constraints, then the effect of increasing numbers of firms is to raise the size of $\Pi_i^D$ relative to $\Pi_i^C$. From Equation (3) it makes it more likely that collusion is not optimal or, equivalently from Equation (4), it increases the size of the discount rate that is required to make collusion stable.

**5-027**     Fifthly, we can simply model the effect of a competition authority's anti-cartel policy. Denote the expected loss to a firm from the competition authority's policy as $CA_i$. This will be an expected value made up of the likelihood that the authority will catch the cartel multiplied by the expected fine (and possibly third-party damages) that would then result. Equation (3) then becomes:

(5)   $\Pi_i^C + \delta\Sigma_i^C - CA_i \geq \Pi_i^D + \delta\,\Sigma_i^{Comp}$

And Equation (4) becomes:

(6)   $\delta \geq \frac{\Pi_i^D - \Pi_i^C + CA_i}{\Sigma_i^C - \Sigma_i^{Comp}}$

Equation (6) indicates that the possibility of competition authority action increases the discount rate that is necessary to make the cartel stable. This is because it becomes necessary for the firm to value future profits by more in order to counteract the negative effect of the competition authority. From Equation (6) we can see the cartel cannot be stable if:

(7)   $\Pi_i^D - \Pi_i^C + CA_i > \Sigma_i^C - \Sigma_i^{Comp}$

because this would require a discount rate of greater than one.

## The role of economic analysis in cartel investigations

In order for firms participating in a cartel to be held to infringe Article 81, **5–028** the Commission need only establish that firms have engaged in illegal co-ordination with the aim of restricting competition. Usually the Commission establishes this with reference to documentary evidence of meetings between firms at which prices, customers and/or market-sharing allocations are discussed. Since an infringement of Article 81 does not require an analysis of the actual impact of any cartel activities, this would appear to make economic analysis in cartel cases redundant. However, economic analysis can play a useful role in two ways.[63] First, it can play a role in providing evidence as to whether it is plausible that an industry was cartelised. Secondly, it can provide estimates of the impact that a cartel has had on price. We deal with these issues in turn.

### Plausibility of collusion

It should be clear that economics can offer insight into whether it is **5–029** plausible that a cartel is operating in a particular industry. There are a number of structural aspects to an industry that, if not present, suggest that cartelisation is not plausible. For instance, if the product is heterogeneous, then cartelisation is unlikely. If the market is subject to a considerable

---

[63] However, we note that it is incorrect as a matter of economics that the mere attempt to engage in cartel behaviour will lead to an increase in prices above the counterfacutal competitive level.

amount of volatility, then cartelisation is unlikely. If entry is easy or there is a competitive fringe with low barriers to expansion, then again we would not expect collusion to be possible. Evidence of market share volatility is hard to make consistent with collusion. So economics can suggest that it is unlikely that a particular industry is cartelised. Turning this round, it can suggest industries where cartelisation is plausible and therefore where further investigation may be warranted.

Alternatively, a competition authority might observe that some firms were active only in one geographical area while others firms are only active in another and seek to argue that this is evidence of a market-sharing agreement. However, it is possible that such market behaviour is consistent with normal competitive behaviour. In this case, an economic analysis of the characteristics of the industry under consideration can provide useful insights as to the appropriate explanation.

This is uncontroversial. More controversial is whether economics can go further and show, even in the absence of a "smoking gun", that collusion has taken place. Our view is that in general economics cannot go this far, although it can provide some useful tests that should be seen as complementary to the "smoking gun" evidence.[64] We discuss some examples below.

5–030    One useful question that economics can try to answer is whether the observed behaviour of firms is inconsistent with competition. If it is, then this is one piece of evidence that firms may be colluding. An example of this is provided by suspected collusion in asphalt auctions in Oklahoma in the period 1954 to 1965. For most of this period, prices were constant at 10.25 cents per gallon. Arguably, this constancy in itself was suspicious, but it certainly is not inconsistent with competition. However, during the same period prices in neighbouring areas were only 6 cents per gallon and were not constant. Even allowing for transport costs from these areas (up to 2.5 cents per gallon), prices in Oklahoma were such that it would have been profitable for operators selling at 6 cents per gallon in neighbouring areas to switch their sales to Oklahoma. In a competitive market, this is what we would have expected to see. Another example is provided by Porter and Zona (1999). They analysed school milk auctions in the Cincinnati area. They were able to divide providers into those who were suspected of collusive behaviour and those that were not. The aim was to see if the process of price formation differed between the two types of firm. Porter and Zona found that they did. One interesting finding was that the relationship between bids and the distance between the relevant supplies processing plant and the school district varied between the suspected colluders and the other firms. The relationship between distance and price

---

[64] One exception to this statement might be the discovery of the US market-makers collusion by Christie and Schulz as a result of their noticing a suspicious lack of odd-eight quotes for NASDAQ securities (Christie and Schultz (1994)).

for the "competitive" firms was as we would expect: as distance between the processing plant and the school district rose, the firms' bids rose. However, for the colluding firms the opposite was true. Their bids fell as distance increased. It is hard to understand this within a competitive setting.

A similar question is simply to ask whether there is a difference in the behaviour between those firms suspected of collusion and those not. This does not require that we show that the behaviour of the suspected colluders is inconsistent with competition, but merely that it differs in some significant way from the behaviour of the "competitive" firms. This is a relatively weak test, but it may throw up interesting empirical observations that may lead investigators to fruitful lines of inquiry.

Another useful question is to see if there is a structural break in the market data that might indicate a change in regime from competition to collusion, or vice versa. The most obvious type of structural break is a change in the price formation process, which could be shown by a significant increase or decrease in prices that is unrelated to changes in underlying costs. For instance, if there is a concern that a cartel started at date X, then an econometric model of the price formation process before date X could be estimated and then it could be tested whether this model also worked after date X. In addition to looking for structural breaks in the price formation process, it could also be useful to look for structural breaks in the level of price variation or market share variation, both of which we would expect to be lower when an industry is cartelised.[65]

Some economists argue that another useful test is to see if a collusive    **5–031** model of the industry "fits" better than a competitive model of the industry. The idea is to specify a model of how the industry would work if it was competitive and how it would work if a cartel was operating. The test is then to see whether the empirical data fits the competitive model or the cartel model best. We are dubious as to the likely efficacy of this approach in practice since it involves a number of embedded hypotheses. First, the model of competition has to be correct. Secondly, the model of how collusion would work has to be correct. Thirdly, the data needs to be able to correctly distinguish between the two. However, there is an interesting theoretical literature on this area[66] and it is possible that there might be a case in which this approach provides some useful information.

One approach to detecting cartels that has been suggested but one which we would reject as being fundamentally flawed is to consider price cost margins. The argument is that cartels raise the price cost margin for an industry and so one way to find cartels is to look for high price cost margins. The reason that this is not right is that price cost margins will vary

---

[65]   This raises the issue of whether the start and/or end date of the cartel can be clearly established.

[66]   For instance, Baldwin, Marshall and Richard (1997), Banerji and Meenakski (2004) and Bajari and Ye (2003).

across industries depending on the cost structure of the industry. Specifically, industries with high fixed costs and low marginal costs will tend to have high price cost margins even under competition.[67]

## Impact of a cartel

**5–032** Economic analysis is often used to assess the impact of the cartel. The mere fact that a cartel has been in operation does not imply that it was successful in increasing prices above the level that would have been observed under conditions of effective competition. This has been accepted by the courts.[68] For example, although the participants of a cartel might announce publicly the agreed price increase, this does not necessarily mean that those price increases are actually implemented in the sense that customers obtain products or services at those announced prices. This is particularly the case where the prices paid by customers are subject to non-uniform discounts off the announced list price.

Although participation in an ineffective cartel does not provide a defence against an adverse finding against the cartel's participants, an analysis of the actual impact may have a bearing on the size of fine issued by the Commission. Moreover, such analysis often provides a precursor to more detailed work that is undertaken in response to the third-party damages claims that are pursued following the Commission's decision.

Chapter 17 deals in detail with the issue of estimating the impact of a cartel and of the resulting damages. For this reason, we do not consider this issue further here.[69]

---

[67] See the extended discussion on this issue in Chapters 2 and 3.

[68] See *Cascades v Commission* (T-308/94) [1998] E.C.R. II-925.

[69] There is a considerable amount of economic literature that argues that many cartels are able to raise prices successfully and hence that they do cause consumer harm. Porter and Zona (2001) studied the school milk auctions in southwestern Ohio between 1980 and 1990. Although they found that the average overcharge due to the cartel behaviour was only 6.5%, they also found that for some school districts the overcharge was as high as 49%. Froeb, Koyak and Werden (1993) found an average overcharge of 27% in the US Department of Defence procurement auctions for frozen perch. Kwoka (1997) looked at collusion among bidders in real estate auctions in Washington DC. This was a buyer cartel and so the cartel led to lower prices, not higher prices. He found evidence of an undercharge of about 30%. Howard and Kaserman (1989) estimated overcharges of about 40% in city sewer construction contracts.

These studies all looked at specific cartels. There have also been a number of meta-studies carried out looking at average overcharges across a range of cartels. Connor and Bolotova (2006) looked at 395 cartel episodes. They estimated that the mean overcharge was 29%, with a median overcharge of 19%. In an earlier paper, Connor (2007) distinguished between the level of cartel overcharges in domestic (i.e. US) cartels as opposed to international ones and found that the median overcharge was 18% for domestic cartels and 32% for international ones. He also found that the overcharge was above 20% in about 60% of cases. Levenstein and Suslow (2006) looked at 35 international cartels and estimated that the mean overcharge was 25% and that it ranged between 10% and 100%.

## Conclusions

Whether an industry becomes cartelised or not depends on how great the **5–033** incentives are for the firms in the industry to form a cartel and how sustainable the cartel is. The incentives to create a cartel depend on the potential difference between the profitability of the firms in the presence of a cartel and in the absence of a cartel. A key determinant of the sustainability of the cartel depends on whether the incentives the firms have to cheat on the cartel agreements are outweighed by the likelihood of cheating being detected and punished. This section has discussed the factors that determine the outcome of these various trade-offs.

However, the supply-side responses by non-cartel members can undermine the cartel. Where entry into a market is easy, or it is easy for non-cartel members to expand their output in response to the cartel members raising their prices, a cartel will not be sustainable. In this sense, these supply-side responses "trump" the other factors discussed above. Furthermore, many industries are not structurally suited to cartelisation. We have discussed the relevant factors that imply that cartel behaviour is more likely to be effective. We have also discussed the role of competition authorities in deterring cartels and the scope for economic analysis to play a role in cartel investigations.

# VERTICAL RESTRAINTS

## Introduction

Vertical agreements are agreements between firms at different levels in the **5–034** production and supply chain and include agreements between manufacturers and retailers, manufacturers and distributors, distributors and retailers and so on. Vertical agreements in general contain restrictions imposed by one party on another. On occasion, these restrictions can fall foul of Article 81. Figure 5.2 illustrates the difference between vertical and horizontal relationships.

## Figure 5.2 The difference between vertical and horizontal relationships

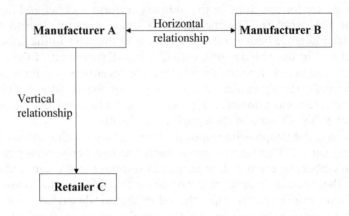

Figure 5.2 shows that manufacturer A and manufacturer B are active at the same stage of the production process (namely, manufacturing) and are competitors in the supply of their products.[70] The relationship between them is deemed to be a horizontal relationship so that any agreement between them would be a horizontal agreement. In contrast, the relationship between manufacturer A and retailer C is a vertical one since they are active at different stages of the production process: manufacturing and retailing, respectively. Manufacturer A supplies product to retailer C that retailer C then sells on to its customers after either using the product as an input in its production process or providing retailing services. Rather than being competitors to one another, the products or services supplied by manufacturer A and retailer C are complementary to each other. Manufacturer A requires the services of retailer C to sell its products, whilst retailer C needs manufacturer A to supply it. Manufacturer A is normally termed the upstream firm and retailer C is termed the downstream firm (the production process of the upstream firm precedes that of the downstream firm).

There are a wide variety of vertical restraints employed by firms that may or may not give rise to competition concerns. Some manufacturers distribute their products to selected outlets only ("selective distribution"). This is typically the case with branded products where the manufacturer is concerned with the environment in which its product is sold. Some retailers sell the products of only one manufacturer ("exclusive dealership"). Some retailers are given a guarantee by the manufacturer that no other retailers within their geographic area will be supplied by that manufacturer ("exclusive territories"). On occasion, manufacturers insist that their

---

[70]  This assumes that the products produced by firm A and firm B form part of the same relevant market.

product is sold for a certain minimum amount ("resale price maintenance").[71] Other manufacturers may insist that the retailer sells a certain minimum amount of their product ("quantity forcing").

Vertical integration is where the activities at different levels of the vertical **5–035** chain are undertaken by the same firm. In the above example, the activities of manufacturer A and retailer C are assumed to be undertaken by different firms. However, in principle both activities could be undertaken by the same firm, in which case manufacturer A and retailer C would be said to be vertically integrated. This is illustrated in Figure 5.3. Here firm A and firm C are part of the same firm, firm D, and so are said to be vertically integrated.

## Figure 5.3 Vertical integration

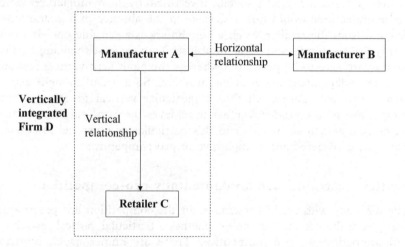

Many of these restrictions (resale price maintenance, quantity forcing, exclusive territories and exclusive dealership) are substitutes, albeit in some cases imperfect ones, for vertical integration. For example, selective distribution is only a partial substitute for vertical integration. Both vertical integration and selective distribution lead to a restriction in the number of retailers being supplied with the product. However, whereas a vertically integrated firm might choose not to retail the products of its rivals, under selective distribution retailers would be free to select products from a number of different manufacturers.

Inherent in the notion of vertical integration is the elimination of contractual or market exchanges and the substitution of internal exchanges within the boundaries of the firm. Vertical integration can be pro-

---

[71]   The Commission has condemned resale price maintenance on various occasions and has been endorsed in this by the European Court of Justice. See, e.g. *Pronuptia de Paris v Schillgalis* (161/84) [1981] E.C.R. 353; [1986] 1 C.M.L.R. 414. However, as we discuss below, the approach to RPM on both sides of the Atlantic appears to be becoming more receptive towards the possibility that RPM can be pro-competitive on some occasions.

competitive in the sense that it allows a firm to improve the efficiency of its operations either through creating transaction cost efficiencies[72] or through enabling a firm to overcome difficulties in contracting with an external party.[73]

**5–036** Before discussing the impact on competition of various vertical restraints, it should be noted that many vertical agreements have a similar impact on competition as vertical integration. For example, exclusive purchasing agreements may have the same pro-competitive effect as vertical integration between manufacturing and retailing stages of production. In general, where a vertical restraint can be shown to achieve the same pro-competitive outcomes as vertical integration, then the vertical restraint can be said to be pro-competitive. For instance, exclusive purchasing agreements can stimulate retailer-specific investment by the manufacturer which the manufacturer would not undertake in the absence of a guarantee of demand from the retailer. Such a benchmark is a sensible one. It would clearly be economic and legal nonsense if efficiency-enhancing vertical integration were to be permitted whereas the equivalent vertical restraint between independent undertakings was not. So a useful thought experiment when considering whether a particular vertical restraint is anti-competitive is to consider whether it achieves the same result as vertical integration and, if so, whether in this particular case vertical integration would be considered anti-competitive or pro-competitive.

## Vertical restraints are fundamentally pro-competitive

**5–037** The difficulty with vertical restraints for the competition law practitioner arises from the need to determine whether a particular vertical restraint is anti-competitive or pro-competitive. There are numerous Commission decisions that have stated that, unless the object of an agreement has a clear anti-competitive intent, the applicability of Article 81(1) to a vertical restraint cannot be determined simply by taking into account its formal terms.[74]

---

[72] Transaction cost efficiencies arise when it is cheaper to carry out a transaction within a single firm rather than between firms. For instance, when a transaction takes place between firms, the firm selling the product may need to expend resources checking that the buying party is creditworthy. This is not true when the transaction takes place within the same firm. See Williamson (1979) and Klein, Crawford and Alchian (1978) for a discussion of these issues.

[73] This problem arises from the inability of firms to contract for every eventuality. Contracts are therefore said to be "incomplete" in the sense of not being able to specify what happens in every eventuality. This can lead to problems if some eventualities dramatically alter the relevant bargaining power of the two parties and allow one party to exploit the other (e.g. by charging excessive prices for products that have become essential to the other party). See Holmstrom and Hart (1989) or Hart (1988) for good introductory surveys and Tirole (1999) for a discussion of the state of the research agenda.

[74] See, e.g. *Société Technique Minière v Maschinenbau Ulm GmbH* (56/65) [1966] E.C.R. 235; [1966] C.M.L.R. 357 and *Brasserie de Haecht SA v Wilkin* (23/67) [1967] E.C.R. 407; [1968] C.M.L.R. 26.

Agreements between firms that are competitors (e.g. horizontal agreements such as collusion and mergers) can often be anti-competitive. This is particularly likely to be true when the two firms both have market power. However, this is not necessarily true when the agreement is a vertical agreement between an upstream and a downstream firm. Agreements of this type can have economic efficiency rationales even when both firms have market power. This is because in a vertical relationship the two firms produce complementary products, whereas in a horizontal relationship the two firms produce substitute products.[75] The demand for a product declines as the price of substitute products falls, but rises as the price of complementary products falls and this gives rise to a difference in the relationship between firms. Where products are substitutes, each firm would prefer the other firm to increase the price of its product and thereby soften price competition. But where products are complementary, each firm would prefer the other to lower the price of its product. Referring back to Figure 5.2, for any given price set by firm A, he will sell more product the higher firm B's price is. Thus, firm A wants firm B to raise his price. But for any given price, firm A wants the downstream firm, firm C, to price low as this maximises demand for the product. So the upstream firm wants the downstream firm to price low. Equally, the downstream firm wishes the upstream firm to price low as the price set by the upstream firm is the downstream firm's input price.

It is therefore often the case that in a vertical relationship, both firms want the other firm to reduce prices. This has the effect of lowering prices to consumers and hence of raising consumer welfare. In this situation, a vertical restraint imposed by one firm on the other may well be pro-competitive as it is likely to be designed to elicit a lower price from the other firm in the vertical relationship, which is precisely what consumers want. This difference in the incentives of firms engaged in a vertical relationship from those engaged in a horizontal relationship is acknowledged in the Commission's Guidelines on vertical restraints.[76] The Guidelines state that in:[77]

"[h]orizontal relationships the exercise of market power by one company (higher price of its product) may benefit its competitors. This may provide an incentive to competitors to induce each other to behave anti-competitively. In vertical relationships the product of the

---

[75] This assumes that the relevant horizontal agreement is between firms selling products in the same product market. If they are not, then the horizontal agreement is not, in general, troubling from an antitrust perspective.

[76] European Commission, "Commission Notice: Guidelines on Vertical Restraints" [2000] OJ C291/01.

[77] Guidelines on Vertical Restraints at para.100.

one is the input for the other.[78] This means that the exercise of market power by either the upstream or downstream company would normally hurt the demand for the product of the other. The companies involved in the agreement therefore usually have an incentive to prevent the exercise of market power by the other."

**5-038** The pro-competitive nature of vertical restraints can be illustrated with reference to the so-called double marginalisation problem. Suppose that both firms in a vertical relationship have market power in the academic sense (i.e. they can price above marginal cost).[79] The upstream firm will set his wholesale price above the marginal cost of production and the downstream firm will set price above his input price (i.e. the wholesale price). The result is that the retail price is marked up over the marginal cost of production twice, leading to a higher price, and lower output, for the upstream firm's product.[80] Given the wholesale price that he sets, the upstream firm would prefer the downstream firm not to add another mark up as this lowers the demand for the product and hence the upstream firm's profits. In this situation a vertical restraint imposed by the upstream firm on the downstream firm that prevented the downstream firm marking up over marginal cost could increase not only the upstream firm's profits, but also consumer welfare.[81] There are a number of vertical restraints that could be used in this case. For instance, the upstream firm could impose the restraint that the downstream firm was not able to price above his marginal cost (a maximum price cap). Or he could impose the restraint that the downstream firm had to buy a certain given number of units from the upstream firm where the number of units was set equal to the level that would push the retail price down to the downstream firm's marginal cost.

There are two points that should be noted here. First, although this is an example in which a vertical restraint is pro-competitive, it is not the case that the vertical restraint ensures that the retail price is at the competitive price. By assumption, the manufacturer has market power (in the academic sense: see fn.80) and so will set his selling price (the wholesale price) above

---

[78] The recently released draft update to the Guidelines (Draft Commission Notice: "Guidelines on Vertical Restraints" (July 2009)) at this point adds the phrase "in other words the activities of the parties to the agreement are complementary to each other".

[79] For the avoidance of doubt, we are not suggesting that market power in the sense relevant to competition law is about the ability to price above marginal cost. As we argued at length in Chapters 2 and 3, many firms can price above marginal cost without having market power in a sense that is relevant to competition law.

[80] This provides the answer to the question, "What is worse than a monopolist?" The answer is: "A chain of monopolists".

[81] It is assumed here that the manufacturer imposes the vertical restraint on the retailer. The general result (that a vertical restraint can increase consumer welfare) holds equivalently if instead it is assumed that the retailer imposes a vertical restraint on the manufacturer.

his marginal cost.[82] Secondly, the effect of the vertical restraints in this case is to remove the market power of the retailer. If the retail sector were perfectly competitive so that retailers did not have market power, the vertical restraint would not be needed. This implies that when assessing the competitive effect of a vertical restraint, it is important to understand the nature of competition at each vertical level.[83]

---

### BOX 5.2: DOUBLE MARGINALISATION

We can present the double marginalisation problem in a more formal setting. Assume we have a monopoly manufacturer supplying a monopoly retailer, so both have market power. Further assume that the retailer's only marginal cost is the wholesale price at which the manufacturer sells to him. We know from Chapter 2 that firms set their price so that their marginal cost is equal to their marginal revenue.[84] So the manufacturer knows that the retailer will price so that its marginal cost is equal to its marginal revenue. This means that the amount of product that the retailer demands from the manufacturer will be determined by where the retailer's marginal cost (i.e. the manufacturer's wholesale price) cuts the retailer's marginal revenue curve. So the manufacturer will treat the retailer's marginal revenue curve as his demand curve and so the manufacturer will set his marginal cost equal to his marginal revenue curve as defined by the retailer's marginal revenue curve (i.e. the manufacturer's demand curve). This is shown in Figure 5.4.

---

[82] Of course, if the retailer imposed the restraint on the manufacturer, it would be the retailer who priced above his marginal cost. The fundamental point is the same: the retail price would be above the competitive price level.

[83] Steiner (1996) is particularly scathing of the assumption of perfect competition at the retail level and of the length of time it has taken for the full implications of dropping this assumption to become apparent. He writes that "[t]he death of the unrealistic single-stage [of market power] paradigm has been effectively delayed because those who develop and apply the theory seldom have operated in the field and have not acquired the intuition, borne of experience, that sounds an alarm when the theory has run off the track." (p.409). He goes on to say that "[m]any economists freely admit that they prefer to work with models that assume either monopoly or pure competition because the math becomes so complex and messy with imperfect competition at both stages. Unfortunately, business people operating in an imperfectly competitive climate are not similarly relieved of their responsibility to figure out their firm's profit-maximising policies under these messy conditions" (p.409).

[84] As noted earlier, this is not true in the special case of cartels.

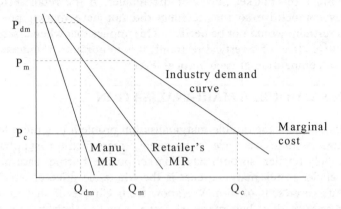

Figure 5.4 Double marginalisation

5–039   The price under perfect competition, where the industry demand curve cuts the marginal cost curve, is $P_c$ and the competitive output is $Q_c$. As a result of double marginalisation, the manufacturer charges the retailer $P_m$ and the retailer charges a price of $P_{dm}$, with output at $Q_{dm}$. However, if the manufacturer could force the retailer to sell at the retailer's marginal cost, then the retailer would charge $P_m$ (the manufacturer's wholesale price) and output would be $Q_m$. That is, output under the vertical restraint would be larger, and price would be lower, than in the absence of the vertical restraint. Vertical restraints that could achieve this include the manufacturer imposing a maximum retail price at which the retailer is allowed to sell ($P_m$) or imposing a minimum amount of product that the retailer must sell and setting this at $Q_m$. Note that even with vertical restraints, the market power of the manufacturer means that the retail price is above the competitive level (i.e. at $P_m$ rather than $P_c$). Note also that although we have assumed monopoly at both vertical levels, this is not necessary: the double marginalisation problem arises whenever there is market power (in the academic sense: see fn.80) at both levels. It is therefore likely to be pervasive and so may be a benefit of many vertical restraints that are agreed. The importance and potential frequency of double marginalisation is recognised in the Commission's Non-Horizontal Merger Guidelines.[85]

There are two important implications of the discussion so far. The first is that vertical restraints can be pro-competitive. The second is that since the vertical aspect of the relationship tends to align the incentives of firms with those of society, this suggests that any potential anti-competitive effects of vertical agreements arise from their effects at a horizontal level. It turns

---

[85]  For a detailed discussion of these, see Chapter 8.

out, and is now generally accepted, that this is indeed the case. Whether a given vertical restraint turns out to be anti-competitive or not turns largely on the question of whether the vertical restraint reduces competition at the horizontal level. Vertical restraints can be used to reduce both inter-brand competition (competition between different brands) and intra-brand competition (competition between the same brand sold in different outlets). When vertical restraints reduce the level of inter-brand or intra-brand competition significantly, they may be anti-competitive. A loss of inter-brand competition is usually more concerning than a loss of intra-brand competition. As the Commission noted in its Green Paper on vertical restraints as far back as 1997[86]:

"The heated debate among economists concerning vertical restraints has calmed somewhat and a consensus is emerging. Vertical restraints are no longer regarded as *per se* suspicious or *per se* pro-competitive. Economists are less willing to make sweeping statements. Rather, they rely more on the analysis of the facts of the case in question. However, one element stands out: the importance of market structure in determining the impact of vertical restraints. The fiercer is inter-brand competition, the more likely are the pro-competitive and efficiency effects to outweigh any anti-competitive effects of vertical restraints. Anti-competitive effects are only likely where inter-brand competition is weak and there are barriers to entry at either producer or distributor level."

This view is also reflected in the approach set out in the Guidelines[87]:

"In the assessment of individual cases, the Commission will adopt an economic approach in the application of Article 81 to vertical restraints. This will limit the scope of application of Article 81 to undertakings holding a certain degree of market power where inter-brand competition may be insufficient. In those cases, the protection of inter-brand and intra-brand competition is important to ensure efficiencies and benefits for consumers."

The draft of the updated Guidelines makes the same point when it is stated that:

"[I]f inter-brand competition is fierce, it is unlikely that a reduction in intra-brand competition will have a negative effect for consumers."[88]

---

[86] European Commission, "Green Paper on Vertical Restraints in EC Competition Policy" (1997), p.iii.
[87] Guidelines, para.102.
[88] Draft Commission Notice: "Guidelines on Vertical Restraints" (July 2009), para.98.

and

> "the loss of intra-brand competition can only be problematic if inter-brand competition is limited"[89]

**5–040**     However, even when a particular vertical restraint can be shown to affect competition negatively by harming inter-brand competition, it is not necessarily the case that it should be prohibited since vertical restraints can have efficiency benefits that might outweigh the anti-competitive effects. As already discussed, vertical restraints might remove the problem of each firm in the vertical relationship pricing higher than is optimal for the other firm in the relationship (i.e. the double marginalisation problem). There are a number of other economic inefficiencies that may arise in a vertical relationship that vertical restraints can be used to alleviate or solve.

In many instances, the imposition by a manufacturer of a vertical restraint on downstream customers is motivated by the need to align the interests of that downstream customer to that of the manufacturer himself. There are a variety of circumstances in which the behaviour of the retailer, whilst optimal from the retailer's perspective, is disadvantageous to the manufacturer. This can result in a situation which is sub-optimal not only for the manufacturer, but also for society in general. Many of these instances are the result of the retailer not being able to appropriate all of the benefits of investment that he undertakes in his store. This leads the retailer to under-invest relative to the level that he would invest if he could appropriate all of the benefits of the investment. This under-investment might be harmful to the manufacturer, and to society, particularly if it leads to a lower demand for the products.

A classic example of this type of inefficiency arises when consumers value pre-sales service in a shop. Pre-sales service can increase the demand for some products, particularly if they are rather complex goods whose quality is not immediately apparent (e.g. expensive consumer electronics). Manufacturers want retailers to offer pre-sales service, such as knowledgeable sales staff, as it increases the demand for their products. However, if most retailers offer pre-sales service, it is profitable for some retailers to offer no pre-sales service and to free-ride on the service offered by other retailers. Consumers can get pre-sales service at one retailer and then buy the product at another retailer that is able to offer a lower price because it does not offer any pre-sales service and so does not incur the cost of offering pre-sales service. The problem for the manufacturer is that this type of behaviour reduces the incentive of any retailers to offer pre-sales service. The result is that too little pre-sales service, from the manufacturer's and society's perspective, is offered. In this case a vertical restraint may be able to remove this problem. If the manufacturer only supplies retailers who

---

[89] Guidelines on Vertical Restraints, para.149.

offer pre-sales service, the problem disappears. The manufacturer can solve the problem by selectively distributing his product only through outlets that offer pre-sales service.[90]

A similar problem can arise in retailer advertising. If advertising by a **5–041** retailer of a particular brand of, say, DVD player raises the demand for that brand from all retailers in the area, each retailer is likely to try and free-ride on the advertising of other retailers. But if each retailer attempts to do this, little or no promotional activity will be undertaken. Certainly, there will be less promotional activity than if there was no incentive to free-ride. The result is that the particular brand of DVD player will be under-promoted and sales will be lower than in the presence of advertising. The manufacturer could solve this problem by making advertising a condition of the selective distribution agreement. A vertical restraint of this type can therefore facilitate the entry of a new product that would otherwise struggle to compete due to a lack of advertising and hence a lack of consumer awareness of the new product.[91]

Note that selective distribution might be anti-competitive. If a manufacturer uses selective distribution to reduce significantly the number of outlets that sell his products, this may reduce intra-brand competition significantly. If there is also relatively weak inter-brand competition, this may allow prices to rise above the competitive level. Selective distribution is likely to enhance economic efficiency when the relevant products genuinely require pre-sales service or there is a need to protect the brand from inappropriate distribution and when either intra-brand competition is not significantly reduced or inter-brand competition remains strong.

Economic inefficiencies can also arise when the manufacturer cannot appropriate all of the benefit of an investment that he makes. Suppose a manufacturer invests in training the retail staff that sell his product. It may be that this training allows these staff not just to sell the manufacturer's product better, but may also allow them to sell the products of other manufacturers better. Since the manufacturer will not take account of this in his calculations, or may even factor it in as a negative effect of the

---

[90] Although this may lead to another inefficiency. There may be consumers who do not want pre-sales service (e.g. because they are already well-informed about the product) but who have to pay more for the product as a result of the manufacturer insisting that all his retailers offer pre-sales service. Selective distribution in this case is imposed by the manufacturer in order to avoid the free-riding problem and hence raise sales. It is therefore aimed at encouraging marginal consumers to buy the product. It may hurt some consumers who would buy the product even in the absence of selective distribution (inframarginal consumers).

[91] An alternative vertical restraint in this case might be exclusive territories. If the exclusive territories are large enough, they can reduce the extent to which retailers can free-ride on the pre-sales service or advertising of other retailers. However, the Commission has traditionally taken a very dim view of territorial restrictions. This is because they are not only potentially anti-competitive (i.e. they reduce intra-brand competition) but they are also anathema to the Commission's single market programme. See, e.g. *Newitt/Dunlop Slazenger* (IV/32.290) [1993] 5 C.M.L.R. 352; [1992] OJ L131/32 and *GlaxoSmithKline v Commission* [2006] E.C.R. II 2969; [2006] 5 C.M.L.R. 29.

training, he will tend to under-invest in training. This inefficiency can be cured by the manufacturer selling his products in outlets that stock only his products (i.e. exclusive dealership). Again, note that exclusive dealership may be anti-competitive. It reduces inter-brand competition within each outlet. If inter-brand competition is already relatively weak, this may allow prices to rise.

**5–042** Vertical restraints may also be used to allow the manufacturer to capture economies of scale. A manufacturer may want to avoid supplying many outlets with a small amount of stock and would instead prefer to supply only a few outlets but with more stock each. A vertical restraint such as a quantity forcing requirement can solve this problem. Note that although this seems to be a legitimate use of a vertical restraint, it may be anti-competitive if the result is that so few retailers are supplied that intra-brand competition is significantly reduced in a market where inter-brand competition is weak.[92]

Vertical restraints can also be used to avoid opportunistic behaviour by one or other party to a vertical relationship. Where the vertical relationship requires relationship-specific investment, parties may be unwilling to make that investment unless they can be reassured that the other party will not try to expropriate the value of the investment ex post. An example of opportunistic behaviour might be the electricity generation plant built next to a steel plant that decides to raise prices to the steel plant because, once the steel plant's location decision has been made, the steel plant has no alternative suppliers. Knowing this danger, the steel company will not build its plant unless it is sure that it will not suffer from opportunistic behaviour. A long-term supply agreement could be used to avoid this problem.

## Potential anti-competitive effects of vertical restraints

**5–043** The discussion so far has focused on examples of vertical restraints being used to remove economic inefficiencies that may arise as a result of the vertical relationship, although it has been noted that even efficiency enhancing vertical restraints may also have anti-competitive effects. However, it is also the case that vertical restraints can be used for anti-competitive purposes. Vertical restraints can harm competition in three ways. First, they can be used to foreclose the market to competitors. Secondly, they can be used to soften price competition between competitors. Thirdly, they may be used to facilitate (usually tacit) collusion.

There are two main reasons for a firm wanting to foreclose a market through using vertical restraints. One reason is simply that a firm may wish to avoid any increase in inter-brand competition due to new entry. For example, an incumbent manufacturer might attempt to foreclose the

---

[92] In effect, quantity forcing in this situation may be akin to exclusive territories.

market to new manufacturers, particularly if they are potentially more efficient than the incumbent, by signing exclusive dealership agreements with all the retailers. If there are barriers to entry into retailing, then the manufacturer might be able to ensure that any new manufacturer would not be able to distribute its product.[93] Equally, a retailer might try to foreclose the market to new retail entry by signing exclusive distribution contracts with all the manufacturers.[94] The key point is that a manufacturer (or retailer) may be able to use a vertical restraint to prevent a rival from being able to trade with other parties, such as retailers or manufacturers, that the rival needs to trade with if it is to enter successfully. The result is that vertical restraints can on occasion be used to deter entry.

The second reason for using vertical restraints to foreclose the market is that an upstream monopolist may wish to reduce intra-brand competition downstream, even when the downstream market is competitive.[95] The standard Chicago argument is that the upstream monopolist can set the wholesale price so as to capture the entire monopoly profit. The monopolist offers this wholesale price to all retailers and thus mimics the vertically integrated solution. However, contrary to the standard Chicago argument, the monopolist may not be able to take the entire monopoly profit. The Chicago argument does not work if there is scope for the monopolist to offer different prices to different retailers at different times (i.e. if contracts are secret and are not signed simultaneously). Once the monopolist has offered one price to one retailer, the monopolist's profit-maximising behaviour is to offer a lower price to the next retailer.[96] However, the first retailer knows this and so would not accept the earlier higher price. Unless the monopolist can commit to a common price for all retailers, the monopoly price will not be credible. This implies that the monopolist will be unable to extract the monopoly profit that is in theory available.[97] A solution to this is for the monopolist effectively to "tie his

---

[93] A slightly attenuated form of this foreclosure would be for the manufacturer to sign up the "best" retailers (e.g. those retailers whose premises are in the best locations). This would not foreclose the market entirely to new entry, but it would make entry harder. In effect, it would raise the cost of entry because the entrant would have to invest more in order to counteract the disadvantage of having weaker retailers (e.g. more brand advertising, refurbish retailers and so on).

[94] Or, at least, with all the best ones.

[95] Hart and Tirole (1990) consider this issue in the setting of Cournot competition, whilst O'Brien and Shaffer (1992) assume price competition in a differentiated products setting.

[96] The logic underlying this is the same as in the case of the durable good monopolist discussed in Chapter 2.

[97] The logic of this argument implies that competition law interventions that impose non-discrimination terms on monopolists may raise consumer prices. We discuss the welfare implications of price discrimination in more detail in Chapter 6.

hands" by signing an exclusive distribution agreement with just one retailer or by giving retailers exclusive territories.

---

**BOX 5.3: THE COMMITMENT PROBLEM**[98]

5–044

Suppose that the upstream monopolist faces just two retailers. Assume that the vertically integrated profit maximising output and price are $Q_M$ and $P_M$. Further, assume that the retailers' costs, apart from the wholesale price, are zero. The inverse demand curve is $P = P(Q)$. The monopolist's constant marginal cost is c. There are no fixed costs. Then the standard Chicago argument holds that the monopolist will offer the product to the retailers at $P_M$ and each retailer (assuming symmetry) will sell $Q_M/2$. Now assume that there is scope for secret contracts, so the retailers are not guaranteed the same price as each other and they do not know the price offered to the other retailer. Denote the two retailers as $R_i$ where i = 1 or 2. Suppose that $R_1$ expects that $R_2$ will purchase $q_2$ units from the manufacturer. $R_1$ will then be prepared to pay a price of $P(q + q_2)$ for any amount of product q. The monopolist's profit-maximisation problem with respect to $R_1$ is then to maximise $[P(q + q_2) - c]q$. The situation is symmetric with the other retailer, so we have the standard Cournot maximisation problem. This implies that the monopolist is unable to make more than the Cournot profits, which by definition are below the vertically integrated monopoly profits. The intuition here is that a retailer will only buy q units at price p subject to the requirement that this is profit maximising for the monopolist only if all other retailers get the same terms, since only then is it credible that the monopolist will not offer lower prices to other retailers. But this is the definition of the Nash equilibrium under Cournot competition (see Chapter 2 and particularly Figure 2.5).

---

The Commission has shown itself to be wary of vertical restraints that may lead to foreclosure. An example of Commission action in this regard was the decision regarding the Irish impulse ice-cream market.[99] The Commission found Unilever guilty of abusing its dominant position on the grounds that it had foreclosed the market to new entry by supplying freezers to retailers on the condition that they were used to stock only Unilever products. The Commission argued that many retailers either cannot or do not wish to install two or more freezers in their outlet. This implied that in many retail outlets, freezer exclusivity was akin to exclusive

---

[98] This treatment follows that of Rey and Tirole (1996).

[99] *Masterfoods Ltd v HB Ice Cream Ltd* [2001] All E.R. (EC) 130; [2001] 4 C.M.L.R. 449. The following discussion is not intended to condemn or condone the Commission's analysis in this decision.

dealing. That is, once Unilever had installed an exclusive freezer in the outlet, no other manufacturers could supply the outlet, so the outlet became a de facto exclusive dealership.

Some commentators have argued that vertical restraints should only be subject to competition law intervention where they can be shown to lead to foreclosure. For instance, London Economics[100] argued that:

"Overall, the contribution of the economic literature on vertical restraints has been to establish that there should be no competition policy intervention, except where they are used strategically by the incumbent to foreclose the market to a new entrant, essentially by reducing rival manufacturers' access to downstream distributors."

However, this is too strong a statement. Although the ability of firms to use  **5–045** vertical restraints to foreclose markets represents a major anti-competitive concern, vertical restraints can also be used as a way of softening price competition between manufacturers and/or facilitating collusion. It is frequently alleged by consumer bodies that this is the intended effect of selective distribution. The argument is that selective distribution can be used by the manufacturer to increase his prices by reducing intra-brand competition. Increased prices may then encourage rival manufacturers to increase their prices (i.e. a reduction in inter-brand competition). On this view, selective distribution by a group of rival manufacturers is akin to tacit collusion. Exclusive distribution may have a similar effect as it also reduces intra-brand competition. Exclusive dealership has a more direct effect on inter-brand competition by removing other brands from the outlet. Again, if all manufacturers used exclusive dealerships, this might be considered akin to collusion. Resale price maintenance (RPM) is another vertical restraint that can be akin to collusion if a number of major manufacturers use it. RPM directly reduces both intra-brand and inter-brand competition.

RPM does not fall within the scope of the Block Exemption Regulation. Traditionally the Commission has been very hostile towards RPM and it was very unlikely that an individual exemption under Article 81(3) would

[100] London Economics (1997).

be granted for it.[101] However, this is an area where policy may be changing, as we discuss in Box 5.4 below.[102]

---

**BOX 5.4: EMERGING POLICY TOWARDS RPM—A TRIUMPH FOR ECONOMICS**

Resale price maintenance provides a good example of the effect of economic analysis on antitrust rules. RPM has been designated by the European Commission as a "hardcore" vertical restraint, which means that it is effectively per se illegal. The United States has also had a per se rule against RPM for many years. However, the US position has softened after the recent *Leegin* case. Leegin is a manufacturer of leather goods and fashion accessories. It competes in a market with many other competitors and so inter-brand competition is strong. Since 1997 Leegin has had an explicit policy of refusing to supply retailers who discount its product below the price recommended by Leegin. One of its customers, Kay's Kloset, took Leegin to court after Leegin had stopped supplying Kay's Kloset because it was selling below the prices recommended by Leegin. A lower court found in favour of Kay's Kloset on the grounds that RPM was per se illegal. The case ended up at the Supreme Court, which overturned the per se ban on RPM and substituted a rule of reason approach instead.[103]

The Supreme Court accepted the argument that RPM could on occasions be pro-competitive. It noted that RPM could be justified on similar grounds to other vertical restraints: "absent vertical price restraints, the retail services that enhance inter-brand competition might be underprovided." This is not to say that RPM cannot also be anti-competitive. The Court was clear that RPM could be anti-

---

[101] There are occasions when RPM can be efficiency-enhancing, although they may be relatively rare. Publishers have traditionally argued that books are an example where RPM is beneficial to society. The argument appears to be that RPM allows publishers to cross-subsidise books that are "worthy", but would not be published if they had to make a profit on their own behalf. However, the Commission has not been impressed by this argument. The Commission ruled against the book-pricing cartels within Belgium and the Netherlands and within the United Kingdom and Ireland. After issuing a Statement of Objections, it accepted undertakings that ensure that the German book cartel (the "Sammelrevers") does not affect trade between Member States.

[102] An example of where it was argued that RPM was efficient is the UK OFT's decision against John Bruce (UK) Ltd (CA/12/2002 *Price Fixing Agreements involving John Bruce (UK) Ltd, Fleet Parts Ltd and Truck and Trailer Components*). The Director General of Fair Trading concluded that Bruce (UK) Ltd, Fleet Parts Ltd and Truck and Trailer Components (a subsidiary of the Unipart Group of Companies) infringed the Competition Act 1998 by entering into price-fixing agreements. All of the above-named undertakings were engaged in the supply of the MEI brand of automatic slack adjuster. However, it was argued that RPM was necessary in order to provide retailers with a sufficient margin for them to promote the John Bruce brand of product, which was a new entrant to the market.

[103] This position was supported by an amicus curiae brief submitted by 25 antitrust economists.

competitive, such as when it is used to facilitate a cartel. Importantly, the Court argued that the following three factors would be important in any inquiry into RPM.

1.  How many other firms were using the same practice?

2.  What was the driving force behind the restraint? The Court argued that RPM is more likely to be anti-competitive if it is driven by retailers rather than by manufacturers.

3.  Does the manufacturer or retailer have market power?

The economic logic behind these factors is clear. If only a few firms **5–046** were using RPM and they did not have market power, then the practice is unlikely to be anti-competitive. This is because it is unlikely to have a significant adverse effect on inter-brand competition. If RPM was driven by the retailers, then this is consistent with retailers wanting to soften downstream competition. However, manufacturers typically want to encourage efficient downstream distribution of their product as their incentives are aligned with that of consumers.

The *Leegin* decision has caused considerable debate, and it should be noted that the Supreme Court itself split 5/4 on the issue. It is noticeable that the Commission's draft new Guidelines on vertical restraints already indicate a softening of its stance against RPM. The Commission proposes to keep RPM as a "hardcore" restraint, but it now offers the possibility that it could nonetheless be exempted under Article 81(3). Thus the new draft Guidelines now state that[104]:

> "[T]his is a rebuttable presumption which leaves open the possibility for undertakings to plead an efficiency defence under Article 81(3) EC in an individual case. In case the undertakings substantiate that likely efficiencies result from including the hardcore restriction in the agreement and that in general all the conditions of Article 81(3) are fulfilled, this will require the Commission to effectively assess—and not just presume—the likely negative effects on competition before making the ultimate assessment of whether the conditions of Article 81(3) are fulfilled."

Furthermore, the draft Guidelines accept that "RPM may not only restrict competition but may also sometimes lead to efficiencies" and list a number of such examples, such as facilitating the entry of a new brand. As with the Supreme Court's decision in *Leegin*, there is no suggestion that RPM will generally be pro-competitive. It remains the

---

[104] Para.47 (and repeated at para.219).

> case that the Commission will treat RPM with great suspicion. However, it appears that the Commission is moving to a "rule of reason" approach based on economic analysis of the particular facts of the case, consistent with both the US *Leegin* decision and with its general attitude since 2000 towards vertical restraints.

## The Commission's policy on vertical restraints

**5–047** The Commission implemented the Block Exemption Regulation governing vertical agreements in June 2000 and at the same time issued a Notice providing Guidelines in which the principles for assessing vertical agreements under Article 81 are set out.[105] The Block Exemption Regulation creates a presumption of legality for those vertical agreements implemented by firms with a market share below 30 per cent.[106] Where a firm has a market share above 30 per cent the Commission will carry out an effects-based analysis to examine whether the relevant vertical restraint has anti-competitive effects in practice. The Commission reserves the right to remove the block exemption from vertical agreements where market shares are below 30 per cent on rare occasions and in particular to do so when 50 per cent of a market is covered by a network of similar restraints imposed by firms which individually have less than 30 per cent of the market. Finally, as noted above, some restraints, such as resale price maintenance, are termed as "hardcore" restraints and so fall outside the scope of the Block Exemption Regulation.

The Block Exemption Regulation addressed three major shortcomings associated with the previous policy approach towards vertical agreements. These were as follows.

1. The then current block exemption Regulations were seen as comprising rather strict form-based requirements and as a result were considered to be too legalistic and to work as a straightjacket.

2. There was a real risk that the then current block exemptions were exempting agreements that actually did distort competition.

---

[105] European Commission, "Commission Notice: Guidelines on Vertical Restraints" [2000] OJ C291/01. These guidelines divide vertical restraints up into four categories and discuss the potential efficiencies and anti-competitive aspects of each. As a reference source, the guidelines are very useful and are included as an Annex to this book. The new draft Guidelines were issued shortly before this book went to press, but they are only draft and are subject to revision after the deadline for comments of late September 2009.

[106] Usually the upstream firm, but the downstream firm where appropriate, such as with exclusive supply agreements.

3.  The block exemptions covered only vertical agreements con-
    cerning the resale of final goods, not intermediate goods or
    services.

In assessing vertical agreements that do not benefit from the exemption,
the Guidelines state that "the Commission will adopt an economic
approach that is based on the effects on the market"[107] and that:

> "[T]he Commission will adopt an economic approach in the appli-
> cation of Article 81 to vertical restraints. This will limit the scope of
> application of Article 81 to undertakings holding a degree of market
> power where inter-brand competition may be insufficient".[108]

This sentiment is echoed in the new draft Guidelines, which state that[109]:

> "For most vertical restraints, competition concerns can only arise if
> there is insufficient competition at one or more levels of trade, i.e. if
> there is some degree of market power at the level of the supplier or the
> buyer or at both levels."

The use of a 30 per cent market share threshold is consistent with the focus **5–048**
only on vertical restraints imposed by firms (or groups of firms) with some
degree of horizontal market power. The Commission has proposed
extending this market share threshold to both parties to the agreement, i.e.
both the upstream and downstream party. Previously the assumption was
that the market share threshold referred only to the firm imposing the
vertical restraint (usually the upstream firm). The Commission has specifically flagged this change as one that they want to receive comments on
as part of the consultation process over the new Block Exemption. Our
view is that the market share threshold should refer only to the party
imposing the vertical restraint and that it is generally very clear which party
this is.

The change in Commission policy towards a more economically focused
and coherent policy is to be applauded. It has been argued that the new
approach provides less legal certainty than the previous more form-based
approach. However, even if this were the case, companies are freed from
the straightjacket on commercial practices which the old interpretation of
Article 81 often implied. The new policy therefore represented in our view
an unambiguous improvement in the Commission's competition policy.
The Commission has recognised that vertical restrictions can only harm
competition in the presence of horizontal market power and the

---

[107]  Guidelines, para.7.
[108]  Guidelines, para.102.
[109]  Para.6 of the draft Guidelines.

Commission's more economically coherent policy makes it much more likely that it will focus on vertical restraints that raise market power concerns than under the old system. There is a widespread acceptance that the policy has been a success. This is reflected in the fact that the Commission's current consultation on the revision of the Block Exemption and the Guidelines, which is required to be completed by May 2010, envisages little change to the policy.

There are, however, a number of issues arising from the Commission's approach that should be highlighted. First, the Commission continues to make use of the concept of "hard-core" vertical restraints. These are vertical restraints that are considered always to fall outside the scope of the proposed block exemption and have been presumed to be illegal. We have discussed RPM at some length above, but there are also four other "hardcore restraints". These relate to:

- restrictions concerning the territory into which, or customers to whom, the buyer may sell;

- restrictions on active or passive selling to end-users by authorised retail distributors in a selective distribution system;

- restrictions on authorised distributors in a selective distribution system selling or purchasing from other members of the network; and

- restrictons on the sale of components as spare parts by the manufacturer of the component to end-users, independent repairers and service providers.

**5–049** What is interesting about these restrictions is that they relate to restrictions on intra-brand competition and they do not seem to be motivated by a concern about inter-brand competition. Instead, they are motivated by a concern that these restraints can lead to segmented markets and an opportunity for price discrimination. The Commission's concern is therefore less a competition concern than a market integration concern. The Guidelines are explicit that this is one of the aims of the Commission's policy. At para.7 the Guidelines state that:

> "Market integration is an additional goal of EC competition policy. Market integration enhances competition in the Community. Companies should not be allowed to recreate private barriers between Member States where State barriers have been successfully abolished."

The concept of hardcore vertical restrictions has no corollary in economics: the competitive effects of vertical restraints need to be assessed on the facts of the particular case. While the prohibition of some of the hardcore restraints may be justified by the market integration goal of EC competition law, it should be understood that a policy of blanket prohibition will also include some efficiency-enhancing agreements.

Secondly, the Guidelines divide vertical restraints into four groups on the basis of their possible negative effects. These are:

- the "single branding group", i.e. non-compete agreements, quantity forcing, tying and so on. The common element is that these restraints directly affect inter-brand competition;

- the "limited distribution group", i.e. selective distribution, exclusive distribution and so on. These restraints directly affect intra-brand competition, although they may also in some circumstances indirectly affect inter-brand competition;

- the "resale price maintenance" group, i.e. minimum prices, maximum prices, recommended resale prices and so on. The concern here is that these may in practice become de facto RPM; and

- the "market partitioning group", i.e. territorial resale restrictions, exclusive purchasing and so on. The concern here relates to the market integration objective.

The Guidelines hold that RPM and market partitioning are more likely to **5–050** be anti-competitive and to have fewer efficiency benefits than the other two groups. This is consistent with the Commission's approach to "hardcore" restrictions, but the inclusion of the market partitioning group as being of more concern than the "single branding" or "limited distribution" groups is not well grounded in competition economics. The pursuit of market integration will sometimes clash with the pursuit of economic efficiency and consumer welfare.

Thirdly, in the Guidelines the Commission for the most part takes the view that combinations of vertical restraints are worse than individual vertical restraints. Thus at para.119(6) it is stated that:

"In general, a combination of vertical restraints aggravates their negative effects. However, certain combinations of vertical restraints are better for competition than their use in isolation from each other."

It may well be true that in general combinations of vertical restraints are worse than single vertical restraints, but it is important to note that the Commission is right that this is not always the case. There is no per se rule to follow here and each combination of vertical restraints should be analysed in the particular market context in which it arises.

Fourthly, the 2000 Guidelines adopt a hostile stance towards vertical agreements employed by dominant firms.[110] According to the Guidelines, dominant firms are unable to obtain an exemption under Article 81(3)[111]:

> "Where an undertaking is dominant or becoming dominant as a consequence of the vertical agreement, a vertical restraint that has appreciable anti-competitive effects can in principle not be exempted."

The Guidelines' reasoning on this point appears to be motivated by a belief in a consistent trade-off between inter- and intra-brand competition, i.e. an absence of inter-brand competition can be remedied through intra-brand competition and vice versa. However, if there is an absence of inter-brand competition, that failure is not generally solved by increasing intra-brand competition—making downstream firms compete more fiercely does not generally resolve a lack of competition between upstream firms. Similarly, there are no general presumptions that restrictions on intra-brand competition will weaken inter-brand competition. As noted above, where there is vigorous inter-brand competition, there is no reason to be concerned about the lack of intra-brand competition that vertical restraints might imply. But it is incorrect to extend this to argue that where inter-brand competition is ineffective (i.e. where there is a dominant firm) vertical restraints cannot be permitted. This fails to acknowledge that dominant firms have many of the same pro-competitive rationales for implementing vertical restraints as non-dominant firms.

5–051    We note that the new draft Guidelines do not include the wording quoted above. This may be indicative that the Commission has softened its stance on dominant firms and vertical restraints. However, the Commission states at para.123 that:

> "A restrictive agreement which maintains, creates or strengthens a market position approaching that of a monopoly can normally not be justified on the grounds that it also creates efficiency gains".

Although much obviously hangs on the meaning of "normally" in this sentence, it seems that the Commission's policy stance has not softened much, if at all, and so the concern remains that vertical restraints used by a dominant firm may not be allowed even when their net effect is to increase consumer welfare.

One response to the Guidelines' hostility towards dominant firms is to argue that the restraints fall outside the scope of Article 81(1).[112] This is

---

[110] This discussion draws heavily on Bishop and Ridyard (2002) and Bishop (2003).
[111] Guidelines, para.135.
[112] See Peeperkorn (2002), who also discusses the reasoning behind the Commission's policy in this area.

precisely the approach adopted by the Dutch Competition authority, the NMa, in its decision assessing the competitive impact of exclusive supply agreements employed by Heineken, the large Dutch brewer, when supplying draught pilsner beer to those pubs and other licensed outlets ("on-premises") to which it provided financial and commercial support.[113]

In assessing whether Heineken's agreements fell outside the scope of **5–052** Article 81(1), the NMa stresses the importance of examining the overall impact of those agreements on competition and notes that such an assessment cannot be inferred from a firm's market position:

> "The position of Heineken on the relevant market is of importance because the stronger that position is, the larger is the risk of anti-competitive effects ... The question whether Heineken has a dominant position (and whether exclusivity in that case is objectively justifiable) is only relevant, if it can be established that the agreements can have appreciable anti-competitive effects."[114]

In other words, the fact that a firm might be held to be dominant does not necessarily imply that the vertical agreements which it employs give rise to appreciable anti-competitive effects. In this particular instance, the NMa found that whilst Heineken's market position justified individual scrutiny, its new supply agreements did not have anti-competitive effects and fell outside the scope of Article 81(1).[115]

## Empirical evidence on vertical restraints

There is a remarkable dearth of empirical analysis of the effects of vertical **5–053** restraints, particularly when compared to the large theoretical literature. Lafontaine and Slade (2008) have surveyed the existing empirical literature. This literature covers a number of industries, such as beer and spirits distribution, car distribution, gasoline, contact lenses, railroads, cable TV, film distribution and crude oil refining. Although the authors are quick to point out that this is a narrow group of industries and so may not be representative of the economy as a whole, they also argue that this literature consistently points to two quite clear conclusions. First, vertical restraints entered into voluntarily by firms tend to be pro-competitive. This is consistent with the fundamental insight that products in a vertical chain are complements, not substitutes, and so we should expect vertical restraints to often have pro-competitive rationales. Secondly, when vertical restraints are imposed on manufacturers as a result of government action,

---

[113] NMa decision of May 28, 2002, *Heineken – Horecaovereenkomsten* (2036).
[114] See para.85 of the decision, unofficial translation from Dutch.
[115] This interpretation accords with the narrower, more economic interpretation of Article 81(1) discussed in the introduction to this section.

they are usually anti-competitive and tend to raise prices and lower service levels. Lafontaine and Slade argue that:

> "It appears that when dealers or consumer groups convince the government to 'redress' the unfair treatment that they allege to be suffering, the consequences are higher prices, higher costs, shorter hours of operation and lower consumption as well as lower upstream profits."[116]

## Conclusions

**5–054** Two key conclusions are apparent from the above discussion of vertical restraints. The first is that whether a given vertical restraint is anti-competitive in a given situation depends, in particular, on the degree of inter-brand competition. Where inter-brand competition is vigorous, it is unlikely that a vertical restraint will have a significant anti-competitive effect even if it reduces or removes intra-brand competition. Where both inter-brand and intra-brand competition are vigorous, there is even less danger of a vertical restraint having an anti-competitive effect. However, where inter-brand competition is weak, vertical restraints can potentially lead to foreclosure or to a softening of price competition.

Table 5.2 provides a non-exhaustive list of vertical restraints and indicates which directly affect which type of competition. This table looks at the direct effects of each vertical restraint. Thus, selective distribution directly reduces intra-brand competition, but not inter-brand competition. This is not to deny that selective distribution may be used to lower inter-brand competition if it is used as an instrument of tacit collusion by a number of manufacturers acting in concert.

**Table 5.2 Effect of selected vertical restraints on competition at the retail level**

|  | Reduces intra-brand competition | Reduces inter-brand competition |
|---|---|---|
| Selective distribution |  | X |
| Exclusive dealership |  | X |
| Exclusive distribution | X |  |
| Price ceiling |  |  |
| Exclusive territories | X |  |
| Resale price maintenance (RPM) | X | X |
| Full-line forcing |  | X |
| Non-compete |  | X |

---

[116] Lafontaine and Slade (2008), p.408.

There are three points to make about this table. First, those restraints listed in Table 5.2 above that reduce inter-brand competition are generally treated more harshly by the Commission than those that reduce only intra-brand competition. Thus RPM is a "hardcore" restraint whilst exclusive dealership, full-line forcing and non-compete clauses all come under the Commission's "single branding" umbrella. Secondly, price ceilings do not directly reduce either intra-brand or inter-brand competition. Our discussion of the complementary nature of vertical relationships suggests that in general price ceilings should be a pro-competitive way of avoiding double marginalisation problems. Given this, it is surprising that they have sometimes been found to be anti-competitive. The argument has been that maximum resale prices can be used as "focal points" for manufacturers to collude around.[117] Although the argument is not entirely without merit from a theoretical point of view, our experience is that in practice it has usually been a weak argument.[118] Hence we think that Table 5.2 conveys the generally right message with respect to price ceilings. Thirdly, this table is only indicative. The exact effect of each vertical restraint is likely to be context specific.

The second key conclusion from this section is that the complementary   5–055
nature of vertical relationships means that vertical restraints will usually increase economic efficiency. Thus even vertical restraints that have some anti-competitive effect can still have a net social benefit if there are significant efficiencies associated with them. Of course, good policy is to ensure that where there are anti-competitive effects as well as efficiencies, the vertical restraints chosen should be those with the least anti-competitive effects amongst those vertical restraints that would safeguard the efficiencies.

# HORIZONTAL AGREEMENTS

Horizontal agreements include agreements such as joint ventures, licensing   5–056
agreements between firms and co-operative standards setting. Joint ventures can cover a number of different activities, such as R&D, production or marketing. Unlike vertical agreements, horizontal agreements are

---

[117] Para.226 of the Vertical Guidelines state that "[t]he possible competition risk of maximum and recommended prices is firstly that the maximum or recommended price will work as a focal point for the resellers and might be followed by most or all of them. A second competition risk is that maximum or recommended prices may facilitate collusion between suppliers."

[118] For instance, the European Commission dismissed the argument in *Repsol CPP* (see paras 18–20 of the Market Test Notice (OJ C258 (2004)). On the other hand, the UK Monopoly and Mergers Commission invoked it against recommended retail prices in consumer electronics (UK MMC inquiry into "Domestic electrical goods" (Cm. 3675)). The idea of tacit collusion being sustainable when there is as much product differentiation as there is in consumer electronics can best be described as a very "challenging" argument to make.

usually between competitors who supply substitute products. This means that there is a fundamentally different relationship between the contracting parties in horizontal agreements compared to vertical agreements and it raises a natural concern that horizontal agreements are anti-competitive. However, as is also the case with vertical agreements, horizontal agreements can often have pro-competitive efficiency effects and so it is necessary to weigh any potential anti-competitive concerns against the likelihood of significant efficiency benefits on a case-by-case basis. From an economic perspective, a horizontal agreement should qualify for an exemption under Article 81(3) if it can be shown to have an overall pro-competitive or at worse neutral impact on the effectiveness of competition.

Some horizontal agreements are examined under the Merger Regulation. These are known as *full function joint ventures* and are defined as joint ventures that perform on a lasting basis all the functions of an autonomous economic entity.[119] Joint ventures of this type are discussed in Chapter 7 below. But even where horizontal agreements are assessed exclusively under Article 81, the economic assessment of whether they qualify for an exemption under Article 81(3) is in a certain sense often akin to that undertaken under the Merger Regulation. The Commission is often required to assess the likely impact on competition of a new joint venture and so the analysis is forward-looking.[120] This can be contrasted with the economic assessment in some Article 81 cases, such as cartel cases, where the issue relates to whether an agreement has already had an adverse impact on effective competition.

The typical competition concern with a horizontal agreement is that it may allow the parties to raise their prices. This can happen either because the horizontal agreement allows firms to fix prices (i.e. collude) or because it leads to a loss of rivalry between firms (actual or potential) that leads to a softening of price competition. We consider these two issues in turn.

**5–057**     There are a number of ways in which horizontal agreements can make it easier for firms to collude. A marketing joint venture may involve firms directly fixing prices as part of the agreement. A production joint venture may become a vehicle for information flows between the parties and this may make collusion easier. For instance, it would be easier to sustain collusion if a production joint venture meant that each party knew accurately the output of the other firm, since then it would be simple to detect if a firm was cheating by pricing below the cartel price and selling more than its "quota" of output. Or it may be that because the joint venture requires regular contact between the parties in the joint venture, the parties can meet together to set prices without the competition authorities being able

[119] Article 3(4) of the ECMR states that "[t]he creation of a joint venture performing on a lasting basis all the functions of an autonomous economic entity shall constitute a concentration within the meaning of Article 3(1)(b)."

[120] This is also true, of course, of the analysis of cases involving the possible imposition of a new vertical restraint.

to detect collusion. Production joint ventures may make collusion easier if they increase the similarity of the cost structures of the firms. As we noted in para.5–014 above, it can be hard to reach agreement on a cartel equilibrium when the firms involved have significantly different cost structures. An R&D joint venture may lead to a reduction in product heterogeneity, and this again may make it easier to agree on a cartel equilibrium. In general, horizontal agreements that affect the vertical chain at a relatively early stage (e.g. R&D or production joint ventures) are less likely to facilitate collusion than agreements that are at a late stage (such as marketing joint ventures).

Horizontal agreements can reduce rivalry between actual or potential competitors. Suppose that firms A and B are currently competing against each other and sell product X and Y respectively. This means that each will take into account the price of the other firm when setting its price. Now suppose the two firms delegate their pricing decision to a joint venture which will set the prices for the products of both firms. This joint venture will not face as much competition from other firms as the two firms did as individuals as the rivalry in prices between products X and Y has been removed. Whereas previously the price of product X (Y) was partially constrained by the concern that sales would be lost to product Y (X), this is no longer the case.[121] This may allow prices to rise, depending on the competitive constraints imposed by other firms. This issue is clearly more likely to arise as a result of a marketing or distribution joint venture than as a result of a production or R&D joint venture. For instance, in *Lufthansa/ SAS*,[122] the Commission found that the joint venture would remove competition between two actual competitors on routes between Germany and Scandinavia. To ensure that potential competition remained a possibility, the Commission imposed conditions to safeguard market access to new entrants on these routes.[123] Similar concerns arose in *Austrian Airlines/ Lufthansa*[124] with respect to routes between Austria and Germany. The joint venture parties were present on 32 out of the 33 routes between Austria and Germany and were the only airlines present on 27 of them. In response to this clear reduction in competition, the Commission imposed a number of remedies designed to facilitate new entry.[125] These remedies included undertakings to divest slots to a new entrant; a commitment not

---

[121] Note that this form of analysis is similar to that for unilateral effects in a horizontal merger. For more details, see Chapter 7.
[122] IV/35.545 [1995] OJ C141/9.
[123] These conditions were potential take-off and landing slot divestments to new entrants.
[124] COMP/37.730—*Austrian Airlines/Lufthansa* (2002).
[125] Similar remedies were imposed in *Air France/Alitalia* (COMP/38.284/D2, 2002).

to increase the frequency of flights for two years after new entry on a route; to offer interlining to a new entrant; and to make capacity available on the joint venture's flights to the new entrant (thus increasing the frequencies available to a new entrant's passengers).[126]

The loss of rivalry caused by a horizontal agreement may not lead to immediate consumer harm but instead may lead to a loss of potential future competition.[127] This is a potential danger with R&D joint ventures.[128] An R&D joint venture between firms A and B may mean that the parties jointly produce one product rather than separately producing two products. By potentially reducing the number of firms in the market, this may reduce the level of effective competition. In *Pasteur Mérieux/Merck*[129] the Commission was concerned, inter alia, that joint R&D would lead to a loss of future competition in a variety of paediatric vaccines.[130] However, the Commission is generally well-disposed towards R&D joint ventures, as is testified by the dearth of enforcement decisions in this area.

**5–058** This raises the key question of whether a horizontal agreement removes competition that *would otherwise have taken place*. Horizontal agreements can be pro-competitive by creating competition that would not otherwise take place. This is recognised in the Commission's Guidelines on Article 81(3).[131] Under the heading "The basic principles for assessing agreements under Article 81(1)" in its "Guidelines on the application of Article 81(3) of the Treaty"[132], the Commission states:

> "The assessment of whether an agreement is restrictive of competition must be made within the actual context in which competition would occur in the absence of the agreement with its alleged restrictions". (para.17)

At para.18 the Commission states that a "useful framework for making this assessment" is to ask the following question:

---

[126] The Commission also imposed a novel pricing remedy. If the joint venture reduced its prices on a route where it faced competition, then it also had to impose the same price cut on three routes (of its choice) where it did not face competition. The aim of this remedy was to protect a new entrant by increasing the cost to the joint venture of engaging in predatory behaviour.

[127] See para.98 of the Commission's Horizontal Guidelines (2001).

[128] See paras 61–67 of the Commission's Horizontal Guidelines (2001).

[129] IV/M159; [1993] 5 C.M.L.R. 118; [1993] OJ C188/10.

[130] Specifically, the Commission was concerned by the potential loss of competition in multivalent measles, mumps, rubella, varicella and monovalent Hepatitis A and varicella vaccines.

[131] Commission Notice: Guidelines on the Application of Article 81(3) of the Treaty (2004/C 101/08). These are appended as Appendix F to this book.

[132] Commission Notice: Guidelines on the application of Article 81(3) of the Treaty (2004/C 101/08). These are appended as Appendix F to this book.

"Does the agreement restrict actual or potential competition that would have existed without the agreement? If so, the agreement may be caught by Article 81(1)."

In *Ford/Volkswagen*,[133] the Commission held that the co-operation between Ford and Volkswagen would not lead to an elimination of competition in the car segment for multi-purpose vehicles. Neither Ford nor Volkswagen were currently in the market and it was thought unlikely that either party would enter by themselves since the minimum viable scale of entry was larger than the likely sales of either party acting on their own. As a result, the Commission argued that the joint venture would actually be pro-competitive by enhancing choice, creating a more balanced market structure and increasing price and quality competition. In *Exxon/Shell* the Commission allowed a joint venture to build a LLDPE/HDPE plant.[134] The Commission argued that neither Exxon nor Shell would have built the plant unilaterally because of the scale of the investment needed.

## Licensing[135]

The licensing of intellectual property rights is an important, beneficial **5–059** feature of the modern economy. However, there are two competition concerns that are frequently raised with respect to licensing. The first is that a firm might refuse to license its intellectual property. On the assumption that competition policy should in general respect property rights, a refusal to license should not generally be considered anti-competitive. There are occasions where this may not be true and these come under the heading of *essential facilities* cases. We deal with these issues in Chapter 6 and so do not address them further here. The second competition concern with licences that is often raised is that the particular terms of a licence are anti-competitive. This is an issue that we consider in more detail here.

When assessing whether the terms of a licence are anti-competitive, it is important to identify the relevant counterfactual. When assessing a particular agreement, the question that needs to be answered is whether the market outcome under the agreement is worse from a competition policy perspective than the market outcome under the likely alternative if the licence is proscribed. If absent the licensing agreement the likely alternative is that no licence would be granted, then it needs to be assessed whether

---

[133] IV/33.814; [1993] 5 C.M.L.R. 617; [1992] OJ L20/14.
[134] IV/33.640 *Exxon/Shell* (IV/33.640) (2004).
[135] This sub-section and the next draw heavily from Lind, Muysert and Walker (2002), "Innovation and Competition Policy", *Office of Fair Trading Economic Discussion Paper 3*. Another good source for a discussion of the issues in this section is "Antitrust enforcement and intellectual property rights: promoting innovation and competition" US DoJ and FTC (April 2007).

that alternative produces a better market outcome than would have occurred under the proposed licence agreement. This is consistent with the US guidelines on licensing intellectual property,[136] which argue that a licence may harm competition if it harms competition that *would have occurred in the absence of the licence*. Thus at para.3.1 those guidelines state that:

> "[A]ntitrust concerns may arise when a licensing arrangement harms competition among entities that would have been actual or likely competitors in a relevant market in the absence of the licence."

Two broad categories of restriction that are frequently included in an intellectual property licensing agreement can be distinguished.

1.  A restriction on the use to which the intellectual property can be put (e.g. a territorial restriction or field of use restriction).

2.  A restriction that in some way impedes the licensor's rivals, such as limiting the ability of the licensee to deal with the licensor's rivals.

The first type of restriction appears at first sight to be anti-competitive, but this is unlikely to be the case. If the alternative to the restriction is that the intellectual property will not be licensed, then licensing subject to such limitations on use are likely to represent a better, and therefore pro-competitive, outcome relative to no licensing. Suppose a licence restricts the licensee to using the intellectual property only in a limited geographical area, such as the United States. If the licence has not removed competition that would otherwise have occurred, the fact that the licence does not increase competition in, say, the EU is not a reason for concluding it is anti-competitive. An example may make this clearer. The "float glass" production process developed by Pilkington significantly lowered production costs and raised quality. Pilkington licensed the technology, but included in many of the licences restrictions on the geographic areas in which the technology could be used. This was not anti-competitive. Pilkington did not have the financial resources to use the technology on a worldwide scale, so its licences, even with territorial restrictions, increased the use of the new technology worldwide and did not harm any competition that would have taken place if Pilkington had chosen not to license the technology.

**5–060**   The second type of restriction however raises more potential concerns of anti-competitive outcomes. A licence that restricts the ability of the licensee to deal with rivals of the licensor may well restrict competition that

---

[136] Joint DoJ/FTC Antitrust Guidelines for the Licensing of Intellectual Property (1995).

would have taken place in the absence of the licence. For instance, licensing software developers to write applications for a particular operating system may be anti-competitive if the licence also requires those developers not to write applications for rival operating systems. Equally, a licence that restricts current rivals' ability to compete with the licensor may be anti-competitive. Returning to the Pilkington example, it would likely be anti-competitive if the licence stipulated that a current rival selling products in the EU could use the new technology only in the United States *and must simultaneously withdraw from the EU glass market.*

Cross-licensing and patent pools can also raise competition policy concerns. Cross-licences arise where one firm licenses its IP to another firm on the basis that the other firm reciprocates. Such licences are often royalty-free. Patent pools arise when a number of IP holders license their patents to a pool that then allows downstream licensees to license all the IP directly from the pool (rather than having to approach each IP holder separately). The pool will set a single price for the pooled IP.[137] Where there are multiple IP holders (i.e. a so-called "patent thicket"), cross-licences and patent pools can be pro-competitive in a number of ways. First, they can dramatically reduce the transactions costs for firms wishing to license the patents. Secondly, they can be used to solve a "blocking patents" problem. Blocking patents problems arise when the patents necessary to produce a product are held by a number of different firms, so no one firm can produce the product without access to the patents of the other firms. In this situation the holder of an essential patent, even if it is only one of many patents that are essential to the relevant technology, may be able to demand a disproportionately high royalty because of the ability to "block" licensors from gaining access to all the IP they need. Thirdly, patent pools can be used to lower royalty rates by avoiding "royalty stacking". The issue is equivalent to that of double-marginalisation. The price set by a monopolist (i.e. the pool) of complementary assets will be lower than the sum of the prices set by the individual owners of the complementary assets. In the extreme, royalty stacking might lead to a product not being produced due to royalty rates being too high.

However, it should be noted that cross-licensing and patent pools can on occasions be anti-competitive. First, they may facilitate collusion if they become a vehicle for the exchange of information between firms that provide complementary IP but who are horizontal competitors downstream. Secondly, where IP is licensed exclusively to a pool, this may stop rival technologies from being able to combine with some of the IP in the pool to produce a set of IP that competes with the pool. Thirdly, pools that include substitute IP, rather than just complementary IP, may be anti-competitive as they may reduce the number of rivals to the pool.

---

[137] On occasion it may be possible to get licences to only part of the pool's IP (so-called "partial licences") at a lower royalty rate, but this is rare.

**5–061**     A good example of an anti-competitive patent pool is given by the *Summit/VISX* case.[138] Summit Technology and VISX competed in the market for equipment and technology employed in photorefractive keratectomy (PRK), a form of eye surgery. Summit and VISX were the only two firms legally able to market laser equipment to be used for PRK in the United States. Summit and VISX had originally developed their own technology for performing the laser eye surgery, and had each sought patent protection. However, rather than exploiting their technology separately, they formed a patent pool in 1992. The pool established a $250 licensing fee to be paid to the pool each time a laser produced by either firm was used to perform PRK. The proceeds from these licence fees were then split between the two firms. The pool's terms also prevented either Summit or VISX from licensing its own technology to any other party without the approval of the other.

The FTC argued that the arrangements restrained competition in two ways. First, the firms no longer competed on price. The $250 licensing fee to be paid to the pool each time a laser produced by either firm was used to perform PRK had the effect of ensuring that neither firm had an incentive to charge doctors less than $250 per procedure. Secondly, the firms no longer had any incentive or ability to compete in the licensing of PRK technology, as neither firm could license its own technology without the approval of the other. It seems clear that this pool involved substitute IP and that it removed competition that would otherwise have taken place between Summit and VISX.

### Co-operative standard setting

**5–062** Another form of horizontal co-operation that can have competition policy implications is co-operative standard setting. This occurs when a group of firms agree to work to a common standard. This can be important when products have to be compatible with each other. For instance, video recorders need to be compatible with videos, CDs with CD players, DVDs with DVD players and so on. The competition policy question is whether setting a common standard benefits consumers, or whether it leads to a loss of potentially welfare-enhancing variety in standards.

A co-operative standard can have three effects.[139] It can lead to a different standard being adopted than would have been adopted under competition. This will involve consumer harm if the adopted standard is worse than the one that would have appeared under competition. It can avoid a "standards war" in which different standards compete with each other before one finally wins and becomes the standard (e.g. VHS against BetaMax). This avoids consumers who make the "wrong" choice being left

---

[138] FTC *Summit-VISX* complaint.
[139] Katz and Shapiro (1998).

with useless products (i.e. it avoids "stranded" investments) and reduces costs by avoiding duplicated R&D. But it also means that consumers miss out on the benefits of the period of intense standard competition. Finally, a co-operative standard allows many firms to compete in the market.

Whether co-operative standard setting is pro-competitive or anti-competitive in a particular case depends on the facts of the case. A number of considerations should be taken into account. First, do the firms engaged in collective standard setting jointly have market power, or are they likely to obtain it as a result of the co-operation? Secondly, is co-operation necessary to the product being launched (e.g. existence of blocking patents, too high a risk for a single firm to launch the product)? Thirdly, will the standard be open (potentially leading to fierce competition in the product market) or closed (limiting competition to just those setting the common standard)? Fourthly, what restrictions are imposed on the parties that affect their incentives and ability to compete with each other?

# THE ROLE OF MARKET DEFINITION IN ARTICLE 81

Traditionally, the definition of the relevant market has not played a sig- **5–063** nificant part in the competitive assessment in Article 81 decisions. While the Court of First Instance in its *Italian Flat Glass*[140] judgment argued that an analysis of the market, contrary to the Commission's view, would not have been superfluous, Article 81 decisions have in the past tended to pay lip service to the definition of the relevant market.

However, the definition of the relevant market potentially has a similarly important role to play in Article 81 decisions as it does in decisions taken under Article 82 or the Merger Regulation. Relevant market definition when conducted properly helps to focus attention on the nature of the competitive constraints which exist between products and helps to understand the various ways in which products do or might compete with one another.

In addition, the Commission's policy on vertical restraints and horizontal agreements under Article 81 both include market share thresholds. Thus the vertical restraints block exemption does not apply to firms with market shares above 30 per cent, whilst the block exemptions for R&D and specialisation contain market share thresholds of 20 per cent and 25 per cent respectively.[141] Also, the guidelines on vertical restraints and on horizontal co-operation both make reference to the Herfindahl-Hirschman index, which requires a market to be defined before it can be calculated. So

---

[140] *Societa Italiano Vetro SpA v Commission (Italian Flat Glass)* (T-68/89, T-77/89 and T-78/89) [1992] E.C.R. II-1403; [1992] 5 C.M.L.R. 302), CFI Judgment of March 10, 1992.
[141] Whish (2009) provides a complete list of the various market share thresholds used in EU and UK competition law.

despite some of the Commission's past practice, market definition does have an important role to play in Article 81 cases.

**5–064** Although the issue of market definition was discussed at length in Chapter 4, it is worth briefly reiterating some of that discussion. Where the focus of concern is a joint venture under Article 81, the standard hypothetical monopolist test approach to market definition is reasonable. The concern is forward-looking and in general the question is whether the post-joint venture competitive situation will be worse than the current one. In this case there is an obvious benchmark against which to apply the hypothetical monopolist test: the current situation.[142] The same is true of some vertical restraints cases. Where the vertical restraint has not yet been put in place, the current situation can act as a benchmark for the implementation of the hypothetical monopolist test.

However, many Article 81 investigations are concerned with the question of whether the current market situation is already anti-competitive. This is true of cartel cases and vertical restraint cases where the restraint is already in place. In these cases relevant market definition is harder because there is no benchmark and there is the danger of falling foul of the *Cellophane* fallacy. However, three points are salient here. First, in these cases it is still important to understand the nature of competitive constraints at the current price level, even though this will not directly define the relevant market.[143] Secondly, the Hypothetical Monopolist Test still provides a useful framework, which helps to focus attention on what matters: the competitive interactions between products and regions. Thirdly, there are empirical techniques available for market definition that are valid even in the presence of the *Cellophane* fallacy and so on occasions market definition can still be possible even when the current price cannot be used as a benchmark.[144]

## SUMMARY

**5–065** In the past, economic analysis has tended to play a less significant role in the competitive assessment of Article 81 cases than in Article 82 or merger cases. This stemmed primarily from the view that effective competition should be equated with freedom of action rather than focusing on market outcomes. However, this view has now changed and the explicit use of economics in this area of European competition law has increased

---

[142] Some joint ventures under Article 81 are concerned about losses of potential competition. In these cases there is a significant difference between the current situation and the situation in the absence of the joint venture (i.e. possible future entry) and so the current situation may not provide a reasonable benchmark.

[143] See Chapter 4 for a discussion of the importance of checking that products are substitutes at current price levels even when *Cellophane* fallacy issues arise.

[144] See Chapter 4 and Part III of this book for more details.

significantly in recent years. Economic analysis is now routinely applied in assessing whether the application of Article 81(3) is justified. This is leading to a tension between the competitive analysis under Article 81(1) and that under Article 81(3).

The past view that Article 81(1) applies to almost all agreements between undertakings has not only given Article 81 an extremely wide scope, but has also resulted in inconsistent analyses. Since the arguments used to justify exemptions under Article 81(3) are typically based on the pro-competitive effects of the agreement, the Commission in granting an exemption under Article 81(3) is effectively seeking to argue that the agreement both restricts and promotes competition. Such a position is neither justifiable nor sustainable. The Commission's policy initiatives in the area of vertical and horizontal agreements recognise the need for a more economically coherent approach. The Commission's guidelines now explicitly acknowledge the central role market power plays in the ability of an agreement to affect competition adversely and its use of market share thresholds represents a step towards a more consistent application of the law.

This chapter has considered the economic issues arising from three potential competition concerns that fall primarily under Article 81: cartels, vertical restraints and horizontal agreements. Cartels can allow firms to exercise market power jointly in cases where individually they cannot. This can be done either explicitly or implicitly. Although from a theoretical perspective, there are no significant differences between these two alternatives, a distinction can be drawn from a policy perspective. Since it is very difficult to discriminate between competitive interactions and implicit collusion, Article 81 should focus primarily on explicit co-ordination. The most effective weapon against tacit co-ordination is likely to be merger control. We have discussed the conditions under which collusion is possible and have shown how economics can be used to show whether there is likely to be scope for successful collusion in a given market. We also discussed how economics can be used to estimate the actual impact of a cartel on prices.

The economics of vertical restraints are complex. However, the com- **5–066** plementary nature of most vertical relationships means that vertical restraints often have pro-competitive efficiency-enhancing rationales. The key conclusion that stands out from a survey of the economic analysis of vertical restraints is that serious competition concerns arise when inter-brand competition is weak. When inter-brand competition is strong, then restraints that restrict intra-brand competition are unlikely to be anti-competitive. When inter-brand competition is weak, vertical restraints can potentially be used to foreclose markets to new entry or to soften price competition.

Horizontal agreements tend to be between competitors or potential competitors and as such can potentially be anti-competitive. They can facilitate collusion and they can reduce or eliminate competition between actual or potential competitors. Collusion is more likely to arise with marketing and distribution joint ventures than with production only or R&D joint ventures. However, the latter form of joint ventures has scope for eliminating potential competition and should be treated accordingly.

Many horizontal agreements take the form of licensing intellectual property. These licences often include restrictions on the licensee that can appear anti-competitive. The key question to ask when assessing such a licence is whether it will lead to the elimination of competition that would have taken place in the absence of the licence. If it does not, then the licence restrictions are unlikely to be anti-competitive.

In the past market definition has often played only a small part in Article 81 cases. The increasing use of market share thresholds for block exemptions, and the general increase in the level of economic analysis under Article 81, has changed this.

# 6. Article 82

## INTRODUCTION

Article 82 of the EC Treaty covers the behaviour of individual firms and **6–001** seeks to prevent firms engaging in anti-competitive behaviour.[1] Article 82 states that:

> "Any abuse by one or more undertakings of a dominant position within the common market or in a substantial part of it shall be prohibited as incompatible with the common market in so far as it may affect trade between Member States.

> Such abuse may, in particular, consist in:
> 
> (a) directly or indirectly imposing unfair purchase or selling prices or unfair trading conditions;
> (b) limiting production, markets or technical development to the prejudice of consumers;
> (c) applying dissimilar conditions to equivalent transactions with other trading parties, thereby placing them at a competitive disadvantage;
> (d) making the conclusion of contracts subject to acceptance by the other parties of supplementary obligations which, by their nature or according to commercial usage, have no connection with the subject of such contracts."

As set out in the Commission's Guidance on the Commission's Enforcement Priorities in Applying Article 82 EC Treaty to Abusive Exclusionary Conduct by Dominant Undertakings (hereafter, "Article 82 Guidance"),[2] there are essentially two steps to be followed in establishing whether a firm has infringed Article 82. The first step establishes the degree of market

---

[1] Article 82 may also cover situations in which firms are jointly dominant. This is discussed below.
[2] Guidance on the Commission's Enforcement Priorities in Applying Article 82 EC Treaty to Abusive Exclusionary Conduct by Dominant Undertakings (2008).

power that the firm under investigation holds in order to assess whether it enjoys a dominant position.[3] The case law relating to Article 82 holds that dominance cannot exist in the abstract.[4] Instead, a dominant position must exist in relation to a market and this necessarily implies that the relevant market or markets in which the firm competes need to be determined. Once the relevant market has been defined, the market shares of both the firm under investigation and its competitors can be calculated. Although both the Commission and the Community Courts have conceded that market shares by themselves do not automatically indicate dominance[5] and that there are other factors that are pertinent to a finding of dominance, the most important factor in determining dominance is usually a firm's market share.[6] The ECJ has held that a market share in excess of 50 per cent can be considered to be so large that except in exceptional circumstances such an undertaking could be presumed to be dominant.[7] The Commission has stated that it takes the view that a dominant position can generally be taken to exist when a firm has a market share greater than 40 or 45 per cent, although it cannot be ruled out for undertakings with a lower market share.[8,9] Indeed, in *Virgin/British Airways*, the Commission held that BA enjoyed a dominant position despite its having a market share below 40 per cent.[10]

A reasonable approach to adopt is that a low market share of a properly defined relevant market indicates a lack of dominance, whilst a high market share is a necessary, but not sufficient, condition for dominance. In assessing market shares, particular attention is also given to the market

[3] Article 82 Guidance, para.9.
[4] *Europemballage Corp and Continental Can Co Inc v Commission* (6/72) [1972] E.C.R. 215; [1973] C.M.L.R. 199.
[5] *Hoffmann-La Roche v Commission* (81/76) [1979] E.C.R. 461.
[6] See Whish (2009) and Faull and Nikpay (1999) for a discussion of the role of market shares in identifying dominance. See also Landes and Posner (1981) and Vickers (2006) for a discussion of the limitations of using market shares to infer a firm's market strength.
[7] *Engineering and Chemical Supplies (Epsom and Gloucester) Ltd v Akzo Chemie UK Ltd* (IV/30.698) [1982] 1 C.M.L.R. 273; [1981] OJ L374/1.
[8] European Commission, Tenth Report on Competition Policy (1981). The Commission stated at para.14 of the Article 82 Guidance that:

> "The Commission's experience suggests that dominance is not likely if the undertaking's market share is below 40% in the relevant market. However, there may be specific cases below this threshold where competitors are not in a position to constrain effectively the conduct of a dominant undertaking, for example where they face serious capacity limitations. Such cases may also deserve attention on the part of the Commission."

[9] Reference is sometimes made to the concept of "super-dominance", i.e. firms that possess market shares of around 90% (e.g. Whish (2009), Chapter 5). For example, the ECJ in *Tetra Pak* noted that Tetra Pak's market share in the market for aseptic cartons and carton-filling machines was in the region of 90% to 95%; in *Compagnie Maritime Belge* the conference's market share was 90% or more; in the *IMS* case the Commission noted that IMS was in a "quasi-monopoly situation"; and in *Microsoft*, the Commission stated that Microsoft with a market share above 90% had an "overwhelmingly dominant position".
[10] IV/D-2/34.780 *Virgin/British Airways* (1999).

position of competing firms; the smaller the market shares of competitors, the more likely it is that the Commission would hold that the largest firm is dominant.

In one respect, the definition of the relevant market can therefore be seen as providing a useful filter for determining whether there is a case to be heard under Article 82. By defining the relevant market in the appropriate manner,[11] market shares can be calculated which provide an initial proxy of the level of market power the undertaking possesses. Only cases where firms possess a high share of the market would require a further second stage of investigation. However, as we noted in Chapter 4, and discuss further below, defining the relevant market in Article 82 cases is often problematic and so recognition of these problems needs to be reflected in the due weight that can be properly placed on the definition of the relevant market and hence on the role of dominance in the overall competitive assessment.

Once a firm has been held to enjoy a dominant position, the second stage **6–002** of the investigation asks whether that firm's conduct represents an abuse of a dominant position. Article 82 does not prohibit firms from holding dominant positions, only from abusing such positions. Article 82 gives some examples of abusive behaviour but that list is by no means exhaustive, and a wide range of business practices have been investigated as potentially constituting an abuse. In general, a firm in a dominant position "has a special responsibility not to allow its conduct to impair undistorted competition on the common market".[12] This raises the question of how to determine whether a dominant firm's conduct represents normal competitive behavior or abusive behavior.

The enforcement of Article 82 has given rise to significant discussion and debate in recent years.[13] This debate led to the publication by the Commission of a Discussion Paper in 2005 and was followed by Article 82 Guidance in 2008.[14] Critics of the current approach to enforcing Article 82 note that dominance has tended to be used as more than a filter; once a firm has been held to enjoy a dominant position, any conduct of that firm

---

[11]  See Chapter 4 for a discussion of the appropriate basis for defining relevant markets.
[12]  See *Michelin v Commission* (322/81) [1983] E.C.R. 3461; [1981] 1 C.M.L.R. 282.
[13]  The following references provide only a small number of the extensive literature that contributed to this debate. Hovenkamp (2007) Werden (2006); Elhauge (2003); Melamed (2006); RBB Economics (2006); and Vickers (2005) as well as the DG Competition discussion paper on the application of Article 82 of the Treaty to exclusionary abuses.
[14]  The distinction as to the proper enforcement policy towards the unilateral conduct of large firms has also taken place in the US. The DoJ and FTC held joint hearings on Section 2 of the Sherman Act. The DoJ then issued a paper in September 2008 entitled "Competition and monopoly: single-firm conduct under Section 2 of the Sherman Act". The FTC promptly disavowed the report, saying it took a too non-interventionist stance. On May 11, 2009 Chrstine Varney, the Assistant Attorney General of the DoJ's Antitrust Division, withdrew the report.

that is held to harm competitors is necessarily inferred to harm competition.[15] The policy debate has therefore centred on whether the current prosecution of Article 82 (if not its strict application) is too formalistic and as a result has tended to be more effective in protecting competitors rather than protecting competition. Critics of the current approach argue that a more effects-based approach to the assessment of a dominant firm's conduct is required to give substance to the statement of the Commission that the aim of Article 82 (as indeed all European competition law) is the protection of competition and not the protection of competitors[16]; rather than assuming that the conduct of a dominant firm harms competition, the impact of that conduct on competition needs to be closely assessed before concluding that it should be proscribed. In short, a case-by-case assessment of the effects of a dominant firm's business conduct is warranted.

The remainder of this chapter is organised as follows. We first discuss the correspondence between the legal concepts of dominance and abuse with their corresponding economic concepts. Dominance can be equated with the concept of significant market power. Abusive conduct can be placed into two categories: excessive pricing and foreclosure. Excessive pricing relates to a direct increase in prices above competitive levels and foreclosure relates to conduct which results in an indirect increase in prices via the exclusion of equally efficient competitors.[17] We then consider the role of market definition and dominance in the assessment of Article 82 cases, noting that, in our view, dominance plays an inappropriately prominent role in the competitive assessment: under one interpretation, little or no competitive assessment of the likely effects of its conduct is required once a firm has been found to be dominant. We then discuss in turn the economic issues arising from the assessment of various types of conduct that might be held to be abusive. We briefly discuss the scope of Article 82 to cover the coordinated behavior of two or more firms.

## THE ECONOMIC MEANING OF DOMINANCE AND ABUSE

**6–003**  The practical implementation of Article 82 requires an assessment of the meaning of the terms "dominance" and "abuse". While the European Court of Justice has provided an interpretation of both terms (see discussion below) it has done so with reference to other concepts, such as "effective competition" and "normal competition", that are themselves only very loosely defined in law. The precise meaning of these legal terms is

---

[15]  See, for example Opinion of Advocate General Kokott, Case C-95/04 P *British Airways Plc v Commission* (2006), para.87.

[16]  See Kroes (2008).

[17]  See Rey and Tirole (2007) for an academic discussion of the economic theory of foreclosure.

unclear and consequently they do not provide a clear benchmark against which competing claims can be assessed. However, as we discuss, each of these terms has an obvious correspondence with basic economic concepts.

## Dominance

The definition of a "dominant position" was established by the European  **6–004** Court of Justice in *United Brands v Commission*. The Court stated the following:

> "The dominant position thus referred to [by Article 82] relates to a position of economic strength enjoyed by an undertaking which enables it to prevent effective competition being maintained on the relevant market by affording it the power to behave to an appreciable extent independently of its competitors, customers and ultimately of its consumers."[18]

The legal definition of "dominance" therefore relates to the ability of an undertaking to prevent effective competition being maintained by acting independently of competitors, customers and consumers. As the Article 82 Guidance notes, this notion of independence should be interpreted as relating to the degree of competitive constraint exerted on the firm under investigation.[19] A firm is therefore said to be dominant if these competitive constraints are not sufficiently effective and as a result the firm in question enjoys substantial market power.[20, 21] The legal concept of dominance can therefore be equated with the economic concept of significant market power.[22] The equating of dominance with significant market power is explicitly recognised in the Article 82 Guidance.[23]

---

[18] *United Brands Co and United Brands Continental BV v Commission* (27/76) [1978] E.C.R. 207; [1978] 1 C.M.L.R. 429.

[19] Article 82 Guidance, para.10.

[20] See Chapter 3 for a discussion of the concept of market power.

[21] Distinguishing in practice between firms that possess significant market power from those that merely possess market power is problematic and ultimately the distinction plays a limited role in the practical application of competition law. See Chapter 2 for a discussion of this issue. The legal approach makes the distinction between market power and significant market power with reference to market shares.

[22] To an economist, the idea of defining whether a firm could exercise market power and then proceeding to ask whether it is actually doing so appears slightly odd since the standard assumption of profit maximisation implies that a firm will always exercise market power if it possesses it. However, the discussion here attempts to put the economic reasoning into the existing legal context.

[23] Article 82 Guidance, para.10.

---

### BOX 6.1: MAKING ECONOMIC SENSE OF DOMINANCE

From an economic perspective, the concept of acting independently does not provide an adequate basis for discriminating between dominant firms and non-dominant firms. No firm can act to an appreciable extent independently of its consumers or customers.[24] This is because each firm is constrained by the demand curve facing them. Firms typically face downward sloping demand curves, indicating that a firm can only charge a higher price if it is willing to make fewer sales. It is not open to the firm to raise prices and sell the same quantity as before. This is true of a dominant firm just as much as it is true of a non-dominant firm.

Although it makes more sense to think of firms acting independently of their competitors than it does to think of them acting independently of their customers or consumers, there are still serious problems with using the concept of independence as a useful indicator of dominance. As is the case for acting independently of customers and consumers, every firm, except for true monopolists, is constrained in its commercial behaviour to some extent by competitors since the presence of these competitors affects a firm's residual demand curve.[25] Although this is by definition true for firms operating in a competitive market, it is also true for a dominant firm. All firms, including those that are held to be dominant, will increase prices above the competitive level to the point at which further price increases would be unprofitable. In this sense, competitors do constrain the behaviour of firms so that even a dominant firm does not act independently of its competitors.

**6–005**  However, there is an important sense in which a dominant firm can act to an appreciable extent independently of its competitors. Since a dominant firm is able to increase its price above the competitive level, one might hold that the dominant firm was able to act independently of competitors at the competitive price. As Whish notes, "the ability to restrict output and increase price derives from independence or, to put the matter another way, freedom from competitive constraint."[26] However, as we note at paras 6–014 et seq below, it is usually not possible to identify the competitive price and so the assessment of dominance is usually based on indirect measures of the ability to price above the competitive level.

---

Defining dominance with reference to market power in this way has two attractive features. First, and most importantly, it provides a definition that is consistent with the economic principles which underpin the rationale for

---

[24] Or at least not on a sustainable basis.
[25] See Chapter 3 for a fuller discussion.
[26] Whish (2001), p.153.

competition law. Secondly, it provides a testable benchmark against which competing claims can be made and against which to assess whether certain factors indicate the existence of a dominant position or not.

The Article 82 Guidance states that market shares provide a useful first indication of the market structure and the relative importance of the various undertakings active on the relevant market; the higher a firm's market share, the more likely it is that that firm enjoys a dominant position. However, the Article 82 Guidance correctly states that competition is a dynamic process and an assessment of the competitive constraints on a firm cannot be based solely on the existing market structure.[27] The potential for existing competitors to expand or for new firms to enter the market can represent effective competitive constraints on the conduct of even firms that possess large market shares.[28] Finally, account must also be given to the potential for customers to exercise countervailing buyer power.[29] However, in practice, as noted in the introductory remarks to this chapter, the assessment of dominance is often made primarily with reference to the firm's market share.

## Abuse

Article 82 does not prohibit a firm from holding a dominant position, but **6–006** only from abusing that position. The legal test for abuse was set out in *Hoffman-La Roche*[30] and restated in *Michelin*[31]:

> "[I]n prohibiting any abuse of a dominant position on the market in so far as it may affect trade between Member States, Article 8[2] covers practices which are likely to affect the structure of a market where, as a direct result of the presence of the undertaking in question, competition has been weakened and which, through recourse different from those governing normal competition in products or services based on trader's performance, have the effect of hindering the maintenance or development of the level of competition still existing on the market."[32]

As with dominance, the legal definition of "abuse" is hard to follow.[33] However, it appears to state that abusive behaviour is likely to affect the structure of the market and to weaken competition and involves the dominant firm behaving in a manner different from "normal competition".

[27] Article 82 Guidance, para.16.
[28] See Chapter 3 for a discussion of these sources of competitive constraint.
[29] See Chapters 3 and 7 for a discussion of buyer power.
[30] (81/76) [1979] E.C.R. 461; [1979] 3 C.M.L.R. 211.
[31] (322/81) [1983] E.C.R. 3461; [1981] 1 C.M.L.R. 282.
[32] op. cit. at para.12.
[33] Valetine Korah has stated that it "is difficult to understand" (Korah (2001)).

This definition suggests that business conduct can only be said to be abusive if it differs from normal competitive behaviour.

In discriminating between normal competitive and anti-competitive behaviour, it is necessary to establish an appropriate benchmark. When a dominant firm exercises market power, it harms consumers by charging prices above the competitive level and/or by reducing the quality of products or services supplied.[34] This implies that a definition of abuse ought to focus directly on consumer harm. "Abuse" can therefore be defined as a dominant firm adopting a particular mode of behaviour that significantly reduces consumer welfare relative to the alternative of the firm not adopting that mode of behaviour.[35] Where it cannot be shown that the behaviour of a dominant firm adversely affects consumers, either immediately or in the longer term, such behaviour should be considered as constituting normal competitive behaviour.[36] This definition of abuse is consistent not only with the economic goals of EC competition law but also with various policy statements made by the EC Commissioner for Competition and senior officials from DG COMP.[37]

Abusive conduct can be divided into two broad categories: exploitative abuses and exclusionary abuses. Exploitative abuses are generally synonymous with the charging of excessive prices. Such abuses represent a manifestation of significant market power that *directly* harms consumers. Exclusionary abuses, in contrast, harm consumers *indirectly* by excluding or foreclosing competitors and as a result increasing that firm's ability to increase prices to consumers.

**6–007**  For the reasons discussed in para.6–019, Article 82 is primarily concerned with exclusionary abuses. Indeed, the Article 82 Guidance only covers exclusionary abuses. The Article 82 Guidance states that the aim of the Commission's enforcement activity in relation to alleged exclusionary conduct is to ensure that dominant firms do not impair effective competition by foreclosing their rivals in an anti-competitive manner and thereby adversely affecting consumer welfare.

The Article 82 Guidance places exclusionary conduct into one of the following four categories.

---

[34] The latter consumer harm is equivalent in analytical terms to an increase in price. For this reason, when economists normally talk of harm deriving from price increases, this is to be interpreted widely to include harm resulting from a reduction in quality.

[35] Note that the behaviour can either harm consumers immediately by raising prices and/or lowering quality, or in the longer run by reducing the level of competition (e.g. excluding a rival) and hence leading to higher prices and/or lower quality.

[36] This approach to abuse is consistent with that adopted by the UK OFT. In its guidelines on the Competition Act, the OFT states that "[c]onduct may be abusive when, through the effects of conduct on the competitive process, it adversely affects consumers directly (through the prices charged, for instance) or indirectly (for example, conduct which raises or enhances entry barriers or increases competitors' costs)." (para.4.2 of OFT 402 (1999) *The Chapter II Prohibition*).

[37] See para.2–004 in Chapter 2 for a discussion of the focus in EU competition law on harm to consumers (rather than harm to competitors).

1. **Exclusive dealing**: the use of exclusive purchasing obligations or rebates to potentially hinder the ability of competitors to sell to customers.[38]

2. **Tying and bundling**: the practice of relating the selling terms of one product to another product, thereby potentially making it harder for competitors to compete.[39]

3. **Predation**: conduct that involves deliberately incurring losses in the short run to foreclosure competitors.[40]

4. **Refusals to supply and margin squeeze**: conduct that results in the "vertical foreclosure" of downstream rivals.[41]

We discuss the economic issues that each of these categories of abuse raises. As we discuss, while each of these forms of conduct can in some circumstances represent anti-competitive behavior, in others they can represent "normal" competitive behavior even when practised by a dominant firm. A common issue that therefore arises in the competitive assessment of each of these types of conduct is how does one discriminate between conduct that is pro-competitive and conduct that is anti-competitive?

The primary competition concern arising from exclusionary abusive conduct arises from the potential for the dominant firm to foreclose its competitors and in so doing lead to an increase in prices to end consumers.[42] Under this definition, the conduct of a dominant firm can only be said to be foreclosing competitors if it has adverse consequences for consumers. Hence, in principle it is insufficient to establish that the business conduct of the dominant firm results in sales being shifted away from competitors to the dominant firm. Such harm to competitors represents a necessary step for concluding that the conduct is abusive but is not sufficient. Furthermore, and in correspondence with the competitive assessment of non-horizontal mergers, it cannot be assumed that share-shifting conduct inevitably results in adverse consequences for consumers.[43]

Distinguishing conduct that represents legitimate competitive behavior **6–008** (and which harms competitors) from conduct that represents anti-competitive behavior (i.e. harms competitors and, as a result, leads to adverse outcomes for consumers) is not straightforward. This is particularly so

---

[38] Article 82 Guidance, paras 31 to 45.
[39] Article 82 Guidance, paras 46 to 61.
[40] Article 82 Guidance, paras 61 to 73.
[41] Article 82 Guidance, paras 73 to 89.
[42] Article 82 Guidance, para.19.
[43] However, as we discuss in the next section, the interpretation of dominance implies that there is a presumption in European competition law that the conduct of a dominant firm that harms competitors necessarily harms competition. Such a stance implies that there is limited scope for a genuine effects-based assessment under Article 82.

when considering price-based exclusionary conduct. Vigorous price competition is generally beneficial to consumers and therefore caution should be exercised before intervening to moderate price competition.[44] Furthermore, intervention is only appropriate if such pricing conduct is capable of foreclosing competitors that are as efficient as the dominant firm.[45] In order to determine whether competitors can be considered as efficient as the dominant firm, reference is made to cost benchmarks.[46] If the pricing conduct of the dominant firm implies that the dominant firm fails to cover the relevant cost benchmark then the Commission will conclude that the dominant firm is sacrificing profits in the short run in order to foreclosure an as efficient competitor.[47] Adverse consequences for consumers are presumed in such circumstances.

## THE APPROPRIATE ROLE OF DOMINANCE IN ARTICLE 82

**6–009** The establishment of dominance not only lies at the heart of the current competitive assessment of Article 82 but in practice represents practically the only important consideration in the whole investigation. There are two fundamental problems with the current approach.

First, establishing dominance is itself highly problematic. Dominance in most cases is primarily determined by a firm's market share, and consequently the definition of the relevant market plays a critical role in the competitive assessment under Article 82.[48] Even though the Hypothetical Monopolist Test provides the appropriate framework for defining relevant markets, this does not imply that defining relevant markets is always a straightforward task. Indeed, experience shows that this is rarely the case and that a detailed case-by-case assessment is usually required. The difficulties of defining the relevant market in Article 82 investigations are compounded by the existence of what is commonly termed the "*Cellophane* fallacy".[49] Importantly, the *Cellophane* fallacy implies that in many cases the available evidence will simply be unable to discriminate between two

---

[44] It is often forgotten that over-intervention carries costs for consumers that are as significant and more likely to be much more so than under-intervention. Errors of over-intervention leads to a chilling effect on competition and, in contrast to under-intervention, the market process has no scope for correcting those errors. As a US judge noted: "[j]udicial errors that tolerate baleful practices are self-correcting;, while erroneous condemnations are not" Easterbrook (1984).

[45] Article 82 Guidance, para.22.

[46] See Annex at para.6–143 for a full discussion of cost benchmarks.

[47] Article 82 Guidance, para.25.

[48] Given the ruling of the European Court of Justice that a dominant position cannot exist in isolation, the definition of the relevant market plays a central role in the Commission's competitive assessment in Article 82 cases.

[49] See Chapter 4 for a detailed discussion of the *Cellophane* fallacy and its implications for the practical implementation of the Hypothetical Monopolist Test.

plausible and therefore competing definitions of the relevant market; the available evidence can be consistent with both a narrow definition of the relevant market and with a wide definition of it. This effectively means that in many cases we simply cannot know with any degree of certainty whether a firm is or is not dominant based solely on an assessment of market shares.[50] Neither the parties nor the competition authorities can definitively prove their case.[51]

Similar issues arise with respect to the assessment of barriers to entry and the strength of the competitive constraint posed by potential entry. The fact that the firm under investigation is prevented from increasing prices above prevailing levels by the threat of new entry does not imply that potential competition provides an effective competitive constraint at competitive levels. However, if potential entry were considered not to provide an effective competitive constraint even at prevailing levels, then it is unlikely that it would do so at a lower level of prices.

---

**BOX 6.2: AN ALTERNATIVE APPROACH?**

These practical difficulties with defining the relevant market have led some commentators to argue that in some circumstances it is possible to identify directly whether conduct has harmed consumers and consequently that market definition is not necessary to the analysis of the case.[52] The US Supreme Court has on occasion approached competition law issues in this way.[53] In *Kodak* the Court stated that:

> "It is clearly reasonable to infer that Kodak has market power to raise prices and drive out competition in the aftermarkets, since respondents offer direct evidence that Kodak did so."[54]

In *Indiana Federation of Dentists*[55] the Court made the same point, but related it explicitly to the need, or lack of need, to assess market power:

**6–010**

---

[50]   For a comprehensive discussion of the additional difficulties of defining relevant markets in Article 82 investigations, see Bishop and Baker (2001).

[51]   Due to the existence of the *Cellophane* fallacy, market evidence may in some cases be construed in such a way that it suggests a market definition that is too wide; one should therefore exercise caution in interpreting such evidence. Unfortunately, as the *Aberdeen Journals* case illustrates so well (see fn.213), the *Cellophane* fallacy is often invoked to unreasonably dismiss all evidence.

[52]   Salop (2000).

[53]   The quotations in this paragraph are taken from Salop (2000).

[54]   *Eastman Kodak Co v Image Technical Serv. Inc*, 504 US 451 (1992).

[55]   *FTC v Indiana Fedration of Dentists*, 476 US 447, 460–61 (1986).

> "Since the purpose of the inquiries into market definition and
> market power is to determine whether an arrangement has the
> potential for genuine adverse effects on competition, 'proof of
> actual detrimental effects, such as a reduction of output', can
> obviate the need for an inquiry into market power, which is but a
> 'surrogate for detrimental effects'."

For the legal reasons noted above, a finding of a dominant position
necessarily requires the relevant market to be defined. Where conduct
truly has an adverse impact on competition, it should be possible to
define a relevant market in which the firm under investigation possesses significant market power. However, if one were to adopt a so-
called "first principles" approach, then considerable care needs to be
taken against using prejudgments as to the competitive effects of
certain conduct to infer dominance. In many instances, dominance
and market power have been inferred from conduct alleged to constitute abusive behaviour without there being good evidence that the
abuse should actually be considered an abuse (i.e. without evidence
being adduced that consumers were harmed by the behaviour). A
good example of this type of analysis is provided by the Commission's
reasoning in *Michelin*.[56]

Secondly, and perhaps more importantly for the overall competitive
assessment under Article 82 are the conclusions that are typically inferred
from a finding of dominance. As noted in para.6–006, the harm to consumers from exclusionary conduct arises indirectly; exclusionary conduct
marginalises competitors (i.e. harm to competitors) and in consequence
results in higher prices to consumers (i.e. harm to competition). But harm
to competitors cannot be assumed to lead to harm to competition. In other
words, harm to competitors represents a necessary but not a sufficient
condition for establishing that conduct represents an exclusionary abuse; a
proper competitive assessment would explain and establish how the harm
to competitors translates into higher prices for consumers.

**6–011**  But in practice the actual competitive effects of the conduct of the
dominant firm, to the extent that they are considered at all, are assumed
rather than assessed. For example, in *British Airways*, the Advocate General stated that any adverse impact on competitors of a firm held to be
dominant can be presumed to harm "competition as such (as an institution)".[57] This approach has been and continues to be supported by the
Courts.[58]

---

[56] *Michelin v Commission* (322/81) [1983] E.C.R. 3461; [1981] 1 C.M.L.R. 282.
[57] Para.68.
[58] See Case C-45/04 P, *British Airways v Commission* (2007) E.C.R. I-000, paras 106 and
107.

The assertion that harm to competitors necessarily translates into harm to competition is at odds with the economic literature and also at odds with the case law in other, but related, areas of policy, particularly in the assessment of non-horizontal mergers. Indeed, it is important to be clear about what is meant by the marginalisation of competitors. In general, the loss of volumes will only marginalise a competitor if it adversely affects the pricing decisions of that competitor, for example by leading to an increase in short-run marginal costs. If this is not the case, then conduct can only give rise to anti-competitive exclusion if its constitutes predatory conduct.[59, 60]

In other words, there can be no presumption that the share-shifting which might arise from the conduct under investigation actually results in the marginalisation of competitors. Indeed, in its Non-horizontal Merger Guidelines, the Commission states (in accordance with established economic literature) that non-horizontal mergers predominantly give rise to benign or pro-competitive effects. This raises an important policy issue; namely, the discrepancy between the assessment of foreclosure under the Merger Regulation as set out in the Non-horizontal Merger Guidelines and its assessment under Article 82. Whereas the presumption set out in the Non-horizontal Merger Guidelines recognises that harm to competitors does not necessarily, or even often, translate into harm to competition, the competitive assessment under Article 82 often takes quite a different stance: anything which a dominant firm does to harm competitors is necessarily assumed to harm competition.

For example, any loyalty rebate scheme employed by a firm held to be **6–012** dominant is assumed to harm competition.[61] But loyalty rebate schemes can provide the kind of efficiency-promoting roles that have been identified with vertical restraints and vertical mergers; loyalty rebate schemes can be employed to eliminate double marginalisation, provide incentives for customers and reduce the divergence between the incentives of suppliers and those of the distributors that sell their products. Having markedly different approaches to assessing the issue of foreclosure is unjustified from the perspective of the underlying economics. It will be interesting to see whether the declared intention to move towards a more effects-based approach in applying Article 82 will lead to the elimination of this discrepancy.

Rather than relying on legal precedents, the assessment of abuse therefore ought to be focused on identifying adverse impact on consumers.

---

[59] See paras 6–084 et seq for a detailed discussion of predatory conduct.

[60] Nota bene, in the context of assessing likely foreclosure arising from non-horizontal mergers, theories of harm predicated on post-merger predatory conduct are not normally considered since such behaviour would be illegal under and therefore caught by Article 82. For example, the CFI in *General Electric v Commission* considered that the Commission should have taken into account the deterrent effect of Article 82 when assessing the incentives to engage in anti-competitive bundling.

[61] See, e.g. the Opinion of Advocate General Kokott in *British Airways*, cited at fn.15 above.

Presuming that a given form of conduct always results in anti-competitive behavior is incorrect. For example, although in certain circumstances the business conduct of offering additional payments for reaching certain targets (i.e. loyalty rebates) may foreclose competition, with adverse consequences for consumers in many if not most other circumstances the same business conduct yields significant benefits to consumers. Similarly, although aggressive price competition might be detrimental in some circumstances, in general it is to be welcomed. The fact that these same business practices are routinely adopted by non-dominant firms demonstrates clearly that they often represent normal competitive practices; the fact that non-dominant firms engage in such conduct demonstrates that such conduct can be pursued for benign or pro-competitive reasons.

This is not to say that such business conduct when practised by a dominant firm cannot lead to anti-competitive outcomes. Rather, it simply implies that a case-by-case assessment is essential if over-intervention, and all of its associated costs, is to be avoided.

**6–013**  The issue of dominance and the role that it plays in the assessment of Article 82 might be characterised as the elephant in the room.[62] Dominance and what role it should play in the competitive assessment under Article 82 is an issue which urgently needs to be addressed, especially given the increasingly recognised difficulties associated with defining relevant markets in Article 82 cases. Unfortunately, the current policy debate largely ignores them. This is surprising since the implications of a finding of a dominant position under the current approach represent a significant and perhaps insurmountable obstacle to the implementation of a genuine effects-based approach in the enforcement of Article 82. A genuine effects-based approach recognises that the same business conduct, even when practised by dominant firms, can in some circumstances be anti-competitive and in others pro-competitive.[63]

In summary, there is no economic support for the legal presumption that any harm to competitors arising from the conduct of a dominant firm necessarily harms competition. The definition of the relevant market and any conclusions on dominance derived from that market definition should therefore be limited primarily to a screening role to eliminate from consideration the activities of those firms that are not dominant under any plausible market definition. Article 82 inquiries should focus predominantly on whether the conduct under investigation constitutes an abuse. The following outlines the economic issues arising in both exploitative and exclusionary abuses.

---

[62]  For a more detailed discussion of this issue, see Bishop (2007).

[63]  This is also recognised in the law—even dominant firms are able to engage in what is termed "normal competition". Unfortunately there has been no attempt by either the Commission or the European Courts to provide an operational definition of that term.

# EXCESSIVE PRICING

Excessive pricing occurs where a dominant firm exercises its market power    6–014
by raising prices above the competitive level. Since a dominant firm is
defined as a firm possessing significant market power, and market power is
the ability to raise prices profitably above the competitive level, then
excessive pricing represents perhaps the most intuitive form of abuse; the
dominant firm increases its price to consumers and in so doing increases it
profits. However, there have been very few pure excessive pricing cases
under Article 82.[64] Instead, excessive pricing has tended to be subsumed
into aftermarket cases where higher prices are charged to consumers that
are locked-in. We consider the economics of aftermarkets in the next
section.

The most well-known excessive pricing case is *United Brands*.[65] The
European Court of Justice indicated in *United Brands* that prices would be
considered excessive for the purposes of Article 82 where the profit margin
demanded by the dominant firm was excessive in comparison to the cost of
providing the good or service:

> "In this case charging a price which is excessive because it has no
> reasonable relation to the economic value of the product supplied
> would be such an abuse.
>
> This excess could, *inter alia*, be determined objectively if it were
> possible for it to be calculated by making a comparison between the
> selling price of the product in question and its cost of production,
> which would disclose the amount of the profit margin." (at [250]–
> [251])

The basic economic reasoning is clear: market power results in prices
above competitive levels thereby allowing higher profits to be earned.
However, determining in practice whether a price is excessive is extremely
difficult if not impossible given the need to identify the competitive price
level.[66] Furthermore, assessing the profitability of a firm as a proxy for
excessive pricing is also very difficult and economic theory does not provide
straightforward answers.

It is important to note that economic theory does not hold that prices are
driven down to costs, or economic profits are driven down to zero, for all
firms in an industry. Economic theory holds that the marginal firm in an
industry should earn zero economic profits, so that more efficient firms will

---

[64] It is also interesting to note that under US Federal law there is no excessive pricing offence.
[65] (27/76) [1978] E.C.R. 207; [1978] 1 C.M.L.R. 429.
[66] See Chapter 3 for a discussion of the difficulties in determining the competitive price in
practice and why short-run marginal cost does not provide a useful proxy for policy
purposes.

by definition earn positive economic profits. This translates into: the price of a product should just cover the average total costs of the marginal firm, but will be more than the average total costs of the infra-marginal firms.[67]

**6–015**    Furthermore, there are some types of industry where it is very difficult to measure the relationship between costs and prices. For example, it is extremely difficult to attempt to give meaning to the concept of excessive pricing in industries with intellectual property rights. In such markets, price typically exceeds the unit cost of production by a significant amount. This is necessary to recover the costs, including those costs associated with risky investment, incurred in bringing the product to market. For example, pharmaceutical companies invest heavily in the research and development of new drugs, the music industry invests in new talent and computer companies invest in developing software. In all cases, these upfront investment costs can be recovered only if the price of the products exceeds unit costs.[68] Given the dynamic nature of competition in these industries, it appears impossible to implement in any meaningful way the test of whether the price has a "reasonable relation to the economic value of the product supplied".[69] Indeed, it is far from clear that excessive pricing should be an issue in such markets. Intellectual property rights, such as patents and copyright, are designed to allow firms to price substantially above unit costs so that they can recover their up-front investments. For example, consider a pharmaceutical company with a patent over a new drug. Even though the firm may charge a price significantly above the unit cost of production, this should not in itself be considered as constituting an abuse of a dominant position. It merely reflects the competitive rewards to an innovation. A similar reasoning can be applied to other industries in which firms have engaged in activities with significant ex ante risks.

Finally, in industries in which demand is cyclical prices may fluctuate around costs depending on the level of demand for the product. When demand is significantly below the industry capacity, prices are likely to be below total costs (although probably above variable or avoidable costs). Conversely when demand is significantly above industry capacity, prices can be expected to increase above total costs, possibly by a substantial margin. Where capacity is fixed in the short-run, such price fluctuations reflect normal competitive behaviour. Indeed, it is optimal for changes in demand to be reflected in prices as this allows the price mechanism to ensure that those who value the product most highly are the ones who purchase it. It would not be economically optimal to seek to stop such price

---

[67] For simplicity we are here assuming that firms are single product firms. The pricing issues that can arise in multi-product firms are considered in the following section.

[68] This assumes that the investment actually results in a new product being brought to market. In many cases, R&D projects will be unsuccessful. This means that revenues earned from successful projects will also need to cover these costs as well as those associated directly with bringing that product to market.

[69] *United Brands v Commission* (27/76) [1978] E.C.R. 207; [1978] 1 C.M.L.R. 429.

changes, even if prices were substantially above costs in the short-run. Also prices and profits are a very efficient way of sending signals to potential new suppliers. High prices and corresponding high profits are likely to attract new entry, which will tend to lead to prices, and profits, falling. This implies that a finding of excessive pricing should at a minimum be based on evidence that prices have been persistently significantly above cost and there is little or no prospect of new entry driving them down.[70]

## Testing for excessive prices

In *United Brands* the Commission concluded that United Brands was **6–016** charging excessive prices based on a comparison of prices between different countries. For instance, the Commission found that prices were 80 per cent higher in Belgium than in Ireland and 138 per cent higher in Denmark than in Ireland. Comparing prices of the same product across regions can be instructive and in Chapter 14 we discuss at some length the use of price-concentration studies. These studies investigate the relationship between prices (or margins or profits) and the level of concentration across various regions to see if there is a systematic relationship between higher concentration and higher prices (or margins or profits), which might suggest a link between concentration and market power. However, using simple price comparisons across regions to deduce the existence of excessive prices is fraught with difficulty. First, there may be significant cost differences across regions that need to be taken into account. Secondly, and more importantly, different prices may reflect price discrimination that is welfare enhancing. This issue is discussed in detail in para.6–029. The important point is that a policy by a dominant firm of pricing differently across regions does not necessarily imply consumer harm and therefore does not necessarily represent abusive behaviour.

Another approach sometimes suggested (and used in *United Brands*) is to compare prices across different firms. This is not usually a good approach. If one firm charges higher prices than other firms, and yet consumers still buy the product, this indicates that consumers consider the product in question to be superior in some respect to the products of other firms. If this is the case, a simple price comparison is not comparing, in the eyes of consumers at least, apples with apples but rather apples with pears. Only if consumers are in some sense "locked in" to buying the higher-priced product might such a simple price comparison make sense. This issue may arise if consumers purchase a durable product that then requires on-going purchases of a proprietary consumable product. "Aftermarket" cases such as this are discussed in para.6–020 below and so we do not consider them

---

[70] This is the approach that the UK OFT advocates. To be abusive, prices must be "consistently excessive" and it must be "clear that high profits will not stimulate successful new entry within a reasonable period." (paras 2.12 and 2.13 of OFT 414 (1999) *Assessment of Individual Agreements and Conduct*).

further here, except to note that in para.6–027, we argue that issues of dominance arising from being the sole supplier of specific complementary products are less common than a naïve application of the law might presume.

Finally, a comparison of prices can be made across various services offered by the dominant firm. In *Deutsche Post AG.* the Commission considered that Deutsche Post's prices for onward transmission of cross-border mail were excessive.[71] Since a detailed analysis of Deutsche Post's costs was not possible, the Commission compared Deutsche Post's prices for cross-border mail with its domestic tariff and on that basis found that cross-border prices were excessive. Such an approach raises a number of difficulties, in large part because of the need to allocate fixed and common costs across various products. As noted in para.6–029, when firms incur fixed costs, it will rarely be efficient to impose the same mark-up on each product offered; in other words, it is efficient and a feature of normal competition for a firm to charge different prices and/or mark-ups for different products. Hence, a comparison of prices and/or mark-ups across products is unlikely to provide any meaningful insights into whether prices are excessive.

**6–017**     In *Scandlines* the Commission rejected a complaint that port charges to ferry operators were excessive at the port of Helsingborg, following the Courts' approach in *United Brands.*[72] The Commission did not simply consider the costs incurred by the port in order to determine whether the port charges were excessive; the Commission considered that a simple cost-plus approach provided an insufficient basis for determining whether observed prices were abusive. Instead, it sought to compare whether the prices charged for port services were high relative to the prices charged for other services at the same port and also with prices charged to ferry operators in other ports. The Commission noted that in assessing whether prices can be considered to be excessive, it is important to note that the test set out by the ECJ in *United Brands* focuses on the price charged, and its relation to the *economic value* of the product. While a comparison of prices and costs, which reveals the profit margin, of a particular company may serve as a first step in the analysis (if at all possible to calculate), this in itself cannot be conclusive as regards the existence of an abuse under Article 82.[73] The Commission concluded in this case that there was no

---

[71]  COMP/C-1/36.915 *Deutsche Post AG—Interception of cross-border mail* (2001).

[72]  COMP/A.36.568/D3 *Scandlines Sverige AB v Port of Helsingborg* (2004).

[73]  The Commission stated at para.232 that:

> "In the present case, the economic value of the product/service cannot simply be determined by adding to the approximate costs incurred in the provision of this product/service as assessed by the Commission, a profit margin which would be a predetermined percentage of the production costs. The economic value must be determined with regards to the particular circumstances of the case and take into account also non-cost related factors such as the demand for the product/service."

infringement of Article 82.[74] Another relevant case here is the UK case *Attheraces*.[75] In this case, the UK Court of Appeal said that evidence that a firm was pricing above cost did not provide sufficient evidence to conclude that prices were excessive: above cost pricing was held to be a necessary but not sufficient condition for excessive pricing.[76] We endorse this view.

A further approach to testing for excessive prices is to use rates of profit to infer abuse. As noted above, the theoretical link between high profits and the exercise of market power is not unambiguous for a number of reasons. In addition, there are often serious practical difficulties. Most attempts to measure profitability rely on accounting measures of profitability. These do not usually reflect the relevant economic concepts.[77] Comparisons across firms, particularly across regions, can be biased by the use of different accounting conventions.[78] Profitability measures are usually based on rates of return on some measure of capital. Measuring capital appropriately is difficult where a significant proportion of the asset base is not made up of physical assets, but of intangible assets, such as human capital.[79] If intangibles are not properly accounted for, it leads to estimates of supra-normal profits that in reality are merely a reflection of a mis-measured capital base. Finally, the question of what constitutes too high a rate of return is also not an easy question to answer. There is a tendency to relate *accounting measures* of profitability to *market-based* estimates of the required rate of return.[80] But this does not constitute a like-for-like comparison and hence is not a valid approach.

The difficulties of distinguishing between excessive prices and those implied by conditions of effective competition are reflected in the paucity of decisions in this area. It is noticeable that apart from *United Brands* there are few instances of the Commission dealing with pure excessive pricing cases outside of cases where firms possess statutory or what are often held to be de facto monopoly positions. Thus, for instance, the issue of excessive pricing arose in the context of telecommunications, where fixed-line operators often have statutory or de facto monopolies. In 1997 the Commission took action against Belgacom for excessive pricing of access to subscriber data for publication in telephone directories in Belgium. In the

---

[74] The Commission also adopted this approach in its investigation of international mobile roaming charges by comparing international roaming charges with domestic roaming charges.

[75] *Attheraces Ltd v British Horseracing Board Ltd* [2005] EWHC 3015 (Ch.); [2005] UKCLR 757, Ch D.

[76] *Attheraces Ltd v British Horseracing Board Ltd* [2007] EWCA Civ 38; [2007] UKCLR 309, CA.

[77] Edwards, Kay and Mayer (1987).

[78] The initial listing of Daimler-Benz on the New York Stock Exchange provides a good example. Under German accounting conventions, Daimler was profitable. But under US accounting conventions, it was loss-making.

[79] For a complete treatment of these issues, see Fisher McGowan (1983).

[80] These are usually based on the capital asset pricing model, which itself is open to serious criticism on both theoretical and empirical grounds.

same year the Commission investigated Deutsche Telekom's prices for offering network access to competitors. As a result of the investigation, Deutsche Telekom lowered its prices. In 1998 the Commission investigated interconnection charges of fixed-line and mobile telecoms operators and found evidence of excessive pricing. This has led to a combination of actions by various national telecoms regulators and the Commission. One of these was an Article 82 inquiry into the international roaming charges levied by mobile phone operators. When a consumer takes their mobile abroad, it "roams" on one of the domestic networks of that country. International roaming charges are the charges levied by the domestic operator on the operator of the customer. Thus, if a UK Vodafone customer uses their mobile in France and roams on the France Telecom network, then France Telecom will levy a roaming charge on Vodafone, who will pass this on to the customer. The Commission sought to find various operators guilty of excessive pricing in the United Kingdom and Germany. It is indicative of the difficulties that excessive prices raise that the Commission spent several years on the cases before finally dropping them in 2007 despite issuing a Statement of Objections and holding an oral hearing. The Commission then regulated the mobile operators directly in 2007 through a Regulation.[81] This approach was an example of a regulator "knowing an abuse when I see one" even though they were unable to show it analytically (and hence dropped the Article 82 case). It was not the Commission's finest hour.

**6–018**    These issues are not confined to European competition law, as evidenced in a South African case, *Harmony v Mittal*.[82] Mittal, a flat steel producer, was accused by Harmony, a gold producer for whom steel was an input to its operations, of excessive pricing on the South African market. Mittal sold domestically in South Africa at the import parity price, meaning that it was priced at the level at which imports were priced. It sold its production that was not sold domestically into the international market. South Africa is a considerable distance from the main steel producing and consuming regions of the world and so there are significant transport costs for Mittal to incur when exporting out of South Africa. The result is that Mittal earns substantially less on its exports than on its domestic sales. In general, it appeared that Mittal's export covered their variable costs of production but not total costs.

The original complaint was dismissed by the South African Competition Commission in 2004, but Harmony then took its case to the South African Competition Tribunal. Both parties presented evidence that was consistent

---

[81]   Regulation (EC) 717/2007 of the European Parliament and of the Council of 27 June 2007 on roaming on public mobile telephone networks within the Community and amending Directive 2002/21/EC. This was updated in July 2009.

[82]   *Harmony Gold Mining Company Ltd and Durban Roodepoort Deep Ltd v Mittal Steel South Africa Ltd and Macsteel International BV*, Case 13/CR/Feb04, Competition Tribunal of South Africa (2007).

with the previous case law: profitability analysis and various price comparisons. The profitability analysis indicated that over the steel cycle, Mittal was not making economic profits (i.e. it was not covering its cost of capital). The price comparisons were aimed primarily at seeking to show that Mittal priced lower where it faced more competition and higher where it did not face competition.

However, the Tribunal took a very different approach. The Tribunal argued that it was not a price regulator and that it was not in a position to identify the competitive price or, therefore, whether a price was excessive (i.e. significantly above the competitive price level).[83] The Tribunal therefore chose to take a structural approach to excessive pricing. It argued that[84]:

"[T]he power to price 'excessively' is the preserve of firms of overwhelming size relative to the market in which they are located and which are, in addition, markets characterised by unusually high entry barriers. That is, the market share enjoyed by the firm in question should approximate 100% and there should be no realistic prospect of entry—*in other words the market should be both uncontested and incontestable*." (italics in the original)

After deciding that Mittal held a market share of close to 100 per cent in an "uncontested and incontestable", the Tribunal went on to argue that[85]:

"[I]f the price is the product of a market structure and of ancillary conduct that reflects precisely the *absence of cognisable competition considerations* then that price will be excessive in relation to the economic value because it will not have been determined by '*the free interaction of demand and supply in a competitive market*'."

In other words, the Tribunal deduced excessive pricing from the structure  **6–019** of the market, reasoning as follows: a firm with a very large share of a market protected by very high barriers to entry must be pricing excessively and so Mittal must be engaging in excessive pricing. Although it was unsurprisingly struck down on appeal,[86] the decision does raise four important issues. First, it highlights the dangers of basing competition assessments on purely structural indicators. The Tribunal found Mittal

---

[83]   Indeed, the Tribunal refused to engage with the evidence to the extent that it even dismissed the capital asset pricing model, the bedrock of investment analysis, as being arcane and controversial. By no stretch of the imagination is either of these characterisations correct.

[84]   *Harmony v Mittal*, para.96.

[85]   *Harmony v Mittal*, para.147.

[86]   *Mittal Steel South Africa Ltd, Macsteel International BV and Macsteel Holdings (Pty) Ltd v Harmony Gold Mining Company Ltd and Durban Roodepoort Deep Ltd*, Case 70/CAC/Apr07, Competition Appeal Court of South Africa (2009).

guilty of excessive pricing despite being presented with evidence that over the steel cycle Mittal was not even making economic profits, let alone making excessive ones. It also left Mittal in the very odd position of having been found guilty of excessive pricing without knowing what the non-excessive price was that it was allowed to charge. Secondly, it is indicative of the difficulty that competition authorities and courts have with excessive pricing and with the requirements often imposed on them in such cases (e.g. price regulation). It is hardly surprising that there have been so few cases and that excessive pricing is not even a federal offence in the United States. Thirdly, it highlights the importance of engaging with the empirical evidence. Failure to engage with the available empirical raises the prospect of an "I know abuse when I see it" approach. Fourthly, it illustrates the practical difficulty presented by the *Cellophane* fallacy. The Tribunal decided that Mittal had a very high share of the relevant market and so must be pricing excessively, without noticing that it could not define the relevant market in this case without first identifying the competitive price, which it explicitly said it could not do. The result was that the Tribunal's logic was circular.

In some respects, the conclusion of this section might appear surprising. Even though excessive pricing would seem to be the most direct form of abuse (i.e. exercising substantial market power to raise prices), there are few pure excessive pricing cases in the case law. Both economic theory and practice indicate that testing for whether prices are excessive is extremely difficult. Given these difficulties, the observation of high prices relative to unit production costs should not in isolation be seen as being indicative of abusive behaviour. Rather, a detailed assessment of the market characteristics is required to determine whether the firm is subject to effective competitive constraints or not and whether its behaviour is likely to be harming consumers.

Finally it should be noted that a finding of excessive pricing logically implies that the Commission should insist that the firm in question lowers its price to a non-excessive level. This requires the Commission to have some idea of what this price level is, which implies detailed price regulation.[87] Given that the Commission has said on numerous occasions that it does not wish to act as a price regulator,[88] we expect pure excessive pricing cases to remain rare in the future.

---

[87] This issue has also been recognised by the UK courts. See *Attheraces Ltd v The British Horseracing Board Ltd* [2005] EWHC 3015 (Ch.); [2005] UKCLR 757, Ch D.

[88] For instance, at para.77 of its XXVIIth *Report on Competition Policy* (1997), in relation to the *Deutsche Telekom* case mentioned in the main text above.

# AFTERMARKETS[89]

In many industries, the initial purchase decision of consumers can have **6–020** long-run effects on their future choices. This occurs where consumers purchase durable products that also require the purchase of some complementary products, at least some of which are purchased at a later date than the purchase of the durable product. There are numerous industries in which this is the case.

## Table 6.1 Industries with aftermarkets

| Industry | Primary Product | Secondary Product |
|---|---|---|
| Video games | Games console | Video game |
| Cars | Car | Spare car parts |
| Computers | Hardware | Hardware and software maintenance services |
| Printers | Printer | Toner cartridges |
| DVDs | DVD player | DVDs |
| Mobile Telephony | Mobile phone/ network | Mobile telephony calls |

The peculiar competitive feature of these types of industry lies in the competitive interaction between the primary durable product and the secondary or "aftermarket" for associated complementary products or services. Often due to technical differences between the durable primary products, the choice of complementary products compatible with a particular primary product is limited. This implies that once the primary product has been purchased, consumer choice is confined to those aftermarket products or services compatible with that primary product. For example, the owner of a Ford motor car needs to purchase spare parts which are compatible with that type of car. In the case of video games, once a consumer has purchased a particular games platform, this can only be used to play games compatible with that platform. In other words, consumers are to a greater or lesser extent locked in to certain aftermarket suppliers.

Where consumers' future purchasing decisions are essentially locked in, this raises the possibility that the firms supplying aftermarket products or services can profitably engage in anti-competitive behaviour with regard to the supply of the complementary product by pricing it at excessively high levels.

The Commission has investigated a number of industries with this **6–021**

---

[89] We also discuss aftermarkets in Chapter 4 in the context of market definition. That discussion is complementary to the one here.

aftermarket feature.[90] Cases include *Hugin/Liptons*,[91] *AB Volvo v Veng*[92] and *Hilti*.[93] In *Hugin/Liptons*, the Commission found that Hugin, despite having only a 12 per cent share of the European cash register market, enjoyed a dominant position in respect of spare parts for its cash registers. The spare parts for Hugin cash registers were not interchangeable with those of other cash registers. Hugin cash registers could not therefore be maintained, repaired or rebuilt without Hugin parts. The European Court of Justice confirmed that Hugin enjoyed a dominant position in relation to those who owned a Hugin cash register. Similar judgments were made in *AB Volvo v Veng* and *Hilti*.

However, the existence of switching costs by themselves is not sufficient to imply that anti-competitive behaviour in the supply of secondary or aftermarket services is possible.[94] Whether the price of secondary products or services can be raised above the effectively competitive level will depend on the extent to which consumers will be deterred either from purchasing secondary services or in making the initial primary purchasing decision. A firm selling in both the primary and secondary markets faces a trade-off when it sets its aftermarket price. A higher price will allow it to earn more profits on aftermarket sales to consumers who have already purchased the equipment. On the other hand, a higher aftermarket price will also reduce sales of the equipment, because potential buyers will take into account this higher expected cost of purchasing the associated aftermarket products. If high prices in the aftermarket deter a sufficient number of consumers from making primary product purchases, then anti-competitive pricing can be deterred.[95] However, where the strength of this competitive constraint is weak—perhaps due to consumers having incomplete information about future costs in the aftermarket—anti-competitive practices in the aftermarket could be profitable.

The strength of the competitive constraint and hence whether anti-competitive behaviour is possible or profitable in an aftermarket depends on several factors. This typically requires examination of the following characteristics of an industry.[96]

---

[90]   The classic US case on this issue is *Kodak* (*Eastman Kodak Co v Image Technical Serv. Inc*, 504 US 451 (1992)).

[91]   *Liptons Cash Registers and Business Equipment Ltd v Hugin Kassaregister AB* (IV/29.132) [1978] 1 C.M.L.R. D19; [1997] OJ L22/23.

[92]   (238/87) [1988] E.C.R. 6211; [1989] 4 C.M.L.R. 122.

[93]   *Hilti AG v Commission* (T-30/89) [1991] E.C.R. 1439; [1992] 4 C.M.L.R. 33.

[94]   The Commission's practice is consistent with this statement. In *Hugin* and *Digital* (XXVIIth *Report on Competition Policy* (1997), pp.153–154) the Commission found that there was scope for abuse in the secondary market, whilst in *Kyocera* (XXVth *Report on Competition Policy* (1995) p.87) it concluded that there was not.

[95]   In *Swan Solutions Ltd/Avaya ECS Ltd* (March 2001) the UK telecoms regulator, Oftel, decided that Avaya would not be able to behave anti-competitively in an aftermarket for these reasons. The UK Office of Fair Trading came to a similar conclusion in *ICL/Synstar* (July 2001).

[96]   See Shapiro (1995).

## The ratio of "locked-in" consumers to new purchasers

Anti-competitive behaviour on the part of suppliers of secondary products  **6–022**
or services compatible with a particular primary product is more likely the
smaller the number of new consumers is relative to the size of the installed
base. Where new customers are important, e.g. in a growing industry, this
will provide a significant competitive constraint on aftermarket pricing.

## The ability to price discriminate in favour of new purchasers

The ability to price discriminate in the secondary market in favour of new  **6–023**
consumers facilitates anti-competitive pricing in aftermarket products,
since low competitive prices could be charged to new consumers to
encourage them to enter the market and higher prices charged to existing
consumers once they face costs of switching to other primary products.
However, the circumstances in which such price discrimination can take
place are likely to be fairly limited. As casual empirical observation usually
shows, the price of secondary products or services is often the same to
potential new consumers as to consumers who have already committed
themselves to a particular system through the purchase of a primary product. For example, in the video games industry the ability of software
publishers to price discriminate in favour of new consumers is at most
extremely limited. Furthermore, there is likely to be a credibility issue here.
Given that the firm is exploiting its installed base, new consumers should
be concerned about how credible it is that the firm will not do the same to
them once they become part of the installed base.

## The magnitude of switching costs

The mere fact that some consumers face high switching costs does not in  **6–024**
itself imply that a firm with a large market share in an aftermarket has
genuine market power. Moreover, it should be noted that different consumers will face different levels of switching costs. In addition, the
switching cost that consumers face typically changes over time. For
example, it is clear that a consumer who has just invested in a new car will
face higher costs of switching to an alternative new car than a consumer
who purchased the same type of car several years earlier.

In particular, switching costs tend to be lower, *ceteris paribus*, in markets
with rapid technological progress. If new equipment has superior performance to installed equipment, these performance advantages effectively
give rise to a "switching benefit" in the form of superior equipment. The
existence of "switching benefits" is borne out, for instance, by the fact that
consumers willingly incur switching costs to upgrade their video games
systems.

### *The quality of information available to marginal consumers*

**6–025** Whether the supply of secondary products or services compatible with a given primary product could profitably be distorted or restricted would also depend on whether consumers made their decisions to purchase the relevant primary product without regard to the terms of supply for secondary products or services compatible with that primary product. If information was not available about the conditions of supply in the aftermarket, this would sever or at least weaken the link between aftermarkets and the primary product markets and would potentially permit a firm in a competitive equipment market to have aftermarket power. However, this potential source of market power clearly could arise only in equipment markets in which buyers were relatively poorly informed about the aftermarket costs associated with various brands of equipment. In a market where information about the total costs of a system—so-called "life-cycle" costs—was difficult or costly to obtain, buyers might make their equipment purchases with poor information about the aftermarket costs. If most buyers were ignorant of these aftermarket costs when buying equipment, then competition between equipment manufacturers might do little to ensure that buyers received competitive prices in aftermarkets. In general, the greater the significance of the aftermarket products to the total system, the more likely it is that consumers will invest in securing information on life-cycle costs, thus making it harder for a single supplier in the aftermarket to engage in anti-competitive practices. Furthermore, not all consumers need to be well informed to ensure an effectively competitive outcome: what matters is that there are enough well informed marginal consumers.[97] Finally, it is common in markets where there are information asymmetries between buyers and sellers for specialist magazines or, more commonly nowadays, internet sites to act as information providers (the myriad car magazines and internet sites is a good example of this).

### *The number of markets in which the selling firm competes*

**6–026** The extent to which a supplier of secondary products or services could profitably engage in anti-competitive practices is also affected by its participation in other markets, including markets unrelated to the industry under investigation. This is because a firm that engages in opportunistic behaviour, such as attempting to charge prices above the competitive level to locked-in consumers, will develop a reputation for doing so. A reputation for charging high prices for secondary products may adversely affect not only the firm's sales of the primary product but also sales of its other products. For some companies, the adverse consequences from developing

---

[97] Assuming sellers cannot price discriminate between informed and uninformed consumers.

such a reputation provide a significant competitive constraint on after-market pricing.

### Strength of system competition

It is often not possible to judge the degree of competition in the secondary   6–027
market without also taking account of the degree of competition in the
primary market. Consumers typically want to purchase the bundle of
services provided by the combination of the primary product and the
secondary product and so it is the total cost of these that matters. In such a
framework, it is not uncommon for manufacturers to earn a relatively small
(or even negative) margin on the primary product and a relatively larger
margin on the secondary product (e.g. mobile phone handsets and calls). It
has been argued that this can be a highly efficient way for firms to operate.[98, 99] For instance, the lower price of the primary product may make it
easier to introduce new products to the market as consumers are more
likely to be willing to "take a risk" when prices are lower.

# EXCLUSIVE DEALING

The first category of exclusionary abuse considered in the Article 82   6–028
Guidance covers exclusive dealing.[100] Exclusive dealing describes an
arrangement whereby the willingness of one firm to deal with another is
contingent upon that latter firm either dealing with it exclusively (exclusive
purchasing) or purchasing a large share of its requirements from the supplying firm. Exclusive dealing is commonly observed and can take
numerous forms. Abusive behavior arising from exclusive dealing relates to
the foreclosure of competitors through the use of either exclusive purchasing obligations which hinder their ability to sell to customers or conditional or loyalty rebates schemes which have the same effect on
competitors.[101] A loyalty rebate encompasses a wide range of discount
schemes which have the key characteristic in that it makes the offer of the
discount conditional on customers reaching certain target purchase
thresholds.[102] Rebates can either be incremental whereby the discount
applies to all units purchased above the threshold or retroactive whereby
the discount applies to all units purchased once the threshold has been
reached.[103] In both categories of exclusive dealing, the competitive

---

[98]   Katz and Shapiro (1994).
[99]   See also paras 6–063—6–083 for a related discussion on tying and bundling.
[100]  See Rey (2008) and Melamed (2008) for a discussion of exclusive dealing.
[101]  Article 82 Guidance, para.31.
[102]  A loyalty rebate need not necessarily be conditional on reducing purchases from rival
       suppliers. Whether this is the case depends on the precise form of the rebate scheme
       employed.
[103]  Retroactive rebate schemes are also known as rollback rebate schemes.

assessment focuses on whether exclusive purchasing or conditional rebate schemes by denying a certain part of overall market demand renders rival firms less effective competitors. The competitive analysis of both types of behavior is therefore effectively the same.

The remainder of this section is organised as follows. Since the price paid by customers depends on their purchases, loyalty rebates involve price discrimination.[104] We therefore first provide a brief overview of the economics of price discrimination. We then discuss the incentive properties of loyalty rebate schemes. This section helps to explain the Commission's historically hostile (but inappropriate) stance towards loyalty rebates with reference to a few of the main cases in this area. We then outline the key issues that need to be addressed in a proper assessment of the competitive effects of loyalty rebates and discuss the likely circumstances in which loyalty rebates might give rise to anti-competitive outcomes.

## Price discrimination

**6–029** Loyalty rebate schemes represent a form of price discrimination in the sense that different buyers face different prices according to how much they buy in relation to their total needs. Although Article 82(c) specifically refers to the application of dissimilar conditions to equivalent transactions as an abuse, price discrimination is not only ubiquitous, it is in most instances pro-competitive.

It is sometimes said that price discrimination cannot occur if a market is competitive. This is not true, except in the uninteresting sense in which an industry is only held to be competitive if it is *perfectly* competitive in the theoretical sense.[105] In reality, price discrimination is rife even in industries subject to effective competition. For example, price discrimination is observed in the airline industry, other transport industries, the pricing of cinema tickets and so on. This fact is acknowledged by a former Director General of the OFT who states:

> "The fact of price discrimination does not by itself allow an inference of market power, still less dominance. There are ample circumstances in which competition and price discrimination are quite consistent".[106]

---

[104] As we will see, loyalty rebates give rise to *second-degree price discrimination*, i.e. where certain selling practices are used to induce consumers to self-select themselves to reveal whether they have a high or low willingness to pay.

[105] As discussed in Chapter 2, using the theoretical model of perfect competition does not provide a useful basis for making policy decisions.

[106] Vickers (2001).

It is difficult to provide a satisfactory economic definition of "price discrimination".[107] However, the definition that is generally used in competition policy is that price discrimination occurs when a product is sold to different consumers at different prices that do not reflect differences in the costs of supply.[108] Economists generally believe that the relevant costs are the marginal or variable costs of supply.

Economists distinguish between three types of price discrimination.[109]   **6–030**

1.  First degree price discrimination occurs when a firm is able to discriminate perfectly between its customers. First degree price discrimination is likely to be extremely rare in practice due to the possibility consumers have for arbitrage behaviour. A customer who has a low valuation for the firm's product can re-sell the product at a higher price to a high valuation customer, while still undercutting the manufacturer. Moreover, first degree price discrimination assumes that the firm has complete knowledge of its customers' willingness to pay—an assumption unlikely to be met in most markets.

2.  Second degree price discrimination occurs when certain selling practices are used to induce consumers to self-select themselves to reveal whether they have a high or low willingness to pay. The most common form of second degree price discrimination are volume discounts. Another common form is the use of two part tariffs where consumers pay a lump sum up front and then a per usage charge thereafter. This type of pricing is common in network markets such as telecoms, water, gas and electricity. As a consumer uses the service more (e.g. uses more electricity), the average price per unit declines. Many rebates and discounts are based on volumes purchased and so are a form of second degree price discrimination.

3.  Third degree price discrimination occurs when firms use information about their consumers (e.g. age or location) to price discriminate. Common examples are firms charging less to children or old age pensioners (e.g. buses and cinemas) or to those willing to travel at off-peak times (e.g. trains and buses).

Competition policy is concerned with second and third degree price discrimination since first degree price discrimination is virtually never possible. The difference between second and third degree price discrimination relates to the fact that in the latter the firm uses directly observable

---

[107] Tirole (1998), Chapter 3.
[108] In theory, selling a product to different consumers at the *same* price when the costs of supply are different is also price discrimination.
[109] Pigou (1920).

information about consumers to price discriminate between them, whereas in the former price discrimination takes place via consumers self-selecting different options.

## The welfare effects of price discrimination

**6–031** The interesting question from a competition policy perspective is what are the welfare implications of price discrimination relative to a policy of uniform prices. The answer is that they are generally not a priori clear and so depend on a case-by-case analysis.

The welfare implications of first degree price discrimination depend entirely on the welfare standard that is used.[110] First degree price discrimination allows the firms to price to each consumer at exactly their valuation of the product. This means the firm will sell products up to the point at which consumers' valuation is below marginal cost, which is precisely the *social* welfare optimising solution that occurs under perfect competition. However, unlike under perfect competition, there is no consumer surplus under first degree price discrimination, so *consumer* welfare is zero. So this is one place where the policy prescription depends crucially on the welfare standard adopted. However, since first degree price discrimination is exceptionally rare, this is one policy dilemma that we can safely ignore.

The welfare implications of second and third degree price discrimination are also ambiguous, but this is true whichever welfare standard is used. In general, where price discrimination leads to an increase in total sales, consumer welfare is likely to be improved relative to the benchmark of uniform prices.[111]

**6–032** We concentrate first on third degree price discrimination. The intuition behind third degree price discrimination is that firms charge higher prices to those who have a higher willingness to pay, and lower prices to those with a lower willingness to pay. In economic terms, this translates into higher prices for consumers with a lower elasticity of demand, and lower prices for consumers with a high elasticity of demand. Clearly, moving from a situation in which price discrimination is practised to one where it is not will generally involve trading off the gains to one group (those with a low elasticity of demand, who now pay a lower price) against the losses of the other (those with a high elasticity of demand, who now pay a higher price). In general, third degree price discrimination reduces welfare if it does not increase total output.[112]

Relative to the welfare optimum of price equal to marginal cost, third degree price discrimination involves two types of economic inefficiency.

---

[110] See Chapter 2 for a discussion of different welfare standards.
[111] See Schmalensee (1981) and Varian (1985).
[112] Tirole (1988), Chapter 3.

First, prices are not equal to marginal cost, but as discussed in Chapter 2, marginal cost pricing is an ideal that can rarely be achieved in the real world. Secondly, if different groups of consumers are charged different prices, there are likely to be some consumers in the higher-priced group who would be willing to pay what the lower-priced group pay, but not what the higher-priced group pay. This will lead to some consumers not buying the product whilst other consumers, who value the product less, do buy it. This is not economically efficient: economic efficiency is best served by those who value a product highest buying it. This effect is in general outweighed when the alternative to price discrimination, uniform prices, leads to lower total output.[113]

A case where third degree price discrimination is particularly likely to increase welfare is where it allows a firm to supply a group of consumers that would not otherwise be supplied. For example, consider a firm that sells branded goods in a low income country at much lower prices than it sells those same goods in a high income country. It may be that if a firm has to charge a uniform price to two groups of consumers with different levels of willingness to pay, the group with a low willingness to pay would make no purchases. This would occur if the price that it would have to charge to continue to supply this group would involve reduced profits from the high willingness to pay group that outweigh the profits from the low willingness to pay group. A hypothetical example should make this clear.

Suppose a cinema charges €2 to children and €10 to adults and would not   **6–033** sell any children's tickets if the child price was above €2.50. Further, suppose the marginal cost of an extra consumer, whether child or adult, is €1. Under this pricing structure, assume that 50 adults and 50 children turn up to a film, the cinema earns revenue of €600 and incurs costs of €100, leading to a profit of €500.[114] Now suppose the cinema was not allowed to price discriminate between adults and children and so had to set the same price to each. If the cinema wants to continue to sell tickets to children, it will have to have a uniform price of no more than €2.50. This means that it will earn a margin above marginal cost of at most €1.50 on each adult, rather than the €9 it earned under price discrimination. It is very unlikely that the firm would prefer to sell tickets to children and earn at most only €1.50 margin per adult. Instead, it will stop selling tickets to children altogether and continue to earn a higher margin on adults. Assuming that €10 was the profit-maximising price to set to adults under price discrimination, the

---

[113] A third possible source of inefficiency arises if consumers with a high willingness to pay expend resources pretending to have only a low willingness to pay. For instance, airlines frequently charge more for a Friday evening return flight than for one on a Sunday, on the basis that business people buy the former and leisure travellers the latter. If a business person stays over on a business trip until Sunday in order to get a lower fare, this involves a cost to the business person (e.g. more time away from family) which is driven by the desire to signal that they are a low willingness to pay customer.

[114] We are excluding fixed costs here for analytical ease. In reality, the €500 will be needed to help cover the fixed costs of hiring the cinema and film and employing staff.

cinema will continue to set this price under uniform prices and will sell no children's tickets. This will harm welfare. The children who no longer buy tickets lose out. The adults do not gain anything (they pay the same price).[115] And the firm loses a positive margin on children of €1 per child. So in this case, price discrimination is clearly welfare enhancing because it ensures that a group of consumers is served that would not otherwise be served.

Another example arises with train travel. Peak train travel typically costs substantially more than off-peak train travel, meaning that peak time travellers contribute more to the recovery of the fixed costs of running trains than do off-peak travellers. If train companies had to charge a uniform price throughout the day, off-peak travellers might well switch to alternative modes of transport or not travel at all. This would mean that off-peak travel no longer made any contribution to fixed costs and so peak time travellers would have to shoulder all the burden. This might lead to higher prices for peak time travellers.

Similar issues arise with second degree price discrimination. Forcing a firm to charge a uniform price (e.g. stop offering volume discounts) may not benefit consumers if total output falls. This is likely to happen if the move to a uniform price leads to prices rising above the willingness to pay of some consumers, who therefore stop buying the product.

**6–034**   Micro-economics does not usually take positions on issues of "fairness", but instead concentrates on economic efficiency. Nonetheless, it is worth noting that those customers who pay more under third degree price discrimination are likely to be on average wealthier than those who pay less. So moving from price discrimination to uniform prices may have adverse distribution consequences.

---

**BOX 6.3: RAMSEY PRICING**

Many firms incur joint costs when they sell products in more than one market. This can be either when there are joint fixed costs of producing different products, or joint costs of selling the same product in different markets. Joint fixed costs can include overheads such as company management, or the fixed costs of a plant used for producing more than one type of product, or brand advertising aimed at increasing demand for all a brand's products, rather than just one particular product. In cases such as these the joint fixed costs need to be recovered from revenues earned on the various products. The most economically efficient way of doing this is called Ramsey pricing[116] and virtually always involves price discrimination.

---

[115] The adults might even have to pay more, if the lost revenue from children was such that the cinema now made losses at the original adult prices.

[116] So called because the underlying theory comes from a 1927 paper on optimal taxation by Frank Ramsey, a Cambridge mathematician, Ramsey (1927).

The basic intuition behind Ramsey pricing is that when marginal cost pricing is not possible due to the presence of joint fixed costs, prices should be set so as to minimise the loss in output caused by pricing above marginal cost. This implies that a relatively larger proportion of the joint fixed costs should be recovered in markets where the elasticity of demand is lower and a relatively higher proportion should be recovered in those markets where the elasticity of demand is higher. Thus the mark-up of prices over marginal cost should be in inverse proportion to the elasticity of demand.

The natural behaviour of firms will involve a form of Ramsey pricing. In order to maximise profits in the presence of significant joint fixed costs, they will mark up above marginal costs on the basis of elasticities. However, whilst to achieve the social optimum, prices should be marked up on the basis of *market* elasticities of demand, individual firms will respond to *firm* elasticities of demand. As we discussed in Chapter 2, these are higher than market elasticities. To the extent that the ratio of a firm's elasticities across markets differs from the ratio of market elasticities across markets, the structure of prices that a firm sets will not be the same structure as Ramsey prices. Equally, if the ratio of firm elasticities is the same as that of market elasticities, they will set the same price structure as Ramsey prices.

**6–035**

To the extent that firm elasticities tend to be higher where market elasticities are higher, and lower where market elasticities are lower, we might expect firms to approximate quite closely to the structure of Ramsey prices. Of course, whether the *level* of prices, as opposed to just the *structure* of prices, are at the social optimum depends on whether the firms have market power.

Several conclusions follow from this discussion. Where there are joint fixed costs, price discrimination is almost certainly optimal. Only if the market elasticities of demand are the same across all the relevant markets will price discrimination not be optimal. Firms will naturally use a form of Ramsey pricing and may well set a structure of prices that is close to the social optimum. Whether they set prices at levels close to the social optimum will depend on how competitive the market is.

Price discrimination is likely to be welfare enhancing in those industries which are characterised by high fixed costs but low marginal costs.[117] When marginal costs are close to zero, any positive price provides the firm with a contribution to fixed costs. However, if the firm charges all consumers a low price (i.e. below average cost), it will not be able to cover its fixed costs. In this case the firm may well have to price discriminate in order to recover

**6–036**

---

[117] The software and pharmaceuticals industries provide good examples, but the same is true of many "old economy" industries as well.

its fixed costs: there might not be a uniform price that allowed the firm to recover its costs. In this scenario, the firm would only produce the product in the first place if it believed it would be able to price discriminate later, so the price discrimination is clearly welfare enhancing.[118]

So far we have not discussed the effect of price discrimination on competitors. Price discrimination can be anti-competitive if it leads to the exclusion of competitors (or potential competitors) which as a consequence reduces the intensity of competition and thereby leads to an increase in the level of prices. In this sense price discrimination can have similar effects to predation, which is discussed at length in paras 6–084 et seq. Given this later discussion, we do not discuss in detail the economics of predatory behaviour here. However, the exclusionary effect of price discrimination has been one of the main concerns that the Commission has had with price discrimination and so it is discussed in the following subsection on the Commission's policy with respect to price discrimination.

The main conclusion from this section is that a blanket prohibition of price discrimination is not warranted. In particular, the assessment of such practices should consider what impact the practice has on total output. This is consistent with the UK OFT stated approach to price discrimination[119]:

> "Where marginal costs are below average costs, however, discriminatory pricing arrangements are likely to be preferable to (that is, more efficient than) uniform prices, as explained above. The more that price discrimination results in increased output or indeed opens up new markets (for example, off-peak rail travel for price sensitive travellers such as students, pensioners, families), the more likely it is to have a beneficial impact on economic welfare." (para.3.13)

### Loyalty rebates and the "suction" effect

**6–037** The term "loyalty rebate" is capable of encompassing a wide class of discount schemes. However, a key characteristic of a loyalty rebate that differentiates it from other discount schemes or forms of price discrimination is that it makes the lower price conditional on increasing purchases from the supplier in question.[120]

One type of loyalty rebate explicitly makes the offer of a rebate conditional on purchase of a certain share of requirements from the supplier. For example, buyers might be offered a discount conditional on purchasing 90

---

[118] This analysis provides an explanation for price discrimination in products such as software, where different versions of the same fundamental software are sold at different prices despite having essentially the same marginal costs.

[119] OFT 414 (1999) *Assessment of Individual Agreements and Conduct*.

[120] A loyalty rebate need not necessarily be conditional on reducing purchases from rival suppliers. Whether this is the case depends on the precise form of the rebate scheme employed.

per cent of their requirements from a given supplier. Such a discount depends not on absolute quantities purchased but quantities purchased relative to total requirements.

The following stylised discount types can all be viewed as loyalty rebates.

- **An exclusivity discount:** The buyer obtains a discount only by purchasing all its needs from the supplier.[121, 122]

- **An individualised quantity discount:** Each buyer is offered a discount conditional on purchasing a given quantity within a particular reference period. In this case the targets may differ for buyers of different sizes.

- **A growth discount:** The buyer receives a discount if its purchases in the current period exceed its purchases in the relevant past period by a given amount. A growth target does not necessarily imply that meeting the threshold target entails an increase in the supplier's market share; if the target growth threshold is set at a level lower than the growth in the overall market, then the threshold can be met without diverting share from competing suppliers.

- **A bundled discount:** The target relates to purchases across a range of products. In this case, it might be necessary for the buyer to purchase a certain amount of another product supplied by the firm in question in order to qualify for the rebate where the target amounts to a large portion of its needs of that product.

The term "loyalty rebate" therefore covers a wide range of discount schemes. What each of these different schemes have in common is that they provide incentives for customers to purchase more product or services from the firm offering the loyalty scheme. Put simply, all loyalty rebate schemes create incentives for customers to purchase more from the firm employing the loyalty rebate scheme, and they are therefore likely to result in share-shifting.

The loyalty-inducing effects of a loyalty rebate scheme can be seen in the **6–038** following hypothetical representation. Firm X has a variable unit cost of production of €1 and annual fixed costs of €1 million (which for the purposes of this discussion we can assume to be sunk).[123] This firm is assumed to set a list price of €2 per unit sold but also offers a 5 per cent

---

[121] Effectively, this is a market share discount where the threshold is set at 100%.
[122] See Ridyard (2008) for a discussion of this type of loyalty rebate.
[123] It is worth noting that the analysis presented here does not assume dominance. This by itself should make it clear that the competitive assessment needs to go beyond a consideration of the incentive properties of a loyalty rebate scheme even when operated by a dominant firm.

discount on all units purchased if the customer reaches a certain target threshold.[124] Its effective price per unit purchased then falls to €1.90 per unit.[125] As the customer increases its volume of sales from the firm offering the loyalty rebate, the incentives to purchase even more from that firm also increase. Indeed, at some point, the effective price for purchasing additional volumes becomes negative. This is the so-called "suction effect". This can be illustrated graphically in Figure 6.1.

**Figure 6.1 Incentive properties of loyalty rebate schemes**

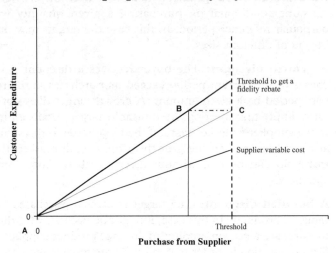

Figure 6.1 shows three diagonal lines sloping up from the origin (point A).[126]

- The steepest line (running from A through E) shows the customer's expenditure when buying at the list price of €2 per unit; the customer's total expenditure increases as it purchases more units. Under the loyalty rebate scheme, this is the price the customer pays until it can show that the number of units purcashed reaches the target threshold set by the dominant supplier. At that point, the customer qualifies for a rebate equivalent to the discount of 5 per cent on all purchases, which is shown as the vertical distance from the top of the list price line to point C.

- The middle line (from A to C) shows the amount that the customer actually pays if it agrees and adheres to the terms of the loyalty rebate, i.e. the effective unit price falls to €1.90.[127]

---

[124] A similar analysis would apply if we were to consider an incremental rebate scheme, i.e. one where the discount applies on all units purchased above the target threshold.
[125] This example assumes that the threshold is based on a share of total purchases but the analysis would be similar if the target threshold were based on year-on-year growth or on achieving an absolute level of sales.
[126] Note, the lines in the above figure are not drawn to scale.
[127] For ease of reference, we have not drawn the line AC to scale.

- The bottom line indicates the total variable costs incurred by the supplier in supplying the required volume of goods or services. The slope of the line indicates the marginal cost.

Figure 6.1 shows that once the customer has purchased volumes equivalent to or greater than B then the effective unit price for purchasing the rest of its requirements from Firm X becomes negative; the value of the prospective year-end rebate is greater than the price the customer needs to pay for the extra units. This implies that, viewed from the perspective of a customer that has already purchased B from Firm X, the incentives to make additional purchases from Firm X are so great that rival firms would find it extremely hard to contest the customer's demand above B; in effect, rival firms would need to offer negative prices to contest such sales. This is the so-called "suction effect" or "loyalty-inducing effect" of such rebate schemes.[128] It is this "suction" effect that underpins the hostile approach of EC competition law towards loyalty rebates.

---

**BOX 6.3A: INCENTIVE PROPERTIES OF INCREMENTAL REBATE SCHEMES**

Figure 6.2 illustrates the incentive properties of a retroactive rebate scheme. Here we illustrate the incentive properties of an incremental rebate scheme. Under such schemes, customers receive a discount on all purchases above the target threshold.

**6–039**

**Figure 6.2 Incentive properties of incremental rebate schemes**

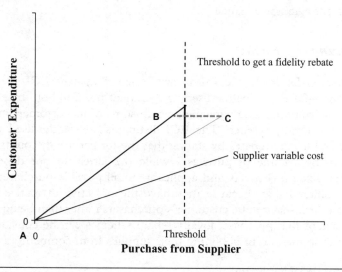

---

[128] For a formal depiction of the suction effect, see Maier-Rigaud (2006).

Even though the rebate only applies to units purchased after the target threshold, the incentive properties are similar to those of a retroactive rebate scheme. Suppose a customer has requirements of purchasing C units. Then once that customer has purchased B units, the effective price of additional units between B and C becomes negative.

## THE COMMISSION'S POLICY TOWARDS LOYALTY REBATES

**6-040** The Article 82 case law can fairly be characterised as being extremely hostile towards any dominant firm offering a loyalty rebate scheme. For example, in *Michelin*[129] the Commission held that Michelin had abused a dominant position in replacement tyres for trucks and buses in the Netherlands through the provision of off-invoice discounts and end-of-year rebates based on performance targets. The Commission stated that:

"[W]ith the exception of short term measures, **no discount should be granted unless linked to a genuine cost reduction in the manufacturer's costs**. The compensation paid to Michelin dealers must be commensurate with the tasks they perform and the services they actually provide, which reduce the manufacturer's burden. In addition the system of discounts and bonuses agreed must be clearly confirmed to each dealer when the sales contract is presented and concluded." (emphasis added).

This section provides a brief summary of two cases that have helped shape this current aggressive stance.

### *Hoffmann-La Roche*[130]

**6-041** In *Hoffmann-La Roche* the European Court of Justice (ECJ) held that Hoffmann—La Roche had abused its dominant position both by entering into exclusive purchasing agreements with some of its customers and also by offering loyalty rebates. The ECJ distinguished standardised volume rebates and loyalty rebates by stating that the former are discounts linked solely to the volume of purchases while the latter do not depend on quantities fixed objectively and applicable to all possible purchasers. The ECJ considered that, because they have the objective of increasing the dominant firm's share of a customer's purchasers rather than being related to the size of that purchase, loyalty rebate schemes can be considered to prevent customers from obtaining their supplies from competitors.

[129] (322/81) [1983] E.C.R. 3461.
[130] *Hoffmann-La Roche & Co AG v Commission of the European Communities* [1979] E.C.R.

The stance taken in this case towards loyalty rebates has led the Commission to argue that loyalty rebates are necessarily exclusionary when implemented by a firm held to be dominant unless the offered discounts reflect genuine cost savings associated with additional sales. The case law in this area has therefore developed with no regard being given to whether the competitors can match the offers or whether it is possible for such loyalty rebate schemes to foreclose a sufficient part of the market to reduce the competitive threat offered by competitors or whether consumer harm is likely.[131]

## *BA/Virgin*[132]

In its decision against British Airways (BA) regarding Virgin Atlantic **6–042**
Airways' complaint concerning BA's marketing agreements with travel agents, the Commission held that BA had used its travel agent incentive scheme to foreclose the market for air travel services from and to the United Kingdom.

The Commission held that the travel agent incentive schemes employed by BA had the following effect.

> "Travel agents are encouraged to remain loyal to BA rather than to sell their services to competitors of BA by being given incentives to maintain or increase their sales of BA tickets which do not depend on the absolute size of those sales". (at [102]).

The decision goes on to state:

> "The exclusionary effect of the commission schemes affect all of BA's competitors and any potential new entrants. They therefore harm competition in general and so consumers, rather than only harming certain operators who cannot compete with BA on merit". (at [106]).

Furthermore, the Commission stated that no analysis of the actual impact on competition was required.[133]

> "Despite the exclusionary commission schemes, competitors of BA have been able to gain market share from BA since the liberalisation of UK air transport markets. This cannot indicate that these schemes have had no effect. It can only be assumed that competitors would

---

[131] The ECJ also pointed to the discriminatory characteristic of the loyalty rebates. This theme was later developed in other cases as a secondary anti-competitive effect of loyalty rebates by the Commission, see for example *BA/Virgin*.

[132] IV/D-2/34.780 *Virgin/British Airways* (1999) and *British Airways v Commission* (C-95/04 P).

[133] See [107] of *BA/Virgin*.

have had more success in the absence of these abusive commission schemes".

This statement is nonsensical. Clearly, if BA did not employ the incentive schemes, competitors would have benefited. But this "observation" amounts to nothing more than saying competitors would be better off if BA chose to compete less aggressively. Furthermore, the competition concern here relates to the *exclusion* of rival firms. The fact that the market shares of rivals were growing suggests strongly that they were not excluded. Indeed, it could be argued that where competitors' market shares are growing there should be a (rebuttable) presumption that the loyalty rebate has no exclusionary effect.[134]

**6–043** Unfortunately, the CFI confirmed this "analysis".[135] The CFI noted the loyalty building character of BA's incentives and indicated that demonstrating concrete effects of the abuse is unnecessary to establish an infringement of Article 82 EC. Following this observation, the CFI subscribed to the Commission's view that whether BA's rivals had grown their market shares during the period of the alleged abuse was irrelevant and absent BA's incentives the rivals would have grown more. No explanation was provided why the current rate of growth of Virgin indicates an absence of effective competition. Indeed, this statement provides no basis for discriminating between harm to competition and harm to competitors. The fact that a loyalty rebate creates incentives for customers to buy more from a particular supplier cannot by itself be used to imply that competition is adversely affected. This is a key theme that lies at the heart of the current debate on the need for reform of the competitive assessment of alleged abuses under Article 82.[136]

## Summary of case law

**6–044** The current policy in European competition law towards loyalty rebates under Article 82 can be summarised very simply: if a firm is found to be dominant, then any loyalty rebate scheme is very likely to be deemed to represent an abuse of that dominant position. This hostile policy stance

---

[134] See Bishop (2008) and roundtable discussion in Ehlermann and Marquis (2008).

[135] This line of reasoning is also present in the CFI *Michelin II* judgment; see for example [241] and [245] of that judgment.

[136] The CFI also accepted the Commission's argument that BA's incentives were harming competition in the travel agency services market by creating discrimination. The fact that the Commission argued for distortion of competition by discrimination by merely showing the dissimilar conditions that applied for similar transactions and not by providing insight or information on the harm caused to competition or consumers did not prevent the CFI from dismissing BA's challenge on this point. Considering "discrimination" as a separate violation of competition rules because it distorts the competition amongst retailers is contrary to any economic logic. This reasoning fails to answer a basic question: why would a dominant undertaking try to harm the competition between its retailers given that tougher retail competition implies more sales for its product?

translates into an effective per se prohibition on dominant firms employing such schemes. In so doing, the law will in many instances be detrimental to competition and hence to consumers.

## Examining the competitive effects of loyalty rebates

The foregoing discussion reveals that loyalty rebates can provide powerful **6-045** incentives for a firm's downstream customers to purchase additional volumes from that firm. In principle, such incentives can make it more difficult for competitors to increase sales since it becomes less attractive for customers to switch volumes away from the dominant firm if this would lead to the loss of the retroactive rebate.[137] The Article 82 Guidance states that the "potential foreclosing effect of retroactive rebates is in principle strongest on the last units purchased of the product before the threshold is exceeded".[138]

But as the hypothetical example above clearly demonstrates, *all* loyalty rebates have these properties, regardless of whether the firm offering the rebate scheme is held to be dominant. This necessarily implies that the existence of the "suction effect" provides an insufficient basis for concluding that a loyalty rebate scheme gives rise to anti-competitive outcomes and that a more complete analysis of the competitive effects of loyalty rebates is therefore required. We first consider the pro-competitive rationale that firms have for employing loyalty rebates. Following that discussion, we explain why, despite the "suction effect", loyalty rebates do not necessarily foreclosure competitors and, in particular, why the competitive assessment needs to go beyond an analysis of the "static" incentives of customers. Having set out why a simplistic approach to the competitive assessment of loyalty rebates is inappropriate, we then consider the circumstances in which loyalty rebates can genuinely foreclose competitors with potential detriment for final consumers.

## *Pro-competitive Benefits of Loyalty Rebates*

The underlying pro-competitive business motivation for employing loyalty **6-046** rebates is to sell more products or services at prices which increase profits. Seeking additional sales so as to increase profitability is a standard motivation for all firms. The proposition that there are pro-competitive motivations for employing loyalty rebate schemes is clearly demonstrated by the fact that such pricing practices are also employed by firms that are not dominant. As is well accepted in competition economics, any business

---

[137] *Nederlandsche Banden Industrie Michelin v Commission (Michelin I)* (322/81) [1983] E.C.R. 3461, [70] to [73].
[138] Article 82 Guidance, para.39.

practice employed by a firm that does not possess significant market power cannot give rise to anti-competitive outcomes.

The various pro-competitive rationales can be categorised as follows:

- providing incentives for customers to supply complementary services;

- inducing customers to lower prices to end consumers (i.e. reducing double marginalisation); and

- efficient fixed cost recovery (Ramsey pricing).[139]

The first two reasons are akin in many respects to vertical restraints.[140] The third rationale is to enable the firm to increase output via price discrimination.[141] We examine each of these in turn.

*Providing incentives for customers to supply complementary services*

**6–047** A key pro-competitive rationale for a firm to employ loyalty rebates is to align the incentives of customers with that of the supplying firm.[142] Customers can add substantial value to a supplier's products or services by providing additional complementary services. These complementary services include promoting the product in store, providing detailed product information to customers (sometimes including a demonstration of how to use the products or services), keeping an appropriate stock of product so that at any time final consumers are able to purchase the product they require, or simply putting more effort into selling the products or services of the supplier.

These services create benefits for the supplier while their costs mainly accrue to the supplier's customers. These intermediate customers choose the level of these complementary services by considering their own marginal benefit received from and their own marginal cost from providing such services. Since the intermediate customer has no inherent incentive to take into account the supplier's interest in deriving such benefits, in general a lower level of services will be provided than the supplier would wish.

A direct solution to this problem would involve the supplier writing a contract with the customer specifying the level of services to be provided and the reimbursement from the supplier to the customer. However, there

---

[139] Ramsey (1927).

[140] See Chapter 5 for a detailed discussion of the economics of vertical restraints.

[141] A firm might seek to achieve higher sales volumes by lowering the price of its product. However, an across-the-board price reduction might not be attractive due to its effect on the profitability. This is particularly true where production involves significant fixed costs and low variable costs. Loyalty rebate schemes provide one method that permits firms to make greater sales to customers without reducing the prices on all units sold.

[142] The need to align the interests of suppliers and customers is sometimes referred to as the principal-agent problem. This issue was first addressed by the Nobel Laureate, James Mirrlees. See Mirrlees (1975).

are several concerns with this method. First, specifying service levels in a contract is difficult because such services often cannot be measured objectively. Secondly, it is costly for the supplier to engage in direct monitoring of the provision of these services. Thirdly, even if monitoring is achievable, enforcement in case of contract breach has additional costs. Finally, and importantly, the customer has an informational advantage over the supplier for determining the appropriate combination of these services to expand demand, as local demand conditions for the product might be highly variable.

Any method that aligns customers' incentives with those of the supplier   **6–048** would allow the supplier to achieve efficient levels of service provision at different locations in a decentralised manner. A loyalty rebate scheme provides an efficient method to achieve this goal. Greater effort by the customer may be necessary to increase the supplier's share of its customer's total purchases of that product. Provided the customer achieves the target threshold set by the supplier, the supplier shares with the customer the benefits of the sale expansion achieved. In short, the discounts made available in the rebate scheme seek to align the incentives of the customer with those of the supplier.

*Inducing customers to lower prices to end consumers (i.e. reducing double marginalisation)*

In many settings, the customers of suppliers employing loyalty rebates (in   **6–049** particular, retailers) add a margin to the wholesale price of products or services when they set their own prices. This margin includes the profit margin of the supplier's customer as well as the customer's costs. Since the supplier's wholesale price already includes a profit margin, the price to the end consumer ends up suffering from *double marginalisation*. As a result, the price to the end consumer is too high compared to what the supplier would choose if it had its own integrated network, to the detriment of both the supplier and end consumers.[143]

Double marginalisation could be eliminated if the supplier charged a wholesale price equal to the marginal cost of producing its products or services. In that case, each customer of the supplier would make the same retail pricing decision that the supplier would make if the customer were vertically integrated with the supplier. But of course, in that case, the supplier would be left with either lower profits or (most likely) significant losses.

A loyalty rebate scheme allows the supplier to disentangle the average wholesale price from the marginal wholesale price to a specific customer. Any customer of the supplier knows that reaching the target will imply a lower price. The customers will therefore have incentives to moderate their

---

[143] See Chapter 5 (para.5–038 and Box 5.2) and Chapter 8 (para.8–045 and Appendix 8.1) and Appendix 8 for a more detailed discussion of double marginalisation.

mark-up over the wholesale price, and in consequence output will be expanded. The customer thereby increases the likelihood of reaching the target threshold, upon which the supplier shares part of the benefits it realises with the customer.

*Efficient fixed cost recovery (Ramsey pricing)*

**6–050** Charging different prices to different customers (i.e. price discrimination) can represent an efficient way for a firm to recover its fixed costs of operations. Loyalty rebate schemes provide one method of price discrimination that permits the efficient recovery of fixed costs. Many industries are characterised by high fixed costs and (relatively) low marginal costs of providing goods and/or services. In consequence, firms in industries with fixed costs charge prices in excess, often well in excess, of short-run marginal costs. The likelihood that such pricing will entail some loss of static efficiency (i.e. certain consumers will be dissuaded from consuming the product even though they value it higher than the marginal cost of supply) must be traded off against the risk that the product would not exist at all if investors were not offered the prospect of fixed cost recovery at the time when the necessary investments were made. Where businesses face this problem of fixed cost recovery, and where they also face a number of markets or market segments in which they sell their product, it becomes likely that they will charge different price-cost margins on different transactions or in different segments of the markets they serve, i.e. firms will engage in price discrimination. For this reason, industries characterised by price differences that cannot be fully explained by differences in the costs of supply are an extremely pervasive phenomenon in real world markets.

## Loyalty rebates do not inevitably foreclose competitors

**6–051** The hostile policy stance towards loyalty rebate schemes stems primarily from focusing solely on the incentive properties of a rebate scheme at or around the threshold of eligibility for the rebate. This section explains why that focus on the "static" incentives of the scheme is inappropriate. Focusing on the last unit means that the competitive assessment fails to address other important issues, and in so doing fails to reflect the actual competitive dynamics observed in many industries. This section addresses two critical issues which lie at the core of an effects-based competitive assessment but which are absent from the current analysis of the competitive effects of loyalty rebates undertaken by the Commission and the Courts.

First, we explain why loyalty rebate schemes do not necessarily have exclusionary effects even when offered by dominant firms. Secondly, we provide a more complete analysis of the incentives at or around the threshold.

### *Loyalty rebate schemes are not necessarily exclusionary*

We presented above an analysis of a loyalty rebate scheme offered by Firm X. Figure 6.3 reproduces Figure 6.1 and considers how the effective prices facing a customer and therefore the incentives of that customer change as the volume of purchases increases. Assuming that a customer has already purchased volumes greater than B, the ability of rival firms to compete for volumes between that amount and the customer's total annual requirements will be extremely limited; the effective price for making additional purchases above B (but below C) is negative. **6–052**

## Figure 6.3 Incentive properties of loyalty rebate schemes

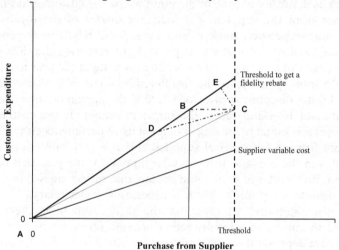

But rather than focusing on the incentives of the rebate scheme at a particular point in time (e.g. once the customer has purchased volumes greater than B), it is interesting and, indeed, more appropriate to consider the way in which this loyalty rebate scheme affects the customer's incentives throughout the period to which the loyalty rebate applies. As we shall see, a customer's incentives depend critically on the point at which the customer is making its purchase decisions throughout the qualifying period.

Once the customer has reached point B, the marginal price of buying the remainder of its requirements from the dominant firm is zero, so rival suppliers would need to work very hard to contest this slice of business. Beyond point B (at point E, for example), the effective marginal price to the customer of buying the remainder of its requirements from the dominant firm is actually negative, since the value of the prospective year-end rebate is greater than the price the customer needs to pay for the extra units.

267

6–053     But if one considers the choices available to consumers at some lower level of purchases, such as D on the dominant firm's list price curve, the incentives are less powerful. Although it is true that at this point it becomes expensive for the customer to contemplate shifting demand to a rival because to do so might result in the forfeit of the opportunity to earn the substantial loyalty rebate at the end of the year, the price for additional purchases is still positive. Figure 6.3 illustrates this incentive effect by reference to the slope of the line drawn between (in this case) point D and the discounted end-period point C. Having bought the majority of its requirements from the dominant firm at list price, the full value of the prospective year-end loyalty discount should be spread across the remaining purchases, giving a lower marginal price. Point D in Figure 6.3 has been constructed so that this marginal price (the slope of the line from D to C) is the same as the dominant firm's variable costs.

Going back further in time to the point where the customer has made no purchases from the supplier, the incentive effects of the loyalty rebate scheme might be even weaker, and indeed the rebate may provide no incentives to divert sales at all. At point A (representing the time prior to the agreement of a supply contact or the beginning of the year to which the threshold applies), the price that is offered by the loyalty rebate scheme is essentially the discounted price of €1.90 if the customer stays "loyal" to the dominant firm and meets the target threshold. If the customer can easily meet this target by buying enough of its requirements either from the dominant firm or from a rival supplier, this is a very simple choice. The rival will win the business if it can offer a price for the year that beats the dominant firm's offer of €1.90, and the fact that the rebate is expressed as a loyalty deal does not imply that it is necessarily exclusionary.

This discussion makes it clear that the likely competitive effects arising from the incentives of a loyalty rebate scheme (even a retroactive rebate scheme) are dependent on the customer's available effective options. First, if customers are in a position to evaluate the offer from the origin (point A), and if they have the clear option to trade off the dominant firm's loyalty rebate offer against similar offers made by rival suppliers, then the shape of the discount profile tells us nothing about its effect on competition. As long as the customer can credibly threaten to buy enough of its requirements from the dominant firm's rivals, it will be able to assess the value-for-money offered by the dominant firm's loyalty rebate offer against the alternative of switching demand to the dominant firm's rivals. In terms of Figure 6.1, the customer will simply compare the dominant firm's discount offer (shown by point C in Figure 6.1) with the alternative offer made by rival suppliers. Having done so, the particularly powerful incentives that come into play at or close to the "last unit" may not arise; customers respond to the incentives provided by the scheme as a whole rather than those that arise as their level of purchases approach the threshold.

*Incentive properties of loyalty rebates are more complex than just considering the "last unit"*

As noted above, both the Commission and the European Courts presume **6–054** that loyalty rebate schemes inevitably involve customers switching part of their requirements to the dominant firm offering the loyalty rebate scheme.[144] But underlying this strong presumption are three assumptions as to the behaviour of customers.

1. First, customers are able to disregard the interests of their own clients (i.e. the final consumers).

2. Secondly, the use of target thresholds gives each customer an "overwhelming incentive" to favour sales of the products of the dominant firm over sales of products supplied by other firms.

3. Thirdly, what is true for an individual customer applies to the market as a whole.

We address each of these issues in turn.

*Intermediate customers are unlikely to be able to disregard the interests of final consumers*

It should be noted that in most industries loyalty rebates apply to inter- **6–055** mediate customers and those intermediate customers possess some ability to influence the purchase decisions of their own customers. This might take the form of pre-sales advice, in-store placement or retail discounts (i.e. price inducements). It is for precisely this reason that suppliers seek to provide appropriate incentives to their customers to promote their products rather than those of a competitor. The use of discount schemes simply represents in many industries only one form of competition between suppliers.[145] Focusing only on one parameter of competition (i.e. the incentive effects of loyalty rebates) will ignore other important, often much more important, parameters of competition. For example, in the *BA/Virgin* case,[146] the Commission effectively assumed that the only parameter of competition between airlines was the incentive schemes provided to travel agents; the price of air travel, the quality of service and other forms of competition (e.g. advertising and in-flight service quality) were simply not considered to be relevant.

Moreover, in many industries, a supplier's customers will themselves

---

[144] Neither the Commission nor the Courts have explained why the same "loyalty inducing" effects of such rebate schemes do not apply equally to non-dominant firms.
[145] Where all firms in the industry employ loyalty rebates, regardless of whether they are large or small, this ought to give rise to a presumption that there is a pro-competitive rationale for such conduct.
[146] Cited at fn.132 above.

operate in a competitive market. A supplier's customers compete with one another to deliver the best possible service to their own clients. Competition may take place with respect to quality of product or service, the ability to meet consumer requirements and, of course, the price of those products or services. An intermediate customer that is unable to fulfil final consumers' requirements will be unlikely to retain that business over time.

*Intermediate customers do not necessarily have an "overwhelming incentive" to promote the sales of the dominant firm*

**6–056** Even if it were supposed that a supplier's customers were able to exercise considerable control over the purchases of their own clients, it is not clear that the structure of loyalty rebate schemes necessarily results in the dominant firm being favoured over competitors. If a customer can choose among suppliers, with no adverse effects on its business, its preference will accord with its expectations as to which products will contribute to the highest revenue possible over the year. But this does not imply that the customer *will always* necessarily choose to buy from the dominant firm.

This can be seen in the following simple example. In this example, it is assumed that, in this case, intermediate customers can, with no adverse effects on their business, sell products or services that yield the highest revenue for themselves. Consider two suppliers, a dominant supplier A and a competing but smaller supplier B. Both suppliers operate loyalty rebate schemes which are based on customers reaching a target threshold. Once that target threshold has been reached, a retroactive discount is granted on all purchases.

Table 6.1 shows the target thresholds set by two competing suppliers. In this simplified example, the loyalty rebate scheme of each supplier contains only one target threshold for each retailer.[147] The threshold for Supplier A is set at 220 which, reflecting its larger size of operations, is four times the threshold set by Supplier B. The price per unit is assumed to be the same for both suppliers at €20 per unit up to the threshold. We also assume that the revenue earned by the customer on each unit sold is constant and the same for the products purchased from each supplier. If a customer reaches the target threshold set by a supplier, it receives a discount on all sales of €10 per unit.

---

[147] The consideration of multiple thresholds does not significantly alter the conclusions to be drawn from this example.

## Table 6.2 Incentives for customers under different sales scenarios

|  | Supplier A | Supplier B |
|---|---|---|
| **Target Threshold** | 220 | 55 |
| Cost per unit (€) | 20 | 20 |
| Discount per unit if threshold is met (€) | 10 | 10 |
| **Current Sales** | | |
| Scenario #1 | 210 | 50 |
| Scenario #2 | 230 | 50 |
| Scenario #3 | 230 | 60 |

Table 6.2 shows the current level of sales of a particular customer in three **6–057** different scenarios. In scenario #1, the customer has not yet reached the target threshold for either supplier. In scenario #2, the customer has already exceeded its target for Supplier A but not for Supplier B, and in scenario #3, the customer has exceeded the target thresholds for both suppliers.

Now suppose the customer has the option of choosing between purchasing an additional 10 units from supplier A or B. As the following shows, it is not necessarily the case that the customer will choose to buy additional units from the larger supplier. Rather, the customer's choice of which supplier to use will clearly depend on which scenario we are considering. Assuming that the list price is the same for the products of both suppliers, the customer will seek to direct sales towards the supplier that generates the greatest increase in discount arising from the structure of the loyalty rebate scheme.

Table 6.3 shows the additional cost of purchasing these additional 10 units relative to the assumed level of sales under the three scenarios described in Table 6.2.

## Table 6.3 Choices of customers under different sales scenarios

|  | Supplier A | Supplier B |
|---|---|---|
|  | **Incremental Cost** | **Incremental Cost** |
| Scenario #1 | – €2,000 | – €400 |
| Scenario #2 | €100 | – €400 |
| Scenario #3 | €100 | €100 |

In scenario #1 in Table 6.3, purchasing an additional 10 units of Supplier **6–058** A's products will imply that this customer will increase its purchases from Supplier A to 220 and therefore meet the target threshold which implies a rebate of €10 on all units purchased. Purchasing the additional 10 units costs €200 (i.e. €20 times 10 units) but results in a rebate of €2,200 (i.e. €10 times 220 units). In other words, purchasing an additional 10 units from Supplier A results in a rebate of €2,000. This can be compared with the additional cost of choosing to purchase an additional 10 units from Supplier B. In this case, total purchases from Supplier B increase to 60 and therefore the customer would also meet the target threshold set by Supplier B. Purchasing the additional 10 units costs €200 (i.e. €20 times 10 units) which is the same as selling the products of Supplier A. The customer also benefits from the rebate from meeting the target threshold. But in this case, the rebate is much smaller; the customer only receives a rebate of €600 (i.e. €10 times 60 units). In other words, purchasing an additional 10 units from Supplier B results in a cost saving of €400, compared to a saving of €2,000 if buying from A. In this case, the customer will choose to purchase from Supplier A, the larger firm.

But in scenario #2, this is no longer the case. The customer has already reached the threshold target for Supplier A. This implies that purchasing an additional 10 units from Supplier A does not trigger the retroactive discount; although the customer still receives the rebate on these additional sales, there is no additional benefit to be had on previous purchases. Purchasing an additional 10 units from Supplier A results in an increase in costs of €100 (i.e. €10 times 10 units). But purchasing another 10 units from Supplier B in scenario #2 implies that the customer meets the target threshold set by that supplier. This implies that although the costs associated with purchasing the additional 10 units is higher at €200 (since unlike purchasers from Supplier A, the customer has not yet reached the threshold), the customer receives a rebate of €10 on all 60 units purchased from Supplier B. This implies that in choosing to purchase an additional 10 units from Supplier B results in a rebate of €400. This is clearly a more attractive option than choosing to purchase from Supplier A.

In scenario #3, where the customer has met the threshold targets of both suppliers, the customer will be indifferent as to which supplier's products he purchases; the cost will be €100 (i.e. €10 times 10 units).

**6–059** This simple example highlights another important element of the analysis which is typically totally disregarded in the competitive assessment of loyalty rebates, namely, the level at which the target is set. If suppliers set too high a target then its customers' purchasing decisions will not be affected; why should customers bother to direct sales to the dominant entity if they have no prospect of reaching the target? Conversely, if the supplier sets the target threshold too low then the customer may be able to reach the target without engaging in any directional selling or other efforts on behalf of the dominant supplier. In this case too the target threshold has no effect on customer incentives. It is by no means obvious that the customer will always seek to favour the larger supplier even when the strong assumption is made that the customer can choose, without detriment, which products to purchase.

Hence, with respect to the second assumption, despite the Commission's presumption that loyalty rebate schemes necessarily bind customers to the dominant firm, a much more careful analysis than is suggested by the approach adopted by both the Commission and the Courts is required. In assessing the competitive effects of loyalty rebate schemes, the assessment must go beyond merely stating that the scheme gives customers incentives to purchase greater volumes from the dominant firm; that should be self-evident. As the above simple examples demonstrate, this is true even for retrospective rebate schemes that set certain targets for customers and grant those customers that meet such targets a discount that applies to all units and not just the additional ones purchased above the target.

*It is the aggregate effect of customers that matters*

The Article 82 Guidance states that the Commission will consider **6–060** whether:

> "[T]he rebate system is capable of hindering the expansion or entry even of 'as efficient' competitors *by making it more difficult for them to supply part of the requirements of individual customers*" (emphasis added).[148]

But it is incorrect to assume that what applies to an individual customer necessarily applies to the market as a whole. The concept of foreclosure relates to the market as a whole; what matters is whether there is sufficient room for a rival to operate efficiently. This can occur if either: the loyalty rebate covers only part of each customer's requirements; or rival firms can obtain sufficient volumes from those customers that choose not to respond to the incentives provided by the loyalty rebate of the firm held to be dominant. Indeed, in many markets in which firms offer loyalty rebates, some customers will choose to purchase primarily from the market leader and others will choose to purchase primarily from rival firms. Moreover, the choices that individual customers make as to which products they purchase in any given year may vary.[149]

## Circumstances when loyalty rebates become exclusionary

The above analysis indicates that it cannot be assumed that a loyalty rebate **6–061** scheme employed by a dominant firm gives rise to anti-competitive outcomes. However, this is not to say that such practices are *never* anti-competitive. This section considers the circumstances in which loyalty rebates employed by a dominant firm might be held to be abusive.

---

[148] Article 82 Guidance, para.40.
[149] This was a feature of the UK travel agency industry in terms of which airline each travel agent chose to promote in any given year.

The analysis corresponding to Figure 6.3 stated that, at the beginning of the rebate scheme, equally efficient rivals can compete effectively against the dominant firm. But a different analysis might apply if the appeal of the dominant firm's brand is such that the customer has a strong pre-disposition to buy a substantial proportion of its requirements from the dominant firm, and therefore the best outcome that a rival supplier can realistically expect to achieve is to secure, say, one-third of the customer's requirements. Such sales might be called the dominant firm's *assured base*.[150] In the presence of an assured base, a loyalty rebate scheme can have a significant effect on a customer's choices. Starting from a point part-way along the customer expenditure profile, the effective price for additional purchases from the firm can be much lower. If that effective price falls below a supplier's marginal cost of supply, the fear of exclusionary effects becomes greater because the rebate scheme involves pricing those contestable units below the supplier's avoidable costs.[151] The Article 82 Guidance considers foreclosure to arise if the effective price is below average avoidable cost. This does not in itself establish that the rebate scheme is abusive, since a finding of some prices below variable costs does not in itself establish an exclusionary economic effect. It does, however, begin to build a picture of exclusionary effects.

To see the impact of such an assured base of sales for the competitive effects of a loyalty rebate scheme offered by a firm held to be dominant, consider Figure 6.4.

**Figure 6.4 The impact of an assured base of sales on the competitive effects of rebate schemes**

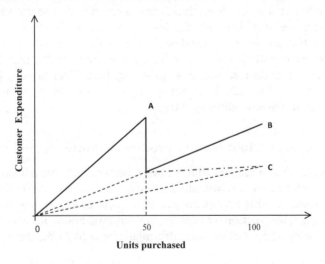

[150] See Article 82 Guidance, para.41.
[151] Article 82 Guidance, para.43.

Figure 6.4 shows a loyalty rebate scheme in which the firm charges €20 per **6-062** unit for all purchases up to 50 units and then offers a retrospective rebate of €10 per unit for all sales above 50. Marginal costs are assumed to be constant at €5 per unit. Overall, the loyalty rebate scheme involves above-cost pricing—at any volume of sales, total revenue exceeds total cost of production. For example, at 100 units, revenues equal €1,000 and costs equal €500.

However, it is clear that if the firm has an assured base of sales of 30 units (for whatever reason) then the overall loyalty rebate scheme can be seen to be exclusionary in the sense that the additional revenues earned on an extra 20 units of sales are below the incremental costs of making those sales (incremental revenues equal −€100, whilst incremental costs are €100).[152] In effect, the loyalty rebate provides a mechanism for the firm to target the effective discount on those volumes that are "open" to competition.

Although an assured base of sales may be very difficult to identify in practice and may differ across customer types, this stylised framework nevertheless provides a useful starting point. First, it demonstrates that a loyalty rebate scheme can, in principle, be used to target a lower price on a range of sales open to competition in the same way that a dominant firm can selectively reduce prices in one market where it faces entry but leave prices high in another market where it does not face the prospect of competition.[153]

Secondly, it provides a framework for assessing the likelihood of fore-closure by "allocating" the discount inherent in the loyalty rebate scheme to the range open to competition. In the above example, the entire rebated discount is allocated to the last 20 units and excludes the assured base of 30 units. This approach allows safe harbours to be devised on the assumption that: (a) an assured base of sales exists; (b) sales could be made at the list price for that assured base; and (c) the appropriate measure of cost does not vary significantly according to the identification of the assured base. These assumptions permit the whole of a discount to be attributed to the range of sales assumed to be open to competition. The larger the assumed assured base, the easier it will be to engage in exclusion. If we are confident that the discount has been "over-allocated" to that range and the implied price for sales in this range *exceeds* average avoidable cost this will typically indicate that the discount scheme does not give rise to foreclosure concerns.

In summary, reference can be made to the same economic principles that have been used to analyse predatory pricing by considering whether the

---

[152] Incremental revenues are −€100 because total revenues fall from €600 to €500. Incremental costs are €100 because this is the cost of producing an extra 20 units at €5 per unit.
[153] There is also a link to the tying and bundling literature. The discount on the range open to competition can be thought of as being conditional on the pre-purchase of the assured base.

discounted price lies above the appropriate measure of cost.[154] If so, the loyalty rebate scheme most likely represents a form of price competition, and an equally efficient rival could match the discounted price.

## TYING AND BUNDLING

### Introduction

**6–063** This section sets out the economic principles of tying and bundling. Tying and bundling refer to sales strategies where firms offer a combination of distinct products. It is useful to differentiate between the following strategies.

- pure bundling;
- mixed bundling; and
- tying.

If two products A and B are only sold as a bundle then the practice is referred to as pure bundling. Mixed bundling refers to a situation where A and B are available separately but are offered at a discount if bought together. Tying usually refers to a situation in which customers that purchase product A are also required to purchase product B; product A is known as the *tied product* and Product B as the *tying product*.[155]

Table 6.4 illustrates the differences between these concepts.

### Table 6.4 Options available to buyers under tying and bundling

|  | Options available to buyers |
|---|---|
| **Tying** | X + Y<br>Y |
| **Pure bundling** | X + Y |
| **Mixed bundling** | X + Y<br>X<br>Y |

The potential competition concerns raised by tying and bundling practices relate to the ability of a dominant firm to use such practices strategically to

---

[154] See paras 6.84 et seq for a detailed discussion of identifying predatory conduct.
[155] The Article 82 Guidance also considers multi-product rebates under the heading of tying and bundling. See paras 58 to 60. The analysis of multi-product rebates is similar to single product rebate schemes considered in paras 6.37 et seq.

foreclose rivals or soften competition in the tied product market. The Article 82 Guidance state[156]:

> "[A]n undertaking which is dominant in one product market (or more) of a tie or bundle (referred to as the tying market) can harm consumers through tying or bundling by foreclosing the market for the other products that are part of the tie or bundle (referred to as the tied market) and, indirectly, the tying market."

The competition concern in the context of bundling and tying is therefore a   **6–064** theory of harm whereby a dominant firm can *leverage* (i.e. extend) its dominance in one market to a related but separate market which would otherwise be competitive. As a result of such leveraging that second market would be less competitive and, in some theories, the firm's dominant position in the tying market would also be protected to the ultimate detriment of consumers. Under such leveraging theories of harm, a dominant firm can combine two products and achieve higher profits from the bundle or tie than the sum of the profits that can be earned by selling each product separately. An early example of the Commission investigating this issue is provided by *Hilti*, where the Commission expressed concerns that Hilti was using its monopoly of nail gun cartridges (the tying good) to increase prices in the market for nails for nail guns (the tied good).[157]

However, tying and bundling are common business practices that are routinely engaged in by firms, including non-dominant firms. As noted above, that fact alone indicates that there are pro-competitive reasons for firms to engage in tying and bundling. Indeed, the bundling of different components to create a product that is preferred by consumers to assembling the components themselves is an ubiquitous feature of practically all manufacturing industries. A good example of such a "value-adding" "bundle" would be a car, which comprises a bundle of an engine, wheels, and many other components ranging from satellite navigation systems to cup-holders. The production process of mass market car assembly makes it prohibitively expensive for consumers to buy and assemble a car from individual components; scale and scope economies make a centralised production process by the car manufacturer more efficient and is the main reason for bundling in this case.

As in the case of other potential exclusionary abuses, therefore, it cannot be assumed that tying and bundling represent per se abusive conduct even when undertaken by dominant firms. This section therefore discusses in more detail the pro-competitive rationales for these practices before

---

[156] Article 82 Guidance, para.48.
[157] *Eurofix-Bauco v Hilti* (IV/30.787) [1989] 4 C.M.L.R. 677; [1988] OJ L65/1, December 22, 1987.

turning to those circumstances in which tying and bundling can lead to the foreclosure of competitors and to the detriment of consumers.

## Pro-competitive rationales for tying and bundling

**6-065** A number of efficiency reasons for why firms bundle have been advanced.[158] In addition to the assembling benefit noted above, efficiencies arising from tying and bundling include providing a form of price discrimination, quality improvement and addressing pricing inefficiencies.[159]

As discussed in paras 6–029—6–036, price discrimination typically has ambiguous effects on social welfare and on consumer welfare. An example of tying acting as a form of price discrimination arises where the tying product requires an input that can potentially be competitively supplied (e.g. computer games consoles require games, printers require ink and photocopiers require paper). If a monopolist ties sales of the tied product (e.g. games, ink or paper) to sales of the tying product, he can use his sales of the tied product effectively to charge more to those consumers who are heavy users of the tying product than to those consumers who are light users of the tying product (hence this practice is often referred to as *metering*). In this way he can potentially increase his profits. The social and consumer welfare effects of this practice can be ambiguous. However, to the extent that tying of this form leads to more consumers buying the tying good, it is likely to increase both social welfare and consumer welfare. If the monopolist prices the tied product above the competitive price level and prices the tying product below the competitive price level, then he may be able to increase the total number of sales of the tying product.

**6-066**

> **BOX 6.4: METERING AS WELFARE-ENHANCING PRICE DISCRIMINATION**[160]
>
> The key in the following example of metering is that the tying allows the monopolist to price discriminate between consumers and so provides the monopolist with an incentive to set prices which allow more consumers to be supplied. In other words, not being able to price discriminate can lead to the exclusion of some consumers. The result is that in this example tying raises social and consumer welfare.
>
> Suppose that there is only one type of computer games console and that it is supplied by only one firm at a production cost of 2. Assume that the market for the software games for the console is perfectly competitive and that the marginal cost of production of games is zero.

---

[158] See Nalebuff (2003).
[159] The pricing efficiencies that can be achieved via bundling parallel the efficiency arguments in vertical mergers where a double mark-up problem can be mitigated.
[160] This discussion owes much to Viscusi, Vernon and Harrington (1995).

This implies that the price of the games is also zero. For expositional ease, we assume that there are only two consumers (A and B). The demand curves for games of these two consumers are $Q_A = 8 - 2p$ and $Q_B = 16 - 4p$ where $Q_i$ is the demand for games of consumer i and p is the price of games. Under perfect competition, the games are priced at zero and so all the area under the demand curves is consumer surplus. This consumer surplus dictates the maximum amount that a consumer would be willing to pay for the games console. A consumer will not pay more for a games console than the consumer surplus he derives from the games. Figure 6.5 illustrates the level of consumer surplus for the two consumers.

**Figure 6.5 Consumer surplus of two computer games buyers**

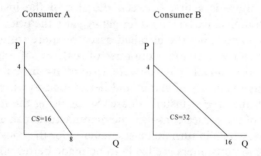

The consumer surplus figures in Figure 6.5 indicate that the best strategy for the monopolist is to set a price of 32 for the consoles. Consumer A will not buy a console since the maximum he would pay for one is 16. However, Consumer B will buy a console. This will provide the monopolist with a profit of 30 (i.e. the price of 32 minus the production cost of 2). If the monopolist wished to sell consoles to both consumers, the highest price he could charge would be 16. This would yield a profit of only 28 (i.e. the price of 16 minus the production cost of 2, twice).

Now suppose that the monopolist will only allow games that he supplies to be used on his console (e.g. via some licensing procedure or technical tweak to the console). The monopolist would be the sole supplier of games and so would not have to price them at marginal cost. The profit-maximising price of consoles is now 9 and the profit-maximising price of games is now 1. Both consumers buy consoles, Consumer A buys 6 games and Consumer B buys 12 games. Total revenue to the monopolist is 36, costs are 4 and so profits are now 32. In effect, the monopolist sets prices so that consumer A is now served.

Tying can also give rise to another potential efficiency where the products **6–067** supplied are durable. Consider a durable good (e.g. a printer) in which the production of the inputs to that durable good (e.g. ink cartridges compatible with the printer) is subject to economies of scale. A monopolist of the durable good (the tying good) could create a technical tie so that he is the only supplier of the input (the tied good). He could then increase the price of the input good and use the extra profit earned to lower the price of the durable good. This will increase demand for the durable good, which in turn will increase demand for the input good. If there are economies of scale in the input good, this will lower the average cost of the input good and may allow its price to fall, thereby increasing demand for the input good, and potentially increasing demand for the durable good.

Computer games consoles provide another example of this phenomenon.[161] Here the tie is technical: games in the format specific to the manufacturer's console must be purchased in order to use the console. In these markets, there is a link between the size of the installed base of consoles, which then drives demand for games, and the price and variety of games available. The larger the installed base, the more software is written for that format as the extreme economies of scale of software (effectively zero marginal cost) mean that software writers are primarily concerned about selling large volumes of games and hence tend to write primarily for the format with the largest installed base. So by using the technical tie to lower the price of the games consoles, the manufacturer can ensure a better supply of games, which in turn increases demand for the consoles. Both the manufacturer and consumers are likely to be made better off by this. This type of approach is not uncommon in markets where there is consumer resistance to the initial cost of buying the consumer durable. Mobile phones are another example of this, where mobile phone handsets are typically subsidised by network operators, who then recoup the revenue from the increased number of calls that result from having a larger installed base of subscribers.

Bundling can also be used to engage in pro-competitive price discrimination. By selling two products both separately and as a bundle, a firm can capture the demand not just of those that value one or either product highly, but also the demand of those who value both products somewhat less. An example should make this clear. Suppose a firm prices Products A and B at €10, but the bundle of A plus B at €15. Those who value either A or B at more than €10, but the combination of both at less than €15, will buy one or other product. Those who value neither product at more than €10, but do value the combination at more than €15, will buy the bundle. These are consumers who would not buy any product in the absence of the bundling, so they gain from the bundling. The manufacturer may also gain. He gains extra sales by selling the bundle but does not lose any sales that he previously made. The only way in which he may lose out is that consumers who previously bought both products for €20, now buy

---

[161] See Katz and Shapiro (1994).

them for €15. But it is clear that mixed bundling can potentially increase the welfare of the manufacturer and consumers.

Bundling can also be pro-competitive when it allows firms to protect **6-068** their reputations and brand names. Where complex products have to work together with other complex products, firms may be concerned that they will get blamed when one of the complementary products malfunctions because consumers may not be able to tell which part of a system of complementary products has malfunctioned. In cases such as these, a firm may prefer to bundle all the complementary products together. This is particularly likely to be the case in high technology markets such as software. However, it should be noted that this justification for bundling is not always plausible. There are many examples of complex complementary products being sold separately (i.e. not as part of a system). Examples include software and expensive hi-fi equipment.[162]

Finally, tying and bundling can give rise to pricing efficiencies. Where the competitive relationships between two firms can be described as complementary, the sales of each product increases if the price of the other is lowered. This relationship is known as the *Cournot effect* and is equivalent to the issue of double marginalisation that arises in the context of vertical relationships.[163] The importance of the Cournot effect is due to its very broad applicability. In order to fully reap the benefits of the internalisation of this pricing externality, complementary products need to be sold jointly through tying or bundling. The reason for this is that, if products are sold individually, customers are free to "mix and match" components of different brands, so that rival firms may appropriate part of the gains from a price reduction. In those cases, the magnitude of the efficiency gain will depend on the portion of customers who buy the products together even without a tie.

This is not to deny that tying and bundling when engaged in by a dominant firm can under some circumstances result in the foreclosure of rivals or the softening of competition in the tied product. However, any such theory of harm needs to address the simple and powerful "Chicago school" argument, to which we now turn.

## Chicago school argument

Any theory of harm based on leveraging market power in one market into **6-069** another must address the question of whether a firm with significant

---

[162] AT&T in the United States used to have a monopoly over the manufacture and installation of telephone equipment, in addition to its monopoly of the network. It justified maintaining these monopolies on the grounds that it was necessary to ensure the equipment worked with the network and did not damage it. When AT&T was broken up it became clear this was an unnecessary concern. Rather than the result being widespread system problems, the result was the growth of an innovative and competitive telephone equipment market.

[163] See Chapter 8 for further discussion of the Cournot effect.

market power in one market can increase its profits by combining this product with a product that is sold in a competitive market. The Chicago school response to this question is negative; a monopolist can only earn a "single monopoly profit".

Consider the situation where only a monopolist supplies product A, which is used by consumers in combination with a complementary product B that is supplied competitively. By tying A and B, the monopoly supplier could easily "extend" its monopoly position from A to A+B in that its share of sales of B could be increased. However, since a monopolist of A should already have set a price for A that maximised the profits from doing so, after imposing the A+B tie the monopolist should not be able to command more than the competitive margin on sales of B (see Box 6.5 for a more detailed explanation of this point). Hence, the artificial "monopoly" over B created by the tie with A does not deliver an additional monopoly profit. Moreover, if there is a possibility that B can be supplied by a third party at a cost below that which the monopolist could achieve, or if rivalry between suppliers of product B creates diversity and/or innovation that the monopolist would not have offered, then the monopolist of A would strictly prefer not to engage in tying. In that case, the demand for A increases if B is sold at a lower price, and therefore the value of the monopoly of A also increases. A tie which excludes a more efficient supplier of B would therefore lead to lower profits for A compared to a scenario without the tie.

**6–070** 

---

**BOX 6.5: THE CHICAGO CRITIQUE**

Assume that there are two products, Product X and Product Y, that are consumed in fixed proportions and that all consumers have exactly the same preferences (i.e. homogeneous consumers).[164] Assume that Product X is monopolistically supplied and consumers value it at $P_X$. That is, consumers are willing to pay up to $P_X$ for Product X but no more. Conversely, assume that the market for Product Y is perfectly competitive with many suppliers able to supply the product in the absence of tying and that all consumers value Product Y at $P_Y$. For simplicity, it is assumed that Product Y is supplied with constant unit costs $C_Y$. Given that the market for Product Y is perfectly competitive in the absence of tying, this implies that the price for Product Y in the absence of tying would be $C_Y$.

What does this imply about the price of Product X in the absence of tying? Since the two products are consumed in fixed proportions, any

---

[164] The assumption that all consumers have exactly the same preferences is made for simplicity. It is not central to the underlying result.

consumer who buys Product Y must also need to buy Product X. Consumers are willing to pay up to $P_X + P_Y$ for the two products, so if they are paying $C_Y$ for Product Y, they will be willing to pay $P_X + P_Y - C_Y$ for Product X. Hence consumers will pay a total of $P_X + P_Y$ for the two products in the absence of tying (i.e. $P_X + P_Y - C_Y + C_Y$). Now consider what happens if the monopolist ties sales of Product X to sales of Product Y. The monopolist now effectively charges just one price for the two products. Given that consumers value the two products at $P_X + P_Y$, this is the most that the tying monopolist can charge for the two products. So consumers pay the same amount under tying or in the absence of tying.[165]

Accordingly, the Chicago school argument holds that firms engage in tying and bundling behaviour for efficiency reasons and not for anti-competitive strategic reasons. Any market power that firms may have is, according to that argument, already fully exploited in the absence of tying and bundling.

## Post-Chicago arguments

The Chicago school argument that firms can only earn a single monopoly **6–071** profit has an appealing simplicity. However, that argument relies on assumptions which if they do not hold may serve to undermine the logic of the Chicago school argument. Post-Chicago theories of harm essentially build on the simple Chicago view by adding more complexity by considering situations where the tied market is not characterised by perfect competition and also including a dynamic perspective to the analysis.[166]

Depending on the exact nature of competition, tying and bundling can be used both to soften price competition and to exclude or deter rivals from remaining or entering the market. However, in practice, the main competition concern relates to the alleged exclusionary impact of tying and bundling. For that reason, we consider this concern first.

### *Exclusionary behaviour*

The first category of post-Chicago theories of harm concerns the classic **6–072** leverage of market power argument. According to this view a monopolist of A can use a tie of A and B to force competitors in B out of the market. This could occur if a stand-alone provider of B finds it more difficult to compete with the monopolist who can make an integrated offering.

Consider the case of a firm that currently sells more of a product that it monopolises (X) than of a product that it does not monopolise (Y).

---

[165] It is simple to confirm that the monopolist's profits are the same under the two scenarios (i.e. $P_X + P_Y - C_Y - C_X$ where $C_X$ is the unit cost of Product X).

[166] See, for example, Whinston (1990) and Carlton and Waldman (2002).

Further, assume that Y is subject to imperfect competition, i.e. prices exceed short-run marginal cost.[167] What happens if the firm decides to bundle X and Y together so that consumers must purchase Y if they want to also purchase X? Whereas previously the firm could sell more of X than of Y, it now, by definition, has to sell the same number of each. This gives the firm an incentive to lower the effective price of Y in order to maintain sales of X (where the firm earns monopoly profits). Previously, failing to sell a unit of Y damaged the firm by an amount equal to the profit on each unit of Y.[168] In the presence of bundling, however, failing to sell a unit of Y damages the firm by an amount equal to the profit on each unit of Y plus the monopoly profit on each unit of X. The firm will therefore price Y more aggressively (lower) than in the absence of bundling. This will tend to benefit consumers unless the reduction in price results in other firms being driven from the market and, in consequence, permits prices to increase in the longer term to the long-run detriment of consumers.

If the firm ties Y to X, rather than bundling them (i.e. consumers can still buy Y separately), the firm still has an incentive to compete more aggressively in the market for Y because each sale of Y also leads to a sale of X, but the incentive is reduced because a lost sale of Y does not automatically imply a lost monopoly profit on X. Consumers who choose not to buy Y might still buy X separately.

**6–073** Related to the "classic" theory of harm, another post-Chicago theory of harm relates to the protection of monopoly power in one market. Suppose there is a possibility that a monopolist's position may erode over time as competitors in a related market B would find it easier to use their position as suppliers of product B as a platform from which to enter market A at some point in the future. Then the dynamic incentives of the monopolist are changed.[169]

According to the Chicago view a monopoly supplier in one market (market A) has an interest in the competitive provision of complementary products (market B). If the supply of those complementary products is competitive, then this boosts demand for not only those products but also for the monopoly product. However, if at some point in the future an efficient supplier of the complementary products would be in a position to enter the market A and compete against the monopoly supplier, then a post-Chicago view would introduce the possibility that the monopolist might seek to bundle the monopoly product with the complementary products and in so doing restrict competition in market B by foreclosing rivals in that latter market. This may not necessarily lead to higher profits in market B, and indeed if the monopoly supplier's product offering in market B is less attractive to consumers relative to the products offered by

---

[167] Whinston (1990).

[168] Given the assumption of imperfect competition (i.e. downward-sloping demand curves), this is not precisely correct. However, the fundamental point should be clear.

[169] Nalebuff (1999).

competing firms, that might reduce demand in market A. But by delaying or foreclosing rivals' development in market B, the monopolist might be able to protect its monopoly position by strategically tying products in market A with those in market B.

Bundling can also be used to make it harder for firms to enter markets (or to remain in markets). Assume a firm is currently a monopolist of two goods, X and Y, and bundles them together as well as selling them separately.[170] An entrant who wishes to enter just one of the markets, say the market for X, may be at a significant disadvantage to the incumbent. This is because consumers who value both X and Y highly will likely prefer to buy the bundle rather than buying from the entrant. The entrant will only be able to win sales from those that value X highly but do not value Y much. If demand for the two products is complementary (i.e. those who value X tend to value Y and vice versa), there may be only a limited part of the market for X that is available to the entrant. If, in addition, there are economies of scale in production, entry may not be viable.[171]

An alternative response in this case would be for the entrant to enter two **6–074** markets simultaneously. However, this may be very difficult, more risky or even impossible. It may be impossible if the entrant does not have a product that he can offer to compete in both markets and is not able to find a partner with whom he can create a bundle. Where one of the products is protected by intellectual property rights, entering with a bundle may not be possible as the entrant may not have access to the relevant intellectual property rights. This suggests that this sort of entry deterrence strategy may be particularly successful in high technology markets that are based on intellectual property rights which have very severe economies of scale (e.g. effectively zero marginal costs). Also, entry is typically risky and two-product entry is likely to be riskier than single-product entry in that both firms have to pass the "market test" of meeting the demands of consumers, rather than just one.

Another relevant factor is that competition between bundles of products may be fiercer than between individual products for reasons similar to those outlined above.[172] Where both products sold in a bundle are priced above their respective marginal costs of production, each lost sale of the bundle of products increases the costs to the bundling firm. The intuition for this is similar to the intuition outlined above. In such circumstances, a

---

[170] This analysis is based on Nalebuff (1999).

[171] The *Microsoft Internet browser* case may have been an example of this. It is alleged that Microsoft bundled its internet browser with its Windows operating system in order to deter entry into the browser market. Demand for the Windows operating system and an internet browser is likely to be highly complementary. Note that when demand is highly complementary, it may well be rationale to integrate products, as Microsoft did with Windows and the browser, because consumers typically want both "functionalities" and would prefer them in a seamless product. This is a pro-competitive rationale for bundling or tying.

[172] Nalebuff (2001).

lost sale represents a loss of two margins rather than just one. This induces firms to price lower than if a lost sale represented a loss of only one margin.

It should be noted that bundling can also be a costly strategy for firms to adopt. Offering products in a bundle is likely to be costly if consumers typically do not want both products. In this case sellers cannot price the bundle much above the cost of the products separately and so they incur the marginal cost of the extra product without earning much revenue to cover this cost. That is why the assumption of complementarity between products was important in the analysis above. However, where marginal costs are low, as in information markets such as software, the cost of including extra products in the bundle is very low. This means incumbents may be able to price the bundle at very close to the price of the products separately, which makes single-product entry hard with even a small amount of complementarity.

### Softening price competition

**6-075**  Tying and bundling can also lead to a softening of price competition.[173] Consider an example in which there is a homogeneous product supplied by two firms (i.e. a duopoly). In the absence of tying under conditions of effective competition we would expect to observe fierce price setting competition. However, if one of these firms enjoys a monopoly over the supply of another product, a tie between this product and the competitively supplied product will lead to an increase in the price of the tied product. This price increase arises because the impact of tying is to make the tied product a differentiated product (i.e. it is no longer equivalent to the other product in the tied market). This reduces the amount of direct competition that the other duopoly product faces from the now tied product. So the other duopoly product will increase its price, which in turn allows the price of the tied product to increase.[174] The result is that profits of both firms increase to the detriment of consumers.[175] If the firm engages in mixed bundling instead of tying, the effect on prices will be lessened as the degree of differentiation between the products offered by the duopolists will be less. There are now two homogenous products and one differentiated product, rather than just two differentiated products.

---

[173]  See, e.g. Whinston (1987 and 1990), Carbajo, De Meza and Seidmann (1990), Seidmann (1991) and Kobayashi (2005).

[174]  It is a standard result in the literature that prices under differentiated products Bertrand competition are higher than those under homogeneous products Bertrand competition.

[175]  Although there is nothing wrong with the analysis here, we would be surprised if antitrust authorities were ever in a position to take action against behaviour of this type. There is no exclusion and competitors are unlikely to since they benefits from the behaviour of the tying firm. It will therefore be very difficult to identify such behaviour.

## *A framework for evaluating tying and bundling*

A useful initial screen for determining whether bundling or tying might give   **6–076**
rise to anti-competitive outcomes is as follows.[176] First, the firm must have
substantial market power, i.e. it must be dominant. Secondly, there must
be demand complementarity between the products in the bundle. If there
is not complementarity and instead the products are independent in
demand, then it is very difficult to create theories of harm that are profitable to the dominant firm. Bundling products that are independent in
demand is likely to reduce sales significantly. Thirdly, there must be significant asymmetries in the product lines of the firms, with the dominant
firm having a longer product line than its competitors. If the product lines
are not asymmetric, then competition between the similar bundles will be
very fierce.

If these three conditions hold, then it is at least plausible that bundling
by a dominant firm could be anti-competitive. It would then be necessary
to provide a coherent theory of harm under which bundling lowers either
current or future competition and to provide some empirical evidence that
the theory of harm is likely to be true. For instance, have prices increased
since the bundling started? Has exclusion occurred? Has rival firms' R&D
expenditure declined?

Finally, it is important to understand whether there are reasons for the
bundling that do not rely on anti-competitive exclusion or a softening of
prices. If a dominant firm cannot provide such a rationale for its bundling,
then this increases the concern that the bundling is anti-competitive.

## Case law criteria for establishing that tying and bundling conduct is abusive

The primary decision in applying Article 82 to tying and bundling practices   **6–077**
is *Microsoft*.[177, 178] Tying and bundling issues were also addressed in a
number of non-horizontal mergers, most notably in *Tetra Laval/Sidel* and
*GE/Honeywell*.[179] In determining whether tying or bundling infringes
Article 82, the Court of First Instance laid down five conditions in
*Microsoft*.[180]

These conditions are:

---

[176] Kuhn, Stillman & Caffarra (2005).
[177] Case T-201/04 *Microsoft Corp v Commission* (T-201/04) [2007] E.C.R. II-3601; [2007] 5
C.M.L.R. 846.
[178] See also *Tetra Pak v Commission* (C-333/94 P) [1996] E.C.R I-5951; [1997] 4 C.M.L.R
662.
[179] COMP/M 2416 *Tetra Laval/Sidel* (2001) and on appeal *Commission v Tetra Laval BV* (C-
12/03 P) [2005] E.C.R. I-987; [2005] 4 C.M.L.R. 573 and COMP/M 2220 *GE/Honeywell*
(2001) and on appeal *General Electric v Commission* (C-210/01) [2005] E.C.R. II-5575;
[2006] 4 C.M.L.R. 686.
[180] See *Microsoft*, fn.177 above, at paras 842, 859–867 and 869.

1.  there must be dominance in the supply of the tying product;

2.  the tying and tied good must be two separate products;

3.  the tying product is not offered without the tied product;

4.  the act of tying forecloses stand-alone competitors; and

5.  the tying conduct cannot be "objectively justified".

We consider each of these conditions in turn.

### Dominance in tying product

**6–078**  The first condition to establish tying or bundling as abusive conduct is to find the undertaking dominant in the supply of the tying product. It is not required to establish dominance in the tied market.

### Separate products

**6–079**  The second necessary condition of a tying abuse is that the tying and the tied product are "separate products". In *Microsoft*, the Court upheld the Commission's reasoning in this regard.[181] The Commission essentially relied on existing case law where the criterion of independent stand-alone providers emerged to define separate products. Specifically, the Commission noted that in the previous *Hilti*[182] and *Tetra Pak II*[183] cases, the Court:

> "[P]ointed out that there existed independent manufacturers who specialised in the manufacture of the tied product, a fact which indicated that there was separate consumer demand and hence a distinct market for the tied product."[184]

This might seem at first glance to be a simple "common sense" approach. However, defining separate products is not a trivial matter and the focus on actual competitors (or stand-alone demand) in the tied product as part of the process of distinguishing tying from other value-added combinations raises many problems that are not fully appreciated by the CFI Judgment.

The Article 82 Guidance defines products as distinct with reference to customer demand[185]:

[181]  See para.44 of the judgment.
[182]  Judgment of the Court of First Instance in *Hilti v Commission* (T-30/89) [1991] E.C.R. p.II-1439.
[183]  Judgment of the Court of November 14, 1996 in *Tetra Pak v Commission* ("*Tetra Pak II*") (C-333/94 P) [1996] E.C.R. I-5951.
[184]  Commission Decision at para.802.
[185]  Article 82 Guidance, para.50.

"Two products are distinct if, in the absence of tying or bundling, a substantial number of customers would purchase or would have purchased the tying product without also buying the tied product from the same supplier, thereby allowing stand-alone production for both the tying and the tied product."

But as noted above, practically all manufacturing industries involve a degree of "bundling" of separate components, and virtually every product or service supplied by profit-seeking firms can be decomposed into various elements that have been "bundled" together in the manufacturing or supplying process. However, no economic principles exist to determine where one product should end or another begins. This is problematic because it means that the line between tying (which is perceived as problematic) and normal value-adding economic activity (which is not) is hard to draw.[186]

### Tying product not offered separately

The third criterion applied by the Court concerned whether the tying and   **6-080** tied products are offered separately. In *Microsoft*, the Commission noted that Microsoft's licensing model required that Windows Media Player (WMP) is pre-installed within the Windows operating system.[187] Moreover, it was also impossible to uninstall the WMP from Windows due to the high degree of integration with other components of the operating system.[188] For those reasons, the Court held that the consumer was coerced into "purchasing" Media Player even though there was no additional cost to doing so. Moreover, rival media players were (and remain) available to consumers to download free of charge. It is at least arguable that the tying of the Windows operating system to WMP did not preclude rivals from continuing to offer their media players in competition to WMP; the problem for rival media player suppliers was not that the bundling of WMP into Windows put them at a price disadvantage, but rather that it increased the convenience to consumers of opting for WMP, and that this added convenience might tip the market towards WMP and against competing products.

### Foreclosure

The fourth, and the most important, criterion to assess anti-competitive   **6-081** tying is concerned with foreclosure of stand-alone providers. It is important to note that tying and bundling conduct that harms competitors does not

---

[186] For example, it is possible to buy shoelaces as a stand-alone product in grocery stores and many shoe shops, but that does not make it suspicious that sellers of new shoes typically deliver their products bundled with shoelaces.

[187] Commission Decision at para.827.

[188] Commission Decision at para.828.

necessarily harm competition. As the approach set out in the Article 82 Guidance makes clear, tying and bundling conduct even when undertaken by dominant firms should not be condemned unless it can be shown that consumers are harmed. In establishing that such practices are anti-competitive it is therefore critical that a coherent explanation of how harm to competitors translates into harm to consumers.

In *Microsoft*, the CFI agreed with the Commission's finding that the inclusion of WMP in the Windows operating system led to the foreclosure of the market.[189] In addition to noting the disincentives of customers to download and of OEMs to install competing media players, the CFI accepted the Commission's arguments relating to "dynamic" foreclosure arguments. By denying rival media player suppliers sufficient market penetration, software developers would stop using the format of these competitors and that would make them even less attractive to consumers and ultimately they would be forced to leave the market.[190]

*"Objective justification"*

6–082　The final criterion to consider when evaluating tying practices is the existence of an "objective justification", the precise meaning of which remains unclear. However, it would appear to cover a range of possible factors such as safety considerations and maybe some efficiency arguments in defence of tying. In *Microsoft*, the CFI considered that there was no objective justification for tying WMP to the Windows operating system.[191]

## Conclusions

6–083　Despite the Chicago critique, the intuitive concern that tying and bundling can be anti-competitive is a legitimate concern under some circumstances. The Chicago critique relied on there being perfect competition in the tied good market and on the products being used in fixed proportions. When competition in the tied good market is imperfect, tying and bundling can lead to the exclusion of rivals and to the softening of price competition. Post-Chicago theories therefore show that uncertainty about the future (e.g. erosion of monopoly power) or foreclosure of competitors by committing to compete fiercely in a related market can overturn the traditional view that there exists only a single monopoly profit in any one transaction.

However, it is important not to lose sight of the fact that tying and bundling often represent pro-competitive practices even when engaged in by dominant firms. Indeed, describing a theory of anti-competitive leveraging is not the same as establishing actual competitive harm to consumers. Economic analysis indicates that tying and bundling can have both pro-

---

[189] See *Microsoft*, fn.177 above, at paras 1031–1096.
[190] *Microsoft*, fn.177 above, at para.1060.
[191] *Microsoft*, fn.177 above, at paras 1144–1167.

competitive and anti-competitive effects. This implies that each case should be considered on its merits and there should not be per se rules against tying and bundling even when such conduct is engaged in by dominant firms.

## PREDATORY BEHAVIOUR

One of the benefits of competition is the downward pressure it provides on **6-084** firms' pricing strategies. Loosely speaking, competition prevents firms from profitably increasing prices above competitive levels. In general, therefore, low prices ought to be welcomed. However, in some instances prices can be so low as to be detrimental to competition. Such pricing behaviour is deemed to be predatory. Predation is said to occur where aggressive competition, normally in the form of low prices, either induces firms to exit the market or deters new firms from entering.[192]

The Article 82 Guidance states that:

> "[A] dominant undertaking engages in predatory conduct by delib- erately incurring losses or foregoing profits in the short run ... so as to foreclose one or more of its actual or potential competitors with a view to strengthening or maintaining its market power, thereby causing consumer harm".[193]

A number of points can be made regarding this definition of "predation". First, the predating firm should enjoy substantial market power.[194] In other words, predation is unlikely to be feasible if a firm only possesses market power. Without dominance, the possible exclusion of some competitors generally does not weaken competition, and therefore it is unlikely that the firm would be able to recoup the losses incurred in pricing low. Secondly, it needs to be demonstrated that the predating firm has accepted a reduction in its short-run profits, i.e. its pricing conduct has involved a sacrifice of short-run profits. Thirdly, the firm's sacrifice should lead to the foreclosure

[192] Various definitions of "predatory behaviour" have been advanced in the academic lit- erature. Ordover and Willig (1981) define predatory actions as those that are unprofitable without the exit of a competitor that it causes. Evans and Schmalensee (2001) define predatory acts as those that are rational only if they chasten or eliminate competition. Fisher (2000) suggests that predation involves the deliberate sacrifice of profits in order to gain or protect a dominant position. Viscusi, Vernon and Harrington (2005) define pre- datory conduct as behaviour "calculated to exclude from the market an equally or more efficient competitor". These various definitions differ. For example, whereas Ordover and Willig and Viscusi et al. all require the exit of a competitor, Evans and Schmalensee require only that competition is "chastened", whilst Fisher focuses on the acquisition or main- tenance of a dominant position.

[193] Article 82 Guidance, para.62.

[194] See paras 6–004—6–005 where we discuss the correspondence between the legal concept of dominance and the economic concept of significant market power.

of competitors and as a result the dominant firm's market power is strengthened with consequent adverse effects for consumers.

It can immediately be seen that identifying predatory behaviour raises the difficulty of distinguishing between low prices that are the product of competition and low prices that harm competition. As noted in para.6–006 abusive conduct is conduct that not only harms competitors but also harms competition; and harm to competition involves, as the Article 82 Guidance definition of "predatory conduct" acknowledges, harm to consumers in the form of higher prices.[195] Since harm to competitors is a necessary consequence of competition, it is not sufficient in allegations of predatory pricing to show that rival firms are losing share in response to keen pricing by more efficient or innovative firms.

**6–085** For this reason, the key element in determining whether low pricing conduct represents normal competition or predatory conduct relates to whether the dominant firm is pursuing business conduct that involves foregoing or sacrificing short-run profits. However, as we shall see, determining whether short-run profits are being sacrificed is itself a difficult and complex task.[196] Given these difficulties, it is appropriate to take into account those other factors that constitute a complete assessment of predatory conduct, in particular the likelihood of recoupment.

The remainder of this section is organised as follows. We first provide an expanded discussion of the basic intuition underlying predatory conduct; predatory conduct essentially involves "investing" in short-run losses in order to benefit from higher prices in the future. Although its intuition is clear, the concept of predatory conduct has been subject to criticism on theoretical grounds. We therefore consider three possible theories of predation that have been advanced to address these theoretical criticisms. We then turn our attention to the critical issue of how to identify when pricing conduct can be correctly characterised as being predatory. We then summarise the case law covering predatory conduct with reference to some of the most important cases. Since predatory conduct does not always involve low prices, we consider potential non-price forms of predatory conduct. Finally, we consider predatory conduct in hi-tech industries.

---

[195] Harm to consumers can also arise if predatory conduct prevents new attractive products becoming established on the market. Of course, this raises the question of whether the firm failed due to predatory conduct or because the products were not as attractive to consumers as claimed.

[196] Reflecting on this difficulty, Bork (1978) has stated that:

"It seems unwise, therefore, to construct rules about a phenomenon that probably does not exist or which, should it exist in very rare cases, the courts would have grave difficulty distinguishing from competitive price behaviour. It is almost certain that attempts to apply such rules do much more harm than good." (p.154)

## The intuition of predatory conduct

The simple predatory pricing argument has two stages. In the first stage, a **6–086** predating firm (usually assumed to be dominant) reduces prices to such levels for a sustained period of time that its competitors leave the market.[197] In the second stage, the predating firm raises prices to such an extent that it earns higher profits; the short-run losses associated with predatory pricing are outweighed by the long-run excess profits. In other words, the short-run loss arising from the low pricing strategy represents an investment in market power.

The time path of profits to the predating firm is shown in Figure 6.6.

## Figure 6.6 Current and net profits from predating

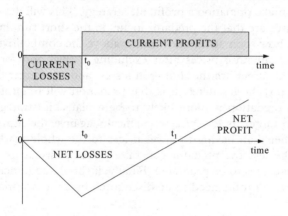

Figure 6.6 shows that the predating firm suffers increasing losses until time $t_0$, at which point the rival firm leaves the market. The predating firm is then able to raise prices above the competitive level and therefore make profits over the long run sufficient to outweigh any short run losses. In Figure 6.6 the predatory strategy leads to net losses up to time $t_1$, and to net profits thereafter.

A profitable, and therefore credible, predatory strategy requires that **6–087** once competing firms have been forced to exit the market, re-entry does not occur when the predating firm seeks to increase prices. In other words, a credible predatory strategy requires there to be barriers to entry. If there were no barriers to entry or to re-entry, then once the predator raised prices, firms would enter the market and undercut the price rise.[198] The

---

[197] However, the Commission argues that predatory conduct does not require the exit of competing firms. See Article 82 Guidance, para.68 and, for a case example, *Wanadoo Interactive* [2005] 5 C.M.L.R. 120.

[198] Note that if the assets of the firm that was predated upon had not degraded significantly since exit, re-entry may be relatively easy, either by the original owner of the assets or by a new owner. For this reason, it might pay the predating firm to buy these assets, so that they cannot be used by a rival for entering the market.

implication of this is that the (allegedly) predating firm would not be able to make excess profits even if it did drive its competitors out of the market. In terms of Figure 6.6, the "Current Profits" box would never outweigh the "Current Losses" box and so the firm would never move into net profit from engaging in predation. Predating would not represent a profitable, and therefore not a credible, strategy. Note that under these circumstances, any attempt at predation would only serve to increase consumer welfare. Consumers benefit from low prices in the short run and do not face anti-competitively high prices in the longer run. However, as we discuss below, a predating firm may be able to create barriers to entry endogenously and thus make predation a possible strategy that does cause consumer harm.[199]

It should also be noted that even if a predating firm can raise prices above the competitive price level after excluding a rival, this may not be sufficient to make predation a profitable strategy. This will depend on how great the losses are that the predator incurs in the short run, how long the short run is, how soon and by how much above the competitive price level the predator can raise prices after excluding a rival and for how long. Obviously, the larger are the short-run losses, and the longer they have to be incurred for, the less likely it is that predation will be profitable. This implies that predation is more likely to be a plausible strategy when the predator can target its low prices specifically against the firm it wants to exclude, rather than having to lower prices to the whole market. Equally obviously, the less the predator can raise prices post exclusion, the less likely the strategy is to be profitable. Finally, it should be remembered that future uncertain profits need to be discounted by an appropriate discount rate.[200]

---

[199] An example of an attempt at predatory pricing that was unsuccessful due to a lack of entry barriers is given by the Empire Gas Corporation in the 1970s. Empire Gas Corporation set very low prices (below the wholesale price) in some of its markets in order to drive competitors out of the market. In many cases, it was successful in driving out competitors or in convincing them to raise their prices. Unfortunately for the Empire Gas Corporation, the lack of entry barriers meant that where competitors exited, other firms entered and where prices rose initially, they soon returned to their previous (pre-predation) levels. Overall, the strategy is said to have lost money. This example is reported in Tirole (1988), who cites Easterbrook (1981).

[200] As McGee (1980) argued:

"If we look at predation as an investment to achieve or increase future monopoly profits, we should keep the arithmetic straight. Future monopoly profits must be discounted appropriately, and may be a long time in coming, if they come at all. Near-term costs weigh more heavily and are more certain.

A one-dollar loss incurred today costs one dollar. At a 10% discount rate, an additional dollar profit three years hence is worth about 75 cents. A dollar profit deferred for five years is worth only 62 cents. If it cannot be realized in 10 years, it is worth only 38.5 cents."

## Economic theories of predation

Traditional arguments regarding a firm's incentive to predate centred on **6–088** the idea that the predator might have access to greater financial resources than the prey (which might be a small firm or new entrant) and might therefore be able to sustain the losses incurred by predating for a longer time period than the prey could sustain the losses incurred by competing given the predatory price. The profit achieved by charging a high price in the recoupment period after the small firm had left the market could justify the profit sacrifice incurred by the predator to induce exit.

Whilst this "deep-pockets" story has intuitive appeal, it is far from satisfactory, in its traditional form, as a theory of predation. The problems with the traditional view of predation were set out by McGee (1958). The greatest challenge to "the 'deep pockets' story" focused on the central assumption that the predator has access to greater financial resources than its prey.[201] Without this assumption in place it would not be possible for the predator to sustain losses for longer than an (equally efficient) prey. Predation would ultimately fail to eliminate a non-financially constrained equally efficient rival and so would not be attempted in the first place. In this rebuttal of the "traditional" theory of predation, sources of finance (e.g. banks) would understand that predation of the efficient rival could not be successful absent a financial constraint, and so would be willing to lend to the prey. Critics of the traditional theory of predation noted that it provided no sound reasons why the target of predatory conduct should be subject to financial constraints.[202]

This critique helped to focus attention on the issues that would need to be addressed by any coherent economic theory of predation. Three potential theories of predation have been advanced. Each of these theories shows that in the presence of imperfect information predation may indeed be profitable.

---

[201] Other elements of the critique included the observation that the costs to the larger firm resulting from predation should be greater than those to the smaller firm because of its larger output base; the observation that the small firm could re-enter once the price rise had taken place; and the observation that the large firm could eliminate its rival in a less costly way simply by acquiring it. These challenges were subsequently largely addressed by those pointing out that the large firm could reduce prices selectively so as not to incur costs over its entire output base; that entry and re-entry might not be possible as a result of sunk costs; and that predation could form part of a strategy to reduce the acquisition price of a rival. In addition, merger control may mean that a firm does not have the option of acquiring a rival.

[202] In addition to McGee, other economists offering critiques of the traditional view included Bork (1978) and Easterbrook (1981).

### *"Deep pockets" or financial market models of predation*

**6–089** Deep pocket or financial market models of predation focus on explaining how the financial constraint described above may indeed arise for the prey in the presence of imperfect capital markets. Imperfect information on the side of financial institutions is shown to give rise to the possibility that predation affects the perceived risk of lending money to the prey and, therefore, endogenously creates a financial constraint.

Financial institutions may not be able to observe how a firm will use the funds they make available. To protect themselves, they may only provide credit to a firm which has an asset base of a certain size. By predating, the dominant firm can reduce the prey's profits, erode its assets and therefore reduce its ability to borrow.

The key assumption that makes this possible is that the financial institution cannot observe the actions of the managers of the borrowing firm.[203] If it could, the financial institution might be able to stop predation from occurring by announcing that it will make funds available to the prey no matter how much its profits are adversely affected. However, without being able to observe the prey's actions, the financial institution cannot be sure in the event that profits turn out to be low whether this is because managers performed poorly (for example by spending funds inefficiently) or whether this is because the firm fell victim to predation. Knowing that the financial institution will not find it optimal to commit to providing unlimited funds to the prey no matter how poorly it performs, and that it can affect the willingness of the financial institution to lend to its rival by engaging in predation, the dominant firm may successfully eliminate its rival by engaging in predation.

### *Signaling models of predation*

**6–090** Signaling models of predation are based on the idea that firms do not have knowledge of each other's costs.[204] Due to this lack of information, a dominant firm may have an incentive to "signal" its costs to rivals through prices. If the incumbent charges prices that are lower than those that would maximise its profits in the short run, potential entrants may interpret this as a signal that the incumbent has low costs. As a result, the potential entrant may conclude that the incumbent would be able to compete fiercely in case of entry and may consequently refrain from entering altogether. The

---

[203] Telser (1966) was one of the first to suggest that a sound financial base (i.e. deep pockets) may be associated with predation. This idea was further developed in a series of economic models by Benoit (1984), Bolton and Scharfstein (1987) and Fudenberg and Tirole (1986).

[204] The first signaling model of this kind was developed by Milgrom and Roberts (1982) in the context of market entry. Their work was further extended by Roberts (1986) and Scharfstein (1984), who provide models of post-entry predation.

incumbent knows this and hence may, under certain circumstances, find it profitable to sacrifice short-run profits in order to deter entry by influencing the entrant's beliefs about the strength of post-entry competition.

The model assumes that the incumbent may be of two types: strong (if its costs are low) and weak (if its costs are high). The entrant does not know the incumbent's costs, but can observe prices charged by the incumbent before deciding whether to enter the market. The entrant would prefer to enter if it knew the incumbent was weak, but would rather stay out if it knew the incumbent was strong.

The model shows that two different types of scenario are possible. In the first, a low cost incumbent finds it profitable to set a price below its short-run profit-maximising level that, crucially, is just low enough for it not to be profitable to charge were it to have high costs. By pricing in this way the incumbent sends a clear signal to the entrant that it is indeed strong, which, in turn, precludes entry. The entrant will only enter if it observes the higher price that would be chosen if the incumbent was weak. It is important to note that whilst in this scenario the strong firm sets a price below its short-run profit-maximising level, deters entry and earns higher profits in the future as a result, this behaviour is socially beneficial. The entrant would have, in any case, not wanted to enter if it had known the firm was strong. The signal provides the potential entrant with valuable information and results in higher welfare for consumers during the period of reduced pricing.

In the second scenario, predation takes place. A weak incumbent finds it **6–091** profitable to set a price below its short-run profit-maximising level that is equal to the price a strong incumbent would have chosen if it were profit maximising. As such, the weak incumbent mimics a strong incumbent. The price the potential entrant observes in the market conveys no information about the costs of the incumbent, and the entrant must therefore rely on some prior belief about whether the incumbent is strong or weak. If on the basis of those prior beliefs the entrant prefers not to enter, the weak incumbent can successfully deter entry by pricing in this way. In this case, the predatory behaviour deters entry that would (under full information) have taken place. To the extent that the gains to consumers from the lower initial price (which the weak incumbent had to charge to hide its high costs) do not outweigh the losses to consumers from the subsequent elimination of competition, then this type of predation can lead to consumer harm.

## Reputation models of predation

A firm may be able to establish a reputation for being "tough" or aggressive **6–092** when it comes to defending their markets from entry. Despite the fact that building this reputation may be costly in the short term, it may pay off in the long run. The reason is that, once established, the reputation serves as an "asset" that helps to discourage future entrants.[205]

Thus, even if there are no structural barriers to entry that would prevent firms from entering once the predator raises prices, the fear of a predatory response to entry may lead to a behavioural barrier to entry. This deterrence effect makes it easier to recoup the short-run losses by raising prices in the future and may thus reinforce the incentive to predate.

Reputation models typically consider a situation in which the incumbent has to defend a number of similar markets from a series of entries. The original example used in the economics literature is that of the incumbent owning a chain of stores in several different cities, with one potential entrant in each city.[206] Where a firm operates in a number of markets, it can establish a reputation for engaging in predatory behaviour by competing aggressively in those markets where it faces entry. The benefit of this "investment" in predatory behaviour is not limited to the market where entry occurred: the aggressive response will deter potential future entrants in all markets and therefore facilitate the maintenance of high prices in all markets. As a result, competition authorities often regard predation as a feasible strategy if a large, multi-market firm responds aggressively to a smaller, start-up entrant. This is frequently alleged in liberalised industries where large incumbents face entry by smaller, newly established rivals.[207]

**6–093** The following example can be used to illustrate how aggressive responses to new entry can be designed to establish a reputation that deters future entry. Consider a firm that is currently a monopolist. Consider also the decision facing a new entrant and how the monopolist should respond to such entry.

Figure 6.7 shows three possible outcomes. If the entrant decides not to enter, the monopolist continues to earn monopoly profits. However, if the entrant decides to enter, then the monopolist must decide whether to price aggressively in response to such entry or to accommodate it.

---

[205] Kreps and Wilson (1982) and Milgrom and Roberts (1982).

[206] This example is originally due to Selten, who called it "the chain–store paradox"; see Selten (1978).

[207] Although, of course, all behaviour that deters entry is not thereby predatory. The announcement of a new technology that drastically cuts production costs in an industry and is patented by the incumbent would lower potential entrants' expectations of the profitability of entry. However, introducing a new technology and putting a patent on it would not normally be termed predatory.

## Figure 6.7 Possible incumbent responses to entry

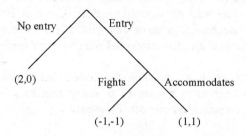

The numbers in brackets at each end point indicate the profits of the incumbent and the potential entrant. If the potential entrant does not enter, the incumbent gets profits of 2 and the potential entrant makes 0. If the potential entrant enters and the incumbent "fights" this entry, then both make profits of −1 (i.e. losses). If the potential entrant enters and the incumbent "accommodates" entry by adjusting his prices to reflect the new competitive environment, then they both make profits of 1. If this was a one-off situation, clearly the potential entrant would enter and the incumbent would accommodate such entry. Predating (i.e. fighting) would make no sense, the potential entrant would know this and so he would enter.

But now suppose instead that the incumbent firm is a monopolist in 10 **6–094** separate relevant geographic markets. In this case, what happens in one market can potentially affect competition in other markets. Suppose that there is just one potential entrant in each market (i.e. 10 potential entrants in total). If a potential entrant enters in market one and the incumbent predates (fights), what is the response of the potential entrants in the other nine markets likely to be? It is plausible that the response of entrants will be to stay out of the industry, because they are concerned that the incumbent, who has already shown a propensity to fight, will respond aggressively to any entry. Depending on the exact pay-offs, it may well make sense to fight (predate) in more than one market. In the example above, accommodating entry in 10 markets gains the incumbent 10, whilst predating in three and being a monopolist in the other seven gains him 11.[208] Note that this theory does not rely on predatory pricing in particular. Any form of predation is adequate. Predation might take a number of other forms.

A possible example of aggressive responses to entry designed to create a reputation for predatory behaviour is provided by General Foods in the United States in the 1970s. General Foods was the producer of Maxwell

---

[208] A similar analysis applies when instead of facing potential entry in different geographic markets, the monopolist faces the possibility of entry into a given market at various different times in the future. Thus predating in response to entry in a particular market now might allow the monopolist to create a reputation for predation that deters potential entrants from trying to enter that market in the future.

House Coffee. At the time General Foods had a market share in the eastern states of about 45 per cent. When Folger's, a brand based in the western states, tried to enter various eastern markets General Foods responded with sharp price decreases in those markets where Folger's had entered. This strategy successfully discouraged Folger's from further entry in the eastern states.

In the *Microsoft* case Judge Jackson concluded that Microsoft had earned a reputation for aggressive responses to entry that had led to firms not trying to compete against Microsoft. He wrote:

> "Most harmful of all is the message that Microsoft's actions have conveyed to every enterprise with the potential to innovate in the computer industry. Through its conduct toward Netscape, IBM, Compaq, Intel, and others, Microsoft has demonstrated that it will use its prodigious market power and immense profits to harm any firm that insists on pursuing initiatives that could intensify competition against one of Microsoft's core products. Microsoft's past success in hurting such companies and stifling innovation deters investment in technologies and businesses that exhibit the potential to threaten Microsoft. The ultimate result is that some innovations that would truly benefit consumers never occur for the sole reason that they do not coincide with Microsoft's self-interest." (Findings of Fact, paras 411–412)[209]

**6–095** Another potential example of predation is provided by the airline industry. In the mid- and late-1990s there were a number of instances where low-cost carriers entered routes in the United States, where the incumbent major carrier on the route drastically lowered its prices and where the new entrant was as a consequence forced to leave the market. The US Department of Transportation (DOT) issued a consultative document devoted to precisely this problem. The DOT stated that:

> "DOT believes that the responses of some large, established carriers at their hub cities to service by small, new-entrant airlines have inhibited competition, resulting in higher prices for many passengers and preventing a large sector of air travel demand from being efficiently served. These responses, which protect major carriers' ability to charge higher prices in local hub markets, involve temporarily selling such large numbers of seats at low fares, comparable to new-entrant

---

[209] United States District Court for the District of Columbia, Civil Action No.98–1232 (TPJ): *United States of America v Microsoft Corporation; State of New York et al. v Microsoft Corporation; Microsoft Corporation v Eliot Spitzer, attorney general of the State of New York, in his official capacity, et al.*

fares, that by sacrificing profits in the short term, they force the new-entrant carriers to exit from the local market."[210]

Note that this example may well include elements of both reputation effects and financial muscle effects. The large carriers were likely to have a much greater ability than the new entrants to sustain short-run losses. The fact that there were virtually no new start-ups in the United States over a prolonged period at least raises the possibility that the major airlines built up a reputation for predation that successfully deterred new entry, although of course it may just have been that the degree of competition within the industry made entry unattractive.

## Identifying predatory conduct

As noted above, low prices are normally a beneficial feature of the com-   **6–096** petitive process. Identifying predatory conduct therefore raises the critical need to distinguish between low pricing conduct that is to be welcomed as a normal outcome of competitive behaviour and low pricing conduct that, despite delivering short-term benefits to consumers, is detrimental to the competitive process in the long run. This is far from straightforward. For example, how can one determine whether a price reduction in response to entry represents predatory behaviour or a normal competitive response? New entry will affect the demand curve of the incumbent so that for any given price the demand for the incumbent's product is likely to be lower than it was prior to entry. The incumbent's profit-maximising response to entry is therefore likely to involve a reduction in its prices, regardless of any predatory intent.[211] It is therefore clear that a price reduction in response to entry by itself cannot provide dispositive evidence of predatory behaviour. Note, however, that we should expect the price reduction to be associated with reduced sales if it is genuinely a profit-maximising response to the demand curve shifting in. An increase in sales compared to pre-entry levels is generally not consistent with short-run profit maximising behaviour.

The difficulty of distinguishing between competitive and anti-competitive price reductions is well recognised in both the economics literature and in the legal practice of the Commission and the Courts.

---

[210] US Department of Transportation (1998).

[211] Furthermore, the incumbent's price cut can be short-run optimal (i.e. not predatory) but still result in losses. For instance, new entry may drive the short-run competitive price below cost. The incumbent then needs to decide whether to make short-run losses or exit the market. If re-entry into the market is costly, it may well be optimal for the incumbent to remain in the market even though it is making losses. The real issue in this sort of case is that the entry is inefficient in the sense that it leads to there being too many firms in the industry given the prevailing cost and demand conditions. See *Aberdeen Journals* for an example of conduct that arguably fits this description. This case concerned the entry of a local weekly free newspaper and the responses of the incumbent newspaper publisher that competed with both a daily paid-for title and a weekly free newspaper.

When considering how to test for predatory pricing, it is important to remember that predation involves a short-run sacrifice of profits,[212] with the expectation of future increases in profits due to the exclusion of a competitor leading to a less competitive market structure. A complete economic assessment of predatory conduct therefore involves an analysis of the following three issues:

1. whether short-run profits are being sacrificed;

2. whether the strategy is likely to lead to the exclusion of a competitor; and

3. whether short-run losses will be recouped in the long run (i.e. it is plausible that the resulting long-run profits will more than compensate the alleged predator for the short-run profits that are sacrificed.)

We address these in turn.

### Sacrifice of short-run profits

**6–097** Predatory pricing involves the deliberate sacrifice of profits in order to induce a rival to exit the market. It is argued that the incurrence of these losses is irrational except as part of a predatory strategy. Such losses are "deliberately" incurred in the sense that alternative actions would have resulted in lower losses (or higher profits). The Article 82 Guidance considers that conduct involves a sacrifice of profits in the following circumstances[213]:

> "Conduct will be viewed by the Commission as entailing a sacrifice if the dominant undertaking, by charging a lower price for all or a particular part of its output over the relevant time period, or by expanding its output over the relevant time period, incurred or is incurring losses that could have been avoided".

Determining whether conduct involves sacrifice usually involves a comparison of observed pricing with an appropriate cost benchmark.[214] Following Areeda-Turner,[215] it is usually held that prices below the costs of production (i.e. short-run marginal cost) necessarily involve deliberate sacrifice; since each sale involves a loss, profits could be increased by reducing sales or ceasing to sell completely. Areeda-Turner proposed average variable costs as providing a reasonable approximation to short-run

[212] We note below that there are exceptions to this.
[213] Article 82 Guidance, para.63.
[214] We consider the scope for "above cost" predation in paras 6–099—6–100 below.
[215] Areeda and Turner (1975).

marginal costs. The assumption that short-run marginal costs and average variable costs are equivalent only holds in the long run. In the short run there can be considerable differences between them. For instance, in an industry that is currently characterised by considerable over-capacity, short-run marginal costs may be very low and considerably below average variable costs. Conversely, when capacity is very tight, short-run marginal costs may be considerably above average variable costs. A test that over-estimates the cost floor for predation in a slump (when there is excess capacity) and under-estimates it in a boom is clearly far from perfect.

However, the Article 82 Guidance proposes Average Avoidable Cost (AAC) as the appropriate benchmark for assessing whether a firm is deliberately sacrificing profits.[216, 217] Avoidable costs are those costs that a firm avoids if it stops carrying out a particular activity.[218] If the revenues that a firm derives from a particular activity are less than the costs that the firm would save (avoid) if it ceased that activity, then the firm would be better off ceasing the activity. So if a firm is pricing below average avoidable costs, then it is making short-run losses relative to the alternative of not carrying out the activity at all. In general average avoidable costs will be above average variable costs because avoidable costs include fixed costs that are avoided by ceasing an activity.[219] Thus, the Commission will hold that a price below AAC should be considered as involving a sacrifice of short-run profits and therefore as being predatory.

However, tests of sacrifice based on a cost benchmark raise a number of difficulties. First, over what time period do we consider costs to be avoidable? The longer the time period considered, the more categories of a firm's cost of operations will become avoidable.[220] For example, over a one-week period, staff costs might not be considered as avoidable but over a **6–098**

---

[216] Article 82 Guidance, para.63.

[217] The Article 82 Guidance states at fn.40 that:

> "In most cases AVC and AAC will be the same, as often only variable costs can be avoided. However, in circumstances where AVC and AAC differ, the latter better reflects possible sacrifice: for example, if the dominant firm had to expand capacity in order to be able to predate, then the sunk costs of this extra capacity should be taken into account in looking at the dominant firm's losses. These costs would be reflected in AAC, but not in AVC".

[218] The adoption of AAC provides two main advantages over the use of AVC. First, it avoids the problem of having to achieve a precise distinction between fixed and variable costs within the specific period. Secondly, it provides a more accurate measure of the avoidable losses than AVC since it also includes the product-specific fixed costs that could be avoided by stopping the production of the product or service in question. As a result, it provides a closer reflection of whether it would be more profitable for the firm to terminate the production than to engage in predatory pricing, i.e. it identifies those costs (variable plus fixed) which dictate the decision of whether to continue production.

[219] Avoidable costs differ from total costs in that they do not include common costs (i.e. costs that are jointly incurred across a range of products) or costs that are sunk over the relevant time period.

[220] See the decisions of the Commission and the European Court of Justice in *Akzo Chemie BV* [1982] 1 C.M.L.R. 273; [1981] OJ L374/1 for an arcane debate about what constitutes a variable cost.

one-year period, they might become avoidable. So the determination of AAC requires an assumption to be made about the relevant time period. There is no widespread agreement over the relevant time period and the Article 82 Guidance refers to the "relevant time period" but does not provide a precise definition of how such a period ought to be defined.

Defining the relevant time period as the period in which the alleged predatory conduct took place has some intuitive appeal.[221] But even here there are practical difficulties. Suppose a large firm lowers its price aggressively in response to a new entrant and that the new entrant exits in response to that pricing response. Whether that behaviour was held to be predatory would depend on how long it took for the entrant to exit the market. If the entrant exits almost immediately, then the period during which the "predation" took place is rather short because by assumption the entrant exited almost immediately. Given this short time period, few costs are likely to be avoidable and so the behaviour is less likely to be found to be predatory under the AAC cost test. But if the entrant remains in the market for a longer time period, more costs become avoidable and the AAC benchmark will increase, making it more likely that the behaviour would be found to be predatory. But it would not be satisfactory for the relevant cost benchmark for predation to depend at least partly on how much "fight" the entrant has.

Even if the above measurement issues could be adequately addressed, using AAC cost benchmarks to assess whether pricing behavior represents predatory conduct raises another issue; namely, there are a number of benign reasons why prices might be below AAC. These include promotional pricing, using spare capacity in an economic downturn, learning by doing, product obsolescence, short-run promotions and so on. Also, inefficient entry can lead to incumbents being forced to price below avoidable costs. Where a new firm enters a market that cannot in fact sustain further entry or where the new entrant enters with an unsustainable business model, it is likely that prices will be driven down to a point at which no firms earn profits and may even be pricing below avoidable cost. It would be absurd in such a case to insist that an incumbent firm must price above its avoidable cost in this case, particularly if this would imply its exit. Such a policy would effectively allow entrants to drive incumbents, and potentially more efficient rivals, out of markets. In other words, prices that result in short-run losses may indicate predation but not necessarily. It should also be recognised that companies can make mistakes; and hence

---

[221] The OFT in the United Kingdom holds that the time period is the period during which the price in question was in force or might have been expected to be in force.

"In general, the Director General will consider that the relevant timescale for the analysis of costs in assessing allegations of predation is the time period over which the alleged predatory price or set of prices prevailed or could reasonably be expected to prevail." (para.4.6 of OFT 414 (1999) *Assessment of Individual Agreements and Conduct*).

firms may seek to amend their strategies with the benefit of hindsight. While retrospection might indicate that an alternative course of action would have been more profitable, firms' decisions are necessarily based on an on-going, forward-looking perspective. In other words, what appeared to represent the most profitable strategy ex ante might turn out to be less attractive ex post.

For these reasons cost tests of predatory behaviour are recognised in the economics literature as providing a one-tailed test.[222] This implies that even when these cost tests are failed, allegations of predatory behaviour still require further substantiation.

### Above cost predation: prices above AAC

According to the Article 82 Guidance, the concept of sacrifice includes not **6–099** just pricing below AAC. The Commission may also assess whether "the allegedly predatory conduct led in the short run to net revenues lower than could have been expected from a reasonable alternative conduct".[223] The Article 82 Guidance states further that "[n]ormally only pricing below LRAIC[224] is capable of foreclosing as efficient competitors from the market".[225] In other words, prices above AAC could still be held to be predatory. We refer to this as *above cost predation*. It raises a number of difficult issues.

The first is that selling part or even all output at prices below LRAIC (or average total cost (ATC)) but above short-term AAC represents commonly observed pricing behaviour by firms (including non-dominant firms) in a wide variety of competitive markets. It is not uncommon for firms to incur losses from time to time for reasons other than as part of a predatory strategy. Indeed, many businesses are accustomed to making periodic losses and few have the option of closing for these periods and reopening when profits return. It is the nature of most businesses that they should remain operating even in periods of loss.[226] Such pricing behaviour can only raise competitive concerns in the long term, to the extent that an "as efficient" rival is unable to fully recover fixed costs and is forced to exit the market (or operate inefficiently) as a result of its financial constraints. It should be noted that these commercial realities were explicitly recognised by Areeda and Turner in their formulation of rules designed to detect predatory behaviour which has held that price above average variable costs but below average total costs may indicate predation but that other evidence is required.

Secondly, there can be difficulties in the calculation of LRAIC or ATC.

---

[222] See, for example, Rapp (1990). See also Posner (2001).
[223] Article 82 Guidance, para.64.
[224] LRAIC stands for long-run average incremental cost. It is similar to average total cost, although not exactly the same. See the cost annex to this chapter for further explanation.
[225] Article 82 Guidance, para.66.
[226] See Baumol (1996).

Specifically, where some costs are common across a number of products, there is no single economically correct way to allocate them and it would not be reasonable to find a firm guilty of predation on the basis that it is pricing below some essentially arbitrary measure of total product costs. Our view is that the test should at most include only those costs that are genuinely incremental to the product. This should be the logic of the LRAIC calculation.

**6–100** A third difficult issue arises when a new entrant initially has higher variable costs than an incumbent firm. This might be because there are significant learning-by-doing effects that allow firms to reduce costs once they have been in the market for some period. Or it might be that the variable costs associated with large-scale activity are lower than those associated with smaller scale activity.[227] In such a situation an incumbent might be able to drive an entrant out by pricing below the entrant's variable costs, not below its own variable costs. In this case a test based on the costs of the predator would not capture the predation. But equally, a test based on the costs of the rival would also be nonsensical: are firms to be accused of predatory behaviour whenever a rival finds itself unable to make any profit?

---

**BOX 6.6: ILLUSTRATING THE PROBLEMS WITH ABOVE COST PREDATION**

Suppose Domco makes widgets and gadgets from the same factory and is dominant in both. The factory has an overhead cost of 250 (in the form of a depreciation charge). Widgets and gadgets both cost 1 per unit to manufacture, and Domco makes 100 units of both, selling both products at 3 per unit. Hence total factory costs are 450, the ATC of widgets and gadgets is 2.25, revenues are 600 and profits are 150.

How can Domco respond if an entrant starts producing widgets at a price of 2? If it is constrained to price so as to cover ATC, its lowest admissible price is 2.25. In that case Domco might have to give up all its widget sales, and thus its widget business will make no contribution to overheads. As a result, its gadget sales become loss-making. Does it have to raise price there as well? Maybe it has to exit both markets? None of this makes any economic sense. Although Article 82 does permit a "meeting competition" defence that might apply to these circumstances; why should Domco be required to justify its behaviour where there is a no reason to suspect an abuse in the first place?

---

[227] It could be argued that competition policy should not protect inefficient entry of this type. However, entry of this type that had the potential to blossom into large scale activity might be desirable in a market with a dominant firm already in place.

Our view is that where a dominant firm prices above AAC, it is likely to be extremely difficult to distinguish harm to competition from harm to competitors. The use of above cost theories of predation therefore raises the real prospect of chilling competition unless there is a presumption that above cost pricing is not predatory. The corollary to this is that any competition authority that wishes to argue an above cost predation case should be put to a high burden of proof.

### *Likelihood of excluding "as efficient" competitors*

In determining the appropriate cost benchmark, it is the costs of the **6–101** dominant undertaking that are relevant rather than the costs of the new entrant. This is appropriate since, as the Article 82 Guidance states, consumers are generally not harmed if inefficient competitors are forced to exit the market; that is a beneficial hallmark of the competitive process. Rather, the object of concern is anti-competitive foreclosure, that is, foreclosure of "as efficient" competitors which is driven by anti-competitive behaviour and which is likely to result in consumer harm. According to the Article 82 Guidance, only pricing below long-run average incremental cost (LRAIC) is capable of foreclosing as efficient competitors from the market.[228] Although we agree that the benchmark should relate to as efficient competitors, we consider the LRAIC concept to be less appropriate for identifying and assessing predatory conduct than the AAC concept (see above).[229]

If there is no prospect of a firm being excluded, then predation is not a rational strategy that will harm consumers. An example should make this clear. In the United Kingdom the cable companies were accused of predatory pricing. The allegation was that by bundling TV and telephony together and pricing them jointly at almost the same price as they sold them separately, they were predating because the incremental prices of each service when offered with the other were below the incremental cost of each service. However, there was no need to go into great detail to understand the implausibility of the allegation. The firms that faced the alleged predatory pricing were British Telecom and BskyB. There was clearly no prospect of either of these firms being excluded from the market by the pricing of the cable companies, nor of them being disciplined into raising their prices. Where the claim that the behaviour will lead to exclusion is not plausible, it should not be necessary to analyse whether short-run losses are being incurred.

However, the Article 82 Guidance states that in identifying predatory conduct it is not necessary to show that competitors have exited the market

---

[228] Article 82 Guidance, para.66.
[229] See Annex to this chapter for a detailed discussion of the various cost concepts and their merits and de-merits in identifying exclusionary behaviour.

in order to show that there has been foreclosure.[230] To the extent that current conduct may not yet have succeeded in driving out rival firms but will likely do so in the future, this policy approach is sensible. However, the Article 82 Guidance appears to envisage going further than this:

> "It cannot be excluded that the dominant undertaking may prefer to prevent the competitor from competing vigorously and have it follow the dominant firm's pricing, rather than eliminate it from the market altogether".[231]

While in theory, this might represent a legitimate concern, in practice it will be highly speculative and almost impossible to prove (or disprove) since it requires one to establish that low prices today will lead to all firms pricing higher than the competitive (or pre-entry) price in the future. There is a real danger that this line of argument leads to translating harm to competitors necessarily into harm to competition.

### Recoupment

**6–102** Implicit in the definition of predation is the sense that the alleged predator is trading off short-run losses for long-term gains. Indeed, it is widely accepted (at least in the economics literature) that predatory pricing is an investment in enhanced market power: predating firms "invest" by incurring short-run losses in order to maintain a dominant position in the long run. But that trade-off implies that predation will be a rational strategy for a firm if and only if there is an expectation that the additional long-run benefits from operating in a market with one fewer competitor outweighs the losses incurred in inducing the exit of a competitor. In other words, a predatory strategy is only rational if short-run losses can be recouped.[232]

The recoupment of short-term losses depends not only on the ability of the alleged predator to induce the exit of efficient entrants but also that post-exit market conditions permit the increase of prices to levels that permit the "predatory investment" to be recovered. Whether that is the case will depend on a number of factors, including the ease with which firms can enter the market and also the response of customers to those price increases.

Hence, predation will only take place in those markets that have a structure conducive to the recovery of the predatory "investment". Unless the characteristics of competition permit the recovery of short-run losses, any predatory strategy will necessarily lead to a decrease in the net present value of the future profits of the firm. For this reason, the ability of the

---

[230] Article 82 Guidance, para.68.
[231] Article 82 Guidance, para.68.
[232] We note below that it appears that EU jurisprudence does not require a recoupment test.

alleged predator to recoup its investment (i.e. losses made in the short run) following the exit of the prey is a central feature of the economic literature on predatory pricing. Unless there is an expectation that any short-run losses can be recouped in the long run, low prices should not be held to be predatory. For example, Areeda and Turner state the following[233]:

> "Predatory pricing would make little economic sense to a potential predator unless he had ... (2) a very substantial prospect that the losses he incurs in the predatory campaign will be exceeded by the profits to be earned after his rivals have been destroyed".

Other commentators have expressed similar views and it is therefore generally agreed that recoupment is a necessary condition for a finding of predatory behaviour.[234]

Notwithstanding the economic literature, the Article 82 Guidance has **6–103** re-iterated case law that proof of recoupment is not a requirement for a finding of predation.[235] According to the Article 82 Guidance, in order to show consumer harm it is sufficient that the predator "is in a position to benefit from the sacrifice." (para.69). Thus the Guidance reiterates the old approach followed by the Commission in *Tetra Pak II*, and upheld by the CFI, according to which proof of recoupment is not a requirement for a finding of predatory pricing. Indeed the Guidance states that proof of overall profits is not required, and likely consumer harm can be demonstrated by a number of factors such as the presence of barriers to entry associated with likely foreclosure effects of the conduct.[236] In the Commission's view, it is sufficient that the predator is likely to benefit from the sacrifice without having to prove how future profits will achieve supracompetitive levels and thereby recover any losses.

This is in contrast to the approach followed in the United States where a general scepticism towards the rationality of predatory behaviour prevails and recoupment is an essential element for a finding of predatory behaviour.[237] A key US case in defining the need to establish recoupment was *Matsushita Electric Industrial Co v Zenith Radio Corp* in 1986. In that case, the domestic TV manufacturers in the United States accused Matsushita of selling its TVs at predatory prices in the United States, subsidised by sales in their domestic market in Japan. This claim was rejected on the grounds that the alleged period of predation was a number of years and therefore the losses incurred by Matsushita must be so large that they could never hope to recoup them, even if they succeeded in attaining a monopoly.

---

[233] Areeda and Turner (1975).
[234] Baumol (1996). See also Rapp (1990).
[235] Article 82 Guidance, para.70.
[236] See Hemphill (2001).
[237] See Emch and Leonard (2009).

Therefore, the predatory explanation made no economic sense and was rejected.

The *Brooke Group* decision also held that evidence of recoupment was essential for proof of predation.[238] Despite demonstrating that the defendant was pricing below costs, the absence of any possibility of recoupment led the court to reject the claims. In its own words, the Court found[239]:

> "The second prerequisite to holding a competitor liable under the antitrust laws for charging low prices is a demonstration that the competitor had a reasonable prospect ... of recouping its investment in below-cost prices."

**6–104** More recently, in its *linkLine* decision[240] of February 2009, the US Supreme Court reiterated its findings in the *Brooke Group* decision by stating that the alleged predator should be able to recoup its "investment" in below-cost prices.[241]

In summary, a strategy that involves lower prices to consumers in the short run with no corresponding higher prices in the longer run should not be considered anti-competitive. Indeed, even in the absence of a formal requirement, we believe that, at the very least, antitrust authorities should undertake a recoupment test as a robustness check of their conclusions.

### Incremental profits and losses

**6–105** It is doubtful whether any cost concept can provide a wholly defensible definition of the "predatory price". For this reason some economists prefer a test based on the incremental profitability of an activity carried out by a dominant firm. The question this test asks is: "Is this policy carried out by the dominant firm incrementally profitable compared to the alternative in the absence of exclusion?" If a dominant firm lowers its price and this conduct would only increase its profits if it leads to the exclusion of a rival, then the behaviour can be considered to be predatory. On the other hand, behaviour that leads to incremental profits even in the short run should not be condemned. The UK OFT describes the test in the following way:

> "Predation is strategic behaviour where an undertaking accepts short term losses in order to eliminate a competitor so as to be able to charge excessive prices in the future. It follows that the alleged predatory strategy should lead to incremental losses for the undertaking in the short term. If the alleged behaviour results in higher profits (or lower

---

[238] *Brooke Group Ltd v Brown and Williamson Tobacco Corp*, 113 US 2758 (1993).
[239] Cited in Gifford (1994).
[240] *Pacific Bell Telephone v linkLine Communications*, 555 US (2009).
[241] Note that in the United States, although recoupment is a necessary condition for a finding of predation, dominance is not required for antitrust action.

losses) than it otherwise would, that behaviour would be legitimate competition and would not be an abuse. Thus, where an undertaking can demonstrate that its behaviour is increasing its profits (or reducing its losses) that particular behaviour should not be treated as predatory."[242]

Two difficulties arise with a test of this sort. What is the correct counter-factual? How do you carry out the calculations? Any attempt to measure incremental profits clearly needs to be based on a comparison with a defined alternative. The obvious alternative is the level of profitability before the firm engaged in the allegedly predatory behaviour. So if a firm cut its prices dramatically and a competitor alleges predation, the com-parison would be between the profits the dominant firm was earning before the price cut and the profits after the price cut. But many situations do not lead to such obvious counterfactuals especially since most allegations of predation arise in the context of a response to new entry.

A particular difficulty arises in trying to understand whether the response of an incumbent to a new entrant is predatory or not. As noted above, a normal competitive response to entry will generally involve the incumbent cutting price below the pre-entry level. This is because the new entry will lead to the incumbent's demand curve shifting in, which will lower the profit-maximising price for the incumbent. Distinguishing between this response and a predatory price cut is difficult for the reasons explained above and there is consequently considerable scope for mis-diagnosing a competitive price response as predation or a predatory price response as a competitive price response.[243] Certainly, undertaking the incremental profitability test by comparing the profits of the incumbent at the old price and the new price does not represent the correct test.

The difficulty that arises with an incremental profitability test is just that **6–106** in practice it is hard to do. It requires detailed information on the shape of the demand curve of the incumbent and on the structure of his costs. In almost all circumstances, a competition authority will not be able to undertake this type of analysis. However, it is reasonable for a competition authority to ask dominant firms to explain the justification for any sig-nificant pricing changes that lead to allegations of predatory pricing. If the firms themselves cannot justify the changed price policy as being incre-mentally profitable without leading to exclusion, then it is more likely that the pricing behaviour raises legitimate predatory concerns.[244]

As mentioned above, the sacrifice test put forward in the Article 82

---

[242] Para.4.15 of OFT 414 (1999) *Assessment of Individual Agreements and Conduct.*
[243] See Joskow and Klevorick (1979).
[244] In *Compagnie Maritime Belge Transports SA and Others v Commission* (T24–26 & 28/93) [1997] 4 C.M.L.R. 273 the fact that the parties accepted that their behaviour had reduced their profitability (i.e. had led to incremental losses) was treated as evidence of abusive conduct.

Guidance entails an assessment of whether the firm's conduct resulted in lower revenues than could have been attained by following an alternative viable strategy: in other words, whether the losses incurred could have been avoided by adopting an alternative conduct.

Inevitably, this approach suffers from some fundamental problems similar to those highlighted above. These derive from the inherent difficulty of identifying feasible alternative (counterfactual) strategies for the firm in question and assessing their profitability vis-à-vis that of the conduct under investigation. Such an approach is liable to be subject to a wide margin of error. Indeed, a strategy which generates losses in the very short run due, for example, to significant investments, could be highly profitable in the long run, in a period not included in the Commission's assessment. On the other hand, in the period investigated by the Commission an alternative strategy might have generated higher profits in the short run despite not being the best long-run strategy. In such circumstances this compounds the risk of false positives, i.e. the risk of falsely concluding that the conduct was anti-competitive.

**6–107**    Given the difficulties in testing for predation, it would be useful if there was a remedy that could be imposed that would affect a firm that was engaged in predation but not one that was engaging in normal competitive behaviour. Such a remedy has been suggested by Baumol. Suppose a firm (Firm X) lowers its prices and the result is that a rival firm exits the market but the antitrust authorities are not sure whether Firm X has set a predatory price (or is merely more efficient than its rival). In this case the authorities could insist that Firm X continues to price at the new low level for a given period of time even after its rival has left the market. This protects consumers from the possibility of an anti-competitive price rise after the rival has exited. If instead of lowering prices, Firm X caused his rival to exit by flooding the market with new capacity, this problem could be dealt with in a similar way. In this case, the antitrust authorities could insist that Firm X continued to use the new capacity for a given period of time.[245] In both cases the remedy protects consumers without unduly harming an incumbent who was not acting predatorily but instead was acting competitively. However, although this can be a useful response to potential predatory behaviour (for a start, it raises the cost of predation and so makes it less likely), it is far from perfect. First, under this rule a firm that responds to inefficient entry that lowers its demand by reducing its prices is not predating, but would have to keep its prices inefficiently low even after the entrant has exited. Secondly, such a rule will not deter a multimarket firm who wants to deter entrants from all its markets by predating in one or a few. Such a firm will be willing to incur lower prices

---

[245] This type of remedy is likely to be particularly effective in transport markets (e.g. airlines and buses) where incumbents can flood the market with capacity in response to new entry. The MMC in the United Kingdom used this remedy in 1996 on two bus companies (Stagecoach and Go-Ahead).

in one market even after the exit of a rival if by doing so it ensures other firms do not try to enter its other markets.

## The Commission's assessment of predatory conduct

The legal approach to identifying predatory pricing is set out in the deci- **6-108** sions of the Commission and the European Court of Justice regarding predatory behaviour in *AKZO Chemie BV*,[246] *Tetra Pak II*[247] and *Wanadoo*.[248] In *AKZO Chemie BV*, the Commission held that AKZO had abused its dominant position on the market for organic peroxides by predatory pricing in order to eliminate a competitor. The Court confirmed that pricing policies of dominant companies could be caught by Article 82 and provided two tests for prices to be predatory.

First, it regarded prices below average variable costs as predatory. When a dominant undertaking sells its products at below average variable cost prices, there is a presumption of predatory intent since, it is argued, such an undertaking:

> "[H]as no interest in applying such prices except that of eliminating competitors so as to enable it subsequently to raise its prices by taking advantage of its monopolistic position, since each sale generates a loss, namely the total amount of the fixed costs and at least, part of the variable costs relating to the unit produced".[249]

Secondly, the Court considered that:

> "[P]rices below average total costs but above average variable costs must be regarded as abusive if they are determined as part of a plan for eliminating a competitor".[250]

Therefore according to *AKZO*, prices above average variable cost can be held to be predatory if it involves pricing below average total costs *and* there is evidence of a plan to drive out a competitor.[251]

The Court reaffirmed these two tests of predatory pricing in *Tetra Pak II*. **6-109** In addition, this judgment rejected Tetra Pak's claim that its pricing strategy could not be regarded as predatory since it had no reasonable prospect of recouping the losses thereby incurred. Instead, the Advocate

---

[246] *Engineering and Chemical Supplies (Epsom and Gloucester) Ltd v AKZO Chemie UK Ltd* (IV/30.698) [1982] 1 C.M.L.R. 273; [1981] OJ L374/1 and Case C-62/86 *AKZO v Commission* (C-62/86) [1991] E.C.R. I-3359; [1993] 5 C.M.L.R. 215.

[247] *Tetra Pak International SA v Commission* (C-333/94P) [1997] 4 C.M.L.R. 662.

[248] *Wanadoo Interactive* (COMP/38.233) [2005] 5 C.M.L.R. 120.

[249] op. cit., para.71.

[250] op. cit. para.72.

[251] See Bavasso (2005) for arguments as to why evidence of intention should not be used to establish abusive conduct under Article 82.

General stated that it was not desirable that the European Court of Justice should lay down the prospect of recouping losses as a new prerequisite for establishing the existence of predatory pricing. A number of reasons were given including:

> "—[S]elling at a loss in order to eliminate a competitor would be suicidal if it were used by a dominant undertaking with no prospect of recouping the losses incurred;
>
> —the economic potential of the dominant undertaking and the weakening of competition on the dominated or related market will in principle ensure that losses are recouped;
>
> —proof of a prospect of recouping losses is difficult to define and requires complex market analyses, as is clear from the [US] Supreme Court's own case law;
>
> —recouping losses is the result sought by the dominant undertaking, but predatory pricing is itself anti-competitive, regardless of whether it achieves that aim."[252]

In *Wanadoo*, the Commission also applied a test comparing prices with an AVC cost benchmark. The Commission found that Wanadoo's prices did not cover an appropriate measure of cost for the provision of high-speed internet access, namely asymmetric digital subscriber line (ADSL) services to residential customers in France. It concluded that this pricing conduct was part of a plan to preempt the market for high-speed internet access.[253] The Commission found that Wanadoo priced initially significantly below AVC and then close to AVC but significantly below ATC. This pricing conduct was designed, in the Commission's view, to take "the lion's share of a booming market". The decision was upheld on appeal to the CFI.

**6–110**  The case raises a number of important issues. First, how does one define AVC? An important issue concerned whether customer acquisition and marketing costs represented a variable cost or a fixed cost. This debate highlights the importance of determining the extent of the relevant time period. Whereas Wanadoo argued that these costs were largely invariant to the number of subscribers, i.e. were fixed and therefore not relevant for the calculation of AVC, the Commission treated some fixed costs as avoidable.

> "Even if advertising costs may be regarded as fixed costs in the very short term because they do not have an absolutely immediate effect on sales, they do have a clear impact in the short term—in any event less than a few weeks."

[252] *Tetra Pak International SA v Commission* [1997] 4 C.M.L.R. 662, at [78].
[253] *Wanadoo Interactive* [2005] 5 C.M.L.R. 120, at [368].

The Commission considered only a 48-month time period for assessing the profitability of these costs whereas Wanadoo argued that these investments are properly considered over their entire lifetime. The CFI upheld the Commission's determination of AVC, stating that the analysis of costs involves a complex economic assessment and that the Commission "must be afforded a broad discretion".

Wanadoo also argued before the CFI that the Commission had not properly determined whether its conduct represented predatory conduct on three grounds.

- First, Wanadoo should be permitted to "meet competition" by aligning its prices with those of competitors.

- Secondly, there was no plan of predation.

- Thirdly, the Commission should have been required to establish that Wanadoo would be able to recoup its losses.

The CFI rejected each of these arguments. The CFI rejected the notion that a dominant firm should be permitted to align its prices with that of competitors. The CFI also noted that the Commission had correctly produced evidence of intent. With respect to the third element of the appeal relating to recoupment, the CFI reiterated the approach taken in *AKZO* and *Tetra Pak* that the recoupment of losses was not a precondition to making a finding of predatory pricing.[254]

## Commentary on legal analysis of predatory pricing

A number of comments should be made about this legal approach. First, **6–111** identifying profit sacrifice is at the core of the competitive assessment of predatory conduct. The primary step in the competitive assessment is based on a test akin to the Areeda-Turner test, i.e. comparing observed prices with a cost benchmark.[255] However, as explained in the discussion above, the presumption that prices below AAC are per se predatory is not supported by the economic literature, although an explanation of such pricing behavior should be provided. As noted above, there are several reasons why an incumbent might legitimately price below AAC. For practical purposes, the most important of these is likely to arise from the inefficiency of the new entrant, where inefficiency applies either to entry into a market which is unable to sustain further entry or, more likely, the entrant employs a business model that is unsustainable. In both instances,

---

[254] *Wanadoo Interactive* [2005] 5 C.M.L.R. 120, at [228].
[255] As we have seen, the cost benchmark used in European competition proceedings was previously AVC and is now AAC or LRAIC.

such inefficient entry may force incumbents to price below average avoidable costs.

Secondly, the use of ATC as a benchmark when combined with evidence of exclusionary intent has some superficial intuitive appeal, as well as some theoretical support. However, as discussed, above cost predation is extremely difficult to distinguish from normal pricing behaviour. Moreover, internal documents should be interpreted carefully, and certainly much more carefully than is usually the case. Firms usually mean to harm their competitors, so documents that talk of an intention to harm a competitor, or to drive them out of a market, are equally consistent with effective competitive behavior as with predatory conduct. For example, when facing a downturn in demand that gives rise to excess capacity in the industry, firms may find it optimal to price below average total cost and at the same time express a desire to see their competitors leave the market. This does not represent predatory conduct since it is unclear as to what pricing conduct would have increased profitability. This illustrates the importance of clearly defining the counterfactual against which the allegedly predatory behaviour is judged. Without knowing the competitive responses, it is in general hard to argue that a particular response is not competitive.

Thirdly, the case law appears largely resistant to the notion that recoupment represents a necessary element in the test for predation.[256] The case law explicitly rejects the need to establish recoupment. The economic definition of "dominance" is that a firm has substantial market power and so can raise prices significantly above the level that would exist under conditions of effective competition. It might be thought that that fact alone would ensure that recoupment was possible.[257] However, this is not an adequate analysis. The fact that a firm already has substantial market power does not therefore mean that it will gain enough *extra* market power to recoup its short-run losses if it excludes a competitor. Also, if the allegedly predatory activity takes place in a market that is separate from the market in which dominance is alleged, a finding of dominance in one market is not necessarily enough to imply an ability to recoup in another market. Nor is the fact that assessing whether recoupment is possible often requires complex analysis adequate grounds for not undertaking such an analysis.

**6–112** However, there is some support in European case law for the need to analyse the scope for incumbents to recoup alleged short-run losses when assessing whether observed pricing behavior constitutes predatory conduct.

---

[256] This approach contrasts with the approach adopted in the United States. It has been stated that recoupment provides an important reality check on assessing whether low prices constitute predation (see US Department of Justice (2008), Chapter 4).

[257] Indeed, this is the approach adopted by the OFT in its guidance on the Competition Act 1998 ("Guidelines to the Competition Act", para.2.10 of *Assessment of Market Power* (OFT 415)).

In *Compangie Maritime Belge*, Advocate-General Fennelly stated the following.[258]

> "In *Tetra Pak II* the Court upheld the judgment of the Court of First Instance in which the approach laid down in *AKZO* had been applied in circumstances where the abuses were found to have occurred on a market other than that on which Tetra Pak was dominant but on which it held a leading position. The appellants in that case challenged – largely by reference to United States Supreme Court case-law – the refusal of the Court of First Instance to require the Commission to demonstrate '. . . a reasonable prospect of recouping losses so incurred'. The Court upheld the finding that the appellant had engaged in below-cost predatory pricing but held that 'it would not be appropriate, *in the circumstances of the present case*, to require in addition proof that Tetra Pak had a realistic chance of recouping its losses'. I shall revert (paragraph 136 below) to the significance of that expression in the circumstances of the present appeal."

In [136], Advocate General Fennelly continues.

> "The sharing of loss of revenues prompts me to revert briefly to the possible need to establish an intention or a possibility of recoupment. The process of sharing revenue losses is in essence a form of recoupment. The strategic purpose of the fighting rates carries with it the unspoken implication that rates will not be reduced for any sailings, current or future, where that is not necessary to meet competition. Furthermore, once the competitor was eliminated, they would clearly no longer be justified. Thus, to the extent that it is necessary, I believe that the present case passes the test of recoupment. At the same time, I would say that some such requirement should be part of the test for abusively low pricing by dominant undertakings. It is implied in the first paragraph of the quotation from *AKZO* (see paragraph 126 above). It is inherent in the *Hoffmann-La Roche* test (see paragraph 124 above). The reason for restraining dominant undertakings from seeking to hinder the maintenance of competition by, in particular, eliminating a competitor is that they would thus be enabled to charge abusively *high* prices. Thus, an inefficient monopoly would be reinstated and consumers would benefit only in the short run. *If that result is not part of the dominant undertaking's strategy it is probably engaged in normal competition.*" (emphasis added).

---

[258] *Compagnie Maritime Belge NV and Dafra-Lines v Commission of the European Communities* (C-395/96P) [2000] E.C.R. I-1365 at para.127 (Case law file, Vol.2, No.18).

However, as we have seen, the Article 82 Guidance rejects the need to establish recoupment. This is to be regretted for the reasons provided at paras 6–102—6–104. The introduction of a recoupment test would have brought EC competition policy not only more into line with economic reasoning but also with the assessment of predatory pricing in the United States where the analysis of recoupment is an established part of predatory pricing cases.

## Non-price predatory conduct

**6–113** While complaints of predation normally arise in the context of aggressive pricing, predation can also take place using means other than price. A few possibilities are discussed briefly. As for predatory pricing, the main issue is to distinguish predation from competition. We note that cost-based tests cannot be used to analyse non-price predatory behaviour such as investing in excess capacity with predatory intent, scheduling in a predatory manner in transport markets or engaging in brand proliferation.

### *Scheduling*

**6–114** Scheduling can be used in a predatory manner in transport industries. There are two mechanisms by which this can happen, but both have the same aim: reducing the demand of a competitor or potential competitor to the extent that they decide not to remain in or not to enter the market. One mechanism is to schedule services just before those of rivals. Scheduling a service just before your rivals' services ensures that you get more of the demand.[259] Predation of this sort has been held to have occurred in the UK bus industry on a number of occasions in the recent past, along with more standard predatory pricing.[260] Note that predation of this sort does not lead to consumer benefit even in the short run. All customers effectively have a smaller choice of departure times, whilst customers who do not know the timetable face longer average waiting periods. To see this, suppose there are two bus companies, Bus A and Bus B, and that they each run two services an hour. This means there should be a service every 15 minutes and average waiting times for those who do not know the timetable should be 7.5 minutes, with a maximum of 15 minutes. However, suppose that

---

[259] An even more aggressive approach to predating via scheduling is to schedule a service just after your rival's service as well as just before. This ensures that anyone who turns up and finds that the next service is from your rival would not have to wait much longer for one of your own services. This makes it easier to sell return tickets without having to interline.

[260] For details, see UK Office of Fair Trading research paper, "The Effectiveness of Undertakings in the Bus Industry", written by National Economic Research Associates. This focuses on nine OFT and MMC inquiries into various local bus markets in the UK. For a recent UK case, see *Chester City Council v Arriva* [2007] EWHC 1373 (Ch). Chester City Council accused Arriva of proposing "to flood Chester with loss making bus services". Arriva prevailed in court.

Bus A now runs its services one minute before those of Bus B. Now average waiting times are just over 14 minutes, with a maximum wait of 29 minutes.

The other mechanism for predating via scheduling is to respond to entry by scheduling even more services so that the entrant cannot profitably run a service. "Swamping" a route in response to entry will often be unprofitable as load factors (the number of passengers per bus) go down. This would then suggest that the incumbent decided to deliberately forego profits in order to drive out the rival.

## Excess capacity

Another possible form of predation is predation through excess capacity. **6–115** The argument is that excess capacity lowers the marginal cost of increasing output and so lowers the cost of responding to entry aggressively by increasing output. By lowering this cost, it makes a predatory increase in output post-entry cheaper and thus more likely. Observing the excess capacity, the potential entrant concludes that entry would be met by a very aggressive response and so does not enter. Excess capacity coupled with a reputation for predation may be a very effective form of entry deterrence.

## Brand proliferation

Entry deterrence can also take the form of introducing a large number of **6–116** different product brands. The US FTC argued that Kellogg, General Mills and General Foods had engaged in this type of predation when they introduced about 150 new breakfast cereal brands over a 20-year period.[261] This was held to be predatory because it filled up the "product space" and left no room in the "product space" for other companies to introduce new brands. This argument has some intuitive appeal. If the incumbents have introduced many slightly differentiated brands into a market, it may be that there is no new brand that potential entrants can introduce for which there would be a high enough demand for entry to be profitable. Under relatively strict assumptions, it turns out that entry is deterred if the number of brands already in the market is just over half the number of brands that the market could theoretically support.

In assessing the scope for broad proliferation to deter entry, it is important to assess to what extent the market positioning of incumbent brands is fixed. If incumbents wish to deter entry, their strategy is likely to be more credible if they engage in some sort of commitment activity that makes it expensive to relocate their brand. Otherwise, they have the option of accommodating entry by repositioning their brands. One possible form

---

[261] For further details, see Schmalensee (1978). The following discussion relies heavily on this paper.

of commitment device would be to advertise heavily so that the brand becomes associated with a particular image and therefore repositioning becomes difficult. Of course, another way for an incumbent to make his strategy credible is to earn a reputation for not repositioning brands in response to entry, even though it might appear to be the best short-run response to entry.

## Predatory behaviour in hi-tech industries[262]

**6–117** Predatory behaviour can be particularly important in hi-tech industries, but at the same time testing for predatory behaviour can be particularly difficult. The first point to note is that non-price predation is likely to be particularly important in many hi-tech industries. The numerous interfaces and interdependencies that are critical to making products work successfully mean that by denying a firm access to information about new platform characteristics or critical interfaces, a dominant firm can effectively stifle competition without resorting to any price predation. For instance, a software company that produces platform software (e.g. an operating system) might be able to exclude rivals in the related market of software to run on the platform by denying those rivals access to the information necessary to write software for the platform.[263] Allegations of this sort were at the heart of one of the two abuses that Microsoft was found guilty of in 2004.[264] Microsoft was found guilty of refusing to supply interoperability information to firms developing work group server operating system products, thus hindering their ability to compete with Microsoft and hence causing consumer harm. The Commission wrote that:

> "Microsoft's refusal limits technical development to the prejudice of consumers, in contradiction in particular with Article 82(b). If competitors had access to the refused information, they would be able to provide new and enhanced products to the consumer. In particular, market evidence shows that consumers value product characteristics such as security and reliability, although those characteristics are relegated to a secondary position due to Microsoft's interoperability advantage. Microsoft's refusal thereby indirectly harms consumers."[265]

It should be noted that predatory behaviour of this type does not lead to consumer gains even in the short run as there is no period of low prices, unlike with standard price predation. Another difficulty that arises with

---

[262] For a fuller discussion of the issues covered in this section, see Lind et al (2002).
[263] See paras 6–119—6–135 for a more detailed discussion of the circumstances under which a refusal to supply might constitute abusive conduct.
[264] *Microsoft* (COMP/C-3/37.792) (2004).
[265] *Microsoft* (COMP/C-3/37.792) (2004) para.18.

predation in hi-tech industries is that their cost structure means that cost-based tests of predation are particularly ill-suited to uncovering predatory pricing. Many hi-tech industries are characterised by very high fixed costs but very low variable costs (e.g. software, pharmaceuticals and tele-communications). This means that firms need to earn a substantial margin above their variable costs if they are to be viable. A test for predation that allowed pricing down to variable cost would not be a good test of predation as it would potentially allow predatory behaviour to go unchecked. Generally, where intellectual property is concerned, a cost-based test of predation will not work. In such cases tests that focus on incremental profitability are better.

Hi-tech industries often feature "winner takes all" type competition. This occurs where there will only be one standard that wins (e.g. Microsoft Windows) or one firm that can win the patent race. In such markets, competition takes place *for* the market and the equilibrium for the market will be a single dominant player, which is likely to be highly profitable and to face either no competitors or just a few fringe firms. In such markets, competition to be the winner is extreme and the strategy of each firm is to eliminate the other firms since only by doing this can they be the winner. Also, in such markets we often see very low "penetration pricing" in the competitive stage. So firms often price below variable cost with intent to eliminate rivals. But it would usually be wrong to treat this as predatory behaviour: it is part of the nature of competition in markets of this type.

This has led some commentators to argue that regulatory intervention **6–118** against the pricing behaviour of firms in the "new economy" is never justified[266]:

> "Despite that fact that new economy firms in an innovation race satisfy the AKZO test (i.e. they price below average total cost and intend to eliminate their competitor(s)) a finding of abuse of dominance and an intervention by the Commission in such circumstances would be unnecessary, harmful and futile. An intervention would be unnecessary because many new economy markets are very competitive despite being highly concentrated: competition just takes a different form from competition in old industries. It would be harmful because any intervention is likely to restrict competition between new economy firms and slow down the innovation race. And it would be futile because the ultimate market structure (i.e. a fragile monopoly) is not the result of the behaviour of the surviving firm (although the identity of the survivor may well be), but the result of the cost structure and network effects that characterise the industry."

[266] Ahlborn et al. (2001).

However, this does not imply as some have argued that the pricing behaviour of firms in "new economy" industries never justifies intervention. It should be noted that in "winner takes all" markets it may be possible for firms to engage in predatory behaviour for only a short period, and yet have a significant effect on the final competitive outcome provided the market is characterised by strong network effects. In such markets a small initial lead might snowball into a winning position and this might justify intervention on the part of competition authorities to ensure that competition takes place on the merits. However, any claims of extreme tipping required by such theories need to be carefully examined with reference to the facts.

## REFUSALS TO SUPPLY: ESSENTIAL FACILITIES AND MARGIN SQUEEZES

### Introduction

**6-119** As a general rule, firms, regardless of their market position, should have the right to choose their trading partners and to dispose freely of their property. Deviations from this fundamental principle of property rights will generally serve to undermine firms' incentives to invest and to innovate, with consequent adverse effects for competition and, therefore, consumers.[267] However, interventions on a firm's right to exercise its property rights may, in exceptional circumstances, be justified where a dominant firm also competes in a "downstream" market and refuses to supply competing firms in that market.[268] In addition to an outright refusal to supply, a dominant firm might set prices to downstream firms at such levels that even efficient competitors are unable to compete profitably in the downstream market.[269]

We first consider the economic issues and case law relating to a refusal to supply and then consider margin squeezes.

### The basic economics of the essential facilities doctrine

**6-120** Much of the case law relating to refusals to supply takes place within the analytical framework of the "essential facilities doctrine".[270] The term "essential facilities doctrine" originated in commentary on US antitrust case law. In such situations, owners of an "essential" or "bottleneck"

---

[267] Article 82 Guidance, para.74.
[268] See for example, refusal to supply products to existing or new customers. *Istituto Chemioterapico Italiano and Commercial Solvents v Commission* (6/73 & 7/73) [1974] E.C.R. 223; [1974] 1 C.M.L.R. 309.
[269] Article 82 Guidance, para.79.
[270] See, for instance, the Commission's *Notice on the application of the competition rules to access agreements in the telecommunications sector* [1997] OJ C265/2.

facility are required by law to provide access to that facility at a reasonable price.[271] For example, a competition or regulatory authority might insist that competitors be granted access to a telecommunications network and might set the terms on which such access is to be granted. The use of the concept of an essential facility has had a significant role in the Commission's liberalisation programme being implemented in network industries such as telecommunications, gas, electricity and transport. However, the doctrine has also been invoked in other industries that are not generally considered to be characterised by natural monopoly. Such industries include newspaper distribution, port facilities and marketing data.

The competition issues potentially raised by a refusal to deal on an alleged essential facility arise where a firm is active in the supply of two related activities (that is, it is vertically integrated), both of which form components of the product that is purchased by the end consumer. These two components are usually denoted "upstream" and "downstream" activities. The potential competition concern arises when the firm active in both upstream and downstream activities refuses to provide access to the facility or services to other firms who wish to provide either upstream or downstream services only. Figure 6.8 illustrates this. It shows that in order for B to supply final consumers, B requires access to a downstream asset which is controlled by A.

## Figure 6.8 Example of a downstream bottleneck

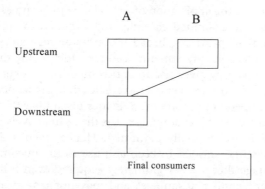

In Figure 6.8 the potential competition law concern arises when B demands access to the downstream facility of A and A refuses to provide such access. The question then becomes whether the competition authorities should insist that A provides access.

The basic argument that sees a refusal to supply as anti-competitive  **6–121** stems from a view that the refusal to supply prevents third party firms from

---

[271] We discuss in para.6–128 what a "reasonable" price might be.

entering the market and that this has the effect of lessening competition. This line of argument raises two issues. First, it should be established why the third party requires supply of the particular product or service. It is not sufficient merely to state that a refusal to supply prevents a firm competing or alternatively that the product being withheld constitutes an essential facility. Indeed, the definition of an essential facility put forward by the Commission in *Sealink* illustrates the difficulties. The Commission defined an essential facility as "a facility or infrastructure without access to which competitors cannot provide services to their customers".

But such a definition raises a number of questions. For example, must it be physically impossible for competitors to replicate the facility through their own endeavours irrespective of cost? Or must it simply be commercially unattractive for competitors to replicate the facility? The former interpretation would confine the concept of essential facilities to cases where there was an insurmountable barrier to replicating the facility, such as a legal prohibition. This seems extreme and appears to risk the danger of potentially inefficient duplication of assets. But the latter definition potentially leads to any asset which it would be inconvenient for competitors to duplicate being defined as an essential facility. In this case, the essential facility doctrine could be applied to those cases where the incumbent firm was simply more efficient than the competitor.

Since the concept of an essential facility runs contrary to that of property rights, it is critical to find an approach that is able to discriminate between a refusal to grant access that merely involves the lawful exercise of property rights and a refusal to grant access that harms competition and hence consumers. Hence, the application of refusal to supply and essential facility arguments must be examined carefully and confined to appropriate conditions, rather than providing broad grounds for regulatory intervention which might undermine investment incentives. Identifying those rare cases where refusal to supply gives rise to anti-competitive outcomes requires a careful analysis of those market characteristics that enable one firm to anti-competitively impede the economic activities of another.[272]

**6–122**    Any company, even if it is dominant, has the right actively to compete by all methods that are normally permitted. Hence, even a dominant firm should in general be entitled to keep and use to the maximum any competitive advantage that it has legitimately acquired even if its competitors do not have any similar advantages and may not realistically be able to

---

[272] Despite the many cases involving refusal to deal and essential facilities, they provide little guidance on either of these central issues. In his review of US essential facility cases Areeda (1990) summarised the essential facilities doctrine as follows:

> "You will not find any case that provides a consistent rationale for the doctrine that explores the social costs and benefits or the administration costs of requiring the creator of an asset to share it with a rival. It is less a doctrine than an epithet indicating some exceptions to the right to keep one's creations to oneself, but not telling us what those exceptions are".

obtain them. Legitimate competition in general includes obtaining and keeping exclusive access to resources such as patents or physical facilities that confer competitive advantages. The returns that a firm earns from such investment, particularly where the initial investment is highly risky, are very important for providing firms with the correct incentives to invest in the first place. Without such returns, much economically efficient investment would not take place. The expropriation of some or all of these returns through mandatory access requirements can act to reduce such investment with consequent serious adverse effects on dynamic efficiency. As the Commission notes in its Article 82 Guidance, this harm to investment incentives can affect not just the dominant firm, but also its competitors.[273] If they know that they can get access to the dominant firm's assets, this reduces the incentive for competitors to invest.

Secondly, it is necessary to examine how the refusal to supply lessens competition. The potential that a refusal to supply will lessen competition and harm consumers only arises if the downstream market is not already subject to effective competition. It is insufficient for a firm to suffer a competitive disadvantage for access to be mandated. What distinguishes an essential facility from a non-essential facility is the impact of the refusal to deal on competition and consumers in the related market. This requires a case-by-case analysis of the particular situation of concern. It is not sufficient to substitute a label (that of "essential facility") for such analysis.

The issues of refusal to supply and essential facilities have generated considerable attention. For a long time, foreclosure was seen as endemic and therefore the vertical links inherent in these cases were subject to considerable scrutiny. Opposition to this view came from the Chicago school. The basic argument of the Chicago school is that there is only one monopoly profit to be had. A monopolist at one stage of production can fully extract the monopoly profit without recourse to foreclosing efficient competitors in the downstream market place (see Chapter 5 for a fuller discussion of the Chicago critique).

The Chicago critique can be illustrated by the following simple tele- **6–123** communications example. Suppose there are three towns A, B and C. Telecommunications operators X and Y compete to offer services between A and B, but operator X owns the telecommunications network between B and C and is therefore in a position to prevent Y from offering services from town A to town C. Can X increase its profits by refusing to supply Y? The answer in this simple example is no for the following reasons.

---

[273] Article 82 Guidance, para.75.

## Figure 6.9 Illustrating a potential bottleneck

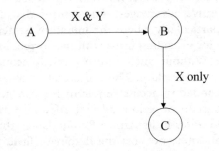

A monopolist over one link of the production chain—here the network between B and C is a critical input into the service from A to C—can fully exploit that monopoly power by setting access charges so that all of the potential monopoly rents are recovered from the network between B and C. In this example, X could exercise its market power over the BC network by insisting on a large enough share of Y's revenues to realise full monopoly profits. In the process, however, Y is not foreclosed from the market (assuming that it is at least as efficient as X).

Assume that €2 was the maximum charge obtainable for a call between A and C. Any higher charges can be assumed to lead to consumers switching to alternative forms of communication. Assume that the marginal cost of carrying a call is the same between A and B and between B and C and that this is equal to €0.50. If operator X handles the call it earns a profit of €1. This is made up of revenues of €2 but less costs of €1. But X could equally earn this amount by allowing Y access to its network between B and C but charging Y €1.50. Under this scenario, Y is not foreclosed. X earns revenues of €1.50 and incurs costs of €0.50, leaving him with a profit of €1, and Y's revenues are sufficient to cover its costs of €2 (i.e. €1.50 paid to X plus costs of €0.5 for the AB leg). Only if Y were less efficient than X in providing the service between A and B would Y be foreclosed from the marketplace. This would not be a competition policy concern: Article 82 recognises that dominant firms should not be forced to assist inefficient competitors.

**6–124**   A question that this analysis raises is why would firms refuse to offer access if it did not have a negative impact on their profits? One explanation may be that the monopolist is subject to price regulation in the supply of the access service (here, the network between B and C) and so wishes to transfer the monopoly profit to the unregulated AB market. Under these circumstances, X may refuse access to Y. The Commission recognises this possibility in the Article 82 Guidance, where it states the following[274]:

---

[274] Article 82 Guidance, para.88.

"[A] refusal to supply may lead to consumer harm where the price in the upstream input market is regulated, the price in the downstream market is not regulated and the dominant undertaking, by excluding competitors on the downstream market through a refusal to supply, is able to extract more profits in the unregulated downstream market than it would otherwise do."

Moreover, especially in industries with network characteristics, foreclosure may provide a less transparent way in which firms can extract monopoly rents and therefore reduce the possibility of detection from competition authorities. In network industries, marginal costs are typically well below average costs so that the price one must charge to extract the monopoly rent will appear to be very high and that would likely lead to scrutiny from competition authorities. Foreclosure on the other hand achieves the same results but may do so in a less visible fashion.[275]

Another possible reason for a refusal to supply is that it may form part of a strategy to extend a monopoly position in one market into another, or to protect a monopoly position. For instance, in *Microsoft* (see below for further details), the Commission argued that Microsoft's refusal to supply interoperability information was designed to extend Microsoft's market power in the PC operating system market into the related workgroup server market.[276]

These considerations give rise to five main economic conditions that an **6–125** asset should satisfy before it should be considered an essential facility. First, it must be impossible or at least uneconomic for any other firm to replicate the asset and not just that the mere retention of that asset for its own use confers an advantage on a dominant firm over competitors.[277] By this we mean that it is not possible for another firm to develop a similar facility that could supply the product or service at a low enough cost to supply the downstream market at a competitive price. In *Oscar Bronner*, the ECJ argued that for a facility to be considered an essential facility it would "at the very least" be necessary to show that it would not be viable for an entrant to create a second such asset even if it operated at the same scale as the incumbent.[278] If it is possible and economic to replicate the asset, then the firm wishing to compete on the relevant market should carry out its own investment in such an asset. Mandating access to another firm's assets is not a step that should be taken lightly. If it became widespread to mandate such access, then firms would lose the incentive to carry out their own potentially risky investment since they would be able to "free-ride" on the investment by other firms. Firms would often prefer to use the

---

[275] Carlton and Klamer (1983).
[276] See the discussion on tying and bundling at paras 6–063 et seq for a more detailed discussion of this potential theory of harm.
[277] See the Advocate General's Opinion in *Oscar Bronner*, at [57].
[278] In *Oscar Bronner* (C-7/97), at [45]–[46].

infrastructure of their competitors rather than invest in their own infrastructure, but as the Advocate General in *Oscar Bronner* notes, this would have a detrimental impact on dynamic incentives to compete:

> "[I]f access to a production, purchasing or distribution facility were allowed too easily there would be no incentive for a competitor to develop competing facilities. Thus while competition was increased in the short-term it would be reduced in the long-term. Moreover, the incentive for a dominant undertaking to invest in efficient facilities would be reduced if its competitors were, upon request, able to share the benefits."

Secondly, there should be no alternative means of entering the relevant market at a reasonable cost. If there are alternative methods of entering a market, then mandating access to an asset is not necessary for the protection of competition. Mandating access is a serious step and should not be taken when it is not necessary to protect competition.

Thirdly, there must be spare capacity on the asset in question. The essential facilities doctrine should not be invoked unless doing so will clearly and substantially increase the level of competition in the downstream market. If there is no spare capacity on the asset in question, then mandating access does not increase the level of competition in the market. Any product sold by the new entrant using the asset would merely be substituting for a product previously sold by the asset owner. This means that the total supply of the product would not have been increased and so price would not have fallen. Accordingly, there would have been no improvement in the level of competition in the market.[279]

**6–126**   Fourthly, there must be a lack of effective competition downstream and a reasonable expectation that mandating access will significantly improve the level of downstream competition. As argued above, if competition is already effective downstream, there is no consumer harm arising from the refusal to supply and so no reason to mandate access. Equally, if there is no reason to believe that mandating access will significantly improve the level of competition downstream so that benefits to consumers outweigh the

---

[279] An objection to this condition might be that if the entrant's downstream product will be of better quality than the incumbent's, then there would be benefit from having the entrant supplying downstream. As a matter of economic theory, there is clearly some merit in this argument. However, as a matter of practical competition policy, we think it would be very dangerous if the Commission, or any competition authority, started making ex ante judgments about the likely quality of rival products and then used these judgments not just to mandate access, but to mandate access when this requires a reduction in output downstream by the dominant firm. This is not the type of micro-management that competition authorities are in general well suited to undertake.

costs associated with mandating access, then access should not be mandated even in the absence of effective downstream competition.[280]

Fifthly, the owner of the asset must compete in the same relevant market as the entrant wishes to compete in. This is more a reality check than an additional condition. If the new entrant is not going to compete directly with the asset owner, then the asset owner has no incentive to refuse supply if the new entrant is prepared to offer a reasonable price for access. If there is no potential anti-competitive explanation for the refusal to supply, then access should not be mandated. There are after all many entirely legitimate reasons for refusing to supply, such as concerns over the credit-worthiness of the entrant or a lack of spare capacity.

It is interesting to note the parallels between essential facility type arguments and some issues that arise with tying and bundling (discussed above at paras 6–063—6–084). In both potential competition concerns, market power in one product can be used to exclude rivals. In the same way that tying and bundling issues need to be dealt with on a case-by-case basis to understand whether a particular practice is harming, or is likely to harm, consumers, so too do essential facility claims.

The Article 82 Guidance is consistent with the analysis presented above. **6–127** At para.81, the Commission states that a refusal to supply raises concerns when all three of the following conditions hold:

- "The refusal relates to a product or service that is objectively necessary to be able to compete effectively on a downstream market;

- The refusal is likely to lead to the elimination of effective competition on the downstream market; and

- The refusal is likely to lead to consumer harm."

## Mandating access implies detailed price regulation

Even where an essential facility can in those rare instances be identified, **6–128** this raises a further issue; namely, on what terms should access be granted. Indeed, mandating access necessarily involves detailed price regulation since it is not sufficient to mandate access. In the absence of price regulation, the owner of the essential facility can effectively deny access by requesting too high a price. Indeed, theory would predict that the upstream monopolist will offer access to downstream competitors at a price that results in him earning monopoly profits upstream. This is the same result

---

[280] The case law appears to go further and to require that, in the absence of access being granted, all competition on the downstream market is eliminated (see, for instance, the *Bronner* judgment (C-7/97)). However, the Article 82 Guidance states that what matters is the elimination of "effective competition", not of all competition.

as we discussed in Chapter 5 in the context of vertical restraints imposed by an upstream monopolist on downstream retailers.[281]

Hence, if the aim of mandating access is to lead to lower prices to consumers, then mandating access will need to be coupled with other conditions. A common condition is to say that the owner of the essential facility must supply downstream rivals at the same price as he supplies his own downstream division. However, this does not avoid the upstream monopolist pricing at the monopoly level. He will sell at the monopoly price to his own division as well as to rivals, content in the knowledge that even though his downstream division earns no profits, his upstream business earns monopoly profits.[282]

The inescapable conclusion from this discussion is that mandating access to an essential facility should be coupled with price regulation. This is implicitly accepted in the case law which refers to supplying on terms that are both non-discriminatory and "reasonable".[283] However, "reasonable" prices must be reasonable relative to some benchmark. How this should be calculated is not specified in the case law.[284] Regulatory authorities usually calculate it on the basis of some form of costs. However, there are serious difficulties with this. First, the information difficulties associated with calculating costs are large, which is why we usually leave it to industry-specific regulators to do. Secondly, there are difficult issues to be considered about what type of costs should be covered (total costs, variable costs, marginal cost or some other measure?) Thirdly, where the incumbent took a considerable risk in investing in the asset in the first place, mandating access at cost is likely to severely damage investment incentives. The need to regulate the price of access rather than just mandating it, and the difficulties involved in doing this, highlight why the essential facilities doctrine should be used very sparingly. We agree with the US Supreme Court's comment in *Trinko*:

> "Compelling [firms with unique facilities] to share the source of their advantage is in some tension with the underlying purpose of antitrust law, since it may lessen the incentive for the monopolist, the rival, or

---

[281] See paras 5–001—5–065.

[282] There is one potentially attractive aspect to this remedy. If the remedy is that the price should be non-discriminatory and must allow the downstream division of the upstream monopolist to at least cover its costs (i.e. it must not make losses), then an entrant downstream that is more efficient than the incumbent downstream will make positive profits. Further, it should be able to undercut the monopolist's downstream division, which will be good for consumers (lower prices) and may spur the monopolist's downstream division to become more efficient. Thus, this remedy has the effect of encouraging efficient downstream entry.

[283] In *Sealink*, the Commission asserts that access prices should be "fair and non-discriminatory" without providing any guidance as to how such prices should be determined.

[284] The UK OFT states that it "would expect competitors to have access at economically efficient prices", but omits to mention how these might be calculated, OFT 414 (1999), *Assessment of Individual Agreements and Conduct*, para.7.5.

both to invest in those economically beneficial facilities. *Enforced sharing also requires antitrust courts to act as central planners, identifying the proper price, quantity, and other terms of dealing—a role for which they are ill-suited.*[285] (emphasis added)

## The case law on refusal to supply and essential facilities

The leading case in this area is *Commercial Solvents*[286] in which the Eur- **6–129** opean Court of Justice held that the company held a dominant position for the production of a raw material used to produce a chemical because the company had a world monopoly. The Court held that Commercial Solvents abused its dominant position by refusing to supply a downstream competitor, stating that:

> "[I]t follows that an undertaking which has a dominant position in the market in raw materials and which, with the object of reserving such raw material for manufacturing its own derivatives, refuses to supply a customer, which is itself a manufacturer of these derivatives, and therefore risks eliminating all competition on the part of this customer, is abusing its dominant position within the meaning of Article 82."

The first case in which the Commission used the phrase "essential facility" was *B&I Line Plc v Sealink*.[287] The decision made it clear that it was based on the decision in *Commercial Solvents*. Sealink was both a car ferry operator and the owner of Holyhead Harbour. B&I was another ferry operator using Holyhead Harbour to compete with Sealink on ferry services between Wales and Ireland. The issue concerned the location of the berths allocated to B&I. The structure of the harbour was such that B&I vessels had to stop loading and unloading whenever a Sealink vessel entered or left the harbour. The issue arose when Sealink altered its sailing times so that B&I was affected in this way more frequently. While recognising that the new Sealink schedule was an improvement from the perspective of consumers, the Commission held that its adverse impact on B&I represented an abuse given that Sealink was using its monopoly position in the supply of the essential facility—the harbour:

> "[T]o strengthen its position in another related market, in particular, by granting its competitor access to that related market on less favourable terms than those of its own service".[288]

---

[285] 540 US 396 (2004) at para.407.
[286] *Instituto Chemioterapico Italiano Spa and Commercial Solvents Corp v Commission* (6 & 7/73) [1974] E.C.R. 223; [1974] 1 C.M.L.R. 309.
[287] *B&I Line Plc v Sealink Harbours Ltd and Sealink Stena Ltd* (IV/34.174) [1992] 5 C.M.L.R. 255.
[288] *B&I Line Plc v Sealink*, above.

**6–130** A disappointing aspect of this case was that there was no focus on consumer harm. The Commission stated that[289]:

> "A dominant undertaking which both owns or controls and itself uses an essential facility ... and which refuses its competitors access to that facility ... thereby placing the competitors at a competitive disadvantage, infringes Article [82]".

The Commission focused on harm to a competitor, rather than harm to competition. As we have argued on numerous occasions above, this is the wrong approach to competition policy and so it is a welcome development that the Commission, if perhaps not the Courts, have accepted in the Article 82 Guidance, and elsewhere, the need to focus on consumer harm. Moreover, it is interesting to note that three years after the Commission's decision in the related *Sea Containers v Sealink* case in which the Commission also deemed Holyhead port to be an essential facility, Sea Containers, rather than taking up the option to operate services from Holyhead, the alleged essential facility, instead began competing services to Ireland from another port (Liverpool).

Another important essential facilities case is *Magill*.[290] This case focused on intellectual property (IP) rights. The need for an economic analysis of a refusal to deal is particularly important in cases involving IP rights.[291] It is in cases involving IP rights that there is the greatest danger of misuse of the essential facility doctrine. The scope for misuse stems from the fact that IP rights are exclusive rights. It is then an easy but usually fallacious step to conclude that the IP right is essential for competitors to compete. But one must be extremely careful in making this step. Instead, a detailed analysis of the market should be undertaken.

**6–131** In *Magill*,[292] the Commission, the Court of First Instance and finally the European Court of Justice ruled that TV listings were an essential facility and that Independent Television Publications Ltd and the BBC should be obliged to license other magazine publishers. If it is justified to treat TV listings as an essential facility, it is important to be clear what is special about these IP rights to distinguish them from the usually benign treatment of IP rights. Failure to make such a distinction would justify competition law intervention for all IP rights.

The answer appears to lie in the fact that TV listings are merely a by-product of television broadcasting and are not a creative activity in their

---

[289] *B&I Line Plc v Sealink*, above, at para.41.
[290] *Magill-Radio Telefio Eirann (RTE) v Commission* (C-241 & 242/91P) [1995] E.C.R. 743; [1995] 4 C.M.L.R. 178.
[291] The reader is referred to Ridyard (1996) for an excellent exposition of the relevant economic issues. For more recent treatments, see Melamed, Stoeppelwerth and Blank (2008) and Hovenkamp, Janis and Lemley (2006).
[292] *Magill-Radio Telefio Eirann (RTE) v Commission* (C-241 & 242/91P) [1995] E.C.R. 743; [1995] 4 C.M.L.R. 178.

own right. It is not possible for publishers to develop rival listings without also entering the television market (even if this were possible). Moreover, the obligation to license has no effect on the incentives to create TV listings. The production of TV listings will be the same regardless of whether the broadcasters are protected from listings competition or not since they depend on the production of TV programmes and these will not be affected by listings competition. This is not true in general for most other economically useful IP rights.[293]

In *Oscar Bronner*[294] the case law on the issues raised by essential facilities moved closer into line with economic thinking.[295] This case involved a publisher (Bronner) of a daily newspaper, seeking access to the nationwide home-delivery system of Mediaprint, a significantly larger competitor. The ECJ concluded that the delivery system was not an essential facility. First, the Court argued that there were other ways that Bronner could gets its product distributed (which it was already using) and so access was not essential to Bronner being able to compete. Secondly, it argued that the hurdle for it being impossible to duplicate the asset was very high and that at a minimum it was necessary for Bronner to show that even operating at the scale of Mediaprint it would be uneconomic to duplicate the asset. Bronner was unable to show this. In his Opinion,[296] Advocate General Jacobs also stressed the damaging effect on investment incentives if assets were too frequently designated as essential facilities[297]:

> "In the long-term it is generally pro-competitive and in the interest of consumers to allow a company to retain for its own use facilities which it has developed for the purpose of its business. For example, if access to a production, purchasing or distribution facility were allowed too easily there would be no incentive for a competitor to develop competing facilities. Thus, while competition was increased in the short term it would be reduced in the long term. Moreover, the incentive for a dominant undertaking to invest in efficient facilities would be reduced if its competitors were, upon request, able to share the benefits."

Advocate General Jacobs also stressed the importance of focusing on harm to competition, not to competitors[298]:

---

[293] It is worth noting that in *Bronner*, the ECJ said that *Magill* involved "exceptional circumstances" at [40], thus suggesting that it should not be interpreted as leading to widespread essential facility issues in IP markets.
[294] (C-7/97) [1998] E.C.R. I-7791; [1999] 4 C.M.L.R. 112.
[295] See Bishop and Ridyard (1999) for a discussion of the implications of this judgment.
[296] Opinion of Advocate General Jacobs, May 28, 1998, *Oscar Bronner v Mediaprint*.
[297] Opinion of Advocate General Jacobs, above, at para.57.
[298] Opinion of Advocate General Jacobs, above, at para.58.

"[I]t is important not to lose sight of the fact that the primary purpose of Article [82] is to prevent distortion of competition—and in particular safeguard the interests of consumers—rather than to protect the position of particular competitors."

**6–132** In the *IMS* interim measures decision, the Commission concluded that IMS Health, a provider of pharmaceutical regional sales data services in Germany, abused a dominant position in refusing to license the use of its "1860 brick structure" to NDC, a competing supplier of these services.[299]

Regional sales reports are based on data delivered by pharmaceutical wholesalers to report providers, such as IMS, NDC and AzyX. The data provided by wholesalers are broken down in a predefined structure. IMS's structure—the 1860 brick structure—is licensed to wholesalers only for the reporting of their data and not for other uses. Pharmaceutical companies use regional data services to build their sales territories in order to develop and implement incentive schemes for their sales representatives and to gain knowledge of market developments (for example, changes in market shares of their products). The brick structure in which regional sales data are reported is therefore important to pharmaceutical companies.

NDC and another competitor AzyX both entered the German market in 1999 and offered regional sales reports which could be aggregated to the 1860 brick structure. However, following a copyright case before the German courts, IMS obtained a judgment preventing NDC and subsequently AzyX from employing the 1860 brick structure. NDC claimed that without this licence it could not compete in the supply of pharmaceutical regional sales data in Germany.

**6–133** The Commission's decision states that the criteria for the establishment of abuse under Article 82 in cases relating to the exercise of property rights, taking into account *Oscar Bronner*, are as follows[300]:

- "[T]he refusal of access to the facility is likely to eliminate all competition in the relevant market;

- such refusal is not capable of being objectively justified; and

- the facility itself is indispensable to carrying on business, inasmuch as there is no actual or potential substitute in existence for that facility."

As such the Commission's assessment of essential facilities is broadly in line with underlying economic principles discussed above.

In conducting its assessment, the Commission focused its analysis on

---

[299] *NDC Health/IMS Health: Interim measures* (COMP D3/38.044), July 2001. This decision was overturned by the Court of First Instance. *IMS Health v Commission* (T-184/01).
[300] *NDC Health/IMS Health: Interim measures* (COMP D3/38.044), July 2001, at para.70.

whether there was a realistic possibility for rivals of IMS to offer regional sales data services in Germany that employed a different brick structure that did not infringe IMS's copyright of the 1860 brick structure. The Commission argued that the answer to this question depends critically on whether customers would consider regional sales data sold in another structure as an effective alternative. The Commission held that this was not the case partly due to the function of the 1860 brick structure as an industry standard and the requirement of customers to compare data over time. Moreover, although some customers could modify data supplied in another structure this would be costly in terms of both time and expense.[301] The Commission therefore concluded that the refusal of IMS to license its 1860 brick structure raised a risk of serious and irreparable harm and damage to the public interest and ordered IMS to license its 1860 brick structure on a non-discriminatory basis to NDC and AzyX.[302] Regardless of whether the Commission was correct in its conclusions, in addressing this issue, it is important to draw a distinction on the one hand between consumer preferences in the market at the time of investigation which are likely to indicate a preference for the incumbent's product and on the other hand whether it is feasible for competitors to overcome any incumbency advantages. In other words, before mandating IMS to grant a licence it is not sufficient merely to identify that IMS enjoyed an advantage by retaining its brick structure for its own use or that customers currently preferred the 1860 brick structure.[303]

The *IMS* decision also illustrates the difficulties associated with designing an effective remedy: it is one thing to mandate access (or in this case, to mandate the granting of a licence) and another to establish the terms at which that access is granted. *IMS* provides few pointers to how such terms should be established. The Commission merely states that:

> "[I]n any agreements in which IMS licences the use of the 1860 brick structure, it is important to ensure that any fee which is charged is reasonable, and that the process does not take an undue amount of time".

The decision delegates the task of determining whether fees meet these requirements to IMS and the party requesting the licence. In those circumstances where mutual agreement cannot be reached, the fees are to be set with reference to one or more independent experts.[304]

*Microsoft*[305] illustrates two important aspects of refusal to supply cases.   **6–134**

---

[301] *IMS* at [118]–[123].
[302] *IMS* at [215].
[303] Another important issue is the extent to which dynamic incentives are affected by mandating access.
[304] *IMS* at [215].
[305] *Microsoft* (COMP/37.792) (Commission Decision of March 24, 2004).

Microsoft was found to be dominant in the market for PC operating systems and to be abusing this dominance by refusing to supply competitors with interoperability information between Windows and non-Microsoft work group server operating systems. A key issue in assessing whether the refusal to supply raised genuine competition concerns is whether the interoperability information supplied by Microsoft was truly a "must stock" item. Although it is essential for servers to be able to work with Windows PCs, so some form of interface between the PC and the server is required, it is less obvious that Microsoft is the only *possible* supplier of that interface. For example, it is arguably the case that server software suppliers themselves are able to achieve some degree of workable inter-operability between their servers and Windows PCs even if that communication is not as good as can be achieved with access to Microsoft's own codes.

This case also serves to illustrate a number of interesting issues that arise from refusal to supply cases. First, Microsoft argued that any compulsory licensing regime would have detrimental effects on its investment incentives. The Commission argued that the relevant test is not whether mandatory access would harm the investment incentives of the dominant firm, but whether it would harm the investment incentives for the industry as a whole. The Commission argued that compulsory licensing would likely increase the incentives for Microsoft's rivals to invest in work group server products. Secondly, the case illustrates the need to price regulate and the corresponding difficulties. After the decision, there were prolonged discussions between Microsoft and the Commission over the price at which Microsoft should license the interoperability information. The dispute was over whether Microsoft was offering the information at genuinely "reasonable and non-discriminatory" terms. In February 2008 the Commission fined Microsoft €899 million for charging unreasonable prices in 2006 and 2007.

## Conclusions on essential facilities

**6–135** Essential facility cases must have reference to the facts and in particular reference to the basic economics of the particular case in question. As Temple Lang (1994) noted:

> "In all of these cases, competition law may oblige the dominant owner of the essential facility to cooperate with its downstream competitors, on competition grounds. These cases can only be resolved by reference to basic principles of antitrust economics."

The requirement of an economic analysis of the impact of refusal to deal will help contain the application of the essential facilities doctrine to those few industries where competition problems do arise. It will always be tempting for a competition authority to respond favourably to firms that complain about the lack of access to new markets and there are certain cases where refusal to supply or essential facilities arguments may have some merit. However, it is important to remember that the purpose of competition law is to protect competition not competitors and in the majority of cases the blind application of the essential facilities doctrine will only serve to undermine the incentives for dynamic efficiency that underpin the competitive process. The risk that regulatory intervention does more harm than good is high in essential facilities cases, and for this reason the burden of proof on the authorities to show consumer welfare benefits from any intervention should be correspondingly high.

It should also be remembered that in those rare circumstances where there are good grounds for requiring firms to provide access to their assets, the inevitable implication is the need to impose price regulation on access terms to that monopoly asset. Recognition of this fact illustrates the seriousness of any proposed intervention.

## Margin squeeze

A form of behaviour that is closely related to a refusal to supply is a **6–136** "margin squeeze". As we noted earlier, one way of refusing to supply a downstream competitor is to charge a price to the competitor that is so high that it effectively amounts to a refusal to supply. A margin squeeze occurs where a dominant firm sells to competing downstream firms at a wholesale price that, given prevailing retail prices, does not allow even efficient downstream firms to cover their costs.

Figure 6.10 illustrates. The dominant upstream firm supplies its own downstream arm and also a number of competing downstream firms. It charges a price of W to these downstream competitors. The downstream firms then compete for final customers. The dominant firm sells at a retail price of P. Assuming that the products offered by the various firms are essentially the same, the downstream competitors to the dominant firm cannot charge a price of more than P. This means that the downstream firms have a per unit sum of P—W with which to cover their costs. A margin squeeze is said to occur where P—W is less than the costs of an efficient downstream firm, thus meaning that such firms cannot remain in the market without making losses.

## Figure 6.10 Margin squeeze

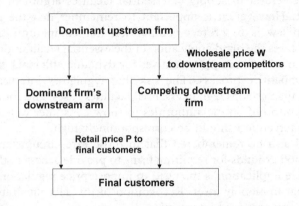

An important question is how to calculate the costs of an efficient operator. The standard approach is to use the "as efficient competitor" test. This implies that a margin squeeze occurs when P—W is less than the costs of the dominant firm's downstream arm. This still leaves open the question of which cost concept is relevant. The Article 82 Guidance states that the Commission will generally use the long-run average incremental cost (LRAIC). This is reasonable, although it should be noted that LRAIC is a per unit cost concept and so an efficient competing firm operating at a smaller scale than the dominant firm may have higher LRAIC if fixed costs are significant. In these circumstances competition authorities, and regulators, sometimes use a "reasonably efficient operator" test. This would hold that the relevant costs are the LRAIC of a firm that is cost minimising given its lower scale. There is in principle a *coherent* argument that efficient but sub-scale entry should be protected, but only if it is likely that the entrant will be able to grow to an efficient scale. Sub-scale entry should not, in general, be protected.

6–137   The observation that P—W is too small to allow an efficient competitor to survive is consistent with either P being too small or W being too large. Therefore, it is sometimes said that a margin squeeze can be characterised as either predatory pricing at the retail level or excessive pricing at the wholesale level. The two cases that we discuss below illustrate this difference well.

However, it is insufficient to show a margin squeeze by a dominant firm to show an abuse. As with other abuses, it is necessary that the behaviour of the dominant firm is likely to cause consumer harm, i.e. it is necessary for there to be a coherent theory of harm. That coherent theory of harm would include showing that access to the dominant firm's assets was necessary to allow competing downstream firms to compete effectively. It would also be necessary to show that the exclusion of the downstream competitor will harm effective competition downstream. If downstream competition is effective then the fact that a particular firm is excluded should not harm consumers, unless it can be shown that the firm would offer an innovative product or service.

## The case law on margin squeeze

The two leading margin squeeze European cases are *Deutsche Telekom*[306]    **6–138** and *Telefonica*.[307, 308] In *Deutsche Telekom* (DT) the Commission found DT guilty of a margin squeeze in the retail fixed line telephony market. DT was actively selling calls to retail customers but also providing wholesale capacity to other firms that allowed those firms also to offer retail telephony. The Commission found that between 1998 and 2001 the retail price charged by DT was below the wholesale price that DT charged, which clearly meant that competitors could not profitably match DT's retail prices. After 2002 DT's retail prices were above its wholesale price, but not by enough to cover DT's own retail costs. An oddity about this case was that both DT's retail prices and its wholesale prices were regulated. The wholesale price was fixed by the German regulator and so DT could only have avoided a margin squeeze by raising its retail prices. It would have needed the regulator's permission to do this.

The margin squeeze in *Telefonica* occurred in the residential broadband market. The Commission held that the gap between Telefonica's retail and wholesale prices in the period 2001 to 2006 was not enough to allow an operator as efficient as Telefonica to compete.[309] Although this case was also in a telecoms market, there was an important difference between this case and the *DT* case. In *Telefonica* the Commission noted that Telefonica's retail broadband prices were the highest amongst the EU-15 countries. So this is a margin squeeze case where the Commission found that the problem was that retail prices were too high. This should be contrasted with *DT*, where the Commission found that retail prices were too low.

## Conclusions on margin squeeze

A number of the comments that apply to refusal to supply and essential    **6–139** facilities cases apply to margin squeeze cases. Lowering the price at which competing downstream firms are supplied will also have adverse effects for incentives to invest. Furthermore, margin squeeze cases also require

---

[306] *Deutsche Telekom AG* (COMP/C-1/37.451, 37.578 and 37.579) (May 21, 2003).
[307] *Wanadoo Espana v Telefonica* (COMP/38.784) (July 4, 2007).
[308] See also *Genzyme Ltd* OFT Decision (2003) UKCLR 950 for a case where a dominant firm has been held guilty of a price squeeze. See Ridyard (2004) for a commentary and critique of the competitive analysis conducted by the UK Office of Fair Trading in this case.
[309] Although this ignored the fact that there was an established competing cable operator in Spain.

complex and difficult decisions to be made regarding the "appropriate" price at which supply should be mandated.

## COLLECTIVE DOMINANCE UNDER ARTICLE 82

**6–140** The ECJ's judgment in *Compagnie Maritime Belge* confirmed that Article 82 applies to firms that can be held to be collectively dominant.[310] In principle, the concept of collective dominance in Article 82 cases is consistent with economic theory. If dominance is equated with "significant market power", there is no reason why two or more firms cannot collectively possess significant market power, even where individually they do not. For collective dominance to exist requires that there exist a group of firms that: (a) do not face significant competitive constraints from other firms outside the group; and (b) these firms are able to adopt a mode of parallel behaviour that reduces the effectiveness of competition between themselves. Under these circumstances, it is possible that prices would be increased above the competitive level. There is therefore a close correspondence between the concepts of collective dominance and tacit coordination.

However, the concept of collective dominance raises a number of practical issues in the context of Article 82 investigations. As noted in Chapter 7, it is extremely difficult in practice to distinguish between competitive conduct that is consistent with tacit co-ordination but which is not consistent with competitive behaviour. Although the economic theory of behaviour in oligopolistic markets recognises explicitly that firms understand their interdependence, this does not imply that all or even most such markets warrant regulatory intervention. Indeed, most market outcomes that are consistent with firms engaging in tacit co-ordination are also consistent with those firms competing aggressively. For example, the parallel movement of prices over time is entirely consistent with firms competing aggressively against one another.[311] One should therefore be extremely cautious in moving from a theoretical possibility to a policy proscription in which normal market conduct becomes subject to regulatory intervention. It is simply far too easy to construct a case in which tacit collusion is a possible outcome but being unable to rule out alternative competitive possibilities.[312] For an extended discussion of how to analyse

---

[310] *Compagnie Maritime Belge NV v Commission* (C-395/96 and C-396/96P) [2000] 4 C.M.L.R. 1076.

[311] As discussed in Chapter 7, the immense difficulties associated with discriminating between conduct unambiguously constitutes tacit coordination from conduct that constitutes normal competitive behavior imply that in practice merger control focuses, or at least ought to focus, on what the merger changes, i.e. the competitive assessment is on the *creation* of tacit coordination rather than on the *strengthening*.

[312] For this reason, it is sometimes argued that such investigations should be conducted on a "no fault" basis. Such an approach used to be possible under UK competition law, which previously allowed for industry-wide investigations under the Fair Trading Act 1973.

whether a market is potentially subject to collective dominance concerns, the reader is directed to Chapter 7.

## SUMMARY

There is a strong alignment between the legal terms used in the application **6–141** of Article 82 and economic principles. In particular, there is a close alignment between the legal concept of dominance and the economic concept of market power, although dominance is normally be seen as applying only to firms that possess substantial market power.

"Dominance" is traditionally defined mainly with reference to market shares. This places a premium on the correct definition of the relevant market. However, market definition in Article 82 cases is fraught with difficulty. This implies that investigators need to recognise that market shares are likely to provide an even less perfect measure of a firm's market power in Article 82 cases than is usual.

When analysing whether the behaviour of a firm is abusive it is necessary to focus on the potential for the behaviour to harm competition and hence consumers, not to focus on harm to competitors. Harm to competitors is a natural result of fierce competition and so in general should not be condemned.

The abuse of a dominant position can potentially take numerous forms. **6–142** We have discussed both conduct that might be held to be exploitative and exclusionary. We argued that whether a given practice constitutes an abuse of a dominant position depends less on its form and more on the outcomes it produces. Since the outcomes that a particular form of behaviour produces will differ depending on the precise market facts of each particular case, this implies that each case requires a detailed analysis. In short, there are no grounds for a policy of per se rules prohibiting certain forms of business conduct even when undertaken by dominant firms.

## ANNEX 6.1: COST BENCHMARKS

The principles set out in the Article 82 Guidance for assessing exclusionary **6–143** conduct are based on the premise that, in general, only conduct that would exclude a hypothetical "as efficient" competitor is abusive. The "as efficient" competitor is a hypothetical competitor that has the same costs as the dominant company. It therefore follows that foreclosure of this hypothetical competitor can only result if the dominant company prices below its own costs.

However, in order to apply the "as efficient" competitor test, it is necessary to establish which measure of costs should be used as the appropriate benchmark for assessing the competitive effects of observed conduct of a dominant firm. This annex provides an overview of various cost concepts with reference to a hypothetical example.

Domco enjoys a very high market share, and is likely to be considered to be dominant. Domco's business comprises a large factory and the costs it faces consist of two elements. First, Domco must pay repayments on a loan it took out to finance the construction of the factory. This repayment amounts to €100K per annum for the 20-year life of the loan (which is also the life of the factory) and does not vary according to the level of the factory's output. Secondly, Domco incurs costs for each unit of output it produces. Specifically, it costs Domco €5 to produce each of the first 10,000 units of output and €7 to produce each unit beyond the first 10,000 in any given year.[313] The capacity of the factory is 20,000 units per annum.

## Average Total Cost (ATC) and Marginal Cost (MC)

**6–144** Figure Annex.1 shows how the marginal and average total costs of Domco vary with production in a given year. The dotted line shows marginal costs and the solid line shows average total costs.

### Figure 6A.1 Illustration of how marginal and average total cost vary with production

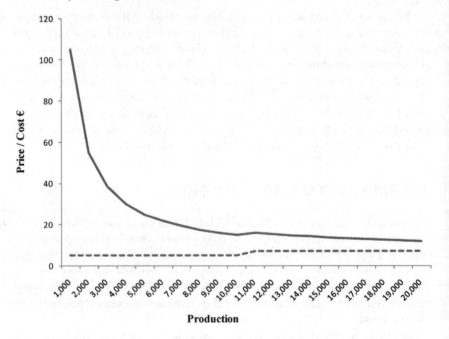

---

[313] This could happen, for instance, if the company would need to pay workers overtime wages to produce more than 10,000 units.

The marginal cost is the cost of producing an additional unit of output. In our example, Domco's marginal cost depends on its level of output. If Domco's output is between 0 and 10,000 units, its marginal cost is €5. That is to say, as long as Domco is producing fewer than 10,000 units, the extra cost that would be incurred if one extra unit were to be produced is €5. However, if Domco produces an output of 10,000 units or above, its marginal cost is €7. The change in cost incurred resulting from producing 10,001 rather than 10,000 units is equal to €7.

Average total cost is the average of all variable and fixed costs. Given the presence of fixed costs, as production increases, average costs will tend to fall as production is increased. Only if price is above average total cost will the firm make positive profits each year.

## Average Variable Cost (AVC)

The average variable cost is defined as total variable costs (i.e. those costs **6–145** that would increase if a firm chose to increase its output) divided by the total number of units produced. Typically variable costs include raw materials, fuel and energy.

In our example, we assumed that the first 10,000 units of Domco's output can be produced for €5 each but that the next 10,000 units would cost €7 each. An implication of this cost structure is that Domco's average variable cost varies according to the level of output it produces. In particular:

- If Domco chooses to produce 10,000 units then its AVC will be €5 (i.e. total variable cost of €50,000 (€5 × 10,000) divided by 10,000);

- If Domco chooses to produce 15,000 units then its AVC will be €5.67 (i.e. total variable cost of €85,000 (€5 x10,000 + €7 x6 5,000) divided by 15,000;

- If Domco chooses to produce 20,000 units then its AVC will be €6 (i.e. total variable cost of €120,000 (€5 × 10,000 + €7 × 10,000) divided by 20,000.

## Average Avoidable Costs (AAC)

Average avoidable cost is the average cost per unit that could have been **6–146** avoided if the company had not produced a discrete amount of (extra) output. In other words, it is the total cost that could be saved by foregoing the production of a certain number of units, divided by that number of units. For instance, let us compute Domco's AAC for expanding production from 9,000 to 12,000, i.e. an expansion of 3,000 units.

Given the cost assumptions outlined above (i.e. €5 for the first 10,000 units and €7 for each unit up to an additional 10,000 units), the total avoidable cost of increasing output from 9,000 to 12,000 units equals: (€5 × 1,000 units + €7 × 2,000 units) = €19,000. The average avoidable cost is therefore €19,000/3,000 units = €6.33.

In Domco's case, AAC would indeed be identical to AVC because the avoidable costs it faces when deciding whether to increase output are all clearly captured by the notion of variable costs. However, there are instances where AAC could also include costs that might be considered fixed as well. To illustrate this, suppose that Domco currently produces 9,000 units at a cost of €5 per unit, and it can produce up to another 10,000 units by using a more expensive technology costing €7 per unit. Assume further that the use of this technology requires Domco to purchase a permit, which costs €10,000. This outlay may not be captured by the notion of variable costs because it does not vary with output. In this case if Domco decides to use the more expensive technology in order to increase its production to 12,000 units, Domco's AAC will be equal to ((€5 × 1,000 units + €7 × 2,000 units + €10,000)/3,000 units = €9.67. The logic hinges on the fact that Domco could well choose *not* to expand its capacity (i.e. by acquiring the permit). Hence, the increase in fixed costs that are associated with acquiring the permit are avoidable as well.

**6–147**   The AAC depends on the time period over which costs are assessed. For example, suppose instead that Domco has to pay a licence fee every six months in order to operate. On a day-to-day basis, that would not change Domco's AAC, but if we were considering Domco's costs over a period longer than six months, then that licence fee becomes avoidable since Domco could avoid such costs by ceasing production.

These examples illustrate the importance of timing when assessing whether to include certain costs in the measure of AAC. Naturally, the extent to which costs are avoidable tends to increase as the time period over which output decisions are viewed increases. AAC is typically an increasing function of the time period chosen for the assessment of a firm's behaviour.

## Average Total Cost (ATC)

**6–148** As noted above, average total cost incurred by a firm varies with production. Consider the ATC for Domco at various levels of output at which it might chose to produce, recalling that Domco must pay €100,000 annually to cover the loan on its factory.

- If Domco chooses to produce 8,000 units, its ATC equals (€100,000 + €5 × 8,000 units)/8,000 units = €17.50.

- If Domco chooses to produce 10,000 units, its ATC equals (€100,000 + €5 × 10,000 units)/10,000 = €15.00

- If Domco chooses to produce 11,000 units, requiring the purchase of the permit costing €10,000 for the use of the more expensive technology, its ATC equals (€100,000 + €10,000 + €5 × 10,000 units + €7 × 1,000 units)/11,000 = €15.18

Therefore, if Domco produces at 10,000 rather than 8,000 units, its ATC falls because the higher level of output would allow the fixed cost associated with the loan to be spread over a broader output base. However, if Domco chooses to produce 11,000 rather than 10,000 units, its ATC increases as it incurs the incremental cost of acquiring the permit necessary to produce above 10,000 units.

Note that at each output level the ATC is higher than a measure of AAC that focuses on the time period over which the loan repayment is unavoidable. This is because ATC includes sunk costs, which would normally be excluded from the AAC as this is normally applied over a shorter time period. For example, the AAC associated with the production of 10,000 units would not include the €100,000 loan repayment and so would be (€5 × 10,000 units)/10,000 units = €5 as opposed to the ATC of €15 in the example above.

## Long-Run Average Incremental Costs (LRAIC)

In many instances, firms produce more than one product and, importantly, **6-149** the production of those various products involves common costs, i.e. costs that are incurred in the production of more than one product. The existence of common costs raises severe problems with the use of ATC since it requires some method for allocating common costs to the various products.

For an illustration of these ideas, let us reconsider the example of Domco. Suppose it produces two products: widgets at a cost of €5 per unit and gadgets at a cost of €10 per unit (regardless of the quantity produced). Assume further that both widgets and gadgets are produced at the same factory, for which Domco has to repay a loan of €100,000 per annum. If Domco produces 10,000 widgets and 10,000 gadgets, the ATC of widgets will be (€5 × 10,000 units + a part of €100,000 loan)/10,000 units, while the ATC for gadgets will be (€10 × 10,000 + remaining part of €100,000 loan)/10,000 units.

Therefore, the ATC for each product depends on how the common loan cost is eventually split between the two products. But there is no sound economic logic that would lead one to prefer one allocation of common costs over any other. As a result, any rule for allocating common costs between products is essentially arbitrary.[314]

---

[314] This is not to say that there is no economically efficient way to recover these fixed costs. As discussed at Box 6.3, the optimal recovery of fixed costs involves charging higher prices to customers with relatively inelastic demand and lower prices to customers with relatively elastic demand.

**6-150**     To address this problem of common costs, consideration is therefore given to the concept of *long-run* average incremental cost (LRAIC). LRAIC is defined as the average of all the costs that a company incurs to produce a particular product, assuming that it starts afresh. Returning to the Domco example above, the LRAIC of producing widgets is simply €5, since the loan costs would be incurred by Domco irrespective of whether it chose to produce widgets as well as gadgets, and is therefore not a cost that is incremental to widget production.[315]

For multiproduct firms, the LRAIC will be lower than ATC because the latter cost concept includes costs that are common to the production of all products, whereas LRAIC excludes these costs because they are not incremental to the production of a particular product.

---

[315] The LRAIC of gadgets is €10, based on similar reasoning.

# 7. Economics of Horizontal Mergers

## OVERVIEW OF EC MERGER CONTROL

The EC Merger Regulation (hereafter, "the Merger Regulation"), first 7–001
came into force in 1990.[1,2] European merger control is now a key element
of EU competition law. Indeed, the increasing importance of economic
analysis in EU competition law stems largely from the use of economics
and subsequent developments in EU merger control.

Article 2(1) of the Merger Regulation states that:

> "Concentrations within the scope of this Regulation shall be appraised
> in accordance with the objectives of this Regulation and the following
> provisions with a view to establishing whether or not they are com-
> patible with the common market. In making this appraisal, the
> Commission shall take into account:
>
> (a) the need to preserve and develop effective competition within
>     the common market in view of, among other things, the
>     structure of all the markets concerned and the actual or
>     potential competition from undertakings located either within
>     or without the Community;
> (b) the market position of the undertakings concerned and their
>     economic and financial power, the opportunities available to
>     suppliers and users, their access to supplies or markets, any
>     legal or other barriers to entry, supply and demand trends for
>     the intermediate and ultimate consumers, and the development
>     of technical and economic progress provided that it is to con-
>     sumers' advantage and does not form an obstacle to
>     competition."

---

[1] Regulation 4064/89 [1989] OJ L395/1.
[2] Until 2004, mergers were assessed by the Mergers Task Force, a specialist unit within DG
COMP of the Commission. However, reforms introduced in the wake of CFI judgments
annulling three merger decisions saw the abolition of the Merger Task Force and mergers
are now assessed within the various units of DG COMP.

**7–001**  Economics of horizontal mergers

At its introduction, mergers with a Community dimension were assessed with respect to whether the merger created or strengthened a dominant position. However, in January 2004, the substantive test of the Merger Regulation was changed to whether a merger gives rise to a significant impediment to effective competition (hereafter, SIEC).[3] The SIEC test is analogous to the "substantial lessening of competition" test (SLC test) that is used to assess mergers in some other jurisdictions, such as the United States, the United Kingdom, Ireland and Australia. The implications of this change in the substantive merger test were heavily debated at the time and the debate is still on-going. The implications of the change are discussed below in paras 7–010—7–012.[4] Article 2(3) of the Merger Regulation states that:

> "A concentration which would significantly impede effective competition in the common market or in a substantial part of it, in particular as a result of the creation or strengthening of a dominant position, shall be declared incompatible with the common market."

**7–002**  The Merger Regulation only covers those mergers and joint ventures which have a significant Community dimension. A merger (or concentration in the parlance of the legislation) is said to have a Community dimension where:

(a) the combined aggregate worldwide turnover of all the undertakings concerned is more than EUR 5 000 million; and

(b) the aggregate Community-wide turnover of each of at least two of the undertakings concerned is more than EUR 250 million, unless each of the undertakings concerned achieves more than two-thirds of its aggregate Community-wide turnover within one and the same Member State.

A merger that does not meet the above thresholds is also said to have a Community dimension where:[5]

(a) the combined aggregate worldwide turnover of all the undertakings concerned is more than EUR 2 500 million;

(b) in each of at least three Member States, the combined aggregate turnover of all the undertakings concerned is more than EUR 100 million;

---

[3] This and other changes to the Merger Regulation are set out in Council Regulation (EC) No 139/2004 on the control of concentrations between undertakings (the EC Merger Regulation).

[4] See articles by Heimler (2008) and Werden (2008) for a good overview of the opposing views and arguments.

[5] Mergers that do not meet these criteria are assessed by the competition authorities of one or more Member States.

(c)  in each of at least three Member States included for the purpose of point (b), the aggregate turnover of each of at least two of the undertakings concerned is more than EUR 25 million; and

(d)  the aggregate Community-wide turnover of each of at least two of the undertakings concerned is more than EUR 100 million, unless each of the undertakings concerned achieves more than two-thirds of its aggregate Community-wide turnover within one and the same Member State.

Subject to being designated as having a Community dimension, all categories of mergers fall with the scope of the Commission's jurisdiction, i.e. it covers *horizontal mergers*, *vertical mergers* and *conglomerate mergers*. The Commission's approach to assessing mergers is set out in two guidelines: Horizontal Merger Guidelines and Non-horizontal Merger Guidelines.[6] Graphical illustrations of each category of merger are provided in Figure 7.1.

## Figure 7.1: The difference between horizontal, vertical and conglomerate mergers      7–003

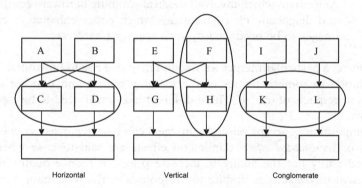

| Horizontal | Vertical | Conglomerate |

- *Horizontal mergers* involve companies that operate at the same level of the supply chain, producing substitute goods. Two products are termed substitutes if an increase in the price of one good induces an increase in demand for the other. For example, in the above figure, the left-hand panel illustrates a horizontal merger involving companies C and D. Horizontal mergers therefore bring together firms active in the same relevant market. Mergers that fall into this category include for instance Friesland/Campina (both parties active in the production of various dairy products), MÁV Cargo/Rail Cargo Austria (both parties are active in the provision of rail freight transport and freight forwarding services)

---

[6]  Guidelines on the assessment of horizontal mergers (2004) and Guidelines on the assessment of non-horizontal mergers (2008).

and StatoilHydro/ConocoPhillips (both parties' activities overlap in the downstream market of retailing motor fuel).[7]

- *Vertical mergers*, in contrast, involve companies that operate at different levels of the supply chain. A common example is a merger between a wholesaler and its retailer, or a manufacturer and its input supplier. In terms of the above figure, this can be illustrated as a merger between companies F and H. Examples of vertical mergers considered by the European Commission are the Tom Tom/Tele Atlas and Nokia/Navteq mergers.[8] In both cases, one of the merging parties (Tele Atlas and Navteq) produced navigable digital map databases, which served as an input for the other merging party (Tom Tom and Nokia) to produce portable navigation devices and applications.[9]

- *Conglomerate concentrations* involve companies that, although they operate in different markets, produce complementary goods, e.g. companies K and L in Figure 7.1. Examples of conglomerate mergers are Proctor & Gamble/Gillette, which involved different non-overlapping oral products sold to the same retailers, and GE/Amersham which involved medical scanning hardware equipment and diagnostic pharmaceuticals which either enhance or enable images to be produced by such scanning hardware.[10]

Of course, a particular merger transaction may give rise to horizontal issues in relation to some activities of the merging parties and non-horizontal issues in respects of others. These different issues will need to be assessed in turn.

**7–004**   Competition concerns raised by mergers can be categorised as *unilateral effects* or *coordinated effects*. Unilateral effects are said to arise when the merged entity has the ability to increase prices or reduce quality to the detriment of consumers despite the responses of the remaining competitors.[11] In marked contrast, the adverse effects associated with coordinated

---

[7]   COMP/M.5046 *Friesland Foods/Campina* (2008), COMP/M.5096 *RCA/MAV Cargo* (2008) and COMP/M.4919 *StatoilHydro/ConocoPhillips* (2008).

[8]   COMP/M.4854 *TomTom/Tele Atlas* (2008) and COMP/M.4942, *Nokia/Navtec* (2008).

[9]   Related to vertical mergers, the Commission has also considered "diagonal" mergers, where the merging parties do not operate in markets that are directly horizontally or vertically related; for instance where one of the firms is a provider of an input into a supply chain the end product of which competes with the other merging party's product. The clearest example of such "diagonal" effects is the Google/Doubleclick decision. As discussed in paras 8–027—8–029, the analysis in these cases does not substantively differ from the standard vertical analysis.

[10]   COMP M.3732 *Proctor & Gamble/Gillette* (2005) and COMP/M.3304 *GE/Amersham* (2004).

[11]   As para.8 of the Horizontal Merger Guidelines makes clear, "increased market power" means the ability of one or more firms to profitably increase prices, reduce output, choice or quality of goods and services, diminish innovation, or otherwise influence parameters of competition. The expression "increased prices" is therefore used as shorthand for these various ways in which a merger may result in competitive harm.

effects depend on one or more competitors to the merged entity choosing to compete less vigorously post-merger. In principle, all categories of merger can give rise to both concerns, but in practice, as discussed in Chapter 8, coordinated effect concerns arise only rarely in non-horizontal mergers.

The Merger Regulation also provides for a fixed timetable in which decisions are made (subject to "stop the clock" provisions, which are discussed below). The fixed timetable to which merger investigations are conducted and the fact that a decision is published for each case, whether positive or negative, are widely seen as one of the main advantages of merger inquiries over inquiries under Articles 81 and 82.[12]

Formally, the Commission's assessment of mergers takes the form of a short initial assessment, usually termed Phase I. Phase I formally lasts one month from the date of notification.[13] Where the Commission considers that the proposed concentration is likely to give rise to significant competition concerns so that it raises serious doubts as to its compatibility with the common market, a second more detailed Phase II investigation is undertaken. Phase II formally lasts for up to four months at the end of which a decision is made. During Phase II, the Commission may issue a Statement of Objections in which the Commission's formal case is meant to be set out. After the Statement of Objections is issued, the merging parties are offered the opportunity of an Oral Hearing at which the parties, and commonly also complainants, are represented.

However, it should be noted that the actual length of many merger **7–005** investigations can be considerably longer than indicated by the statutory timetables for Phase I and Phase II. Many mergers are subject to lengthy periods of pre-notification discussions with the Commission, during which many of the substantive issues are addressed prior to the formal commencement of Phase I. Moreover, it is also increasingly common for the timetable to be subject to a "stop the clock" period, either to allow the Commission more time to assess complex issues, perhaps to provide more time to assess the requested information, or because the Parties are unable to produce the requested information within the timeframe of the formal request.[14]

Since the introduction of the Merger Regulation in 1990, 4,189 mergers have been notified to DG COMP.[15,16] The majority of these were cleared at Phase I, with only 191 mergers (approximately 5 per cent of all notified mergers) progressing to a Phase II inquiry.[17] For a merger subject to a

[12]   See Bishop (2008).
[13]   An extension to six weeks is possible where parties have offered commitments to address the Commission's concerns.
[14]   See Whish (2009) and Lindsay (2009) for a discussion.
[15]   This was as of end September 2009.
[16]   125 of these notifications were withdrawn, 91 in Phase I and 34 in Phase II.
[17]   This figure excludes the 34 Phase II investigations of mergers that were withdrawn and for which there is therefore no decision.

Phase II investigation, there are three possible outcomes.[18] First, the merger can be cleared in its entirety (Article 8(1)). Secondly, the merger can be cleared subject to the parties giving undertakings to remedy the competitive concerns raised by the investigation (Article 8(2)). Up to the end of September 2009, 46 Phase II investigations have been cleared without conditions and a further 91 with undertakings. Article 8(3) provides for a third outcome, namely prohibition. The first merger subject to prohibition was Aerospatiale/de Havilland in 1991. Between then and the end of September 2009, in total 20 concentrations were prohibited, although a number of other mergers which faced the prospect of being prohibited following a Phase II investigation have been withdrawn.

**7–006** **Table 7.1 ECMR Statistics September 1990 to September 2009**

| Type of case/investigation | Number of cases |
|---|---|
| Phase I Investigations* | 4,097 |
| Phase II Investigations* | 191 |
|     Cleared unconditionally (art.8.1) | 46 |
|     Cleared with commitments/divestments (art.8.2) | 91 |
|     Prohibited (art.8.3) | 20 |

\* Excludes cases withdrawn in Phase I; 35 cases have been withdrawn in Phase II.
*Source: DG Competition Website*

A number of the Commission's prohibition decisions have been challenged before the European Court of First Instance. Prominent examples in which substantive elements of the Commission's decision were challenged include *Airtours/First Choice*, *Tetra Laval/Sidel*, *GE/Honeywell* and *Sony/BMG*.[19] The Court of First Instance's decisions can be further appealed to the European Court of Justice (ECJ). The decisions of the latter are final. However, it is important to note that both CFI and ECJ are largely concerned with procedural issues, basing their decisions on the same evidence as the Commission's initial assessment while at the same time granting the Commission a wide degree of discretion in the interpretation of that evidence. In short, the courts do not provide an effective constraint on the Commission's economic analysis.

The remainder of this chapter is concerned with the economic issues raised by horizontal mergers, with the economic issues raised by non-horizontal mergers being discussed in the following chapter. We first provide a discussion of the relationship between the economic issues

---

[18] There is a fourth outcome, under Article 8(4) to restore effective competition. This applies only to concentrations that have already been implemented prior to a Commission decision. This outcome has occurred four times.

[19] The Commission's decision in *Sony/BMG* was to clear the merger unconditionally and the case was brought by dissatisfied complainants. This case is discussed in more detail in para.7–074.

potentially raised by horizontal mergers and their relationship to the legal concepts. This includes a brief discussion on the implications of the change in the substantive test from a dominance test to one of substantial impediment to effective competition.

We then turn to the substantive economic analysis of horizontal mergers. **7–007** Given the continued importance of structural analysis in the assessment of horizontal mergers, paras 7–013—7–018 considers the role of market definition and measures of changes in concentration. Paragraphs 7–020—7–024 consider the key economic principles that underlie the assessment of unilateral effects. Paragraphs 7–024—7–038 outlines the key issues to be addressed in assessing whether unilateral effects are likely. In particular, a decision to raise price (and therefore restrict output) involves both benefits and costs to the firms involved and a proper assessment of unilateral effects involves an examination, most likely an empirical assessment, of this trade-off: do the benefits from restricting output outweigh the costs associated with that restriction? Even where post-merger market shares are high, a merger may not give rise to unilateral effects for a number of reasons. First, competitors already active in the market may respond to any output restriction so as to mitigate and possibly eliminate any benefit to the merged entity from restricting output. In particular, existing competitors can respond either by expanding or re-positioning their product offerings. In addition to the dynamic response of actual competitors (i.e. the ability of existing competitors to expand their sales and/or reposition their product offerings), it is also possible for potential competitors to respond to any output restriction by entering the market. The competitive constraint provided by entry and how it is assessed is discussed in paras 7–039—7–045. Paragraphs 7–046—7–048 then discusses the scope for the actions of customers to undermine the benefits of output restrictions; namely, the scope for buyer power. Buyer power refers to the ability of customers to take actions to alter the structure of the market upstream by sponsoring either expansion by existing firms or by sponsoring the entry of new firms. A dynamic assessment of the likely effects of a horizontal merger is therefore central to a complete assessment of horizontal mergers, even if only conducted in an ad hoc manner.

Paragraphs 7–049—7–074 address coordinated effects arising from horizontal mergers. We address first the ability of firms to reach a coordinating strategy and then their ability to sustain that coordinating strategy. Particular emphasis is given to the need to address how the structural change arising from the horizontal merger changes the ability of firms to successfully moderate their competitive behaviour. In particular, how does the merger enable firms to reach a tacit understanding to moderate their competitive behaviour? In assessing the likelihood of a horizontal merger giving rise to coordinated effects, the competitive constraints provided by supply-side responses of competing firms, new entry and buyer power are also relevant but we do not repeat the discussion provided in paras 7–039—7–048.

Paragraphs 7–076—7–081 then discusses the treatment of efficiencies in the competitive assessment of horizontal mergers. Paragraphs 7–082 and 7–084 consider particular issues arising in the assessment of mergers in industries characterised by network effects and two-sided markets, respectively. Although these two types of industry have peculiarities which need to be taken into account, when assessing the likely impact of a merger the standard economic analyses of unilateral and coordinated effects are still applicable. Finally para.7–087 discusses the failing firm defence.

## 7–008   ECONOMICS AND THE LAW

Article 2(3) of the Merger Regulation prohibits horizontal mergers which would significantly impede effective competition, in particular as a result of the creation or strengthening of a dominant position. The Commission's approach to assessing whether a horizontal merger results in a significant impediment to competition is set out in its Horizontal Merger Guidelines.[20] A detailed commentary on these guidelines is provided in the relevant sections below which describe the economic issues raised by horizontal mergers. As noted in the introduction to this chapter, a merger is said to be *horizontal* if the parties involved undertake directly competing activities. Horizontal mergers produce two consequences that do not arise in either vertical or conglomerate mergers. They reduce the number of firms active on the relevant market and they result in an increase in market concentration. Although specific horizontal mergers each raise their own particular competition issues, the structural changes brought about by horizontal mergers can result in a significant impediment to competition in two potential ways; either the merger gives rise to unilateral effects or the merger gives rise to coordinated effects.[21]

By eliminating the competitive constraint which currently exists between the merging parties, a horizontal merger may weaken to a significant degree the strength of the overall competitive constraints acting on one or both of the two parties. As a result, the prices charged by the merged entity may increase relative to their pre-merger level despite the competitive response of rival firms. A merger which has these characteristics is said to give rise to a situation of *unilateral effects*. Such price increases are known as *unilateral price increases* as they do not rely on the merged entity's remaining competitors adopting a particular mode of conduct. The Commission

---

[20]   Guidelines on the assessment of horizontal mergers under the Council Regulation on the control of concentrations between undertakings, (2004/C 31/04).

[21]   Some commentators consider there to be a third category of potential competition harm; namely *non-unilateral effects*. According to Scheffman and Coleman (2003) "[n]on-unilateral" is broader that coordinated interaction". However, the examples put forward by Scheffman and Coleman, on a proper analysis, fall either into unilateral effects or coordinated effects. We do not therefore subscribe to this "third way".

often refers to unilateral effects as non-coordinated effects. There is no practical analytical difference between the two terms and the two terms can be used interchangeably. However, in this chapter we tend to use the term unilateral effects, reflecting the economics literature.[22]

Alternatively, a horizontal merger may lead to a reduction in the effectiveness of competition if the change in market structure creates a competitive environment which is more conducive for two or more firms to collectively adopt a mode of competitive behaviour that reduces the intensity of competition and thereby increase prices above the levels that would have prevailed but for the merger.[23] A merger which has these characteristics is said to give rise to *coordinated effects*.[24] Such price increases are termed *coordinated effects* since the price increase depends on a number of firms, and not just the merged entity, altering its behaviour.

There is therefore a clear distinction to be drawn between unilateral **7–009** effects and coordinated effects: the former is not predicated on one or more rival firms adopting a particular mode of competitive behaviour, whilst the latter is. It is important not to confuse the possible responses of rival firms to a post-merger unilateral price increase as a coordinated effect. In many instances, a unilateral price increase by the merged entity will lead to the remaining competitors responding to the merger and possibly also increasing their prices. But that behaviour does not properly constitute coordinated effects since the initial price increase is optimal for the merged entity even if competing firms do not alter their competitive behaviour.

However, this is not to say that there is no overlap in the competitive analysis of the two potential concerns. The analysis of factors that constrain the behaviour of the merged entity and the other firms that constitute the alleged coordinating group is similar to the analysis necessary to assess whether unilateral effects are likely in the sense that such an analysis comprises an assessment of inter alia the ease of entry, the ability of smaller competitors to react to any attempted post-merger price increase, the extent of supply-side substitutability and the ability of large buyers to counteract the market power of the coordinating group.

Importantly, it is the case both for unilateral effects and coordinated effects that the respective competition concerns are predicated on the notion that the merging firm will restrict output in the sense that in order to

---

[22] Proponents of the use of "non-coordinated effects" argue that this term indicates that rivals may also alter their pricing behaviour in response to the unilateral effect. However, in terms of deciding whether the merger is anti-competitive, focusing on whether unilateral effects arise is sufficient. In short, the concern as to how rivals alter their pricing behaviour is primarily of academic interest.

[23] The change in market structure might also lead to more favourable conditions for explicit collusion.

[24] This is also known as *conscious parallelism*.

increase prices, the merged entity must accept a loss of sales.[25] In assessing whether a horizontal merger is likely to give rise to anti-competitive effects (either unilaterally or in a coordinated manner), the competitive assessment is normally undertaken in a two-step approach: first, define the relevant market and calculate pre- and post-merger market shares and the change in market concentration; second, assess the likely impact on competition arising from that change in concentration.[26] Paragraphs x.xx to x.xx provide more detail on how these two steps are implemented in practice.

## The substantive impact of the SIEC test in EU merger control

**7–010** As noted in the introduction, the substantive test of the Merger Regulation was changed in 2004 from a dominance test to an SIEC test. Before discussing the reasons put forward in support of the change in the substantive merger test, we note that the concept of unilateral effects is closely linked to the old concept of *single firm dominance* as can be seen once dominance is interpreted as being synonymous with significant market power. Moreover, the concept of coordinated effects can be seen as synonymous with the concept of collective dominance. In the past, there was a debate as to whether the concept of collective dominance was wider than the concept of tacit coordination that underpins the notion of coordinated effects. At the European level this debate is effectively over; it is generally accepted that the concepts of collective dominance and tacit coordination are equivalent from an economic perspective.[27]

Notwithstanding this correspondence between the "old" and "new" concepts of competitive harm, various arguments were presented in favour of switching EC merger control from the dominance test to an SIEC-based test. First, such a change would allow for an alignment towards a global standard for merger assessment by competition authorities and courts.[28] However, this would only represent a significant improvement if there were significant differences between adherents to the SIEC or SLC tests on the one hand and adherents to the dominance test on the other. Provided dominance is interpreted as referring to significant market power, and "strengthening" of a dominant position explicitly relates to assessing the

---

[25] This is a consequence of the downward-sloping nature of demand curves: given the demand schedule for a particular product, higher prices necessarily imply lower output levels. Output could be restricted in terms of production, capacity and product range.

[26] As we discuss in detail below, market shares can under- or overstate the pre-merger competitive constraints between the merging parties. It is important to take this possibility into account when using market shares as a filter for determining whether a merger warrants further investigation.

[27] The same is true for most Member States. Even in Germany where the presumption of collective dominance is based on market shares, it has been recognised by economists working within the Federal Cartel Office that collective dominance should be equated with coordinated effects.

[28] See Werden (2008) and Vickers (2002).

likely actual effects on competition arising from the merger in question, there is either no or little significant difference between the two types of merger test.

Secondly, it has been argued that the introduction of the SIEC test introduces a clearer separation between the ex ante competition test applied in the context of merger control and the ex post concept of dominance under Article 82 on the abuse of dominance. The concern here is that the use of the concept of dominance designed for Article 82 leads to an inappropriate threshold in merger control; what is appropriate for Article 82 differs from what is appropriate for merger control. In particular, it was argued that the threshold for a finding of dominance under Article 82 was too low,[29] but that any increase in the threshold for finding dominance would necessarily spill over to merger control. Introducing a different test, it was argued, allows for the possibility of a much higher threshold for intervention under Article 82 than under EC merger control.[30]

However, practice since the introduction of the SIEC test tends to suggest that the outcome of the change in the substantive merger test may have had the direct opposite effect; namely, the threshold for intervention has decreased below 40 per cent. Indeed, there is no lower limit to when the Commission will ex ante rule out intervention.[31] In consequence, the introduction of the SIEC test arguably raises a real danger of a more (some might say overly) intrusive merger regime that is not only costly for the merging parties but for the competitive process as a whole and therefore for consumers.[32]

The reduction in the threshold for intervening against a merger with a   **7–011** market share below the standard dominance threshold of 40–50 per cent can be justified on the grounds that even at relatively low levels of concentration, horizontal mergers might remove an "important" competitive constraint.[33] But this raises an important issue as to how to distinguish "important" competitive constraints from "unimportant" ones. By definition, all horizontal mergers involve firms active in the same relevant

[29]   As Werden (2008) notes, in the US, courts have indicated that a market share below 50% precludes the inference of market power and many in the United States argue that a market share in excess of 70% for 5 years is necessary for an inference of market power.

[30]   It should, however, be noted that there are good analytical grounds for defining the relevant market more widely in some merger cases relative to the definition that would be appropriately applied in an Article 82 investigation. See Chapter 4 for a discussion of this point.

[31]   The Horizontal Merger Guidelines state that a combined market share of below 25% provides only "an indication" that a merger does not give rise to competition concerns.

[32]   The SLC test has been a feature of US merger control since 1914. During the 1960s, applying the SLC test, resulted in a number of mergers being prohibited in extremely fragmented markets. See, e.g. *United States v Von's Grocery Co 384 US* (1966) and *United States v Pabst Brewing Co 384 US* (1966).

[33]   See, e.g. Vickers (2004) who states that "numerous mergers could seriously jeopardise competition without crossing the threshold of dominant market power".

market and therefore remove some competitive constraint. In most cases, in line with the traditional analysis of single firm dominance, the importance of the pre-merger competitive constraint can be assessed with reference to a firm's market share. However, as the Horizontal Merger Guidelines note, where firms supply differentiated products some firms may be closer competitors than others in the sense that market shares understate the competitive constraint between the two merging parties.[34] The closer competitors the merging parties are, the more likely it is that a merger will give rise to significant unilateral effects.[35]

It has therefore been argued that, because the dominance test relies on a structural approach to the competitive assessment of horizontal mergers, it places too much emphasis on market definition and market shares, and may therefore fail to capture an anti-competitive merger where the two firms are particularly close competitors. The concern is that relying on market shares when analysing a merger involving highly differentiated products may obscure the possibility that two firms are particularly close competitors and, consequently, despite each having only a small share of total sales, the merger would give rise to unilateral effects. In such cases, anticompetitive mergers of this type would only be caught if the market were defined narrowly. Capturing unilateral effects therefore requires markets to be defined narrowly.[36] Advocates of the SIEC test argue that this narrow market definition would then affect the analysis of future mergers in that industry. However, this is a "formalistic" rather than economic or "effects-based" argument. It ignores both the fact that this "narrow" market definition might indeed be the appropriate one for assessing future mergers and the fact that different mergers even within the same industry can raise different concerns.

Furthermore, these arguments are, in practice, largely empty since a structural analysis continues to play an important role in the competitive assessment of mergers involving highly differentiated products, as the experience of EU merger control subsequent to the change in the substantive test demonstrates.[37] Indeed, the additional complexities of assessing the likely competitive impact of a merger in industries with highly differentiated products derives less from difficulties of defining the relevant market but rather with the interpretation of the resulting market shares.

**7–012**     Thirdly, in addition to potentially setting the market share threshold too high under the dominance test, the dominance test is also said to include "blind spots" or "gaps" since it is alleged that there exist certain anti-

---

[34]  Closeness of competition is defined with reference to the propensity of the customers of one of the merging parties to switch to products supplied by the other merging party. The greater that propensity, the *closer* competitors the two firms are said to be. See para.28, EC Merger Guidelines.

[35]  See para.7–026 for a more detailed discussion of the closeness of competition and how to assess it in practice.

[36]  It could be argued that this is the approach taken by the US courts in *Office Staples*.

[37]  The same is true for US merger control.

competitive mergers that could not be categorised as creating or strengthening a position of either single firm dominance or of collective dominance, where collective dominance is confined to encompassing anticompetitive outcomes arising from an increased likelihood of tacit collusion, i.e. coordinated effects. A number of hypothetical examples have been put forward which it is claimed would fall outside the scope of single firm dominance. The oft-cited example of a blind spot under a dominance test is the proposed acquisition by Heinz, the third largest producer of baby food in the United States, of Milnot Holding Corp, whose primary subsidiary was Beech-Nut, the second largest baby food producer. The merger would have given the combined firm 33 per cent of the market. Almost all of the remainder of the market was accounted for by the market leader, Gerber, with a market share of 65 per cent. The relevant market was prepared baby food, in particular jarred baby food, in the United States (with the possibility of there being regional markets though this makes no difference to the assessment).

This merger was held to give rise to unilateral effects because supermarkets preferred to stock only two brands of baby food, with Gerber almost always being chosen as one of them; Gerber was found in 90 per cent of supermarkets, Beech-Nut and Heinz at 45 per cent and 40 per cent respectively. In other words, there was alleged to be intense competition between the two merging parties to be the *second brand* on the shelf. The two firms were also found to have had a history of competing on innovation in product development and differentiation. This competition between the two firms "forced Gerber as well to compete on price and innovation for sales."[38] The deal was abandoned after the Court of appeals reversed the district court's denial of an injunction. Many commentators argued that this case could not have been caught under the old dominance test since it involved the second and third largest firms and therefore (it is argued) this makes it unlikely that the merger could have been said to create or strengthen a position of single firm dominance.[39]

The Commission's decision in *T-Mobile Austria/tele.ring* is presented as "proof" that there were indeed gap cases under the old dominance test.[40] That case involved a merger between the second largest and fourth largest mobile phone operators in Austria. Although the merger increased T-Mobile Austria's market share to about a third of the market, the company

[38]   *FTC v H.J. Heinz Co and Milnot Holding Corp*: Memorandum in Support of Preliminary Injunction (2000).
[39]   We note that the alleged blind spot only arises if dominance is defined solely with reference to market shares and, importantly, on the appropriate definition of the relevant market. In this case, given that the competitive concern was a reduction in competition to be the *second brand on the shelf* defining the relevant market to reflect this concern cannot be ruled out. Moreover, even to the extent that this case would not have been caught under the old dominance test, there would appear to be no other or at most, extremely few cases that would have fallen into the "gap".
[40]   COMP/M.3916 *T-Mobile Austria/tele.ring* (2005).

remained smaller than Mobilkom, the largest operator in the Austrian mobile telephony market. However, although it was argued that the theory of harm in this case related to unilateral effects and that such a case would have been difficult to fit within the concept of single firm dominance, the decision indicates that the main concerns arose from the alleged "maverick" behaviour of *tele.ring*.[41] But such concerns are relevant to a theory of harm relating to coordinated effects rather than unilateral effects and, as such, it is unconvincing (to the authors at least) that this case provides a genuine example of a gap case.

In summary, there should therefore in practice be little to distinguish either the competitive analysis undertaken or the outcome of that analysis under the two tests, especially since, as noted above, a structural analysis continues to play an important role in the practical assessment of mergers under the SIEC test.[42] Moreover, if dominance is defined as "significant market power", as many would advocate, then the differences between the dominance test and the SIEC test are at most negligible.[43] Indeed, we would argue that the change in the merger test has had little if any impact on the outcome of merger decisions since 2004.[44,45]

## THE ROLE OF THE RELEVANT MARKET IN MERGER ANALYSIS

**7–013** Under the old dominance test, it was unsurprising that the definition of the relevant market played an important part in the Commission's decision-making process. However, even under the new SIEC test, market definition continues to play an important role in the competitive assessment of mergers, not least because the Commission continues to place significant

[41] See para.7–066 on coordinated effects for a discussion of mavericks.
[42] It should also be noted that the concept of dominance continues to be central to the Commission's assessment of horizontal mergers; the Merger Regulation and the Horizontal Merger Guidelines state that the Commission determines "whether the merger would significantly impede effective competition, *in particular through the creation or the strengthening of a dominant position*" (emphasis added).
[43] Indeed, the debate may simply arise from the lack of a precise economic definition of "the creation or strengthening of a dominant position". See Kolasky (2002): "prior to 1982 we did not have a clear definition of what the Clayton Act meant by a 'substantial lessening of competition.' One of the key innovations in the 1982 [US Merger Guidelines] was to define "lessening of competition" in purely economic terms as a merger that is likely to "create or enhance market power or to facilitate its exercise." The guidelines went on to define "market power" as "the ability of one or more firms profitably to maintain prices above competitive levels for a significant period of time." By incorporating these economic concepts into our test for substantial lessening of competition, the guidelines firmly rooted merger policy in economic science.".
[44] It should also be noted that the Commission continues to apply the old dominance philosophy whereby any increase in a dominant firm's market share is presumed to give rise to competition concerns. This is at odds with the economic approach to the assessment of unilateral effects that is discussed below.
[45] For a discussion of the impact of the change, see Röller and de la Mano (2006).

weight on post-merger market shares. In addition, experience of the assessment of horizontal mergers under the new substantive test reveals that whether a merger is considered to raise serious doubts continues to be driven primarily by a structural assessment.[46] Moreover, from a practical perspective, defining the relevant market continues to provide a useful filter for determining whether a more detailed assessment of the merger is required;[47] put simply, mergers involving firms with low market shares in a properly defined relevant market cannot give rise to competition concerns and therefore do not require a detailed assessment.[48] Finally, it is worth noting that disregarding market definition raises a real danger that important competitive constraints are ignored from the competitive assessment entirely. Consequently, the definition of the relevant market continues to represent an important analytical step in the competitive assessment.[49]

As explained in Chapter 4, the definition of the relevant market allows an assessment of market structure, including inter alia the calculation of market shares and how these are affected by the merger and the identification of those suppliers that provide the most effective competitive constraints on the commercial activities of the merging parties. The Commission's Notice on market definition states clearly that the interpretation of the guidance notes to defining the relevant market contained in Form CO is to be made in accordance with the approach presented in the Notice.[50]

It is also worth reiterating that the assessment of mergers is concerned with whether the structural change implied by the horizontal merger will result in prices increasing post-merger (i.e. a forward-looking analysis), and therefore differs from the competitive assessment conducted in most Article 81 and Article 82 investigations which are concerned with the current market situation and are often backward looking. This difference has not only important ramifications for the use and interpretation of empirical analysis employed in the respective competition inquires, but also in relation to market definition. In assessing horizontal mergers, the appropriate benchmark for assessing the hypothesised price increase is the

---

[46] As a result, the basic concept of dominance, or significant market power, is still relevant to the competitive assessment under the SIEC test. Indeed, in the majority of cases, the practical approach adopted by the Commission mirrors exactly the competitive assessment under the old substantive merger test. The Commission even continues to argue that where a firm possess a large pre-merger market share even a very small market share increment will give rise to competition concerns.

[47] However, as noted above, market shares can both under- and overstate the importance of the competitive constraint between the merging parties when products are significantly differentiated.

[48] See para.10, Horizontal Merger Guidelines.

[49] Moreover, the notification procedure requires the parties to complete Form CO s.6 of which requires the parties to define relevant product and geographic markets.

[50] European Commission's *"Notice on the Definition of the Relevant Market for the Purposes of Community Competition Law"* [1997] OJ C372/5; [1998] 4 C.M.L.R. 177 para.9.

prevailing price level. This means that in relation to horizontal mergers, the Cellophane fallacy is extremely unlikely to apply in the context of a horizontal merger; arguments to the contrary are simply wrong.[51] In consequence, it is entirely consistent for a relevant market for the purposes of assessing a horizontal merger to be different to the relevant market defined in the context of Article 81 and Article 82 investigations.[52]

**7–014**     The importance of a continued structural assessment is evidenced by the use of market share thresholds and concentration measures based on the Herfindhal-Hirschmann Index (HHI).[53,54] The Horizontal Merger Guidelines state that "[m]arket shares and concentration levels provide useful first indications of the market structure and of the competitive importance of both the merging parties and their competitors".[55]

The purpose of providing market share thresholds is (or should be) to provide a clear one-tailed test; if the merging parties' market share is not in excess of the threshold then all competition concerns can be readily dismissed without the need for detailed investigation. In setting the safe harbour threshold, explicit account needs to be given to the likely impact on enforcement. Setting the threshold too "high" would permit anti-competitive mergers; whereas setting the threshold too "low" would imply that more mergers will be subject to detailed scrutiny. This, in itself, does not necessarily raise any serious concerns (other than resource constraints) providing that these market share thresholds are not perceived as giving rise to a presumption (albeit a rebuttal one) of competition concerns.

The Horizontal Merger Guidelines state that mergers where the post-merger entity would have a limited market share are unlikely to impede effective competition. This is particularly the case where the market share of the merging parties does not exceed 25 per cent.[56] This threshold is similar to the (unofficial) threshold employed by the US Department of Justice and Federal Trade Commission which states that a merger is unlikely to give rise to significant unilateral effects unless the post-merger firm has a market share in excess of 35 per cent.[57] The Horizontal Merger Guidelines state that mergers that give rise to a combined market share above 50 per cent are normally considered to be problematic absent

---

[51] COMP/M.5096 *RCA/MAV Cargo* (2008) provides a good example of the erroneous application of the Cellephone fallacy reasoning. See Chapter 4 for a discussion of this case and the perils of unthinking appeals to the cellophane fallacy to dismiss "unhelpful" evidence.

[52] Chapter 4 provides an example of the different market definitions that might arise under Article 82 and under the Merger Regulation.

[53] The HHI index is calculated by summing the squares of the individual market shares of all firms in the market. See Chapter 3 for a discussion of HHI measures.

[54] The use of market share thresholds is a common feature of merger control regimes around the world including the US, Germany, Australia and the UK.

[55] para.14, Horizontal Merger Guidelines.

[56] This market share threshold applies to the assessment of unilateral effects and not to the assessment of coordinated effects. See Horizontal Merger Guidelines fn.24.

[57] See, for example, Section 2.211 US Horizontal Merger Guidelines (1997).

evidence to show that actual or potential competitors are able to expand their sales sufficiently.[58] The Horizontal Merger Guidelines also contain thresholds based on HHI levels and the change in HHI where the Commission is unlikely to intervene. These are as follows.[59]

- HHI below 1,000;[60]

- HHI lies between 1,000 and 2,000 and the delta (i.e. the change in the pre-merger and post-merger HHIs) is below 250;[61] and

- HHI lies above 2,000 and the delta is below 150.[62]

These HHI thresholds are illustrated in Figure 7.2 below. Horizontal **7–015** merger cases that fall within the white area are "unlikely" to create horizontal competition concerns. The cases that fall within the grey area may be identified as "potentially problematic" cases where a detailed analysis may be required.

**Figure 7.2: Graphical illustration of the HHI thresholds in the 7–016 Horizontal Merger Guidelines**

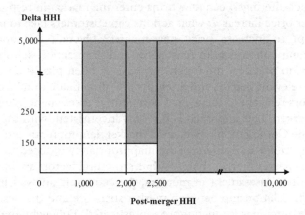

These thresholds are set at levels such that many horizontal mergers are likely to exceed them. For example, a relevant market in which there are ten firms each with a 10 per cent market share (i.e. a very fragmented market structure) would have an HHI of 1,000. Furthermore, a merger between two firms in an eight-firm symmetric market (i.e. pre-merger each

---

58   para.17, Horizontal Merger Guidelines.
59   These HHI thresholds mirror closely those contained in the DoJ/FTC horizontal merger guidelines.
60   para.19, Horizontal Merger Guidelines.
61   para.20, Horizontal Merger Guidelines.
62   A number of exceptions are provided. See para.20, Horizontal Merger Guidelines.

firm has a 12.5 per cent market share) would also exceed these thresholds.[63] But such mergers are extremely unlikely to give rise to either unilateral effects or coordinated effects.

It is therefore important to recognise, as the Horizontal Merger Guidelines clearly state, that these thresholds only provide an initial indicator of the likelihood of competition concerns and do not give rise to a presumption of either the existence or the absence of competition concerns.[64]

Although market shares, and therefore the definition of the relevant market, play an important role in the competitive assessment of mergers, it is important that this role is not overstated. First, the definition of the relevant market forms merely the first step in a two-step analysis. In loose terms, the first stage involves a "macro" consideration of the interaction of groups of products affected by the horizontal merger. The type of questions one attempts to answer at this stage of the inquiry do not relate to individual firms. The second stage involves a "micro" consideration of the competitive position of firms within the defined relevant market. This micro consideration includes addressing such questions as the following: are some firms closer competitors to one another?; are rival firms able to expand in response to any putative price increase?; can rival firms alter their product offerings?; can new firms enter the market in response to any post-merger price increase?; what actions can customers take to undermine any attempt to increase price post-merger? Overall, this approach to assessing competition is both reasonable and, in practice, sensible.

**7–017**    However, in practice, too much emphasis is often placed on the definition of the relevant market and attempts are often made to take account of all the factors relevant to the overall competitive assessment in defining the relevant market. This approach is not only inconsistent with the approach set out in the Commission's Notice on market definition but can also result in the competitive assessment being inappropriately reduced to a calculation of post-merger market shares. While structural factors are important in the competitive assessment of mergers, the economic analysis involved in assessing the relationship between market structure and the desirability of competitive outcomes is much more sophisticated. Following the criticisms of the structure-conduct-performance (SCP) paradigm, it is now accepted that high levels of concentration need not preclude a market from operating effectively. In contrast to the SCP model, modern economic analysis does not infer that high concentration necessarily leads to poor competitive outcomes.[65] Rather, it merely states that high levels of concentration are in general a necessary condition for such outcomes.

---

[63]  The pre-merger HHI is 1,250 and the delta is 312.5.
[64]  para.21, Horizontal Merger Guidelines. The fact that a horizontal merger exceeds these HHI thresholds does not establish a "presumption" that the merger is anticompetitive.
[65]  For instance, a high level of concentration in a perfectly contestable market (i.e. a market with no barriers to entry or exit) would not lead to an anti-competitive outcome.

It is often argued that defining the relevant market is neither necessary nor appropriate in industries that are characterised by competition among highly differentiated products since it is more difficult to draw a distinction between products that are "in" the market (because they provide an effective competitive constraint on the other products included in the market) and those held to be "outside" the relevant market (because they do not provide an effective competitive constraint).[66] However, it is important to note that the Hypothetical Monopolist test is inherently designed to deal with differentiated products.[67] It explicitly recognises that products can be imperfect substitutes and is designed to address the important issue of what degree of substitution between products is necessary in order for them to be included in the same relevant market.[68] Put simply, the fact that products in an industry are differentiated does not mean that the Hypothetical Monopolist test cannot be usefully applied.

The potential issues raised by differentiated product markets are not therefore in relation to the appropriateness of seeking to identify the source of important competitve constraints (this is after all what defining the relevant market entails). Rather, the potential issues relate to the extent to which market shares can convey information regarding competitive constraints in markets with differentiated products and whether the resulting market shares provide a misleading picture of the post-merger competitive environment. That possibility arises since market shares are unable to discriminate between "close" competitors and "not so close" competitors. Implicitly, an analysis based on market shares assumes that the magnitude of the competitive constraints provided by each product in the relevant market is related to that product's market share. But that assumption ignores the very essence of competition between differentiated products where the strength of the competitive constraints that exist between the various products may depend more on the closeness of substitutability between them than on the share of total sales for which they account. In consequence, an analysis based purely on market shares will have even more limitations in markets with differentiated products than in markets with homogeneous products.[69]

However, notwithstanding the additional complexities of interpreting   **7–018** market shares where products are highly differentiated, the exercise of defining the relevant market and calculating market shares provides a useful filter for assessing whether a merger raises serious competition

---

[66] The distinction between homogenous and differentiated products should not be taken too literally since most industries are characterised to some extent by differentiation, e.g. even where products are truly homogenous, the existence of transport costs may mean that plants located close to one another are closer competitors than plants located further apart.

[67] For further discussion of this point, see Chapter 4.

[68] See Scheffman and Simons (2003).

[69] For a detailed discussion of the implications of differentiated products for the role of market share in merger analysis, see Baker and Coscelli (1999) Farrell and Shapiro (2008), Shapiro (1996) and Carlton (2007).

concerns. In the presence of highly differentiated products, if even within a narrowly defined relevant market the combined share of the two merging parties is relatively low, it is extremely unlikely that the merger will give rise to serious competition concerns. Moreover, even where market shares by themselves do not provide a good guide to assessing the likely competitive impact of a merger, the competitive assessment still requires the identification of the sellers of close substitutes. For example, economic modelling of unilateral effects often requires estimating the proportion of the acquiring firm's customers that consider the acquired firm's product as their second choice. The results produced are likely to be erroneous if close substitutes are omitted from the analysis. Accordingly, one outcome of the market definition process, the identification of the sellers of close substitutes, remains important even if one were to consider that market shares by themselves contribute little to merger analysis in highly differentiated markets.[70]

## UNILATERAL EFFECTS[71]

**7–019**   A horizontal merger is said to give rise to unilateral effects if the merged firm finds it profitable to increase price regardless of the reactions of the remaining competitors.[72] This section outlines the key economic issues to be addressed in assessing whether a horizontal merger gives rise to unilateral effects and the type of evidence that should be presented in order to establish such a theory of harm. Central to establishing any theory of unilateral effects is the notion of restricting output; an inevitable consequence of increasing price is that the merged firm must accept a reduction in the volume of sales.[73] The following sections provide more detail on the analysis of unilateral effects.

First, we discuss the necessary conditions for unilateral effects to arise, i.e. for the merged firm to have an incentive to increase price, restrict output (or, more generally reduce its service levels or product quality offering). We then discuss why market shares, and the increment arising from the merger, form the appropriate cornerstone of the competitive assessment of unilateral effects. We then consider the concept of closeness

---

[70]   Baker (1997).

[71]   As noted above, although the Horizontal Merger Guidelines talk of non-coordinated effects rather than unilateral effects, we prefer to use the standard economics terminology.

[72]   When the primary competitive focus is on product innovation, rather than price competition, the main potential competitive concern with a merger will be that it will reduce the rate of innovation and the speed with which new products are brought to the market.

[73]   As noted above, this is a consequence of the downward-sloping nature of demand curves: given the demand curve for a particular product, higher prices necessarily imply lower output levels. Output could be restricted in terms of production, capacity, product range or product quality. In the majority of cases the focus is on a potential restriction of production.

of competition in both differentiated and homogeneous product markets, and then in industries characterised by bidding competition. Finally, and importantly, we consider the importance of taking into account the dynamic responses of firms, both actual and potential competitors, and of customers.

## Key principles of unilateral effects

A merger will give rise to unilateral effects if and only if the merged entity 7–020 would find it profitable post-merger to increase price (or restrict output) acting unilaterally; namely, independently of its competitors.[74] Any increase in price (or equivalently a restriction of output) is always associated with both benefits and costs.[75] The profitability of restricting output will depend on these two countervailing factors. The benefits arise primarily from the increase in price.[76] The costs of price increases or equivalent output restrictions arise from the loss of the margins that would have been earned absent the loss in sales. The greater the margin earned on each sale, the greater the opportunity cost associated with a given price increase or output restriction, and the more likely that such a strategy is unprofitable.[77]

Figures 7.3 and 7.4 illustrate these costs and benefits associated with a restriction of output.

Figure 7.3 considers the implications for one of the merging firms of increasing price pre-merger. The left-hand panel shows the profits of this firm, Firm 1, at pre-merger prevailing price levels. At the prevailing price level p1, Firm 1 earns a margin over and above the incremental costs associated with producing an additional unit, i.e. the difference between the price at which the good is sold and its incremental cost. Total operating profits are given by the margin times the number of units sold.[78] The right-hand panel illustrates the impact of any attempt to increase price pre-merger.

By increasing price, Firm 1 would increase the margin earned on each

---

[74] Note, this is not to say that competitors will not respond to the merger. Typically, post-merger competitors will adjust their commercial behaviour. However, the profitability of the unilateral price increase does not require that competing firms react in a certain manner. This is in contrast to coordinated effects, where the profitability of the post-merger output restriction depends on the competitive behaviour of competing firms.

[75] Some authors, e.g. Motta (2004), argue that all horizontal mergers, absent efficiencies, give rise to price increases. As a matter of theory, these authors are correct in a static world in which firms do not respond to the merger. But, as a practical matter, we disagree with this position; because such arguments disregard the dynamic aspects of competition that are prevalent in most real-world markets.

[76] If one is concerned with capacity as the relevant description of output, the benefit will also extend to deferred capital expenditure costs.

[77] This insight is analogous to that provided by critical loss analysis. See Chapter 4 for a more extensive discussion.

[78] This ignores any fixed costs. In many industries, firms earn high margins on each unit sold but earn very low profits due to the need to cover large fixed costs.

unit sold. The increase in the margin is shown by the increase in price from p1 to p2. However, that increase in price is necessarily associated with a reduction in the volume of sales. Hence, there are benefits and costs. The benefits are shown in Figure 7.3 as the top box (Box B); the increase in the margin on all sales "retained" following the price increase. The costs are shown as the lower box (Box A); this cost is given by the pre-merger margin times the volume of sales lost.

**7–021 Figure 7.3: Pre-merger price increases are unprofitable**

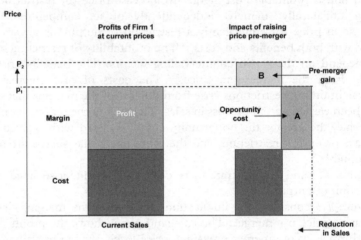

Absent the merger, the level of price and/or output must be optimal for the merging parties; any increase in price will be insufficient to offset the losses associated with that output restriction.[79] We therefore know that, pre-merger, Box A must be larger than Box B.[80]

However, a horizontal merger alters the calculus of the trade-off between the benefits and the associated costs. The calculus alters following a horizontal merger since, post-merger, some of the sales that would have been lost pre-merger following an increase in one of the merging parties' prices may be "captured" by the combined firm (i.e. sales lost by one of the merging firms to the other, and vice versa, are no longer losses to the combined firm). The greater the propensity of the customers of one of the merging firms to switch to the other firm's products, the greater potential there will be for the merger to give rise to unilateral effects. This can be seen in Figure 7.4.

[79] As explained in Chapter 2, this must be true by definition. If it were not true then, under the assumption of profit maximisation, the firm would have already increased price.

[80] If firms are able to adjust output in a continuous fashion and price is a continuous function of output then pre-merger it will be the case that the opportunity cost associated with restricting output will be equal to the marginal benefit associated with that output restriction, i.e. Box A will be equal in area to Box B.

**Figure 7.4: Horizontal mergers lead to an increase in the**  7–022
**benefit of price increases**[81]

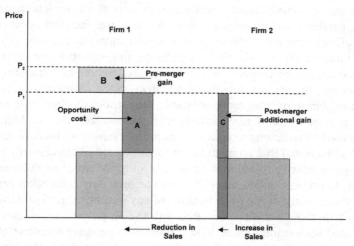

The left-hand panel replicates the right-hand panel of Figure 7.3, i.e. it shows the implications if one of the merging parties were to increase price; the benefits and costs are the same as pre-merger. The right-hand panel shows the impact on the other merging party. Following an increase in the price of Firm 1, sales of Firm 2 increase and this implies that the merger between Firm 1 and Firm 2 gives rise to an additional benefit; namely, the margin earned on the increase in the sales of Firm 2. The larger the increase in the sales of Firm 2 (i.e. the greater the extent to which consumers of Firm 1 would switch to Firm 2), the more likely it is that the total benefits (i.e. Box B plus Box C) will exceed the costs (i.e. Box A).[82]

Of course, Figure 7.4 only considers the change in the pricing of products sold by Firm 1 following the merger. It is also possible, indeed likely, that the pricing of products sold by Firm 2 would also change. This would have the following effects:

- Increasing the margins on retained sales of Firm 2.

- Reduction in the loss of sales experienced by Firm 1 following an increase in its price.

- Reduction in the increase in sales experienced by Firm 2 following an increase in the price charged for products produced by Firm 1.

[81]  We assume here for expositional reasons that the prices of both firms are the same.
[82]  If firms can adjust output in a continuous manner and price is a continuous function of output, then ignoring the dynamic responses of competitors and customers, the benefits from restricting output (i.e. Box B plus Box C) will exceed the opportunity costs associated with that restriction (i.e. Box A). If firms cannot adjust output continuously and/or price is not a continuous function of output, then this is no longer necessarily the case.

The first two effects represent an increase in the benefits to the merged entity whilst the third would represent a decrease.

**7–023**　　The above considerations represent only part of a complete assessment of the likelihood of unilateral effects. In assessing the likely post-merger trade-off between costs and benefits of a price increase, account also needs to be taken of the response of competitors. For example, the more likely competitors are to respond to the output restriction by expanding their own output, the greater the mitigating effect on the ultimate price increase achieved. Similarly, the more able are competitors to alter their product offering to compete more effectively with the merged firm, the higher will be the level of switching to competitors in the event of an increase in price. It should be noted that competitor responses would not necessarily need to offset completely any attempt to restrict output (either in volume or in timing) to prevent unilateral effects from arising. Any competitor response will serve to mitigate the price benefits of any output restriction. Unilateral effects arise if the benefits associated with the output restriction exceed the associated opportunity costs. The greater the aggregate response of competitors, the lower the benefits and hence, all else equal, the lower the likelihood that the output restriction would be profitable. Paragraph 7–039 provides further discussion of the need to take into account this, and other, dynamic responses.

　　The following outlines the basic approaches to assessing whether a horizontal merger is likely to give rise to unilateral effects, and in so doing highlights the type of evidence that can be used to inform the analysis. As the above discussion ought to have made clear, determining whether the benefits will outweigh the costs of a price increase necessarily involves an empirical analysis. The simple fact that the benefits associated with a given output restriction increase post-merger is an insufficient basis for concluding that a horizontal merger will give rise to unilateral effects.

### Standard approach to assessing unilateral effects: market share analysis

**7–024**　The standard approach to determining whether a horizontal merger is likely to give rise to unilateral effects involves an assessment of post-merger market shares. This traditional assessment of mergers implicitly measures the key factors discussed in the previous section. *Ceteris paribus*, the higher the merged firm's market share, the greater is the benefit on the installed customer base of a price increase or an output restriction.[83] Furthermore, market shares may provide a useful proxy for the strength of competitive constraints provided by each firm in the relevant market, i.e. the larger the

---

[83]　Of course, the higher the demand and supply elasticity in a given market, the less likely the firms are, even if they enjoy high market shares, to find an attempted increase in price profitable.

market share of a merging party, the greater its pre-merger competitive constraint is assumed to be.

As a result, in general, the larger the post-merger market share of the merged entity, the more likely the merger is, *ceteris paribus*, to give rise to unilateral effects. However, it is also important to consider the increment arising from a merger. A merger that gives rise to a post-merger market share of 60 per cent arising from combining a firm with a 57 per cent market share with one with a 3 per cent market share is likely to have a substantially different effect on post-merger competitive conditions than a merger between two firms both with 30 per cent market share; the latter being more likely to give rise to unilateral effects concerns. The substantial difference arises because of the impact of these two mergers on the trade-off between the benefits and costs arising from a price increase or a restriction of output. In the former case, where the increment in market share is only 3 per cent, the benefits to the merged firm are only increased marginally; whereas in the latter case where the increment in market share is 30 per cent, there is a significant impact on the benefits arising from a restriction of output.

Under the dominance test, combined market shares above 40 per cent were usually seen as providing a threshold below which no competition concerns were raised. However, since the change in the merger test, the market share threshold above which a merger might be held to give rise to unilateral effects has decreased to 25 per cent.[84] This change has been introduced to capture the possibility that market shares significantly understate the competitive constraint that exists pre-merger between the merging parties. As noted above, where products are highly differentiated, market shares do not always provide a good indicator of the likely competitive effects of a merger since some products are "closer" competitors than others. The concept of closeness of competition can also arise in industries where (a) firms sell homogeneous products but are distinguished primarily by their capacities and (b) in markets characterised by bidding for tenders.[85] In assessing the likelihood of a horizontal merger giving rise to unilateral effects, it is therefore important to assess whether market shares over- or understate the magnitude of the competitive constraint between the merging parties.

However, regardless of its level, the market share threshold is merely a  **7–025** filter and it ought not to be presumed that mergers exceeding the threshold necessarily give rise to competition concerns. As noted above, it is now widely recognised that the scope for a merger to give rise to unilateral effects depends not just on market shares but also on other factors and in particular on the ease with which rival firms can expand output and the

---

[84] See para.18, Horizontal Merger Guidelines.
[85] See paras 7–034—7–035 for a discussion of these two concepts of closeness of competition.

dynamic responses that those rivals might make (for example, through the repositioning of existing products) in response to attempts by the merged entity to increase price.[86] In other words, it is important to extend the competitive assessment beyond a simple static analysis (i.e. one based primarily on current market shares) to one that explicitly adopts a dynamic assessment (i.e. one that takes into account inter alia the scope for firms to expand output and/or to reposition their respective product offerings, including the introduction of new products).[87]

We discuss the assessment of closeness of competition and then the importance of taking into account dynamic responses in turn.

## Closeness of competition with highly differentiated products

**7–026** Potential variations in the "closeness" of competition between competing firms that arises from product or geographical differentiation raises a number of additional complications in applying the traditional approach to assessing whether a merger gives rise to unilateral effects.[88] As noted in the discussion of the role played by the relevant market in the assessment of horizontal mergers, it is often argued that defining the relevant market is much more problematic in industries characterised by a high degree of differentiation. But, as we have seen, the Hypothetical Monopolist Test is well-suited to addressing such issues. This implies that any additional complications that arise in industries with highly differentiated goods and services relate to the interpretation that can be drawn from market shares rather than the definition of the relevant market. Interpreting market shares in highly differentiated industries is rendered more difficult since the very essence of competition between differentiated products implies that consumers do not consider all products to be equally substitutable. In consequence, products do not all impose the same strength of competitive constraint on each other. Where this is the case, market shares provide a poor proxy for discriminating between "close" competitors and "not so close" competitors.[89]

A competitor will be said to be, loosely speaking, "close" if following a relative price increase a significant proportion of the resulting lost sales would be gained by that competitor. The concept of "closeness of

---

[86] The *Pirelli/BICC* merger provides a good example of a competitive assessment that went beyond merely assessing post-merger combined market shares. The Commission noted that high market shares at a national level reflected previously state-controlled purchasing decisions in the affected energy utility industries. Following the liberalisation and privatisation of these industries, the Commission concluded that non-domestic firms now represented an effective alternative to domestic customers. See COMP/M.1882, *Pirelli/BICC* (2000) and Bishop and Lofaro (2001).

[87] Unfortunately, these factors are often given little weight in the Commission's assessment.

[88] Vellturo (1997).

[89] In addition, product differentiation makes coordinated effects less likely. See para.x.xx below for a discussion of coordinated effects.

competition" when a merger concerns highly differentiated products can be thought of in terms of product characteristics and geographical location. For example, a premium ice cream, say, is likely to face "closer" competition from another supplier of a premium ice cream brand than from a supplier of an own-label product. Similarly, where transportation costs are important, a supplier is likely to face "closer" competition from suppliers located nearby than from those located further away.

The concept of "closeness" of competition is illustrated in the following **7–027** example. Suppose there are four firms, A, B, C and D, each with sales of 100. Suppose that if A raises its price by 5 per cent, it will lose 20 per cent of its sales, which makes the price rise unprofitable. These sales would be diverted to the other three firms as shown in Table 7.2. This Table shows that 15 consumers divert from A to B, three divert to C and two divert to D. In this sense, B is a closer competitor to A than either C or D; the extent to which consumers would divert from A to B is understated by B's market share. If A and B were to merge, then an increase in the post-merger price of products supplied by A would lead to the combined firm, AB, losing only five units of sales. In consequence, increasing the price of A by 5 per cent is more likely to be profitable than a merger between A and D, where the same increase in the price of products supplied by A would lead to the loss of 18 units of sales.

**Table 7.2:   An illustration of unilateral effects**   **7–028**

| Firm | Sales at current prices | Sales if A raises price by 5 per cent |
|------|------------------------|---------------------------------------|
| A | 100 | 80 |
| B | 100 | 115 |
| C | 100 | 103 |
| D | 100 | 102 |
| **AB** | **200** | **195** |

This example illustrates that the degree to which a merger in a differentiated product market might result in a unilateral price increase depends on the relative "closeness" of the merging firms to one another. Based on market shares alone, B, C and D all appear to be providing an equally strong competitive constraint on A. However, examination of the diversion of sales from A to these firms shows that in this hypothetical example, B provides a much stronger pre-merger competitive constraint on A than either C or D since most of A's lost sales went to B, indicating that A and B are in some sense particularly "close" competitors.[90]

However, it is important to understand that the concept of closeness of

---

[90]   Where the degree of competition between products in a market varies across the products, competition is sometimes said to be "localised". Hotelling (1929) provided the first formal treatment of this subject.

competition cannot be divorced entirely from an assessment of market shares. In the above example, B is said to represent a particularly close competitor because the proportion of sales lost to B exceeds that predicted by market shares alone; on the basis of market shares, we would predict that six or seven units[91] would be diverted to B whereas in reality the number of units diverted (in this hypothetical example) would be 15. Assessing whether a merger will result in a reduction in the effectiveness of competition therefore requires an assessment of whether market shares provide a good proxy for the degree of pre-merger competitive constraint or whether they understate or overstate the importance of that competitive constraint. In the case where market shares understate the competitive constraint, we can properly consider two firms to be "close" competitors.

When assessing closeness of competition, it is important that the source of that closeness is clearly articulated and closely examined. All too often, it is asserted that two firms are particularly close competitors without reference being made to the alleged source of that closeness. Assessing whether two firms represent particularly close competitors is an empirical question and cannot (or should not) be determined solely with reference to physical or geographical attributes of the firms concerned. For example, consider a straight road on which four petrol stations are located. On one level, it might appear intuitive that the petrol stations adjacent to one another provide "closer" competitive constraints than non-adjacent petrol stations. But that is not necessarily the case. If all potential customers drive past all of these four petrol stations on their way to work from home then all the petrol stations could be equally close.[92] Similarly, the fact that two firms have more similar offerings than some other competitors cannot by itself be determinative that they represent particularly close competitors.

**7–029**   Furthermore, the identification of the "closest" competitor itself cannot be determinative of the likely effects of a merger. For example, suppose Firm A, a firm with a large market share, represents the next best alternative to the largest number of customers of one of the merging parties but the proportion of switchers is less than indicated by market shares. In contrast, another firm, Firm B, with a small market share, may account for a proportion of switchers in excess of that predicted by market shares. In this hypothetical example, Firm B represents a closer competitor to one of the merging parties than Firm A in the sense that its market share understates the degree to which consumers of the merging parties would switch to it in response to a relative price increase; but the magnitude of the competitive constraint provided by Firm A may well still exceed that provided by Firm B. Moreover, there will be other situations in which while it is strictly speaking true to say one firm is the closest competitor,

---

[91]   Strictly speaking, 20/3 units would be diverted.
[92]   Indeed, two petrol stations located on opposite sides of a motorway are unlikely to represent close competitors.

this does not mean that other firms cannot provide important, indeed almost equally close, competitive constraints.[93] Although a merger is more likely to give rise to unilateral effects in highly differentiated markets if a significant proportion of customers regard the products of the two merging firms as their first and second best choices,[94] the merger is unlikely to give rise to anticompetitive price increases if the product offerings of other competitors are nearly as close alternatives to the merging parties since this will act to limit the extent of any post-merger increases.[95]

Moreover, a focus on "closeness of competition" can result in important competitive constraints being ignored entirely in the competitive assessment. There is therefore a danger that ignoring market definition entirely (or deferring the definition of the relevant market to the end of the competitive assessment) reintroduces an ad hoc subjective analysis of competition of the type that the Hypothetical Monopolist Test was designed to counter, i.e. determining closeness based solely on differences in product characteristics of the merging parties' product offering rather than assessing competitive constraints. Whilst differences in product characteristics may result in product differentiation, such differences do not necessarily imply that two products with similar product characteristics are close competitors in the sense that market shares understate the pre-merger competitive constraint, nor that products with dissimilar characteristics necessarily impose an insignificant pre-merger competitive constraint on one another.[96] Such fallacious reasoning often arises in retailing markets where it is often alleged that competition between specialist high street retailers is often much more intense than that between a specialist high street retailer and either supermarkets or internet retailers. This may be the case, but it cannot be asserted merely on the basis of product characteristics. For example, the fact that the two merging parties are both specialist high street retailers whereas supermarkets and internet providers are not does not necessarily imply that they are "particularly close competitors" in the sense that consumers would switch between them in greater proportion than indicated by their respective market shares.[97] Furthermore, even if it were correct that specialist high street retailers are closest competitors, one still needs to consider the aggregate of the remaining competitive constraints before concluding that unilateral effects are likely.

---

[93] Werden (1998).

[94] See s.2.21 of the US Guidelines for a discussion of this issue.

[95] It is also important to take account of the ability of firms to reposition their product offerings post-merger. See para.7–037 below.

[96] This is analogous to defining relevant markets solely on the basis of differences in the physical characteristics of the products concerned. Such an approach is to be severely criticised for the reasons given in Chapter 4.

[97] Good examples are provided by UK investigations into specialist high street retailing of video games and into book retailing. See *Game Group Plc and Gamestation Ltd: A report on the completed acquisition by Game Group Plc of Gamestation Ltd*, (2008) and *HMV Group Plc and Ottakar's Plc: Proposed acquisition of Ottakar's plc by HMV Group Plc through Waterstone's Booksellers Ltd*, (2006).

The assessment of the closeness of competition can take one of three forms of analysis each of which seek to focus directly on the extent to which the merging parties supply products that provide effective competitive constraints on one another. The three approaches are (a) structural demand analysis; (b) the calculation of diversion ratios; and (c) econometric analysis. Structural demand analysis covers a range of different modelling approaches. These include examining detailed price and sales data for the merging parties (e.g. the AIDS model);[98] price and sales data on the merging products and detailed industry-specific and product-specific cost data (residual demand analysis);[99] or market share and pre-determined elasticity estimates (Antitrust Logit Simulation Model).[100] Each of these approaches enables, in principle, the likely impact of the merger to be simulated.

**7–030**  Unfortunately, each of these approaches to conducting structural demand analysis requires extensive data to be available and in most merger inquiries sufficient data will not be available (see Chapter 10 for a discussion of these techniques). In response to such data limitations, attention has been focused on the calculation of so-called *diversion ratios*. The degree of closeness between two products can be captured to some extent in the diversion ratio. The diversion ratio from Firm A to Firm B (denoted $D_{AB}$) is defined as that proportion of sales lost by Firm A when the price of Firm A increases that are captured by Firm B. For example, suppose the price of Firm A rises by 10 per cent and that as a result sales fall by 1,000 units. If 400 of these lost sales are captured by Firm B, this means that Firm B captured 40 per cent of the sales lost by Firm A and so the diversion ratio from A to B ($D_{AB}$) is 0.4.

In principle, a reliable diversion ratio approach dispenses with any need to define the relevant market because it purports to measure directly the extent of the pre-merger competitive constraints. However, there are a number of pitfalls in using diversion ratios to make predictions of the impact of a merger on competition.[101,102]

First, estimating the diversion ratio properly requires data on the substitution patterns of consumers. In the case of differentiated product markets, there is no benefit to the standard shorthand of calculating diversion ratios with reference to market shares.[103] Using market shares to estimate diversion ratios assumes that the strength of each of the competitive constraints posed by other products on Firm A is proportional to the

---

[98]  Hausmann, Leonard & Zona (1994).
[99]  Baker and Bresnahan (1992).
[100]  Werden and Froeb (1994a, 1994b, 1996) and Werden, Froeb and Tardiff (1994).
[101]  For a critique, see Walker (2006) and RBB Economics (2006).
[102]  See Chapter 11 for a more extensive discussion of these issues.
[103]  Under this approach the diversion ratio from Firm A to Firm B is approximated by the market share of Firm B divided by one hundred minus the market share of Firm A. So if the market share of Firm A is 40%, and that of Firm B is 15%, the diversion ratio from A to B would be 0.25 (i.e. 15/(100–40)).

market shares of those firms. The key issue under consideration—namely the potential that certain products represent closer competitors than others—is therefore not taken into account.[104]

Furthermore, it is difficult to obtain survey analysis of customers'    7–031 switching options that truly captures the behaviour of "marginal" consumers as opposed to "inframarginal" consumers. Differentiated products arise in part because consumers have heterogeneous preferences. For any Product A produced by Firm A there will be purchasers of Product A that would place considerable value on Product A relative to all available alternatives and would continue to buy Product A even if the relative price of Product A were to increase. Such consumers are referred to as inframarginal consumers. There are also purchasers of Product A that buy Product A at current prices but would choose an alternative product if relative prices were to change. In evaluating the relevant diversion ratio between Firms A and B in a merger involving differentiated products it is the importance of Firm B as a destination for the marginal consumers of Firm A that represents the effective measure of the price-constraining effect that Firm B has on Firm A. If a significant number of marginal consumers of Firm A consider Firm B to be their next best alternative then the loss of sales to Firm B which served to constrain the price of Firm A prior to the merger would no longer be "losses" and would instead be retained by the merged firm. In this situation, the merged firm may have an unilateral incentive to raise prices post-merger.

Limiting a diversion ratio analysis to the next best alternative of marginal consumers is therefore not the same as considering whether B is the next best choice to A for all consumers of A. Inframarginal consumers of Firm A will continue to buy Firm A even if relative prices change by a small amount. It is the behaviour of marginal consumers, those who will stop buying A when its price rises, that matters for the competitive assessment. Since by definition, inframarginal and marginal consumers do not have similar preferences, the alternative purchasing preferences of inframarginal consumers may not provide useful information on the preferences of marginal consumers (i.e. the second choices of inframarginal consumers may differ from the second choices of marginal consumers).

Even in the absence of appropriate data, however, the analysis of diversion ratios is incomplete. Diversion ratios consider the proportion of customers that would switch to Firm B from those customers that would switch away from Firm A in response to a price increase. However, it is silent on the question of the number of customers that would switch away from A in the first place. If a large number of customers would switch from A in response to an increase in price, even if a significant proportion of these customers switch to B, the merger between A and B may not be sufficient to enable A to increase price post-merger. For instance, if 90 per

---

[104] Velturo (1997).

cent of customers would switch away from A in response to a 5 per cent price increase, then the fact that 40 per cent of them ($D_{AB}$=0.4) would go to B would not make a merger between A and B profitable. This is a key dynamic in determining the likelihood of unilateral effects that cannot be captured solely by the assessment of diversion ratios and requires further data as to the propensity to switch.

**7–032**     Finally, an assessment of diversion ratios is not dynamic and cannot properly capture the ability of customers to respond to entry or product repositioning. As noted above, such dynamic responses often represent an important source of post-merger competitive constraint, but are often given insufficient weight.

Econometric analysis can also be used in certain circumstances to assess the closeness of competition.[105] The degree of closeness of competition between merging parties can be assessed by considering how the prices earned on sales made by one party when it faces competition from the other merging party compare to the prices earned on sales when it did not face competition from the other merging party. In order to make a like-for-like comparison, it is necessary to take into account other factors that might affect prices in the two samples (i.e. the sample where the two merging parties competed and the sample where they did not). Econometric analysis using multiple regressions is ideally suited to address such questions since it isolates the impact of the presence of one of the merging parties on the prices offered by the other and vice versa.[106] If the results of the econometric analysis were to show that each merging party offers relatively lower prices whenever the other merging party competes compared to the price offered when the other party does not compete, then this would indicate that the merging parties currently exert an important competitive constraint on one another. This would in turn suggest that the proposed merger may be expected to lead to a post-merger price increase. Alternatively, if the results of the econometric analysis were to show that the variation in prices offered by each merging party is largely unaffected (after taking into account all other relevant factors such as the size of the contract and the number of competitors) by the presence of the other merging party, this would indicate that there is nothing unique about the competitive constraint that the two merging parties exert on one another and that,

---

[105] Note, the use of econometrics here is not equivalent to simulation models that have been proposed. The difference is that in the latter case a particular mode of theoretical competition is imposed upon the data. This is done in order to provide estimates of the actual price effects of a merger. However, this is at the cost of making strong assumptions as to the actual nature of competition in the industry at hand and often the results of these models do not conform to industry reality ie they are unable to explain observed outcomes. See Chapter 15 in Part III for a more detailed discussion.

[106] See Part III for a more detailed discussion of the use of econometrics in competition law, in particular "Econometric Annex" which provides an overview of econometric methods and techniques.

therefore, the proposed merger would be unlikely to give rise to significant unilateral effects.[107]

The use of econometrics to assess closeness of competition can be illustrated by the *Oracle/PeopleSoft* case.[108] Both companies were active in design, development, manufacture and distribution of software, in particular enterprise application software (EAS). This software is widely used in business for instance for accounting, supply chain management and human resources. One of the key questions in the Commission's competitive assessment was how closely the merging parties' products competed. Since most of the EAS contracts were individually negotiated between the developer and customer, the prices were represented by individual bids.

The Commission conducted a number of econometric analyses to investigate whether the discounts offered by the winning bidder depended on either the number of bidders or the identity of the final round bidders. The Commission generally found that there was a very strong relationship between the size of the deal and the discount offered. However, no general pattern emerged regarding the impact of the number or identity of final round competitors on the discounts offered by Oracle. Based on this analysis, and the fact that buyers are sophisticated and can exert competitive pressure on bidders (e.g. by re-inviting bidders previously excluded or concealing who else is bidding), the Commission concluded that Oracle was not likely to be in a position to profitably increase prices after the merger.

The closeness of competition can also be assessed using data drawn from **7-033** one or more of the following sources: switching studies, consumer surveys, win/loss reports, and an assessment of market share/sales shifting patterns. Data drawn from these sources can provide useful insights into the closeness of competition between two products (or regions) and can therefore provide important insights into the likely competitive effects of a merger.[109]

## Closeness of competition where firms are distinguished primarily by capacity

So far we have discussed closeness of competition in the context of dif- **7-034** ferentiated products. In general, there is no concept of closeness of competition where products are homogeneous since the products of all firms are near perfect substitutes. In such cases, market shares also do not necessarily provide a good proxy for the competitive strength provided by each competitor. Even competitors that have a comparatively small market share pre-merger can provide an important competitive constraint if they would be in a position to expand sales post-merger, i.e. have excess

---

[107] See Bishop and Lofaro (2005) for a practical discussion of these issues.
[108] COMP/M.3216 *Oracle/PeopleSoft* (2004).
[109] See para.29, Horizontal Merger Guidelines.

capacity pre-merger or are able to relatively quickly (within one or two years) expand capacity. In such instances, barriers to expansion are low and any analysis based solely on market shares will again provide a poor indicator of the merger's impact on competition.

However, if some firms are capacity constrained, this will prevent them expanding output in response to a relative price rise by the merging parties. The existence of capacity constraints therefore reduces the scope for customers of the merging parties to switch away from their products and in consequence increases the possibility of a post-merger price increase being profitable.[110] Whether that is indeed the case will depend on which firms are capacity constrained and how much excess capacity firms currently have. Where a merger involves the only two firms with excess capacity in a homogeneous products market this is likely to lead to a unilateral post-merger price increase unless there are off-setting factors to be taken into account, most notably the ability and speed with which competing firms would be able to add additional production capacity and the presence of any cost efficiencies as a result of the merger.[111]

The importance of potential capacity expansion by competitors is reflected in the *Bertelsmann/Springer* joint venture case.[112] The parties are active in publishing, printing and distribution of newspapers and magazines. The proposed joint venture created a clear market leader in the German market for the printing of magazines with market shares in the range 45–50 per cent, while the next two biggest competitors Schlott and TSB had around 20–25 per cent market share each. The Commission's analysis showed that a significant volume of printing capacity could be made available by competitors for the printing of German magazines if the proposed joint venture were to undertake a price increase for the printing of magazines. Specifically, the capacity to print magazines can be switched away from catalogue and advertising printing. Furthermore, the competitors would have incentives to do so because profit margins in advertisement printing are lower than in magazine printing. The Commission therefore concluded that it was unlikely that the Parties could profitably increase prices post merger.

---

[110] Technically, it has been shown that where firms compete by first setting capacity and then setting prices, this is equivalent to competition according to the Cournot assumption which, as discussed in Chapter 2, leads to higher prices when the number of competitors falls, unless marginal costs also fall significantly. See Kreps and Scheinkman (1983).

[111] It is important to note that whereas so-called green-field investments are often infeasible due to their cost, capacity expansion can also take place via the removal of bottlenecks or through minor infrastructure investment. Indeed, in many industries, capacity is expanded in this incremental way.

[112] COMP/M.3178 *Bertelsmann/Springer/JV* (2005).

## Closeness of competition when firms bid for tenders[113]

A win/loss analysis can be usefully undertaken in those markets in which   **7-035**
competition between suppliers takes the form of bidding for contracts
placed by customers, and where, as well as the name of the winning bidder,
the identification of the runner-up can be identified. Such win/loss data
offers complementary information to that provided by market share data
because they help identify the strength of the competitive constraints on
each of the merging parties provided by each existing competitor. If the two
merging firms represent the closest competitors for one another, then one
may expect the merging firms to face each other in bidding contests more
frequently than they face other competitors, or the data may show that in
those bids won by one of the merging parties, the other is usually the
runner-up.

In most circumstances, it is the second-placed bidder that effectively
determines the price that is the result of a bidding contest. In order to win,
a firm has to set a price that is just slightly more attractive to a customer
than the next-best alternative. Of course, there are often important practical difficulties in undertaking a proper win-loss analysis. In particular, it is
necessary that the parties are able to provide sufficiently reliable data on
those bids in which they participated (or at least won) and which supplier
was ranked second in those bids.[114] This might suggest that the merger may
eliminate an important constraint that, absent any product repositioning
on the part of the remaining suppliers, could allow the post-merger entity
to raise prices.

Where it can be shown that other firms provide an equal or more
important constraint on each of the merging parties, then the merger is
unlikely to raise competition concerns. Such an analysis was accepted by
the Commission in *Philips/Marconi Medical Systems*.[115] This case concerned
the supply of various different types of medical diagnostic imaging
equipment supplied primarily to hospitals. The Commission accepted a
"win/loss" study prepared on behalf of the parties which showed that in
each of the relevant product markets—computed tomography, magnetic
resonance and nuclear medicine—Philips faced closer competition from
other suppliers, in particular GE and Siemens, than from Marconi Medical
Systems. On that basis, the Commission concluded that the merger would
not give rise to anticompetitive effects.

In *GE/Instrumentarium* the Commission also considered a win/loss ana-   **7-036**
lysis for each of the affected products and for each European country. In
the relevant markets for critical care monitors, C-arms and mammography
devices, the Commission accepted the results of these analyses as providing

---

[113] See Chapter 12 for a discussion of empirical techniques that can be used to assess competition in such markets.
[114] The Commission may be better placed to obtain such information.
[115] COMP/M.2537, *Philips/Marconi Medical Systems*, (2001).

evidence that the two parties were not each others' closest competitors. For example, para.244 of the decision, which refers to the C-arm market, states:

> "On the basis of bids where GE won, at the EEA level Siemens is reported as runner-up in [40–50] per cent of all cases, followed by Philips ([30–40] per cent) and Instrumentarium ([0–10] per cent). [Instrumentarium] occurs as runner-up less frequently than one would expect if all suppliers were equally close substitutes."[116]

The Commission therefore concluded that "the bidding data presented by the notifying party tend to indicate that market shares in this case overstate the impact of GE's and Instrumentarium's combined market power to the merger."[117] In other words, the Commission found that GE and Instrumentarium were not particularly close competitors.

The Commission also considered an econometric analysis of the discounts offered by both parties on the tenders in which they were successful focusing on the impact on the magnitude of those discounts when the other merging party was also present in the tender.[118] Consistent with the win/ loss analysis, the results of the econometric analysis for the critical care monitor, C-arms and mammography markets showed that neither party had a significant impact on the size of the discount offered by the other party[119]:

> "The results of this extended empirical assessment were that the presence of Instrumentarium as a bidder in the auction ... does not appear to have had any systematic influence over the size of the discount offered by GE in its bids. In none of the models that the Commission estimated was the coefficient of the ... variable capturing the presence of Instrumentarium in the auction statistically significant."

In the perioperative monitoring market, however, the results of the various econometric studies were at odds. The study presented by GE's economic experts showed that the presence of GE in those bids won by Instrumentarium did not have a significant effect on the discount offered by Instrumentarium. That study also showed that Philips exerted the main competitive constraint on Instrumentarium's price. Conversely, the study presented by a third party showed that its own discounts were higher when both GE and Instrumentarium were participating in the bid than when either GE or Instrumentarium was present. As the merger would eliminate

[116] COMP/M.3083 *GE/Instrumentarium* (2003) para.244.
[117] op. cit. para.245.
[118] See Werden (2008) for a commentary.
[119] op. cit. para.248.

the competition between GE and Instrumentarium, this study indicated that the merger would result in the third party (and presumably also GE) increasing its price post-merger.[120]

## The importance of a dynamic assessment

Even horizontal mergers that give rise to high market shares and/or involve   **7–037** particularly close competitors may not give rise to unilateral effects due to the responses of rival firms. The potential for firms to respond to the merger is therefore an important, indeed essential, aspect in assessing the likelihood of unilateral effects. Dynamic responses from existing firms can take numerous forms.

First, smaller rival firms may be able to expand production to mitigate or even undermine any attempts to increase price. Such competitive responses do not necessarily require that firms have existing excess capacity; in some instances, the threat that such firms would expand their own production capacity in response to an attempted price increase would provide sufficient competitive constraint on the merged entity.

Secondly, rival firms can alter their competitive offerings, e.g. by offering a new service that previously only the merging parties offered. Changes in competitive offerings can take the form of extending the range sold; for example, a retailer might respond to a merger by increasing the range of products stocked. Alternatively, competing firms might re-position their product offerings by beginning to produce or make available product offerings that are closer to those provided by the merging parties. A good example of firms re-positioning their offerings in response to a merger is provided by the retailing of video games. In *GAME/Gamestation*, the UK Competition Commission expressed concerns that the two parties were the only firms offering pre-owned titles for sale alongside new games (so called "mint" games).[121] The merging parties argued that existing retailers of mint games could respond to an increase in the price of pre-owned titles by offering their own pre-owned titles since retailers of mint games already possessed an established customer base, the necessary stock management tools and would simply need to reallocate a proportion of their shelf space to display pre-owned stock. The UK Competition Commission rejected such arguments. However, less than a year after taking that decision (i.e. within the timeframe for assessing such dynamic competitive responses), a competing retailer began to make pre-owned games available.[122]

In short, as a study prepared for the UK Office of Fair Trading con-   **7–038** cluded, mergers do not take place in a vacuum.

---

[120] As an aside, one might question why a competing supplier would complain about a merger effect that would raise its margins and wonder what this implied about the credibility of the evidence.

[121] See *GAME/Gamestation*, op. cit.

[122] See Murgatroyd, Majumdar and Bishop (2008) for a discussion of this case.

"The dynamic responses that take place after mergers underline the fact that post-merger predictions based purely on clues from demand-side relationships tell only part of the story. Thus, although models of unilateral effects provide useful insights into possible danger areas, they must be supplemented by an attempt to assess how the market may respond to structural changes caused by mergers."[123]

In addition to the dynamic responses of actual competitors, there are two other sources of dynamic responses that increase the competitive constraints on the merged entity. These are the entry of new firms and the exercise of buyer power by customers of the merged entity. These two dynamic responses are examined in the following two sections.

## ENTRY[124]

**7–039** The Horizontal Merger Guidelines correctly state that "[w]hen entering a market is sufficiently easy, a merger is unlikely to pose any significant anti-competitive risk."[125] Assessing the likelihood of new entry is therefore an important element of the competitive assessment of unilateral effects.[126] However, while the assessment of the possibility of effective entry into a market is an important part of the merger assessment, it is important to put this assessment in its correct context. In particular, it is important not to work backwards by inferring that a merger will give rise to unilateral effects simply because barriers to entry are high. It is quite possible that even with high-entry barriers, competition post-merger between existing firms will continue to be strong. Indeed, where competition between existing firms is vigorous, one would not expect to see entry taking place even if barriers to entry were low. The consideration of ease of entry should therefore be undertaken *after* one has assessed the likely level of competition post-merger in the absence of entry. If this is considered to be sufficient, then no assessment of ease of entry is required. For instance, who cares whether entry is difficult, if there are still five firms competing vigorously in the market?[127] Hence, the consideration of entry is necessary only if one considers that the merger may give rise to competition concerns in the absence of entry.

We can assess entry under two different categories. The first is entry that can occur quickly with no, or very low, sunk costs. This is what the

---

[123] Office of Fair Trading Research Paper (1999).
[124] See also the discussion on entry in Chapter 3.
[125] See para.68, Horizontal Merger Guidelines.
[126] Entry also forms an important element of the competitive assessment of coordinated effects as explained in para.7–063.
[127] Similarly, it makes no sense to argue that barriers to entry are high due to prices within the relevant market being low.

literature has termed "hit-and-run" entry.[128] The firm enters because it believes that there is a profit opportunity (for instance, because a merger has raised prices) knowing that it can exit the market relatively costlessly if that profit opportunity disappears. If firms are able to engage in hit-and-run entry, then potential competition would provide an effective competitive constraint; if prices were to increase post-merger, hit-and-run entry will occur. As long as the entrant has enough capacity, this ought to drive prices back down to the pre-merger price level.[129] This type of entry has been referred to as a "trump": however bad the rest of the competitive assessment looks for the merger, entry of this type means that the merger will not be anticompetitive.[130]

Supply-side substitutability can be characterised as a form of hit-and-run entry.[131] If there are firms that can easily divert their production into the product in question, then this will tend to defeat any anticompetitive price rise.[132] Note that supply-side substitutability will only represent an effective competitive constraint if the opportunity cost for the relevant firm of substituting out of its current product is low, or if the firm currently has excess capacity. A firm will be less likely to reduce the production of Product A in order to increase the production of Product B in response to a short-run rise in the price of Product B if this will lead to the loss of high margins on the sales of Product A.

The second category of entry is the category usually encountered in the **7–040** assessment of horizontal mergers. We term this long-term entry. Long-term entry usually involves firms incurring sunk costs and therefore entry will be undertaken by firms that aim to remain in the market in the long-term.[133] Most entry requires sunk costs (e.g. advertising, research and development and investments in unrecoverable assets). Entry of this type can be sufficient to defeat an anti-competitive price rise post-merger, but the analysis is not as clear cut as for hit-and-run entry.

The Horizontal Merger Guidelines state that in order for entry to be considered a sufficient competitive constraint, entry must be shown to be *likely, timely and sufficient.*[134]

---

[128] It is similar to what the US Guidelines call *uncommitted entry.*

[129] Such entry is unlikely to drive prices down below the pre-merger price level. If there were profits to be made at this level, the entrant would have already entered pre-merger.

[130] Baker (1997).

[131] As noted in Chapter 4, supply-side substitution can be taken into account when defining the relevant market.

[132] See para.73, Horizontal Merger Guidelines.

[133] This type of entry is similar to what the US Guidelines call *committed entry.*

[134] The Horizontal Merger Guidelines' assessment of entry mirrors that contained in the US horizontal merger guidelines.

*Likelihood*

**7-041** For entry to be considered to be likely, it must be sufficiently profitable taking into account the price effects of adding more output into the market and the potential responses of the incumbents. A firm will only incur sunk costs associated with entry if the entry will be profitable in the long run. As noted in Chapter 3, a rational firm deciding whether to enter a market will be influenced not by the prices currently prevailing in the market, but by the prices that can be expected to prevail once entry has taken place. In some situations, the current market price may be expected to provide a reasonably accurate picture of the likely post-entry price. In other cases, however, the post-entry price may be expected to be substantially below the prevailing price. This will be the case if the addition of a further firm to the industry results in a significant intensification of competition and, therefore, in a very substantial fall in prices. It is therefore possible for a firm to continue to set inflated prices and earn substantial profits without attracting entry, provided prices would be expected to fall sharply if further entry occurred. Under these circumstances, the threat of entry, and the expected level of post-entry prices, cannot be considered to constrain pre-entry prices.

However, the relevant benchmark for assessing all horizontal mergers is the prevailing price level:[135] the concern is whether the elimination of a potential competitor would permit the merged entity to increase prices above that benchmark. For potential competition to provide an effective competitive constraint post-merger, it is only required that a sufficient number of customers would be able to switch to the new entrant to render any attempted price increase by the merged entity unprofitable.

**7-042** For example, any attempt by the merged firm to raise prices from 100 to 110, say, would be unprofitable provided that customers could respond by switching their business to a new entrant at a price of 100 in sufficient numbers to make that entry viable. Put simply, the new entrant does not need to be viable at prices below but only at prevailing prices for it to represent an effective competitive constraint.[136]

One way of judging the likelihood of entry is to consider the *minimum viable scale* of entry. The minimum viable scale of entry is the smallest amount that the entrant needs to sell at pre-merger prices in order to break even. That amount can in principle be estimated.[137] If it is large relative to

---

[135] See Baker (1997).
[136] UK Competition Commission, *Acquisition of Adsteam Marine Ltd ("Adsteam") by Svit-zerWijsmuller A/S*, (2007) provides a good example of the assessment of entry as a post-merger competitive constraint, including a debate as to the appropriate post-entry price level for the competitive assessment. See Lewis and Lofaro (2007) for a commentary on the UK Competition Commission's reasoning.
[137] The *Adsteam/Svizter* transaction, op. cit., provides a good example of such analysis.

the size of the market, this suggests that entry is unlikely; whereas if it is small this might suggest that entry is likely.[138]

## *Timeliness*

In order to deter or counteract any perceived increase in prices following 7–043 the merger, entrants must be able quickly to affect prices in the relevant market to a significant degree. This raises the issue of what time period is appropriate. The Horizontal Merger Guidelines consider entry to be timely if it can affect prices in the relevant market within two years.[139] Even though entry would not occur for, say, 12 months, potential competition can still provide an effective competitive constraint and so eliminate all concerns of unilateral effects. If new entry takes place this has an adverse effect on the merged entity for all subsequent periods after entry occurs. The "losses" to the merged entity following this new entry can outweigh the "benefits" of a short-lived price increase.

## *Sufficiency*

The Horizontal Merger Guidelines state that entry must be of sufficient 7–044 scope and magnitude to deter or defeat the anti-competitive effects of the merger.[140] Small-scale entry, for instance into some market "niche", may not be considered sufficient.

## Conclusions on entry analyses

Two conclusions flow from the above discussion. The first is that it is not 7–045 enough to argue that barriers to entry are high or are low. Indeed, in some sense we are not interested in this question. What matters is whether entry is likely to prevent prices rising post-merger. As we have noted, this depends on factors such as the likelihood of entry and the nature of competition post-entry. The second conclusion is that unless hit-and-run entry is likely, the hurdle for successfully making an "entry defence" is quite high and requires substantive analysis to establish that entry arguments are strong. Certainly, the mere possibility of entry, or even probability of entry of some sort, is not enough to "trump" the anti-competitive effects of the merger.

---

[138] See para.69, Horizontal Merger Guidelines for a discussion of economies of scale and other potential sources of barriers to entry.
[139] See para.74, Horizontal Merger Guidelines.
[140] See para.75, Horizontal Merger Guidelines.

## BUYER POWER[141]

**7–046**   Buyer power refers to the ability of buyers to take actions to alter the structure of the supply market. As the Horizontal Merger Guidelines note, buyer power can be exercised by threatening to resort to alternative sources of supply.[142] There are potentially two strategies that can be used by buyers to thwart attempts to increase prices post-merger.

The primary strategy involves the sponsoring or threat of sponsoring the expansion of existing competitors to the merging parties or sponsoring new entry (including the possibility of buyers engaging in vertical integration). Such expansion of existing firms or new entry is said to be sponsored if buyers are able to underwrite the expansion of capacity including the building of green-field capacity, perhaps through entering into long-term supply contracts. In this way, the risks associated with such investments are dramatically reduced. The threat that buyers are able to sponsor new entry can be a potent post-merger competitive constraint even where such capacity expansion can only arise with some delay. Where suppliers have made significant sunk investments, the prospects of increasing prices even for a number of years to buyers would not be sufficient to outweigh the losses that they would suffer were entry to occur in the future. Since the investment in any new capacity would also be sunk and hence committed to the market for several years, the time delay in bringing forth such investment would be offset by the length of time such capacity would compete with the merged entity.

It is important to distinguish these genuine sources of buyer power from mere appeals to the fact that customers are large. It is often argued that where firms face large, sophisticated buyers any scope for the merger to result in an increase in the exercise of market power is offset by the countervailing buying power of consumers. For example, in *Metallgesellschaft/Safic Alcan*, the Commission concluded that buyer power was significant since tyre manufacturers accounted for two-thirds of worldwide consumption of solid natural rubber.[143] Conversely, the Commission has argued that buyers do not possess buyer power because they are less concentrated than their upstream suppliers.[144] This is clearly an inadequate basis for dismissing buyer power arguments.

**7–047**      However, for buyer power to exist it is not sufficient to show that buyers are concentrated. It is not concentration per se that matters but rather the ability of buyers to take actions that undermine any attempt by suppliers to increase prices and for the buyer power argument to be convincing, a more

---

[141] See paras 64 to 67, Horizontal Merger Guidelines, and the discussion on buyer power in Chapter 3.
[142] See COMP/M.1882 *Pirelli/BICC* (2000), COMP/M.1245 *Valeo/ITT Industries* (1998) and COMP/M.1225 *Enso/Stora* (1998).
[143] IV/M146, *Metallgesellschaft/Safic Alcan* (1991).
[144] See, e.g. COMP/M.5046 *Friesland Foods/Campina* (2008).

sophisticated analysis is required which takes into account whether the structure and other characteristics of the industry in question make the exercise of countervailing buyer power likely. In particular, it is necessary to demonstrate strategies that the buyer could undertake to thwart any attempt to increase prices post-merger. It is the availability of these options and not mere size alone which is the source of buyer power that might conceivably be sufficient to counterbalance the increase in market power created by the merger.

*Enso/Stora* provides a good example of the potential for buyer power to offset concerns of high post-merger market shares.[145] Enso and Stora were two leading European producers of pulp, paper and packaging board. In 1999, their merger would have created the largest paper and board manufacturing company in the world with high post-merger market shares in a number of markets affected by this transaction (50–70 per cent), while the other competitors were small and fragmented (for instance, on the market for liquid packaging board (LPB) the only other players, Korsnäs and Assi-Domän, accounted for 10–20 per cent of EEA sales each). Moreover, concerns over the high post-merger market share were heightened by apparently high barriers to entry, very modest demand growth and the absence of effective potential competition from EEA-based producers of other board products, such as MoDo and Metsa-Serla, and non-EEA producers.

The Commission recognised that the buying-side of this market was also extremely concentrated. In particular, at the time of the merger Tetra Pak accounted for 60–80 per cent of total demand, the remainder being purchased by Elopak and SIG Combibloc with 10–20 per cent each. In recognition of the degree of concentration amongst the customers, the Commission analysed whether the buyers could sponsor new entry. The Commission found that Tetra Pak purchased such large volumes of LPB that it would have the option of developing new capacity with other existing or new suppliers. In short, irrecoverable investments, or sunk costs, that would be considered too risky if the suppliers faced a fragmented demand side are made much less risky when they can be made in effective collaboration with a large customer. The Commission concluded that in this case Tetra Pak would be able to sponsor expansion or even new entry to thwart any attempted post-merger price increase and consequently cleared the merger despite high post-merger market shares.

The second strategy that customers can employ is to switch at least part **7-048** of their demand to other existing suppliers.[146] The effectiveness of this threat will be most potent where buyers are able to take actions that affect the attractiveness and/or availability of suppliers' products. For example,

---

[145] IV/M1225, *Enso/Stora* (1998).
[146] The possibility of turning to non-Spanish suppliers was an important factor in the Commission's decision to approve the *Alcatel/Telettra* merger (IV/M42) (1991).

supermarkets are often able to exercise buyer power by threatening to reduce the shelf space that they allocate to branded products and increase that allocated to private label products. However, it should be noted that the Commission has not generally accepted such arguments in retail markets. In *SCA/Metsa Tissue*, the Commission argued that customers had limited switching alternatives due to the high post-merger market shares and the merged entity would, moreover, be able to price discriminate between different customers.[147] Hence, it was argued, even if the largest customers would be able to exercise countervailing buyer power this would not be the case for smaller customers.[148]

In summary, a proper assessment of the countervailing buyer power arguments should therefore include looking not only at the concentration of buyers, but also at whether these buyers can influence the terms of supply. Under certain circumstances buyer power can undermine attempts by even very large firms to increase prices above prevailing levels. However, in examining such arguments it is very important to assess whether suppliers are able to engage in price discrimination between those buyers that possess buyer power and those that do not.

# COORDINATED EFFECTS

## Overview

**7–049** A merger is said to give rise to coordinated effects concerns when the consequent change in market structure, including the reduction in the number of firms and the greater combined market share held by the merging party, better enables the merged firm and at least one of its remaining competitors to reach and sustain a tacit agreement not to compete effectively with one another and thereby raise prices.[149] Such price increases are termed *co-ordinated effects* because they result not from the actions of the merged entity alone but rather from the realisation amongst a number of firms (i.e. the merged entity and at least one of its remaining competitors) that the returns to competing less vigorously with one another are higher than competing vigorously.[150] In other words, co-ordinated effects rely on one or more of the remaining competitors *also restricting their output* when the merged entity restricts its output. This is in marked

---

[147] COMP/M.2097 *SCA/Metsa Tissue* (2001).
[148] Similar arguments were deployed by the Commission to dismiss claims that customers had significant buyer power in the Dutch dairy merger between Friesland Foods and Campina. COMP/M.5046 *Friesland Foods/Campina* (2008).
[149] See para.39 Horizontal Merger Guidelines.
[150] Under a unilateral effects theory of harm, competing firms may also respond to the higher post-merger prices charged by the merged entity by increasing prices. But such responses do not represent an "accommodating" response. Rather, the resulting higher prices are a consequence of unilateral profit maximisation, reflecting an increase in their respective residual demand.

contrast to unilateral effects, where the post-merger price increase is profitable for the merged entity regardless of the responses of competing firms.

Coordinated effects can arise since, as noted in Chapter 2, in many industries, firms recognise that the desirability of a given commercial decision depends to a degree on the commercial decisions taken by other firms in the industry. For example, the profitability of a given action depends on the commercial decisions adopted by other firms. For example, a firm would prefer, *ceteris paribus*, to charge its customers a high price rather than a low one but does not do so if it expects rival firms to charge low prices; a high price will merely result in a reduction in sales and therefore lower profits. But if all firms could reach an understanding to charge high prices (i.e. not to compete aggressively), then the high-price strategy would become profitable. This understanding does not involve explicit communication between firms (such behaviour would be illegal under Article 81) but relies only on two or more firms recognising the competitive interaction between themselves and competing firms and adjusting their mode of competition accordingly. The change in the mode of competitive behaviour is therefore normally termed tacit coordination or tacit collusion to distinguish it from explicit coordination. The differences between tacit and explicit coordination are discussed below.

However, as also noted in Chapter 2, whenever firms attempt to coordinate their competitive behaviour, there are always incentives for individual firms to deviate from that understanding. In other words, even if firms have an incentive to moderate their competitive behaviour, such outcomes are far from inevitable due to the incentives to deviate.

To establish a persuasive theory of harm based on coordinated effects, it **7–050** must be established that firms in the coordinating group are able to achieve the following[151]:

- First, firms in the coordinating group must be able to reach a tacit understanding as to which parameters of competition they will moderate their competitive behaviour.

- Secondly, firms must be able to sustain any tacit understanding. This requires them to be able to (a) monitor that the tacit understanding is being adhered to by the other firms in the coordinating group and (b) if a firm does deviate from the tacit understanding, the other firms must be able to respond effectively (i.e. retaliate) to punish that firm.

---

[151] This assumes that the identity of the firms in the coordinating group can be readily established.

- Thirdly, for the tacit understanding to be sustainable, it must be immune from the potentially destabilising reactions of firms outside the coordinating group.

We consider these in turn.

### *Firms must be able to reach a tacit understanding*

7–051   Any theory of harm based on coordinated effects must explain in what ways firms in the coordinating group moderate or can be expected to moderate their competitive behaviour so as to achieve higher prices. In principle, firms can moderate their competitive behaviour in numerous ways. Such moderating behaviour might take the form of raising prices directly; limiting production; limiting the amount of new capacity brought to the market; dividing the market by, for instance, geographic area or other customer characteristics; or by allocating contracts in bidding markets.[152] However, regardless of the precise mechanism through which firms coordinate their competitive behaviour, the outcome of that coordinated behaviour is the same: higher prices than would prevail absent the merger.

For it to be feasible for firms to reach such a tacit understanding, firms must have similar views as to how to moderate their competitive behaviour. For this to be the case, firms must have reasonably common incentives, which are usually affected by their respective costs and capacities. Where firms' incentives diverge, it is less likely that firms can reach a tacit understanding as to how to moderate their competitive behaviour. Furthermore, reaching a tacit understanding requires the market environment to be sufficiently simple. Sufficient simplicity is required in order to enable firms to reach an understanding as to how to moderate the degree of competition between them. It is easier for firms to reach a tacit understanding where firms need to reach an understanding over only a few competitive parameters rather than many and where the market environment is relatively stable.[153] For example, if typical transactions in the industry involve complex terms that vary across customers and/or across products, then reaching a tacit understanding as to the appropriate mode of competitive accommodation with respect to price is unlikely.[154] Tacit coordination is also more likely to occur when demand and supply are relatively stable over time, rather than if they are constantly changing. Although establishing that firms in the coordinating group can reach a tacit understanding as to how to moderate their competitive behaviour is clearly

---

[152] See para.40, Horizontal Merger Guidelines.
[153] See para.41, Horizontal Merger Guidelines.
[154] Of course, it might be possible for firms to coordinate their competitive behaviour and thereby affect price indirectly in another manner; for example, by coordinating over capacity expansions or allocation of customers.

important, this step in the competitive assessment, in common with the academic literature, is often ignored.[155]

## *Firms must be able to sustain the tacit understanding*

Second, while most firms may have an *incentive* to coordinate their behaviour, this is not to say that coordination actually takes place in most markets. Hence, even assuming that firms in the coordinating group are able to reach a tacit understanding, that would by itself be an insufficient basis for concluding that a merger will give rise to coordinated effects. It is well established in both the economic and legal literature that successful tacit coordination between firms is not inevitable. This is true even in highly concentrated industries protected by insurmountable barriers to entry.[156] The key to this insight is the recognition that individual firms are prone to act in a self-interested fashion. If all firms tacitly reach an understanding to compete less vigorously by charging high prices, then this raises the scope for one firm to increase its profits by "deviating" from the understanding by charging a low price. Hence, there is always a tension between a firm's desire to compete less effectively by coordinating its commercial behaviour and the ability to abide by that coordination once the agreement is in place. This implies that for tacitly coordinated behaviour to be successfully exercised and sustained over time, each participant in the coordinating group must be convinced that the other participating firms will also adhere to the agreement.

It will be easier for firms to sustain any tacit understanding where the industry is characterised by sufficient transparency. Sufficient transparency is required so that firms can monitor the competitive behaviour of the other firms in the coordinating group and to identify deviations from the tacit understanding when these occur. If the market is not transparent, then it will be possible for firms to deviate without being detected.

Even if they can be rapidly spotted, deviations from the tacit understanding will only be deterred if the other firms in the coordinating group are able to respond effectively (i.e. retaliate) to punish the deviating firm. For coordination to be sustainable there is therefore a need for some sort of a threat mechanism that can be activated if deviation is detected. Furthermore, this threat must be credible in the sense that once a deviation is detected, there is sufficient certainty that other coordinating firms have an

7–052

---

[155] e.g. in the first COMP/M.3333 *Sony/BMG* (2004) investigation the Commission failed to articulate, let alone establish, on what pricing parameters the major record companies were moderating their competitive behaviour.

[156] This result is seen in the concept of the "prisoners" dilemma in game theory models (see Chapter 2 for further details).

incentive to activate the mechanism and punish the deviator.[157] Determining whether such a credible punishment strategy is available is not straightforward. However, in general, the most credible punishment response is one which involves rival firms engaging in an individually short run profit-maximising response to the deviation that renders the deviation unprofitable.

### *Firms external to the coordinating group are unable to destabilise the tacit understanding*

**7–053**   For tacit coordination to be stable over time it must be immune from the potentially destabilising reactions of outsiders. This refers to the actions of existing competitors not participating in the coordinating group, the possibility of new firms entering the market and the actions of customers.[158] For example, if firms are attempting to tacitly coordinate over capacity[159] expansions, this will only have adverse effects for consumers if non-coordinating firms are unable or have no incentive to respond to this decrease by increasing their own capacity expansion plans.

In summary, successful coordinated interaction therefore entails reaching terms of coordination that are profitable to the firms involved and an ability to detect and punish deviations that would otherwise undermine the coordinated interaction. Detection and punishment of deviations ensures that coordinating firms will find it more profitable to adhere to the terms of coordination than to pursue short-term profits from deviating. The analysis of coordinating effects must therefore be focused on these two elements: the ability to reach an understanding to compete less effectively without engaging in explicit coordination; and the ability to sustain that mode of competitive behaviour again without engaging in explicit coordination.[160]

The following sections consider two analytical approaches to assessing whether a merger is likely to give rise to coordinated effects. First, we consider the traditional approach, often referred to as the "checklist" approach. This approach assesses whether the characteristics of the industry are conducive to reaching and sustaining tacit coordinated behaviour. However, although the checklist approach identifies industry characteristics that facilitate or hinder tacit coordination, this analytical approach provides neither a systematic framework for assessing the relative

---

[157]   Numerous game theoretic models exist in the economics literature that explore different scenarios of coordination, cheating and enforcement. See, e.g. Green and Porter (1984). The Green and Porter model relies on periodic (damaging) price wars as a means by which cheating from the co-operative price is discouraged.

[158]   See para.56, Horizontal Merger Guidelines.

[159]   See the discussions on entry (paras 7–039—7–045) and on buyer power (paras 7–046—7–048).

[160]   This analytical approach mirrors the US Merger Guidelines which state that: "Successful coordinated interaction entails reaching terms of coordination that are profitable to the firms involved and an ability to detect and punish deviations".

importance of the various factors nor does it address how the merger affects the mode of competition other than in the obvious sense of reducing the number of suppliers and changing the distribution of market shares. To remedy these deficiencies, we present an analytical framework that organises the competitive assessment into three categories: examination of the ability of the firms in the coordinating group to reach and sustain a tacit understanding assuming that these firms face no other competitive constraints (internal factors); examination of the competitive constraints provided by firms outside the coordinating group, including potential new entrants and the possible reactions of customers (external factors); and assessing how the merger affects the likely mode of competition.

## The "checklist" approach

Traditionally, the assessment of the likelihood of a merger giving rise to  **7–054** coordinated effects has been based on a number of characteristics that have been identified as hindering or facilitating tacit coordination. Many of these factors are the same as those factors which are conducive to the formation of cartels.[161] In addition to market concentration, the following industry characteristics are often considered to indicate the likelihood of tacit coordinated behaviour post-merger.

- *Inelastic market demand.* If market demand is inelastic, then if all firms lower prices, demand will not increase much. This makes cheating unlikely because any punishment stage (i.e. lower prices) will probably involve a considerable reduction in profits.

- *The availability of key information concerning market conditions, transactions and individual competitors.* The more transparent the market, the easier it is to police the coordination.

- *The extent of firm and product heterogeneity.* The more homogeneous are firms and products, the easier it is to agree on the collusive output.

- *The presence of maverick firms.* It may be difficult to convince a maverick firm to collude and so the maverick firm may undercut the collusive price. If the maverick firm has a reasonably large capacity, this can undermine the collusive behaviour of the other firms.

- *The characteristics of buyers.* The more sophisticated are the buyers, the harder it is to raise prices post-merger. Also, if there are

---

[161] See Chapter 5 for a fuller discussion.

some large buyers with a large amount of buyer power, they can put pressure on the collusive price.[162]

- *The presence of excess capacity.* If firms have excess capacity, this gives them more of an incentive to raise output and undercut the collusive price. However, it also makes retaliation more plausible and effective.

- *The presence of a competitive fringe.* This will tend to limit the scope for co-ordination.

- *The characteristics of typical transactions.* If transactions in the market tend to be large and infrequent, then tacit collusion is harder to sustain than if transactions are small and frequent.

- *The ease of entry.* The easier it is for new firms to enter the market, the less likely it is that a merger will lead to coordinated effects.[163]

However, the major drawback with the "checklist" approach is that it does not provide a systematic framework in which to assess the relevant factors. It should be stressed that the checklist does not constitute a "points system" whereby the number of characteristics of a market that are held to be conducive to tacit coordinated behaviour (so-called "oligopoly plus" factors) are weighed on a one-for-one basis against those characteristics that are held to hinder successful tacit coordinated behaviour (so-called "oligopoly minus" factors).[164] The fact that the "pluses" outweigh the "minuses" in no way implies that coordinated effects are to be expected. For example, a merger in a market which fulfils many of the "oligopoly plus" conditions but is characterised by easy entry or easy expansion by existing smaller firms is unlikely to give rise to concerns of coordinated effects.

The checklist approach therefore provides only a reference point for the analysis, listing those characteristics that are pertinent to the competitive assessment of coordinated effects but without providing a framework for analysing that list of characteristics. By itself, the checklist provides no basis for assessing those industries in which both plus and minus characteristics are present. Moreover, and importantly, the checklist approach is unable to provide any insights into how a merger affects competition other than by reducing the number of firms active in the relevant market.

---

[162] Paras 7–046—7–048 provide a more detailed discussion of buyer power.
[163] Paras 7–039—7–045 provide a detailed discussion of entry.
[164] Bishop (1999).

## A more economic analytical framework

A better analytical framework for thinking about coordinated effects is to   **7–055**
organise the competitive assessment into three categories:[165]

- Internal factors

- External factors

- What does the merger change?

*Internal factors* refer to the ability of firms that are alleged to form part of the coordinating group to act as if they were a single entity. This assessment examines first whether the characteristics of the industry are such that these firms are able to reach a tacit understanding so as to reduce the effectiveness of competition between themselves (without recourse to explicit coordination). The competitive assessment then considers whether even if these firms are able to reduce the effectiveness of competition between themselves by reaching such a tacit understanding, those same firms are able to sustain that tacit understanding. As noted above whenever firms enter into coordinated agreements to charge higher prices (whether tacit as is the case here, or explicit as is the case with cartel agreements) there are always short-run incentives for individual firms to deviate from the agreements by charging a low price. Whether a tacit agreement can be sustained therefore requires that long-term considerations outweigh the short-run incentives to deviate by competing more vigorously.[166] The ability to sustain the tacit understanding depends both on how quickly attempts at price competition or other departures from the "agreed" mode of conduct can be identified and on the speed with which retaliatory actions can be implemented. Proving that a merger is likely to give rise to coordinated effects therefore requires showing that not only do firms have incentives to compete less effectively with one another but also that those incentives can be translated into sustainable anti-competitive actions.

But even assuming that the characteristics of the industry indicate that the internal factors permit those firms that are alleged to form part of the coordinating group to coordinate their behaviour and to sustain such coordination over time, those firms do not necessarily enjoy a position of coordinated effects. Even if these conditions exist, the firms forming the alleged coordinating group can be undermined by competition from other suppliers in the industry (i.e. by *external factors*)

The final element of the competitive assessment is to examine how the   **7–056**
structural changes brought about by the merger make it more likely for two or more of the remaining firms to reach and sustain a tacit understanding. Although a merger clearly involves a reduction in the number of suppliers

---

[165] For a more detailed analysis of this analytical framework, see Bishop and Lofaro (2005).
[166] The economics literature talks of firms *cheating* on the tacit understanding.

and also results in an increase in market concentration, many of the characteristics of the industry will remain the same as pre-merger. For example, if a market is characterised by transparent pricing pre-merger, then it is likely that the market will continue to be characterised by transparent pricing post-merger. The key issue to understand therefore when arguing that a merger gives rise to coordinated effects is why the industry characteristics were not sufficient for co-ordination pre-merger but would be post-merger.[167] It is this latter analysis that is often missing from the Commission's assessment of coordinated effects.

The following provides a more detailed discussion of each of the three necessary elements of the analysis.

## Internal Factors

**7–057** Even if it could be assumed that the firms that form the alleged coordinating group faced no other competitive constraints (i.e. there are no other market participants and there are no potential new entrants) the characteristics of the industry may still prevent those firms from achieving and sustaining a tacit understanding to compete less vigorously. Factors that affect whether that is the case fall into the following categories:

- the stability of the market;

- the transparency of market conditions; and

- the degree of symmetry between the various suppliers in the market.

These factors are called *internal factors* since they affect the ability of the firms in the coordinating group to reach and sustain a tacit understanding.

### Stability

**7–058** A stable market is necessary if a tacit understanding to compete less vigorously is to be sustained over time. Where market conditions are changing continually over time, the ability of suppliers to coordinate their behaviour from one period to the next becomes more difficult. Conversely, if market conditions are relatively stable, this makes is easier to coordinate behaviour. In addition, if the size of the market is relatively stable, then firms will be aware that competition amongst them is unlikely to increase the size of the market much, but will involve significant costs in terms of foregone revenues. This increases their incentives to co-ordinate rather than compete.

---

[167] As discussed below, the Commission often seeks to avoid this issue by arguing that the market is already subject to tacit coordination and that the merger will enhance that coordination.

Two main conditions should be met in order for the market to be sufficiently stable to offer a realistic prospect of a merger giving rise to coordinated effects. First, demand and prices should be relatively stable or at least change in a predictable manner so that any deviations can be rapidly identified. Suppose a firm finds that the demand for its product has fallen. When market demand is stable, this makes it easier for the firm to identify whether its demand has fallen due to a market-wide reduction in demand (i.e. a negative demand shock) or because of deviating behaviour on the part of one or more firms in the coordinating group. Secondly, the elasticity of industry demand should be low. A high elasticity of industry demand implies that it is more difficult for a tacit understanding to be enforced since the benefits of deviating from the tacit understanding will be relatively large; price cuts will lead to a relatively large increase in sales.

## *Transparency*

In order for the firms in the coordinating group to be able to sustain a tacit **7–059** understanding over time, it is necessary that each of these firms is able to observe the behaviour of the others in respect of their prices, outputs or, ideally, both. When this is not the case, firms in the coordinating group will be more likely to be tempted to deviate from the tacit understanding since it is less likely that their deviations will be detected by the other coordinating firms. In other words, in markets not characterised by transparency, there is unlikely to exist a credible punishment mechanism.

Whether a market is transparent depends on both the ability of firms to observe transaction prices and the level of sales of competitors and the degree of market concentration. The easier it is for firms in the coordinating group to observe the actual transaction prices charged by the other firms in the coordinating group and/or the level of their sales, the easier it is for firms to monitor the other firms' competitive behaviour and thereby identify and respond rapidly to any deviations from the tacit agreement to compete less vigorously. However, it should be noted that even if transaction prices are fully observable, it may still be difficult to reach and sustain a tacit understanding if products are highly differentiated. Finally, the presence of many small customers also makes it more difficult for firms to sustain a tacit understanding. The ability to detect deviations is reduced since it is more difficult to infer that a rival has deviated simply because one customer has changed supplier.

The level of market concentration affects the transparency of an industry. In concentrated markets deviations from the tacit understanding are more easily identified, and consequently the incentives to deviate in the first place are reduced. This is because deviations by a large firm are more likely to be noticed than deviations by a small firm since deviations by the former would likely have a significant impact on total market sales.

*Symmetry*

**7–060**   The ability of firms in the coordinating group to reach and sustain a tacit understanding over time will be enhanced if they have similar views as to the appropriate level of prices (or equivalently the level of output reduction). Where firms in the coordinating group have very different motivations and incentives, this will tend to reduce both the ability to reach a tacit understanding and the ability to sustain that understanding over time given that there may be no common price that is acceptable to all parties.

There are at least four factors that affect the symmetry of firms and therefore the ability to reach and sustain a tacit understanding to compete less vigorously. First, if firms produce at different costs, this will make it more difficult for firms to reach and sustain a tacit understanding over time. Where firms have different costs, they will find it more difficult to agree to a common pricing policy. Indeed, firms with a lower marginal cost will want lower prices than the other firms would wish to sustain. More generally, the diversity of cost structures may rule out any "focal point" in pricing policies and so exacerbate coordination problems. In addition, technical efficiency would require allocating market share to low-cost firms, but this would clearly be difficult to sustain in the absence of explicit agreements and side payments.

Furthermore, even if firms can reach a tacit understanding, low-cost firms will be prone to deviate, both because they might gain more from undercutting their rivals and because they have less to fear from a possible retaliation from high-cost firms: the low-cost firm has less to fear from a price war, since it could serve the market profitably at a price (slightly) below the other firms' cost. More generally, retaliation will be less effective when exercised by a relatively inefficient firm than when exercised by a relatively efficient one. In particular, the relatively inefficient firm will be less able to impose a substantial profit loss on the relatively efficient one without at the same time itself incurring substantial losses. This means that the retaliations that the relatively inefficient firm will be rationally willing to implement will impose little discipline on the relatively efficient firm. Thus the incentive of the relatively efficient firm to deviate from the tacit understanding will be larger than if it faced competition from equally efficient firms.

**7–061**   Asymmetries in capacities will also tend to undermine firms' ability to reach and sustain a tacit understanding. Compared to a situation where all firms face the same capacity constraints, increasing the capacity of one firm at the expense of the others both increases the first firm's incentive to undercut the others and limits these other firms' retaliatory power. Overall, therefore, introducing such asymmetry hinders collusion.

Secondly, where products are differentiated, it will be more difficult for firms in the coordinating group to reach agreement (tacitly) on a fair schedule of prices to be adopted for the different types of product. Product customisation particularly makes it harder to maintain a tacit understanding since every order could represent the creation of a new product whose place in the fixed schedule of prices is unclear.

Thirdly, in industries in which product quality is important, tacit coordination will be more difficult to reach and sustain since competition need not take place solely on price but also on the quality of the products. Fourthly, in the presence of a high pace of innovation, the products supplied by the competitors as well as the market positions of each firm change over time. This implies that the "game" played by the competitors continuously changes over time, making it more difficult to sustain a tacit understanding.

A number of the Commission's decisions have concerned coordinated effects that arise through what are termed *multimarket contacts*.[168] This theory of competitive harm is based on the notion that where firms compete in more than one market (this can be across a number of product markets or a number of geographical markets), it is easier for firms to maintain a tacit understanding because their incentives to deviate are changed.[169] Where a firm competes in a number of markets, a price cut in one market could in theory be met by rival firms retaliating in not only that specific market but also in the other markets in which they compete with one another. In effect, multimarket contacts increase the size of retaliation punishment. It is argued that by retaliating across a number of markets, the losses that can be inflicted on the deviating firm will be increased and that this will consequently reduce the incentives of firms to deviate in the first place.

The Commission has considered the issue of multimarket contacts in a **7–062** number of its decisions. These include *Air Liquide/BOC*[170] and *Solvay/ Montedison-Ausimont*.[171] The Commission considered whether increased geographical scope in the former case and an increased range of products in the latter case would lead to increased likelihood of tacit coordination since disciplining deviations would be easier.

However, in applying such theoretical arguments it is important to remember that the fact firms can respond to deviations in one market by cutting prices in several markets does not mean that they will actually do so. Although retaliating across a number of markets does indeed increase the severity of the punishment, it also increase the costs to those administering the punishment for now prices and hence short-run profits are reduced in more than one market. In some cases, responding across a number of markets may not be credible and the extent of multimarket contact will not affect the ability of firms to engage in tacit coordination.

---

[168] In principle, these theories of competitive harm can arise where the merger has little or no impact on horizontal overlaps.
[169] Bernheim and Whinston (1990).
[170] IV/M1630 *Air Liquide/BOC* (1999).
[171] COMP/M.2690 *Solvay/Montedison-Ausimont* (2002).

The importance of multimarket contacts in any particular case is an empirical question that can only be answered by case-specific analysis.

### External Factors

**7–063** Even assuming that the internal factors suggest that the firms in the coordinating group are able to reach and sustain a tacit agreement not to compete aggressively, coordinated effects can still not be assumed. Indeed, for anti-competitive tacit collusion to be possible, a necessary condition is that members collectively must have market power, i.e. they should be able to increase prices above their current level without being sufficiently constrained by factors that are external to the coordinating group. This makes the assessment of external factors similar to the analysis one ought to undertake in the assessment of unilateral effects. That analysis should consider the following:

- the ease with which existing firms can expand and/or new firms enter the market (see paras 7–039—7–045); and

- the ability of buyers to exercise countervailing buyer power (see paras 7–046–7–048).

It should be noted that examining external factors provides a useful policy filter for the assessment of coordinated effects concerns. If external factors are sufficient to prevent a group of firms from increasing prices, then coordinated effects concerns can be dismissed. Even if one were to assume that those firms were able perfectly to co-ordinate their behaviour, they would still not possess the ability to raise prices above the prevailing level.[172]

### How does the merger change matters?

**7–064** The key issue in assessing the likelihood that a horizontal merger will give rise to coordinated effects is to assess why a merger might make it more likely that tacit coordination is likely to occur post-merger or whether existing tacit coordination will be made more stable post-merger. For the purposes of this discussion, we consider first how to determine whether a merger "creates" conditions that permit sustainable tacit coordination and then consider the competitive assessment under the alternative hypothesis that holds that firms are already tacitly coordinating their commercial decisions. As we will discuss, the latter approach, although superficially appealing, is fraught with difficulties.

---

[172] A good example of the destabilising effect of smaller firms on the alleged coordinating group is provided by COMP/M.2498: *UPM-Kymmene/Haindl*, (2001), see paras 140 to 148 inclusive.

*Determining whether a merger "creates" tacit coordination*

In general, we assume that pre-merger firms are competing effectively with **7–065** one another and the issue is therefore to determine whether the merger will result in firms adopting a less aggressive mode of competition. However, although economic theory has provided many useful insights into the conditions that are *necessary* for reaching and sustaining a tacit understanding, it has been less successful in identifying the characteristics of an industry that are *sufficient* for such tacit coordination to be reached and sustained.[173] A particular problem for the practical application of merger control is that neither the theoretical nor the empirical economics literature provides much guidance as to when a merger, by reducing the number of suppliers in a particular industry, will cause an industry to "tip" from not being tacitly collusive to being tacitly collusive. This is a particular issue when attempting to assess the likelihood of coordinated effects using the checklist approach; apart from the number of firms post-merger, all the other market characteristics will be the same pre- and post-merger.

Economists generally agree that there is a relationship between the size, size distribution and number of firms in a market and the likelihood of collusion. Since most horizontal mergers increase both concentration and reduce the number of firms operating in the relevant market, these changes in market structure potentially alter the conditions for tacit coordination from being unfavourable to being favourable. In general, the greater the level of concentration in the market post-merger and the lower the degree of inequality between the shares of the larger firms, the more likely it is that firms will be able to coordinate their behaviour.[174] Another finding of the theoretical literature is that the welfare loss to consumers from coordinated behaviour also rises with the level of concentration.[175] So mergers in more concentrated markets are not only more likely to lead to price rises due to post-merger coordination, they are also more likely to lead to significant consumer welfare losses.

However, from a practical point of view, there are no rules of thumb and certainly no consensus as to the level of concentration at which concerns of tacit coordination arise. The characteristics of industries differ significantly from each other to such an extent that while tacit coordination might be possible between four firms in one industry, in a different industry that would not be the case. Assessing whether a merger is likely to result in a change in the mode of competition therefore requires an assessment of the characteristics of the industry under consideration. As with unilateral effects, the likelihood of there being coordinated effects following a

---

[173] It could also be argued that economic theory has focused more on the mechanism by which coordination is sustained rather than the mechanism through which coordination is reached in the first place.
[174] See Sleuwaegen (1986).
[175] See Willig (1991).

horizontal merger will depend on many factors in addition to the change in concentration. It is therefore important to consider carefully how the structural changes brought about by the merger increase the likelihood of firms engaging in sustained tacit coordination post-merger beyond merely pointing to a reduction in the number of suppliers.

**7–066**    In practice, the competitive assessment tends to focus on the following two issues.

First, the merger can affect the degree of asymmetry of the market shares of the various firms. As noted above, economists recognise that the size distribution of firms affects the likelihood of tacit coordination being sustainable. This suggests that the likelihood of tacit coordination arising from the merger will depend in part on whether it increases or decreases the symmetry between firms. In general, the greater the degree of symmetry, the greater the likelihood of a merger giving rise to coordinated effects. Conversely, where a merger increases the degree of asymmetry between firms, the lower the likelihood that the merger will give rise to coordinated effects. Symmetry can be assessed with respect not only to market shares but also to other factors. For example, a merger may give rise to differences in the distribution of excess capacity.[176] Mergers may also affect the relative cost structures of firms and, to the extent that they affect marginal costs, therefore affect the ease with which firms can reach and sustain a tacit understanding to compete less vigorously.

Secondly, the removal of a firm that can be characterised as a "maverick" is often held to increase the likelihood of a merger raising concerns of coordinated effects. Sustained coordinated behaviour ultimately relies on the firms in the market playing along with a (tacit) agreement not to "rock the boat". If one player has a reputation for pursuing a different commercial strategy—that is, it adopts a maverick commercial approach—this can make coordination to reduce the effectiveness of competition less likely. For that reason, if the merger involves the acquisition of a maverick player by an existing large player, this can, subject to the analysis of internal and external factors, increase the likelihood of a merger giving rise to coordinated effects. Conversely, where the merger does not involve a maverick player it is less likely, subject to other changes implied by the merger, that the risk of coordination will be increased. Moreover, a merger can also reduce the likelihood of tacit coordination if it were to create a maverick supplier. Such a possibility may arise if the merger creates substantial efficiencies (i.e. reductions in marginal costs) so that the post-merger firm's commercial incentives become less aligned with other suppliers.[177]

The US Merger Guidelines note that the role that mavericks can play is

---

[176] See Compte, Jenny and Rey (2002) for a detailed discussion of these issues.
[177] See Baker (2002) for a discussion of the assessment of maverick firms.

to reduce the likelihood that a merger gives rise to coordinated effects. Those guidelines state that:

> "where capacity constraints are significant for many competitors, a firm is more likely to be a maverick the greater is its excess or divertable capacity in relation to its sales or sales in the relevant market".[178]

It should be noted however that this is not to say that only small firms that have sufficient excess capacity to expand sales rapidly in response to any post-merger price increase are potential candidates for being maverick firms. Large firms can also act as maverick suppliers particularly where such firms are able to deviate from the tacit understanding by having a greater ability to secretly expand sales, as might be the case for a vertically integrated firm.[179]

### *Determining whether a merger "strengthens" tacit coordination*

In a number of cases, the focus of the Commission's competitive assess-   **7–067** ment has been focused not on how the merger permits firms to moderate their competitive behaviour but rather how the merger makes existing tacit coordination more stable. The argument is a rather simple one: if firms are currently able to engage in tacit coordination, the reduction in the number of firms ought to make sustaining that tacit understanding easier.[180]

In *ABF/GBI Business*, the Commission adopted the stance of seeking to demonstrate that pre-merger competition in the market was characterised by tacit coordination. The Commission argued that the competition for compressed yeast in Spain and Portugal was characterised by tacit coordination pre-merger with reference to a number of market characteristics including few active suppliers, elasticity of demand "likely to be low", high barriers to entry and expansion, homogenous products and transparency over important parameters of competition, such as price and capacity decisions. It can therefore be seen that the conclusion that competition in the market was already characterised by tacit coordination was reached primarily on the basis of applying the checklist approach.[181]

But as discussed above, the checklist approach has a number of deficiencies. In particular, strictly applied, the checklist provides no scope for the parties to present rebuttable evidence. For example, if a market is

---

[178] Section 2.12, US Department of Justice and Federal Trade Commission, Horizontal Merger Guidelines (1997).

[179] Kolasky (2002).

[180] In principle, one could argue the opposite of the symmetry point noted above; namely, that the merger gives rise to more asymmetric outcomes and this leads to a destabilising of any tacit understanding.

[181] The Commission also noted that the prices of the alleged coordinated group tended to move in parallel (see paras 223 and 318). However, as discussed below with reference to the CFI *Impala* judgment (T-464/04) July 2006, such evidence is entirely consistent with firms competing effectively.

characterised by homogenous products, it cannot be denied that products are indeed homogenous. But the fact that a market is characterised by homogenous products cannot by itself imply that firms are tacitly coordinating. Indeed, the existing suppliers of those homogenous products could be competing intensely.

In short, applying the checklist approach to determine pre-merger tacit coordination necessarily raises the critical issue: how to discriminate between pre-merger outcomes that reflect effective competition and those that reflect tacit coordination? Unfortunately, it is extremely difficult in practice to distinguish between commercial conduct that is consistent with tacit coordination but which is not consistent with competitive behaviour. Indeed, most market outcomes that are consistent with firms engaging in tacit coordination are also consistent with those firms competing aggressively. For example, the parallel movement of prices over time is entirely consistent with firms competing aggressively against one another. This fact implies that discriminating between the two modes of outcomes is extremely difficult and so theories of coordinated effects that rely on pre-merger tacit coordination should be used sparingly, if at all.[182,183]

### The distinction between tacit co-ordination and explicit co-ordination

7–068   The foregoing discussion has been concerned with firms reaching and sustaining tacit coordination. That analysis focused on the ability of firms (a) to reach an agreement and (b) to sustain that agreement over time. But that same analysis applies equally to the assessment of explicit coordination discussed in Chapter 5. Indeed, for the most part, the economics literature has not tended to draw a distinction between explicit and tacit coordination, and the same factors that are listed in the checklist above are said to be equally applicable to the assessment of explicit and tacit coordination.

However, there are important differences between the two categories of coordination.[184] Explicit coordination may be useful initially to reach an agreement and it may allow the cartel members to coordinate on a price higher than the one that could have been achieved under tacit coordination. Moreover, where the market lacks transparency (i.e. if firms cannot observe their rivals' behaviour in terms of their prices and outputs), explicit collusion may also have a stabilising effect to the extent that firms are

---

[182] It has been argued that where firms have engaged in explicit coordination, then it can more easily be assumed that current observed behaviour represents tacit coordination. However, the counter argument is that if firms needed to engage in illegal explicit collusion then this would indicate that tacit coordination was not feasible.

[183] We discuss below some flaws in the analytical reasoning of the CFI on this issue in its *Impala* judgment.

[184] Indeed, if there were no difference, it would be hard to understand why firms are willing to engage in illegal behaviour when they could achieve the same outcomes through tacit collusion.

willing to report the correct market information to the other members of the cartel. Furthermore, explicit agreements may make it easier to reach and sustain coordination with a larger number of firms than would be possible absent such explicit communications.

## The evolution of the Commission's assessment of coordinated effects

This section provides a brief commentary on the evolution of the Com-   **7-069** mission's assessment of coordinated effects.

### *Early decisions*

The Commission's early use of coordinated effects tended to be confined   **7-070** to those mergers that resulted in a reduction in the number of leading suppliers from three to two. For example, in *Nestlé/Perrier*, the Commission argued that the nature of the post-merger relations between the merged party, Nestlé-Perrier, and the other leading firm in the industry, BSN, would more likely be cooperative than competitive. The Commission found that Nestle-Perrier and BSN would be jointly dominant in the French market for bottled water. As a consequence, Nestlé was required to divest a number of lesser brands to a single purchaser.[185]

The other leading early cases applying the concept of coordinated effects were *Gencor-Lonrho* and *Kali-Salz*.[186] *Gencor-Lonrho* was the first case where the Commission prohibited a merger on the grounds that it created or strengthened a position of collective dominance such that effective competition was impeded (i.e. in current terminology, gave rise to coordinated effects).

Both decisions were appealed to the CFI. The judgments of the CFI confirmed not only that coordinated effects fell within the jurisdiction of the Merger Regulation but also (in *Kali-Salz*) that structural links were not a necessary condition for a finding of coordinated effects. Prior to the CFI judgment in *Kali-Salz*, it was argued that coordinated effects required a structural link between the members of the collectively dominant group. Such structural links normally took the form of cross-shareholdings between these firms. In its *Gencor* judgment, the CFI states that[187]:

> "[I]n its judgment in the 'Flat Glass' case [the CFI] did not lay down the existence of structural links as a requirement or restrict the notion of economic links to the structural links required on by the applicant. The Commission is therefore entitled to understand that notion as

---

[185] Nestlé sold nine brands to Castel. Nestlé also sold the Volvic brand to BSN, although this was part of the original merger proposal.
[186] COMP/M308. *Kali Salz* (1993) and COMP/M.619 *Gencor/Lonhro*, (1996).
[187] *Gencor v Commission*, (T-102/96) (1999) para.270.

including the relationship of interdependence which exists between the members of a tight oligopoly."

**7-071**  The CFI judgment also states that their independence would enable firms to "anticipate one another's behaviour" and to be "strongly encouraged to align their conduct in the market, in particular in such a way as to maximise their joint profit by restricting production with a view to increasing prices". This indicates that the CFI viewed the concept of coordinated effects as matching that of the economic concept of tacit coordination.

### *Airtours/First Choice and the establishment of "economic" criteria*

**7-072**  As noted above the early decisions all related to mergers that reduced the number of competitors from three to two and the establishing coordinated effects was reached by adopting effectively the checklist approach to the Commission's competitive assessment. The *Airtours/First Choice* decision represented the first occasion on which the Commission prohibited a merger on the grounds of coordinated effects where the merger reduced the number of firms from four to three. This decision concerned the package holidays market in the United Kingdom. The Commission argued that the merger between Airtours and First Choice would reduce the number of leading firms from four to three and that small providers of package holidays would not provide an effective competitive constraint on the coordinating group consisting of the leading three firms.

The Commission's decision was controversial on a number of grounds and was severely criticised by the CFI following an appeal by the merging parties.[188] These related, inter alia, to the mechanisms through which coordination was said to have worked and to the absence of any retaliation mechanism. Given the heterogeneous nature of foreign package holidays, it was infeasible to argue that firms would be able to coordinate on price. As noted above, the more a market is characterised by product differentiation the more difficult it is for firms to reach an understanding as to the appropriate prices that each should be charging and also to monitor that those prices are actually charged. The Commission therefore argued that coordination would need to take place on the level of capacity put in place for each season. The Commission argued that following the merger, the three leading providers of foreign package holidays would be able to coordinate their activities in restricting the supply of capacity. This restriction of capacity would lead to an increase in price since capacity would be set at a level such that even operating at full capacity, output was

---

[188] See *Airtours Plc v Commission* Case T-342/99 (2002) ECR II-2585. For commentary on this judgment see, inter alia, RBB Economics (2002).

lower than pre-merger and so prices would be higher than would be the case absent the merger.

However, as the CFI subsequently noted, this argument can be rejected for two reasons. First, capacity decisions in this industry do not involve merely increasing or decreasing overall capacity. On the contrary, account needs to be taken of the differences between the various categories of package holidays, which are differentiated by inter alia destination, departure airport, and the quality of accommodation.[189] These factors, coupled with a high degree of demand volatility, imply that the development of capacity decisions are complex and, in consequence, are likely to represent a major impediment to reaching and maintaining a tacit understanding. Secondly, the Commission's theory of coordinated effects requires a high degree of transparency in the setting of capacity by the other firms in the coordinating group. The CFI held that this was not the case stating that:

> "in a market in which demand is on the whole increasing, but is volatile from one year to the next, an integrated tour operator will have difficulty in interpreting accurately capacity decisions taken by the other operators concerning holidays to be taken a year and a half later."[190]

In overturning the decision, the CFI set out the following criteria against    **7–073** which any theory of harm based on coordinated effects should be satisfied with regard to a sufficiently cogent and consistent body of evidence. First, it must be established that the firms in the coordinating group are able to reach a common understanding as to terms of coordination. Secondly, any such tacit understanding must be shown to be sustainable. This requires the following three conditions to be established[191]:

- there must be sufficient market transparency so that each member of the alleged coordinating group has the ability to know how the other members are behaving in order to monitor whether or not they are adopting the common policy;

- there must be a means for other members of the coordinating group to retaliate against any departures from the common policy, so that members have an incentive not to depart from the common policy;

- the foreseeable reaction of current and future competitors, as well as consumers, would not jeopardise the results expected from the common policy.

---

[189] para.166.
[190] para.169.
[191] para.62.

## Sony/BMG and the CFI

7–074    Following *Airtours* and the above criteria set out in the CFI's judgment in that case, there has been a marked (and unwelcome) shift in the Commission's approach to assessing the likelihood of coordinated effects. Rather than seeking to establish whether a merger will lead to firms moderating their competitive behaviour and competing less aggressively post-merger, the Commission has focused instead on seeking to demonstrate that the industry under investigation is already characterised by tacit coordination and that the merger will make such coordination more stable.

This line of argument was pursued in *Sony/BMG*.[192] *Sony/BMG* involved the creation of a joint venture between two of the five so-called Major record companies. The Commission's primary theory of harm held that the merger would enable the five Majors to better coordinate on wholesale prices and the level of discounts/rebates granted to retailers. Even though the wholesale prices/rebates were not observable per se, the Commission's theory stated that the latter could be inferred from retail prices, which were observable. However, the investigation showed that in reality:

(i)    there is a significant level of dispersion in retail CDs' prices (e.g. no standard mark-up for the same album across retailers); and

(ii)    there is not a fixed relationship between retail price, wholesale price and discounts granted to retailers.

Therefore, even if all retail prices were in principle easily available to producers, the producers would not be able to "reverse engineer" the level of wholesale price based on the knowledge of their own discount only. The Commission therefore concluded that the market was not characterised by sufficient transparency and hence there was limited scope for the merger to give rise to coordinated effects.

The first *Sony/BMG* clearance decision was appealed by the Independent Music Publishers and Labels Association (Impala), and annulled by the CFI[193] in 2006 (so-called *Impala* decision). The CFI sought to argue that the Airtours criteria could be inferred indirectly using observed market characteristics. In particular, the CFI stated[194]:

"Thus, in particular, close alignment of prices over a long period, especially if they are above a competitive level, together with other factors typical of a collective dominant position, might, in the absence

---

[192]    Following the *Impala* appeal, the Commission was required to re-examine the case and therefore there are two decisions in this case. COMP/M.3333 *Sony/BMG* (2004) and (2007).

[193]    *Impala v Commission* (T-464/04) July 2006.

[194]    op. cit., para.251.

of an alternative reasonable explanation, suffice to demonstrate the existence of a collective dominant position, even where there is no firm direct evidence of strong market transparency, as such transparency may be presumed in such circumstances."

This line of argument is, however, severely limited in practice for a number of reasons. First, it assumes that prices are above the competitive level. As we have discussed at numerous places in this book, it is extremely difficult to conclude that prices are at or above competitive levels purely on the basis of observed prices. Secondly, as noted at the beginning of this section, observed market outcomes that are consistent with tacit coordination are nearly always also consistent with effective competition. For example, the "close alignment of prices over a long period" is entirely consistent with firms competing effectively. This implies that in practically all cases there will be "an alternative reasonable explanation" and so this type of analysis will be of little practical use.

It is noteworthy that the European Court of Justice (ECJ) did not concur with the CFI judgment and set it aside.[195] The ECJ stated that when assessing the likelihood of coordinated effects, it is necessary to take into account the overall economic mechanism of the alleged tacit coordination[196]:

> "In that regard, the assessment of, for example, the transparency of a particular market should not be undertaken in an isolated and abstract manner, but should be carried out using the mechanism of a hypothetical tacit coordination as a basis. It is only if such a hypothesis is taken into account that it is possible to ascertain whether any elements of transparency that may exist on a market are, in fact, capable of facilitating the reaching of a common understanding on the terms of coordination and/or of allowing the competitors concerned to monitor sufficiently whether the terms of such a common policy are being adhered to. In that last respect, it is necessary, in order to analyse the sustainability of a purported tacit coordination, to take into account the monitoring mechanisms that may be available to the participants in the alleged tacit coordination in order to ascertain whether, as a result of those mechanisms, they are in a position to be aware, sufficiently precisely and quickly, of the way in which the market conduct of each of the other participants in that coordination is evolving."

In other words, the assessment of coordinated effects needs to be grounded **7–075** in a theory of harm which coherently sets out the parameters of

---

[195] C-413/06 P.
[196] *Bertelsmann and Sony Corp of America v Impala* (C-413/06 P) (2006) para.126.

competition upon which the firms in the alleged coordinating group are meant to be coordinating their behaviour.

.

# EFFICIENCIES[197]

**7–076** Many horizontal mergers are motivated by pro-competitive rationales, either as dynamic responses to changes in the market environment or to better utilise tangible and intangible assets.[198] Efficiencies arising from the better utilisation of tangible assets include rationalisation through the reallocation of the production and/or benefiting from economies of scale or economies or scope.[199] Efficiencies arising from the better utilisation of intangible assets include the sharing of know-how, management expertise, R&D and innovation, adjusting product line and benefiting from increased purchasing power.[200]

In some instances, a horizontal merger will create sufficient cost efficiencies that serve to put *downward* pressure on post-merger prices. These efficiencies may in certain circumstances be sufficient to outweigh any *upward* pressure on prices that results from the potential loss of competition removed by the merger. As is well established in economic theory, a profit maximising firm will produce output until marginal cost is equal to marginal revenue.[201] In other words, the pricing decisions of firms are affected by the marginal cost of production; the additional benefits from selling (and therefore producing) one more unit are greater when marginal costs of production are low. If a merger results in a reduction in the marginal cost of production, this will, *ceterius paribus*, lead to the merged firm increasing output, i.e. lead to incentives to lower price. In some instances, such marginal cost efficiencies can be of sufficient magnitude that, despite the removal of an important competitive constraint, the horizontal merger results in prices at or lower than the pre-merger prevailing price levels. Box 1 provides an analytical illustration of how marginal cost reductions can outweigh a post-merger incentive to increase prices.

---

[197] See s.VII, Horizontal Merger Guidelines.
[198] See Ivaldi (2003) for a discussion on the need to take efficiencies into account in the competition assessment.
[199] See for instance Perry and Porter (1985), Farrell and Shapiro (1990).
[200] See Scherer and Ross (1990).
[201] See Chapter 2.

> **BOX 7.1: A SIMPLE NUMERICAL EXAMPLE OF A MERGER BETWEEN SUBSTITUTABLE PRODUCTS**
>
> The incentive that firms producing substitutable products have to increase prices following a merger can be illustrated by reference to the following simple example. Suppose that in an industry there are only two firms each producing one variety of a differentiated commodity. Inverse demand functions are:
>
> (1)   $p_1 = a - q_1 - dq_2$
>       $p_2 = a - q_2 - dq_1$
>
> where   $a>0$;
>          $p_1$ is firm $1$'s price;
>          $q_1$ is firm $1$'s output; and
>          $d \in [0,1)$ indicates to what extent the two products are differentiated.
>
> If $d=0$, products are unrelated while if $d \rightarrow 1$, products tend to be perfectly homogeneous. Both firms produce at a marginal cost equal to $c$ and face no fixed costs. This implies that each firm's profit can be simply written as follows:
>
> (2)   $\Pi_i = (p_i - c) \, q_i = (a - q_i - dq_j - c) \, q_i$     $i,j = 1,2$ and $i \neq j$
>
> If the two firms compete in price à la Bertrand, then equilibrium prices are:
>
> (3)   $p_1 = p_2 = \dfrac{a(1 - d) + c}{2 - d}$
>
> Following a merger between the two firms, the new entity will maximise joint profits, resulting in the following new price:
>
> (4)   $p_1 = p_2 = \dfrac{a + c}{2}$
>
> It is straightforward to verify that the prices of both products increase after the merger whatever the degree of substitutability between the two products. For instance, if $a=7$, $c=3$ and $d=0.5$, then post merger the equilibrium price would increase from $p_1 = p_2 = 4.3$ to $p_1 = p_2 = 5$. Suppose now that the merger brings about a reduction in the marginal cost of the post-merger entity. In particular, we assume that after the merger the marginal cost decreases from $c=3$ to $c=0$. This implies that post merger the new equilibrium price will be:
>
> (5)   $p_1 = p_2 = \dfrac{a + c}{2} = \dfrac{7 + 0}{2} = 3.5$
>
> In other words, despite the elimination of the competition between firms 1 and 2, due to the reduction in the marginal cost of production, after the merger prices are lower than pre merger.

In order to take account of efficiency claims in the competitive assessment **7–077** of a horizontal merger and be in a position to reach the conclusion that as a consequence of efficiencies, there are no grounds for declaring the merger to be incompatible with the common market, the Commission requires that efficiencies can be shown to benefit consumers, be merger-specific and be verifiable.[202,203] These conditions are cumulative.

### Benefits to consumers

**7–078**   The Horizontal Merger Guidelines state that the relevant benchmark for assessing efficiency claims is that consumers will not be worse off as a result of the merger.[204] In the Horizontal Merger Guidelines, the Commission states that:

> "[f]or that purpose, efficiencies should be substantial and timely, and should, in principle, benefit consumers in those relevant markets where it is otherwise likely that competition concerns would occur."[205]

Since pricing decisions are affected by marginal costs, consumers are more likely to benefit from efficiencies that reduce variable costs rather than fixed costs. However, as discussed below, this raises the critical issue as to the appropriate time period to assess whether costs are fixed or variable.[206]

It should be noted that cost savings that arise from a post-merger reduction in output do not qualify as relevant efficiencies generated by the merger. Clearly, it is true that a reduction in output will be associated with cost reduction, but that cost reduction does not represent an efficiency. The fact that such changes involve cost savings to the merging parties does not mean that they represent legitimate merger efficiencies.

It is also important to note that not all efficiency benefits involve production cost savings. The Horizontal Merger Guidelines state that efficiencies that lead to new or improved products may also directly benefit consumers.

---

[202] para.78, Horizontal Merger Guidelines.

[203] See Kolasky and Dick (2002) for a commentary on the treatment of efficiencies in US merger control.

[204] For a discussion of welfare standards see Chapter 3 and, e.g. Lyons (2002).

[205] para.79, Horizontal Merger Guidelines. The US guidelines, by contrast, require that the agencies will also consider efficiencies in other markets that are "inextricably linked" to the effects in the relevant market. This implies that, in the US, mergers which deliver significant efficiencies in large markets, but have potential anti-competitive effects in a smaller market (in which the consumers are broadly the same as the first), can nevertheless be cleared (see Alfter, Bishop and Mahr, 2004).

[206] Of course, if it is held that competition authorities should aim at maximising social welfare (i.e. consumer welfare plus producer welfare), then the arguments for positively treating efficiencies, even fixed cost ones, that arise from a merger are even more overwhelming. See Chapter 2 for a discussion of alternative welfare standards.

"A joint venture company set up in order to develop a new product may bring about the type of efficiencies that the Commission can take into account."[207]

Such benefits are, by their nature, passed on to consumers, although the benefit may be offset to some extent by increases in price.

## Merger specific

Efficiencies should only be considered to represent a merger benefit if they  7-079
would not be realised except through the merger. If the efficiencies can be attained through the unilateral actions of one or both parties, then the efficiency gains cannot properly be said to be a consequence of the merger. This implies that only efficiency benefits which neither merging party could have achieved by itself pre-merger should be considered. For example, a merger which permits the exploitation of economies of scale in production could represent a genuine efficiency. Equally, rationalisation which involves the transfer of production from a high-cost plant owned by one party to a low-cost plant owned by the other party is a genuine efficiency benefit. The important point is that a necessary condition for taking account of the efficiency is that it is not possible for either firm to achieve such efficiencies unilaterally.

## Verifiable

Finally, any claims of efficiencies arising from a merger need to be verifi-  7-080
able such that the Commission can be reasonably certain the efficiencies are likely to materialise and be substantial enough to counteract a merger's potential harm to consumers.[208] The burden of proof on demonstrating efficiencies lies with the merging parties.

## Marginal cost efficiencies versus fixed cost efficiencies

As noted above, efficiencies arising from a merger that affect marginal costs  7-081
are more likely to benefit consumers than efficiencies that affect fixed costs. Reductions in marginal or variable costs will increase incentives for the merged entity to lower prices and therefore, to the extent that this offsets the effects of the removal of the competitive constraint between the parties, represent direct consumer benefits. In contrast, reductions in fixed costs will not feed directly through to consumer prices and it is therefore more difficult to assess the impact of such efficiencies on consumer welfare.

However, this distinction is not as clear cut as it might seem. Indeed,

---

[207] para.81, Horizontal Merger Guidelines.
[208] para.86, Horizontal Merger Guidelines.

whether costs are characterised as fixed or variable raises a difficulty as to the appropriate timeframe over which to assess which costs are variable and which are fixed. The longer the timeframe considered, the more costs that can be appropriately considered to be variable. For example, efficiencies resulting in reductions in the cost of building new machinery do not affect the short-run variable cost of units produced on old machines. However, in the longer term, they affect the cost of expanding production onto a new machine, and so may be thought of as variable costs over a longer time horizon. In some cases, therefore, such "fixed cost" reductions could also lower consumer prices. In particular, for industries where short-run marginal costs are close to zero, the proposition that long-run marginal costs are not taken into account in price setting does not appear to accord with common sense. The more pragmatic, common sense view would be that reductions in costs that are avoidable, or fluctuate with output in the medium term (say over 12 to 24 months), do affect the price formation process and should therefore be taken into account.

In summary, efficiencies created by horizontal mergers can, in principle at least, offset any otherwise adverse competitive consequences. However, given the role played by such efficiency arguments, namely offsetting identified consumer harm, it is appropriate that the Commission's three conditions for accepting efficiency arguments are stringent. Indeed, in practice efficiency arguments that prevail are extremely rare. Indeed, to date, the Commission has not cleared any horizontal merger based on the efficiencies created by that merger. In practice, therefore claims as to the efficiency benefits of a horizontal merger are more likely to provide a rationale for the merger rather than a substantive argument in itself.

## ASSESSING MERGERS IN NETWORK INDUSTRIES

**7–082** In some industries, the value that consumers place on a firm's product offering depends on the number of other consumers that are using that firm's product. Where this is the case, in general, an increase in the number of consumers using the firm's product increases the value consumers place on that product and hence the more attractive the product becomes, at given prices. Such industries are termed "network industries".

The existence of network effects raises the possibility that a merger will give rise to *tipping* or *snowball effects*. *Tipping* refers to the phenomenon whereby network effects can sometimes lead to the market being dominated by just one product (e.g. Microsoft Windows). The basic argument of such theories is as follows. Due to the existence of network effects, if two networks were to merge, this will make that network more attractive to consumers and as a result more consumers would be attracted to that network, thereby further enhancing its competitive position. Such a virtuous circle, it is then alleged, can lead to the market tipping as all consumers drift towards the largest network operator, ultimately resulting in total monopoly.

This line of argument has been applied by the Commission in a number of cases, including *MCI/Worldcom*,[209] *Vodafone/Mannesmann*[210] and *Microsoft/ Liberty Media/Telewest*.[211] In *MCI/Worldcom*, the Commission argued that the proposed merger would lead to the merged entity enjoying a high share of top level internet connectivity (the so-called "internet backbone") and that this position could be used to degrade the connectivity enjoyed by smaller rivals. In this way, the Commission argued that MCI/Worldcom would be the most attractive internet provider to consumers. Moreover, as more subscribers were attracted to its network, this would serve to reinforce the attractiveness of the network and that this would lead to a *snowballing effect*.[212]

Similar arguments were presented in *Vodafone/Mannesmann* and in *Microsoft/Liberty Media/Telewest*. In *Vodafone/Mannesmann*, the Commission argued that the merger, which involved a number of non-overlapping mobile providers (so that there was no increase in market shares), would permit Vodafone to create the first single pan-European mobile network and that other mobile operators would not be able to replicate it, at least in the medium term. The Commission therefore concluded that:

"[t]he merged entity would be the only mobile operator able to capture future growth through new customers, because new customers would be attracted by the services offered by Vodafone Airtouch/ Mannesmann on its own network."[213]

The Commission held that the merged firm would thereby become dominant. In *Microsoft/Liberty Media/Telewest*, the Commission sought to prohibit Microsoft from obtaining a minority shareholding in the UK cable operator Telewest since it feared that this would permit Microsoft to obtain a dominant position in the supply of software for set-top boxes.

The Commission's analysis in each of these cases can be heavily criti-   **7–083** cised for a reliance on speculative market analysis that placed too much weight on the theoretical possibility of tipping effects without subjecting those theories to empirical reality. For example, in *MCI/Worldcom*, no analysis was presented as to whether the theoretical argument surrounding degradation was likely. Indeed, there was no discussion as to whether a consumer would be able to tell whether the poor services on which the theory so heavily relies arises from the particular website he is accessing or due to being a subscriber to an inferior network. The Commission simply

---

[209] IV/M1741, *MCI /Worldcom* (2000).
[210] COMP/M.1795 *Vodafone Airtouch/Mannesmann* (2000).
[211] IV/JV27, *Microsoft/Liberty Media/Telewest* (2000).
[212] See Cremer, Ray and Tirole (1999).
[213] See *Vodafone Airtouch/Mannesmann* case op. cit. para.45.

assumed the latter.[214] In *Vodafone/Mannesmann*, no empirical evidence was presented that the "internationally mobile customers" represented a significant proportion of customers or that international roaming charges provided the overriding reason for choosing a mobile operator.

Finally, it is important to distinguish between the possibility that network effects are strong enough to lead to tipping and the apparent assumption that network effects inevitably lead to monopoly. To see that monopoly is not the inevitable outcome of network effects, consider the video games market. Although this market is arguably characterised by network effects it has not tipped to monopoly. There are currently three main players: Sony, Microsoft and Nintendo.[215]

# ASSESSING MERGERS IN TWO-SIDED MARKETS

**7–084** A number of industries can be considered to be "two-sided". For a market to be described in economic terms as "two-sided" two conditions must hold. First, the product at the centre of the analysis is a "platform" that allows or facilitates the interaction of two distinct groups of customers. Secondly, the benefit that customers in one group derive from the interaction is larger the greater the number of customers on the other side of the platform (the platform creates indirect network externalities). Examples of markets with two-sided features include the media (where advertisers and audience/readership "interact" through newspapers or television channels) and credit cards (interaction between merchants and customers).

In two-sided markets, a firm's bargaining strength with one group of customers can affect its bargaining strength with the group of customers on the other side of the market. This raises the possibility that a change in market structure brought about by a merger could lead to adverse outcomes for one or both groups of customer. By strengthening the merged entity's position on one side of the market, it may be able to raise prices to consumers on the other side of the market.

In a traditional one-sided market, economic theory predicts that when a firm raises price this has two conflicting effects on the profits of the firm. On one side, it increases the firm's revenues on each unit sold. On the other side, higher prices induce some customers to switch to competing products, thereby reducing the firm's volume of sales. A horizontal merger may give rise to unilateral effects because, post-merger, some of the sales

---

[214] The Commission's analysis can also be criticised on the grounds that if tipping were so likely, then one would have expected to see this trend already emerging unless one argued that the industry was in a precarious state of balance. The Commission did not make this argument.

[215] This reflects the fact that any network benefits that "large" firms have in this market can be overcome by introducing a higher "quality" game system that induces consumers to switch.

lost as a result of a price increase are captured by the other merging party, mitigating the loss of sales volume compared to the pre-merger situation and therefore creating an incentive to raise prices.

In a two-sided market these conflicting incentives also exist, but the **7–085** mechanism is more complicated due to the interaction between the two sides of the market. If a supplier raises its price to customers on one side of the market (call them "downstream"), it may induce some of those customers to switch to its competitors. This would lead to a reduction in the volume of sales made through that firm and therefore reduces revenues. Moreover, the reduction in the number of downstream customers means that the firm would become less attractive to customers on the other side of the market (call them "upstream") and this may weaken the firm's bargaining position vis-à-vis these customers. This additional feedback "interaction" between the downstream and the upstream side of the market, which is a specific characteristic of two-sided markets, reinforces the competitive constraints existing on suppliers but may also create opportunities for suppliers to "leverage" market power from one side of the market to the other side.

The merger of Galileo and Worldspan provides a good example of merger analysis in a two-sided market.[216] These firms operated Global Distribution Systems ("GDS") which are computerised booking systems used by travel agents which allows them to search and compare prices of airlines. A GDS supplier acts as an intermediary in a two-sided market, connecting airlines on the "upstream" side of the market and travel agents on the "downstream" side. The two-sided nature of the GDS market stems from the existence of "indirect network externalities", namely the fact that a GDS is more valuable to travel agents the larger the range of products it offers and, vice versa, the GDS is more valuable to airlines the larger the number of travel agents that subscribe to it.

The Commission identified several possible theories of unilateral effects concerns, of which only one differed from standard unilateral effects analysis.[217] This theory related to the alleged ability of the merged entity to leverage its market power with respect to travel agents in a number of Member States in order to increase prices to airlines; so-called "vertical cross-market effects". According to this theory, post-merger Galileo/Worldspan would have had a large share of the travel agent market in several Member States. As a consequence, if an airline has a particular interest in distributing its content in such countries, it would become more dependent on the merged entity to such an extent that it would represent an unavoidable "gateway" for airlines to reach a substantial part of end-consumers. The merger would therefore improve the bargaining position of the parties vis à vis airlines, leading to higher prices in the upstream market.

---

[216] COMP/M.4532 *Travelport/Worldspan* (2008).
[217] See RBB Economics (2008) for further details of this case.

Moreover, since GDS fees are a marginal cost for airlines (they are paid on a per transaction basis), higher fees could ultimately be passed on to consumers in terms of higher ticket prices, thus reducing consumer welfare. However, it was shown that airlines could take a number of steps to protect themselves against any attempt to worsen their terms of business with the merged GDS supplier. In particular, airlines can withdraw specific content from the GDS and they are able to impose surcharges on travel agents that book through a particular GDS. By using these bargaining tools, an airline can make that GDS less attractive to travel agents, inducing some of them to switch to rival GDS suppliers. Crucially, if a travel agent switches, the GDS loses not only the bookings on the airline in question, but also the bookings made by that travel agent on all other airlines, which could cause a substantial loss of revenues for the GDS supplier.

7–086    In order for this competitive mechanism to be effective, it is particularly important that travel agents have the ability to switch to alternative GDS providers post-merger. Empirical analysis showed not only that travel agents could and do switch GDS supplier but that a disproportionate number of the travel agents that switched away from either Galileo or Worldspan joined Amadeus (the market leader in the EEA) and not the other merging party. The Commission therefore concluded that the merger was unlikely to result in unilateral price increases as a result of "vertical crossmarket effects".

In summary, most cases involving two-sided markets do not involve a substantially different substantive merger assessment. Even though many markets have two-sided features, these are not necessarily the predominant aspect of the market. For example, the possible two-sided aspects of supermarkets do not preclude supermarket mergers from being analysed under the traditional one-sided markets framework. Furthermore, the competitive concerns raised by mergers in one-sided markets generally also apply in two-sided markets and many of the concepts and tools applied in the analysis of mergers in one-sided markets continue to play a key role in markets with two-sided features. Nonetheless, as the Travelport/Worldspan case illustrates, mergers in two-sided markets can raise specific competitive concerns, such as the "vertical cross-market effect" described by the Commission. It also illustrates the importance of taking into account the indirect constraints that may exist because of the interaction between the two sides of the market.

## MERGERS INVOLVING FAILING FIRMS

7–087  Some mergers involve a firm that has been making losses. In such circumstances, it is often claimed that the merger will not adversely affect competition since in the absence of the merger, the loss making firm would go out of business in any event. The merger will therefore not have any long-term effect on the number of firms operating in the relevant market. While such arguments cannot be dismissed, the defence of a merger purely on grounds of a failing firm warrants close scrutiny. The failing firm defence carries most weight when it can be shown that the merger enables productive assets to continue in use that would otherwise exit the market. In most markets, firms that experience losses on an on-going basis will eventually exit the market. However, this does not mean that their productive assets will also leave the market. If other firms (i.e. not the merging party) will buy the assets after a firm has failed, then the failing firm defence of a merger is not valid. Only if productive assets would otherwise exit the market is the failing firm defence reasonable.

The Horizontal Merger Guidelines set out three criteria for the successful application of a failing firm defence.[218] These are as follows[219]:

- First, the allegedly failing firm would in the near future be forced out of the market due to financial difficulties if not taken over by another undertaking.

- Secondly, there is no alternative merger that would be less anti-competitive.

- Thirdly, in the absence of the merger, the assets of the failing firm would inevitably exit the market.

These criteria are appropriately stringent and the failing firm defence is unlikely to prevail in most cases. However, in *Kali-Salz/MdK/Treuhand*[220] the Commission did accept a failing firm defence to clear the merger between the only two German producers of potash. The Commission argued that absent the merger, Mitteldeutsche Kali AG (MdK) would in the near future exit the market, that Kali-Salz would take over the share of MdK and that there did not exist an alternative purchaser who would give rise to less anticompetitive concerns.[221] Under these circumstances, the merger could not be said to lead to the creation or strengthening of a

---

[218] para.90, Horizontal Merger Guidelines.
[219] These criteria are the same as those set out in the *Kali-Salz* decision.
[220] IV/M308, *Kali-Salz/MdK/Treuhand* (1993).
[221] These conditions are similar to those contained in the US *Guidelines*, s.5.1.

dominant position since the same market position would arise in any event.[222]

**7–088**     In contrast the Commission did not accept the failing firm defence in *Aerospatiale-Alenia/de Havilland*[223] arguing that there was no evidence that de Havilland would exit the market and even if it were to do so, the parties were not the only potential purchasers. However, in *BASF/Eurodiol/Pantochim*, the Commission accepted the argument that BASF would achieve a comparable position even in the absence of the merger and that in any event the assets of the businesses in question would exit the market unless the merger were to proceed.[224] In that decision, the Commission applied the three criteria for a failing firm defence, as set out above.

Although the first two conditions were satisfied, it was not the case that BASF would obtain the market shares of Eurodiol and Pantochim. However, the Commission noted that the losses of the productive capacity of the two companies would cause a significant shortage of capacity in a market already operating under tight capacity constraints. The Commission therefore held that the market conditions would be more favourable for customers after the merger since it would maintain that productive capacity in the market rather than allowing that capacity to exit. On that basis, the Commission cleared the merger.[225]

## SUMMARY

**7–089**  This chapter has discussed the main economic considerations that are central to the assessment of the likely competitive effects of horizontal mergers. The main points can be summarised as follows.

All theories of harm arising from horizontal mergers involve some notion of output restriction; a horizontal merger cannot give rise to a price increase, unless the merged entity is prepared to accept fewer sales. This is true whether the theory of harm relates to unilateral or coordinated conduct.

Despite the change in the substantive merger test from a dominance test

---

[222] The Commission stated (para.95) that:

> "the Commission has come to the conclusion that after the proposed merger a dominant position on the German market for agricultural potash will be strengthened. However, it has also concluded that K+S's dominant position would be reinforced even in the absence of the merger, because MdK would withdraw from the market in the foreseeable future if it was not acquired by an undertaking other than K+S; it can be practically ruled out that an undertaking other than K+S would acquire all or a substantial part of MdK."

[223] IV/M53, *Aerospatiale-Alenia/de Havilland* (1991).

[224] COMP/M.2314, *BASF/Eurodiol/Pantochim* (2001).

[225] See also a number of mergers cleared by the UK competition authorities (the Office of Fair Trading and the Competition Commission) on the basis of the failing firm defence, e.g. *British Salt/New Cheshire Salt Works* (2005), *Long Clawson/Millway* (2009), and *HMV/Zavvi* (2009).

to a SIEC test, a structural analysis based on market shares continues to play an important role in the competitive assessment. Such an approach has theoretical support; mergers that give rise to a firm with a low market share are extremely unlikely to give rise to anticompetitive outcomes. Using market shares as a filter for the competitive assessment has much to merit it. However, it is important to consider whether market shares under- or overstate the extent of competition between the merging parties, by, for example, considering the diversion ratios between the parties.

Market shares and diversions ratios provide a static overview of the likely impact of the merger. But it is important before concluding that a merger gives rise to either unilateral or coordinated effects to assess other dynamic factors. These include the ease with which smaller firms already active in the market are able to expand and/or change their product offerings (i.e. the scope for firms to expand); the ease with which new firms could enter the market (i.e. the scope for new entry) and also the ability of buyers to alter the structure of upstream supply, in particular by sponsoring new entry (i.e. the exercise of countervailing buyer power). Each of these factors, either alone or cumulatively, can more than offset any potential problems that might appear to arise from a purely static assessment. In short, a proper competitive assessment of the likely effects of a horizontal merger takes into account the dynamic responses of both competitors and customers. In addition to these factors it is important to take into account the impact of any efficiencies that arise as a result of the merger on post-merger competitive outcomes.

We also discussed the particular issues that can arise in industries **7–090** characterised by network effects or two-sided markets. We showed that although competition in industries with such characteristics does have some different features that need to be taken into account, most cases involving network effects or two-sided markets do not involve a substantially different substantive merger assessment from "standard" industries.

Finally, we considered the failing firm defence. Such a defence relies on establishing that pre-merger competitive conditions do not provide the relevant counterfactual for assessing the competitive effects of the merger since the failing firm would inevitably exit the market. As noted, the conditions that need to be met for establishing a failing firm defence are appropriately stringent.

# 8. The Economics of Non-Horizontal Mergers

## INTRODUCTION

8-001 This chapter completes our overview of the economic assessment of mergers under the Merger Regulation by considering the key economic concepts and potential competition concerns raised by non-horizontal mergers.[1] Whether a non-horizontal merger is deemed to have a Community dimension is subject to the same turnover thresholds that apply to horizontal mergers. The same procedures and timetables also apply. We do not therefore repeat the discussion of these issues which are set out in Chapter 7.

There are two broad categories of non-horizontal mergers; vertical mergers and conglomerate mergers.[2,3] Vertical mergers involve companies that operate at different levels of the supply chain and it is common to denote firms as upstream or downstream of one another. The *upstream firm* produces a product which is used as an input by the *downstream firm*. Common examples of vertical mergers are mergers that involve a wholesaler and a retailer or involve a manufacturer and its input supplier. Conglomerate mergers involve companies that operate in different relevant markets and which are not in a vertical relationship. In practice, conglomerate mergers only arise when the merger involves firms that are active in closely related markets, for example involving producers of

---

[1] The Commission's approach to assessing whether a non-horizontal merger is likely to give rise to competition concerns is set out in its non-horizontal merger guidelines, *Guidelines on the assessment of non-horizontal mergers under the Council Regulation on the control of concentrations between undertakings* (2008/C 265/07) (hereafter, "the Non-horizontal Merger Guidelines").

[2] It is of course possible for a merger to have aspects that fall within more than one of these categories. For example, a merger may affect several markets, with potential concerns being horizontal in some markets and vertical in others.

[3] In COMP/M4731 *Google/Doubleclick* (2008), the Commission also raised a "diagonal" concern. Such diagonal concerns follow essentially the same logic as vertical concerns. See para.8–027 below and Section 7.2 of the Commission's decision, COMP/M4731 *Google/Doubleclick* (2008).

complementary goods or products that belong to the same product range.[4] Importantly, anticompetitive conglomerate effects can only occur if there are common buyers of the various products. In the absence of common buyers, there is nothing to link the products from the perspective of suppliers and hence no potential for any anticompetitive effects.[5]

In common with horizontal mergers, non-horizontal mergers are prohibited if they give rise to a significant impediment to effective competition. However, as this Chapter explains, there are important differences between horizontal and non-horizontal mergers which determine both the type of potential competition concern and the frequency with which such competition concerns are likely to arise. Importantly, non-horizontal mergers are much less likely to give rise to anticompetitive outcomes than horizontal mergers since, whereas horizontal mergers involve producers of substitute goods or services, non-horizontal mergers involve producers of complementary goods or services.[6,7] This means that non-horizontal mergers do not entail the loss of direct competition and any adverse competitive effects are necessarily the result of *indirect effects*.[8,9] Furthermore, reflecting the fact that they involve complementary products, non-horizontal mergers tend to give rise to a direct incentive to reduce price and/or improve quality, i.e. non-horizontal mergers tend to give rise to efficiency gains.

The remainder of this chapter considers the main economic issues raised **8–002** by non-horizontal mergers in practice, taking into account these fundamental differences between non-horizontal and horizontal mergers. We first discuss in para.8–003 a general framework for the type of competition issues that might arise from non-horizontal mergers. Whereas horizontal mergers, in practice, give rise to concerns of both unilateral effects and

---

[4]  Para.5 Non-horizontal Merger Guidelines. Examples include IV/M938 *Guinness/Grand Met* (1997) (spirits) and COMP/M.2220 *GE/Honeywell* (2001) (inputs to aircraft).
[5]  For a good overview discussion of conglomerate effects, see Neven (2008).
[6]  Non-horizontal Merger Guidelines para.11.
[7]  It should be noted that there is a close analogy between vertical relationships and the relationship between producers of complementary products. Indeed, vertically related products can also be thought of as complements, in that an increase in the price of a downstream product will decrease the demand for upstream inputs. The main difference between vertical and conglomerate mergers is the identity of who combines the two products: in the case of vertical mergers, it is the downstream firm that combines the two products, whilst in the case of a conglomerate merger involving complementary products, the integration of the products is normally left to the consumers (absent product tying by firms).
[8]  Non-horizontal Merger Guidelines para.12.
[9]  In this sense, there are parallels in the competitive assessment of non-horizontal mergers and unilateral exclusionary conduct under Article 82. See Chapter 6 for a discussion of the competitive assessment under Article 82.

coordinated effects, the potential competition concerns arising from non-horizontal mergers are, in practice, nearly always of a unilateral nature.[10] Moreover, such competition concerns relate to the foreclosure of rival firms that results in adverse consequences for consumers. We discuss what constitutes foreclosure and then present a general framework for assessing whether such concerns are likely to arise, including a discussion of the three-step approach presented in the Commission's Non-Horizontal Merger Guidelines.

Paragraph 8–008 discusses briefly the role played by market definition in the competitive assessment and, in particular, its role in assessing whether the merged entity would possess the *ability* to foreclose. This corresponds to Step 1 in the Commission's three-step analytical approach discussed in para.8–006. Paragraph 8–009 then provides a detailed discussion of the likelihood that a vertical merger will create the *incentive* to engage in practices designed to foreclose rival firms and if so whether such commercial practices give rise to adverse consequences for consumers, i.e. assess Steps 2 and 3 of the Commission's analytical approach. Paragraph 8–030 provides a mirror discussion for assessing the likelihood that conglomerate mergers give rise to competition concerns. Paragraph 8–043 briefly addresses potential concerns of coordinated effects raised in the Non-Horizontal Merger Guidelines. Paragraph 8–044 then provides an extended discussion of efficiencies that might be created by non-horizontal mergers and how such efficiencies ought to be integrated into the competitive assessment.

## ECONOMICS AND THE LAW

**8–003** Article 2(3) of the Merger Regulation prohibits non-horizontal mergers which would significantly impede effective competition, in particular as a result of the creation or strengthening of a dominant position. The Commission's approach to assessing whether a non-horizontal merger results in a significant impediment to competition is set out in its Non-horizontal Merger Guidelines. A detailed commentary on these guidelines is provided in the relevant sections below which describe the economic issues raised by vertical and conglomerate mergers, respectively.

There are significant differences between horizontal and non-horizontal mergers in the manner in which competition concerns can arise. Horizontal mergers involve firms that supply substitute products: if, pre-merger, one

---

[10] Although unilateral effects resulting from the foreclosure of competitors represent the primary potential competitive concern arising from non-horizontal mergers, theories of harm based on coordinated effects are also possible. Coordinated effects might arise if the non-horizontal merger reduces the number of effective competitors via foreclosure (see Non-horizontal Merger Guidelines paras 83 and 120) or if a non-horizontal merger increases the degree of symmetry between market participants, perhaps by aligning the degree of vertical integration in the industry or in the product offerings of firms. We discuss this issue in more detail below.

of the merging parties raised the price of its products, this would cause some of its customers to switch to suppliers of substitute products, including those supplied by the other merging party, and as a result the demand faced by those firms will increase.[11] Post-merger, some of those lost sales are "internalised" and this can give rise to a post-merger incentive to raise the price of that product. The possible harmful effects of a horizontal merger between two competing producers can be understood in the context of these cross-price effects.

In contrast, non-horizontal mergers bring together suppliers of complementary (or unrelated) products. This implies that non-horizontal mergers do not eliminate a direct competitive constraint. Moreover, such mergers also generally give rise to an incentive for the merged firm to lower its own prices and/or improve the quality of its products. Where firms supply complementary products, an increase in the price of one firm's product will have adverse consequences not only for the demand for its own product but also for the demand for complementary products.[12] As a result, where the competitive relationships between two firms can be described as complementary, each firm would benefit from increased sales if the other *lowered* the price of its product. When producers of complementary goods are under separate ownership, the beneficial effects that a price decrease of one product has on the demand for the other complementary product is not taken into account. However, if the two parties merge, consideration of such effects will be internalised and would provide an additional incentive to lower price. This is sometimes referred to as the Cournot (complements) effect. The complementary relationship between two products therefore gives rise to an "externality" and, in consequence, by internalising this externality, a merger between the suppliers of complementary products provides an incentive to reduce prices post merger (even when both parties have market power), thus raising consumer welfare.[13,14]

Put simply, whereas horizontal mergers tend to lead to upward pressure **8–004** on prices, non-horizontal mergers tend to lead to downward pressure on prices. The externality effect is not restricted to prices. Improvements in, for example, quality, promotion or distribution can also have a positive effect on the suppliers of complementary products.

This is not to say that no non-horizontal merger can give rise to anti-competitive outcomes. But it does highlight the fact that competition

[11] In economic terms, substitute products are characterised by a positive cross-price elasticity.
[12] The cross price elasticity between complementary products is negative: an increase in the price of one good reduces the demand for a complementary good.
[13] This difference in the incentives of firms engaged in a non-horizontal relationship from those engaged in a horizontal relationship is acknowledged in the Commission's Non-Horizontal Merger Guidelines (2008).
[14] In relation to vertical mergers in particular, the internalisation of this externality is referred to as the elimination of "double marginalisation".

concerns only arise if the merger leads to the marginalisation or exclusion of competitors which in turn leads to higher prices. Sometimes, such marginalisation of competitors is a direct result of lower prices; the non-horizontal merger results in the merged entity lowering prices and as a result competitors find it harder to compete. In such cases, the "source" of the potential competition problem is a direct result of a merger efficiency. For this reason, theories of harm in such cases are sometimes referred to as an "efficiency offense".[15] It should also be noted that in such cases, the merger produces direct short-run benefits to customers that cannot be disentangled from the potential indirect long-run competition concerns. It is therefore important, when assessing theories of harm based on short-run price reductions that are alleged to result in the foreclosure of rival firms, to carefully specify the conditions that permit the merged entity to translate short-run price decreases into long-run price increases, going beyond a mere theoretical assessment by accounting for observed industry characteristics and behaviour.

In practice, the primary source of competition concerns in relation to non-horizontal mergers relates to "*foreclosure*" of rival firms, where the merged firm reduces the ability or incentive of competitors to compete to such an extent that they are marginalised or driven from the market altogether.[16] In such circumstances, foreclosure can lead to increased prices.[17] Although there exists a large academic literature that posits competitive harm arising from non-horizontal mergers,[18] it should not be assumed that non-horizontal mergers ubiquitously give rise to competition concerns; many of these theoretical models are either very sensitive to underlying assumptions and/or are non-testable since they rely on parameters of competition that are simply not observable.[19]

**8-005**  A non-horizontal merger between two suppliers may create the incentive and ability to foreclose rivals for two primary reasons. First, the merged firm may be able to *leverage* market power in one market into another. By using its existing market power in one market to foreclose competitors in a related market, the merged entity may be able to reduce competition in that second market also, thereby resulting in an increase in price to the detriment of consumers. In the case of vertical mergers, the leveraging can take place from the upstream market into downstream markets or vice versa. Such vertical leveraging generally arises by refusing to deal with rival

---

[15] For a critique of such theories of harm, see Patterson and Shapiro (2001).
[16] Non-horizontal Merger Guidelines para.18.
[17] Alternatively, entry or expansion may be deterred, allowing the firm to preserve its market power.
[18] See Church (2004) for a comprehensive review of the academic literature.
[19] See ICC Submission to DG Competition (2005) and Cooper, Froeb, O'Brien and Vita (2005) on the dangers that the academic literature in general and the Church report in particular could be misinterpreted by practitioners as supporting an aggressive stance towards non-horizontal mergers. See also the response of Professor Church to the Cooper critique, Church (2005).

firms, either upstream or downstream firms, or by only dealing with these rival firms on terms less favourable compared to the pre-merger situation. By foreclosing rival firms, such practices can reduce competition in either the upstream or downstream markets thereby resulting in an increase in price to the detriment of consumers. In the case of conglomerate mergers, leveraging generally arises from the bundling or tying of products. Such practices can foreclose rival firms and thereby reduce competition in a number of related markets to the detriment of consumers. Secondly, particularly in relation to conglomerate effects, foreclosure in related markets may be used to protect market power, rather than to leverage it into related markets. By tying or bundling related products, the merged firm may be able to deter entry into the market in which it has market power.

It is tempting to consider that any commercial practice that reduces the options for rival firms or adversely affects the ability of an individual firm to compete can be deemed to represent a foreclosure strategy.[20] This viewpoint would consider any commercial practice that makes commercial life harder for a competitor as representing foreclosure and would result in a very hostile, interventionist approach towards non-horizontal mergers.[21] Such a wide definition of foreclosure is unjustified.[22] Competitive market conduct, such as a policy of reducing prices to obtain market share, is, after all, harmful to rival competitors, as they either lose sales or have to reduce their prices to remain competitive. It is therefore extremely important to understand precisely conduct that can be said to result in *foreclosure*. The Non-horizontal Merger Guidelines define foreclosure as follows:

> "any instance where actual or potential rivals' access to supplies or markets is hampered or eliminated as a result of the merger, thereby reducing these companies' ability and/or incentive to compete. As a result of such foreclosure, the merging companies—and possibly, some of its competitors as well—may be able to profitably increase the price charged to consumers".[23]

It is important to stress the second part of this definition of foreclosure; only if prices can be expected to increase to consumers will a non-horizontal merger give rise to genuine competition concerns.[24] The fact that

---

[20] Such thinking (*sic*) underpinned earlier decisions of US competition authorities in the 1950s. See, e.g. *Brown Shoe*. Such cases were the catalyst for the Chicago critique which had, and continues to have, an important effect on shifting the policy on non-horizontal mergers towards a much less interventionist approach.

[21] This viewpoint would mirror the "formalistic" interpretation of vertical agreements under Article 81(1).

[22] See also Chapters 5 and 6 for the discussion of vertical restraints and tying respectively. These chapters provide an overview of the Chicago critique.

[23] Non-horizontal Merger Guidelines para.18.

[24] Throughout the chapter, the concept of price increases is used broadly to capture any worsening of a suppliers "price quality range or service (PQRS)" offering.

rival firms might be denied access to a source of supply or an outlet for their products by a non-horizontal merger does not by itself provide grounds for finding a competition concern. Showing harm to competitors represents only a necessary but not a sufficient condition for establishing harm to competition and hence to consumers.[25]

**8–006**   Given this definition of foreclosure, how does one determine the circumstances under which harm to competitors gives rise to adverse consequence for consumers? The Non-horizontal Merger Guidelines provide for a three-step approach to assessing competition. The three steps are as follows:

- Step 1: does the merged firm have the ability to foreclosure competitors?

- Step 2: does the merged firm have the incentive to engage in business conduct that forecloses competitors?

- Step 3: what is the overall impact on competition, i.e. consumers?

Step 1 effectively represents a substantive screen for significant market power, i.e. does one or both of the merging parties enjoy significant market power in a relevant market? Such a step makes intuitive sense since it is commonly accepted that where firms do not possess significant market power, their actions cannot give rise to anti-competitive outcomes. In the context of conglomerate mergers, for example, the step that assesses ability can also be extended to consider whether alleged post-merger practices (e.g. bundling) are possible.[26] For example, although a merger may bring together products that are sold to the same customers, it may be that bundling is not possible because the products are purchased at different times.

Step 2 considers whether, even if the merged firm had the ability to adopt a strategy that might affect rival firms' access to inputs or to customers, the merged firm would have the incentive to engage in such behaviour. The need to assess whether such an incentive exists arises because any potential foreclosing strategy involves costs as well as potential benefits. For example, a decision of the upstream firm to stop supplying its rival downstream suppliers involves a loss of profit on all of the sales to its downstream competitors. The consequence of this loss of sales may more

---

[25]   The issue of identifying under what circumstances harm to competitors translates into harm to competition also lies at the heart of the competitive assessment of exclusionary abuses under Article 82. See Chapter 6 and Bishop (2008) for a detailed discussion of this issue and potential conflicts in approach between the application of Article 82 and merger control.

[26]   The Non-horizontal Merger Guidelines extend the assessment of incentives beyond a simple market share test and also take into switching costs and network effects. See COMP/M4731 *Google/DoubleClick* (2008) for an example of how these factors are taken into account.

than offset the benefits to the merged firm of any price increase in the downstream market.

Step 3 considers the impact of the foreclosing strategy on consumers. Only if the non-horizontal merger results in increased prices to final consumers can it properly be deemed to be anti-competitive. The Non-horizontal Merger Guidelines state that this step involves an assessment of buyer power and the likelihood of new entry, as well as the impact of efficiencies.[27] As is the case with the competitive assessment of horizontal mergers, the burden to prove efficiencies is placed squarely on the parties. However, given that, as acknowledged by the Non-horizontal Merger Guidelines, non-horizontal mergers give rise to significant scope for efficiencies, in practice the hurdle for proving efficiencies in non-horizontal mergers ought to be much lower than in the case of horizontal mergers.[28]

The Non-horizontal Merger Guidelines state that these three steps are often examined together since they are closely intertwined.[29] In practice, Step 2 and Step 3 are always assessed together. As explained in more detail below, the incentives to engage in a strategy that is potentially foreclosing will depend in part on its impact on prices to final consumers. In other words, in conducting a complete analysis of the merged entity's incentives to engage in such practices, it is necessary to assess whether prices to final consumers are increased, so examining Step 2 necessarily involves undertaking an assessment of Step 3. If the assessment of incentives incorporates a price increase, then Step 3 is unnecessary; it can be assumed that the strategy will result in anticompetitive outcomes.  **8–007**

Therefore a useful interpretation is to treat Step 2 as a "static" analysis and Step 3 as a "dynamic" analysis. Step 2 would consider whether a foreclosure strategy would be profitable taking into account only the static responses of rivals and consumers and includes an assessment of the likely impact on prices to final consumers. If it is found that the merged entity would have the incentive to engage in potentially foreclosing behaviour, Step 3 would then consider whether potential "dynamic" responses of competitors and consumers would undermine such a strategy. Step 3 would continue to consider the scope for buyer power and new entry. Importantly, Step 3 would in particular consider the scope for rival firms to adopt counter strategies, such as to engage in a merger themselves in response to a vertical or conglomerate merger.[30]

Paragraphs 8–009—8–042 consider how this modified three-step

---

[27]  See paras 51 and 52, Non-horizontal Merger Guidelines.
[28]  See Bishop (2008) for a discussion of this issue. Moreover, just as is the case with horizontal mergers, it is unlikely that in practice any efficiency argument would be sufficient to overturn a well-founded theory of harm.
[29]  para.32 Non-horizontal Merger Guidelines.
[30]  It is also possible that the "counter strategy" response for rival firms falls short of a full responsive merger.

framework can be applied to assess whether vertical mergers and conglomerate mergers, respectively, give rise to anticompetitive outcomes.

## ASSESSING ABILITY: THE ROLE OF THE RELEVANT MARKET AND MARKET SHARES

**8–008** As is the case with the competitive assessment of horizontal mergers and also, as one would expect given their analytical similarity, the competitive assessment of vertical restraints, market shares play an important role in the competitive assessment of non-horizontal mergers. Non-horizontal mergers can only give rise to competition concerns if the merged entity has a significant degree of market power in at least one of the markets concerned.[31] Again mirroring the assessment of horizontal mergers, market shares and concentration levels are used as a first indicator of the existence of market power and the competitive importance of both the merging parties and their competitors. In order to calculate market shares and levels of concentration, it is a necessary pre-condition that the relevant market is first defined.[32]

The Non-horizontal Merger Guidelines state that a non-horizontal merger is unlikely to give rise to competition concerns where the market share of the merged entity in each of the markets concerned is below 30 per cent and the post-merger HHI is below 2,000.[33] The threshold for a firm to be held to possess significant market power is below that traditionally associated with dominance and is in accordance with the approach taken by the Commission in applying the Vertical Restraints Block Exemption.[34] However, these thresholds, correctly, do not give rise to a legal presumption of a competitive concern, i.e. it cannot be presumed that a non-horizontal merger that exceeds these thresholds necessarily gives rise to competition concerns.[35]

---

[31] The Non-Horizontal Merger Guidelines are explicit in drawing a distinction between market power and dominance; the Commission therefore reserves the right to intervene even if the merging firms are not dominant in any market. See para.23 Non-horizontal Merger Guidelines.

[32] In contrast to the definition of the relevant market in the assessment of horizontal mergers, the definition of the relevant market in non-horizontal mergers can in principle be affected by the Cellophane fallacy since the likelihood of foreclosure depends on *existing* market power pre-merger.

[33] Para.25 Non-horizontal Merger Guidelines. However, the Non-Horizontal Merger Guidelines do set out a number of exceptional circumstances in which the Commission might still seek to intervene below this threshold; see para.26.

[34] See Chapter 5 for more details.

[35] See Bishop (2008) for a critique of the market share threshold and the use of HHIs as a filter.

# ASSESSING THE LIKELIHOOD OF FORECLOSURE ARISING FROM VERTICAL MERGERS

This section examines the specific issues that arise in the assessment of the   **8-009**
likely competitive effects of vertical mergers. The following section mirrors
this discussion in relation to the assessment of the likely competitive effects
of conglomerate mergers.

The primary competition concern arising from vertical mergers is that of
foreclosure which can arise by denying competing firms access to a source
of supply or access to actual or potential customers. Put another way,
theories of harm arising from vertical mergers depend either on raising the
costs of rivals or reducing the revenue of rivals.[36] Two types of foreclosure
can therefore be identified; *input foreclosure* and *customer foreclosure*.

The theory of harm associated with input foreclosure involves raising
rivals' costs. Input foreclosure occurs when the integrated firm either stops
supplying competing downstream firms (complete foreclosure) or does so
only at a higher price (partial foreclosure), resulting in both cases in an
increase in the price of the upstream input post-merger, thereby potentially
raising the costs of competing downstream firms.[37] If the costs of competing downstream firms are increased, this can relax the downstream
competitive constraint on the integrated firm, i.e. enable a downstream
price increase.[38]

The theory of harm associated with customer foreclosure typically
involves reducing rivals' revenues. Customer foreclosure occurs when,
post-merger, the downstream division of the integrated firm no longer
sources supply from independent upstream firms. This reduces the sales
volume of the upstream rival, which can lead to an increase in the average
cost (if economies of scale are important) and/or the marginal cost of
upstream competitors. To the extent that this leads to exit (from higher
average costs) or to reduced competitive vigour (from increased marginal
costs) the competitive constraint these firms exert on the upstream division
of the integrated firm will be reduced, leading to greater market power
upstream and higher input prices. The higher input prices, in turn, can
result in an increase in the costs of non-integrated downstream firms which
in turns leads to an increase in prices to final consumers in an analogous
fashion to input foreclosure.

---

[36] See Church (2004).
[37] Note that unless the merged firm is the only upstream supplier, its decision not to supply
its downstream rivals will mean that these rivals will still be able to purchase the input from
other upstream firms. However, since the available supply is now lower relative to demand,
the prices to downstream rivals would be expected to increase absent any dynamic
responses.
[38] In making this assessment it is important to assess both the "static" and "dynamic"
responses of competing upstream firms in determining whether the cost of inputs to
competing non-integrated downstream firms would increase.

We examine the assessment of the likelihood of a vertical merger giving rise to input foreclosure and customer foreclosure in turn.

### Input foreclosure

**8–010** Input foreclosure arises where post-merger the merged entity is able to restrict the access of downstream competitors to its upstream products or services that it would have otherwise supplied absent the merger. In consequence of this restriction of access, the costs of downstream competitors may be adversely affected. If that is the case, then prices in the downstream market may increase following the merger. Alternatively, input foreclosure can prevent new firms from entering the market and therefore enable the merged firm to preserve significant market power upstream.[39]

**8–011** **Figure 8.1: Input foreclosure**

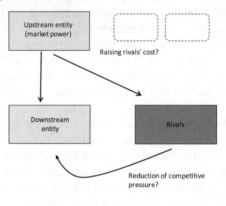

However, as we discussed earlier in the chapter, there is also a countervailing effect present in vertical mergers, since the integrated firm, by bringing together complementary products, enables the merging firm to internalise the positive sales externality between its upstream and downstream divisions, and hence to decrease price. Therefore, the overall effect on consumers is not clear cut and requires careful examination.

For input foreclosure to be a concern, it must be the case that the merged entity enjoys significant market power in the upstream market. It is

[39] There are actually 3 main branches to the academic economic literature that consider input foreclosure. These are as follows: the hypothesis that a vertical merger leads to an increase in the price of the input of the non-integrated firms; the hypothesis that a vertical merger enables the upstream firm to preserve significant market power; and the hypothesis that a vertical merger permits a foreclosure strategy that is not credible pre-merger. For more details on the economic theory relating to input foreclosure, the reader is referred to Church (2004) and the references contained therein. As Church notes, only the first two strands have practical relevance for antitrust policy.

only in these circumstances that the merged entity can be expected to have a significant influence on the supply of the upstream input product. Otherwise, its decision not to supply the upstream product to downstream competitors, or to do so on worse terms, would have little effect on the upstream market price. Where the merged firm enjoys significant market power in the upstream market, the firm is said to have the *ability* to engage in foreclosure.[40]

However, having the ability to engage in foreclosure is insufficient for a finding that the vertical merger will give rise to competition concerns. Rather, it must also be established that the vertical merger will give rise to the *incentive* to engage in input foreclosure. In assessing the likelihood of anti-competitive input foreclosure, it is necessary to take into account that such a restriction involves both costs and benefits to the merged entity. The costs of a foreclosure strategy are the lost margins on the sales of products to downstream competitors that are not made post-merger.[41]

The benefits of the foreclosure strategy have two potential sources. First, to the extent that consumers switch from downstream competitors to the merged entity in response to the foreclosure strategy, the merged entity would earn both the wholesale and the retail margin (i.e. the margin on the sale from the upstream business to the downstream business, as well as to the downstream business) on those additional sales. The greater the extent to which downstream demand is likely to be shifted away from the fore-closed rivals and the greater the share of that diverted demand that the downstream entity of the merged firm will capture the more profitable the strategy will be, all else equal.[42] Secondly, there would be the (potential) increase in margins in the downstream market; reduced competition in the downstream market may permit prices in that market to increase. Of course, competition concerns are only likely to arise if the second benefit arises as a result of the vertical merger.

To illustrate the costs and benefits arising from a strategy of input foreclosure consider the following hypothetical example. Firm A currently supplies its Product A to a downstream distributor, Firm X and also to downstream competitors to Firm X. Firm A faces competition from a number of competing upstream suppliers.

---

[40]   See para.8–008 for a discussion of the market share and market concentration filters applied in the Non-horizontal Merger Guidelines.

[41]   This is analogous to the costs associated with a strategy of restricting output that lies at the centre of the assessment of the likelihood of a horizontal merger giving rise to unilateral effects.

[42]   This phenomenon is known as *share-shifting*.

**8–012  Figure 8.2: Pre-merger upstream and downstream profits**

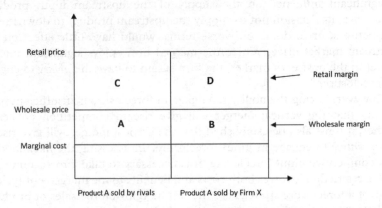

Pre-merger, Firm A earns the wholesale margin earned on sales to Firm X and the wholesale margin earned on sales to other distributors of its products. The wholesale margin is the difference between the wholesale price and the marginal cost of production. In Figure 8.2, the total revenues made by Firm A are given by A + B: the wholesale margin multiplied by the volume of sales to distributors other than Firm X plus the wholesale margin multiplied by the volume of sales to Firm X. The retail revenue earned by Firm X is shown as box D—retail margin multiplied by sales of Product A by Firm X; the retail revenue of its competitors is given by C.

Now consider the implications of a vertical merger between Firm A and Firm X. Pre-merger their combined revenues are A + B + D. At this point, we ignore the incentive for the merged firm to internalise the externality and therefore to lower its retail price—such efficiencies are considered in greater detail later in the chapter. Instead, we assume that A + B + D represents the post-merger revenue to the firm absent any exclusionary practices.

Now consider the effects of a complete foreclosure strategy, where the combined firm refuses to supply its products to competing distributors of Firm X (see Figure 8.3).[43]

---

[43]  The analysis is analytically identical if the foreclosure strategy involves raising the prices at which competing downstream firms are supplied. However, in this case, the degree to which consumers substitute towards the vertically integrated firm will be muted so that the benefits of the foreclosure strategy are less than compared with full foreclosure. But it is also the case that the costs associated with a partial foreclosure strategy are less; the wholesale margin is lost on fewer sales.

**Figure 8.3: Costs and Benefits of Input Complete Foreclosure** 8–013
**Strategy**

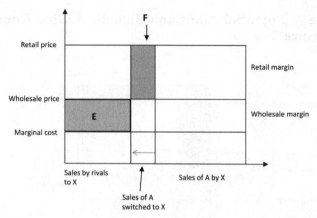

Clearly, there are costs associated with this strategy. The rival downstream distributors now start to purchase from Firm A's upstream competitors, and the merged firm loses the wholesale margin on those sales of Firm A's products that would have been made absent the foreclosure strategy. This cost is equal to the sales switched from Firm A to rival producers multiplied by the wholesale margin, and is shown as E in Figure 8.3.

On the other hand, some customers that previously purchased from competitors of Firm X now switch to Firm X since (assuming complete foreclosure) Firm A's products are now only available from Firm X. This leads to an increase in the sales of Firm X. This is shown in Figure 8.3 by the leftward shift in the sales of Product A by Firm X. This benefit is equal to the increase in sales multiplied by the retail margin (i.e. the difference between the retail price and the wholesale price)—F in Figure 8.3.

However, the above analysis provides only an incomplete assessment of the costs and benefits associated with input foreclosure strategies. The strategy of refusing to deal with downstream rivals might also permit the retail price of the product to be increased. In particular, the refusal of Firm A to supply Firm X's rivals may raise their input costs, since the demand for upstream inputs competing with Product A has increased relative to available supply. As a result, their competitiveness relative to Firm X is reduced.

A number of possible outcomes may result. First, the integrated merged firm might find it profit-maximising to maintain its price advantage, and benefit from higher sales. In and of itself, it is not clear that this would be a disadvantage to consumers.[44] Alternatively, the merged firm might increase its downstream price in line with competitors, leading to higher prices than

---

[44] However, theory posited in some cases is that such a "margin squeeze" on competitors may be sufficient to drive them out of the market, after which the merged firm would be in a position to raise prices. Such theories are however difficult to sustain unless it can be shown that re-entry into the market, once the downstream price increases, is difficult.

would have otherwise prevailed, and therefore potential consumer harm. This case is shown in Figure 8.4 below.

**8–014  Figure 8.4: Potential Additional Benefit Arising from Input Foreclosure**[45]

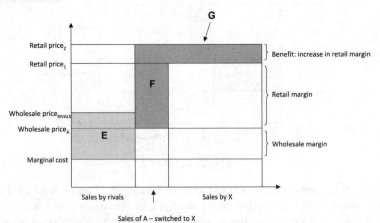

The higher wholesale price faced by competitors leads to an increase in the retail price, from Retail Price$_1$ to Retail Price$_2$. This produces an additional benefit to the merged firm of input foreclosure, as, in addition to benefitting from diverted sales (F), it is also able to increase its retail margin over its entire downstream sales base—this is shown as box G. However, the opportunity cost of not supplying rivals—shown by box E in Figure 4— also increases, with the wholesale margin of third party supply. If E is greater than F and G combined, a strategy of refusing to supply unintegrated downstream competitors would not be profitable, and therefore would not be credible.[46]

Therefore, any proper competitive assessment needs to trade-off these costs and benefits.[47] *Ceteris paribus,* the lower the wholesale margins, the lower the loss from restricting input sales. Similarly, the higher the retail margin, the higher the profit gain from increasing market share downstream at the expense of foreclosed rivals. However, such observations provide only rough and necessarily imperfect guides; a proper assessment of the costs and benefits associated with an input foreclosing strategy necessarily involves an empirical analysis involving, inter alia, not only an assessment of upstream margins and downstream margins but importantly the propensity of consumers to switch from downstream competitors to the merged entity.

---

[45] As drawn, the figure assumes a retail elasticity of zero, i.e. an increase in the retail price does not lead to any reduction in retail demand. This is unlikely to hold in practice and we would therefore expect to see some reduction in the volume of sales made by X.

[46] See, e.g. discussion in COMP/M.4942 *Nokia/ Navteq* (2008).

[47] See, e.g. COMP/M.4300 *Philips/Intermagnetics* (2006) paras 56 to 62.

A key factor in determining whether input foreclosure represents a profitable strategy therefore depends on the ability of downstream rivals to obtain equivalent inputs from other upstream suppliers, and the cost of so doing. If upstream suppliers are in a position to expand their production so as to fill any "gap" resulting from the putative foreclosure strategy, then input foreclosure is unlikely to give rise to any competition concerns. However, if competing upstream firms are capacity constrained, are less efficient (so that they are only able to supply inputs at a higher cost than the merging upstream firm) or branding is important in determining the choices of the customers of downstream firms then downstream firms may find it difficult to obtain equivalent inputs at pre-merger prices. This is precisely why non-horizontal mergers are not expected to lead to anti-competitive effects in the absence of substantial market power in one or more of the affected markets.

The effect on downstream demand will also depend on whether the affected input represents a significant proportion of downstream costs or if it represents a critical input of the downstream product. If the upstream product represents only a small proportion of the overall retail price, even a significant increase in the price of that product is unlikely to materially affect the downstream retail price.[48] Cost pass through of downstream firms is also important—the greater is the incentive of downstream firms to absorb the cost increase, the less effective will be the foreclosure strategy.

Furthermore, in assessing the impact of competitor responses on the profitability of the putative foreclosure input strategy, account needs to be taken of potential dynamic reactions of those competitors. In particular, account needs to be taken of the ability of downstream rival firms to respond by engaging in vertical integration themselves or of the ability of competing upstream firms to expand or for new firms to enter.[49] Account also needs to be given to the possibility of new entry occurring potentially via the scope for customers to exercise buyer power (i.e. buyers sponsoring new entry or vertically integrating themselves). Finally, the overall impact of the vertical merger on competition needs to take into account of the efficiency benefits that may arise from the vertical merger. Paragraph 8–044 below discusses the treatment of efficiencies in non-horizontal mergers.

---

[48] This can again be seen from an examination of Figure 8.4: the smaller is the proportion of the downstream price accounted for by the upstream input, the smaller is box G. For further discussion, see Non-horizontal Merger Guidelines para.42. For an example of the Commission's assessment see COMP M.4561 *GE/Smiths Aerospace* (2007).

[49] If rival firms engage in vertical integration and also adopt a "self-supply" approach, the downstream firm (Firm X in our example) may lose additional downstream sales.

*Commission's assessment of input foreclosure in practice*

**8-015** This section considers two examples of the Commission's assessment of input foreclosure concerns in practice: *TomTom/Tele Atlas* and *Nokia/Navteq*.[50] However, good examples of the application of such "vertical arithmetic" are also provided by *BPB/Saint Gobain* and *Sasol/Engen*. The former involved a vertical merger between BPB, a supplier of plasterboard, and Saint Gobain, a distributor of plasterboard. The Commission cleared this merger in Phase I.[51] *Sasol/Engen* concerned a proposed merger involving a South African oil refinery and a downstream petrol and diesel retailer. In this case, the South African Competition Tribunal found that there was a credible likelihood of foreclosure and prohibited the merger.[52]

*TomTom/Tele Atlas*

**8-016** The acquisition of Tele Atlas by TomTom in 2008 was one of the first cases in which the Commission sought to apply the methodology described in the Non-Horizontal Merger Guidelines. TomTom produces portable navigation devices (PNDs), or satnavs as they are more commonly known. TomTom was the leading PND manufacturer in Europe at the time.[53] Tele Atlas produced the maps that are required by PNDs and was the largest of only two producers of "navigable maps" in Europe at the time.[54] At first glance, this merger might appear to be very problematic; the largest downstream firm was buying the largest upstream firm in an upstream duopoly. However, after a Phase II investigation, the merger was cleared as the Commission decided that there was no plausible theory of harm. Although the Commission investigated both customer foreclosure and input foreclosure, the main competition concerns related to input foreclosure.[55]

---

[50] COMP/M.4854 *TomTom/Tele Atlas* (2008) and COMP/M.4942 *Nokia/Navtec* (2008).

[51] For details see COMP/M.3943 *Saint-Gobain/BPB* (2005).

[52] For details, see decision of the South African Competition Tribunal, 101/LM/Dec04.

[53] Para.177 COMP/M.4854 *TomTom/Tele Atlas* (2008) puts TomTom's EEA market share at between 30% and 50%.

[54] Para.77 op. cit. put Tele Atlas' EEA market share at between 50% and 70%.

[55] The theory of harm associated with customer foreclosure held that the merged entity would be able to harm upstream firms by foreclosing them from access to customers and thus denying them economies of scale. In this case it would imply denying Tele Atlas' upstream rival, Navteq, access to TomTom and to this causing Navteq to lose economies of scale. However, pre-merger Tele Atlas was already effectively the sole supplier to TomTom, so the merger would not change anything in this respect. As a result, the Commission dismissed this theory of harm.

The theory of harm relating to input foreclosure came in two forms: complete and partial input foreclosure. Complete input foreclosure would involve the merged entity no longer supplying maps to TomTom's rivals. The result would be that Navteq would effectively become the monopoly supplier to TomTom's rivals and so would be able to raise its prices.[56] This would cause TomTom's PND rivals to raise their prices and this would benefit TomTom by reducing the competitive pressure it faced from rivals. It could take advantage of this by raising its own prices, or selling more PNDs, or a mixture of both. *Partial* input foreclosure was a similar theory of harm, but under this theory the merged entity would not stop supplying downstream rivals entirely, but would raise its prices to them (or lower the map quality), thus allowing Navteq to also raise its prices and thus reducing the downstream competition faced by TomTom.

This theory of harm is economically coherent, but whether it is applicable in practice is an empirical matter. Applying the "ability, incentive, harm to consumers" methodology, the Commission first concluded that the merged entity would have the ability to engage in input foreclosure. The Commission then considered whether the merged entity had an incentive to do so. The theory implies that the merged entity sacrifices profits from its upstream arm (i.e. it reduces map sales) in the expectation of earning increased profits downstream (from higher PND prices and/or more PND sales) that outweigh the lost upstream profits. One factor that is clearly relevant here is the relative margins upstream and downstream. It turned out that downstream margins were considerably higher than upstream margins,[57] which suggests that the theory might have been applicable. However, the Commission dismissed the concern because it found that the effect of higher map prices on PND prices was likely to be very low. First, maps account for only a small proportion of the cost of a PND (less than 10 per cent[58]), so even a significant increase in map prices would have little effect on PND prices. This implies that there would be little reduction in the competitive pressure on TomTom. Secondly, the Commission carried out an econometric estimation of the cross-price elasticity between TomTom and its rivals and found that it was low, so even a significant increase in the price of rival PNDs would not significantly increase the demand for TomTom PNDs.[59] As a result, the Commission concluded that the merged entity would not have an incentive to engage in

---

[56] In fact, there was some dispute over this claim as it was argued that when Navteq was negotiating with a PND manufactuer, it would not be able to commit not to offer a lower price subsequently to another PND manufacturer and so the first one would not accept a raised price from Navteq in the first place. This issue is similar in principle to the problem faced by a durable goods monopolist and discussed in Chapter 2. This issue is mentioned in the Non-Horizontal Merger Guidelines at fn.40.

[57] Fn.164 of the decision suggests that downstream margins were between 5 and 10 times higher than upstream margins.

[58] para.216 op. cit.

[59] para.221 op. cit.

input foreclosure as it would likely lose more margin from the reduction in upstream sales than it would gain in downstream margin. Given this conclusion, it was clear that the merger was not likely to harm consumers.

**8–017**     The Commission also considered the efficiency claims of the parties. As noted in the Non-Horizontal Merger Guidelines, vertical mergers can lead to pricing efficiencies due to the elimination of double marginalisation.[60] The Commission accepted that there were likely to be such efficiencies in this case, but only after confirming that these efficiencies could not be achieved without the merger. Specifically, the Commission investigated whether maps could be sold on the basis of a fixed fee plus a variable component related to marginal cost. It concluded that such contracts were not used in the industry and so the price efficiencies were merger specific.[61] The parties also claimed non-pricing efficiencies related to the ability of the integrated company to better update their maps on the basis of information provided by TomTom's users. The Commission accepted that the parties' claim that the merger would lead to "better maps—faster" was likely to be correct.[62]

### *Nokia/Navteq*

**8–018** Similar concerns were raised in the parallel *Nokia/Navteq* transaction. In consequence, much of the analysis undertaken in relation to *TomTom/Tele Atlas* was also undertaken in *Nokia/Navteq*. In this case, an analysis of the "vertical arithmetic" of complete input foreclosure showed that a very significant price increase by Tele Atlas would be necessary before sufficient sales would be switched from downstream rivals to Nokia such as to make a complete foreclosure strategy profitable (i.e. a similar conclusion to that reached in *TomTom/Tele Atlas*).

This result, in part, relies on the rate of pass-through of any input price increase into consumer prices. It also relies on the degree to which such price increases would lead to switching towards Nokia handsets, as captured in cross-price elasticities. The Commission's own empirical analysis of the relevant downstream elasticities indicated that Nokia would capture only a limited amount of sales downstream following a foreclosure strategy. The Commission noted that the incentive to engage in complete foreclosure would be further undermined due to the map database accounting for only a small proportion of the final input price of a handset. The Commission then found that:

---

[60]  See para.8–045 and the Appendix to this chapter and Chapter 5 for a discussion of double-marginalisation.
[61]  paras 241 and 242 op. cit.
[62]  para.249 op. cit.

"if TeleAtlas does not raise prices by more than two hundred per cent, a total input foreclosure strategy would not be profitable for Nokia/ NAVTEQ".[63]

The questions then to be considered would be: what would limit Tele Atlas from engaging in a very large upstream price increase; and could NAVTEQ be sure that Tele Atlas would increase its price sufficiently? The Commission concluded that it was "unlikely that NAVTEQ would risk all its map revenue without any guarantee that TeleAtlas would raise prices by such magnitude." Furthermore, the Commission noted the potential importance of entry here. Specifically:

"such a price increase by TeleAtlas does not appear realistic in light of the industry characteristics. In particular, it would increase the prospect for entry, which would defeat the purpose of a total foreclosure strategy".[64]

In *Nokia/Navteq*, a complete input foreclosure strategy was also ruled out **8–019** on the basis that it would not represent a credible strategy. As a result of *Nokia/Navteq* implementing a complete input foreclosure strategy, Tele Atlas would increase its profits upstream. But, this would provide an incentive for NAVTEQ to re-enter into the supply of maps to downstream rivals, given that they are going to be supplied anyway by Tele Atlas. After the merged entity states its intention not to supply downstream rivals, and following an increase in Tele Atlas's price in response to this, Nokia/ NAVTEQ could then slightly undercut Tele Atlas and benefit from higher priced sales to downstream rivals. Nokia/NAVTEQ would also benefit in the downstream market due to these rivals now facing higher map database input costs relative to the period before Nokia/NAVTEQ announced its decision not to supply rivals. These higher input costs would be expected to cause higher prices for non-Nokia handsets and switching of demand to Nokia. Given that NAVTEQ will continue to have, and to upgrade, its maps to be used in Nokia handsets and given that the marginal costs of supplying additional maps to other handset manufacturers are close to zero, the costs of NAVTEQ "re-entering" into the supply of other handset manufacturers would be very low. Therefore, unless Nokia/NAVTEQ was able to make a credible commitment not to "re-enter" into such supply, Tele Atlas would be unlikely to increase its prices. This would then undermine any total input foreclosure strategy. Furthermore, the incentive for Nokia/NAVTEQ to "re-enter" into the supply of downstream rivals would increase with the size of any price increase by Tele Atlas. The Commission therefore recognised that a total input foreclosure strategy

---

[63]   para.346 COMP/M.4942 *Nokia/ Navtec* (2008).
[64]   fn.138 COMP/M.4942 *Nokia/Navteq* (2008).

may "not be credible for the merged entity which would have an incentive to undercut Tele Atlas".[65]

### Customer foreclosure[66]

**8–020** Customer foreclosure arises when an upstream firm vertically integrates with an important downstream customer thereby denying rival upstream firms access to this customer. If this customer is sufficiently large then this may have the effect of reducing the ability of rival upstream firms to compete, in particular by increasing their average costs of supply.[67] This may allow the merged entity to profitably increase prices in the downstream market.[68]

**8–021** **Figure 8.5: Customer Foreclosure**

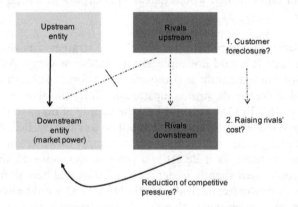

Customer foreclosure can, in principle, either take the form of full foreclosure whereby the merged entity decides to source all of its required goods and services from its upstream entity and as a result stop purchasing from rival upstream firms or partial foreclosure whereby the merged entity chooses to reduce purchases from upstream competitors (often by offering less favourable prices as compared to the pre-merger situation).

For customer foreclosure to be a concern, it must be the case that the vertical merger involves a firm that is an important customer that enjoys significant market power in the downstream market.[69] It is only in these circumstances that the merged entity can be expected to have a significant influence on the supply of the upstream input product. Where the merged

---

[65] op. cit.
[66] For more details on the economic theory relating to customer foreclosure, the reader is referred to Church (2004) and the references contained therein.
[67] This might be the case if economies of scale are particularly important.
[68] para.58 Non-horizontal Merger Guidelines.
[69] See para.61 Non-horizontal Merger Guidelines.

firm enjoys significant market power in the downstream market, the firm may have the *ability* to engage in customer foreclosure.[70]

However, as in the case of input foreclosure, having the ability to engage in customer foreclosure is insufficient for a finding that the vertical merger will give rise to competition concerns. Rather, it must also be established that the vertical merger will give rise to the *incentive* to engage in customer foreclosure.

In assessing the likelihood of anticompetitive customer foreclosure, it is necessary to take into account that such a restriction involves both costs and benefits to the merged entity. The *static* cost associated with a customer foreclosure strategy—or the cost that does not take into account counter strategy mergers of unintegrated rivals—is the lost retail margin on any reduction in the sales of the downstream firm that arise from choosing to supply only the integrated firm's product.[71] Such losses may arise either because the integrated upstream firm is less efficient and/or the products supplied by upstream competitors are more attractive; by choosing not to supply upstream rival's products, the downstream firm may lose sales.

The benefits of the customer foreclosure strategy have two potential **8–022** sources. First, to the extent that the integrated downstream firm replaces purchases from upstream competitors to the integrated firm, the merged entity would earn the wholesale margin (the margin on the sale from the upstream business to the downstream business) on those additional sales. The greater the extent to which downstream demand is shifted away from the upstream foreclosed rivals and the greater wholesale margin the more profitable the strategy will be, all else equal. Secondly, there would be the (potential) increase in margins in the downstream market. If, by denying upstream firms access to an important downstream customer, the wholesale price to non-integrated downstream firms increases, then this can lead to reduced competition in the downstream market and hence higher retail margins. Of course, competition concerns only arise if the second benefit arises as a result of the vertical merger since otherwise there is no harm to consumers.

If the integrated firm is successful in winning sales from its upstream rivals, and if the upstream market is characterised by significant economies of scale, customer foreclosure can also lead to higher input prices. Where this is the case, vertical mergers resulting in customer foreclosure may affect the ability of upstream competitors to compete effectively. For instance, if rival firms are, pre-merger, operating at or close to the minimum efficient scale, then the loss of a significant customer could result in a significant increase in the average cost of these competing upstream

---

[70] See para.8–008 for a discussion of the market share and market concentration filters applied in the Non-horizontal Merger Guidelines.

[71] This is analogous to the costs associated with a strategy of restricting output that lies at the centre of the assessment of the likelihood of a horizontal merger giving rise to unilateral effects.

suppliers and, as a result, lead in the long run to an increase in the prices charged to downstream customers.

To illustrate the costs and benefits arising from a strategy of input foreclosure consider the following hypothetical example. Firm X currently purchases from Firm A and also from upstream rivals of Firm A. Suppose Firm X and Firm A merge.

**8–023  Figure 8.6: Pre-merger upstream and downstream profits**

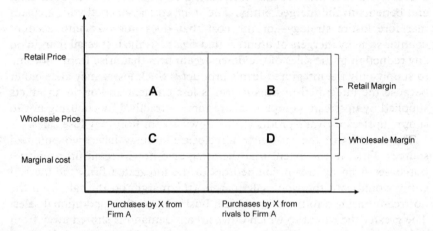

Pre-merger, Firm X earns the retail margin on all of its sales.[72] This leads to revenues of A+B. Firm A earns wholesale margin of C, so pre-merger the two firms earn revenues of A+B+C.

Now consider the effect if post-merger the combined firm were to refuse to purchase its input requirements from competitors to Firm A. Therefore, we are considering complete foreclosure of upstream rivals.[73] Figure 8.7 shows that such a strategy has a number of effects.

---

[72]  Note that, in Figure 8.5, in contrast to earlier diagrams, the sales of X represent the entire horizontal axis.

[73]  The analysis is analytically identical if the foreclosure strategy involves raising the prices at which competing downstream firms are supplied. However, in this case, the degree to which consumers substitute towards the vertically integrated firm will be muted so that the benefits of the foreclosure strategy are less compared to full foreclosure. But it is also the case that the costs associated with a partial foreclosure strategy are less; the wholesale margin is lost on fewer sales.

**Figure 8.7: Costs and Benefits Associated with Customer**    8–024
**Foreclosure**

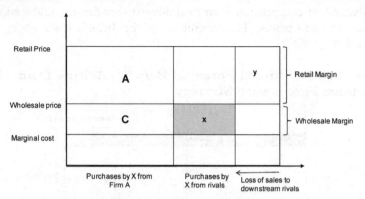

First, consider the potential costs associated with this strategy if Firm A is less efficient than its upstream competitors or produces a less attractive product. In either case, switching to purchasing only from Firm A may result in a reduction in the volumes of sales made by Firm X in the downstream market. Figure 8.7 shows the case where Firm A is as efficient as its upstream competitors (they have the same marginal cost) but supplies a less attractive product, resulting in a leftward shift in the total volume of sales made by Firm X. This loss would be equal to the retail margin on those sales of Firm X's products that would have been made absent the foreclosure strategy. This is shown as $y$ in Figure 8.7.

The benefits associated with customer foreclosure are two-fold. First, the strategy involves share-shifting; the upstream rivals of Firm A lose market share to Firm A since the input requirements of customer X that were previously purchased from competitors of Firm A are now switched to Firm A; assuming complete foreclosure Firm X now only purchases its input requirements from Firm A. This leads to an increase in the sales of Firm A. This benefit is equal to the increase in sales multiplied by the wholesale margin (i.e. the difference between the marginal cost of production and the wholesale price). This is shown as $x$ in Figure 8.7.

However, the strategy of refusing to purchase from non-integrated upstream firms might also permit the retail price of the product to be increased. This may occur if the variable cost of non-integrated upstream firms is significantly increased[74]; such an increase in the marginal cost of non-integrated firms would lead to an increase in the cost of inputs to non-integrated downstream firms, making them less effective competitors to the merged firm. The merged firm would benefit from this increase in the wholesale price to competitors in two ways. First, consumers would switch away from the now relatively less efficient downstream firms to the merged

---

[74] This might occur if upstream marginal production costs are associated with significant economies of scale.

entity, i.e. the merged entity would experience an increase in sales. This benefit is shown as **x\* + y\*** in Figure 8.8. Secondly, the reduction in the effectiveness of competition from rival downstream firms would lead to an increase in retail prices. The magnitude of this benefit is shown as G in Figure 8.8.

**8–025  Figure 8.8: Additional Potential Benefits Arising from Customer Foreclosure Strategy**

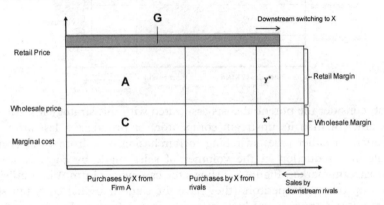

Assessing whether the strategy would be profitable requires establishing whether y minus y\* (the overall loss of retail margin) is less than x plus x\* (i.e. the overall increase in wholesale margin) plus G (i.e. the overall increase in retail margin on retained sales). This is ultimately an empirical question which, as noted above, will depend, *inter alia*, on assessing the magnitude of the wholesale margin, the degree of share-shifting and the likely impact on the retail margin. The extent of the loss of any upstream economies of scale and the substitutability of inputs are important.

However, as a general comment, customer foreclosure is less likely to give rise to competition concerns than input foreclosure, since competition concerns arising from customer foreclosure are likely to require that there is a significant customer in the downstream market that accounts for a very large market share and that input suppliers are subject to significant economies of scale. Only if these two conditions hold, can the loss of sales to the post-merger vertically integrated customer would result in an increase in the variable costs of competing input suppliers, thereby reducing their ability to compete effectively.

A profitable customer foreclosure strategy also assumes that upstream firms are not able to expand sales to other downstream firms. If upstream suppliers are in a position to expand their production so as to fill any "gap" resulting from the putative foreclosure strategy, then customer foreclosure is unlikely to give rise to any competition concerns. Furthermore, in assessing the impact of competitors' responses on the profitability of the putative customer foreclosure strategy, account needs to be taken of potential dynamic reactions of competitors. In particular, account needs to be taken of the ability of upstream rival firms to respond by engaging in vertical integration themselves.[75]

Finally, the overall impact of the vertical merger on competition needs to take into account the efficiency benefits that may arise from the vertical merger. Paragraph 8–044 below discusses the treatment of efficiencies in non-horizontal mergers.

## Commission's assessment of customer foreclosure

Reflecting the fact that customer foreclosure is less likely to give rise to **8–026** competition concerns than input foreclosure, potential concerns of customer foreclosure have arisen less frequently in the Commission's merger assessments than input foreclosure concerns.[76] Moreover, such concerns have yet to be assessed in detail following the publication of the Non-horizontal Merger Guidelines. However, it can be expected that in future the principles of "vertical arithmetic" that the Commission has applied in its assessment of input foreclosure will be applied where appropriate.

## Diagonal mergers

A further potential source of unilateral effect concerns arise in so-called **8–027** "diagonal" mergers. A diagonal merger is one where the two merging firms are not horizontal competitors and are also not in a direct vertical relationship.

Figure 8.9 illustrates this for a merger between Firm A and Firm D. Firm A sells to Firm C, which is at the same vertical level as Firm D, but does not sell to Firm D itself.

---

[75] If rival firms engage in vertical integration and also adopt a "self-supply" approach, the competing integrated firm may gain sufficient sales to maintain cost effectiveness in the wholesale market.

[76] Cases where customer foreclosure issues have been mentioned include COMP/M.1879 *Boeing/Hughes* (2000), COMP/M.2822 *ENBW/ENI/GVS* (2002), and COMP/M.2978 *Lagardere/Natexis/VUP* (2003).

**8–028** **Figure 8.9: Example of a diagonal merger**

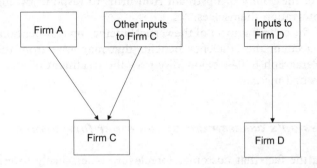

On the face of it one might assume that there are no potential competition concerns in this case. However, there is a coherent theory of harm when the upstream firm supplies a downstream firm that is a competitor to the downstream merging party. The theory of harm is this: post-merger, the upstream firm will have an incentive to raise its prices because this will lead its downstream customers to raise their prices, which will benefit the downstream merging party. Thus in Figure 8.9, Firm A would raise its price to Firm C, and Firm C would therefore raise its price to consumers and this would cause some consumers to switch to Firm D. Whilst before the merger Firm A does not take account of the benefit to Firm D from raising its price, after the merger it does and so this gives it the incentive to raise its price above the pre-merger level. Note that this is a unilateral effect. It does not rely on other firms engaging in the same behaviour (i.e. a coordinated effects concern).

Although the theory of harm is coherent, it relies on three necessary conditions.

1.  Firm A must be able to raise its price to Firm C without other suppliers of the same input undercutting the price rise. This requires that Firm A has market power.

2.  The input sold by Firm A must make up a significant proportion of the input costs of Firm C, since otherwise the effect on Firm C's price would be negligible and hence the potential effect on Firm D's sales would be negligible.

3.  The products offered by Firm C and Firm D must be close substitutes, since otherwise even if Firm C raises its price, there will be little effect on Firm D's sales.

These three conditions are all necessary conditions. These conditions are only likely hold in exceptional circumstances and so we do not expect diagonal merger concerns to arise very often.

An example of diagonal concerns arose in the *Google/Doubleclick* merger   **8-029** investigated by the Commission in 2008.[77,78] The concern arose in the area of online advertising. Google was a supplier of online text advertising. Online text advertising competes with online display advertising (i.e. adverts with either static or animated graphics). Doubleclick was a supplier of "ad serving" technology. This technology is used to deliver an advert from the advertiser to the advertising space. Doubleclick provided ad serving technology for display adverts, but not for text adverts. The theory of harm was that post-merger Doubleclick would increase its prices, this would increase the price of display adverts and this would benefit Google's text advert business as consumers switched from display adverts to text adverts.

This is a perfectly coherent theory of harm. However, the empirical evidence in this case did not support the theory. First, Doubleclick faced fierce competition in the supply of ad serving for display adverts. Indeed, at the time it was both cutting its prices and losing customers due to competition. So there was no likelihood of a significant price rise to online advertisers using display adverts. Secondly, ad serving technology accounts for only a small proportion of the cost of display adverts, so even a significant rise in the price of ad serving would have little effect on the cost of display adverts or, therefore, on the price of display adverts. Thirdly, the evidence was that Google's text adverts were not a close substitute for display adverts. Thus none of the three necessary conditions for competitive harm held in this case. The Commission consequently cleared the merger unconditionally early in the Phase II investigation.

## ASSESSING THE LIKELIHOOD OF FORECLOSURE ARISING FROM CONGLOMERATE MERGERS

Conglomerate mergers are mergers between firms which have no existing   **8-030** or potential competitive relationship either as competitors or as supplier and customer and therefore do not give rise to either horizontal or vertical issues.[79] A distinction can be made between conglomerate mergers that involve *complementary products* and conglomerate mergers that involve *unrelated products*. The definition of complementary products was provided above—these are products where a consumer's increased demand for one product generates increased demand for its complement. Unrelated products are those which have no obvious commonality, i.e. they are neither substitutes nor complements for one another. However, unrelated products may be sold to the same group of customers, and so utilise similar

---

[77]   COMP/M.4731 *Google/Doubleclick* (2008).
[78]   See Lewis and Lofaro (2008) for an excellent discussion of this case.
[79]   para.91 Non-horizontal Merger Guidelines.

promotional strategies and distribution channels. Such products are sometimes said to be in "neighbouring markets" since although the goods may be unrelated from the point of view of the consumer, and thereby not complementary in a strict sense, they can nevertheless be considered complements from the point of view of some firms at a certain level of the supply chain. For example, whisky and vodka can be unrelated for consumers, but a retailer (e.g. a bar) can perceive them as complementary, because if it stocks only one of these products the attractiveness of the bar to consumers as a whole may be reduced.[80] Conglomerate mergers that involve complementary products or products in neighbouring markets are said to be "closely related". Conglomerate mergers that do not involve companies that are active in closely related markets are unlikely to give rise to competition concerns.[81]

Theories of harm arising from conglomerate mergers are typically based on an extension of the merged entity's product offering with the intuition that the merged entity is able to leverage its "strong" brands into increased sales for its "weak" brands. In consequence, such theories of harm are often referred to as *range effects* or *portfolio power*. However, it is important to understand how an extension to the merged entity's product range might give rise to potential competition concerns especially since such extensions are often (indeed, usually) associated with efficiency benefits for consumers of those products.

A conglomerate merger can only give rise to *portfolio power* in those instances where customers (usually, large retailers) typically purchase a range of the affected products. The underlying principle in the application of the concept of portfolio power is that the market power which can be derived from a range of products in separate markets is greater than the sum of its parts. In other words, being present in each of, for instance, five separate relevant markets gives a firm a better competitive position than being present in only one or two of those markets.

To examine the logic of these arguments consider the following example of a merger between Firm A and Firm B. Firm A operates in markets I, II and III while firm B operates in markets III, IV, and V. It is agreed that all five markets are distinct relevant markets. A hypothetical monopoly supplier in each of these markets could therefore profitably increase price. Table 8.2 provides the pre-merger market shares of the two parties and the impact post-merger.

---

[80] According to some authors, it is also useful to identify conglomerate mergers between buyers of the same input which produce non-competing outputs. Although mergers of this type may give rise to specific effects in certain circumstances (most notably buying power increases), it is not clear whether this justifies the introduction of an additional category of conglomerate mergers.

[81] para.91 Non-horizontal Merger Guidelines.

**Table 8.1: Portfolio power**

| | Market | | | | |
|---|---|---|---|---|---|
| | I | II | III | IV | V |
| A | 30 | 30 | 10 | 0 | 0 |
| B | 0 | 0 | 10 | 40 | 40 |
| Post-Merger | 30 | 30 | 20 | 40 | 40 |

The only overlap of the merger is in market III but this gives rise to a post-merger market share of only 20 per cent. We assume that on the basis of a standard competition analysis, this merger does not give rise to any detrimental horizontal competitive outcomes.

There are five potential notions that might underpin the notion of portfolio power.

- The merged firm would be more attractive to buyers because it would offer a range of products.

- The merger would allow economies of scale and scope to be realised in sales and marketing.

- The merged entity will enjoy greater financial resources, thereby strengthening its competitive position vis-à-vis its remaining competitors—the "big is bad" theory of harm.

- The merger increases the threat of a refusal to supply.

- The merger creates greater opportunities for tying products.

The first two of these "sources" of additional market power appear to harm competitors rather than competition. The second "source" in particular appears to be pro-competitive as it involves the merged entity being able to supply consumers at lower costs.

It is also the case that size per se is insufficient grounds for concluding that a conglomerate merger is likely to have an adverse consequence for competition. In the past, the Commission has argued that conglomerate mergers may give rise to competition concerns where the concentration will make available greater financial resources to one of the merging parties, thereby strengthening its competitive position vis-à-vis its remaining competitors. But while size may be an advantage in some circumstances, it is wrong and dangerous to assume that bigger necessarily equals more competitively powerful, or that access to "deep pockets" will necessarily allow a firm to win contests for market share by outspending rivals. Evidence from the real-world indicates that the largest firm—the one with access to the most internally generated funds—does not always enjoy a competitive advantage. One reason that bigger does not necessarily equal more powerful is that capital is fluid and flows to the best investment opportunities. Moreover, it is often the case that where bigness does have an effect on competition, it will be for efficiency reasons, and not anti-competitive ones.

**8–032**     The fourth "source" of adverse portfolio power is only of concern if there is the potential for a significant foreclosure effect. However, this alleged "source" of market power is often unconvincing. There seems to be some idea that in combination the products are so attractive that no buyer can refuse them, even at an anticompetitive price. It is not clear why this should be so. In our example, the outside options open to buyers have not changed in four of the relevant markets and have not changed significantly in the fifth (by assumption), so why does the combination of products mean that buyers now have less ability to not take the products of the merging parties?

The final notion of anticompetitive portfolio power does represent a legitimate source of potential competitive concern. However, while the extension of a firm's product range might provide more possibilities for tying products, only in exceptional circumstances will an extension in product range give rise to competition concerns for the reasons discussed below.[82]

The main theory of harm arising from conglomerate mergers therefore relates to the potential that the extension of the merged entity's product offering enables unilateral conduct that results in foreclosure.[83] Such foreclosure can arise if the conglomerate merger enables the merged entity to leverage a strong market position in one market into another by means of tying or bundling practices. Tying usually refers to situations where a product can only be purchased if another product is purchased. Tying can be "commercial tying" (known as pure bundling), where the supply of one product is predicated on the purchase of another, or technical. Technical tying refers to situations where only certain products are technically compatible with another product. Bundling usually refers to the practice of mixed bundling, i.e. situations where it is possible to buy two products separately, but a discount is obtained if both products are purchased at the same time.[84]

So while under certain specific circumstances conglomerate mergers may give rise to adverse outcomes for consumers, they are even less likely to give rise to competition concerns than vertical mergers. As is discussed in detail in the next section, theories of competitive harm in conglomerate mergers primarily centre on the "efficiency offence". Such theories of harm postulate that the merged firm is able to provide consumers with a bundle of products at a lower price or better quality relative to pre-merger offerings and this means that rival firms experience a reduction in sales to such an extent that these firms are marginalised, i.e. less able to compete effectively

---

[82]  Baker and Ridyard (1999).
[83]  para.93 Non-horizontal Merger Guidelines.
[84]  Bundling can also take the form of pure bundling. This is in practice the same as tying.

against the merged entity. However, it is critically important to understand that such adverse outcomes depend on short-run *direct* benefits to consumers being translated in an *indirect* manner into long-run adverse outcomes for those same consumers. Hence, while such concerns cannot be dismissed on purely theoretical grounds, such conglomerate theories of harm should be subject to a high standard of proof. In its *Tetra-Laval/Sidel* judgment, the ECJ stated the following:

> "[T]he analysis of a 'conglomerate-type' concentration is a prospective analysis in which, first, the consideration of a lengthy period of time in the future and, secondly, the leveraging necessary to give rise to a significant impediment to effective competition mean that the chains of cause and effect are dimly discernible, uncertain and difficult to establish. That being so, the quality of the evidence produced by the Commission in order to establish that it is necessary to adopt a decision declaring the concentration incompatible with the common market is particularly important since that evidence must support the Commission's conclusion that, if such a decision were not adopted, the economic development envisaged by it would be plausible."

We now turn to the analytical steps for assessing the competitive effects of conglomerate mergers.

## *Assessing the ability to engage in bundling or tying*

Conglomerate mergers cannot give rise to competition concerns unless the   **8–033** merged entity enjoys significant market power in at least one relevant market.[85] Furthermore, for foreclosure to be a potential concern, it must be the case that there is a large common pool of customers for the products concerned. If that is not the case, then bundling and tying strategies are unlikely to be effective in switching share away from competitors to the merged entity which is central to the "leveraging" theories of harm.[86] It must also be the case that bundling or tying strategies are feasible. If the concerned products are purchased at different times and/or with different frequency then bundling and tying strategies are unlikely to be feasible.

In assessing the market position of the merging parties, reference is sometimes made to so-called "must have" products.[87] However, both the definition of a "must have" product and the implications for a product

---

[85]   Para.99 Non-horizontal Merger Guidelines.
[86]   See Neven (2008)
[87]   See, e.g. COMP M.3732 *Proctor & Gamble/Gillette* (2005) where the Commission argued that the two parties had a significant number of "must stock brands" (see para.111). However, despite the existence of "must have" brands, the Commission cleared the merger at Phase I in part because retailers stated that they would continue to stock private label products which provide competitive constraints on branded products.

being so designated are unclear. Intuitively, a "must have" product is one which a purchaser (typically, a retailer) needs to stock in order to meet the requirements of its customers. However, the fact that a product is "must have" in this loose sense does not mean by itself that the product enjoys significant market power. Indeed, in many instances, purchasers are able to affect the demand for a product via stocking decisions; it is one thing to stock a product and quite another to stock large quantities of that product and/or give that product favourable location within store and/or to engage in efforts to promote that product over competing alternatives. Instead, the application of the label of "must have" to the products of the merging parties ought to be accompanied by an analysis of why buyers are unable to alter (significantly) the volumes of their purchases of those products. The necessity for such an analysis is particularly required where those same buyers stock competing products, often including private label alternatives, to the products supplied by the merging parties. In such instances, retailers are more easily able to implement one or more of strategies to counter any adverse consequences that might arise from the merged firm's attempts to leverage across its product range. These strategies include reducing the shelf space allocated to branded products (perhaps by expanding the space allocated to private label products); restricting promotions of branded products (by reducing the ability of branded producers to offer price discounts, this will make private label products relatively more attractive to consumers); and by giving branded products less visibility (again making private label products relatively more attractive to consumers).

### Assessing the incentive to engage in bundling or tying

**8–034** As noted above, the primary concern in these cases is that the merged entity might engage in anti-competitive strategies aimed at leveraging its market power in one or more markets in order to foreclose its competitors in a complementary or neighbouring market. The principal mechanism by which a conglomerate merger might, at least in theory, lead to such anticompetitive outcomes arises if the merged entity is able to bundle products and as a result lead to the long-run marginalisation of competitors. Bundling can, in principal, take the form of technical bundling, pure bundling or mixed bundling. However, bundling strategies also entail costs. Pure bundling and tying may entail losses for the merged entity if a significant number of customers are uninterested in purchasing the bundle and instead prefer to buy only one product. In such instances, attempting to bundle one product for which there is demand with another for which there is much less may result in a significant loss of sales of the tying product.[88] Furthermore, consumers who want a bundle may have a

---

[88] Such loss is the most extreme where no complementarity between products exists.

preference for the bundled offering of competing firms. Mixed bundling involves the cost associated with the implicit discount.

In practice, most competition have concerns related to mixed bundling and the following therefore focuses on that form of bundling. To assess the risk that a conglomerate merger might give rise to anti-competitive leveraging effects through mixed bundling, regard must be given to the following two key questions, namely:

- *Would the merged entity be likely to engage in mixed bundling?* Specifically, mixed bundling must be a feasible commercial strategy in the markets in question, and the parties must have an incentive to carry this strategy out.

- *Would mixed bundling result in the marginalisation of rivals?* Even if the post-merger entity were to engage in mixed-bundling, this would have anti-competitive effects only if certain conditions hold so that competing suppliers are marginalised in the medium to long term to such an extent that the post-merger entity is able to raise prices and thereby harm consumers in the long run.

In assessing the merged entity's incentive to engage in mixed bundling, we **8–035** need to consider the following:

- Are the products produced by the merging parties complementary? The potential benefits to firms associated with bundling and tying arise from share-shifting sales from competitors. The extent of such benefits will vary from case to case. The benefits from mixed bundling will depend on the degree of complementarity between the bundled products. If there is limited complementarity, the merged entity's short-term price incentives would not materially change and hence there will be a limited effect on competitor sales. However, the greater is the complementarity, the higher is the post-merger incentive to reduce prices of one good, and thereby increase the sales of the complementary good.

- Even if the products produced by the merging parties are complementary in nature, this would not necessarily give the merged entity an incentive to lower prices significantly. Whether this is the case or not depends on the relative value of the products being bundled. If one of the products has a relatively low value, then the benefits from bundling will likely be limited. In the absence of any significant Cournot effects, mixed bundling—whose main purpose would be to permit the merged entity to benefit from the negative cross price elasticity between the complements—is extremely unlikely to represent a short-term profit maximising strategy.

- Would mixed bundling offer the merged entity greater scope for price discriminating across customers? In some instances, mixed bundling can provide a means for a firm to engage in price discrimination. This is most likely to be the case when commercial terms are not negotiated on an individual basis.[89]

In the absence of any significant Cournot effects and the absence of any greater scope for price discriminating, any theory of harm based on mixed bundling essentially boils down to an allegation of predatory pricing; "foreclosure" of competitors arises not as the result of the merged firm's increased pricing efficiency, but rather from the merged firm's willingness and ability to engage in predatory behaviour (but which neither of the merging parties would be willing or able to engage in). Such a theory of harm would need to explain why predation would be profitable post-merger but not pre-merger and would also need to be assessed against the stringent standards of assessing predatory behaviour under Article 82, including an assessment of the likelihood of recoupment.

### Assessing the competitive impact of any bundling or tying strategy

**8–036** Even if the merged entity has the ability and the incentive to engage in a bundling or tying strategy post-merger, this will have adverse effects for competition and therefore for consumers only if certain conditions imply that competing suppliers are marginalised in the medium to long term to such an extent that the post-merger entity is able to raise prices and thereby harm consumers in the long run.

Although bundling or tying can result in a significant reduction in the sales made by competing firms, that reduction in sales is not of itself an indication of competition concerns.[90] It is important to be clear as to what is meant by the marginalisation of competitors. For example, where a conglomerate merger causes the merged entity to reduce its prices, this will adversely affect competitors in the sense that they will find it harder to make sales at the margins that prevailed prior to the price reduction. But such price reductions can only be said to marginalise competitors if they reduce their ability to compete to such an extent that they are unable to

---

[89] See Chapter 5 for a discussion of price discrimination arising from mixed bundling.
[90] para.111 Non-horizontal Merger Guidelines.

constrain the merged firm from increasing prices in the future.[91,92] In making the assessment of whether this is likely, a distinction needs to be made between harm to competitors (i.e. a reduction in profits) and harm to competition as a result of reducing the ability of rivals to compete effectively. A loss of sales normally only adversely affects a firm's ability to compete if there are significant economies of scale in production.

Furthermore, a conglomerate merger can only result in anticompetitive foreclosure if rival suppliers to the merging parties find it unattractive or impractical to respond by adopting a similar strategy (or "counter strategy") that reduces the impact of the merged party's actions. By merging with other firms or by arriving at equivalent contractual arrangements (so-called "teaming arrangements"), the rival suppliers may be able to deploy strategies that diminish or eliminate the competitive advantages of the hypothesised strategy (e.g. bundling or raising rivals' costs). The act of seeking and implementing such arrangements will often be an important part of the dynamic competitive process that is sparked by non-horizontal mergers. Where such responses to the merged firm's hypothesised strategy are plausible the competitive concern will be mitigated.

We would therefore propose that the assessment of the incentive to **8–037** engage in anti-competitive bundling or tying follows the following sub-steps, each of which would need to hold in order to conclude that the non-horizontal merger would likely lead to anti-competitive exclusionary effects. Since it is acknowledged that non-horizontal mergers do not generally give rise to competition concerns, as noted above and set out in the CFI's *Tetra Laval/Sidel* judgment, the standard of proof on establishing that post-merging bundling strategies will result in foreclosure should appropriately be high; it needs to be proven and not assumed that short-run price decreases will lead to the long-run marginalisation of competitors. The conditions required for non-horizontal mergers to harm competition through foreclosure are as follows[93,94]:

- Condition A: Are rival firms marginalised in the sense above?

- Condition B: Will rival suppliers to the merging parties find it unattractive or impractical to respond by adopting a similar

---

[91] In theory, consumer harm may also arise if the marginalisation of competitors had the effect of permanently reducing investment in new products (by the merged firm or its competitors), if such investment would have had the effect of improving product quality, or lowering costs. However, such a theory of harm is likely to be extremely difficult to prove in practice.

[92] In practice, for this to be the case, one or more competing firms will need to exit the market.

[93] These conditions focus on the foreclosure of *existing* competitors. Analogous conditions can be derived for strategies aimed at excluding potential entrants.

[94] These reflect, in addition to a significant market power screen, the same conditions proposed by one of the authors and accepted by the Commission during the investigation of *GE/Amersham* (COMP/M.3304 *GE/Amersham* (2004)).

strategy (or "counter strategy") that reduces the impact of the merged party's actions.

- Condition C: As a result of the above chain of events, will prices be increased and customer interests harmed? This can only occur if those competitors are marginalised to such an extent that short-run marginal costs are significantly affected or be forced to withdraw permanently from the market so as to permit the merged firm to increase prices in the long run.

### The Commission's assessment of conglomerate mergers in practice

**8-038** This section provides an extended discussion of the Commission's assessment of conglomerate effects. We do so to illustrate the evolution of the Commission's assessment of conglomerate effects through its treatment of three cases involving General Electric; namely *GE/Honeywell* (2001), *GE/Amersham* (2004) and *GE/Smiths* (2007). These cases indicate the shift in the Commission's stance on conglomerate mergers from being hostile to being more in accordance with standard economics.

#### GE/Honeywell

**8-039** The case that has brought the most attention to conglomerate effects was the Commission's decision to block the merger of General Electric and Honeywell. Both the Antitrust Division of the US Department of Justice (DOJ) and the Canadian Competition Bureau approved the proposed merger subject to the certain divestments and commitments. In contrast, the Commission prohibited the merger. Although the case involved horizontal, vertical and conglomerate issues, it was the Commission's assessment of conglomerate issues that was most controversial, and it is on this issue that the following discussion focuses.[95]

General Electric (GE) produces aircraft engines on its own and through CFMI, a 50/50 joint venture with a French company SNECMA. Honeywell produces various avionics components (for aircraft control, navigation and communications) and various non-avionics components (such as auxiliary power units, environmental control systems, wheels and brakes). Both engines and avionic/non-avionic products are used on large commercial and regional jet aircraft. Major customers on this market are airframe original equipment manufacturers (OEMs), including Boeing, Airbus, Bombardier, Embraer and Fairchild Dornier, and airlines. The Commission held that GE was dominant in the market for large

---

[95] However, it should be noted that the CFI in its judgment on the Commission's decision also criticised the Commission's reasoning with respect to the vertical theory of harm.

commercial jet aircraft engines and that Honeywell had "leading" positions in several avionics and non-avionics markets.

The conglomerate concerns relied on the fact that the respective products of GE and Honeywell were complements for one another, which are sometimes, but not always, sold to the same customers. Hence, a fall in the price of engines will lead, all else equal, to more aircraft being built, which translates into higher demand for avionic and non-avionic products. In addition, the Commission considered that GECAS, GE's aircraft leasing business, played a significant role in determining the choices of other customers; by influencing the choice of avionics and non-avionic products installed in aircraft purchased by GECAS, this would induce other customers to make the same choices.[96]

In the Commission's view, the merger would have given GE the ability and the incentive to engage in one or more forms of bundling of engines and avionic products that would lead to a strengthening of GE's market position on the markets for large and regional aircraft engines and would create significant market power in the supply of avionics products.[97,98]

Without providing a detailed discussion of all the Commission's arguments,[99] the following points are worth highlighting. First, the Commission did not appear to consider the scope for competitors to respond to the merger. Secondly, the Commission's assessment of the likely effects of bundling focused on the profitability of rivals. For example, the decision states:

> "The ability of the merged entity to cross-subsidise its various complementary activities and to engage in profitable forms of packaged sales will have an adverse effect on the profitability of competing producers of avionics and non avionics products, as a result of market share erosion."

In the Commission's view this would likely lead to the exit of existing competitors and hence market foreclosure.[100] In short, the Commission appears to have assumed in its *GE/Honeywell* decision that a reduction in profitability can be equated to a reduction in a firm's competitive significance. This viewpoint is very much in line with the "traditional"

---

[96] This theory of harm has been labelled "Archimedean leveraging", in the sense that choices made by GECAS would distort the purchasing decisions of other customers since, it was alleged, airlines prefer to maintain "fleet commonality". See Reynolds and Ordover (2002) for a discussion of this theory and Grant and Neven (2005) for a critique.

[97] COMP/M.2220 *General Electric/Honeywell* (2001) para.341.

[98] The Commission also argued that bundling would assist in the creation of a dominant position in the supply of corporate jet engines. See COMP/M.2220 *General Electric/Honeywell* (2001) paras 443 and 444.

[99] There are numerous critiques of the Commission's decision. See inter alia, Baxter, Dethmers and Dodoo (2006), Nalebuff (2002) and Emch (2004).

[100] See para.398 COMP/M.2220 *GE/Honeywell* (2001).

assessment of foreclosure under Article 82 where any harm to competitors was assumed to be translated into herm to competition.[101] However, as the Non-horizontal Merger Guidelines make clear, this approach is now largely discredited. Thirdly, and contrary to the economic assessment set out above, nowhere in the decision does the Commission assess whether bundling would represent a profitable strategy for the merged firm. Rather, it is assumed that the alleged commercial advantage that the merged entity would possess would inevitably imply that bundling would increase its profitability. The decision states as follows:

> "[T]he Commission does not consider the reliance on one or the other [economic] model necessary for the conclusion that the packaged deals that the merged entity will be in a position to offer will foreclose competitors from the engines and avionics/non-avionics markets".[102]

In effect, the Commission held that there was a consensus that bundling will result in foreclosure. But as explained above, that presumption is at odds with standard economic thinking.

The CFI subjected the Commission's decision to a scathing attack finding that the Commission had failed to show that a merged GE/Honeywell would likely engage in the anticompetitive conglomerate practices alleged in the decision. The CFI concluded that the Commission had not sufficiently established that GE would have either the ability or the incentive to engage in the bundling of engines and avionics/non-avionic products. The CFI reached this conclusion having regard to two main considerations. First, the CFI noted the inherent practical difficulties associated with implementing the bundling practices alleged by the Commission and while this did not preclude the possibility of the merged entity actually attempting to engage in such practices the CFI observed that the practical problems made a bundling strategy less credible.

> "Although those practical problems admittedly do not make bundling less impossible, the fact remains that they make it more difficult to put into practice and, accordingly, make it less likely that bundling will occur".[103]

In short, the Commission failed to establish the ability to bundle.

**8–040**     Secondly, the CFI held that the Commission failed to establish any real likelihood that the merged entity would engage in the alleged commercial practices. In particular, in relation to the possibility of the merged entity engaging in mixed bundling, the CFI stated:

[101] See Chapter 6 for a detailed discussion.
[102] See para.352 COMP/M.2220 *GE/Honeywell* (2001).
[103] *General Electric v Commission*, CFI judgment 2005 para.415.

"in the absence of a detailed economic analysis applying the Cournot effect theory to the particular circumstances of the present case, it cannot be concluded from the Commission's brief mention of that theory ... that the merged entity would have been likely to engage in mixed bundling after the merger".[104]

In short, the CFI held that the Commission had failed to establish that even if GE/Honeywell would have had the ability to engage in such behaviour, it would have the incentive to do so.[105] Given these findings, the CFI did not grapple with the alleged foreclosing effect that might have arisen from a strategy of bundling. In other words, it did not address the central elements in the Commission's theory of harm; namely, that rivals would lose market share *and* that that loss of market share would permit the merged entity to increase prices in one or more markets.

### *GE/Amersham*[106]

The impact of a loss of market share on competitors' ability to compete **8–041** and the impact of that loss of market share on final consumers was, however, directly addressed in the Commission's assessment of General Electric's acquisition of Amersham. The products affected by the merger were medical diagnostic products. GE produces diagnostic imaging (DI) equipment to produce internal images of the body, while Amersham produces diagnostic pharmaceuticals (DPs) to enhance the clarity of the images produced by DI equipment. DI equipment and DPs can therefore be considered to be complementary products.

The Commission considered whether the merged entity might acquire the ability and incentive to foreclose competition "by leveraging its pre-merger market power from one market to another through exclusionary practices, such as bundling and/or tying."[107] The Commission considered possible theories of harm based on bundling of DI equipment and DPs and on technical tying.

In marked contrast to *GE/Honeywell*, where the focus of the competitive assessment was only on the likelihood of the merged entity engaging in bundling strategies post-merger, the *GE/Amersham* decision also addressed the effects of any such bundling. In assessing commercial (or mixed) bundling, the Commission examined whether:

> (1) the merged entity would be able to leverage pre-merger dominance in one market into another;

---

[104] *General Electric v Commission*, CFI judgment 2005 para.462.
[105] The CFI also considered that the Commission should have taken into account the deterrent effect of Article 82 when assessing the incentives to engage in anti-competitive bundling.
[106] COMP/M.3304 *GE/Amersham* (2004).
[107] op. cit. para.31.

(2)   rivals would be unable to respond to the bundling strategy;

(3)   the resulting marginalisation of competitors would result in their exit from the market; and

(4)   following the exit of these competitors, the merged firm would be able to implement unilateral price increases that would not be undermined in the long run either by new entry or by the re-entry of previously marginalised competitors.[108]

As such, the Commission addressed each of the steps set out in para.x.xx. The Commission found that none of these conditions would hold and consequently cleared the merger at Phase I. The decision explicitly notes that even if commercial bundling were to materialise as a result of the merger, it would not result in the foreclosure of competition.[109] The Commission also dismissed concerns of technical tying whereby the merged entity would develop DPs that are only compatible with its DI equipment. In addition to examining whether such a strategy would actually be possible, the Commission also examined the economic incentives to engage in technical tying and concluded that this would not be a profit-maximising strategy since this would deny the merged entity access to the installed base of DI equipment.

In short, *GE/Amersham* represented a marked improvement in the competitive assessment of bundling and tying over that adopted in *GE/Honeywell*.

### *GE/Smiths*[110]

**8-042**   The degree to which the Commission's assessment of bundling and tying has evolved is starkly illustrated by its *GE/Smiths* decision. In many respects, this merger represented a re-run of the arguments presented in *GE/Honeywell* since Smiths was active in the supply of products and engine components for commercial and military aircraft.[111] Since both GE and Smiths sold products to airframers (Boeing and Airbus), the Commission examined the possibility of conglomerate effects in relation to those markets where Smiths had a significant market position.[112] Although the Commission found that GE held a dominant position in the supply for large commercial aircraft engines, it held that the transaction was unlikely to strengthen that market position via the bundling of engines with Smiths' products.

---

[108]   op. cit., para.37.

[109]   op. cit., para.42.

[110]   COMP/M.4561 *GE/Smiths Aerospace* (2007)

[111]   As was the case with COMP/M.3220 *GE/Honeywell* (2001), the transaction involved vertical as well as conglomerate issues.

[112]   These markets were for flight management systems for LCA and for fuel quantity measurement.

First, Smiths' products were of low value compared to GE's engines which implied that a discount on Smiths' products would have very little impact on the demand for GE engines. Secondly, the strategy of bundling these products would be unlikely to be successful since a significant proportion of GE's engines were sold not to airframers but to airlines. This meant that a significant proportion of the customer base for engines would be unaffected by any bundling or tying strategy. Furthermore, there were no concerns of creating significant market power in the supply of products supplied by Smiths as a result of leveraging GE's position in the supply of engines for large commercial aircraft, partly because Smiths Aerospace's products were of low value compared to GE's engines, which implied that any discount on Smiths Aerospace's products would have little effect with respect to the price paid for an engine.[113]

In consequence, the Commission cleared the merger unconditionally at Phase I.

# COORDINATED EFFECTS

As is the case with horizontal mergers, non-horizontal mergers may also **8–043** give rise, at least in theory, to coordinated effects whereby prices to end consumers are increased through a change in the competitive behaviour of not only the merged firm but also one or more of its rivals, either upstream or downstream. A vertical merger can make it easier for firms to reach and sustain a tacit understanding to compete less vigorously, perhaps by increasing the degree of symmetry between firms or by increasing the level of market transparency, perhaps through the scope for increased information flows over the prices charged by rival firms.[114] Vertical mergers may also make a tacit understanding easier to sustain by reducing the ability of firms outside the coordinating group to expand or to enter the market, if entry requires both upstream and downstream market presence.

A conglomerate merger may influence the likelihood of a coordinated outcome in a given market by reducing the number of effective competitors.[115] Further, a conglomerate merger may increase the extent and importance of multi-market competition. Competitive interaction on several markets may increase the scope and effectiveness of disciplining mechanisms in ensuring that the terms of coordination are being adhered to. However, in practice these theories rely on a reduction in the number of firms, i.e. the conglomerate merger results in the foreclosure of one or more

---

[113] COMP/M.4561 *GE/Smiths Aerospace* (2007) paras 116 to 119.
[114] Alternative mechanisms by which non-horizontal mergers may lead to coordinated effects has been the subject of recent economic theory. See, e.g. Nocke and White (2007). However, a persuasive theory has yet to be outlined in practice.
[115] Non-horizontal Merger Guidelines para.120.

rival firms. In practice, therefore, coordinated effects concerns will be subsidiary to the more usual concern of unilateral foreclosure.

# EFFICIENCIES ARISING FROM NON-HORIZONTAL MERGERS

**8–044** As noted in the introduction to this chapter, there is great scope for non-horizontal mergers to give rise to efficiency gains since in numerous instances, non-horizontal mergers give rise to a direct incentive to reduce price or to improve quality post merger as this will increase the sales of complementary products. In addition, as products manufactured by firms in vertical and complementary relationships are, by definition, used together, non-horizontal mergers can give rise to efficiency gains arising from improved interaction between the two products. Such efficiency gains are often not associated with a direct impact on pricing behaviour but may improve quality, increase variety, or increase levels of investment.[116]

The potential sources of efficiency gains from vertical and conglomerate mergers result from a wide variety of mechanisms and occur in a broad range of situations. However, they can be broadly grouped under the following four headings[117]:

- Increasing pricing efficiency;
- Increasing productive efficiency;
- Preventing profit expropriation;
- Overcoming problems arising from incomplete contracts and/or transaction costs.

### Increasing pricing efficiency

**8–045** In many cases, charging a uniform unit price will not be an optimal way of organising a supply chain or of providing complementary products. However, more sophisticated pricing mechanisms may be costly or impossible to introduce. In such cases, by removing the need for external pricing, non-horizontal integration can lead to a more efficient outcome. Pricing efficiencies created by non-horizontal mergers are particularly relevant because they can result in immediate price reductions.

Amongst the pricing efficiencies created by vertical mergers, the *elimination of double marginalisation* has the broadest applicability. This

---

[116] For example non-horizontal mergers can enable firms to overcome so-called "hold-up problems" (see Chapter 5 for further details).
[117] See Bishop, Lofaro, Rosati and Young (2005) for an extensive discussion of the efficiencies created by vertical and conglomerate mergers.

inefficiency occurs when there are multiple mark-ups in a supply chain, causing price to exceed the marginal cost of production at more than one stage in the supply chain. Due to the ubiquitous presence of fixed costs and market power in the economy, prices often exceed short run marginal cost, so mark ups are likely to be an extremely widespread phenomenon.[118] Appendix 8.1 provides a simple theoretical model that relates the intensity of downstream competition to the benefits associated with eliminating double marginalisation. The less intense is competition in the downstream market, the greater the benefits associated with double marginalisation.

The *Cournot effect* is the conglomerate equivalent of the double marginalisation inefficiency arising in vertical industries: where the competitive relationships between two firms can be described as complementary, each firm would benefit from increased sales if the other *lowered* the price of its product. When producers of complementary goods are under separate ownership, the beneficial effects that a price decrease of one product has on the demand for the other complementary product is not taken into account. However, if the two parties merge, consideration of such effects will be internalised and would provide an additional incentive to lower price.

The importance of the Cournot effect is due to its very broad applicability. In general, any two firms which supply complementary products and price at a mark-up are affected by this source of inefficiency. A merger reduces this pricing inefficiency by eliminating the externality between the merging firms. Further, unlike double marginalisation, contractual alternatives to a full merger are not simple and rarely used in practice. Note that, in order to fully reap the benefits of the internalisation of this pricing externality, complementary products need to be sold jointly through tying or bundling. The reason for this is that, if products are sold individually, customers are free to "mix and match" components of different brands, so that rival firms may appropriate part of the gains from a price reduction. In those cases, the magnitude of the efficiency gain will depend on the portion of customers who buy the products together even without a tie.

## Increasing productive efficiency

Non-horizontal integration may result in a more efficient use of inputs and/ **8–046** or productive assets, due to the existence of economies of scope or scale, improved managerial or financial efficiency or supply assurance. For example, a vertical merger might improve productive efficiency by increasing coordination of demand and supply between upstream and downstream firms. Integrated firms may also benefit from *increased*

---

[118] See discussion on vertical restraints in Chapter 5 for a more detailed explanation of double-marginalisation.

*coordination and information flow* in the fields of R&D, distribution, marketing, and from the adoption of new production technologies.

### Preventing profit expropriation

8–047 In some cases, a firm may be unable to appropriate the full benefits of its investments, as these are partly reaped by competitors. This can result in sub-optimal levels of investment. By "internalising" such externalities, non-horizontal mergers can lead to significant efficiency gains. For example, a firm may fear that competitors may be able to *"free ride"* on its investment. This reduces the firm's incentive to invest not only to its own detriment but also to that of its vertical partners (either upstream suppliers or downstream customers). For example, a retailer may be unwilling to promote a manufacturer's product if this benefits competing retailers. In consequence, the service is therefore not provided or is provided at a lower than optimal level, and output falls. If the upstream firm integrates with the downstream suppliers and excludes independent retailers, all the gains are appropriated by the single, integrated entity, and this increases the incentive to invest. Partial expropriation of profits by other firms is also common in *R&D activity*. A firm may be concerned that its competitors will find out about its innovation and know-how, and then copy ("free ride" on) the results. Vertical integration can mitigate such horizontal spillovers, by reducing the chance that "know-how" will be leaked to competitors via other firms in the supply chain, or by providing the opportunity to embed the innovation in the upstream product.

Complementary mergers can also promote efficiency by helping to prevent profit expropriation. First, a merger can facilitate *quality standardisation*. Controlling the quality of both complements may be important when two goods are only used together (as a system good), and if consumers can observe the quality of the system, but not the quality of the single components (i.e. there is asymmetric information between consumers and firms). Secondly, a merger can increase the incentive to invest in innovation by allowing a firm to *internalise R&D benefits*, if those benefits spill over into related product markets.

### Overcoming problems arising from incomplete contracts and/or transaction costs

8–048 Efficiencies arising from the existence of incomplete contracts and transaction costs represent an important pro-competitive motivation for vertical mergers.[119] Where contracts are not fully specified, a party may be able to exploit contractual loopholes to the disadvantage of their vertical partners.

---

[119] For instance, the Commission accepted that the benefits to better product integration in COMP/M.4854 *TomTom/TeleAtlas* (2008) could not be achieved via contractual means.

A specific example of this is the *"hold-up" problem*, where a relationship-specific investment makes one party very dependent on the other. This gives rise to the opportunity for exploitative behaviour once the investment has been undertaken. Where protection from such behaviour is impossible or at least prohibitively expensive when firms are in separate ownership, the investment may be deterred. Clearly, such concerns do not arise under common ownership. At a general level, even where there are no specific incompleteness problems, *transaction costs* are always incurred to a greater or lesser degree in searching for parties and drawing up contracts.

Incomplete contracts and transaction costs play a central role also in the analysis of pro-competitive motivations for conglomerate mergers. For example, a hold-up problem may arise in a conglomerate setting if the profitability of an investment of a manufacturer of one good is dependent on interoperability with complementary goods. As such, the general analysis of incomplete contract issues does not depend on whether the parties are in a vertical or a complementary relationship, and the conditions for realisation of efficiency gains from the elimination are the same as described for vertical mergers.

In addition, conglomerate mergers may reduce transaction costs by providing a *one-stop-shopping opportunity* for customers. This leads to an efficiency gain whenever transaction costs are non-negligible, either for the seller or for the buyer.

## Assessing the impact of efficiencies on the competitive effects of non-horizontal mergers

The fundamental differences between horizontal and non-horizontal **8–049** mergers imply not only significant differences in the types of competition concerns but also in how efficiencies are taken into account in the overall competitive assessment. As discussed in Chapter 7, the competitive assessment of horizontal mergers adopts a two-step approach: first, assess the likely impact on competition and if the merger is expected to reduce competition significantly then assess whether there are any efficiencies that offset those identified competitive concerns. In the context of horizontal mergers, such an approach has a clear logic. Efficiencies arising from horizontal mergers are typically assessed *after* it has been established that the proposed merger will remove an important competitive constraint and, in consequence, prices are expected to increase. The assessment of efficiencies is therefore focused on whether they are sufficient to off-set the identified competitive harm.[120]

The Non-horizontal Merger Guidelines propose that efficiencies are

---

[120] It should be stressed that in practice this approach to assessing the competitive effects of a horizontal merger is only appropriate for (a) assessing unilateral effects concerns and (b) only applies to marginal cost efficiencies.

assessed in a similar way, i.e. under Step 3 of the Guidelines' proposed approach. However, given the indirect nature of the potential theories of harm raised by non-horizontal mergers, the two-step approach to appraising anti-competitive and efficiency implications used in the assessment of horizontal mergers is often inappropriate. When assessing the competitive effects of non-horizontal mergers, it may simply not be possible to separate the assessment of competitive harm and the assessment of efficiencies. Indeed, in many instances, the theory of competitive harm posited in the appraisal of non-horizontal mergers arises *because* the merger generates an efficiency. For example, the standard theories of harm raised by conglomerate mergers usually involve a short-run competitive advantage to the merging parties (often in the form of an ability to offer lower prices) which is alleged to result in the marginalisation of competitors and subsequently to the long-run detriment of competition. But clearly, the short-run price reduction also represents an efficiency that directly benefits consumers. In other words, the source of the potential competitive harm in this case is the same as the efficiency. It is difficult to see how the two effects can be assessed separately.[121]

By corollary, it is also questionable whether the same strict criteria set out in the horizontal merger guidelines for the assessment of these types of efficiency are appropriate in the case of non-horizontal mergers since, as the Non-horizontal Guidelines clearly state, such mergers provide substantial scope for efficiencies. The burden on the parties for proving efficiencies arising from non-horizontal mergers ought to be much lower than those claimed to arise from horizontal mergers. Indeed, where it is necessary to conduct a unified assessment of the efficiencies and potential anti-competitive effects arising from a non-horizontal merger one ought to adopt the stance that observed efficiencies give rise to pro-competitive outcomes *unless* it can be demonstrated otherwise. This is in marked contrast to the approach, often labelled the *efficiency offence*, where efficiencies are viewed as problematic unless it can be demonstrated otherwise.

## SUMMARY

**8–050** This chapter has highlighted some fundamental differences between horizontal mergers and non-horizontal mergers. Horizontal mergers involve suppliers of directly competing products, and, by directly removing a competitive constraint, therefore increase the incentives of the merged

---

[121] This view is (implicitly) shared by economists at the CET. De Conick and Papandropoulos in their review of the COMP/M.4854 *TomTom/TeleAtlas* (2008) transaction note that the merger eliminated double marginalisation and that this efficiency is "an **integral** part of the evaluation of any theory of harm" (emphasis added), De Concick and Papandropoulos (2008) para.28.

entity to raise prices. Non-horizontal mergers in contrast do not involve suppliers of directly competing products. The main competition concerns arising from non-horizontal mergers therefore stem from indirect effects of the merger on the ability of rival firms to compete, i.e. competitive concerns typically arise only if it can be demonstrated that rival firms are foreclosed as a consequence of the merger.

The nature of the competition concern also affects both the stance on efficiency claims and how the effects of those should be both assessed. First, non-horizontal mergers provide great scope for efficiencies; often a direct consequence of such mergers is for firms to lower prices. The standard of proof for accepting such efficiency claims ought therefore to be lower than in the case of horizontal mergers. Secondly, when assessing horizontal mergers, it is possible to separate out the direct competitive effects of the merger and the impact of any efficiency benefits into two discrete steps; first, assess whether the merger will lead to price increases; and if so, whether there are any efficiencies which will offset the incentive to increase price resulting from a loss of competition. In contrast, when assessing non-horizontal mergers, it is often not possible to disentangle the competitive assessment and the impact of efficiencies and this indicates that the assessment of efficiencies needs to be integrated into the competitive assessment.

## ANNEX 8.1: INTENSITY OF COMPETITION AND DOUBLE MARGINALISATION[122]

**8-051** This appendix makes use of simple theoretical economic models to show that the lower the intensity of competition at the downstream level, the higher the benefits from the elimination of the double marginalisation problem that can be achieved through vertical integration. Moreover, we show that in the extreme case of perfect competition in the downstream market, the competitive effects brought about by the vertical merger are neutral, as no double marginalisation occurs pre merger.

### Model

**8-052** The model is based on the following assumptions:

1. In the industry there are n>0 firms operating downstream and one operating upstream;

2. The monopolist produces each unit of output at cost C and it sells it to the downstream firms at price c. Its demand function is given by the output of the downstream firms;

3. The n downstream firms are identical in size and produce a perfectly homogeneous product;

4. Downstream firms use one unit of input (which is the output of the upstream firm) in order to produce one unit of output. They also face an additional cost x per unit sold.

5. Demand function in the downstream market is $p = a - bQ$, where $Q = \sum_{i=1}^{n} q_i$ is the aggregate output, and $q_i$ is firm i's individual output.

Given assumptions 1–5, each downstream firm's profit function can be written as

$$(1) \quad \mathrm{Pi}_i = \left( a - b \sum_{i=1}^{n} qi - c - x \right) q_i$$

and the upstream firm's profit function is

$$(2) \quad \pi = (c - C) \sum_{i=1}^{n} qi$$

---

[122] This annex is taken from Bishop et al (2005).

As common in the literature on vertical restrictions, the timing in our analysis is as follows.

*First stage.* The upstream monopolist chooses c such that (2) is maximised.

*Second stage.* Downstream firms observe c and compete in quantities à la Cournot. In the special case n=1, the downstream firm simply chooses the output that maximises its profit.

Since this is a dynamic game with complete and perfect information, the relevant concept of equilibrium is the subgame perfect equilibrium. Therefore, the game must be solved backwards starting from the second stage, in which for a given value of c, the n downstream firms compete à la Cournot. Then in the first stage, the upstream firm, anticipating the outcome of the next stage, will choose the optimal value of c that maximises its own profit.

## Solution absent vertical merger

In the second stage, each downstream firm i maximises its individual profit, **8–053** given by (1), with respect to $q_i$. The symmetric solution is

$$(3) \qquad q_i = \frac{a - c - x}{b(1 + n)}$$

Then, in the first stage, the upstream firm maximises its profit, given by (2), with respect to c. That is,

$$(4) \qquad \max_{c} (c - C) \sum_{i=1}^{n} q_i = n(c - C)\frac{a - c - x}{b(1 + n)}$$

This leads to

$$(5) \qquad c = \frac{a - x + C}{2}$$

Industry output is then:

$$(6) \qquad Q = \sum_{i=1}^{n} q_i = n\frac{a - x - C}{2b(1 + n)}$$

## Solution in the case of vertical integration

Suppose now that the n downstream firms are acquired by the upstream **8–054** firm. In what follows, we solve the two-stage model described above in the new scenario and then we compare the outcomes with the previous model.

As the upstream firm now owns the downstream firms, the only choice that it needs to make is how much output to produce and sell in the downstream market. In other words, the monopolist maximises:

$$(7) \qquad \max_{Q} = (a - bQ - C - x)Q$$

Note that we have assumed that the monopolist's cost is equal to $C+x$. In other words, we have assumed that the merger does not give rise to any cost synergies.

The solution to the above maximisation problem is:

$$(8) \qquad Q^{**} = \frac{a - C - x}{2b}$$

## Benefits from vertical integration

**8–055** The social welfare benefit from vertical integration can be defined as the difference between $Q^{**}$ and $Q$. This is because, to the extent that vertical integration brings about a social welfare improvement, this will result in an increase in the level of output (or equivalently a decrease in the level of price). The difference between the levels of output in the two scenarios is:

$$(9) \qquad Q^{**} - Q = \frac{a - x - C}{2b} \frac{1}{1 + n}$$

It is easy to prove that the above difference is always positive (i.e. vertical integration always leads to a higher output), as it is increasing in the demand intercept $a$ and decreasing in the cost parameters $x$ and $C$, the demand parameter $b$, and most importantly the number of firms $n$.

The latter result implies that the larger the number of firms, the lower is the social welfare benefit from vertical integration. This is due to the fact that as the number of downstream firms increases, competition also increases. Therefore the double marginalisation problem tends to disappear. As the number of firms $n$ tends to infinity (i.e. the downstream industry moves to perfect competition), the benefit from vertical integration disappears.

Figure 8A.1 below illustrates the behaviour of the relationship between $Q^{**}-Q$ and the number of firms $n$ assuming that $(a-x-C)/2b = 20$ holds.

# Figure 8A.1 Benefits from vertical integration as a function of 8–056 the number of downstream firms

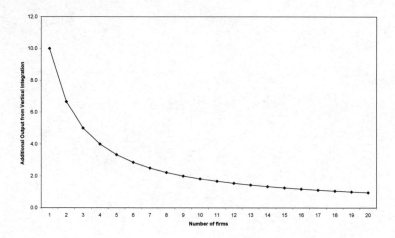

# Part III. Measurement

"Supposing is good, but finding out is better."

Mark Twain

# 9. Introduction to Empirical Analysis

## INTRODUCTION

As Parts I and II of this book have shown, determining whether the **9–001** competitive conduct of firms, in all of its various forms, is anti-competitive is a complex and often difficult task. While economic theory can provide the framework in which the competitive assessment takes place, it is unusual for there to be, a priori, unanimous agreement on all of the critical aspects of the case in question. For example, do own-label products provide an effective competitive constraint on branded products in the same industry? While in some industries, own-label products do indeed provide such an effective competitive constraint, in others they do not. Hence, relying on broad rules of thumb or previous decisions relating to other industries does not provide an adequate or acceptable guide for decisions. Instead, the assessment of the competitive consequences of a firm's conduct needs to take into account those factors relevant to the specific matter in question.

For this reason, empirical analysis plays a central and often critical role in the competitive assessment. By having reference to the facts—that is, the market outcomes that competition in the industry has actually produced— the degree to which unsubstantiated assertion plays a role in the decision process is reduced, resulting in a more objective assessment. This is not to suggest that the whole assessment is reduced to a mechanical process. Rather, reference to the facts provides a check on the claims that both the parties and officials can make.

The use of empirical analysis by the European Commission has increased steadily over the last decade. The advent of the Chief Economist's Team (CET) has been an important factor in this evolution, but the process started well before the CET was set up. The empirical techniques that we discuss in the following chapters are now routinely used by the Commission.

This Part of the book provides an overview of the main empirical tests that are used in competition law investigations and discusses the role that empirical techniques can play in aiding the competitive assessment.

Emphasis is placed on what elements of competition each test seeks to address and, in the light of this, how the results should be interpreted. The strengths and weaknesses of each test as an aid to assessing competition are also discussed.

The aim of the following chapters is to introduce and illustrate the use of various empirical techniques that are available. The presentation of the analysis is made at a level that is generally accessible to the non-economist.[1] The aim is to suggest which empirical techniques can be useful in the competitive assessment, not to provide a "cookbook" of how to carry them out. In general, that is best left to an economic practitioner.

## THE ROLE OF EMPIRICAL ANALYSIS IN EC COMPETITION LAW

**9–002** The critical economic issue for investigations under EC competition law—whether under Article 81, Article 82 or the Merger Regulation—is the existence and exercise, whether current or potential, of market power. Each of the empirical techniques presented in this book is concerned with the same issue: the measurement, either directly or indirectly, of market power. Empirical tests can be loosely divided into two categories: direct methods and indirect methods.

Direct methods assess the degree of market power directly: elasticity estimates and price concentration studies are examples of such tests. Indirect methods examine issues that are indirectly relevant to the question of market power: tests, such as price correlation tests, that seek to define the relevant market are examples of such tests.

All empirical tests of the competitiveness of a particular industry seek to employ data drawn from the market under investigation to test certain hypotheses about the nature of competition. For example, price correlation analysis is often used to test hypotheses about the relevant market. In theory, empirical observations can be used to test any hypothesis about competitive behaviour in the marketplace. It is important in applying such tests to be clear as to what hypothesis is being tested: which test is used depends on what hypothesis is to be tested.

---

[1] However, some parts of the text are aimed more at the economic practitioner than at non-economists. This is true in particular of some parts of Chapters 10 and 15.

## Presenting empirical analysis

### *The wrong approach*

The wrong approach to the presentation of empirical evidence is a "black **9–003**
box" approach that relies on the competition authority or court "trusting"
the expert.[2] So a piece of analysis along the following lines is not
acceptable.

---

1. $\log q_{mt} = \beta \log y_{Bt} + \sum \delta_{mk} \log \pi_{kt} + \alpha_m + \varepsilon_{mt}$
2. $\log u_t = \beta_0 + \beta_1 \log y_t + \beta_2 \log \Pi_t + Z_t \, \delta + \varepsilon_t$
3. $s_{it} = \alpha_i + \beta_i \log (y_{Gt}/P_t) + \sum \gamma_{ij} \log p_{jt} + \varepsilon_{it}$

Therefore plausible parameter values imply the merger is pro-
competitive

---

The evidence is not transparent, it is not accessible and no attempt has
been made by the expert to explain the analysis or how the conclusion
follows from the analysis. The approach is very much of the "I'm an expert,
trust me" form that was unfortunately common amongst economists in the
past and still appears far more often than it should. As an approach to
convincing a competition authority or court of a particular view, it can
appear both lazy and patronising. If an expert submits analysis of this form
then the decision-making body needs to decide whether to accept the
evidence based on the reputation of the expert witness (a leap of faith at
best) or to simply disregard the evidence. Our view is that if the authorities
cannot appraise the evidence properly, then it is reasonable for them to
disregard it. However, it is also true that it is incumbent on the authorities
to respond to empirical analysis that is presented to them and to tell the
parties that they feel unable to appraise it. This then gives the parties an
opportunity to provide further explanation to help the authorities to
appraise the evidence. It is not acceptable for competition authorities to
remain silent as to their views on analysis presented to them and to then
dismiss the evidence in a decision without giving the parties the opportunity to provide further explanation.

A good example of the relevant authority not feeling able to properly
appraise complex econometric evidence arose in the *UK Premier League*
case.[3] One of the issues in this case was whether televising a Premier
League match led to a lower attendance at that match. The economic
expert for the OFT argued that it did not. The economic expert for the
Premier League presented econometric evidence to rebut this claim. The

---

[2]  It should go without saying that the same standards ought to apply to analysis provided by
competition authorities.

[3]  *Televising Premier League Football Matches*, Restrictive Practices Court, January 12–May 5,
July 28, 1999, [2000] E.M.L.R. 78 RPC.

expert for the OFT simply said that the econometric evidence was unreliable but without explaining why. Faced with this conflicting technical evidence, Justice Ferri concluded that:

> "The evidence of the econometricians displayed an enormous degree of expertise and diligence, but we have to say that we found it of limited assistance. . . . Unfortunately there was little common ground between them. . . . we do not feel able to prefer the evidence of one of the experts to that of the other." (para.227)

**9–004** The result was that the judge decided this issue on the basis of his own intuition. The next paragraph of the decision begins:

> "Nevertheless it seems to us to be inherently probable that if football matches are shown on television to a significantly greater extent than hitherto there will be a tendency towards a reduction in attendances at matches." (para.228)

## Criteria for good empirical economic analysis

**9–005** Good empirical analysis is analysis that provides a correct description of reality and that is accessible to the decision making bodies. The necessary criteria for such analysis are that any empirical analysis presented to competition authorities be:

- based on clear economic theory which implies
- testable propositions which are
- intuitive and
- replicable.

First, the underlying economic theory that any empirical analysis is focused on, and the assumptions inherent in this theory, need to be made explicit and clear.[4] Only in this way can the authorities properly appraise the underlying economics. Secondly, the theory must lead to testable propositions that distinguish between competing hypotheses. Thus finding that the cross-price elasticitity between an allegedly dominant firm and a potential competitor is high does not convey useful information. The high-cross price elasticity might be because the potential competitor is an actual competitor that constrains the allegedly dominant firm to price competitively (i.e. the firm is not actually dominant). Or it might be that the allegedly dominant firm is actually dominant and has exercised this

---

[4] Note that when we refer to "economic theory" we do not equate this only with complex economic models. The best economic theory is usually simple and clear.

dominance by raising its price to the point at which the potential competitor begins to impose a competitive constraint.[5] Thirdly, empirical analysis that is intuitive is much more likely to influence a decision maker than analysis that is not intuitive. The UK High Court snooker case provides a good example of analysis that was not intuitively appealing being dismissed.[6] The judge rejected economic analysis related to dominance presented by the World Professional Snooker and Billiards Association because although he stated that it was analytically correct, it was not intuitively appealing and "seem[ed] to me to defy common sense" (para.98). Fourthly, empirical analysis must be replicable: if the authorities cannot replicate the results of the analysis, then they cannot verify the results. In such circumstances it is very hard for them to put much weight on those results.

# COMMON CRITICISMS OF THE USE OF QUANTITATIVE TECHNIQUES

The use of empirical economic techniques in European competition law **9–006** has been subject to a great deal of discussion. A number of objections to their use have been raised.

## The data are not available

The first category recognises in principle the merits of using empirical **9–007** techniques as an aid in the competitive assessment. However, concerns are expressed about the applicability of tests in practice. For example, the following statement is still often heard following presentations of these techniques: "This is all very good, but we do not have the requisite data."

While it is certainly true that the amount and type of data rarely matches the ideal, this should not be taken to mean that there are no useful data available. Data can come from a number of sources: published industry research, commissioned research, from the company under investigation itself and so on. The amount of data available within companies is often surprising. The critical step in finding this data is often the identification of the correct person within a company to talk to. The fact that the chief executive of a large multinational company is unaware of the existence of historic price data on its products does not meant that the data do no exist.

Moreover, the fact that the ideal data set is not available does not mean that no use can be made of the available data. Where data are available, a

---

[5]   It should be noted that in this case a low cross-price elasticity of demand would convey useful information, since it would show that the two firms were not competitors, regardless of whether the allegedly dominant firm was exercising substantial market power or not.

[6]   *Hendry v World Professional Billiards and Snooker Association Ltd* (HC0100813) in the High Court of Justice, Chancery Division, October 5, 2001.

stark choice needs to be made. Either rely solely on theoretical judgments and unsubstantiated claims about consumer behaviour or complement that theory with the best available tools while being aware of its weaknesses. The latter approach is clearly preferable: an assessment based on more information is better (certainly no worse) than one based on less.[7]

Of course, one must be aware of the potential deficiencies of the data. In particular, one must take care that the data are both appropriate in the sense that they relate to the issue of interest and that the data relate to the appropriate time horizon. For example, price data must refer or approximate in a systematic manner to the actual prices paid by customers. List prices will not provide appropriate data if customers actually pay prices discounted in a non-systematic manner from lists prices. Equally, elasticity estimates used in a merger inquiry should relate to what would happen over a period of a year or more, not over a period of just one week.

As with all statistical analysis, it is important to assess how representative the available data are of the whole competitive process. The larger the data set, the more likely it is that the results of any such analysis will be representative. But even partial coverage can be informative. If the data set contains reliable information on a significant proportion of transactions in the market, this will normally be sufficient to produce results representative of the industry in question.

### Is the past a good guide to the future?

**9–008** Merger analysis necessarily involves the use of historic data. This raises the issue of whether analysis using such data can provide a good indicator of the likely impact of a merger on future competition. In assessing the likely competitive effects of a merger, one must have regard to possible changes in behaviour both on the part of suppliers and customers. For example, in assessing the competitive effects of a merger between two differentiated products that are close substitutes, one would need to assess the potential for remaining suppliers to reposition their products. Similarly, the structural change implied by the merger might make tacit co-ordination more or less likely. Empirical analysis cannot usually answer all of these questions. Instead, empirical analysis will form *part* of the overall competitive assessment. This does not imply that empirical analysis should not be undertaken or serves no purpose. Rather, its use should be coupled with knowledge of its potential shortcomings.

---

[7] Although Diamond and Hausman (1994) correctly point out that no inference is better than the wrong inference.

## "Garbage in, garbage out"

A further category of criticism is more fundamental and concerns whether **9–009** empirical techniques have any usefulness in aiding the competitive assessment. This strand of criticism can be summarised in the statement: "garbage in, garbage out".

Clearly, there is a degree of merit in this statement. The results of techniques using inappropriate data cannot be relied upon. For example, using list prices in a correlation analysis when it is known that most transactions take place at varying discounts from the list price would be a good example of garbage in, garbage out. However, one must guard against this type of argument being used simply as a smoke screen, particularly where one party is attempting to discredit the evidence of an opposing party. At a minimum, the opposing party should demonstrate why the data is faulty and explain the ways in which correcting the faulty data would alter the findings of the original study.

# EMPIRICAL TECHNIQUES DISCUSSED IN PART III

The chapters in Part III of this book each consider a different empirical **9–010** technique. The techniques are:

1. Price tests

2. Using elasticities (critical loss and diversion ratios)

3. Bidding studies

4. Shock analysis

5. Price concentration analysis

6. Merger simulation

7. Shipment and transport cost tests

8. Damages estimation

We have also provided an Appendix that includes an introduction to econometric analysis.

Which of these tests can usefully be undertaken will vary from case to case depending upon the issues at hand, the availability and quality of the data and the time available in which to perform the test. Generally speaking, the larger the data set available, the better the quality of the data and the more time in which to undertake the analysis, the more sophisticated the analysis which can be employed.

## Price tests

**9–011** This chapter covers a number of tests that come under the general heading of price tests. These are tests that look at the relationship between different price series in order to try and derive implications for competitive interaction and market definition. The tests covered in this chapter are price correlation, Granger causality, cointegration and tests of stationarity.

Price correlation analysis has two advantages. First, the underlying principles of the test are intuitive. If two products are viewed as substitutable by users or producers and are, therefore, in the same market, then the price of each will constrain the price of the other. The prices of these two products should therefore move together over time. Secondly, the analysis is relatively easy to carry out.

However, price correlation analysis has a number of weaknesses. The results of such analysis cannot be properly used to test directly issues of market power. Moreover, high levels of correlation between the prices of two products can be caused by a number of factors extraneous to any consideration of competitive constraints. The various pitfalls inherent in correlation analysis are discussed. Nonetheless, when used and interpreted correctly price correlation tests can provide useful information.

The other price tests covered in this chapter require econometric analysis and have been advocated as an improvement on the use of less sophisticated price correlation analysis. We argue in this chapter that these apparently more sophisticated tests do not necessarily represent an improvement on price correlation analysis. Like price correlation analysis, they do not directly answer the central question of the Hypothetical Monopolist test, they are often of low power and they can lead to perverse results. It is therefore important to be clear that they do not solve all the difficulties that arise with price correlation analysis.

## Using elasticities: critical loss and diversion ratios

**9–012** This chapter covers the direct application of the hypothetical monopolist test using a technique known as critical loss analysis or critical elasticity analysis. This allows one to answer the hypothetical monopolist question using data only on price-cost margins and elasticities. The analysis is certainly not without its pitfalls (e.g. consistency between firm specific and market elasticities, correct time period for elasticities and costs, etc.), but nor is it particularly technical.

After discussing critical loss and critical elasticity analysis, we then discuss the use of "diversion ratios" in antitrust analysis. Diversion ratios measure the proportion of sales lost by one firm when it raises its price that are won by another firm. Diversion ratios are a useful measure of the relative closeness of competition between a number of products. The higher the diversion ratio between two products, the closer competitors they are. This can be useful, particularly when considering which should be the next product added to the putative market in a market definition exercise. However, the use of diversion ratios to estimate post-merger price rises, as has been advocated by some, is fraught with difficulties and should not be done. We explain why in detail.

## Bidding studies

Bidding markets differ from other markets in that sales are made through a   **9–013** tender process. Each firm bids a price to win the tender and then is either chosen as the winning bidder or not. The implication of this is that bidding markets are often characterised by a high degree of price discrimination, with prices being bespoke for each tender. We discuss three forms of empirical analysis that are particularly well suited to such markets.

The first relates to estimating how many firms are required to ensure effective competition. An analysis of the relationship between price and the number of bidders can reveal how many firms are required for effective competion. Secondly, market shares do not always provide a good proxy for competitive strength in bidding markets. In bidding markets it is often possible to analyse the effect that a small firm has on the competitive outcome by looking at how competitive outcomes vary depending whether or not a particular firm took part in the bidding process. Thirdly, an important question in unilateral effects cases is often how competitive the merging parties are. The type of data available in bidding markets can often be used to determine whether the merging parties are close competitors or not.

## Shock analysis

This chapter discusses a technique called shock analysis. This technique is   **9–014** simple but it can provide a powerful test of competing hypotheses. Shock analysis is a way of thinking about what past events in an industry tell us about the form of competition in that industry. Shock analysis looks at shocks that have occurred to an industry and considers whether the response of the industry to the shock tells us anything of interest about the industry. In truth, this is not so much an empirical technique as the appliance of common sense to data. Shocks to an industry can convey a substantial amount of information about how an industry operates. The types of shock that can be useful include new product launches, exchange rate shocks, input costs shocks and promotional campaigns.

Shock analysis is not rocket science. It involves thinking intelligently about what insights can be drawn from the behaviour of a market after there has been a shock to that market. Its simplicity is a major advantage. The downside to this form of analysis is that it is not always possible to carry it out. If there have not been any useful shocks in the recent past, then the approach cannot be used. However, it should be noted that some shocks such as new product launches, short-term promotions and new advertising campaigns are relatively common.

This chapter also discusses stock market event studies. These are analyses that attempt to glean information about the likely competitive effects of a merger from the movement in the share prices of competing firms when the merger is announced. Our view is that there are serious difficulties with using stock market event studies for predicting the effect of a merger on competition.

## Price concentration studies

**9–015** This chapter discusses a potentially powerful, and intuitively appealing, empirical technique that can be used in a range of antitrust settings. The technique is called a price concentration study. It investigates the relationship between price[8] and concentration, or market share, in a given industry or industry segment. It does this by considering how price and concentration vary over a number of separate "markets".

Price concentration studies are simple but potentially powerful studies. They can provide direct evidence on the question of interest: does increased concentration in a market allow prices to rise? This question is relevant to merger cases (will increased concentration lead to higher prices?), dominance cases (does the firm's high market share allow it profitably to raise prices above the competitive level?) and Article 81 cases (is this an agreement between firms with the ability profitably to raise prices above the competitive level?). This is a considerable advantage, particularly given that several of the other empirical techniques that are discussed in this book (e.g. price correlation analysis and shipment tests) do not *directly* answer the question of interest, but instead answer an intermediate question (i.e. market definition).

However, price concentration studies have been subject to serious criticism and it is true that there are many potential pitfalls that may confront an investigator using one. We discuss these in the chapter. Our view is that despite these criticisms, price concentration can often be very useful, particularly for market definition.

## Merger simulation

**9–016** This chapter considers merger simulation, a quantitative technique that has become significantly more widely used in European merger control in recent years. The purpose of this chapter is not to allow readers to carry out their own merger simulation. As we explain at length in this chapter, carrying out a merger simulation that actually adds value to the decision

---

[8] Or margin or, on occasion, profit.

making process is a technical exercise that requires considerable economic modelling, and ideally also econometric, expertise. Instead, the aim of this chapter is to provide readers with an understanding of when a merger simulation might be useful, and when it is unlikely to be useful, and to enable them to critically appraise a merger simulation that is presented during the course of a case. Whilst elements of carrying out a good merger simulation might be described as "rocket science", understanding whether a particular simulation is likely to be a good guide to the effect of a merger is not rocket science.

We stress in this chapter that even the best merger simulation is not a basis for making a merger control decision on its own. They omit important parts of the competitive effects analysis, such as entry, buyer power, product repositioning and changes in the mode of competition post-merger. This is not to say that merger simulations are therefore not useful, but only to highlight what their correct role is. One important role that they can play is in the assessment of the effect of post-merger marginal cost reductions on prices.

## Shipment and Transport Cost Tests

In many competition investigations, a critical issue is the significance of the   **9–017** competitive constraint posed by firms situated in other geographic regions. This is particularly the case where a firm has a high market share in a given Member State or region but might be subject to competitive constraints not only from other firms located in that Member State or region but also from firms located in other Member States or regions.

Shipment and import penetration tests provide an intuitive test for assessing the strength of competition across regions. As such, they can provide a useful aid in helping to delineate the relevant geographic market and, in particular, in deciding whether domestic firms face significant competition from foreign suppliers. Such tests consider the extent to which sales within a given region originate from outside that region or the extent to which production in a region is exported.

Shipment tests are very attractive for two reasons. First, they are intuitive: it is simple to understand what they imply. Secondly, they are very easy to carry out: they require only quantity data and can be quickly calculated. For these reasons, it is not surprising that shipment tests (or rather, informal versions of them) appear in many Commission decisions. However, they are not without their weakness and we discuss these in the chapter.

Transport cost tests focus on estimating from how far it is feasible to supply into a market from outside that market. This is relevant to understanding the competitive constraints faced by suppliers in a particular region. These tests can be used to show which suppliers that do not currently ship into an area could do so, either at current prices or if prices were to increase after a merger.

## Damages estimation

**9–018** This chapter covers an issue that has become much more prominent in recent years: the calculation of damages arising from anti-competitive behaviour by firms. It is clear that anti-competitive behaviour can harm other firms and consumers. For instance, cartels lead to prices being higher than they otherwise would be and this can harm both consumers and producers who use cartelised products in their production process. Excessive pricing has the same effect. Predatory pricing, and other forms of exclusionary conduct, can harm competitors by driving them out of the market and hence preventing them from earning profits and can harm consumers by raising prices in the longer term.

In this chapter we discuss the broad methodology for calculating anti-trust damages and then describe a number of ways in which this methodology can be implemented. Much of the discussion takes place within the context of calculating the damages arising from cartels, but the methodology and approaches described can be applied to other types of anti-competitive behaviour. Finally, we discuss a number of issues and common pitfalls that arise in calculating damages. We assume throughout that the aim is to calculate compensatory damages, not punitive or restitutionary damages.

## Appendix: Introduction to econometric analysis

**9–019** Assessing the competitiveness of an industry in the context of a competition law inquiry is a complex task. A number of factors, including, inter alia, the number of competing firms, the effectiveness of other products to act as substitutes and the ease with which new firms can enter the market, all need to be taken into consideration. In other words, there are multitudinous, interdependent factors that determine the nature of competition between firms. In undertaking the competitive assessment, a number of different empirical questions often arise, such as: "What is the own price elasticity of demand?", "How large a competitive constraint does Firm A impose on Firm B?", "Are prices higher when concentration is higher?" and "Does new entry lead to lower prices?".

While taking into account all of these factors is complex, in principle at least, econometric analysis is able to do this. Econometric analysis consists of a set of quantitative tools employing statistical methods which are used to construct representational models of real-world competitive relationships and, most importantly, to test these alleged relationships. Econometric models enable one to take into account the numerous factors which are believed to affect competition (subject to data restrictions) and to estimate the economic importance of each of these factors. As such, they offer a very useful empirical method for assisting competition law investigations.

This Appendix is designed to provide an understanding of what is being shown by a particular set of econometric results and to provide the tools for a rudimentary appraisal of the quality of an econometric analysis. While there are good and bad econometric analyses, there is also a whole battery of tests that allow discrimination between good and bad econometric analyses. It is simply untrue to say, as is often claimed, that econometric analysis can be used to prove "anything".

## SUMMARY

The use of empirical evidence can be critical in discriminating between **9-020** competing claims. While it is unusual for a single test to provide definitive results, it is usually the case that empirical evidence will be more supportive of one view than the other. This is particularly the case where several pieces of empirical evidence all point to similar conclusions. When used with care and sophistication, empirical analysis can reduce arbitrariness and greatly improve the quality of the competitive assessment.

Empirical analysis presented in competition law proceedings should not be a "black box" in which results are presented without any explanation of how they were reached or what the economic theory behind them is. In addition, it is incumbent on the presenter of the evidence to ensure that it is understandable to a non-economist.

There are a number of arguments that have traditionally been used against the use of empirical analysis. One of these is that there is rarely the requisite data available for empirical analysis. Our view is that it is virtually never true that there is no useful data available. Another is that the past cannot be used as a predictor of the future. Whilst it is true that the past cannot be used in an unthinking manner, it is also true that the nature of past competition in a market almost always contains helpful information on the likely nature of competition in the future. The third argument that we covered was that poor quality data will lead to poor quality empirical analysis. This is undoubtedly true and investigators should take care to ensure that their data is of the best quality possible. It should be noted that these arguments against the use of empirical analysis are heard much less often today than when we wrote the first edition of this book, which is a welcome development.

# 10. Price Tests

## INTRODUCTION

**10–001** This chapter covers a number of tests that come under the general heading of price tests. These are tests that consider the relationship between different price series in order to try and derive implications for competitive interaction and market definition. The tests covered in this chapter are price correlation analysis, Granger causality, cointegration and tests of stationarity. The latter three tests involve econometric analysis whereas the first, price correlation, does not. Accordingly, we start with a discussion of price correlation analysis.

## PRICE CORRELATION ANALYSIS

**10–002** Price correlation has become a standard tool of European competition law, particularly in the evaluation of mergers. This is because it is a relatively simple technique that can quickly provide useful data for defining the relevant market. Price correlation tests have played a significant role in numerous cases and have been used by both the Commission and by the parties under investigation. It is also one of the first quantitative techniques that European competition authorities started to use. Early major merger cases in which price correlation tests played an important role included inter alia *Nestlé/Perrier*,[1] *Mannesmann/Vallourec/Ilva*[2] (steel tubes), *Proctor & Gamble/VP Schickendanz*,[3] *Lonrho/Gencor*[4] and *Guiness/Grand Metropolitan*.[5,6] It continues to be used on a regular basis and has recently been

---

[1] IV/M190 *Nestlé/Perrier* [1997] OJ L356/1.
[2] IV/M315 *Mannesmann/Vallourec/Ilva* [1994] OJ L102.
[3] IV/M430 *Proctor & Gamble/VP Schickendanz* [1994] OJ L354/2.
[4] IV/M619 *Lonrho/Gencor* [1997] OJ L11/30.
[5] IV/M938 *Guiness/Grand Metropolitan* [1997] 5 C.M.L.R. 760; [1998] OJ L288/24.
[6] Price correlation analysis has also been used in Article 81 and Article 82 cases. However, as will become apparent later in this chapter, it is in general better suited to merger cases (and Article 81 joint ventures), than to Article 82 and most Article 81 cases.

important in cases such as *Ryanair/Aer Lingus*[7] and *BMG/Sony*.[8] Its widespread use stems mainly from its modest data requirements and the speed with which the test can be undertaken. One of the aims of this chapter is to explain the underlying intuition behind price correlation analysis and to evaluate the usefulness of correlation analysis as a tool for market definition.

At the outset, one must recognise that there are several weaknesses associated with the use of correlation analysis in market definition. As a method of analysis its results are less reliable than, for instance, price elasticity estimates based on a well-specified econometric model of an industry. However, despite these weaknesses, price correlation analysis, if used and interpreted correctly, can provide useful information to aid the definition of the relevant market. In particular, given its relatively low information requirements and ease of use, it would be foolish to ignore a technique that can potentially provide useful information. Instead, practitioners must be fully aware of what the potential shortcomings of correlation analysis are and how these affect the interpretation of the results.

This chapter considers the underlying intuitive principle of price correlation analysis and how it can aid the competitive assessment. A brief discussion of the use of price correlation analysis in some Commission decisions is provided. These decisions illustrate the potential usefulness of price correlation analysis in the competitive assessment, particularly when used in conjunction with other analyses. We explain the relationship between the test and the fundamental approach to defining relevant markets.[9]

The potential weaknesses of correlation analysis are highlighted. It is **10–003** widely recognised that price correlation analysis can suggest a narrow market when the true market is wide and a wide market when the true market is narrow. The circumstances in which problems of this type are liable to arise are explained. For instance, the results of price correlation analysis can be subject to spurious correlation. Spurious correlation refers to those circumstances in which the degree of correlation between two price series is high but this has little or nothing to do with the competitive constraints between the two respective products or regions. In many cases, spurious correlation is caused by the existence of common costs in the two price series—a problem which it is possible to solve. Unfortunately, as this chapter shows, the problem of spurious correlation has other sources and these are more difficult to resolve in a satisfactory fashion. Price correlation analysis has also been criticised because its results can be hard to interpret in terms of defining a relevant market. The use of benchmarking

---

[7]   COMP/M.4439 *Ryanair/Aer Lingus* (June 27, 2007).
[8]   COMP/M.3333 *BMG/Sony* (October 3, 2007).
[9]   The fundamental approach refers to the hypothetical monopolist test described in Chapter 4.

techniques in addressing this problem is discussed and, in particular, how the results of benchmarking should be interpreted.

Traditionally price correlation analysis has been routinely applied in European competition inquiries to both product market and geographic market definition. However, it is important to note that when price series are denominated in different exchange rates (e.g. sterling and the Euro), then the use of price correlation analysis raises difficult issues. We therefore include a discussion of the applicability of price correlation analysis to delineating relevant geographic markets across exchange rate areas. The key conclusion of this discussion is that except where exchange rates are very stable and so approximate to fixed exchange rates, price correlation analysis is unlikely to provide a useful test for defining relevant geographic markets. Whilst the advent of the Euro has reduced the incidence of these problems and so increased the scope for using correlation analysis for geographic market definition across Member States, it still remains a problem in a significant number of cases. Although there are now 15 countries in the Euro-zone, plus a number of other countries where the Euro is formally legal tender, there are still a number of significant European countries that do not use the Euro (i.e. Denmark and the United Kingdom within the EC and Norway and Switzerland within the EEA).

## Correlation analysis as an aid for assessing competition

**10–004** The purpose of defining the relevant market is to aid the competitive analysis by identifying the products and/or regions which provide a significant constraint on the competitive behaviour of the products and/or regions under investigation. This implies that the appropriate basis for defining the relevant market is to address explicitly the nature of the competitive constraints which operate between products and regions.[10] This is not the same as defining markets on the basis of physical differences, differences in price levels or some other arbitrary categorisation (as competition authorities still sometimes do). Any approach to market definition that does not explicitly focus on the competitive constraints faced by a product will result in a correct definition of the relevant market only by chance.

The extent to which a product is subject to effective competitive constraints depends on the effect of any price increase on the demand for the product and the supply of the product. If the price of a product increases, we should expect consumers to buy less of that product. This effect is captured by the own-price elasticity of demand for the product. In general, the own-price elasticity of demand for a product is higher (in absolute terms) when there exist close substitute products on the demand side. We should also expect to see an effect on the supply-side. If the price of a

---

[10] See Chapter 4 for a detailed discussion.

product increases, we should expect other firms to be willing to supply more of the product. This effect is captured by the elasticity of supply of the product.

If two products are substitutes for one another, one would expect to observe at least one of two effects following a relative price increase in one of these products: the demand for the relatively more expensive product falls as consumers switch to the other product and/or the price of the substitute product also increases. In other words, any perceived independent movement in the prices of products in the same market ought to be accompanied by a noticeable market reaction. In the case of demand-side substitution, price divergence between such products will lead to consumers switching their purchases towards the relatively cheaper product whose price has fallen (in relative terms). In the case of supply-side substitution, it will take the form of producers switching production to the product whose price has risen in relative terms. It should be expected that the increased demand for the cheaper product will lead, in general, to its price increasing. Equally, it should be expected that the increased supply of the more expensive product will lead in general to its price falling. Prices should be expected to move back towards each other if the two products are genuinely substitutes. Thus the prices of substitutes should be expected to move together over time. Price correlation analysis provides a measure of the extent to which two price series move together over time.

The degree to which the prices of two products move together over time   **10–005** can be measured statistically by the correlation coefficient. The correlation coefficient can be used to provide a measure of the extent to which changes in the price of one product or one region are reflected in changes in the prices of other products or regions.

The correlation coefficient between two series X and Y is defined as follows[11]:

(1) $$\frac{\sum (x_t - \bar{x})(y_t - \bar{y})}{\sqrt{\sum (x_t - \bar{x})^2 \sum (y_t - \bar{y})^2}}$$

where   $x_t$ is the price of product X at time t;
$y_t$ is the price of product Y at time t; and
$\bar{x}$ and $\bar{y}$ are the average values of the two price series.

The correlation coefficient between two series always lies between $-1$ and 1. A positive correlation coefficient between the prices of two products implies that an increase (decrease) in the price of one is reflected by an increase (decrease) in the price of the other. A negative correlation implies that an increase (decrease) in the price of one product is associated with a decrease (increase) in the price of the other product. If the correlation coefficient is 1, this means that every movement in one price series is

---

[11]   Equation (1) can also be written as $\rho = \sigma_{xy} / \sigma_x \sigma_y$ where $\sigma_x$ and $\sigma_y$ are the standard deviations of series X and Y respectively, and $\sigma_{xy}$ is the covariance of the two series.

exactly reflected in the other series.[12] Equally, a correlation coefficient of −1 would mean that every movement in one series is reflected by an exactly opposite movement in the other price series. A correlation coefficient of zero implies that movements in one price series are not reflected in movements in the other price series, in any direction.

Where the prices of two products are positively correlated, a graph of these prices would be seen to move up and down together over time. The greater the positive value of the correlation coefficient, the more closely aligned will such changes be. In general, the higher the degree of correlation between the two price series, the more likely it is that the two products lie in the same relevant market. We discuss this issue in more depth below. Note that the absolute level of prices is not relevant here.[13] It is quite possible that the price of Product A lies above that of Product B and yet they are in the same relevant product market. This might be because there are quality (real or merely perceived) differences between the two products. Thus, private label products may well be in the same product markets as branded goods, even though they are often significantly cheaper.[14] The relevant question is whether the price of Product A is constrained by the price of Product B.[15]

**10–006** Figure 10.1 provides an illustration. It shows the prices of three products over time. Figure 10.1 shows Products A and B moving together relatively closely over time. An increase in the price of Product A is accompanied by an increase in the price of Product B. On the basis of the foregoing discussion, this provides support for the contention that Products A and B are in the same product market. However, although the price of Product C also follows those of Products A and B in some periods, in others there are sharp divergences. Unless these sharp divergences can be explained (for instance, by an unexpected constraint on the available supply of C) this

---

[12] The phrase "exactly reflected" is a bit imprecise. What is meant is that the relationship between changes in one series and changes in the other is constant. So if a one unit increase in one series is associated with a two unit increase in the other, then this will hold for all changes in the price series, so a reduction of 2 in the first series would be associated with a reduction of four in the other. Alternatively the relationship might be in percentage terms, so a 1% change in one series is always reflected by an x% change in the other.

[13] See the discussion in Chapter 4 where it is explained that differences in price levels do not imply separate relevant markets.

[14] For instance, in its *Kimberly-Clark/Scott Paper* decision, the Commission effectively argued that the relevant market consisted of both branded and own-label products even though, as the Commission recognised, a price differential existed between these two sets of products. See Levy (1996). More recently (2007), in the *SCA/Procter & Gamble* decision (COMP/M.4533), the Commission concluded that

"First, private labels and branded product compete at the retail level. Second, the quality of private label products has increased and is now similar to branded products. Nevertheless, branded products are still sold with a price premium over private labels." (para.17).

[15] Although to some this view may appear to be at odds with Form CO, it is very much in the spirit of the Commission's *Notice on the Definition of Relevant Market for the Purposes of Community Competition Law* [1997] OJ C372/5.

would suggest that Product C does not lie in the same relevant product market as Products A and B, even though the prices of Product A and Product C were very similar at the start of the period.

**Figure 10.1: Hypothetical prices of three products over time   10-007**

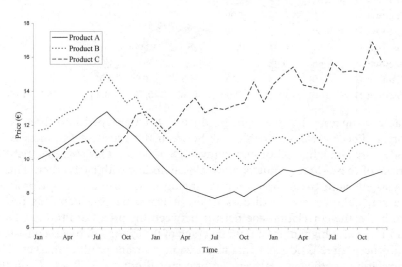

However, using graphical methods to assess the degree to which the prices of two products move together over time does not provide a systematic measure. This can be provided by correlation coefficients. The correlation coefficients associated with the price series in Figure 10.1 are shown in Table 10.1.[16] It can be seen that the correlation coefficient between Product A and Product B is positive whilst those between Product C and Products A and B are negative.

**Table 10.1: Correlation coefficients associated with Figure    10-008 10.1**

|  | Product A | Product B | Product C |
|---|---|---|---|
| **Product A** | 1.00 | | |
| **Product B** | 0.98 | 1.00 | |
| **Product C** | −0.65 | −0.62 | 1.00 |

Table 10.2 provides an example of the results of a (hypothetical) price correlation analysis for eight products.

[16]   Note that correlation analysis is usually carried out using the logarithms of price series. An equal percentage change in two price series will translate into an equal absolute change in the logs of their price series.

**10–009** **Table 10.2: Results of a (hypothetical) price correlation analysis**

| | Product A | Product B | Product C | Product D | Product E | Product F | Product G | Product H |
|---|---|---|---|---|---|---|---|---|
| Product A | 1.00 | | | | | | | |
| Product B | 0.95 | 1.00 | | | | | | |
| Product C | 0.96 | 0.93 | 1.00 | | | | | |
| Product D | 0.89 | 0.87 | 0.90 | 1.00 | | | | |
| Product E | 0.87 | 0.91 | 0.89 | 0.96 | 1.00 | | | |
| Product F | 0.88 | 0.90 | 0.85 | 0.96 | 0.97 | 1.00 | | |
| Product G | 0.10 | 0.13 | 0.13 | 0.05 | 0.03 | 0.02 | 1.00 | |
| Product H | −0.13 | −0.22 | −0.60 | −0.50 | −0.55 | −0.43 | −0.65 | 1.00 |

Table 2 suggests that the eight products can be grouped into three categories. The correlation coefficients between the prices of Products A, B and C are all high: 0.93 or higher (average of 0.95). This suggests that the prices of these three products move closely in line with each other. This is consistent with these three products being in the same relevant product market, although as we discuss below it canot be considered as proof. Similarly, the correlation coefficients between the prices of Products D, E and F are also high: at least 0.96 (average of 0.96). Again, this is consistent with these three products being in the same relevant product market. The correlation coefficient between the prices of Products A, B and C on the one hand and the prices of Products D, E and F on the other also suggest that there are strong competitive constraints between the six products. The average correlation is 0.88. This is consistent with the contention that these two categories of products form part of the same relevant market.

However, Products G and H do not seem to provide a significant competitive constraint on the pricing behaviour of the other six products. The correlation coefficients between the prices of Product G and Product H and the other six products are all low. The highest correlation between Product G and the other six products is only 0.13 (with Products B and C), whilst the highest correlation between Product H and the other six products is actually negative (−0.13, with Product A). These results suggest that Products G and H are not in the same relevant market (or markets) as the other six products.

## The use of correlation analysis in Commission decisions

**10–010** Given its relatively low data requirements and because it provides a straightforward intuitive analysis, price correlation analysis has been used routinely in EC competition law investigations, particularly in merger investigations. In this section, the use of price correlation analysis in the Commission's competitive assessment is illustrated with reference to a number of decisions. The purpose of this section is to illustrate how price correlation has been used in actual cases in order to provide context for the discussion that follows, which looks at some of the issues that need to be considered when analysing a correlation analysis.

### *Nestlé/Perrier*[17]

*Nestlé/Perrier* was the first European case where correlation analysis played   **10–011** a prominent role in the market definition debate. In *Nestlé/Perrier*, an important issue was the degree of competition between bottled mineral water and soft drinks. The proposed merger led to a reduction in the number of leading mineral water firms from three to two with the merged parties having 50 per cent of the sales of sparkling and still mineral water (by volume).[18] Clearly, the concerns raised by the merger would have been considerably less if soft drinks provided an important competitive constraint on the pricing of mineral waters.

It could be argued that there was no separate market for mineral water and that the relevant market in which to assess the proposed merger should have been that for non-alcoholic refreshment beverages, including both mineral water and soft drinks. The Commission at one stage took the opposite view, arguing that there was a distinction between sparkling mineral water and still mineral water from the perspective of competition analysis. Various potential market definitions are depicted in Figure 10.2.

### Figure 10.2: Potential market definitions in the *Nestlé-Perrier*   10–012 case

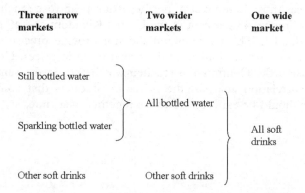

Price correlation analysis played a critical role in settling this dispute.[19] The results of price correlation revealed high correlation coefficients between

---

[17]   IV/M190 *Nestlé/Perrier* [1993] 4 C.M.L.R. M17; [1992] OJ L356/1.
[18]   Commission decision para.133.
[19]   Lexecon Competition Memo (1994).

the various brands of sparkling mineral water and also between the various brands of still mineral water. More importantly, the correlation coefficients between sparkling mineral water brands and still mineral water brands were also high. This suggested that there existed a significant competitive constraint between sparkling and still brands. Conversely, the correlation coefficients between brands of mineral water and soft drinks were found to be uniformly low, indicating the absence of a competitive constraint on mineral waters from soft drinks.[20] From this evidence, in conjunction with other reasoning, the Commission concluded that the relevant product market was defined by mineral source water.[21]

## *Procter & Gamble/VP Schickedanz*[22]

10–013 This case is interesting because it illustrates the use of the underlying logic of price correlation analysis, even when a formal price correlation analysis is not carried out. This investigation was concerned with the impact of the proposed acquisition of VP Schickedanz by Procter & Gamble on the feminine hygiene industry in Germany. An important issue in assessing the potentially anticompetitive effects of the transaction was the extent of the relevant geographic market.[23] The transaction led to high market shares of sanitary towels in Germany and Spain.[24] One piece of evidence that the Commission used in this regard was the evolution of prices in various northern European countries.[25] Specifically, the Commission argued that the prices of sanitary towels in Germany, France, the United Kingdom and the Netherlands did not move together between the beginning of 1991 and the beginning of 1993. Over this period, prices in Germany rose by 10 per cent, whereas those in the rest of northern European rose much faster (24 per cent in France, 43 per cent in the United Kingdom and 45 per cent in the Netherlands). The Commission did not provide precise correlation coefficients, but instead looked at the broad trend in prices. Nonetheless, the conclusion the Commission reached was based on the same logic as underlies correlation analysis: the prices of products that compete with each other should be expected to move together over time.

---

[20] Commission Decision at para.13.
[21] Commission Decision para.19.
[22] IV/M430 *Procter & Gamble/VP Schickedanz* [1994] OJ L354/33.
[23] The extent of the relevant product market was also an issue of contention. The Commission appears to have relied heavily on elasticity estimates to define the relevant product market, although it also used a crude form of price correlation analysis (para.70).
[24] Commission Decision para.119.
[25] para.81.

*CVC/Lenzing*[26]

The competitive concerns in this merger related to the cellulosic staple **10-014**
fibre sector and, in particular, to viscose staple fibres (VSF) and lyocell
staple fibres. The Commission concluded that the merger would lead to
the creation of a dominant position in the EEA markets for commodity
VSF, spun-dyed VSF, lyocell, lyocell production and processing technology, and to the strengthening of a dominant position in the EEA market for
VSF for tampons. As part of its assessment, the Commission carried out
correlation analysis. This analysis provides a good illustration of the pitfalls
that an unthinking use of correlation analysis can raise.

The Commission calculated correlation coefficients between VSF and
cotton, polyester and polypropylene. For each of polyester and polypropylene the Commission used a high price and a low price series. The
high price was described[27] as the list price or that paid by small users, while
the low price was that paid by large users. Table 10.3 shows the results.

**Table 10.3: Price correlations between VSF and other fibres** **10-015**

(Monthly data, January 1991 to May 2001)

| | |
|---|---|
| Cotton | 0.04 |
| Polyester: low price | 0.39 |
| Polyester: high price | 0.44 |
| Polypropylene: low price | 0.06 |
| Polypropylene: high price | 0.24 |

Source: para.74 of Commission Decision

The Commission concluded that these results indicated that none of the
listed fibres could be considered as being in the same relevant product
market as VSF. The problem with this analysis is that the Commission
failed to provide a benchmark for what level of correlation was required to
imply a combined market. As we discuss below, correlation analysis
requires a benchmark and this benchmark will vary depending on the
industry in question and the periodicity of the data. However, the Commission stated that:

> "Even the highest correlation ($\sigma = 0.44$) ... is not high enough to
> justify the assumption of a combined product market." (para.74)

and justified this by saying:

[26] COMP/M.2187 *CVC/Lenzing* (2000).
[27] See fn.61 to COMP/M.2187 *CVC/Lenzing* (2000).

"This conclusion is in line with Commission practice. Correlations higher than those indicated in Table 1 have been considered insufficient in previous decisions, the Commission having regarded correlations of above 0.80 as high and correlations below 0.65 as low." (fn. 59)

The Commission's apparent belief that there was a single standard for a correlation being high enough to imply a wide market that was independent of the industry in question or the periodicity of the data was incorrect. It may be that in this industry with these data 0.44 is too low a figure to suggest a combined market, but the Commission did not present any evidence on this point.

**10–016**  The Commission compounds its errors later in the Decision when it carries out a correlation analysis of three types of VSF (commodity, spun-dyed and VSF for tampons) on cotton, polyester and polypropylene. The Commission finds that the highest correlation is 0.76, which is between low price polypropylene and commodity VSF. The Commission dismisses this as being "below the level that has generally been considered indicative of the existence of a wider product market",[28] again seemingly believing that the benchmark for a correlation analysis is independent of the industry and periodicity of the data. In addition, it appears that the data was list data, not transactions data.[29] Price correlation analysis only makes sense when it is carried out using transactions prices since it is these prices that are driven by actual competitive constraints between products.

### *Ryanair/Aer Lingus*[30]

**10–017**  A recent example of the use correlation analysis by the Commission is the *Ryanair/Aer Lingus* decision. This was the proposed acquisition by Ryanair, a low cost airline, of the Irish airline Aer Lingus. Both use Dublin as their main hub and compete on a number of routes. However, whilst there were some direct overlaps where the two operators flew to the same airports, there were more overlaps where the two operators flew to different airports, but in the same city, or at least to destinations that were close to each other. For instance, Ryanair did not fly to London Heathrow, but instead flew to London Stanstead, Luton and Gatwick. Aer Lingus flew to London Heathrow and Gatwick, but not to Luton or Stansted. The Commission carried out a correlation analysis to look at the price correlations between fares on the same, or close, city pairs but different airports.

This case is interesting because the Commission's correlation analysis

---

[28] COMP/M.2187 *CVC/Lenzing* (2000). para.110.
[29] See COMP/M.2187 *CVC/Lenzing* (2000) paras 111, 114 and 115.
[30] COMP/M.4439 *Ryanair/Aer Lingus* (June 27, 2007).

was much more sophisticated than a standard analysis. In particular, it took account of the following issues:

- The need to provide a benchmark against which to compare the correlation coefficients between different airport pairs. The Commission used as a benchmark the average correlation for those routes where Ryanair and Aer Lingus flew to the same airports. There were six such routes. The average correlation was 0.69. As can be seen in Table 10.4, correlations above this were associated with the Commission deciding that the relevant airport pairs are in the same market.

- The Commission tested for whether the price series were stationary or non-stationary. This is a relatively technical issue (dealt with below in para.10–058), but the key point is that non-stationary price series can lead to spurious correlations and the Commission was right to take this issue seriously.

- The Commission noted that fuel costs account for a significant part of an airline's costs and that this would lead to a common factor being present in the fares across different airport pairs, regardless of whether they were part of the same relevant market or not. The presence of a common cost tends to increase the correlation coefficient between two price series even if the products are not competitively related. The Commission therefore took steps to remove the influence of fuel costs from the correlation analysis. We discuss the issue of common costs at para.10–026 below.

- Airline fares exhibit seasonality and so this was another common factor that the Commission stripped out of the correlations.

- Competitive responses between airlines may not be instantaneous. A price cut by one airline on a route, or city-pair, may not engender a response until the following month or months. Accordingly it is important to take account of this lagged effect when carrying out correlation analysis. The Commission did this. We discuss this issue further at para.10–050.

**10–018**   **Table 10.4: Correlation analysis in *Ryanair/Aer Lingus***

| Airport pair | Correlation coefficient | Market definition |
|---|---|---|
| Alicante-Murcia | 0.90 | One market |
| Amsterdam Schiphol-Eindhoven | 0.45 | Unclear |
| Barcelona-Girona-Reus | 0.92 | One market |
| Birmingham-East Midlands | 0.62* | One market |
| Brussels Airport-Charleroi Brussels South | −0.27 | Unclear |
| Frankfurt am Main-Frankfurt/Hahn | 0.53 | Unclear |
| Glasgow International-Glasgow Prestwick | 0.62 | Unclear |
| London: Stansted-Gatwick-Luton | 0.93 | One market |
| London: Heathrow v others | 0.19 | Unclear |
| Manchester-Liverpool | 0.57** | One market |
| Newcastle-Durham Tees Valley | 0.81 | One market |
| Paris Charles de Gaulle-Paris Beauvais-Tillé | 0.74 | One market |
| Rome Fiumicino-Rome Ciampino | 0.89 | One market |
| Toulouse Blagnac-Carcassonne | 0.95 | One market |

Note: The Commission's correlation Annex included more airport pairs than in the table above. However, this table includes all the airport pairs included in the correlation analysis for which the Commission made market definition findings.
* The figure of 0.62 is an average of 0.80 for Ryanair's flights to Birmingham and East Midlands and 0.45 for the correlation between Aer Lingus' flight to Birmingham and Ryanair's to East Midlands. The Commission noted that the figure of 0.80 indicated that Ryanair, at least, considers the two airports to be substitutes.
** The figure of 0.57 is below the Commission's benchmark of 0.69, but is above the correlation coefficient between Ryanair and Aer Lingus for flights from Dublin to Manchester.

### *ABF/GBI* [31]

**10–019**   The Commission's decision in *ABF/GBI* concerned the Spanish, Portuguese and French markets for compressed yeast. In each of these countries, the merging parties faced competition from Lessafre and a small number of

---

[31]   COMP/ M. 4980 *ABF/ GBI Business*, (2008). This case is the first case since *Airtours* where remedies have been required to address concerns of coordinated effects. See Chapter 7 for a discussion of the Commission's reasoning in concluding that the merger would give rise to coordinated effects.

fringe suppliers, collectively accounting for less than 15 per cent of each national market under consideration. The Commission considered entry to be unlikely. The Commission found that Spain, Portugal and France delineated separate relevant markets. One of the reasons for reaching this conclusion was an assessment of the correlation of prices in Spain with those in Portugal and in France. The Commission first noted:

> "a striking difference is observed between the dynamics of prices in Portugal in comparison with neighbouring Spain in particular. Whereas the average prices in Portugal were in decline between 2003 and mid-2005 and then rose sharply again at the end of 2005 and the beginning of 2006, the evolution of prices in Spain shows a constant increasing trend since 2002." (para.76)

The Commission then reported the results of a correlation analysis:

> "Moreover, correlations of average price movements reconstructed on regional levels show that within all regions of Spain prices moved in a very homogenous manner, whereas the correlation is not as strong when compared to regions in Portugal and France. For example, the graph in Figure 5 depicts the price correlations with the base region of Madrid, the intensity of the colour indicates the strength of the correlation. The graph shows that prices across all regions of Spain are very much correlated with the price in the region of Madrid and to a lower extent with the region outside Spain." (para.77)

## The relationship between price correlation analysis and relevant markets

The Hypothetical Monopolist test (or SSNIP) has been endorsed by the  **10–020** Commission as the appropriate method to define relevant markets in its Notice on relevant market definition.[32] This approach asks whether a hypothetical monopolist over the group of products in question could profitably impose a small but significant non-transitory increase in price (usually thought of as between 5 per cent and 10 per cent) above the competitive price level.[33] With this market definition in mind, it is clear that the fact that two price series are highly correlated does not necessarily prevent one of the products being a relevant market by itself. The fact that there is competitive interaction between Product A and Product B does not necessarily mean that the degree of competition is *enough* to prevent a profitable increase in the price of one product. In other words, Product A

---

[32] See Chapter 4.
[33] As we discussed in Chapter 4, the benchmark in a merger case is usually the current price.

may be worth monopolising in the sense that a single supplier of Product A would be able to increase its profits by raising prices.

If there is a high correlation between the prices of two products, this suggests *at a minimum* that the cross-price elasticities between these two products are positive and therefore suggests that there is some competitive interaction. However, the fact that there is *some* competitive interaction (i.e. the fact that the cross-price elasticities are positive) does not necessarily mean that they form part of the same market. It could be imagined that the cross-price elasticities between mineral water and soft drinks are positive (meaning there are some competitive interactions), but it appears that these interactions are not enough to make the relevant product market mineral water and soft drinks (see the *Nestlé/Perrier* and *Nestlé/San Pellegrino* decisions[34]). Put simply, a positive cross-price elasticity is a necessary, but not sufficient, condition for two products to be in the same relevant product market.

**10–021**

> ## BOX 10.1: AN EXAMPLE OF A HIGH CORRELATION BETWEEN TWO PRODUCTS IN SEPARATE MARKETS
>
> The following example provides an illustration of the fact that a high correlation coefficient does not necessarily imply a wide market. This example is based on the fact that it is not enough to have *some* competitive interaction between products for them to be in the same market: there must be *enough* competitive interaction. Consider a very simple demand system for trucks and cars. Specifically, the demand for trucks depends only on the price of trucks and cars, and the same is true for cars.
>
> (2) $\quad Q_T = 100 - P_T + 0.1P_C$
> (3) $\quad Q_C = 1000 - 5P_C + 0.5P_T$
> where $\quad Q_T$ is the demand for trucks;
> $\quad\quad\quad Q_C$ is the demand for cars;
> $\quad\quad\quad P_T$ is the price of trucks; and
> $\quad\quad\quad P_C$ is the price of cars.
> Further, suppose that the car market is characterised by a homogeneous product Bertrand oligopoly, so the price of a car is equal to its marginal cost. Finally, assume that the truck market is currently a monopoly. The question of interest is what does the level of correlation between the price of cars and the price of trucks tell us about the correct market definition? To answer this question, the equilibrium market prices of cars and trucks are calculated.
>
> The profits of the truck company are:
> (4) $\quad \Pi_T = (100 - P_T + 0.1\ MC_C)(P_T - MC_T)$

---

[34] IV/M190 *Nestlé/Perrier* (1992) OJ L356/1 and IV/M1065 *Nestlé San Pellegrino*; (1998).

where $MC_T$ is a constant marginal cost and there are no fixed costs. Differentiating with respect to $P_T$ yields:

(5)    $\frac{\delta \Pi_T}{\delta P_T} = 100 - 2P_T + MC_T + 0.1MC_C$

Setting this equal to zero and rearranging yields

(6)    $P_T = (100 + MC_T + 0.1\ MC_C)/2$

By assumption $P_C$ equals $MC_C$ and so Equation (6) can be rewritten as

(7)    $P_T = (100 + MC_T + 0.1\ P_C)/2$

If per unit costs of truck manufacture are constant over time, then the correlation between cars and trucks is equal to +1 since any change in the price of cars is immediately reflected in the price of trucks. So on the basis of a standard correlation analysis, one would conclude that cars and trucks are part of the same product market.

But do cars and trucks in the above example lie in the same relevant market? Suppose that the per unit cost of trucks is 20 and the marginal cost of cars is currently 10. This implies that the monopoly price of trucks is currently 60.5. Under the assumption of Bertrand competition, the competitive price is 20 (i.e. marginal cost). Hence, trucks is a market worth monopolising—it is profitable for the monopolist to raise price by more than 5 per cent above the competitive level—and therefore trucks delineate a relevant market by themselves. This example, while highly stylised, indicates that a high correlation coefficient between two price series is not always a sufficient condition for including both products in the same relevant market.

Another problem in interpreting the results of price correlation analysis **10–022** arises once supply responses of different companies are considered.[35] The price mark-up over the competitive price for a product increases as the elasticity of supply of substitute products decreases. For a given increase in the price of Product A, there will be a smaller output response from substitute products the lower is their elasticity of supply.[36] Instead, the substitute products are likely to raise their prices more than if their elasticity of supply was higher (in which case they would increase output by more). This implies that the competitive constraints imposed on Product A by substitutes are lower when their elasticity of supply is lower. Instead of responding to the increase in the price of Product A by increasing output (and potentially causing the price rise to be unprofitable), they will instead be likely to follow the price increase.

But this has potentially perverse implications for price correlation analysis. If substitutes follow the price rise of Product A, this is likely to imply a relatively high correlation between the price series, even though in fact the substitutes are not imposing much of a competitive constraint on Product

[35] See Werden and Froeb (1993).
[36] At the limit, if the substitute products are all supply constrained, then their elasticity of supply is zero and there will be no output response.

A. Conversely, if the elasticity of supply was high and so substitute products did not follow the price rise, this is likely to give rise to a lower price correlation, even though the substitutes are imposing a significant competitive constraint in this case. The implication of this is that the results of price correlation analysis should be considered in the light of potential supply-side responses.

10–023

---

**BOX 10.2: GRAPHICAL ILLUSTRATION OF POTENTIALLY PERVERSE EFFECT**

Consider the competitive constraint between branded colas and own-brand colas. If a change in the price of branded colas led to an outward shift in the residual demand curve for own-brand colas, the extent to which the price of own-brand colas will rise depends in part on the slope of the supply curve of the own-brand cola industry. The steeper is the supply curve, the more the price of own-brand colas will rise for a given rise in the price of branded colas. This implies that the steeper is the supply curve, *ceteris paribus*, the higher will be the correlation coefficient between the prices of branded colas and own-brand colas.[37] On the basis of a correlation coefficient test, this implies that the steeper the supply curve for the manufacture of own-brand colas, the more likely price correlation analysis is to imply that branded colas and own-brand colas are in the same relevant market. But this must be wrong. The steeper is the supply curve for own-brand colas, the smaller is the output response from suppliers of own-brand colas to a price increase in branded colas and so the smaller the competitive constraint imposed on branded colas. The greater the price rise in own-brand colas, the less the competitive impact on branded colas. Figure 10.3 makes this clear.

---

[37] This is not strictly speaking true. Suppose Price B rose or fell by exactly the same amount as Price A, whilst Price C rose or fell by only half the amount Price A changed. The correlation coefficient between Price A and Price B and between Price A and Price C would be the same: one. However, in a world where price series are likely to include random noise, this would not hold as the random noise will remove the perfect correlation between the price series and will do so to a greater extent for the price series (Price C in our example) with the smaller movements. In the limit, if the random noise is very large, it might remove entirely the correlation between the series.

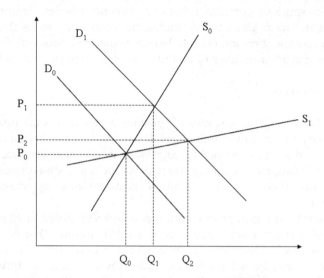

**Figure 10.3: The importance of supply side responses to correlation analysis**

The rise in the price of branded colas shifts the residual demand curve for own-brand colas from $D_0$ to $D_1$. The effect of this on the price of own-brand colas depends on the shape of the supply curve for own-brand colas. If it is $S_0$, then price rises to $P_1$ and quantity rises to $Q_1$. However, if the supply curve is more elastic (e.g. $S_1$) then price rises by less and quantity rises by more (in this case to $P_2$ and $Q_2$). In the second case, own-brand colas impose more of a competitive restraint on branded colas because the output response is larger and the price rise less. However, it is likely that the correlation coefficient between own-brand colas and branded colas will be less in the second case than in the first case. In the extreme, if the supply curve for own-brand colas were perfectly elastic (i.e. flat), the correlation coefficient would be zero, but own-brand colas would impose a very large competitive constraint on branded colas.

### Spurious correlation

**10-025** Price correlation analysis can overstate the extent of the relevant market if there exists spurious correlation between two price series. Spurious correlation is the term given to correlation between price series that is not driven by competitive interaction between the two products.[38] In this section we discuss a number of potential causes of spurious correlation.

### Common costs

**10-026** One well-known potential source of spurious correlation is the problem of common costs or common influences. If two price series have a common input, then they may be highly correlated despite the absence of any competitive relationship between the two. As such, it is always necessary to confirm that there are no common costs driving apparently high correlations.

For example, the European Commission correctly noted in *Ryanair/Aer Lingus* that fuel costs are a major cost faced by airlines that is common across all routes.[39] Thus there is a common cost in the fares from London to New York and from Paris to Moscow. However, it is doubtful that a monopoly supplier of flights from London to New York would be constrained by the pricing of flights from Paris to Moscow.

The problem raised by the existence of common costs can be dealt with through adjusting the price series to remove the common cost or costs. There are two main approaches which can be taken to correct for the influence of common costs.

The first is to remove the influence of common costs by precisely estimating the contribution of the common factor to the total costs of the product. For instance, if we know that a particular product uses 10kg of flat steel and another uses 15kg of flat steel, then we can calculate the cost of the flat steel in each product and subtract this from the price of the product. Thus if the price of flat steel was $7 per kg, then we would subtract $70 from the selling price of the first product and $105 from the selling price of the second product. Since the price of flat steel varies over time, we would subtract differing amounts each time period depending on the prevailing price of flat steel.[40]

**10-027** However, it will often not be possible to calculate the cost of the common factor in such a precise manner. An alternative approach is to econometrically estimate the effect of the common factor on selling prices. The European Commission used this approach in *Ryanair/Aer Lingus*. The

---

[38] Numerous examples of spurious correlations exist. For instance, as far back as 1955 Daniel Suits, provoked by a comment by George Stigler, highlighted high correlation between saws and granulated bulk salt, plows and cotton yarn and Texan hides and medium salt (Suits (1955)).

[39] See para.15 of Annex III of COMP/M.4439 *Ryanair/Aer Lingus* (June 27, 2007).

[40] Arguably, depending on the cost of flat steel at the time at which it was purchased.

approach is as follows. First, carry out a simple regression of the following form for all the price series:

(8)   $Price_t = \alpha + \beta\ Cost\ of\ Common\ Factor_t + \varepsilon_t$

where   $Price_t$ is the price of the product at time t;

Cost of Common $Factor_t$ is the cost of the common factor at time t;

$\alpha$ and $\beta$ are regression coefficients; and

$\varepsilon_t$ is the residual from this equation.

This will then lead to a set of residuals for each price series. The correlation analysis is then carried out on these residuals. The residuals from the regression for Price A are then correlated on the residuals from the regression for Price B and this provides the correlation coefficient between Price A and Price B after the removal of common costs. Finally, these correlations (or "partial correlation coefficients") should then be compared to the correlation coefficients derived from the unadjusted price series. If these "raw" correlations are significantly higher than the partial correlation coefficients, then this implies that the "raw" results were being driven by the presence of common costs rather than by the presence of competitive interaction.

A word of warning is due here. If common costs account for a large proportion of the price of a product, then stripping them out may lead to low correlations which suggest separate markets, even though on the supply side the products are in the same market. Suppose there are two products, A and B, whose prices are highly correlated but that have 90 per cent common costs. Stripping out these common costs might well drastically reduce the correlations between the two products. However, the fact that the two products share such a high proportion of common costs may indicate that the underlying production processes for the two products are very similar and that they should therefore be considered to be supply side substitutes and hence in the same relevant market. An example of this is pet food. Dog and cat food are not demand side substitutes (at least, not for cats: dogs are less choosy), but they are produced on the same production lines. The differences between tinned cat and dog food lies not in the production process but only in the ingredients, and even then many of these are common to both. The result is that the raw correlations between dog and cat food are very high, but they fall dramatically when common costs are removed because they account for such a large proportion of total costs. However, there is no doubt that the products should be considered as part of the same relevant market on the supply side.

The authors have experience of a case where two products were not **10–028** demand side substitutes, but had very high correlations because they were made with almost exactly the same ingredients using the same plant. The raw price correlations were more than 0.90 whilst the adjusted correlations were around 0.20. However, the correct conclusion in this case was not that the two products were in separate relevant markets but that they were very close supply side substitutes.

Before leaving this issue, it is important to stress that the mere fact that there are common costs in two price series does not mean that they are therefore not in the same relevant market. Hence it is important to correct for common costs and re-run the correlation analysis.

### *Seasonality*

**10–029**   Spurious correlation can also arise where the prices of products exhibit a seasonal trend. For example, the price of fresh flowers and the price of fresh fruit tend to increase in winter months (reflecting the increased costs involved in shipping such products from warmer climates). This will tend to induce a degree of positive price correlation between the prices of these two sets of products. But this degree of positive correlation provides little or no information on the degree to which the price of fresh flowers provides an effective competitive constraint on the price of fresh fruit and vice versa. Addressing this problem requires an adjustment to the price series to take account of any seasonal component in prices. This is done by using the differences of the price data with the difference period being the period of seasonality. Thus, if price series exhibit seasonality on an annual basis (e.g. high prices in summer, low in winter), then the correlation analysis should be carried out by first calculating the annual changes in the price data and then corelating this data. An example should make this clear.

Figure 10.4 shows three years of quarterly data for two price series. It is clear that both series are highly seasonal, with peaks in Q1 of each year and troughs in Q3. The correlation between these two series is 0.93.

**10–030**   **Figure 10.4: Effect of seasonality on correlations**

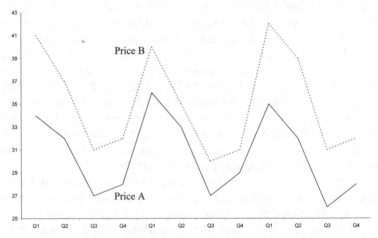

Figure 10.5 shows the annual changes in the two price series. It is clear that these series do not move together over time and this is reflected in the correlation coefficient of −0.78.

**Figure 10.5**                                                    10–031

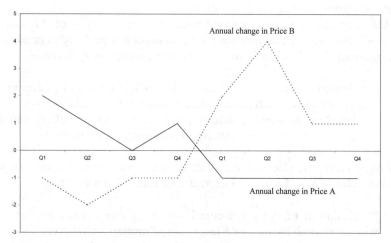

Similar to seasonality, it is also possible that a demand shock (or a business cycle) may influence the prices of unrelated products such that their prices appear correlated over time. For example, an economic boom may induce higher demand for some luxury goods, such as sports cars or jewellery, but the fact that we observe the prices of those luxury goods moving together does not necessarily imply that these products belong to the same relevant market. Similarly, the prices of all inputs into producing steel could increase when faced with an unanticipated spike in world crude steel production even in the absence of competitive interaction between those different types of those inputs.

## *Integrated variables*

Spurious correlations can be driven by non-stationary price series.[41] This is   **10–032** a rather technical issue and the details are discussed in para.10–058 below. However, the important point to note is that if there is a substantial difference between the implications of a correlation analysis carried out on the raw data and a correlation analysis carried out on first differences of the data,[42] then there must be some doubt about the validity of the analysis. If the price series are non-stationary, then they are likely to give rise to spuriously high correlations, but these high correlations will disappear when the analysis is carried out in first differences. So high correlations should always be checked by also carrying out the analysis in first

---

[41]  As we discuss further below, issues related to stationarity have come to the forefront in recent years. However, the issue has been known in the antitrust literature for many years. For instance, it is quite clear that Stigler and Sherwin (1985) were well aware of the issue and took care to avoid it leading to spurious correlations.

[42]  "First differences" are the change in the data each period. Thus if the data is $x_1, x_2, x_3, x_4$ etc., then the first differences are $x_2 - x_1, x_3 - x_2, x_4 - x_3$, etc.

differences. For similar reasons, any common trends should also be removed from the data (e.g. inflation).

The Commission took this into account in its analysis of the *Lonrho/Gencor*[43] merger. In this inquiry the Commission found high correlations but realised that these were due to having non-stationary variables:

> "Although the prices of precious metals like gold and platinum are highly correlated, a high correlation does not in itself imply a causal relationship. Indeed, economic price series data are often non-stationary (i.e. trended) and therefore automatically correlated."[44]

More recently, the Commission dealt with the issue of non-stationarity in *Ryanair/Aer Lingus*. In this decision the Commission argued:

> "Calculation of the price correlation coefficient raises no concerns when the underlying price levels are stationary. However, when the series are non-stationary this would result in spuriously high correlation coefficients even though the series may not be significantly correlated. Notwithstanding this, when price levels are integrated of order 1 it still makes sense (and is valid statistically) to calculate the correlation coefficients of the price changes, that is, correlations of the transformed series $\Delta p_{it} = p_{it} - p_{it-1}$. In this situation the economic interpretation of the correlations differ because it is the price changes rather than the price levels that potentially will correlate. In this case, it is relative convergence that is being tested. A "high" correlation of price changes across products or services for different geographical areas still indicates that these prices co-vary and hence suggests products belong to the same geographical market."[45]

---

**10–033** | **BOX 10.3: NON STATIONARY SERIES**

A stationary series is one that has a constant mean and variance. A non-stationary series is one whose mean and variance vary over time. Many economic variables (for instance, GDP and consumption) are non-stationary. If a variable is stationary, it is said to be integrated of order 0 and this is denoted as I(0). If a variable becomes stationary on being differenced once, it is integrated of order 1 and this is denoted I(1).

It is standard in the statistical literature that regression using I(1)

---

[43] IV/M619 *Lonrho/Gencor* [1997] OJ L11/30.
[44] IV/M619 *Lonrho/Gencor* [1997] OJ L11/30, para.49.
[45] COMP/M.4439 *Ryanair/Aer Lingus* (June 27, 2007) para.24 Annex III.

variables lead to what are called *nonsense regressions*. If two I(1) variables are regressed on each other, then even if they are entirely unconnected,[46] standard regression techniques will reject the null of no statistically significant connection about 80 per cent of the time.[47] In other words, the statistical analysis will suggest a relationship when none exists. A similar problem arises with correlations.

Consider two price series, X and Y, for two products which exert no competitive constraint on one another. Prices are assumed to change over time according to the following processes:

(9)   $X_t = X_{t-1} + e_t$

(10)   $Y_t = Y_{t-1} + \eta_t$

where $e_t$ and $\eta_t$ are normally distributed errors with mean 0 and variance 1. Both variables are I(1) since the first difference of both of them is stationary (i.e. the error terms have constant mean and variance). If we carry out a correlation analysis of these two variables, our mean expectation is that the correlation will be zero because by assumption there is no competitive interaction between the two products.

However, simulation analysis using 5,000 repetitions shows that this is not the result that is actually observed. This is shown in Table 10.5, where the results if both variables are trending are also shown.[48]

### Table 10.5: Correlations between unconnected I(1) variables                            10–034

| Level of correlation | Frequency of result (%) | |
| --- | --- | --- |
| | **No trends** | **Trends** |
| **Over 0.5** | 19.9 | 66.2 |
| **Over 0.6** | 13.8 | 58.7 |
| **Over 0.7** | 8.6 | 49.4 |
| **Over 0.8** | 5.1 | 35.7 |
| **Over 0.9** | 2.7 | 13.8 |

Since there is no competitive constraint between the two products, any correlation between the two price series is spurious. The results of Table 10.5 suggest that there is considerable scope for finding spurious correlations. Cartwright, Kamerschen and Huang suggest that

---

[46]   e.g. they are random walks with independent normally distributed errors.
[47]   See Yule (1926).
[48]   Further details of this analysis are available from the authors on request.

any correlation above 0.5 is indicative of a wide market.[49] On this basis, correlating I(1) variables will give a spurious positive result about 20 per cent of the time even if the two series are entirely unconnected. As Table 10.5 shows, the problem becomes even more serious if the two variables are both trending, as is common in economics. The correlation is above 0.5 in about two thirds of the cases where there is a trend whilst it is above 0.8 in 35 per cent of the cases.

These examples demonstrate the importance of checking the degree of integration of price series before carrying out a correlation analysis. If it is found that they are I(1) (or integrated of a higher order) then the correlation analysis should be carried out on the prices after they have been made stationary by differencing.[50] Equally, if there is a strong common trend (e.g. caused by high inflation) then this should be removed from the data.

### Benchmarking

**10–035** Price correlation analysis is often criticised on the grounds that it suffers from the problem of not having a clear benchmark. How high a correlation coefficient is enough to imply that two products lie in the same relevant market or not? Is 0.5 high enough? What about 0.9? A partial riposte to this criticism is provided by the use of benchmarking techniques. These use the correlation coefficient between the prices of two products or series which one is willing to state on a priori grounds lie in the same relevant market as a benchmark against which to compare other correlations. If the correlation coefficient between two other products lies above the benchmark, this is usually interpreted as meaning these two products lie in the same relevant market.[51]

As an example, consider the (hypothetical) assessment of the competitive constraint between various branded colas (e.g. Coca-Cola and Pepsi) and own-brand colas. A benchmark can be calculated by using the correlation between "Coca-Cola" and "Pepsi". This assumes that there are strong, a priori, reasons to believe that these two brands form part of the same relevant product market. The correlation coefficient between these two brands is then used as a benchmark to assess whether other weaker

---

[49]   Specifically, Cartwright, Kamerschen and Huang (1989) argue that:

> "We do not know of anyone who has been bold enough to put a precise quantitative threshold value on what is a 'high' enough value of the price correlation coefficient ... to constitute strong enough substitutes to form a market. While it is not possible to cite the chapter and verse supporting the suggested quantitative threshold value, we feel a (positive) correlation of 0.5 or higher is consistent with the qualitative statements that are made about market definition." (p.85)

[50]   Stigler and Sherwin (1985) make a similar point when discussing whether correlations should be carried out in levels, first differences, logarithms or first differences of logarithms.

[51]   Of course, the benchmark product must be in the same or a very similar industry.

brands and own-brand colas form part of the same relevant market. Hypothetical results are given in Table 10.6.

**Table 10.6: Hypothetical correlation results for Coca-Cola, Pepsi, a minor brand and own-brand colas**    10–036

|             | Coca-Cola | Pepsi | Minor brand | Own-brand |
|-------------|-----------|-------|-------------|-----------|
| Coca-Cola   | 1.00      |       |             |           |
| Pepsi       | 0.77      | 1.00  |             |           |
| Minor brand | 0.81      | 0.79  | 1.00        |           |
| Own-brand   | 0.34      | 0.27  | 0.35        | 1.00      |

On the assumption that Coca-Cola and Pepsi are part of the same relevant market, the benchmark from Table 10.6 is 0.77 as this is the correlation coefficient between Coca-Cola and Pepsi. On the basis of this benchmark, it appears that the minor brand cola is also part of the same relevant product market as Coca-Cola and Pepsi. The correlation coefficients between the minor brand cola and both Coca-Cola and Pepsi are greater than the benchmark correlation. However, the same is not true of own-brand colas. The correlation coefficients between own-brand colas and the other colas are much less than 0.77 as they range between 0.27 and 0.35. On this basis there is no evidence that own-brands are part of the same relevant product market as branded colas.

## Problems with benchmarking

It is intuitively appealing that if Products A and B are in the same product    10–037
market and have a correlation of, say, 0.8, and Product C is more highly correlated with A, then C is in the same product market as A and B. However, there are a number of issues raised by the use of such benchmarking techniques.

The first of these arises because benchmarking involves making a priori judgments. In some instances, such judgments are clear cut or can be supported through other analysis. However, in other cases, the choice of benchmark is less obvious and leaves the benchmarking analysis open to the criticism of arbitrariness. The force of this criticism will depend on the availability of other evidence used to support the choice of benchmark.

Consider the following example.

**10–038 Table 10.7: Hypothetical product market correlations**

|  | Apples | Oranges | Pears | Bananas |
|---|---|---|---|---|
| **Apples** | 1.00 |  |  |  |
| **Oranges** | 0.88 | 1.00 |  |  |
| **Pears** | 0.89 | 0.94 | 1.00 |  |
| **Bananas** | 0.34 | 0.27 | 0.35 | 1.00 |

Suppose it is argued, a priori, that apples and oranges lie in the same relevant market, so that the correlation coefficient between apples and oranges is chosen as the benchmark (i.e. 0.88). On this basis, pears also lie in this relevant market as the correlation coefficients between oranges and pears (0.94) and between apples and pears (0.89) are higher than the correlation between oranges and apples. So the relevant market contains apples, oranges and pears. But if oranges and pears were chosen for the purposes of benchmarking (i.e. 0.94), then the correlation coefficients between apples and oranges (0.88) and between apples and pears (0.89) both lie below the benchmark threshold, suggesting that apples are not part of the same relevant market as pears and oranges.

This illustrates not only that benchmarking is sensitive to the choice of benchmark, but also the fact that a correlation coefficient below the benchmark does not necessarily imply that the two products do not lie in the same relevant market. This latter point is unsurprising given how the benchmark is chosen. Almost by definition, the correlation coefficient between the two benchmark price series will be high. The chosen benchmark is likely to be between two very close substitutes, hence giving a high benchmark price correlation coefficient of, say, 0.9. But this would not necessarily preclude another product, albeit a less effective substitute, also belonging to the same relevant market solely on the grounds that the price correlation coefficient between one of the benchmarking products and the candidate substitute product is only 0.85. For these reasons, the benchmarking exercise can often be considered as at best a "one-tail" test: it can provide evidence which suggests that a product lies in the same relevant market but is less useful in reaching the opposite conclusion.

**10–039**   This is consistent with the Commission's approach in *Ryanair/Aer Lingus*. The Commission used correlation analysis to help define relevant geographic markets for point-to-point air travel. In particular, they wanted to analyse whether different airport-pairs (e.g. Dublin-Manchester compared to Dublin-Liverpool) were part of the same relevant market. The Commission used as its benchmark the average correlation between the fares charged by Ryanair and Aer Lingus on those routes where they served the same airport pairs (e.g. Dublin-Birmingham, Dublin-Bristol and so on). This gave a benchmark of 0.69. The Commission then decided that correlation coefficients between airport-pairs above this figure provided evidence that the airport-pairs were part of the same market. So the correlation coefficient between Dublin-Newcastle (Aer Lingus) and Dublin-Durham Tees Valley (Ryanair) of 0.81 was considered as providing evidence that these two airport-pairs were part of the same market. However, when the correlation coefficient was below the benchmark of 0.69 then the Commission considered that the result was unclear. Thus the correlation coefficient between Dublin-Amsterdam (Aer Lingus) and Dublin-Eindhoven (Ryanair) was 0.45. The Commission stated that:

> "The Commission's own empirical analysis (price correlation) is not conclusive as to whether services between Dublin and either of the two airports lie within the same catchment area." (para.202)[52]

The alert reader will have noticed that in Table 10.4 above, which reproduces the Commission's results from their correlation analysis in *Ryanair/Aer Lingus*, the Commission held that a correlation coefficient above 0.69 implied "one market" whilst a correlation below 0.69 did not imply "two markets" but was considered "inconclusive".

The conclusion to be drawn from this section is that benchmarking **10–040** provides a response, albeit a partial one, to the criticism that price correlation analysis does not offer a "threshold" value. First, it seems clear that benchmarks can provide a threshold value for a one-tailed test that provides evidence that a particular product or area is part of a relevant market. Secondly, benchmarks can provide a two-tailed test where the benchmark is substantially above the correlations for other candidate products or areas. Thus, if the benchmark is, say, 0.8 and the correlation between two products or areas is, say, 0.3, then this provides evidence that is at least strongly suggestive that the products are in different relevant markets. As with all empirical analysis, ultimately the investigator needs to exercise careful judgement.

## Price correlation analysis and variable exchange rates

In European competition law investigations, a common issue is the degree **10–041** to which producers in one Member State are constrained by producers located in other Member States. This raises the issue of how to take into account the fact that prices in some Member States are denominated in different currencies.[53]

On the face of it, this should not provide any problems. Simply convert all the price series into a common currency and then carry out the correlation analysis on these adjusted series. However, it is not as simple as this.

---

[52] COMP/M.4439 *Ryanair/Aer Lingus* (June 27, 2007).
[53] To our knowledge, this problem has not been the subject of any research, probably reflecting the fact that the majority of papers concerning the use of price correlation analysis in competition law investigations originated in the United States. Clearly, the problem of differing exchange rate regimes does not arise in US antitrust investigations.

The problem is that converting price series into a common currency imposes a common factor on the price series and this has the effect of raising the price correlations artificially. We can demonstrate this with a simple hypothetical example.

First, we generated three prices series that are entirely independent of each other. We call these series France, Belgium and Germany. We then converted them to a common currency by converting the Belgium and Germany series into French Francs using the relevant exchange rates from the period 1996–98 (i.e. before the Euro). The resulting correlations are shown in Table 10.8.

10–042  **Table 10.8: Imposing a common exchange rate on independent series: French francs**

|  | France | Belgium | Germany |
|---|---|---|---|
| **France** | 1.00 |  |  |
| **Belgium** | −0.11 | 1.00 |  |
| **Germany** | −0.07 | 0.82 | 1.00 |

What is striking about these results is the very high correlation between Belgium and Germany, even though the underlying price series are not related. The France/Belgium and France/Germany correlations are much lower, consistent with the price series not being related, because we have not imposed a common factor on them (i.e. the French price series has not been converted unlike the other two price series). We get a similar result if we put all the prices into German marks, but now the high correlation is between France and Belgium. This is shown in Table 10.9.

10–043  **Table 10.9: Imposing a common exchange rate on independent series: German marks**

|  | France | Belgium | Germany |
|---|---|---|---|
| **France** | 1.00 |  |  |
| **Belgium** | 0.72 | 1.00 |  |
| **Germany** | 0.21 | 0.29 | 1.00 |

Finally, we convert the three price series into a third-party currency. We use sterling and get the following results. Now all three correlations are high despite the lack of any underlying relationship between them.

**Table 10.10: Imposing a common exchange rate on indepen-** 10–044
**dent series: Sterling**

|         | France | Belgium | Germany |
|---------|--------|---------|---------|
| France  | 1.00   |         |         |
| Belgium | 0.90   | 1.00    |         |
| Germany | 0.90   | 0.94    | 1.00    |

These results make it clear that using price correlations across exchange rate regimes is likely to lead to spurious correlations because of the imposition of a common factor on at least some of the price series.[54]

The problem identified here would not exist if prices always adjusted to exchange rate shocks instantaneously. In this case, variations in exchange rates would never change relative prices and there would be no problems caused for correlation analysis by exchange rate movements. This implies that the problem lies in the fact the price adjustment to exchange rate shocks is not instantaneous but instead takes place over several periods.[55] Figure 10.6 shows the implication of this. Figure 10.6 shows the variation in the relative price of a product in two countries (Domestic and Foreign). It is assumed that both countries form part of the same geographic market. The figure shows the effect of an exchange rate shock in which the domestic currency depreciates sharply. The short-run effect of the depreciation is that the price of the foreign product in domestic currency increases markedly, with the result that the prices in the two countries diverge markedly. However, over time they readjust back towards equilibrium levels, as one would expect if the two countries form part of the same relevant market.

---

[54] Annex 10.1 to this chapter contains a more technical explanation of why using price correlation analysis across exchange rate areas is not in general valid and is likely to lead to spurious correlations.

[55] Theoretical work incorporating uncertainty into the decisions of firms indicates that firms will be less sensitive to exchange rate fluctuations than traditional theory would suggest. In other words, sluggish adjustment to exchange rate fluctuations are to be expected. The reader is referred to Dixit and Pindyck (1993) for details.

**10–045** **Figure 10.6: Price of foreign goods relative to domestic goods in domestic currency**

It is clear that in this case the correlation coefficient between the price series for the two countries is unlikely to be very informative. The decline in the price of the foreign good after the exchange rate shock and the rise in the price of the domestic price are consistent with the two products being in the same geographic market, but mean that the correlation coefficient will be negative for the period after the exchange rate shock. For the 18 months after the exchange rate shock, the correlation in Figure 10.6 is −0.96. On this basis, the results of price correlation analysis indicate that the two countries lie in separate relevant markets, even though a sensible interpretation of the data is that they lie in the same market.

The effect discussed above assumes that if two products are in the same relevant market, then their exchange rate adjusted prices should move together even in the presence of exchange rate shocks. There is a range of models in which it is not true, including a simple Bertrand differentiated products model. The following example illustrates.[56]

**10–046**   Consider two firms, one domestic and one foreign, that compete in prices in a differentiated products industry. The two firms compete in a two-period model in which exchange rates can change in both periods. Further (and crucially) assume that demand in the second period is positively related to sales in the first period. This assumption can be motivated by the existence of brand loyalty, switching costs, network externalities, customer tie-ins and so on. Consider the effect of a temporary appreciation of the domestic currency on the prices of the foreign good. There are three effects at work here. First, the foreign firm now has lower costs denominated in the domestic currency and so should lower the price it sets in the domestic market. Further, this should increase its sales in the first period and so increase demand in the second period (so the price reduction is an

---

[56]   This example is taken from Froot and Klemperer (1989).

investment in future sales). On the other hand, the fact that the exchange rate appreciation is only temporary (or at least is expected to be only temporary) means that a given level of domestic profits are worth more to the foreign firm now than they will be in future (when the exchange rate has depreciated again). This latter effect suggests that the foreign firm should raise the price that it charges in the domestic market. The domestic firm also faces an incentive to change his price, over and above that created by the change in his rival's price. If the exchange rate appreciation is expected to be only temporarily, then this implies that domestic interest rates will be expected to be higher this period than next.[57] The higher current interest rate increases the value of current revenue and so reduces the incentive to invest in market share via lower prices, and hence raises domestic prices.

It is thus quite possible that the price movements of the two products in terms of the domestic currency will be different. The domestic price might rise (due to the interest rate effect) whilst the lower costs of the foreign firm in domestic terms might lead the foreign firm to reduce prices. Whether the foreign firm will actually lower prices or raise them depends on the relative strengths of the two effects that it faces. The cost effect and investment in future sales effect may be large enough to outweigh the added benefit of current profits, or they might not. If the foreign firm's demand in the domestic market is relatively inelastic, then reducing prices will not increase current sales much and so will not increase future sales much. In this case, the current profits effect is likely to dominate. But if current demand is elastic, then the increase in future sales from a price cut may outweigh the current profits effect. So it is quite possible that with variable exchange rates and future returns to current market share, the prices of two products that are in the same relevant market may not move together over the short run.

## Conclusions on using correlation analysis across exchange rate regimes

It should be clear that, at a minimum, great care should be taken when **10–047** using price correlation analysis to define relevant markets across variable exchange rate areas. Indeed, our view is that this should be avoided wherever possible. Of course, the significance of this issue within Europe has declined with the introduction of the Euro, but even now there are a significant number of European countries outside the system (e.g. Denmark, Norway, Sweden and the United Kingdom). Furthermore, the issue of concern is often whether relevant geographic markets are wider than just

---

[57] Without dealing with the technical macroeconomic theory involved here, suffice to say that lower interest rates next period are necessary to induce the depreciation in the currency.

Europe. In these cases, the warning about price correlation analysis continues to hold.

It might be thought that price correlation analysis is still valid if exchange rates only vary a "little bit". However, it does not appear to be the case that exchange rates vary only a little. The two charts below show the variation in the dollar, euro, yen and sterling in the period from the beginning of 2003 to the end of 2007. The exchange rate series in these charts exhibit considerable volatility. The difference between the lowest and highest exchange rate for each currency is 43 per cent for the Euro-dollar exchange rate, 22 per cent for the Yen-dollar exchange rate and 35 per cent for the sterling-dollar exchange rate.

**10–048**   **Figure 10.7: Euro-US dollar and Sterling-US dollar exchange rates (2003–7)**

Source: *http://www.oanda.com*

**Figure 10.8: Yen-US dollar exchange rate (2003–7)**

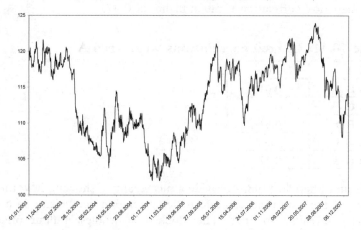

Source: *http://www.oanda.com*

## Periodicity and lags

The correlation coefficient is potentially affected by the frequency of data **10–050** with which it is calculated. In many markets, prices do not adjust instantaneously. Instead, there is often a degree of time lag before prices react to changes elsewhere in the industry. Recognition of this fact is important in determining whether it is appropriate to use daily prices or whether weekly, monthly or even annual prices provide a better reflection of the competitive process.

So an important question for an investigator to answer is what periodicity of data to use and whether to use lags. For instance, should they use weekly, monthly or annual data? Should they correlate current values of one series with lagged values of another? The simple answer is that the data that is used must be appropriate to show any competitive interaction between prices that might exist. Thus, if competitive effects are transmitted only with a delay between price series, perhaps because the prices are for geographically separate areas, then contemporaneous correlations probably will not show this competitive interaction. An example should make this clear.

Consider the following situation. We are concerned with the potential competitive pressure exerted on prices in Area A by prices in Areas B and C. Areas A and B are contiguous, whilst Area C is overseas (e.g. think retail mortgages in the Republic of Ireland, Northern Ireland and Great Britain). Consider the following correlation results. The contemporaneous correlations between Area A and the other two areas are both very low (0.01 and −0.15), but the lagged correlation between Area A and Area B is relatively high (at 0.61). This suggests that competitive effects from Area B impact on Area A with a one period delay. The results for Area C suggest that the

525

delay is longer. The correlation lagged one period is still low (−0.02) but the four period correlation is much higher at 0.47.

**10–051   Table 10.11: Lagged correlations with Area A**

| Area A | 1.00 |
|---|---|
| Area B | 0.01 |
| Area C | −0.15 |
| Area B-1 | 0.61 |
| Area C-1 | −0.02 |
| Area C-4 | 0.47 |

Stigler and Sherwin (1985) provide a nice example showing how the periodicity of the data used can affect the correlation coefficients in a competitively revealing manner. They looked at wholesale flour prices in Minneapolis, Kansas City, Buffalo and Portland (Oregon) over an 11-year period. They had a strong prior belief that Minneapolis and Kansas City were part of the same relevant market and so used the correlation between these two cities as their benchmark. This correlation was 0.92.[58] The correlations using monthly data for the four cities are shown in Table 10.12. This shows that the correlation between Minneapolis and Buffalo is above the benchmark, but the other correlations are all below the benchmark, but still relatively high (0.77–0.88). A reasonable interpretation of these results would be that there is competitive interaction between the four cities, but not in general as close as that between Minneapolis and Kansas. This conclusion is perhaps not surprising. Buffalo is about double the distance from Minneapolis and Kansas City than they are from each other, but much closer than Portland.[59]

**10–052   Table 10.12: Wholesale flour price correlations: monthly data 1971–1981**

| | Minneapolis | Kansas City | Portland | Buffalo |
|---|---|---|---|---|
| Minneapolis | 1.00 | | | |
| Kansas City | 0.92 | 1.00 | | |
| Portland | 0.81 | 0.77 | 1.00 | |
| Buffalo | 0.98 | 0.88 | 0.81 | 1.00 |

[58]   This was the correlation of the first differences of the logarithms of prices.
[59]   Minneapolis and Kansas City are about 440 miles apart, whilst Buffalo is 950 and 1,010 miles respectively from them. Portland is 1,720 miles from Minneapolis, 1,820 from Kansas City and 2,670 from Buffalo.

However, we might expect that correlations using annual data would show significantly different levels of competitive interaction over this longer time period. That is precisely what Stigler and Sherwin's data shows.

**Table 10.13: Wholesale flour price correlations: annual data**   10–053
**1971–1981**

|            | Minneapolis | Kansas City | Portland | Buffalo |
|------------|-------------|-------------|----------|---------|
| Minneapolis | 1.00        |             |          |         |
| Kansas City | 0.98        | 1.00        |          |         |
| Portland    | 0.96        | 0.99        | 1.00     |         |
| Buffalo     | 0.99        | 0.97        | 0.95     | 1.00    |

In general, common sense and the available data will suggest the correct approach. Competitive responses will tend to be quicker when markets are more transparent and more sales are taking place. Thus, one would expect competitive responses to be quicker for fast moving consumer goods than for intermediate goods.

# ECONOMETRIC PRICE TESTS: GRANGER CAUSALITY, COINTEGRATION AND UNIT ROOT TESTS

In recent years there has been an increased focus on the use of econometric   **10–054** tests on price series as complements to correlation analysis.[60] These include tests for Granger causality, unit roots and cointegration. This section focuses on these econometric tests. We explain the logic underlying them and discuss their advantages, and disadvantages, compared to standard correlation analysis.

The econometric tests appear to offer more precise and statistically robust results than mere price correlation tests. However, as we argue below, the advantages of these tests for market definition are more apparent than real. This is partly due to the way in which the tests are typically used and partly due to the nature of the tests. Investigators often seem to confuse the fact that there is a statistically significant relationship between two price series as implying that there is an economically significant relationship between them. Further, in common with many empirical tests, neither Granger causality nor cointegration tests address directly the fundamental issues underpinning market definition. As such,

---

[60]   See, for instance, Forni (2004), Mncube (2007), Boshoff (2007), Coe and Krause (2008), Hosken and Taylor (2004) and various Competition Authority cases such as *Nutreco/Hydro Seafood* in the UK and COMP/M.2187 *CVC/Lenzing* (2000) at the EC.

these tests can only ever provide indicative evidence relevant for market definition.

In the rest of this chapter we first introduce the various econometric price tests and then provide a critique of them.

## Granger Causality

**10–055** Standard regression techniques assume that there is a cause and effect relationship between the dependent variable and the independent variables. In determining the economic model to be estimated, prior knowledge of economic theory is typically drawn upon, taking into account the particular characteristics of the industry under investigation. It is unavoidable, however, that some assumptions about the direction and degree of causality between variables need to be made. The need to examine these assumptions has led to the development of the concept of Granger causality.[61]

A variable X is said to Granger-cause another variable, Y, if taking into account past values of variable X leads to improvements in the predictions of variable Y. There are three dimensions of Granger causality to consider: whether X causes Y; whether Y causes X; and whether there exists instantaneous causality whereby X causes Y and Y causes X.

The use of the concept of Granger causality in competition law inquiries can be illustrated with reference to market definition. If two products, X and Y, form part of the same market, then one would expect the price of X to affect the price of Y and vice versa. This suggests that the predictions of the price of Y obtained using available information on the prices of X and Y will be better than those obtained using only information on the price of Y. The same would be true for predictions of the price of X.

**10–056** At first sight it appears that Granger-causality tests have obvious attractions for market definition and indeed they have been frequently used in the academic literature.[62] If Product X is in the same product market as Product Y, then it would be expected that there is some link between the price series of the two products. For instance, if two regions form part of the same relevant geographic market, a disturbance in one region will spill over into the other region and the data should indicate that the price in one region Granger-causes the price in the other region. In contrast, if the two regions are sufficiently distinct, there should be no spill-over and the data should not indicate Granger causality between the regions.

In order to make the discussion more concrete, consider the example contained in Slade (1986). Slade investigated the extent of the geographic market for wholesale petroleum products in the United States. Specifically,

---

[61] Granger (1969).
[62] See Slade (1986), Cartwright, Kamerschen and Huang (1989), Bessler and Brandt (1982), Howell (1984), Huang (1987), Uri, Howell and Rifkin (1985), Klein Rifkin and Uri (1985), Uri and Rifkin (1985) and Werden and Froeb (1993).

she was primarily interested in whether the South-eastern United States was part of the same geographic market as the North-east and, to a lesser extent, whether both of these areas were part of the same market as the western seaboard. Slade used Granger-causality tests to analyse the extent of the relevant market.

Slade found Granger causality between all the city pairs within the South-east, but for only five of the eight South-east/North-east city pairs for which she had data. She found no Granger causality between the South-east/West Coast city pairs. The conclusion that she draws from this is that:

> "the interior of the South-eastern part of the United States is a local geographic market that is loosely connected to the North-eastern seaboard and is entirely separate from the West Coast".[63]

---

**BOX 10.4: TESTING FOR GRANGER CAUSALITY**     10–057

Letting $P^k$ be the price in region k, the null hypothesis that Slade tested is that $P^k$ is exogenous to the system that determines $P^j$, and vice versa. The following two equations are used to test this hypothesis.

$$(11) \quad P_t^j = \sum_{i=1}^{L} \alpha_{ij} P_{t-i}^j + g_1^j(Z_t) + \varepsilon_t^j$$

$$(12) \quad P_t^j = \sum_{i=1}^{M} \beta_{ij} P_{t-i}^j + \sum_{i=1}^{M} \gamma_{ij} P_{t-i}^k + g_2^j(Z_t) + \eta_t^j$$

where $\varepsilon^j$ and $\eta^j$ are disturbance terms with zero means, $Z_t$ are exogenous variables whose exogeneity is not being tested, $G(Z_t)$ is a linear function of the $Z_t$ and $\alpha_{ij}$, $\beta_{ij}$ and $\gamma_{ij}$ are standard regression coefficients. Any common factors, such as the price of common inputs, which might lead to the appearance of spurious Granger causality if they were omitted are included among the $Z_t$ variables. The test for Granger causality that Slade uses is that the inclusion of the $P^k$ variables in Equation (12) does not significantly increase the explanatory power of Equation (12) relative to Equation (11). This is equivalent to whether the data rejects the restriction that $\gamma_{ij} = 0$ for all i.

---

## Cointegration analysis

A series is said to be stationary if it has constant mean and variance (i.e. **10–058** these do not vary over time). A stationary series is said to be integrated of order zero, or I(0). A series that is not stationary, but becomes stationary

---

[63]  at p.301.

when it is differenced once, is I(1). A series that requires differencing twice before becoming stationary is said to be I(2), and so on. Suppose that a variable x is described by the equation $x_t = x_{t-1} + u_t$ where $u_t$ is a normally distributed innovation with mean zero. Then x is I(1). This is because x does not have a constant mean and variance (indeed its variance is infinite), but the first difference of x (i.e. $x_t - x_{t-1}$) is stationary because it is equal to $u_t$.

Consider two time series, x and y, that are both I(d) where d≥1. In general, a linear combination of the two will also be I(d). However, if there is a linear combination such that $z_t = y_t - a - b\, x_t$ is $I(d-b)$, $b≥1$, then the two series are said to be cointegrated.[64] In general, and throughout this chapter, the term cointegrated is used to refer to I(1) variables which have a linear combination that is I(0). What it means for two variables to be cointegrated is that there is a stable long run relationship between them. In terms of the above cointegrating equation, $z_t$ can be interpreted as the equilibrium error (i.e. the distance that the system is away from the equilibrium at any point in time).

Engle and Granger suggested that substitutes in the same market might be one example of cointegrated variables.[65] Whalen has argued similarly and applied the technique for the delineation of relevant markets.[66]

## Unit root tests

**10–059**  If two products are in the same market, then it is reasonable to expect that there would tend to be a long-run equilibrium relationship between their prices. This implies that if there is a shock that changes one of the prices, this should only have a temporary effect on the relationship between their prices. Thus, if a shock leads to the price of one product (Product A) falling, thereby implying that its relative price is below the long-run equilibrium, then we should expect to see either the price of the other product (Product B) falling, or the price of Product B falling and Product A rising, or the price of Product A rising again. However, if there is no long-run equilibrium relationship then we would not expect to see relative prices returning to an equilibrium level after a shock to one of the price series. A unit root test is a test of whether there is a long-run equilibrium between two price series. As noted below, unit roots tests are very similar to tests for whether price series are cointegrated.

The standard approach to testing for a unit root is to test whether $\rho=1$ in the following equation:

(13)  $P_{A,t} - P_{B,t} = \rho(P_{A,t-1} - P_{B,t-1}) + \varepsilon_t$

where  $P_{A,t}$ is the log of the price of Product A at time t;

[64]  This definition was introduced by Engle and Granger (1987).
[65]  Engle and Granger (1987).
[66]  Whalen (1990).

$P_{B,t}$ is the log of the price of Product B at time t; and

$\varepsilon_t$ is a random variable with mean zero and no serial correlation.

If $\rho$ is greater than or equal to 1, then this implies that any shock this period affects the relationship between the price series permanently. However, if $\rho$ is less than 1, then this means that the effect of a shock dies away over time and so the long-run equilibrium is restored. The test that is most commonly used for whether $\rho=1$ is a Dickey-Fuller test.[67] The null hypothesis is that $\rho \geq 1$ and so the test is whether this null is rejected, in which case $\rho < 0$. If $\rho < 0$ then there is not a unit root and the two price series are considered as part of the same relevant market.[68] If the null is not rejected, then it is not possible to say that shocks do not last permanently and so it is not possible to say that there is a long-run equilibrium relationship between the two series.

It should be noted that this test can only be used if the individual price **10–060** series are not themselves both stationary. If the two price series are stationary then there will be a long-run equilibrium relationship between them even if they are entirely unrelated. This is intuitively clear. If both price series have constant mean and variance, then we would expect the ratio of their prices to tend to a constant (i.e. $\mu_A/\mu_B$ where $\mu_A$ and $\mu_B$ are the means of prices series A and B respectively).

One advantage claimed for this test is that because it looks at the ratio of two price series, it is immune from the problems that bedevil correlation analysis in the presence of variable exchange rates. The logic is that if there is an exchange rate shock leading to a change in relative prices, then the ratio of the two price series will revert to its equilibrium level only if the two products are in the same relevant market. If the ratio does revert, this should be shown by stationarity in the ratio.

## The use of econometric price tests in Commission decisions

The use of price tests employing the econometric concepts of Granger **10–061** causality, cointegration and unit roots in EC competition law is relatively infrequent.[69] However, the Commission has either itself employed or been presented with submissions using both tests. In *Mannesmann/Vallourec/Ilva*,[70] the parties submitted evidence employing the results of Granger causality tests. In *Lonrho/Gencor* and *CVC/Lenzing*,[71] the Commission itself

---

[67] Dickey and Fuller (1979). In fact, an *augmented* Dickey-Fuller test is often used. This is similar to the standard Dickey-Fuller test but is used to remove any serial correlation in the error term of Equation (13).

[68] For technical reasons, Equation (13) is usually estimated using the first difference of the log of the ratio of the price series. This means that the coefficient on the lagged log of the ratio of the price series on the right-hand side of Equation (13) becomes $\rho-1$. The test then becomes whether this coefficient is less than zero.

[69] This is in contrast to the use of price correlation analysis.

[70] IV/M315 *Mannesmann/Vallourec/Ilva* [1994] OJ L102/15.

[71] IV/M619 *Lonrho/Gencor* [1997] OJ L11/30 and COMP/M2187 *CVC/Lenzing* (2000).

employed cointegration tests as an aid to assessing the extent of the relative product market. We also briefly discuss a UK Competition Commission case, *Nutreco/Hydro Seafood*.[72]

### *Mannesmann/Vallourec/Ilva*

**10–062** Granger causality tests were carried out using monthly data from 1979 to 1993 to examine whether the United States, the European Union and Eastern Europe were part of the same relevant market for seamless stainless steel tubes. The test was carried out by examining the following relationship:

(14) $\quad y_t = \beta_0 + \Sigma_s \beta_s x_{t-s} + \varepsilon_t$

where $y_t$ denotes the price at time $t$ in Region Y; and

$\quad\quad x_{t-s}$ denotes the price in Region X at time $t-s$.

The test is essentially a test for whether or not the coefficients $\beta_s$ are jointly zero. If the coefficients are found to be jointly zero, then prices in Region X do not Granger-cause those in Region Y. This is assumed to imply that X and Y are not in the same market.

The results of the Granger-causality tests indicated strongly that all three markets were linked. US and EU prices were shown to Granger-cause each other with a high degree of statistical certainty. Eastern European prices were shown to Granger-cause US and EU prices, although the effect of EU and US prices on Eastern European prices was shown to be less (in statistical terms) than the effect of Eastern European prices on EU and US prices. It was argued that such results indicated that the three regions formed one relevant geographic market.

### *Lonrho/Gencor*

**10–063** The degree of cointegration between price series has also been used as a test of market definition. The Merger Task Force (MTF) used it in its 1996 analysis of the proposed merger between Lonrho and Gencor. The Merger Task Force:

"proceeded with a cointegration analysis of the data set of the prices of platinum, rhodium and palladium as well as gold and silver prices. Cointegration analysis is an econometric method which can test whether there is a system equilibrium (or long-run) relationship between two or more time-series of data. The results of the analysis show that the data do not suggest any equilibrium (or long-run) relationship between the respective price levels of platinum, rhodium, palladium, gold and silver, nor of any subset of these metals. This

---

[72] "Nutreco Holding NV and Hydro Seafood GSP Ltd: A report on the proposed merger", UK Competition Commission, Cm. 5004, December 12, 2000.

econometric analysis of metal prices indicates that platinum, rhodium, palladium, gold and silver prices tend to vary, over the long run, independently of each other, thus confirming the view that platinum, rhodium, palladium, gold and silver are separate relevant product markets."[73]

This quotation from the decision makes it clear that the MTF interpreted the absence of cointegration as confirmation that the five products lay in separate relevant product markets.

## CVC/Lenzing[74]

Co-integration tests were carried out to check the validity of some corre-  **10–064** lation analysis results. The Commission found relatively high correlations between commodity viscose staple fibres (VSF) and spun-dyed VSF and between commodity VSF and polyester. However, the Commission was concerned that these results were driven not by competitive interactions between the three products but by the presence of common costs and trends. To test this proposition they carried out a co-integration analysis. The Commission argued thus:

> "*Common trends*: For this purpose a test of co-integration has been carried out by the Commission. In general terms, a test of co-integration is based on the assumption that two series of data should not diverge in the long run if the products concerned belong to the same market, in which case such series in econometric jargon are called *stationary*. By contrast, if commodity VSF and spun-dyed VSF belong to two different markets, the relative price between the two time-series will have to be *non-stationary*, that is to say a high degree of correlation between the two time-series will be due to a common trend. Indeed, the results of the statistical tests in the present case (see explanations on the Unit-root Test below) have always remained below the critical values. It is therefore justified to conclude that commodity VSF and spun-dyed VSF do not belong to the same market.
>
> *Unit-root Test*: The Commission has used an ADF test and examined the null hypothesis that the relative prices between commodity VSF and spun-dyed VSF are non-stationary. Specifically, if the test result is lower than the critical value, it fails to reject the null hypothesis, that is to say, relative prices do not revert to some long-run equilibrium and two products do not belong to the same relevant market." (fn. 83)

[73] IV/M619 *Lonrho/Gencor* [1994] OJ L102/15 at p.37.
[74] COMP/M.2187 *CVC/Lenzing* (2000).

As we discuss below, this is statistically a very weak test. The Commission says that its test "fails to reject the null hypothesis" and so the price series are not cointegrated. However, a failure to reject one hypothesis (presumably at 90 per cent or 95 per cent confidence level) does not automatically mean that an alternative hypothesis is correct. All it means is that you cannot be 90 per cent sure (or 95 per cent sure) that the null hypothesis was rejected.

### Nutreco Holdings and Hydro Seafood GSP[75]

**10–065**  The UK Competition Commission (CC) case assessed Nutreco's acquisition of Hydro Seafood from Norsk Hydro in the United Kingdom, France, Ireland and Norway. Product market definition was controversial and so the parties submitted, in addition to a correlation analysis, an analysis of stationarity. The parties looked at the relative prices of Scottish and Norwegian salmon in the United Kingdom and in France. They used an augmented Dickey-Fuller test and found that the null hypothesis of no stationarity could be rejected and, thus, that the series were stationary. The implication of this was that Norwegian salmon and Scottish salmon were in the same relevant product market.[76] Note that the test required rejection a null hypothesis and so was much more powerful than the test used by the European Commission in *CVC/Lenzing*, which just involved not being able to reject a null hypothesis.

The Competition Commission noted that this result could have been driven by the presence of common costs, but then found on further investigation that this was unlikely as the most likely common cost, fish feed, had actually moved in different directions in the various geographic markets. In addition, the Competition Commission also carried out a stationarity test for salmon feed pricing in Norway and the United Kingdom and found that the relative prices were not stationarity (or rather, that the null hypothesis of non-stationarity could not be rejected). The Competition Commission concluded that this result was "not consistent with there being competitive interaction between the UK and Norwegian markets" for salmon feed.

---

[75] "Nutreco Holding NV and Hydro Seafood GSP Ltd: A report on the proposed merger", UK Competition Commission, Cm. 5004, 22/12/2000.

[76] Although this was not reported in the decision, it appears that a stationarity test was also carried out by the parties for geographic market definition and that this concluded that there was a wide geographic market covering Europe. For some further details, see Lexecon Competition Memo, June 2001.

**Analytical issues arising in the use of econometric price tests.**

*Granger-causality*

Market definition is not concerned with the concept of Granger causality in   **10–066**
the strict statistical sense of the word. This is because a correctly specified
Granger-causality test may reject the notion that Product B Granger-
causes Product A even though both products are part of the same market.
For example, suppose that there are three products, A, B and C, which all
exert competitive pressure on each other and are in the same product
market on the basis of any sensible antitrust analysis. In order to show this
one might attempt to show that Product C Granger-causes Product A. To
test this a regression of the price of Product A on past prices of A and B and
all other relevant factors is compared with the same regression but with the
addition of the past prices of C. But it might be found that adding in the
past prices of C does not add to the explanatory power of our equation.[77]
On the basis of this approach to Granger-causality, C is not part of the
same market as A and B. The reason for this result is that the price of C
does not contain any additional information on the price of A beyond that
already contained in B. But this clearly does not mean that it is necessarily
in a different market. For instance, if the prices of C and B were perfectly
correlated (because they are perfect substitutes, say) then the price of C
would not add any more information than the price of B. Hence, it would
appear that the price of C did not Granger-cause the price of A.

What this serves to underline is that in fact the literature does not
recommend carrying out a proper Granger-causality test. Instead, it suggests investigating the explanatory power of the lags of one price series on
another (i.e. estimating an autoregressive lag equation). In so doing, the
investigator risks mis-specifying the model and drawing incorrect inferences. A regression of the lags of y on x might lead to a conclusion of
apparent Granger causality because y is highly correlated with z and z does
Granger-cause x. One obvious reason might be that there are common
costs, z, involved in the manufacture of x and y. So the investigator needs
to ensure that the equation is well specified and that his or her results are
not being driven by omitted variables. In other words, an econometric
modelling exercise of the determination of x is required. Slade notes this
when she writes that:

> "For a given application, the determination of the relevant universe of
> information rests on considerations of economic theory and institu-
> tional practice. The choice is no more (or less) difficult than the choice
> of appropriate variables to include in any behavioural equation. And

---

[77] Formally, the correct test of Granger causality would be to run the first regression and then
regress the residuals from this equation on the price of C to see if the residuals are an
innovation relative to the price of C.

just as with structural models, omission of relevant variables leads to mis-specification and results in biased estimators."[78]

In this case, why not estimate formal demand equations and derive elasticities that allow a direct answer to the Hypothetical Monopolist test to be calculated? The practical answer is that in most actual cases there will be insufficient quantity data available and so elasticities cannot be estimated. However, this should not disguise the fact that the estimation of an auto-gressive lag equation is an imperfect substitute for a proper econometric investigation.

## *Statistical significance versus economic significance*

**10–067**  A further, more serious, problem with Granger-causality tests is that they seem to lead to a confusion of statistical significance with economic significance. There appears to be an unwritten assumption in the literature that statistical significance equates to economic significance and so if X Granger-causes Y, then they must be in the same market. For instance, Cartwright et al[79] claim that Granger causality has several advantages over correlation analysis, one of which is that it does not suffer from the problem that "the determination of the price correlation level that is 'high' enough to define a market is arbitrary".

However, the fact that the price of one product appears to Granger-cause the price of another product, and vice versa, does not show that they exert enough competitive pressure on each other to be in the same market. All that it shows is that one can be certain at the 95 per cent level (or whatever significance level is chosen) that the price of one product affects the price of another. The competitive constraint imposed by that product may nonetheless be insufficient to make unprofitable a price rise of 5–10 per cent above the competitive level by a hypothetical monopolist. The prices of two products could Granger-cause each other without their being in the same market and, equally, the prices of two products might not Granger-cause each other even though they are in the same market.

This point is illustrated by the following two examples. In both examples, the question is whether Product X lies in the same relevant product market as Product Y. How useful is Granger causality in answering this question? In both examples three lags of X and three lags of Y are regressed on the price of Y in order to see whether the inclusion of the price of X gives a statistically significantly better estimate of Y. The data used in Table 10.14 is high quality scanner data with high periodicity (i.e. daily) and a long time series. The data used in Table 10.15 is much less high

---

[78]  Slade (1986) p.295.
[79]  Cartwright, Kamerschen and Huang (1989).

quality with low periodicity (i.e. monthly) and significant measurement inaccuracies.

**Table 10.14: Granger causality indicates a wide market**     10–068

|  | Coefficient | t-statistic | Coefficient | t-statistic |
|---|---|---|---|---|
| Constant | −2.22 | −2.00 | −0.22 | −0.24 |
| Y-1 | 0.85 | 183.89 | 0.86 | 183.95 |
| Y-2 | 0.10 | 19.45 | 0.10 | 18.81 |
| Y-3 | 0.02 | 4.76 | 0.02 | 4.97 |
| X-1 | 0.01 | 1.08 |  |  |
| X-2 | 0.01 | 2.51 |  |  |
| X-3 | 0.01 | 1.59 |  |  |
| RSq | 0.997 |  | 0.997 |  |
| RSS | 20.93 |  | 23.23 |  |
| No. Obs. | 100 |  | 100 |  |
| F-test | 3.42 | (97.94) |  |  |

The F-test statistics (of 3.42) indicates that at the 95 per cent confidence level past prices of X Granger-cause the current price of Y. If it is thought that Granger causality is a reasonable indication of the extent of antitrust markets, then X and Y are in the same antitrust market.

**Table 10.15: Granger causality indicates a narrow market**     10–069

|  | Coefficient | t-statistic | Coefficient | t-statistic |
|---|---|---|---|---|
| Constant | −0.18 | −0.01 | 38.65 | 1.35 |
| Y-1 | 0.34 | 2.28 | 0.43 | 2.92 |
| Y-2 | 0.20 | 1.21 | 0.21 | 1.28 |
| Y-3 | −0.04 | −0.24 | −0.02 | −0.12 |
| X-1 | 0.36 | 2.21 |  |  |
| X-2 | 0.09 | 0.64 |  |  |
| X-3 | 0.06 | 0.41 |  |  |
| RSq | 0.10 |  | 0.07 |  |
| RSS | 22262 |  | 23557 |  |
| No. Obs. | 100 |  | 100 |  |
| F-test | 1.80 | (84.80) |  |  |

In this case the F-test shows that past prices of X do not Granger-cause the current price of Y at the 95 per cent level. The question is, should one be happy to decide that in the first case there is a wide market and in the second there is a narrow market? The answer ought to be "no". In the first case the lags of X were statistically significant, but very small and they added very little to the explanatory power of the equation (i.e. less than 0.1 per cent as the $R^2$ remains 0.997). Although there appears to be a statistically valid relationship between X and Y in this case, it is so small that it is doubtful that the application of the 5 per cent test would place both products in the same market. The opposite is true in the second case. The lower quality of the data makes hard statistical inference uncertain. However, the effect of X on Y is greater than in the first case. Specifically, the coefficient on the first lag of X is now quite large (0.36) and statistically different from zero. The inclusion of the three lags of X increases the explanatory power of the equation by nearly 50 per cent (from an R-Squared of 0.07 to one of 0.10). It may well be (although of course our results do not prove it) that a 5 per cent test would put X and Y in the same antitrust market.

McCloskey and Ziliak (1996) have noted that there is a widespread tendency in the economic literature to confuse statistical significance with economic significance.[80] Indeed, they claim that only 30 per cent of the papers using regression analysis that were published in the *American Economic Review* in the 1980s made this qualification in their conclusions. That is, 70 per cent equated statistical significance with economic significance. But, as the example above shows, the two are not equivalent.

### *Power of tests for cointegration and stationarity*

**10–070** Some of the tests used for cointegration and stationarity can be of low power. For instance, the standard test[81] for whether X and Y are cointegrated is to first test whether X and Y are both I(1), then to estimate the linear combination that is most likely to be cointegrated (by a simple regression of X on Y) and then test whether the null that this combination is I(0) can be rejected. The power of this test is low because the initial test for whether X and Y are I(1) is itself a test of low power. Specifically, the test is whether the null hypothesis of a unit root (i.e. that the series is not stationary but its first difference is) can be rejected. If it cannot, then it is assumed that the series are I(1). But to say that one cannot reject the possibility that a series is I(1) rather than I(0) is very different to saying that it is I(1). There is a considerable scope for a Type II error, i.e. there is considerable scope for deciding that two I(0) series are actually I(1), then finding that a linear combination is definitely not I(1), and so concluding they are cointegrated. But of course if the original series are actually both I(0), a linear combination of them must be I(0).

The implication of this is that investigators need to be very careful to clearly specify whether they have rejected a null hypothesis, which is a strong result, or failed to reject a null hypothesis, which is not a strong

---

[80] McCloskey and Ziliak (1996).
[81] See Dolado, Jenkinson, and Sosvilla-Rivero (1990).

result. In *Ryanair/Aer Lingus*, the Commission found that they could not reject the hypothesis of non-stationarity for flights to, amongst others, the regions around Alicante, Barcelona, Rome, Paris and Toulouse by each of Ryanair and Aer Lingus. They then found that they could reject stationarity for the relative prices of Ryanair and Aer Lingus to each region. The Commission then stated that:

> "At the very least this result does not contradict the qualitative evidence that strongly suggests all the above routes constitute city-pair markets".[82]

This is right: the evidence was consistent with the city-pairs constituting markets, but no more than this. The original test of a lack of stationarity was weak and so it is quite possible that the prices for the two airlines were themselves stationarity, in which case the ratio would obviously be stationary. Indeed, in the case of Paris, the original test had shown the Paris routes to be stationary.

## *Cointegration and stationarity in the short run*

Cointegration is concerned with long-run relationships. It is not clear that   **10–071** this is appropriate for market definition where the concern is with price increases in the medium- or short-term. Consider Figure 10.9. This shows hypothetical monthly prices for two commodities (widgets and gadgets) over an eight-year period (January 1987 to April 1995). The two price series are both I(1), but they are cointegrated. Specifically, the cointegrating equation is:

(15)   $z_t = P_{Gt} - 1.2 P_{Wt}$

where   $P_{Gt}$ is the price of gadgets at time $t$ and
$P_{Wt}$ is the price of widgets at time $t$.
The two price series are cointegrated over the whole time period. However, whilst this relationship is relatively clear from May 1990 onwards, it is much less clear before this date. Indeed, up to March 1989 it appears that the two price series are about equal, rather than the price of gadgets being 20 per cent greater than the price of widgets. This suggests that in cointegrated series it is quite possible to have significant deviations away from the long-run equilibrium in the medium term (certainly of two years or more). Given that competition authorities tend to be concerned with the exercise of market power on a shorter time scale, this implies that cointegration may lead to markets being defined too widely.

---

[82]   Para.38, Annex III, COMP/M.4439 *Ryanair/Aer Lingus* (June 27, 2007).

**10–072** **Figure 10.9: Two cointegrated price series**

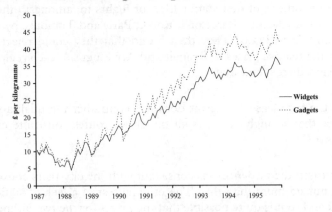

*Econometric price tests bear little relation to the 5 per cent test*

**10–073** It is important to remember that none of these econometric price tests is a direct test of the key market definition question: is this a market worth monopolising? Or, alternatively, how high is the own-price elasticity of the group of products? This is not a criticism that only applies to the econometric price tests: it also holds for correlation analysis. However, in our experience, investigators tend to lose sight of this as soon as they catch sight of an econometric relationship or test statistic. We discussed above the importance of distinguishing between economic and statistical significance. The point here is slightly different. Even if there is a well-defined competitive relationship between two products, that does not necessarily put them in the same relevant market. Perhaps the most obvious example of this would be a Cellophane fallacy case. Suppose a firm with substantial market power has no close competitors at the competitive price level and so has raised prices significantly above the competitive price level. We will refer to this as the "monopolised" product. At some point products that are not close substitutes to this product at the competitive price level will become close substitutes as the price of the monopolised product rises. This is the Cellophane fallacy: cellophane wrapping did not face any close substitutes at the competitive price level but did once DuPont had raised the price of cellophane to a significantly higher level.[83] If we carry out an econometric price test, we might find that these tests suggest that the price of the monopolised product is Granger-caused by other products, or that it is cointegrated with other products, or that its price relative to other products is stationary. However, none of those would mean that the monopolised product was in the same market as these other products if we were dealing with a non-merger case.

[83] *United States v E.I. du Pont de Nemours & Co* 351 U.S. 377 (1956); 76 S. Ct. 994; L. Ed. 1264. See Chapter 4 for a detailed discussion of the Cellophane fallacy.

## *Recent studies on econometric price tests*

An interesting study has been carried out by Forni.[84] It provides an **10-074** interesting insight into the power of cointegration and stationarity tests. Forni tests whether the geographic market for milk in Italy is regional or wider. The data is weekly price data for 105 weeks covering 13 regions of Italy. He tests whether relative prices across regions are stationary, which he believes would indicate a wide geographic market.

He uses two tests. One is the standard augmented Dickey-Fuller test. However, as Forni notes, this has as its null the hypothesis that the series are non-stationary. If the regions are separate relevant markets, then this test would provide a weak test since it would only show that non-stationarity could not be rejected, not that stationarity could be rejected. The other test is that proposed by Kwiatkowski, Phillips, Schmidt and Shin and referred to as KPSS.[85] This has the advantage that the null hypothesis is that the series is stationary and so non-stationarity requires the null to be rejected. However, it should be noted that the small sample properties of the test are not great. First, the test is only asymptotically efficient and the small sample size distortions can be large, particularly in the presence of autocorrelated errors. Secondly, the power of the test is particularly weak in the presence of lags in samples of less than 200.[86]

The results are very interesting. First, stationarity is only not rejected by KPSS in 15 out of the 78 relative price series. This implies that on 63 occasions the relative prices of the regions are not stationary, which is taken to indicate a lack of competitive interaction between them. Of the 15 region-pairs where stationarity is not rejected, non-stationarity is also not rejected by the Augmented Dickey-Fuller test (ADF) on nine occasions. This means that there are six occasions where stationarity was not rejected by KPSS but non-stationarity was rejected by ADF. These are occasions where the evidence would seem to imply that there is competitive interaction between the regions. However, a consideration of the list suggests that the test approach has not worked very well. The six region-pairs are Veneto-Emilia Romagna, Puglia-Piedmont, Puglia-Lombardy, Piedmont-Lombardy, Trentino-Lazio and Tuscany-Calabria. Figure 10.10 illustrates the difficulty.

---

[84] Forni (2004).
[85] Kwiatkowski, Phillips, Schmidt and Shin (1992).
[86] For more details on these issues see, in addition to Kwiatkowshi, Hobijn (1998). See also Elliot, Rothenberg and Stock (1996) and Ng and Perron (2001) for issues related to the efficiency of the ADF test. Hobijn, Franses and Ooms (1998). Elliot, Rothenberg and Stock (1996). Ng and Perron (2001).

**10–075** **Figure 10.10: Map of the Italian regions**

Source: *http://www.goeurope.about.com/cs/italy/l/bl_italy_region.htm*

Four of the six candidate pairs for being part of the same geographic market as each other are not contiguous. It makes no sense to consider Puglia as part of the same market as Piedmont or Lombardy when Puglia is in the south-east and the other two regions are in the north-west. By similar logic, Trentino-Lazio and Tuscany-Calabria make no sense. Veneto-Emilia Romagna and Piedmont-Lombardy do make sense. But it is hard to have much faith in a test that appears to produce nonsensical results.

Another interesting paper is Coe and Krause (2008). They carried out an investigation of the power of a number of price-based tests for market definition. They set up a simulation in which there were three products operating in a differentiated products setting. Two of the products were substitutes, Goods 1 and 2, whilst a third was not. The authors generated 10,000 sets of sample data and then tested the following approaches to market definition: standard correlation analysis; Granger-causality; the ADF test for a unit root; and two tests for cointegration between the logs of the price series.[87]

The results were striking. When the model of competition included firm-specific cost shocks and immediate adjustment to each new equilibrium each period, simple correlation analysis did a very good job of distinguishing between the substitute products and the non-substitute. For

---

[87] These were the Engle and Granger (1987) approach discussed above and the Johansen (1991) procedure.

instance, for T=104 periods, the average correlation analysis between Goods 1 and 2 was 0.76 whilst that between Goods 1 and 3 and Goods 2 and 3 was 0.00. On the other hand, the other approaches all produced very poor results in which there was no difference in rejection rates for the various null hypothesis regardless of whether the products in question were substitutes or not.

As the authors note, however, one would expect the econometric price tests to be more useful on those occasions where competitive responses are sluggish and so price correlation analysis works less well. But the tests do not seem to work well even in the environment for which one would have thought they were designed. Table 10.16 shows the results for Granger-causality for the period length 104.

**Table 10.16: Rejection rates from Coe and Krause: Granger**  10–076
**causality**

| | |
|---|---|
| $GC_{21}$ | 0.456 |
| $GC_{31}$ | 0.055 |
| $GC_{12}$ | 0.460 |
| $GC_{32}$ | 0.055 |
| $GC_{13}$ | 0.053 |
| $GC_{23}$ | 0.056 |

The rejection rate for the null that Good 1 does not Granger-cause Good 2, and vice versa, is 0.46. This is a long way below the correct figure of 0.95 and does not suggest that the test works well.

Table 10.17 shows the results for the ADF test for stationarity. The figure for the ADF test for stationarity is even worse than that for Granger causality. The rejection rate for the relative price of Good 1 and Good 2 being non-stationary is only 0.16, rather than the correct figure of 0.95.

**Table 10.17: Rejection rates from Coe and Krause: ADF test**  10–077
**for stationarity**

| | |
|---|---|
| $ADF_{12}$ | 0.159 |
| $ADF_{13}$ | 0.057 |
| $ADF_{23}$ | 0.063 |

Finally, Table 10.18 shows the results for the two tests for cointegration. The rejection rate for the null of no cointegration is only 0.33 under the Engle-Granger approach and 0.52 under the Johanson approach, again substantially below 0.95. Worse, the Johanson approach over-rejects by more than four times for the cointegration of Good 3 with Goods 1 and 2.

10–078 **Table 10.18: Rejection rates from Coe and Krause: tests for cointegration**

| | |
|---|---|
| $EG_{12}$ | 0.325 |
| $EG_{13}$ | 0.055 |
| $EG_{23}$ | 0.055 |
| $TR_{12}$ | 0.523 |
| $TR_{13}$ | 0.221 |
| $TR_{23}$ | 0.221 |

The authors conclude, with particular reference to the unit root and cointegration tests, that "our results suggest that the application of these tests may not be a fruitful avenue of research in antitrust analysis."[88]

# SUMMARY

10–079 This chapter has focused on the intuition behind price correlation analysis as a tool for defining markets and has highlighted a number of potential weaknesses of the technique. The test has been severely criticised by many commentators, such as Werden and Froeb[89] who criticise the use of price correlation tests on the grounds that such tests do not directly test for market power and therefore can lead to erroneous conclusions. It is true that price correlation analysis does not directly answer the Hypothetical Monopolist test; it can lead to spuriously high correlations unless the analysis is undertaken with care; the issue of benchmarking is not simple; and in general it should not be used across exchange rate regimes. The fact that there are weaknesses places a premium on the evaluation of results and a critical examination of the data used and the assumptions made, particularly in any benchmarking exercise. However, these weaknesses do not imply that price correlation analysis can never be useful. On the contrary, price correlation analysis remains a useful tool for providing preliminary indications as to the extent of competitive relationships between products and regions and hence the definition of the relevant market.

It should be remembered that competition law investigations are usually subject to time and data constraints imposed by a combination of the law, the competition authorities and the parties involved. In such situations, a stark choice needs to be made. Either rely solely on theoretical judgments about consumer behaviour or complement that theory with the best tools available in the relevant time frame while being aware of their weaknesses. The latter approach is clearly preferable.

Of course, if one is able to undertake formal econometric estimates of

---

[88] p.24.
[89] Werden and Froeb (1993).

own-price demand elasticities, it might appear that there is no need to use price correlation analysis. But even in these cases price correlation analysis can provide a useful initial description of the data and can be quickly carried out: if the data is available for an econometric approach, then it is certainly available for price correlation analysis.

Price tests based on the use of econometric techniques have been advocated as an improvement on the use of less sophisticated price correlation analysis. We have argued in this chapter that these apparently more sophisticated tests do not necessarily represent an improvement on price correlation analysis. Like price correlation analysis, they do not directly answer the Hypothetical Monopolist test question, they are often of low power and they can lead to perverse results. It is therefore important to be clear that they do not solve all the difficulties that arise with price correlation analysis.

## ANNEX 10.1: WHY DO VARIABLE EXCHANGE RATES INVALIDATE CORRELATION ANALYSIS?

If the exchange rate between two countries is constant, then standard price **10–080** correlation analysis applies. Denote the constant exchange rate between Country A and Country B as $e$ units of Country A currency to each unit of Country B currency. Then the alternative methods of calculating the correlation between them (i.e. in Country A's currency or Country B's currency) are equivalent. The correlation in Country B currency is:

$$(16) \quad \frac{\sum(\frac{x_t}{e} - \frac{\bar{x}}{e})(y_t - \bar{y})}{\sqrt{\sum(\frac{x_t}{e} - \frac{\bar{x}}{e})^2 \sum(y_t - \bar{y})^2}}$$

whilst the correlation in Country A currency is:

$$(17) \quad \frac{\sum(x_t - \bar{x})(ey_t - e\bar{y})}{\sqrt{\sum(x_t - \bar{x})^2 \sum(ey_t - e\bar{y})^2}}$$

It is simple to confirm that in each case the $e$ terms cancel in the denominator and numerator to give the simple correlation coefficient:

$$(18) \quad \frac{\sum(x_t - \bar{x})(y_t - \bar{y})}{\sqrt{\sum(x_t - \bar{x})^2 \sum(y_t - \bar{y})^2}}$$

However, the same is not true when the exchange rate is allowed to vary over time. In this case:

$$(19) \quad \frac{\sum(\frac{x_t}{e_t} - (\frac{\bar{x}}{e})_t)(y_t - \bar{y})}{\sqrt{\sum(\frac{x_t}{e_t} - (\frac{\bar{x}}{e})_t)^2 \sum(y_t - \bar{y})^2}} \neq \frac{\sum(x_t - \bar{x})(e_t y_t - (e\bar{y})_t)}{\sqrt{\sum(x_t - \bar{x})^2 \sum(e_t y_t - (e\bar{y})_t)^2}}$$

### Extent of the problem

**10–081** We have investigated the potential extent of the problem using Monte Carlo analysis to look at the effect of exchange rate movements within the context of a differentiated products duopoly in which one firm is the domestic firm and the other is the foreign firm.

The simulations presented here assume that demand can be modelled as follows:

(20) $\quad Q_D = \alpha_D - \beta_D P_D + \gamma_F \frac{P_F}{ER} + \varepsilon_D$

(21) $\quad Q_F = \alpha_F - \beta_F P_F + \gamma_D P_D ER + \varepsilon_F$

where: $\quad Q_i$ is output of firm i;

$\qquad ER$ is the exchange rate in terms of the number of units of foreign currency for each unit of domestic currency;

$\qquad P_i$ is the home country price for firm i;

$\qquad \varepsilon_i$ is a demand shock for firm i;

$\qquad \alpha_i, \beta_i$ and $\gamma_i$ are demand parameters; and

$\qquad D$ stands for domestic and $F$ for foreign.

Further, the demand shocks for each firm are made up of an element that is common to the two firms and an element that is firm-specific. Thus:

(22) $\quad \varepsilon_D = \varepsilon_d + \varepsilon_C$

(23) $\quad \varepsilon_F = \varepsilon_f + \varepsilon_C$

where all three shocks ($\varepsilon_d$, $\varepsilon_f$ and $\varepsilon_C$) are normally distributed with constant mean and variance. It is not specified how much of its output each firm sells in its own market and how much is sold abroad. In effect, transport costs are assumed to be zero.

Using randomly generated shocks and a series of parameter values for the demand equations, sets of time series of prices on the basis of a non-co-operative Nash equilibrium in prices and a constant exchange rate were generated.[90] The degree of correlation between these price series depends on the relative size of the two components of the demand shocks that each firm faces: the larger the common shock relative to the specific shocks, the larger the correlation. The correlation coefficient when the exchange rate is constant is treated as the "true" correlation between the two price series. The exchange rate is then allowed to vary and correlations in both the domestic and the foreign currency are carried out. The exchange rate is assumed to be a random walk subject to normally distributed shocks each period.

**10–082** In the first simulation analysis, it was assumed that exchange rates were random walks without trends. The second simulation analysis introduced a trend into exchange rate movements. Some of the results of the first simulation are shown in Table 10.19. Column 1 shows the variability of the

---

[90] In the simulation analysis, the authors set $a_D = 400$, $a_F = 400$, $b_D = 10$, $b_F = 2$, $c_D = 0.4$, $c_F = 2$ and the constant exchange rate equal to 5. Marginal costs were set at 20 for the domestic firm and 100 for the foreign country (i.e. marginal costs were identical, adjusted at the constant exchange rate).

exchange rate as measured by the standard deviation of the normally distributed exchange rate innovation each period. Column 2 gives the "true
correlation" as defined by constant exchange rates. Column 3 gives the
actual estimated average correlations in the simulations. These correlations
were effectively the same whichever currency they were estimated in
(domestic or foreign) and so only the results using the domestic currency
are reported.

## Table 10.19: Effect of exchange rate variability on correlations[91]

(Equal sized firm-specific and general demand shocks)                **10–083**

| ER variability | True correlation | Estimated correlation |
|----------------|------------------|-----------------------|
| 0.002 | 0.64 | 0.63 |
| 0.005 | 0.63 | 0.60 |
| 0.008 | 0.63 | 0.55 |
| 0.011 | 0.63 | 0.53 |
| 0.020 | 0.63 | 0.47 |
| 0.040 | 0.63 | 0.49 |
| 0.060 | 0.63 | 0.54 |
| 0.080 | 0.64 | 0.63 |
| 0.100 | 0.63 | 0.69 |
| 0.120 | 0.63 | 0.74 |
| 0.200 | 0.63 | 0.85 |
| 0.300 | 0.64 | 0.91 |

These results indicate that the effect of exchange rate variability, even in
the absence of a trend in the exchange rate, can be either to reduce the
apparent correlation coefficient below the true value (as defined above) or
to raise it above the true value. Specifically, a small amount of exchange
rate variability reduces the correlation below the true level whilst a large
amount raises it above the true level. When exchange rate movements are
relatively large, they swamp the effects of competitive interaction on correlations, whilst when exchange rate movements are small, they merely
make it harder to discern these competitive interactions.

However, these results apply to exchange rates without a trend. In the
real world, exchange rates often exhibit trends. The results from the second
simulation analysis where there were trends in exchange rate movements
suggest that interpreting the results of price correlation analysis in the
presence of exchange variability is even more problematic. Whereas in the

---

[91]   The results are based on repeated simulations on the basis of randomly generated shocks
and exchange rate innovations. For each level of exchange rate variability 200 simulations
were carried out using 200 time periods.

absence of a trend, the correlations with the varying exchange rate were different from the true value but were largely indifferent to which exchange rate they were calculated in (i.e. domestic or foreign), now the correlations are both different from the true value and differ depending on the exchange rate used. This is shown in Table 10.20.

**10–084** **Table 10.20: Effect of trends in exchange rates on correlations**

| ER variability | Trend | True correlations | Estimated correlation | |
|---|---|---|---|---|
| | | | Domestic currency | Foreign currency |
| 0.06 | −0.0075 | 0.64 | 0.77 | 0.68 |
| 0.06 | 0.0075 | 0.64 | 0.59 | 0.68 |
| 0.08 | −0.0075 | 0.63 | 0.78 | 0.71 |
| 0.08 | 0.0075 | 0.63 | 0.62 | 0.69 |
| 0.10 | −0.0075 | 0.64 | 0.79 | 0.72 |
| 0.10 | 0.0075 | 0.64 | 0.66 | 0.74 |

# 11. Using Elasticities: Critical Loss and Diversion Ratios

## INTRODUCTION

We discussed the Hypothetical Monopolist test in Chapter 4. The Hypo- **11–001**
thetical Monopolist test asks what is the narrowest range of products such
that a hypothetical monopolist of a group of products could permanently
and profitably raise relative prices by a small but significant amount (e.g. 5–
10 per cent). This range of products constitutes a relevant market. In a
merger case, the baseline for the imposition of the possible price rise is the
current price. Many of the empirical techniques discussed in this book are
relevant to market definition (e.g. price correlation analysis, price concentration analysis) but are not direct applications of the Hypothetical
Monopolist test. However, it is possible to implement the Hypothetical
Monopolist test directly. We first demonstrate this below before then
explaining how this relates to an empirical approach referred to as critical
loss analysis or critical elasticity analysis.

After discussing critical loss and critical elasticity analysis, we then discuss the use of "diversion ratios" in antitrust analysis. Diversion ratios
measure the proportion of sales lost by one firm when it raises its price that
are won by another firm. As we argue below, diversion ratios are frequently
misused in competition law cases.

We do not deal with the source of elasticity estimates in this chapter.
Elasticities can be estimated using econometric analysis or via surveys.
Sometimes firms themselves have good estimates of the elasticities in their
industry. For clarity, in this chapter we assume in general that the accuracy
of the elasticity measures is not in doubt. Where we do not assume this, we
make it clear.

# DIRECT IMPLEMENTATION OF THE HYPOTHETICAL MONOPOLIST TEST

**11–002** Suppose that the question we are facing is whether the product "widgets" is a separate relevant product market. Assume that a priori it is plausible that it is not because of competition from a number of other products. The first thing to note is that in order to carry out the Hypothetical Monopolist test, we actually only need to know two things about widgets because there are just two things that will determine whether an increase in the price of widgets would be profitable to a hypothetical monopolist. The first will be the extent to which sales of widgets will fall after the hypothetical price increase. This is measured by the own price elasticity of widgets. The second will be the extent of any cost savings that the hypothetical monopolist will make as a result of sales falling and so production costs falling. It is possible that costs will fall enough that even though total revenues fall after the price rise, it is still profitable for the hypothetical monopolist to raise prices.

Suppose that the current price of widgets is 10, that sales are 1,000 and that the estimate of the own-price elasticity is two. This implies that current revenues are 10,000. What happens if the price is raised by 5 per cent to 10.5? If the elasticity is two, then sales will fall by 10 per cent (i.e. 5 per cent * 2) and so sales will fall to 900. Since price has risen to 10.5, revenues are now 9,450 (i.e. 900 * 10.5), which is a decline in 550. However, this does not mean that the price increase is therefore not profitable, because we have not yet investigated the extent of any cost savings. Costs will have fallen by the variable cost per unit of production times the decline in sales. Suppose that constant variable unit costs are five. This means that costs have fallen by 500 (i.e. 100 * 5). Since revenues have fallen by 550 but costs have only fallen by 500, total profits have fallen by 50 and so the 5 per cent price rise is not profitable. This indicates that the relevant market is wider than just widgets. The numbers are shown in Table 11.1. For expositional ease we have assumed that there are no fixed costs.

**11–003** **Table 11.1: Effect of a hypothetical price rise**

|  | Before 5 per cent price rise | After 5 per cent price rise |
|---|---|---|
| **Price** | 10.0 | 10.5 |
| **Sales** | 1,000 | 900 |
| **Revenues** | 10,000 | 9,450 |
| **Variable unit costs** | 5 | 5 |
| **Total variable costs** | 5,000 | 4,500 |
| **Profits** | 5,000 | 4,950 |

Now suppose that instead of an elasticity of two, the elasticity for widgets is 1.5. This changes the answer to the market definition question. If price is raised by 5 per cent to 10.5, sales now decline by 7.5 per cent to 925 and so revenues fall to 9,712.5, a decline in revenues of 287.5. Since sales have declined by 75, costs have fallen by 375 (i.e. 5 * 75). If revenues fall by 287.5 but costs fall by 375, this implies that total profits have risen by 87.5 (i.e. 375–287.5) and so the 5 per cent price rise was profitable. The numbers are shown in Table 11.2.

**Table 11.2: Effect of a hypothetical price rise**                 11–004

|  | Before 5 per cent price rise | After 5 per cent price rise |
|---|---|---|
| **Price** | 10.0 | 10.5 |
| **Sales** | 1,000 | 925 |
| **Revenues** | 10,000 | 9,712.5 |
| **Variable unit costs** | 5 | 5 |
| **Total variable costs** | 5,000 | 4625 |
| **Profits** | 5,000 | 5,087.5 |

Now suppose that the elasticity is two, but that unit costs are six rather than five. This again changes the result of the market definition question. As in our original example above, sales fall to 900 and revenue falls to 9,450. But now costs fall by 600 (i.e. 6 * 100) rather than by 500. So although revenues have fallen by 550, total profits have actually risen because costs have fallen by more. The numbers are shown in Table 11.3.

**Table 11.3: Effect of a hypothetical price rise**                 11–005

|  | Before 5 per cent price rise | After 5 per cent price rise |
|---|---|---|
| **Price** | 10.0 | 10.5 |
| **Sales** | 1,000 | 900 |
| **Revenues** | 10,000 | 9,450 |
| **Variable unit costs** | 6 | 6 |
| **Total variable costs** | 6,000 | 5,400 |
| **Profits** | 4,000 | 4,050 |

These examples demonstrate that two economic variables are important when defining the relevant market using an elasticity estimate. The first is the elasticity itself as this determines the change in revenue caused by the hypothetical price rise. The second is the amount of costs that will be saved as a result of the lower demand for the product. These examples have also illustrated two important results. First, for any given price-cost margin, the lower is the own price elasticity of demand, the more likely the set of products is a separate relevant market. This is because the lower is the elasticity of demand, the smaller is the loss of sales from the price rise and so the greater are the remaining sales that are sold at a higher price. Secondly, for any given elasticity, the larger are variable costs as a proportion of price, the more likely the price increase is to be profitable. This is because the larger are variable costs, the greater the cost savings due to any reduction in sales.

### Critical loss analysis

**11–006** Critical loss analysis does not so much provide an answer to the Hypothetical Monopolist test as rephrase the question in a more user friendly manner. Returning to our example of widgets, suppose that total widget sales are 1,000, price is 10 and variable costs are 6. This means that gross margins are 4. Critical loss analysis asks how many sales a hypothetical monopolist could afford to lose in response to a price rise before the price rise becomes unprofitable. Suppose that the hypothetical monopolist in our example were to raise prices by 10 per cent to 11. Before the price rise the hypothetical monopolist is making total gross margin of 4,000 (i.e. a margin of 4 on sales of 1,000). After the price rise the hypothetical monopolist's margin rises to 5 (i.e. 11–6). How many sales would it have to make to still make total gross margin of 4,000? The answer is 800 (i.e. 4,000 / 5). So the critical loss in this case is 200 (i.e. 1,000–800). It is the number of sales the hypothetical monopolist can afford to lose before the price rise becomes unprofitable. If the 10 per cent price rise would lead to sales falling by more than 200, then it would not be profitable. If it led to prices falling by less than 200, then it would be profitable, indicating that the relevant market is no wider than widgets.

Note that this approach does not answer the Hypothetical Monopolist test. All it does is tell us what is the necessary condition for the Hypothetical Monopolist test to be passed or failed. In the example above we still need to investigate what effect the 10 per cent price rise would actually have on sales. This is the sense in which critical loss analysis rephrases the Hypothetical Monopolist test. In our example, instead of asking whether a hypothetical monopolist could profitably raise prices by more than 10 per cent, we are now asking whether a 10 per cent "market-wide" price increase would cause sales to fall by more than 200.

The critical loss depends on the size of the posited price increase. In Table 11.4 we show the critical loss in our example for a 5 per cent Hypothetical Monopolist and a 10 per cent price increase. The critical loss for the 5 per cent price increase is 111, whilst for the 10 per cent price increase it is 200.

**Table 11.4: Critical loss for a 5 per cent and a 10 per cent price** 11–007
**increase in our example**

|  | 5 per cent SSNIP | 10 per cent SSNIP |
|---|---|---|
| Price | 10 | 10 |
| Sales | 1,000 | 1,000 |
| Variable cost | 6 | 6 |
| Margin | 4 | 4 |
| Total margin | 4,000 | 4,000 |
| Price after SSNIP | 10.5 | 11 |
| Margin after SSNIP | 4.5 | 5 |
| Sales required to make same total margin | 889 | 800 |
| Critical loss | 111 | 200 |

As noted above, whether a price increase is profitable for a hypothetical
monopolist depends on the pre-price rise margin, the size of the price
increase and the number of sales that would be lost as a result of that price
increase. Algebraically, a price increase is profitable if and only if:

(1)  $(p + \Delta p - c)(q - \Delta q) > (p - c)q$

where   p is the pre-price rise price;
c is marginal cost;
q is pre-price rise market sales; and
$\Delta p$ and $\Delta q$ are the post-price rise changes in p and q.

Simple algebraic manipulation shows that the SSNIP is profitable if and
only if:

(2)  $\dfrac{t}{m + t} > \dfrac{\Delta q}{q}$

where   t is the proportionate price rise (i.e. $\Delta p/p$); and
m is the price-cost margin (i.e. $(p-c)/p$).

The right-hand side of Equation (2) is the proportionate decline in sales
after the price rise. So if $t/(m+t)$ is greater than the proportionate change in
sales, then the posited price increase is profitable. This allows one to calculate the critical proportionate sales loss for any combination of t and m.
This is shown in Table 11.5

**11–008 Table 11.5: Critical loss values as the price increase and price-cost margin vary**

| Price-cost margin | Critical loss (per cent decline in sales) | |
|---|---|---|
| | 5%<br>(t=0.05) | 10%<br>(t=0.1) |
| 0.9 | 0.05 | 0.10 |
| 0.8 | 0.06 | 0.11 |
| 0.7 | 0.07 | 0.13 |
| 0.6 | 0.08 | 0.14 |
| 0.5 | 0.09 | 0.17 |
| 0.4 | 0.11 | 0.20 |
| 0.3 | 0.14 | 0.25 |
| 0.2 | 0.20 | 0.33 |
| 0.1 | 0.33 | 0.50 |

Whether a price increase will lead to sales falling by more than the critical loss is essentially an elasticity question. In Table 11.4, the critical loss for a 10 per cent price increase is 200, which is a 20 per cent decline in sales. So whether or not the posited price increase is profitable depends on whether a 10 per cent price increase leads to a decline in sales of more than 20 per cent. This is equivalent to asking whether the elasticity of demand in response to a 10 per cent price rise is more than two. This suggests that another way of implementing the Hypothetical Monopolist test is through an estimate of the elasticity of demand. We discuss this below.

### The critical elasticity and the critical margin

**11–009** We have discussed above how the answer to the Hypothetical Monopolist test depends on the elasticity of demand for the set of products and the margin over variable costs. It would be useful to have some general formula based on the own-price elasticity and the level of variable costs that would indicate whether a hypothetical monopolist would find it profitable to raise prices or not. Such a formula exists and it has a rather simple form, although as we discuss below there is an important underlying assumption that needs to be tested. If the question is whether a hypothetical monopolist could profitably raise prices by proportion $t$, then the answer is "yes" if and only if the own-price elasticity facing the hypothetical monopolist is less than:

$$(3) \quad \frac{1+t}{m+t}$$

where $m$ is the current-price cost margin (i.e. (p–c)/p); and

$t$ is the proportional amount of the hypothetical price rise.

Note that, as before, t is the proportionate rise in price. So if one is concerned with a hypothetical 5 per cent price rise, then t is 0.05. If one is concerned with a hypothetical 10 per cent price rise, then t is 0.1.

Consider the first two scenarios above where the current price of widgets was 10 and variable costs were five. This means that the price-cost margin was 0.5. If we are concerned with a 5 per cent price increase, then t is 0.05. On the basis of the formula in Equation (3), the critical elasticity is 1.05/0.55, or 1.91. Thus if the elasticity of demand for the product is less than 1.91, then that product is a separate market on the basis of a 5 per cent price increase test. This is consistent with what we found above. When the elasticity was two, the price rise was not profitable, but it was when the elasticity was 1.5.

Now suppose that the price-cost margin was 0.4, as in the third scenario above. Now the formula implies that the critical elasticity is 1.05/0.45, which is 2.3. This is consistent with the fact that we found that when the margin fell to 0.4, then the 5 per cent price increase was profitable even when the elasticity of demand was two. Table 11.6 shows for price increases of 5 per cent and 10 per cent how the critical elasticity varies as the price-cost margin varies.

**Table 11.6: Variation in the critical elasticity as the price-cost** 11–010
**margin varies**

| | Critical elasticity | |
|---|---|---|
| Price-cost margin | SSNIP=5 per cent | SSNIP=10 per cent |
| 0.9 | 1.11 | 1.10 |
| 0.8 | 1.24 | 1.22 |
| 0.7 | 1.40 | 1.38 |
| 0.6 | 1.62 | 1.57 |
| 0.5 | 1.91 | 1.83 |
| 0.4 | 2.33 | 2.20 |
| 0.3 | 3.00 | 2.75 |
| 0.2 | 4.20 | 3.67 |
| 0.1 | 7.00 | 5.50 |

Table 11.6 shows that as the price-cost margin falls, so the critical elasticity rises. If the price-cost margin is 0.9, then the critical elasticity is 1.11 (i.e. the product is not a separate relevant market unless the own-price elasticity of the product is less than 1.11). However, if the price-cost margin is 0.1, then the critical elasticity is 7.00. The intuition for this should be clear. The lower the price-cost margin, the more variable costs are saved when demand (and so output) declines and so the more revenue that can be foregone without the price rise being unprofitable.

So far this discussion has been framed within the context of knowing the price-cost margin and then calculating the critical elasticity. It could, of course, just as easily have been framed within the context of knowing the elasticity and then calculating the critical margin. This is shown in Table 11.7.

**11–011** **Table 11.7: Critical margins**

|  | Price increase | |
|---|---|---|
| Elasticity | 5 per cent | 10 per cent |
| 1.2 | 0.83 | 0.82 |
| 1.6 | 0.61 | 0.59 |
| 2 | 0.48 | 0.45 |
| 2.4 | 0.39 | 0.36 |
| 2.8 | 0.33 | 0.29 |
| 3.2 | 0.28 | 0.24 |
| 3.6 | 0.24 | 0.21 |
| 4 | 0.21 | 0.18 |
| 4.4 | 0.19 | 0.15 |
| 4.8 | 0.17 | 0.13 |

## Elasticity assumptions: Constant elasticities v linear demand

**11–012** The discussion above ignores an important issue concerning the use of critical elasticities in market definition. It has been assumed that the elasticity estimates are what are known as *constant elasticity estimates*. This means that the own-price elasticity of demand for a product, or group of products, is the same whatever the price. This is an assumption that is often made in econometric analysis as it simplifies the analysis considerably. However, it is by no means clear that elasticities are always constant. We often believe that as the price of a product rises, its own-price elasticity of demand rises. If this is the case, then using the critical elasticity formula given above will lead to markets being defined too narrowly because the analysis will assume the posited price increase leads to a smaller loss of sales than in reality it would. This has been referred to as the *reverse Cellophane fallacy* because it leads to markets that are defined too narrowly, unlike the standard Cellophane fallacy that leads to markets being defined too widely (see Chapter 4).[1] An alternative elasticity assumption is to assume that demand curves are linear (i.e. straight lines). The elasticity on a linear demand curve increases as price rises. This is intuitively appealing: we should expect consumers to become more price sensitive as price rises. If we believe that demand curves are linear, then Equation (3) above needs to be replaced with Equation (4) below.

[1] Werden and Froeb (1993).

(4)  $\dfrac{1}{m + 2t}$

It is simple to confirm that for any given margin, the critical elasticity will be higher under the constant elasticity assumption (i.e. Equation (3)) than under the linear demand curve assumption (i.e. Equation (4)), meaning that the constant elasticity formula will tend to define markets more narrowly than the linear demand curve assumption. It is also simple to confirm that for a given elasticity, the critical margin will be higher under the constant elasticity assumption. Again, this implies that the constant elasticity assumption will tend to lead to markets being defined more narrowly.

It is important to stress that the actual form of the elasticity of demand is an empirical matter. We cannot in general say a priori that the demand curve is linear or that it has constant elasticity. If using alternative assumptions leads to a different answer to the Hypothetical Monopolist test, then it is important to test the assumption. This is an issue that arises in merger simulation as well as in critical elasticity analysis and we discuss it in more depth in Chapter 15. If we were willing to assume that the elasticity did not fall as prices increased, then the constant elasticity assumption would give an upper-bound for the correct elasticity. This would imply that using the constant elasticity formulas would give a lower bound on the maximum width of the market.

---

### BOX 11.1: CRITICAL ELASTICITY FORMULAE

The formulae for the critical elasticity for constant elasticity and linear demand curves are derived below. Note that these formulae are derived on the assumption that the firms involved are single product firms. If this assumption is wrong, then so are these formulae, although equivalent ones can be derived for multi-product firms.

**11–013**

#### Constant elasticity[2]

Every profit-maximising single product firm will price so that the price-marginal cost margin (m) is equal to minus the inverse of the own-price elasticity. Thus $(p-c)/p = -1/\varepsilon$ where $\varepsilon$ is the own-price elasticity. Denote the monopoly price as $p_M$. Then $\varepsilon = -p_M/(p_M-c)$. What is of interest is whether the monopoly price is more than proportion $t$ above the current price (denoted by $p_0$),[3] so therefore the question is what elasticity will lead to the monopolist setting $p_M = (1 + t)p_0$. Substituting in, this implies that:

**11–014**

---

[2]  The analysis follows Werden (1998).
[3]  This assumes one is dealing with a merger. In a non-merger/joint venture case, $p_0$ is the competitive price.

$$(5) \quad \varepsilon = \frac{-(1+t)p_0}{(1+t)p_0 - c}$$

Dividing through by $p_0$ gives:

$$(6) \quad \varepsilon = \frac{-(1+t)}{1+t-\frac{c}{p_0}}$$

Since $1 - (c/p_0) = m$, this simplifies to:

$$(7) \quad \varepsilon = \frac{-(1+t)}{m+t}$$

Thus a hypothetical monopolist will raise prices by proportion $t$ above the current price if this would lead to an elasticity of $-(1 + t)/(m + t)$. Since a constant elasticity is assumed, this must also be the elasticity facing the hypothetical monopolist at $p_0$ and so this is the critical elasticity at which the hypothetical monopolist will raise prices by proportion $t$. If the elasticity is larger in absolute terms, the hypothetical monopolist will raise prices by less than this amount. If the elasticity is smaller in absolute terms, he will raise prices by more than proportion $t$.

**11–015** | ## Linear demand

Notice that the logic of the above argument implies that whatever shape of demand curve the hypothetical monopolist faces, he will set prices so that $\varepsilon = -(1 + t)/(m + t)$. However, if the demand curve is linear, the elasticity at $p_0$ that implies this elasticity at $(1 + t)p_0$ will be different. A linear demand curve has the form $p = a - bq$. The elasticity of a demand curve is $-pdq/qdp$, which in this case is $-p/(a-p)$. This implies that:

$$(8) \quad \frac{-(1+t)}{m+t} = \frac{-p_M}{a - p_M}$$

or

$$(9) \quad \frac{1+t}{m+t} = \frac{(1+t)p_0}{a - (1+t)p_0}$$

Rearranging (9) gives:

$(10) \quad p_0(m + 2t + 1) = a$

We know that the critical elasticity (denoted $\varepsilon_0$) is equal to $-p_0/(a-p_0)$. This implies that $a = (-p_0/\varepsilon_0) + p_0$. Substituting, this leads to:

$$(11) \quad \varepsilon_0 = \frac{-1}{m + 2t}$$

Thus the critical elasticities are as follows:

| Constant elasticity demand curve | Linear demand curve |
|:---:|:---:|
| $\dfrac{-(1+t)}{m+t}$ | $\dfrac{-1}{m+2t}$ |

(12)

## Critical loss v critical elasticity analysis

Two main advantages are claimed for critical loss analysis over critical  **11–016**
elasticity analysis.[4] The first is that it is easier to estimate the likely loss of
sales from a hypothetical price rise than it is to estimate elasticities. This is
a rather odd claim since an estimate of the likely loss of sales implies an
elasticity estimate. If it is estimated that sales are likely to fall by 25 per cent
in response to a 10 per cent price increase, then the implied elasticity is
−2.5. The claim seems to be more that estimating elasticities econometrically is often difficult (true), whereas estimating the likely loss of sales is
not (untrue). However, if you feel able to estimate the likely loss in sales,
you *are* estimating an elasticity, so the criticism comes down to no more
than saying, "it is often hard to get precise elasticity estimates". This is
true, but logically it affects both critical elasticity analysis and critical loss
analysis equally.

A better founded claim for critical loss analysis being superior to critical
elasticity analysis lies in the possibility that infra-marginal consumers are
substantially less price sensitive than marginal consumers. It might be that
a 5 per cent price rise would not be profitable because it would lead to 10
per cent of consumers switching away from the relevant products, whereas
a 25 per cent price rise might be profitable because it would still lead to
only 10 per cent of consumers switching. This might be the case if there
was a set of customers who were very price sensitive, but the majority of
customers were very insensitive to price, perhaps because they are in some
way "locked-in" to using the product (e.g. it is an input to some durable
good they already own). Critical elasticity analysis cannot account for this
possibility whenever a single value is estimated for the elasticity. So, in
principle, this claim in favour of critical loss analysis is sound. We should
note, however, that in general we expect elasticities to increase as prices rise
and so in practice we would expect the issue to arise only rarely. However,
it is good practice for analysts to consider whether the nature of the market
under investigation suggests that infra-marginal consumers might be much
less price sensitive than marginal ones.

It should not need saying, but the Hypothetical Monopolist test should
not be used to test whether a single firm is in a separate relevant market of
its own. A firm, regardless of whether it has market power or not, will profit
maximise by setting its price at a level such that any further increase in
price would be unprofitable. If a further increase in price was profitable, we
should expect the firm to have already raised its price to take advantage of
this. This implies that asking whether a firm could profitably raise its price
from the current price should (absent price regulation) always be met with
the answer no. This implies that estimating the own-price elasticity of a
firm in order to see whether it is above the relevant critical elasticity makes

[4]  See, for instance, Langenfeld and Li (2001).

no sense. However, this error has been made by competition authorities that have estimated the own-price elasticity of a firm and, finding that it is low have argued that this implies that the firm is in a separate relevant market. In reality, all this shows is that the elasticity estimates are implausible.[5]

**11-017**   We noted above the apparently obvious observation that if margins in a market are high, then the critical loss is low. But this does not necessarily imply that it is less likely that a price increase would be profitable because it is more likely that the decline in sales as a result of the price increase will be above the critical loss threshold.[6] What matters is the actual loss following the price increase. Indeed, a high price-cost margin for a firm can imply that its own price elasticity is low. The Lerner equation indicates that if a single-product firm has a price cost margin of 25 per cent (i.e. m=0.25), then its own price elasticity is −4. Equally, if its margin is 90 per cent, then its own price elasticity is −1.11.

Of course, the relevant elasticity is the industry own-price elasticity rather than the firm own-price elasticity. The market elasticity is likely to be lower than the firm own-price elasticity, since the market elasticity will in general be less than firm specific elasticities. This is because when a firm raises its price, some of the sales that it loses are won by other firms in the market. That is, not all the lost sales "leave the market". So a high firm-specific margin suggests that the industry elasticity will be low and so any price increase is likely to lead to only a small reduction in market sales. This means that even a low critical loss threshold may not be reached.

An example may make this clearer. Suppose that Firms A and B both make widgets and wish to merge. They face competition from a number of other widget manufacturers. They argue that the relevant market is wider than just widgets. Their basis for this assertion is as follows:

- margins in the widget market are 60 per cent;

- this means that a 5 per cent price increase would not be profitable if sales fell by more than 7.7 per cent (i.e. t/(m+t) = 0.077);

- a 5 per cent price increase would lead to a fall in sales of at least 10 per cent;

- so the 5 per cent price increase would not be profitable and the relevant market is wider than just widgets.

---

[5]   For an example of this mistake, see La Cour and Møllgaard (2003). They analysed the case of the only Danish producer of cement, Aalborg Portland (AP), and found that its own price elasticity was −0.27. This is not plausible, since it implies that AP was not profit maximising. If AP's elasticity really was −0.27, then by raising its price, it would have increased its revenues (as the own-price elasticity was less than one) and lowered its costs (as sales would have declined), which would have increased its total profits.

[6]   Farrell and Shapiro (2007), O'Brien and Wickelgren (2003) and Scheffman and Simons (2003).

The problem with this line of argument is that the parties claim that sales would fall by more than 10 per cent implies an elasticity of −2, but this is not consistent with the parties' own margins. Their margins of 60 per cent imply that their own-price elasticities are −1.67. Since the industry elasticity will be less than the firm specific elasticities, the figure of −2 is not consistent with what is known about the firms' margins.

What is particularly interesting about this line of argument is that it **11–018** actually implies that the higher is the price-cost margin, the more likely the relevant market is narrow. This is because when margins are high, the critical elasticity is very close to the firms' own price elasticities. This is illustrated in Table 11.8. When the price-cost margin is 90 per cent, this implies a firm specific elasticity of −1.11 and, for a 5 per cent price increase, critical elasticities of −1.11 (constant elasticity assumption) and −1.00 (linear demand assumption). Clearly, the critical elasticities are close to the firm specific elasticity, which makes it more likely that the actual industry elasticity is below the critical elasticity and so makes it more likely that the market is narrow. Conversely, when the price-cost margin is 0.1, then the implied firm specific elasticity is −10, but for a 5 per cent price increase elasticities are −7 (CES) and −5 (linear). These elasticities are significantly smaller than the firm specific elasticity and so it is more likely that the actual industry elasticity will be above the critical level.

## Table 11.8: Firm-specific elasticities v critical elasticities as   11–019 price-cost margins vary

| Price-cost margin | Firm elasticity | Critical elasticity | | | |
|---|---|---|---|---|---|
| | | 5 per cent SSNIP | | 10 per cent SSNIP | |
| | | CES | Linear | CES | Linear |
| 0.9 | −1.11 | −1.11 | −1.00 | −1.10 | −0.91 |
| 0.8 | −1.25 | −1.24 | −1.11 | −1.22 | −1.00 |
| 0.7 | −1.43 | −1.40 | −1.25 | −1.38 | −1.11 |
| 0.6 | −1.67 | −1.62 | −1.43 | −1.57 | −1.25 |
| 0.5 | −2.00 | −1.91 | −1.67 | −1.83 | −1.43 |
| 0.4 | −2.50 | −2.33 | −2.00 | −2.20 | −1.67 |
| 0.3 | −3.33 | −3.00 | −2.50 | −2.75 | −2.00 |
| 0.2 | −5.00 | −4.20 | −3.33 | −3.67 | −2.50 |
| 0.1 | −10.00 | −7.00 | −5.00 | −5.50 | −3.33 |

An important question that this discussion raises is: when will the market elasticity be close to the firm specific elasticity? Whether the market elasticity is close to the firm-specific elasticities depends on how many sales "leave the market" when a firm raises its price. If most of the sales that a firm loses are won by other firms in the market, then the overall loss of sales from the market will be small. This means that the market elasticity will be significantly lower than the firm specific elasticity. Conversely, if most of the sales that a firm loses do leave the market, then the market elasticity will be close to the firm specific elasticity.

Note that the line of argument in this section relies on the firms in the industry currently being in a non-cooperative Nash equilibrium (i.e. each firm is maximising its profits given what all the other firms are doing). If they are not, but are instead tacitly colluding, then the Lerner condition does not hold and so it is not possible to derive the firms' own-price elasticities from their margins. Note also that the simple Lerner condition applies only to single-product firms, although equivalent but more complicated equilibrium conditions can be derived for multi-product firms. Finally, if fixed costs are high and marginal costs low, then the short-run non-cooperative Nash equilibrium may not represent a sustainable market outcome. If firms price significantly above marginal costs in order to recover their fixed costs, then it makes sense for each firm to undercut this price and so win more sales. But if all the firms do this, then they will not cover their fixed costs and so it is not sustainable. So it is quite possible that firms cannot operate sustainably according to the short-run Nash equilibrium and in consequence the Lerner condition will not hold even for single product firms.

## Time periods of the elasticities and variable costs

**11-020** An issue to which little attention is given is the appropriate time period of the elasticity estimate. An elasticity measures the response of consumers to a price increase. The immediate response of consumers to a price increase is likely to be different to the longer-run response. For example, there is likely to be a difference in the response of consumers in the week that a price rise takes effect compared to the response that takes place over the two years after the price increase. When using elasticities to delineate markets it is very important that the correct elasticity estimate is used. Use of an elasticity estimate that measures the response over one to two years is recommended.[7] This is approximately the length of time that competition authorities tend to be concerned with: for instance, will this merger allow prices to rise over a period of one to two years? Such a length of time is also consistent with the view of the US Merger Guidelines that for committed entry to be considered "timely" it must be likely to have a significant impact on the market within two years of the merger taking place.

**11-021** It is often argued that short-run elasticities (e.g. the response to a two-week promotion) will tend to be larger than longer-run elasticities because they will include an element of "stocking up". Consumers will stock up

---

[7] In general, there will not be much difference between the 1-year elasticity and the 2-year elasticity.

with a product if they see that its price is temporarily low as a result of a promotion, even if they do not increase their total purchases of the product over the longer term. This "stocking up" effect will lead to the appearance of high short-run elasticities that are not reflected in longer-run elasticities. Identifying the presence of stocking up effects should be relatively easy: if an increase in sales during a promotion is mirrored by an equivalent, or close to equivalent, decline in sales in the weeks after the promotion, this suggests that the increase in sales was largely a stocking up effect, rather than a genuine increase in demand in response to a lower price.

It is also possible that the short-run elasticity will be lower than the long-run elasticity as consumers may take some time to adjust their purchasing habits. Pindyck and Rubinfeld provide an excellent example of how elasticities can vary over time.[8] They report estimates of the price elasticity of petrol and the price elasticity of cars. These are reported in Table 11.9 which shows how the elasticity of demand for petrol and cars increases as the time period increases.

### Table 11.9: The price elasticity of cars and petrol    11–022

|  | 1 | 2 | 3 | 5 | 10 |
|---|---|---|---|---|---|
| **Elasticity of petrol** | −0.2 | −0.3 | −0.4 | −0.5 | −0.8 |
| **Elasticity of cars** | −1.2 | −0.9 | −0.8 | −0.6 | −0.4 |

*Source*: Pindyck and Rubinfeld (2008).

The elasticity of petrol rises in absolute value over time from −0.2 to −0.8. It is quite intuitive why this happens. In the short run, consumers do not have much scope for reducing the amount of petrol they consume, hence a low elasticity of demand. In the longer run, they can substitute out of owning a car and so reduce their petrol consumption markedly. The elasticity of cars works in the opposite direction: it falls in absolute value over time from −1.2 to −0.4. In the short run, consumers respond to a rise in the price of cars by delaying their purchase of a new car. In the longer run, they accept that the price increase is permanent and replace their car. This is likely to be a general result for consumer durables.

The important point to take away from this discussion is that short-run elasticity estimates can vary from longer-run elasticity estimates. It is therefore important to use an elasticity estimate that relates to the time period of concern.

Note that there is an equivalent issue for variable costs. When estimating the potential for a hypothetical monopolist to raise prices profitably, the variable cost figure used should relate to the same time period as the elasticity estimate. More costs are variable over a one- to two-year timescale

---

[8]  Pindyck and Rubinfeld (2008).

than over a one-week timescale, so it would be wrong to use a variable cost figure that related to costs that are variable over a one week, one month or one quarter period if a one-year or two-year elasticity estimate is used.

## DIVERSION RATIOS

**11–023**   The diversion ratio is a concept that is frequently used to measure the closeness of competition between two products in a differentiated products industry. It is also sometimes used as a "simple" way of measuring the likely post-merger price rise in a unilateral effects merger case. The purpose of this section is to explain the limitations of diversion ratios for the latter use.

The diversion ratio between two products is the proportion of the sales lost by one product, when its price increases, that go to the other product. Suppose the price of Product A rises by 10 per cent and that as a result sales fall by 1,000 units. Suppose that 400 of these lost sales are captured by Product B. This means that Product B captured 40 per cent of the sales lost by Product A and so the diversion ratio from A to B ($D_{AB}$) is 0.4.[9]

The sense in which the diversion ratio can be used to measure closeness of competition is clear. If the diversion ratio from A to B is 0.4 and that from A to C is 0.2, then this indicates that twice as many of the sales lost by A go to B as go to C. The implication is that the higher the diversion ratio, the greater the competitive constraint imposed by the relevant firm.

Under special circumstances, the diversion ratio can be used to estimate quickly the likely effect on prices of a merger. Under these special circumstances, the proportionate price increase after the merger is[10]:

$$(13) \quad \frac{p^* - p}{p} = \frac{mD}{1 - m - D}$$

Where   $p^*$ is the post-merger price;
   $p$ is the pre-merger price;
   $m$ is the pre-merger price-marginal cost margin; and
   $D$ is the diversion ratio between the two products.

An example illustrates how easy it is to use this formula. Suppose that two firms are merging whose diversion ratio is 0.2 and whose pre-merger price-

---

[9]   Throughout this chapter we use the standard definition of a diversion ratio: the proportion of sales lost by A that are won by B ($D_{AB}$). This is sometimes referred to variously as the *unit diversion ratio*, the *volume diversion ratio*, the *sales diversion ratio* or the *customer diversion ratio*. An alternative is the *revenue diversion ratio*. This is the proportion of the revenue lost by A that is won by B. Suppose that the price of A is 10 and that in response to a 1% price increase, A loses sales of 100. Suppose that B captures 50 of these sales and its price is 8. Then the unit diversion ratio is 0.5: 50 won sales divided by 100 lost sales. The revenue diversion ratio is 0.4: revenue of 400 won (50 * 8) divided by revenue of 1000 lost (100 * 10). Algebraically, the relationship between the two diversion ratios is:

$$Unit\ DR_{AB} = Revenue\ DR_{AB} \frac{p_B}{p_A}$$

The equations in this chapter are all based on a unit diversion ratio.

[10]   Shapiro (1996).

marginal cost margin is 0.4. Equation (5) implies that the post-merger price will be $(0.2 * 0.4) / (1 - 0.2 - 0.4) = 0.2$ higher than the pre-merger price (i.e. prices will rise by 20 per cent).

Diversion ratios therefore appear to offer a straightforward method of estimating post-merger price increases. However, even a brief consideration of Equation (5) suggests that there are problems with this approach. For instance, suppose the price-cost margin is 50 per cent and the diversion ratio is 0.45, then the formula suggests that post-merger prices will *rise* by 450 per cent! But if the margin was a little higher at 60 per cent, then it would imply that prices would *fall* by 540 per cent! Clearly something is not right.[11] Unfortunately, Equation (5) only holds if: **11–024**

(a)   the two merging firms were symmetric before the merger;

(b)   they were both single product firms before the merger; and

(c)   they face constant elasticity demand curves.

We discussed the plausibility of a constant elasticity assumption above, where we argued that in general we would expect the elasticity of demand to rise as prices rise. However, if we prefer to assume that the demand curve is linear, then it is possible to derive an equally simple formula for the post-merger price rise. This is shown in Equation (6).

$$(14) \quad \frac{p^* - p}{p} = \frac{mD}{2(1 - D)}$$

However, this equation still requires that condition (a) and (b) hold. Condition (b) is a stringent assumption since most firms are multi-product firms. Condition (a) virtually never holds. To the extent that these conditions do not hold, Equations (5) and (6) will at best be only an approximation to the correct answer. Relaxing condition (a) (the most implausible of the conditions) makes Equation (5) significantly inaccurate.

If we continue to assume that conditions (b) and (c) hold, but drop the assumption of symmetry, then the correct formula for the proportionate price rise after the merger, assuming constant elasticity, is considerably more complex than in the symmetric case. The formula for the proportionate rise in the price of Product A $(P_A)$ after the merger is:

$$(15) \quad \frac{P_A^* - P_A}{P_A} = \frac{-D_{AB}(c_B(1 + \varepsilon_{AA}) + c_A D_{BA}\varepsilon_{BB})}{c_A(1 + \varepsilon_{AA} + \varepsilon_{BB} + \varepsilon_{AA}\varepsilon_{BB} - D_{AB}D_{BA}\varepsilon_{AA}\varepsilon_{BB})}$$

where   $p^*_i$ is the post-merger price of firm i:
   $p_i$ is the pre-merger price of firm i;
   $c_i$ is the constant marginal cost of firm i; and
   $\varepsilon_{ii}$ is the own-price elasticity of firm i.

---

[11]   Using Equation (5), the UK Competition Commission found a predicted post-merger price rise in the *Somerfield/Morrison* merger of nearly 2000%! See the case study below for further details.

Equation (7) is clearly a little less user friendly than Equation (5).[12] If the assumption that the firms were single product firms is also dropped, things would become even more complicated. If it is necessary to use Equation (7), which involves estimating own-price and cross-price elasticities, then this is a move away from quick back-of-the-envelope calculations and instead a proper demand analysis and simulation should be carried out. For further details, and a discussion of the pitfalls of this approach, see Chapter 15.

**11–025**     It might be the case that even though Equation (5) is not exactly correct in most situations, it is a reasonable approximation in many circumstances. This is not so. The extent to which Equation (5) gives the wrong answer in the case of single product firms is:

$$(16)\ Error = \frac{-D_{AB}(c_B + c_A \varepsilon_{AA} + c_A D_{BA} \varepsilon_{BB})}{c_A(1 + \varepsilon_{AA} + \varepsilon_{BB} + \varepsilon_{AA} \varepsilon_{BB} - D_{AB} D_{BA} \varepsilon_{AA} \varepsilon_{BB})} - \frac{m_A D_{AB}}{1 - m_A - D_{AB}}$$

Using this equation, it is relatively straightforward to show that the magnitude of the errors from using the wrong equation are economically significant. We provide examples in Annex 11.2.

An interesting question is whether there are any other circumstances in which the simple equations are correct. The answer is that for Equation (5) there is one such circumstance. This is the instance in which all the firms are "equally close" to each other: that is, the diversion ratios can be derived from the market shares of the two firms. By this it is meant that sales lost by a product due to an increase in price are captured by the other firms in the market in direct proportion to their market shares (this is the sense in which all the products are "equally close"). Thus, if Product A has a 20 per cent market share and Product B has a 30 per cent market share, then the diversion ratio from A to B is 0.375 (30 per cent of the 80 per cent of the market not accounted by Product A) and the diversion ratio from B to A is 0.286 (20 per cent of 70 per cent). Under these conditions it is possible to show that Equation (5) is correct. However, Equation (6) is not correct even under the assumption that all firms are equally close.

Moreover, any estimate of a diversion ratio needs to be consistent with the other information that has been obtained about an industry. There is a relatively simple relationship between diversion ratios, elasticities and price-marginal cost mark-ups (see below). It is quite possible (indeed more than likely) that diversion ratios calculated on the basis of market shares will be inconsistent with the elasticities and price-marginal cost mark-ups

---

[12]   For the derivation of this result, see Annex 11.1 to this chapter. Note also that this formula differs slightly from that in previous editions of this book. This is because in the previous editions we switched to assuming that the diversion ratio was a negative number. This is the economically correct approach since, as we discuss below, the diversion ratio is equal to the cross-price elasticity divided by the own-price elasticity, which gives a negative number. In this edition we have maintained consistency with the literature and treated the diversion ratio as a positive number.

of the companies involved. In addition, the correct market definition may well not be uncontroversial, in which case the market shares are not uncontroversial. In general, it seems unacceptable to assume that diversion ratios can be estimated from market shares without good evidence to support that assumption. It might be a reasonable approach if the market definition was uncontroversial and if the products in question were homogeneous, since then it is plausible that volumes would divert in proportion to market shares. But note that in this case it is very unclear what useful role diversion ratios would be playing. If products are homogeneous, then we are unlikely to be concerned about unilateral effects.[13]

Finally, but most importantly, all of the above discussion is predicated on the assumption that there is no new entry or product repositioning after a post-merger price increase. There may well be occasions when these assumptions may reasonably be made, but in general one should be wary of doing this. We discuss this issue in depth in Chapter 15 on merger simulation.

---

### BOX 11.2: DIVERSION RATIOS, ELASTICITIES AND PRICE-COST MARK-UPS

If single-product firms are acting non-co-operatively in a Bertrand setting, their price-marginal cost mark-up should be equal to the inverse of their own-price elasticity of demand. Assuming a Nash equilibrium in prices, it is possible to recover the own-price elasticity of demand for a firm on the basis of their price and marginal costs. The diversion ratio from Product A to Product B $(D_{AB})$ is the cross-price elasticity of demand for A with respect to the price of B $(\varepsilon_{AB})$ divided by the own-price elasticity of demand for A $(\varepsilon_{AA})$. This means that if there is an estimate of the diversion ratio from A to B and an estimate of the own-price elasticity of A, this implies a cross-price elasticity of demand for A with respect to the price of B.

$$(17) \quad D_{AB} = \frac{\varepsilon_{AB}}{\varepsilon_{AA}} \Rightarrow D_{AB}\varepsilon_{AA} = \varepsilon_{AB}$$

So if there are estimates of the diversion ratio from A to B and of the diversion ratio from B to A, and given that the own-price elasticities from the price-marginal cost mark-up can then be recovered, then there are implied estimates of the two cross-price elasticities of demand between A and B. However, it is also known that there is a relationship between the two cross-price elasticities of demand. Specifically, Slutsky symmetry implies that the cross-price elasticity of demand for A with respect to the price of B will be equal to the cross-price elasticity of demand for B with respect to the price of A, multiplied by the ratio of sales of B to sales of A. Algebraically:

11–026

---

[13]   For a further discussion of this issue, see Chapter 7.

$$(18) \quad \varepsilon_{AB} = \varepsilon_{BA} \frac{Sales_B}{Sales_A}$$

The important point is that it is possible to check for the consistency of estimates of the diversion ratios between two firms. If the price-marginal cost mark-ups for two firms are known, then so are their own-price elasticities (on the assumption of a Nash equilibrium in prices). If one of the two diversion ratios is known, or one of the cross-price elasticities, then the remaining cross-price elasticities and diversion ratios can be calculated. However, if one knows the own-price elasticities and has estimates of both diversion ratios, then a check can be made with regard to the consistency of the estimates of the diversion ratios.

An example should make this clearer. Suppose it is known from the price-marginal cost mark-ups that the own-price elasticity of demand for Product A is $-3.5$ and for Product B it is $-4.5$ and that Product A has twice as many sales as Product B. Suppose further that there are estimates (perhaps from survey data) that the diversion ratios from A to B and from B to A are 0.2 and 0.1 respectively. If the diversion ratio from A to B ($D_{AB}$) is 0.2 and the own-price elasticity of A ($\varepsilon_{AA}$) is $-3.5$, then the cross-price elasticity of demand for A with respect to the price of B ($\varepsilon_{AB}$) is 0.7. Given that sales of A are twice sales of B, this implies that $\varepsilon_{BA}$ is 1.4. Given that it is known that $\varepsilon_{BB}$ is $-4.5$, this implies that $D_{BA}$ is 0.31. But this is inconsistent with the estimate for $D_{BA}$ of 0.1.

**11–027**     This inconsistency might occur for two main reasons:

(1) the estimates of the diversion ratios are incorrect; or

(2) the non-co-operative Nash equilibrium assumption is wrong, in which case the estimates of the own-price elasticities from the price-marginal cost mark-ups are unreliable.

Either way, the message in these cases is clear: it is not valid to continue with an analysis that assumes accurate estimates of diversion ratios and non-co-operative Nash equilibrium behaviour.

### Case study: Somerfield/Morrison[14]

**11–028** In 2005, Somerfield sought to acquire 115 stores from Wm Morrison Supermarkets. The merger was referred to the UK's Competition Commission (CC). In addition to a number of other types of empirical analysis, the CC tried to predict potential post-merger price rises using diversion

[14] Competition Commission 2005, "A report on the acquisition by Somerfield plc of 115 stores from Wm Morrison Supermarkets plc".

ratios. This analysis was applied only to those local markets where post-merger there would be four or fewer competing supermarkets. The CC commissioned a survey of 56 of the stores that were going to be acquired. The CC calculated diversion ratios based on the question "If this store had not been available which store would you have used instead?" and estimates of each consumer's spend. The CC then estimated post-merger price increases using these diversion ratios, estimates of the pre-merger price cost margin and the simple formulae discussed above. Stores for which the predicted post-merger price rise was above 5 per cent were identified as providing competition concerns. These are shown in Table 11.10.

**Table 11.10: Predicted post-merger rises in Somerfield-Morrison**                                                                    11–029

| Acquired store | Diversion ratio | Margin | Predicted post-merger price rise (per cent) | |
|---|---|---|---|---|
| | | | CES | Linear |
| Johnstone | 0.72 | 26.9 | 1898.4 | 34.7 |
| South Shields | 0.43 | 25.7 | 36.0 | 9.8 |
| Peebles | 0.36 | 20.8 | 17.5 | 5.9 |
| Middlesborough Linthorpe | 0.34 | 26.0 | 22.4 | 6.8 |
| Frome King St | 0.29 | 25.3 | 16.3 | 5.2 |
| Pocklington | 0.28 | 30.7 | 21.3 | 6.1 |
| Yarm | 0.22 | 28.8 | 13.2 | 4.1 |
| Newark | 0.23 | 25.8 | 11.9 | 3.9 |
| Paisley | 0.21 | 25.4 | 10.3 | 3.5 |
| Filey | 0.21 | 27.8 | 11.1 | 3.6 |
| Poole | 0.19 | 25.3 | 8.5 | 2.9 |
| Whitburn | 0.17 | 24.8 | 7.1 | 2.5 |

*Source:* Table 1 of Appendix E of *Somerfield/Morrison*.

There are two comments to make about this analysis. First, it is based on the simple formulae discussed above. But, as also discussed above, these simple formulae are incorrect except in very limited circumstances.[15] The parties pointed out to the CC that the formulae assumed symmetry between the two merging parties. The CC's response was that in the absence of evidence to the contrary, it was reasonable to assume symmetry. This is not correct. The CC should have checked for symmetry. For instance, were the diversion ratios from Somerfield to Morrison the same

---

[15] Bizarrely, the CC do not mention this fact, even though they footnote the second edition of this book as the source for the derivation of the simple formulae.

as from Morrison to Somerfield? This appears not to have been checked. If you know that particular assumptions are important to your results, then it is incumbent on you to try to confirm that they are reasonable assumptions.

Secondly, the CC argued that the constant elasticity formula was more reliable than the linear demand curve formula. At para.7.26 the CC state:

> "isoelastic demand—i.e. a constant elasticity of demand at difference prices—is as we discuss in Appendix D a realistic assumption: an alternative assumption of linear demand implies elasticity rising as prices increase, which is implausible."

This assertion is surprising, since it is usually assumed that elasticities do rise as prices increase. Furthermore, isoelastic demand implies that the prices of non-merging firms do not respond to the increase in the price of the merging firm's products, which seems unlikely.[16] The assumption of constant elasticity was important since for six of the stores in Table 11.10, the predicted price rise under a linear demand curve was below the CC's chosen 5 per cent threshold for competition concern.

In summary, this approach to using diversion ratios is exactly the type that we think should be avoided. However, we should note that it could have been worse. The CC did at least carry out a survey for estimating the diversion ratios, rather than just assuming that they could be derived from market shares.

## SUMMARY

**11–030** Elasticity estimates can be very useful in market definition. If price-cost margins are known, then elasticity estimates can be compared to the relevant critical elasticity in order to answer the hypothetical monopolist test. The analysis is certainly not without its pitfalls (e.g. consistency between firm specific and market elasticities, correct time period for elasticities and costs, etc.), but nor is it particularly technical.

Critical loss analysis is also useful, but in a rather different way. Critical loss analysis does not answer the hypothetical monopolist test. Instead, it reframes the relevant question in a form that non-practitioners (e.g. business people) are likely to find easier to understand and hence easier to answer.

Diversion ratios are a useful measure of the relative closeness of competition between a number of products. The higher the diversion ratio between two products, the closer competitors they are. This can be useful, particularly when considering which should be the next product added to

---

[16] For a more detailed discussion of this issue, see Chapter 15.

the putative market in a market definition exercise. However, the use of diversion ratios to estimate post-merger price rises is fraught with difficulties and should not be done. If an investigator wishes to estimate post-merger price increases, then this implies the need to carry out a proper merger simulation (see Chapter 15 for details).

## ANNEX 11.1: DERIVATION OF TRUE DIVERSION RATIO FORMULA

In what follows, it is assumed that pre-merger both firms are single product **11–031** firms. If they are not, the analysis is somewhat more complicated, although not different in nature.

The problem that the single product firm faces is to maximise the profit function:

(19) $\quad \Pi = q_i(p_i - c_i) - F_i$

where $\Pi$ are profits, $q_i$ is the output of firm i, $p_i$ is the price of firm i, $c_i$ are (assumed to be) constant marginal costs and $F_i$ are fixed costs. Differentiating this with respect to $p_i$ (i.e. the Bertrand assumption) gives us:

(20) $\quad \dfrac{\delta\Pi}{\delta p_i} = q_i + (p_i - c_i)\dfrac{\delta q_i}{\delta p_i} = 0$

Rearranging this gives us the familiar first-order condition that:

(21) $\quad \dfrac{p_i - c_i}{p_i} = \dfrac{q_i\delta p_i}{p_i\delta q_i} = \dfrac{-1}{\varepsilon_{ii}}$

where $\varepsilon_{ii}$ is the own-price elasticity of demand for Product i.

The problem for the two-product firm is slightly more complicated. The objective function to be maximised is now:

(22) $\quad \Pi = q_i(p_i - c_i) - F_i + q_j(p_j - c_j) - F_j$

Differentiating with respect to $P_i$ gives us:

(23) $\quad \dfrac{\delta\Pi}{\delta p_i} = q_i + (p_i - c_i)\dfrac{\delta q_i}{\delta p_i} + (p_j - c_j)\dfrac{\delta q_j}{\delta p_i} = 0$

The familiar first order condition is now:

(24) $\quad \dfrac{p_i - c_i}{p_i} = \dfrac{-1}{\varepsilon_{ii}} - \dfrac{p_j - c_j}{p_i}\dfrac{\delta q_j}{\delta p_i}\dfrac{\delta p_i}{\delta q_i}$

which can be rewritten as:

(25) $\quad \dfrac{p_i - c_i}{p_i} = \dfrac{-1}{\varepsilon_{ii}} - \dfrac{p_j - c_j}{p_i}D_{ij}$

where $D_{ij}$ is the diversion ratio from i to j. Simple manipulation yields:

(26) $\quad p_i = \dfrac{c_i - D_{ij}(p_j - c_j)}{1 + \frac{1}{\varepsilon_{ii}}}$

By symmetry we can write:

(27) $\quad p_j = \dfrac{c_j - D_{ji}(p_i - c_i)}{1 + \frac{1}{\varepsilon_{jj}}}$

Substituting (27) into (26) yields:

$$(28) \quad p_i \left[ 1 - \frac{D_{ij}D_{ji}}{\left(1 + \frac{1}{\varepsilon_{ii}}\right)\left(1 + \frac{1}{\varepsilon_{jj}}\right)} \right] = \frac{c_i + c_j D_{ij} - \frac{D_{ij}c_j + D_{ij}D_{ji}c_i}{1 + \frac{1}{\varepsilon_{jj}}}}{1 + \frac{1}{\varepsilon_{ii}}}$$

which simplifies to:

$$(29) \quad p_i^* = \frac{c_i \varepsilon_{ii} + c_j D_{ij} \varepsilon_{ii} + c_i \varepsilon_{ii} \varepsilon_{jj} - c_i D_{ij} D_{ji} \varepsilon_{ii} \varepsilon_{jj}}{1 + \varepsilon_{ii} + \varepsilon_{jj} - \varepsilon_{ii} \varepsilon_{jj} - D_{ij} D_{ji} \varepsilon_{ii} \varepsilon_{jj}}$$

where we have replaced $p_i$ with $p_i^*$ to distinguish the new price level ($p_i^*$) from the old one ($p_i$). It follows from (21) that:

$$(30) \quad p_i = \frac{c_i}{1 + \frac{1}{\varepsilon_{ii}}}$$

Using (29) and (30) and simplifying we arrive at:

$$(31) \quad \frac{p_i^* - p_i}{p_i} = \frac{D_{ij}(c_j + c_j \varepsilon_{ii} - c_i D_{ji} \varepsilon_{jj})}{c_i(1 + \epsilon_{ii} + \varepsilon_{jj} - \varepsilon_{ii} \epsilon_{jj} - D_{ij} D_{ji} \epsilon_{ii} \varepsilon_{jj})}$$

## ANNEX 11.2: QUANTIFYING THE POTENTIAL INACCURACIES FROM USING THE SIMPLE DIVERSION RATIO FORMULA

11–032   The main point that we seek to illustrate in this annex is that the simple diversion ratio formula will not be a useful approximation to the correct answer in most cases. There is no substitute to solving the model explicitly in each case. In the case of two single product firms merging, this is just Equation (31) derived in Annex 11.1 and discussed in the main text of this chapter. In the more common case of pre-merger multi-product firms, solving the model is more complicated, although not substantially different from the single product case.

### Variation in sales volumes

11–033   We first allow the relative sales of the two firms to vary, holding the diversion ratios and own-price elasticity of A constant.[17] We set the diversion ratios at 0.15 and the own-price elasticity of demand for A at $-3.33$. The effects of varying the sales volumes on the accuracy of the simple formula are shown in Table 11.A2.1. The first two columns detail the sales volume of the two products. The next two columns contain the post-merger price rises predicted by the model. The next two columns contain the post-merger price rises predicted by the simple formula. It is clear that the predictions using the simple formula can vary substantially from the correct predictions. For instance, when A has a market share of 20

[17]   As discussed in the main text, if we hold the two diversion ratios and the own-price elasticity of demand for one of the products constant, then depending on the sales volumes, this implies the other three elasticities (i.e. one own-price and two cross-price elasticities).

per cent but B has 35 per cent, the simple formula under-predicts the increase in the price of A by 6 per cent and over-predicts the increase in the price of B by 10 per cent.

**Table 11.A2.1: Effect of variations in sales volumes on the** 11–034
**inaccuracy of the simple formula**

| Volumes | | True Price Rise (per cent) | | Formula Price Rise (per cent) | |
|---|---|---|---|---|---|
| **A** | **B** | **A** | **B** | **A** | **B** |
| 20 | 5 | 2.7 | 5.3 | 8.2 | 1.5 |
| 20 | 10 | 4.5 | 6.1 | 8.2 | 3.2 |
| 20 | 15 | 6.3 | 7.0 | 8.2 | 5.4 |
| 20 | 20 | 8.2 | 8.2 | 8.2 | 8.2 |
| 20 | 25 | 10.1 | 9.6 | 8.2 | 11.9 |
| 20 | 30 | 12.1 | 11.5 | 8.2 | 16.9 |
| 20 | 35 | 14.3 | 14.0 | 8.2 | 24.3 |

## Variation in own-price elasticities

We now keep the sales volumes constant and symmetric but allow the own- 11–035
price elasticities between the two products to diverge. Specifically, we keep the sales volumes at 20 for each product, the cross-price elasticities at 0.5, the own-price elasticity of A at −3.33 and just vary the own-price elasticity of B between −2.5 and −4.5. This implies that the diversion ratio from B to A to also varying.

**Table 11.A2.2: Effect of variations in own price elasticities on** 11–036
**the inaccuracy of the simple formula**

| Own-price elasticities | | True Price Rise (per cent) | | Formula Price Rise (per cent) | |
|---|---|---|---|---|---|
| **A** | **B** | **A** | **B** | **A** | **B** |
| −3.33 | −2.50 | 11.6 | 13.9 | 8.2 | 20.0 |
| −3.33 | −3.00 | 9.3 | 9.8 | 8.2 | 11.1 |
| −3.33 | −3.5 | 7.8 | 7.6 | 8.2 | 7.1 |
| −3.33 | −4.0 | 6.7 | 6.1 | 8.2 | 5.0 |
| −3.33 | −4.50 | 5.9 | 5.1 | 8.2 | 3.7 |

It is apparent that the formula will tend to under-estimate the price rise for the higher elasticity product and over-estimate it for the lower elasticity product.

## Variation in marginal costs

**11–037** So far we have assumed that the marginal costs faced by the two firms were the same. In this section we keep everything constant (sales volumes, diversion ratios and elasticities) and vary only the relationship between the marginal costs. We set the sales volumes at 20, the own-price elasticities at $-3.33$, the cross-price elasticities at 0.5 and so the diversion ratios are $-0.15$. Since what determines the degree of inaccuracy of the simple formula is the relative sizes of the marginal costs, not their absolute size, we record below only the ratio of the marginal cost of B to the marginal cost of A.

**11–038** **Table 11.A2.3: Effect of variations in marginal costs on the inaccuracy of the simple formula**

| Ratio of $MC_B$ to $MC_A$ | True Price Rise (per cent) | | Formula Price Rise (per cent) | |
|:---:|:---:|:---:|:---:|:---:|
| | **A** | **B** | **A** | **B** |
| 1.0 | 8.2 | 8.2 | 8.2 | 8.2 |
| 1.2 | 9.6 | 7.1 | 8.2 | 8.2 |
| 1.4 | 10.9 | 6.3 | 8.2 | 8.2 |
| 1.6 | 12.3 | 5.7 | 8.2 | 8.2 |
| 1.8 | 13.6 | 5.2 | 8.2 | 8.2 |
| 2.0 | 15.0 | 4.8 | 8.2 | 8.2 |

Note that this is the symmetric case except for the difference in the marginal costs. It is clear that differences in marginal costs have a significant effect on the accuracy of the formula.

# 12. Bidding Studies

## INTRODUCTION

This chapter looks at three types of analysis that are particularly well suited **12-001** to what are often referred to as "bidding markets". Bidding markets differ from other markets in that sales are made through a tender process. Each firm bids a price to win the tender and then is either chosen as the winning bidder or not. The implication of this is that bidding markets are often characterised by a high degree of price discrimination, with prices being bespoke for each tender. This is different to "normal" markets where prices are typically set by the seller and then buyers decide whether or not to buy. In these markets there tends to be a relatively limited number of different prices (e.g. depending on volume bought) and they do not differ on a customer-by-customer basis.

This chapter is not concerned with the particular economics of bidding markets, but only with the type of empirical analysis that is appropriate for such markets. Nonetheless, before discussing these empirical approaches, we need to dispel some misconceptions about the nature of competition in a bidding market.

It is sometimes argued that in bidding markets market shares are particularly poor indicators of market power. Some have on occasion even gone further and argued that competition concerns do not arise in bidding markets. Klemperer (2008) refers to this as the "consultants' fallacy". We do not subscribe to these views. Whilst it is of course true that market shares can be a poor indicator of market power in bidding markets, this is also true of other markets[1] and so is not a point of distinction between bidding markets and other markets.

Another argument that is often made is that in bidding markets effective competition requires only two or a very few players. The argument runs roughly as follows: in a bidding market, if you do not win a tender then you make no sale to that customer and this "all or nothing" aspect means that

---

[1] For instance, in a perfectly contestable market even a monopolist does not have market power. For more details, see Chapter 3.

firms bid very competitively. This is not an argument that we in general subscribe to. There are bidding markets where the failure to win a tender has very serious consequences for firms and so firms bid very aggressively even when there are only a few competitors. When the size of the tenders on offer is large relative to the size of the total market, there is a particular pressure on firms to be the winning bidder. Failing to win the tender may mean that the firm has to make significant cuts in plant and employees or even that it does not survive. In such markets, the number of firms competing for the market may be a particularly poor indicator of market power. If tenders are large and infrequent, then even with relatively few firms, the serious consequences of failing to win the bid may be enough to ensure that bidding is very competitive. However, most bidding markets do not involve large and infrequent tenders and so this line of argument is not generally applicable (although we do provide an example of such a market below).

**12–002**   A further argument that is sometimes made relates to a comparison between bidding markets and standard differentiated products markets. In a standard differentiated products market, setting a price above what a particular consumer is willing to pay does not lead to no sales at all: unless the price is far too high, there will be some customers who will buy the product. Since it is not usually possible to price discriminate completely between customers, firms in a differentiated product market will set prices above marginal costs and so not serve some customers that it would be profitable to serve (in the sense that the revenue received from them would be above the cost of supply). However, bidding markets are characterised by a high degree of price discrimination (each buyer is offered a different price) and so there is no countervailing benefit to pricing too high for a given customer. It is sometimes argued that this means that competition will necessarily be fierce. This is not correct. If each tender could be characterised as a one-shot homogeneous Bertrand game, then it would be correct. But this is not a good description of most bidding markets. Instead, firms often sell differentiated products and usually compete for many tenders over time. The differentiation of products means that firms do not necessarily have to bid the lowest price in order to win a tender. Buyers may prefer a particular product even though it is not the cheapest available and this allows for winning prices above marginal cost. The fact that firms compete repeatedly means it is possible for them to collude tacitly and thus for prices to be above the competitive level.[2]

We now turn to a description of three forms of analysis that can be used in bidding markets. These are:

- Testing how many bidders are "enough".

- Testing for competitive relevance.

- Testing for closeness of competition.

---

[2]   See Chapters 5 and 7 for further details on explicit and tacit collusion.

# EMPIRICAL ANALYSIS IN BIDDING MARKETS

## Testing how many bidders are "enough"

A reasonable question to ask in a merger in a bidding market is whether **12–003**
there will be enough firms left after the merger to ensure effective competition. One way to consider this question is to look at how prices vary as
the number of bidders varies. Below we present two examples of this type
of analysis. One illustrates a market where only two bidders are needed to
ensure effective competition, whilst the other illustrates a market in which
several bidders are needed.

The first example is the award of advertiser-supported television franchises in the UK television industry. Under the 1990 Broadcasting Act, the
Independent Television Commission (ITC) was required to award 15
regional franchises on the basis of competitive tendering. Each franchise
lasted for at least a 10-year period, so a failure to win a franchise excluded
one from the market for a considerable period. There were 37 applications
for the 15 regional franchises. These applications allow one to investigate
the effect of the number of bidders on the price bid: in three franchises
there was only one bidder; in four franchises there were two bidders; in six
franchises there were three bidders; and in the other two franchises there
were four bidders. The ITC published the number of bidders, their identity
and the amount they bid in a press release.[3] From this it is possible to see
how the size of the bid varied according to the number of bidders.

Figure 12.1 shows the average bid tendered when there was only one
bidder and when there were two, three or four bidders. The bids are
expressed as £s per television household in order to allow for differences in
the size of each franchise area.[4]

---

[3]   "ITC announces Channel 3 licence awards", October 16, 1991.

[4]   Deriving the numbers for Figure 12.1 is not quite as simple as it seems. There are two parts
to the payment that each franchisee had to make to the ITC. In addition to the cash bid,
they had to pay a percentage of their "qualifying revenue" (broadly speaking, their revenue
from advertising, sponsorship and subscriptions). This percentage was set in advance by
the ITC and varied across franchises from 0% to 11%. There is a good argument that this
second part of the franchise fee needs to be taken into account when looking at the cash
bids made since the bidding companies would have been concerned about their total
franchise payments. Figure 12.1 does this and uses the 1998 qualifying revenues.
   Bishop and Bishop (1996) also look at this bidding case study. They derive an even more
striking chart in terms of the difference between one bidder and more than one bidder.
However, it appears that this ignores the qualifying revenue part of the franchise payments
and that it omits bids that the ITC decided were not sustainable (i.e. too high to be
profitable). Both of these omissions may be justifiable, although we prefer not to make
them. Since the qualifying revenue payment is related to the success of the franchisee each
year, it carries less risk to the franchisee than the cash bid part of the franchise fee.
Accordingly, it may be correct to partially discount it. Bids that the ITC deemed unsustainable might be thought of as not being "real bids". The argument would be that such
bids were predicated on the franchisee expecting to be able to renegotiate the cash bid
during the lifetime of the franchise.

**12–004 Figure 12.1: Variation in average bids tendered**

(£ per television household, 1998 prices)

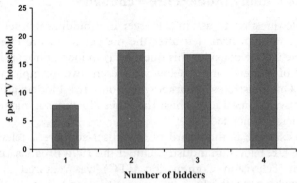

What is striking about this chart is that there is a large difference in the average bid per TV household when there was only one bidder (about £6) compared to when there were two bidders (about £18). Even more interesting, adding extra bidders above two made very little difference to the average bid. Indeed, the average bid when there were three bidders is actually slightly lower than when there were two bidders. The implication of this chart is that in this market two bidders are "enough" to ensure competitive bidding. This explanation assumes that bidders know when they do not face any other bidders: in general, this is unlikely to be a very strong assumption to make. When tendering for a large project, companies will naturally carry out some research as to the number and identity of their rivals.

The results shown in Figure 12.1 are perhaps not surprising. If a firm failed to win a franchise, then it was locked out of the market for at least ten years, which would be expected to encourage aggressive bidding. As it turns out, the ITC[5] has not retendered the franchises, although it has altered the payment terms to remove the large disparities in franchise fees between some franchisees.

Our second example is a hypothetical one and is shown in Figure 12.2. Here firms bid to be the lowest priced supplier. It is apparent from Figure 12.2 that the winning bid falls as the number of bidders increases. The average winning bid falls when we move from one bidder to two bidders (by 15 per cent) and then continues to fall until there are five bidders in the process, at which point the average winning bid is 45 per cent less than when there is only one bidder and 35 per cent less than when there are only two bidders. Increasing the number of bidders above five does not seem to lower prices as prices remain largely unchanged when there are five, six or seven bidders. This suggests that a merger leading to their being only four bidders for a significant number of tenders might be a competition concern.

---

[5] Since the ITC is now part of Ofcom, it is actually Ofcom that has not retendered the franchises.

**Figure 12.2: Variation in average winning bids**                    12–005

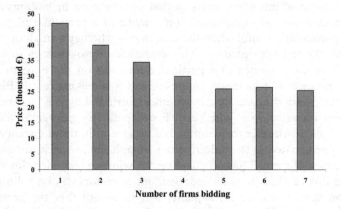

Number of firms bidding

There are two important questions that an investigator needs to ask before drawing firm conclusions from a result such as that in Figure 12.2. The first is to ask if there is a difference in the type of product being sold when there are only a few bidders compared to when there are many bidders. For instance, it might be that there are only a very few firms who are able to produce a high quality product. Assuming that higher quality products cost more to manufacture, it would not be surprising to see an apparent link between the number of bidders and the winning bid even if there was no competition problem.

Secondly, and related to the first question, it is important to ask how many firms the buyer asks to tender. Buyers often limit the number of suppliers that they ask to tender for a contract. This can give some indication of how many bidders are enough since buyers can be expected to ask enough firms to tender to ensure that they receive competitive bids. If buyers only ask for three bidders, then this implies that three is enough. Equally, if buyers insist on six or more, this suggests that fewer bidders (e.g. three or four) are not enough. Further, if a buyer only asks for a few firms to bid for some types of tender but more firms to bid for other types, this may say something about the number of firms that are capable of producing the relevant products. However, evidence of this sort needs to be treated with some care. Klemperer (2008) argues that it is important not to over-estimate the ability of buyers to exercise countervailing power in bidding markets. For instance, if most buyers are small players who buy only infrequently, they may have little ability to exercise buyer power. They may also have little ability to ensure that suppliers stick to the terms of their bids.[6]

---

[6]   Consider, for instance, the relationship between residential customers and builders.

### Testing for competitive relevance

**12–006** Another form of empirical analysis that can be used in bidding markets seeks to estimate the competitive importance of a particular player. This can be particularly useful when the question is whether a small firm has an effect on the market outcome. This empirical approach tries to estimate what effect the presence of a particular firm has on the outcome of the bidding process. For instance, suppose Firm A is seeking to buy Firm B, a small rival, and the question is whether Firm B imposes a competitive constraint on prices (i.e. whether it is competitively relevant). We might want to look at whether the winning bid was lower in those instances when Firm B participated in the bidding than when it did not. If it turns out that the presence of Firm B has no effect on the winning bid, then this suggests that the loss of Firm B as an independent operator may have little or no effect on market outcomes. Equally, if it turns out that the presence of Firm B has a significant effect on the winning bid, then its loss from the market would be more concerning.

There are a number of ways of looking at the competitive relevance of a firm. A very simple approach is just to look at the average winning bid when the firm is involved in the process and the average winning bid when it is not involved in the process. This is illustrated in Table 12.1. Under Scenario 1, the average winning bid is 100 regardless of whether Firm B bids or not. This suggests that the loss of Firm B as an independent player in the market is not competitively significant. However, under Scenario 2 the average winning bid when B does not bid is 10 per cent higher (110 v 100) than when B does bid. This suggests that the loss of B would have a significant effect on the competitive outcome.

**12–007** **Table 12.1: Competitive relevance of Firm B**

|  | Scenario 1 | Scenario 2 |
|---|---|---|
| Average winning bid when B bids | 100 | 100 |
| Average winning bid when B does not bid | 100 | 110 |

This is clearly an unsophisticated approach to looking at the competitive relevance of a firm. In particular, it does not take account of any factors that might affect the winning price except for the presence or absence of Firm B. However, there may be other factors at work that explain why in Scenario 2 the winning bid was higher when B was not present than when it was present. For instance, it might be that Firm B is unable to compete in tenders requiring a particularly high quality of work and this might explain both why the winning bid is high (because the required work is of a high quality) and why Firm B is not in the process.

An alternative approach that does allow for other factors to be taken into account is to use multiple regression techniques. These allow the influences of a number of factors to be taken into account simultaneously.[7] Returning to our example above, suppose the product in question was carbon steel. Carbon steel is differentiated along a number of dimensions: type (flat steel, long steel, etc.), thickness, whether it is galvanised or not and so on. The volume of steel required is also relevant to the unit price. So if we wanted to carry out a more sophisticated analysis of the effect of Firm B on prices, we would carry out a multiple regression analysis in which we estimated the effect on price of each of these factors, plus the presence or absence of Firm B. We might then find that the 10 per cent extra price of winning bids when B was not present in Scenario 2 was explained by these other factors. For instance, it might be that Firm B is unable to produce galvanised steel and so cannot compete in bidding for galvanised steel contracts. Galvanised steel is more expensive than most other carbon steel products as it requires extra processing.

The Commission carried out an analysis of this form in the *Boeing/McDonnell Douglas* merger case.[8] The principal competition concerns arose in the market for large commercial aircraft. Boeing would increase its share of this market by 6 per cent from 64 to 70 per cent. This was made up of an increase in its share of the wide-body segment from 71 to 73 per cent and of the narrow-body segment from 55 to 66 per cent. After the merger, there would only be two competitors in the market: Boeing and Airbus. It might be thought that a market share of 6 per cent meant that McDonnell Douglas was not a credible competitor and so the merger would not lead to a significant loss of competition.

However, the Commission's decision notes that a multiple regression **12-008** study of over 50 bidding competitions suggested that this was not the case. This study compared the price per aircraft realised by the winning bidder when McDonnell Douglas bid and when McDonnell Douglas did not bid and allowed for various other factors that affected price (e.g. type of aircraft, number of aircraft ordered, and so on). The study found that in campaigns where McDonnell Douglas had bid prices were on average 7 per cent lower than when McDonnell Douglas did not bid.

Since it is not discussed in the decision, the precise formulation of the study is not known. However, it is likely to have taken the following general form:

(1)   $Price_i = c + \beta MDC_i + \gamma' \, Otherfactors_i + \varepsilon_i$

where   $Price_i$ is realised price per aircraft in tender i;

$MDC_i$ is a variable reflecting the presence ($MDC_i = 1$) or absence ($MDC_i = 0$) of MDC in the auction;

Other factors$_i$ is a vector of all other factors that are relevant to the

---

[7]   See the Econometric Annex for a description and explanation of multiple regression analysis.

[8]   IV/M877 *Boeing/McDonnell Douglas* [1997] 5 C.M.L.R. 270; [1997] OJ L336/16. The discussion following comes from paras 54 to 58 of the decision.

price (e.g. type of aircraft, number of other bidders, number of aircraft ordered);

$\beta$ and $\gamma$ are regression coefficients.

The coefficient on MDC measures the extent to which the presence of McDonnell Douglas reduces prices.

This study indicated that despite its small market share, McDonnell Douglas was competitively relevant. This is an example of where empirical analysis can provide a better indication of the nature of competition than mere market shares do.

The Commission also spoke directly to various airlines. It found that:

> "Out of the remaining 29 airlines, 20 stated that in those cases where they had placed orders with Boeing or Airbus, MDC had been in competition for all or a part of the orders. Out of the 20 airlines, 13 stated that competition from MDC had an influence on the outcome of their negotiations with the winner of the bid in terms of a better price or better purchasing conditions."[9]

## Testing whether two firms are "close" competitors

**12–009**  As in all markets, market shares are not always a good indication of the strength of competition between two firms. This means that merely adding up market shares in a merger case may not give a good indication of the potential loss of competition. If the two firms are in some sense "competitively close" to each other, then there may be a large loss of competition even if the combined market share is low. Alternatively, if the two firms are not competitively close, then there may be little or no loss of competition even if their market shares are relatively large.[10]

One way to investigate this is to look at the number of occasions on which both firms have bid and to see how often the two firms have put in the first and second most competitive bids. Suppose Firm A and Firm B want to merge in a market where buyers tender for suppliers (i.e. they ask firms to bid their best price and then choose a supplier on that basis). Under what circumstances will this merger lead to buyers paying higher prices? If the two firms are never the lowest and next lowest priced firms in a tender, the buyer will never have to pay a higher price post-merger. This is because there are no tenders in which the winning bid could be higher if the two firms bid as one. Equally, if they were often the lowest and next lowest bidders, then there would be a loss of competition.

Consider the two scenarios in Table 12.2 below. Both of these scenarios show occasions when either Firm A or Firm B has won the tender by

---

[9]  See para.58 of IV/M877 *Boeing/McDonnell Douglas* [1997] 5 C.M.L.R. 270; [1997] OJ L336/16.
[10]  For further discussion of this issue, see Chapter 7.

making the lowest bid. However, there is an important difference between the two. In Scenario 1 the next lowest bid is always by one of the parties. So in the first case in Scenario 1 Firm A bid 100, Firm B bid 105 and the next lowest bid was 110. If Firm A and B had been one firm, then this combined firm would only have had to beat the "Next Lowest" bid of 110 and the result would have been that the buyer would likely have had to pay a higher price. Equally, in the second case in Scenario 1 Firm B made the lowest bid (100) whilst Firm A made the second lowest (105). The next lowest was 120. Post-merger the combined entity would only have had to beat 120, whilst pre-merger Firm B had to beat 105. The implication is that under Scenario 1 a merger of Firm A and Firm B would potentially lead to prices rising.

Conversely, this is not true in Scenario 2. In this Scenario the tender is still won by either Firm A or Firm B, but in each case the next lowest bid is not made by the other party. So in the first case in Scenario 2 Firm A won the bid with 100, Firm B bid 110 but the next lowest bid was 105. So after the merger the combined entity would have to beat 105, which is the same as Firm A had to beat pre-merger. The other cases in Scenario 2 are similar.

## Table 12.2: "Closest substitutes" bidding analysis     12–010

| Scenario 1 | | | Scenario 2 | | |
|---|---|---|---|---|---|
| **A** | **B** | **Next Lowest** | **A** | **B** | **Next Lowest** |
| 100 | 105 | 110 | 100 | 110 | 105 |
| 105 | 100 | 120 | 120 | 100 | 105 |
| 110 | 112 | 115 | 110 | 115 | 112 |
| 95 | 97 | 110 | 95 | 110 | 97 |
| 120 | 115 | 130 | 130 | 115 | 120 |

There are a number of points that should be noted about this form of analysis. First, if the data is available, it is rather simple to carry out. It does not require any sophisticated statistical approaches or modelling. Secondly, it may be difficult for firms to get hold of the data. In a merger case the merging parties will presumably know what they bid on each tender, but they may not know what the next lowest bid was. However, competition authorities may well be able to carry out this analysis even when the parties cannot as they can typically require the various firms in the market to provide the relevant data. Also, buyers may well keep the data on their own tenders and may be willing to hand their data over to a competition authority if they believe the merger may harm them. Thirdly, the logic of the analysis requires that firms have a good idea when they bid as to what other firms are bidding. Thus we assume that in Scenario 1 the parties know they were closest substitutes and so know they could bid higher after the merger. Whilst we might not expect firms to have very detailed knowledge of the bids of the other bidders (i.e. they might not know who was the next lowest in every case), it is likely that over time firms will come to know who their closest competitors are on particular types of tender.

# EXAMPLES OF BIDDING MARKETS

**12–011** The Commission has examined bidding markets in a large number of cases. We discuss some of these below: the joint venture between Group SNECMA and TI Group; the merger between Philips and Agilent; the merger between MCI WorldCom and Sprint; and the merger between GE and Instrumentarium. We also briefly discuss the UK *North Sea Helicopters* case. The *Boeing/McDonnell Douglas* case was discussed above in paras 12–007—12–008.

We start by discussing the GE/Instrumentarium merger because it is an excellent example of two of the three types of analysis discusse above.

## GE/Instrumentarium[11]

**12–012** The *GE/Instrumentarium* decision approved the acquisition by General Electric Medical Systems (GE) of Instrumentarium, a leading hospital equipment manufacturer. The main market segments affected by the transaction included patient monitors, C-arms, and mammography devices. Patient monitors were further distinguished between perioperative and critical care monitors. In each of these markets, the merging parties faced competition from two large suppliers—Philips and Siemens—and a number of smaller firms, which were often present in only some national markets. In each relevant product market, the merged entity would have enjoyed high market shares in a number of national markets (in some cases significantly in excess of 50 per cent).

Sales of these products are made via tenders and so the markets could be characterised as bidding markets. The Commission collected a considerable amount of data from the main players in the various markets and used this to carry out a number of pieces of empirical analysis. We do not discuss all of these below, but instead focus on some of the analysis carried out in two of the markets concerned: the market for mobile C-arms and the market for perioperative patient monitors. The analyses carried out in these two markets provide good examples of two of the types of bidding study described above: analysis of how close two firms are and analysis of whether a firm is competitively relevant. All of the data mentioned below comes from the Commission decision.

[11] COMP/M/3083 *GE/Instrumentarium* (September 2, 2003).

## Mobile C-arms

The Commission estimated that the combined post-merger EEA market  **12–013**
share of the parties in mobile C-arms would be between 45 per cent and 50
per cent. In addition, the Commission identified a number of countries
where the post-merger market shares would be significantly higher, such as
Austria (80–90 per cent for vascular C-arms) and Germany (60–70 per
cent for low-end C-arms). The parties presented an analysis of more than
400 tenders in the EEA between 1998 and 2003 that GE had won. The
aim of the analysis was to see how often Instrumentarium had made the
second lowest bid in those tenders won by GE. The results are shown in
Table 12.3.

### Table 12.3: Runners-up when GE won a mobile C-arm tender  12–014

|  | per cent occasions made second lowest bid |
|---|---|
| Instrumentarium | 0–10 |
| Philips | 30–40 |
| Siemens | 40–50 |

Source: para.244 Case COMP/M/3083 *GE/Instrumentarium* (September 2003).

These results show that on those occasions when GE won a tender, the
second lowest bid was only rarely made by Instrumentarium. The parties
presented a similar analysis of tenders won by Instrumentarium, although
this only covered Germany due to a lack of data for other countries. This
analysis showed that when Instrumentarium won in Germany, GE made
the second lowest bid on only 10–20 per cent of these tenders, whilst the
corresponding figures for Philips and Siemens were 50–60 per cent and
20–30 per cent respectively.[12]

These studies are examples of the "closeness of competition" studies
described above. They suggest that pre-merger there were relatively few
occasions when the binding constraint on GE when it won a tender was
Instrumentarium, and vice versa. Instead, the binding constraint typically
came from Siemens or Philips. Both of these firms would remain after the
merger and so the implication is that in general the binding constraints pre-
merger would remain post-merger, thus indicating that the merger was not
likely to lead to prices rising.

The Commission also carried out an econometric analysis. This used
data from Siemens as well as from the parties.[13] The aim of the analysis was
to measure the effect on the price offered by GE of Instrumentarium being

---

[12] COMP/M/3083 *GE/Instrumentarium* (September 2, 2003) para.245.
[13] The Commission reported in the decision that although it also had data from Philips, the
quality of this data was too poor to be usable.

present in a tender. This analysis is an example of the "competitive relevance" studies that we described above. Price was measured by the discount off the list price offered in each tender. If GE consistently offered lower prices (i.e. higher discounts) when Instrumentarium was present, this would suggest that the loss of Instrumentarium as an independent bidder would lead to GE pricing higher post-merger. However, the Commission found that the presence or absence of Instrumentarium had no effect on GE's prices.

> "The results of this extended empirical assessment were that the presence of Instrumentarium as an independent bidder in the auction and the number of bidders does not appear to have had any systematic influence over the size of the discount offered by GE in its bids. In none of the models that the Commission estimated was the coefficient of the dummy variable capturing the presence of Instrumentarium in the auction statistically significant." (para.248)

The Commission concluded that despite potentially high post-merger market shares, the transaction would not lead to the merged entity being dominant in mobile C-arms, either across the whole of the EEA or in individual countries.

### Perioperative patient monitors

12–015    The Commission found that the post-merger market share of perioperative patient monitors was more than 50 per cent and the increment in market share more than 5 per cent in five countries: France (55–60 per cent[14]), Germany (45–50 per cent), Spain (80–85 per cent), Sweden (70–75 per cent) and the United Kingdom (80–85 per cent).

Using data on more than 3,000 tenders across the EEA between 1998 and 2003, the Commission investigated how often the parties competed against each other. It found that the parties met in 50–60 per cent of the tenders. Of these tenders, the parties faced no other competitor 20–30 per cent of time and only one other competitor 20–30 per cent of the time. It also found that in 30–40 per cent of cases where the parties faced competition, it came from fringe players only and not from Philips or Siemens. The Commission concluded that this meant that post-merger there would be a reduction from two to one in the number of significant players bidding in about a third of tenders.

The Commission also relied on an analysis of tenders won by Instrumentarium between 1998 and 2003. This included more than 2,000 tenders. This showed GE was the runner-up 50–60 per cent of the time in

---

[14]    The figure given in the decision is 55–100%. However, the figures for the two firms separately (5–10% and 45–50%) indicate that the 100% figure is a mistake.

France, 70–80 per cent of the time in Germany and 60–70 per cent of the time in Spain. The Commission concluded that:

"This would therefore suggest that, at least in France, Germany and Spain, GE is the closest competitor to Instrumentarium." (para.147)

For France and Germany this is contrary to what might be expected based only on the market shares. The Commission estimated that Instrumentarium's market share in France was between 45 per cent and 50 per cent. This implies that the market share of all other firms was 50–55 per cent. The Commission estimated that GE has a share of 5–10 per cent. This means that GE had between 10 per cent and 20 per cent of the non-Instrumentarium "market" (i.e. 5 out of 55 per cent is 9 per cent; 10 out of 50 per cent is 20 per cent). So on the basis of market shares alone, one might therefore expect GE to be the runner up to Instrumentarium between 10 and 20 per cent of the time. However, the study showed that the actual figure was more than 50 per cent. The same is broadly true for Germany. This shows that deriving "closeness of competition" from market shares can lead to significant mistakes. Based only on market shares, it would have appeared that both Philips and Siemens were closer competitors to Instrumentarium in France and Germany than was GE. The analysis of the bidding data indicates that in fact GE was the closest competitor in both countries.

The result for Spain is more in line with the market shares. Instrumentarium's market share was 65–70 per cent and GE's was 15–20 per cent. If Instrumentarium's market share was 65 per cent and GE's 20 per cent, then we might expect GE to be the runner up to Instrumentarium in about 57 per cent (20/35) of cases. So the figure for Spain (60–70 per cent) is not so unexpected based on market shares.

The Commission was also able to carry out an econometric analysis of GE's pricing in France.[15] When GE won, its winning bid was on average a discount off list prices of 35–45 per cent when Instrumentarium was also bidding, but only 25–35 per cent when Instrumentarium was not bidding. The difference between these average discounts was statistically significant. This suggested that post-merger GE would raise its prices as it would no longer be constrained by Instrumentarium.

The Commission concluded that the merger would lead to the parties having a dominant position post-merger in perioperative patient monitors. As a result, the parties offered a divestment remedy that cured these concerns.

---

[15] The analysis that we discuss actually looked at Dräger's pricing in France. Dräger was the exclusive distributor of GE's perioperative monitors in the EEA between March 1999 and February 2002.

## Group SNECMA/TI Group[16]

**12–016** This case involved the creation of a joint venture between the two landing gear subsidiaries of SNECMA and TI. This merger reduced the number of major suppliers of landing gear from four to three. On the basis of the value of contracts won during 1993 the joint venture would have created an entity with a market share of less than 30 per cent.[17] The largest competitors remaining in the market were Menasco Aerospace Ltd and Goodrich Aerospace Cleveland Pneumatic Corp. They had shares of total contracts in value terms similar to the merged entity.[18] Competition in the market for landing gear takes the form of bidding to be the long-term supplier of landing gear to each different model of aircraft. The design of landing gear for each model of aircraft is different and so each bidder is offering both a design and a price. This means that once a bidder has been chosen and the contract awarded, the aircraft manufacturer has no substitutes for the supplier and design of landing gear chosen.[19] The landing gear industry therefore provides a good example of competition *for* the market. This was recognised by the Commission which noted that:

> "market share figures for products such as landing gear should be viewed in the perspective of the long product life-cycles of the aircraft manufacturing industry ... Future competition will be for new long-term contracts for new aircraft-specific landing gear units and existing market shares may only be a rough indicator of the relative competitive strengths of companies which will bid for those new contracts."[20]

The Commission defined the relevant market for civil applications as worldwide. The Commission noted that the US suppliers were credible bidders who were expanding their geographical spread, particularly in Europe, and extending the range of landing gear that they intended to produce. On this basis, one could concur with the Commission's decision that the merger did not raise serious competition concerns.

## Philips/Agilent[21]

**12–017** *Philips/Agilent* provides an example of testing whether two firms were close competitors. The competition concern in this case was an overlap in the cardiac ultrasound market. Philips had entered the ultrasound market in

---

[16] IV/M368 *Group SNECMA/TI Group* [1994] OJ C42/12.

[17] IV/M368 *Group SNECMA/TI Group* [1994] OJ C42/12 at para.23.

[18] IV/M368 *Group SNECMA/TI Group* [1994] OJ C42/12 at para.33.

[19] This was perhaps not strictly true but the large switching costs involved in going to another supplier meant that in effect the aircraft manufacturer was locked into the landing gear supplier once the contract had been awarded.

[20] IV/M368 *Group SNECMA/TI Group* [1994] OJ C42/12 at para.25.

[21] COMP/M2256 *Philips/Agilent* [2001].

1998 with the acquisition of ATL and now wanted to buy Healthcare Solutions Group (HSG) from Agilent. The post-merger market share of the merged entity would be around 40 per cent of the EEA market.[22] The Commission concluded that HSG and ATL were not each other's closest competitors. The parties submitted a bidding study of tenders that HSG had taken part in. Using data for 1998–2000, the study found that when HSG won a tender, both GE and Siemens were in second place more often than was ATL. When HSG lost a tender, GE and Siemens were both the winner more often than ATL. The Commission concluded that:

> "for HSG's cardiac ultrasound machines ... GE and Siemens/Acuson are the strongest challengers on both projects won and lost. ATL is generally the third ranked. Therefore, it can be assumed that Philips/ HSG would not be in a position to increase prices for one or both products without facing competitive constraints by the other first-tier suppliers." (para.35).

## MCI WorldCom/Sprint[23]

One of the concerns that the Commission had in this case was that it would **12–018** lead to collective dominance in the market for global telecommunications services (GTS) sold to multinationals. The post-merger market shares calculated by the Commission put the merged parties at between 25 per cent and 40 per cent, and the Concert alliance at between 25 per cent and 45 per cent. The Commission noted that GTS were sold on the basis of bidding contests and suggested that this bidding structure of the market would allow the two leading parties to coordinate their behaviour successfully. The argument was broadly this: each bid consists of two stages; in the first stage firms bid on the basis of quality of services, not price; in the second stage they compete on price; after the merger, MCI WorldCom/ Sprint and Concert could offer at the first stage a combination of services that smaller players could not match and so would be the only firms to reach the second stage; they would then price softly because there would be only two competitors left, bids were frequent and so tacit collusion was possible.

There were many weaknesses in the Commission's analysis of how bidding worked in this market and the parties attacked the Commission's analysis on a number of substantive grounds. However, the key ground was that the Commission was assuming that smaller players such as Equant and Cable & Wireless, with market shares of less than 5 per cent, could not impose competitive constraints on the merged entity or the Concert

---

[22] COMP/M2256 *Philips/Agilent* [2001] at para.24.
[23] COMP/M1741 *MCI WorldCom/Sprint* [2000].

alliance. However, the Commission noted that what matters is a firm's ability to bid credibly, not its market share. Thus the Commission reported:

> "Notably, the parties explained that in bidding markets ... firms with a small market share *e.g.* Equant and Cable & Wireless are able to effectively constrain the behaviour of companies with larger market shares." (para.295)

Smaller players were able to put together credible bids, despite their apparently low market shares, and so the Commission concluded by saying:

> "The Commission recognises that it was not able to show the absence of competitive constraints from actual competitors such as Equant or Cable & Wireless to the merging parties and the Concert Alliance." (para.302)

### North Sea Helicopters[24]

**12-019** In 2000, two supplies of helicopter services to offshore oil and gas facilities in the northern sector of the North Sea, Bond and Brintel, successfully sought to merge.[25] This was a three-to-two merger as the two companies faced only one other competitor pre-merger (i.e. Bristow). This was a bidding market. Oil companies awarded contracts via bidding processes. The contracts that were awarded tended to be long-term contracts of between three and five years duration. There were relatively few buyers and so each contract represented a relatively large proportion of the relevant market. This suggests that competition might be effective even with only two players. In addition, barriers to entry were low and so there was a credible threat of new entry if prices were to rise post-merger. As part of its investigation, the UK Competition Commission received evidence from the parties about the comparison between gross margins in the Norwegian market, where there were only two players, and the northern sector of the North Sea, where there were three players. The comparison was based on gross margins to allow for the fact that costs were higher in the Norwegian market than in the North Sea market. The parties showed that over the period 1995 to 1998, gross margins in the Norwegian market were consistently less than in the North Sea. This is shown in Figure 12.3.[26] The parties argued that this evidence was consistent with the proposition that

---

[24] "CHC Helicopter Corporation and Helicopter Services Group ASA: A report on the merger situation", Cm 4556, January 1, 2000.
[25] The discussion of this case relies on Oldale (2000).
[26] This chart is reproduced from Oldale (2000).

moving from three players to two players would not lead to a loss of effective competition.

**Figure 12.3: Gross margins in the northern North Sea and**   12–020
**Norwegian sectors**

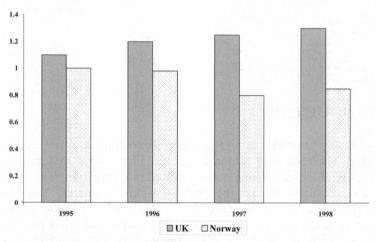

## SUMMARY

There are a number of forms of empirical analysis that can be carried out in   **12–021**
bidding markets. In this chapter we have discussed three of them:

1) Effective competition may only require a relatively small number of firms to be active in a market. An analysis of the relationship between price and the number of bidders can reveal how many firms are required for effective competition.

2) Market shares do not always provide a good proxy for competitive strength. In bidding markets it is often possible to analyse the effect that a small firm has on the competitive outcome.

3) An important question in unilateral effects cases is how "close" are the merging parties. The type of data available in bidding markets (i.e. data on the bids made by the firms that take part in tenders) can often be used to determine whether the merging parties are close competitors or not.

# 13. Shock analysis

## INTRODUCTION

**13–001** It is sometimes said that empirical analysis in competition law cases is too complex. There are two responses to this. First, this simply reflects the complexity of the underlying issues involved in competition law cases; it is therefore unsurprising that the analysis is often complex. Secondly, in many instances, the statement is incorrect. Many empirical tests are neither difficult to undertake nor unintuitive. This chapter discusses a technique called *shock analysis*. Although this technique is simple, properly applied it can provide a powerful test of competing hypotheses.

Shock analysis uses past events in an industry to inform us about the nature of competition in that industry. Shock analysis looks at shocks that have occurred to an industry and considers whether the response of the industry to the shock tells us anything of interest about the industry. In truth, this is not so much an empirical technique as the appliance of common sense to data. Shocks to an industry can convey a substantial amount of information about how an industry operates. The types of shock that can be useful include:

- New product launches: when a new product is launched, from whom does it appear to steal sales? In general, we would expect it to win sales from substitute products and not from products with which it does not compete.

- Exchange rate shocks: when the relative prices of two products are changed by an exchange rate shock, what happens to those prices thereafter? This type of shock can be useful for geographic market definition.

- Differential input cost shocks: when the relative costs of production of two products are changed due to an input cost shock suffered by only one of them (e.g. one of the products is manufactured using oil but the other is not), what happens to their prices thereafter? If the two products are close substitutes, then we should expect the pricing of the product that has not suffered the input cost shock to move in line with the product that has. This might involve the price of the product that has suffered the input cost shock not moving because it is constrained by the price of the substitute product. Or it might involve the price of the substitute product rising in response to a rise in the price of the product that has suffered an input cost shock.

- Effect of advertising campaigns. When one product engages in a new advertising campaign that boosts its sales, from whom does it steal the sales? Which products respond with their own advertising campaigns.

It should be noted that the Commission itself has endorsed the use of shock analysis as being potentially very useful in market definition. At para.38 of its Market Definition Notice[1] the Commission wrote:

"*Evidence of substitution in the recent past.* In certain cases, it is possible to analyse evidence relating to recent past events or shocks in the market that offer actual examples of substitution between two products. When available, this sort of information will normally be fundamental for market definition. If there have been changes in relative prices in the past (all else being equal), the reactions in terms of quantities demanded will be determinant in establishing substitutability. Launches of new products in the past can also offer useful information, when it is possible to precisely analyse which products have lost sales to the new product."

This chapter is organised as follows. In paras 13–002—13–008 we provide three examples of shock analysis. Two of these come from past European Commission cases whilst one is a hypothetical example. We then discuss another form of shock analysis in paras 13–009–13–016: stock market event studies. Paragraph 13–017 concludes.

# CASE STUDIES

## Procter & Gamble/VP Schickedanz[2]

An important competitive issue in this case was whether sanitary towels **13–002** were in the same product market as tampons. The Commission carried out a shock analysis of this issue. In July 1991, Procter & Gamble launched its

---

[1] European Commission *Notice on the Definition of the Relevant Market for the Purposes of Community Competition Law* [1997] OJ C372/5; [1998] 4 C.M.L.R. 177.
[2] IV/M430 *Procter & Gamble/VP Schickedanz* [1994] OJ L354/32.

sanitary towel product, *Always*, in Germany. In its decision the Commission focused on what happened in the sanitary towels and tampons markets afterwards. It first looked at prices and found that in two and half years after the entry of *Always*, other sanitary towel prices hardly changed, whilst tampon prices rose significantly (see Table 13.1).

**13–003 Table 13.1: Price changes following the entry of *Always***

|  | per cent change to price | |
|---|---|---|
|  | Tampons | Towels |
| **Within 6 months** | 0.7 | −3.8 |
| **At February 1994** | 18.2 | 2.3 |

*Source*: para.63 of Commission decision.

This simple evidence suggested that *Always* imposed a competitive constraint on other towels, but not on tampons. The Commission then looked at the effect of the entry on the proportion of women using tampons or towels. If *Always* competed equally with both towels and tampons in Germany, then one would expect it to take market share from both towels and tampons. Table 13.2 shows that this was not the case.

**13–004 Table 13.2: Evolution of penetration ratio in Germany**

|  | *Always* | Other towels | Total towels | Tampons |
|---|---|---|---|---|
| **July 90/June 91** | 0 | 64 | 64 | 36 |
| **July 91/June 92** | 5 | 58 | 63 | 37 |
| **July 92/June 93** | 11 | 52 | 63 | 37 |

*Source*: para.64 of Commission decision.

Table 13.2 indicates that *Always* took market share from other towels, but not from tampons. Again, this implies that *Always* competed with other towels but not with tampons in Germany. The Commission also noted (at para.71) that it appeared that when *Always* entered the Nordic countries, the other towel manufacturers responded by raising their advertising expenditure, but the tampon manufacturers did not.

The evidence provided by this shock analysis around the time of the entry of *Always* into the German market was both simple and powerful. Certainly, the Commission appears to have relied heavily on it in concluding that sanitary towels and tampons were in separate relevant product markets.[3]

---

[3] Para.75 of the decision states that "the Commission concludes that there are indeed clearly separate markets—not only for pantliners but also for pads and tampons."

## Exchange rate shock

Exchange rate shocks can provide useful evidence on geographic market **13–005** definition. Suppose that the question is whether products sold in different countries are part of the same relevant market. Further, suppose that there was an exchange rate shock so that the currency of a country depreciated by around 20 per cent. This would make the price of foreign products, when converted into the domestic currency, about 20 per cent more expensive. The interesting question is then what happens after that. Do the prices of the products in different countries, when converted into a common exchange rate, converge over time or not? Figure 13.1 provides an example in which they do converge. At the start of the period the prices of domestic and foreign product, when converted into the domestic currency, are about the same. There is then an exchange rate shock which led to an immediate increase in the price of foreign product, when converted into the domestic currency, of about 20 per cent. However, over the next 15 months the prices in the two countries converged again. The price of domestic product rises whilst the price of the foreign product falls. The result is that after 15 months both products are priced about 10 per cent higher in terms of the domestic currency. This actually means that the price of the foreign product has fallen since the exchange rate depreciation of 20 per cent means it should be priced 20 per cent higher, when converted into domestic currency, than it previously was.

The implication of this is that these products do impose a competitive constraint on each other. When the price of foreign product rose in domestic currency terms, this appears to have allowed the domestic price of the product to rise. Equally, the competition between the two products has meant that the price of the foreign product has not been able to fully reflect the exchange rate shock.

## Figure 13.1: Example of an exchange rate shock                  13–006

What does this imply about the two products? It implies that they are in the same geographic market as it appears that their prices do not remain out of line with each other in anything but the short-run.

## AstraZeneca[4]

**13–007** The Commission used shock analysis, among a number of other empirical techniques, in its AstraZeneca (AZ) Article 82 decision. This case related to AZ's product *Losec*. This was the first proton pump inhibitor (PPI), which is a class of drug used to treat various acid-related gastro-intestinal diseases.[5] Prior to the introduction of PPIs, the most common type of drugs used to treat the various acid-related gastro-intestinal diseases were histamine receptor antagonists (H2 blockers).

An important question was whether H2 blockers and PPIs were in the same relevant market during the period of the alleged abuse (1991–2000). If H2 blockers were in the same relevant market, then it would have been very hard for the Commission to argue that AZ was dominant and hence very hard for them to run an abuse of dominance case against AZ.

Paragraphs 418 to 437 of the decision deal with market definition in Germany. The Commission refers to four pieces of evidence that are relevant to this question. The Commission states:

> "These 'natural events' constitute important evidence of the existence of significant competitive constraints on the market as they allow for testing of AZ's hypothesis of a common relevant product market containing PPIs and H2 blockers." (para.421)

The four pieces of evidence were:

1    When the second PPI, pantoprazole was launched in Germany in September 1994, the price of Losec fell by 16 per cent, but there did not appear to be any effect on the prices of H2 blockers. The Commission argued that this showed that the new PPI competed with the existing PPI but not with H2 blockers.

2    The entry of a generic version of the H2 blocker Ranitidine in 1995 lead to H2 blocker prices falling substantially (by 40 per cent over three months) but had no effect on the prices of the PPIs. This suggested that the generic Ranitidine competed with other H2 blockers but not with PPIs.

3    The Commission noted that there was a sharp increase in promotional activity of H2 blockers just prior to the entry of generic

---

[4]  COMP/A.37.507/F3 *AstraZeneca* (June 15, 2005).
[5]  Peptic ulcers, gastro-intestinal oesophagael reflux and dyspepsia.

Ranitidine, but no increase in the promotional activity of PPIs. The Commission argued that this showed that an increase in competition in the H2 blocker segment had "no spill-over effect into the PPI market".[6]

4   The launch of generic omeprazole (the active substance in Losec) had a significant effect on sales of Losec, which fell by about 60 per cent. The sales of all PPIs fell, but not by as much. The Commission argued that this showed that Losec was far more constrained by its closest substitute than by H2 blockers.

If it is the case that price competition is an important dimension of com-   **13–008** petition in pharmaceutical markets, then the analysis that the Commission carried out appears to have been both simple and intuitively appealing. For instance, the fact that the entry of a second PPI affected Losec prices but not H2 blocker prices does look like good evidence that PPI competition had little effect on H2 blockers. The reverse appears to be true based on the entry of generic Ranitidine: H2 blocker competition had little effect on PPI competition.

However, it should be noted that the Commission's conclusions are not immune from criticism. In a market in which competition was primarily on price, the Commission's conclusions would seem to be reasonable and then this would be an example of simple analysis providing strong conclusions. However, it may be that in pharmaceutical markets price competition is not a primary dimension of competition.[7]

# STOCK MARKET EVENT STUDIES

Another form of shock analysis is a stock market event study. The idea   **13–009** behind these studies is to use the reaction of the stock market to merger-related announcements to infer information about the likely effect of a merger. The standard test (the so-called "Eckbo-Stillman" test[8]) focuses on the share price movements of rival firms, not of the merging parties. It is standard that merger announcements usually lead to the share prices of the merging parties rising. However, this does not tell us very much about

---

[6]   COMP/A.37.507/F3 *AstraZeneca* (June 15, 2005). para.424.
[7]   We understand that AZ argued that price competition was not the primary dimension of competition. AZ apparently noted that in pharmaceutical markets, doctors determine the choice of drug for a given condition and doctors tend to make decisions on therapeutic rather than financial grounds. This raises a question of how much weight to place on price-based analysis in pharmaceutical markets. We understand that AZ drew on a detailed analysis of prescribing behaviour to argue that PPIs and H2 blockers were prescribed for virtually all micro-diagnoses over the period in question, which it viewed as evidence supporting a wider market.
[8]   So-called because of pioneering work in the application of event studies to antitrust by Eckbo (1983) and Stillman (1983).

whether the stock market believes the merger is anti-competitive or pro-competitive. An anti-competitive merger leading to higher prices and hence higher profits for the merging parties would be expected to lead to the share prices of the merging parties rising. But the same is true of a pro-competitive merger that was expected to boost profits as a result of merger efficiencies lowering costs. So instead the Eckbo-Stillman test looks at the share prices of competing firms. If a merger is expected to lead to higher prices from the merging parties, then this should benefit competing firms and so their share prices should rise. On the other hand, if the merger is expected to lead to the parties becoming more efficient, this will harm competitors who have to compete against a more efficient rival and so should lead to their share prices falling.

An event study compares the actual share price change when the merger is announced to the share price change that would otherwise have been expected. Even without any news, share prices move on a daily basis, so it is necessary to allow for this when carrying out an event study. The usual approach is to assume that the expected return to a stock is

(1)   $r_t = \alpha + \beta \, r_{mt}$

where   $r_t$ is the return to a stock at time t;

$r_{mt}$ is the return to the market portfolio at time t; and

$\alpha$ and $\beta$ are coefficients.

Equation (1) just says that the expected return to a share is equal to a constant plus a proportion $\beta$ of the return on the market.[9] The coefficients $\alpha$ and $\beta$ can be estimated via simple multiple regression analysis using daily data from before the merger announcement.[10] It is then possible to estimate the "abnormal return" ($ar_t$) on the day of the merger announcement:

(2)   $ar_t = r_t - \alpha - \beta \, r_{mt}$

We expect that this will be positive for the merging parties. The Eckbo-Stillman test concentrates on whether for competitors to the merging parties their abnormal return is positive (implying an anti-competitive merger), negative (implying a pro-competitive merger) or neither.[11]

**13–010**   A simple example should help to illustrate the Eckbo-Stillman test. Suppose that Firm A announces that it is going to buy Firm B. Suppose that $\alpha$ is zero and $\beta$ is one for both firms and that on the day of the announcement the stock market rises by 5 per cent. Then the expected

---

[9]   Those familiar with basic finance theory will note that this equation is just the capital asset pricing model with $\alpha = (1-\beta) \, r_{RF}$ where $r_{RF}$ is the risk-free rate of return.

[10]   See the Econometric Annex for an explanation of mutliple regression analysis.

[11]   It has been suggested (e.g. Fee and Thomas (2004)) that a similar approach could be taken to look at the effect of a merger on upstream suppliers. The argument is that if the merged firm can use its increased buyer power post-merger to get lower input prices, which should be pro-competitive, then this would show up in a reduction in the stock prices of upstream suppliers. However, another reason for upstream stock prices falling would be if the merged entity increased its prices and reduced output post-merger, thus requiring fewer inputs from upstream firms. So this approach does not discriminate between a pro-competitive and an anti-competitive explanation.

return for both A and B is 5 per cent. Suppose that Firm C, a competitor to A and B, also has $\alpha$ and $\beta$ of 0 and one, so its expected return is also 5 per cent. Table 13.3 provides two possible scenarios. In both examples the abnormal return to the merging parties is positive: 7 per cent and 11 per cent for A and B in Scenario 1, 18 per cent and 23 per cent in Scenario 2. But the abnormal return for C, the competing firm, differs markedly between the two scenarios. In Scenario 1, the share price of C actually falls by 5 per cent on the announcement of the merger and so its abnormal return is $-10$ per cent. According to the Eckbo-Stillman test, this indicates that the merger is pro-competitive. In Scenario 2, the share price of C rises by 17 per cent and so its abnormal return is 12 per cent. This indicates that the merger is anti-competitive.

## Table 13.3: Example of an event study           13–011

|  | Scenario 1 | Scenario 2 |
|---|---|---|
| Expected return for A, B and C | 5% | 5% |
| Actual return to A | 12% | 23% |
| Abnormal return to A | 7% | 18% |
| Actual return to B | 16% | 28% |
| Abnormal return to B | 11% | 23% |
| Actual return to C | −5% | 17% |
| Abnormal return to C | −10% | 12% |

There are a number of problems with the Eckbo-Stillman test. First, the basic logic of the test only works when the anti-competitive concern is that the merged entity will raise prices and that this will allow other firms to also raise their prices. This is the standard concern in a horizontal merger. However, if the competition concern is that the merged entity will engage in post-merger exclusionary behaviour, then the Eckbo-Stillman test does not work. This is because when the concern is exclusionary, then competitors to the merging parties suffer harm both if the merger is anti-competitive and if it is pro-competitive. Exclusionary concerns arise most often in vertical mergers,[12] but have also arisen in horizontal mergers (e.g. *GE/Honeywell*[13]).

Secondly, the *power* of the test may be very low. What this means is that it may be very difficult to identify any effect on the share prices of competing firms even when the merger is anti-competitive. There are a number of reasons for this. Perhaps the main one is that most firms are multi-product firms and so even if their expected profitability in one product is altered significantly by a merger announcement, this might have little effect

---

[12] See Chapter 7 for a discussion of theories of harm in vertical mergers.
[13] COMP/M.2220 *General Electric/Honeywell* (July 3, 2001).

on the overall profitability of the firm. Suppose an announced merger was anti-competitive and would lead to the profits of a competitor rising by 10 per cent. If the product in question only accounted for 25 per cent of that firm's profits, then this only translates into a 2.5 per cent increase in the share price. Given that share prices tend to be volatile, it may well be difficult to identify movements of this size in daily data. There are also technical reasons why the Eckbo-Stillman test may have low power. One of these is that it may be difficult to test whether any abnormal return is statistically significant.[14]

McAfee and Williams (1988) argue that event studies are unlikely to be able to detect anti-competitive mergers. They carry out an event study of a merger that was known to be anti-competitive and show that share price movements did not show this. McAfee and Williams look at the acquisition of Kalvar Corp by Xidex Corp. Both firms produced non-silver duplicate microfilm. Three months after the merger, Xidex closed down Kalvar's only plant and sacked its entire staff. McAfee and Williams estimate that this allowed Xidex to raise its prices and that this led to a significant increase in Xidex's profits in the following two years that was larger than the acquisition price. However, they find that the share prices of rival firms showed no evidence of this anti-competitive effect. That is, they were unable to find any positive abnormal returns for competitors around the time of the merger announcements. Indeed, if anything the abnormal returns tended to be negative (although not statistically significant). McAfee and Williams suggest that the main problem with event studies is that firms tend to be multiproduct firms and merger effects typically only affect a subset of those products.

**13–012**   A further reason why event studies may have low power is that it may not be clear when news of the merger reached the stock market. There are often rumours of mergers before they are formally announced. If the stock market factors these rumours into share prices before the formal announcement of the merger, then there may be relatively little share price reaction on the day of the announcement. If it is not clear when the information reached the market, it is not possible to test what effect the information had on share prices.

There is also a logical problem with the Eckbo-Stillman test. The idea is that the stock market will understand when a merger is anti-competitive (in the sense of leading to higher prices) and so will factor this in to share prices. But if the stock market knows that a merger is anti-competitive, then why does it not also expect that the competition authorities will block it, or at least remedy the anti-competitive effects of the merger? Alternatively, if the stock market knows the merger is anti-competitive, why

---

[14]   The issue here is that standard significance testing requires that daily stock market returns are normally distributed. This is generally not the case. For further details, see Ford and Kline (2006).

does it think the competition authority will nonetheless clear the merger? If the share price of competitors rises on the announcement, it cannot be because the stock market expects the merger to be anti-competitive unless the stock market also believes that the competition authority will not block the merger. It seems more reasonable to assume that the competition authority will block the merger and that the stock market will expect this outcome, in which case the Eckbo-Stillman test cannot work.

Finally, it should be noted that one reason that the share prices of competing firms may rise on the announcement of a merger is that the stock market may believe that these other firms may also become takeover targets and that this belief leads to their share prices rising.

## Examples of event studies

### Staples-Office Depot

Warren-Boulton and Dalkir (2001) carried out an event study of the **13–013** Staples-Office Depot merger. This merger involved two of the three office superstores in the United States (OfficeMax was the third) attempting to merge. The FTC was granted a preliminary injunction blocking the merger and the parties subsequently abandoned the merger.[15] Warren-Boulton and Dalkir looked at six events, from the original announcement of the merger to the court decision to grant the preliminary injunction. The effect of the announcement of the merger and the combined effects of the FTC announcement of its challenge and then the court decision are shown in Table 13.4.

## Table 13.4: Staples-Office Depot event study                         13–014

|  | Abnormal returns (per cent) | | |
|---|---|---|---|
|  | **Staples** | **Office Depot** | **OfficeMax** |
| **Announcement of merger** | −2.8% | 30.0% | 10.6% |
| **FTC challenge and court decision** | 6.5% | −59.3% | −15.3% |

*Source*: Warren-Boulton and Dalkir (2001)

The effect of the merger announcement on the parties is relatively common: the share prices of acquiring firms often fall when a merger announcement is made,[16] whilst the share price of the target virtually always rises. However, what is interesting about Table 13.4 is the effect of

---

15  For further details of this merger, see Chapters 14 and 15.
16  Explanations for this tend to focus on the possibility that the acquiring firm is paying more for the target than it is worth or on the possibility that the merger will cause the management of the acquiring firm to stop focusing on running their existing business properly.

the merger announcement, and then the subsequent blocking of the deal, on OfficeMax. OfficeMax abnormal return was more than 10 per cent on the day of the announcement, which is consistent with the hypothesis that the merger was anti-competitive and would have led to price rises. The effect on OfficeMax's share price of the blocking of the merger seems to confirm this as OfficeMax suffered a negative abnormal return of −15 per cent. The authors conclude that:

> "the financial market expected that this merger would lead to a price increase for products in markets where OfficeMax currently competes with Staples and Office Depot."[17]

## UK cases

**13–015** Beverley (2007) carries out event studies of various decisions by the UK Competition Commission. The overall impression from the sample is to confirm that event studies tend to be of low power. For instance, Beverley looked at the *HMV/Ottakar's*[18] merger and the effect of various announcements on the share price of a major competitor in the retail book market, WH Smith. Beverley found that WH Smith's share price did react positively to one event and that this was consistent with an anti-competitive theory of harm. But she also found that the positive reaction was not statistically significant and so discounted it. WH Smith's share price did not seem to react to other events in the study.

In the *Baggeridge/Wienerberger*[19] merger there were two quoted firms who were reasonably specialised in the relevant market (i.e. the UK brick market), which suggests that this might have been a good market in which to use an event study. However, Beverley found no share price reactions from either of the competitors to any of the bid events.

## Microsoft

**13–016** Bittlingmayer and Hazlett (2000) carried out an event study of the US enforcement action against Microsoft between 1991 and 1997. They identified 159 other quoted firms operating in the computer industry. These constituted a mixture of competitors to Microsoft, customers of Microsoft and sellers of products complementary to those of Microsoft. They identified 54 events related to the litigation against Microsoft. They

---

[17] Warren-Boulton and Dalkir (2001) p.480.
[18] "HMV Group plc and Ottakar's plc Proposed acquisition of Ottakar's plc by HMV Group plc through Waterstone's Booksellers Ltd" (May 12, 2006) Competition Commission, Final Report.
[19] "Wienerberger Finance Service BV and Baggeridge Brick plc: A report on the anticipated acquisition by Wienerberger Finance Service BV of Baggeridge Brick plc" (May 10, 2007) Competition Commission.

characterised 29 of these as being pro-enforcement against Microsoft, eight being anti-enforcement against Microsoft and 17 being unclear. For instance, the day on which the FTC announced that it was investigating Microsoft was a "pro-enforcement" day whilst the day on which the DoJ said it would take no action prior to Windows 95 shipping was an "anti-enforcement" day. The hypothesis that Bittlingmayer and Hazlett investigated was whether pro-enforcement actions aimed at restraining Microsoft's alleged market power had a positive or negative effect on the rest of the computer industry. They found that pro-enforcement actions consistently had a negative effect on Microsoft's share price and on the share prices of the other firms in the industry (on average, to the tune of about $3bn per event for Microsoft and more than $1bn per event for the other 159 firms in total). Conversely, they found that anti-enforcement actions led to increases in Microsoft's share price and the share prices of the other firms. The authors conclude that the study provides strong evidence against the proposition that enforcement action against Microsoft between 1991 and 1997 benefited the rest of the computer industry.

## CONCLUSIONS

Shock analysis represents a relatively unsophisticated empirical analysis. At **13–017** one level, it simply requires thinking intelligently about what can be learnt from the behaviour of a market after there has been a shock to that market. Its simplicity is a major advantage and we hope that the examples we presented above show that analysis using empirical evidence need not be complex in order for it to provide useful information. The examples show that shock analysis can be both simple and effective.

The downside to this form of analysis is that it is not always possible to carry it out. If there have not been any useful shocks in the recent past, then the approach cannot be used. However, it should be noted that shocks such as new product launches, short-term promotions and new advertising campaigns are common. We also accept that even when there have been shocks in a market, this does not always mean that useful information can be derived from them. For instance, it may be difficult to disentangle the effect of a shock to a market from the effect of other factors affecting the market at the same time. It may also be difficult to derive useful information from past shocks if there is evidence that the nature of competition in the market has changed more recently.

Our view is that there are serious difficulties with using stock market event studies for predicting the effect of a merger on competition. Part of this relates to technical issues to do with the power of the test. But the more substantive concern is that stock markets will not react to news of a merger without also thinking about the likely enforcement action that will be carried out by competition authorities. This means that the standard logic of the Eckbo-Stillman test is likely to be flawed when used as a predictor of merger effects.

# 14. Price Concentration Studies

## INTRODUCTION

This chapter discusses price concentration studies, a potentially powerful, **14–001** and intuitively appealing, empirical technique that can be used in a range of antitrust settings. Price concentration studies investigate the relationship between price[1] and concentration, or market share, in a given industry or industry segment. It does this by considering how price and concentration vary over a number of separate "markets".

Price concentration studies can potentially be used to answer a number of questions.

- Market definition. If price and concentration are positively correlated across a number of markets, this suggests that a hypothetical monopolist of one of these markets could profitably raise prices. The extent of the correlation between concentration and price can give an indication of the amount by which a hypothetical monopolist could raise prices. One of the attractive aspects of finding that price and concentration in a given "market" are unrelated is that this is consistent with at least three propositions. It may be that products that are demand substitutes have been left out of the market definition; it may be that there are geographic areas that impose a competitive constraint on the "market" that have been left out of the market defintion; or it may be that supply-side constraints have been omitted and that entry into the "market" is very easy. It is not necessary to know which proposition is correct in order to be able to draw a conclusion about market definition from a price concentration study.

- Dominance. The legal concept of dominance is equivalent to the economic concept of substantial market power. We should expect a firm with substantial market power to be able to price above the

---

[1] Or margin or, on occasion, profit. We discuss below the relative merits of these alternatives.

competitive level. One test of whether a high market share in a given market leads to dominance could be whether prices are systematically higher the higher is the market share of the leading firm. This would be consistent with the dominant firm model discussed in Chapter 2.

An attractive property of price concentration studies is that they can potentially be used in Articles 81 and 82 cases as well as in merger cases without suffering from the Cellophane fallacy that makes the interpretation of elasticities and price correlations so problematic in non-merger cases. If prices are not systematically higher where one firm has a large market share compared to where there is no dominant firm, this suggests that the dominant firm has not been able to raise prices above the competitive level and so a market definition exercise is not subject to the Cellophane fallacy.

- Merger analysis. A positive correlation between concentration and prices might suggest that a merger could lead to coordinated effects as it is consistent with the proposition that increased concentration within a market makes it easier for firms to collude tacitly and hence to raise prices. Equally, a positive correlation between the market share of the leading firm and prices might suggest that a merger would lead to unilateral effects.

There are, therefore, a number of ways in which price concentration studies can be useful. However, price concentration studies have been subject to serious criticism and it is true that there are many potential pitfalls that may confront an investigator using one. We discuss these below. Our view is that despite these criticisms, price concentration can often provide useful insights for the competitive assessment, particularly in relation to the definition of the relevant market.

The remainder of this chapter is organised as follows. Paragraphs 14–002—14–006 discuss the mechanics of a price concentration study. Paragraphs 14–007—14–016 contain some case studies illustrating the use of price concentration studies in actual cases. Paragraphs 14–017—14–026 discuss the various pitfalls that can arise in the use and interpretation of price concentration studies. Paragraph 14–027 contains our conclusions.

## THE MECHANICS OF A PRICE CONCENTRATION STUDY

**14–002** Consider a merger between two retailers that each have a large number of outlets. Suppose that the competition authority has identified a number of local markets in which both parties have outlets and that it claims that in these local markets prices will rise after the merger due to the increase in concentration (i.e. a coordinated effects concern). The parties dispute this, believing that they do not operate in local markets but in wider markets, in which the accretion of market share is negligible. One way for the parties to show that a high market share of a local "market" does not confer market power would be to carry out a price concentration study to show that prices and market shares are not systematically related across local markets.

A starting point might be to look at a simple graph of average price in each area plotted against concentration in that area. In our example, the price variable will be an index of the prices of a number of goods since the parties are multi-product retailers. The chart in Figure 14.1 relates price to the four-firm concentration ratio (CR4) in each of 38 areas.

**Figure 14.1: A positive relation between price and concentration** 14–003

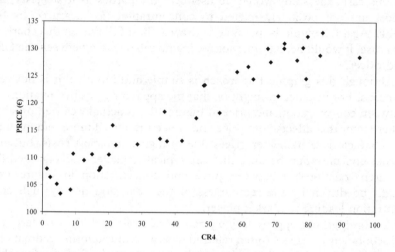

In this example, the price concentration analysis tells a clear story. It appears that prices are systematically high in areas where the CR4 is higher. This implies that the merger, which will increase the CR4 in a number of areas, can be expected to result in price increases in these areas. By drawing a "best fit" line on the chart, it would be possible to provide a very crude estimate of the amount that prices rise, on average, as the CR4 rises. In the case illustrated in Figure 14.1, the "best fit" line would have a gradient of about 0.3, indicating that prices rise by €0.3 for each percentage point rise in the CR4.

The chart in Figure 14.2 again relates the CR4 to price in 38 areas, but this time there does not appear to be a systematic relationship between concentration and price.

**14–004** **Figure 14.2: No relation between price and concentration**

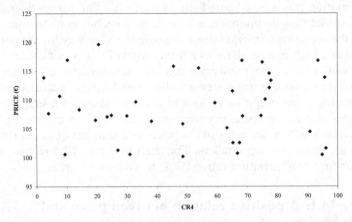

In this case, the study would be useful to the parties as it suggests that prices are not positively related to concentration (as measured by the CR4). Again, it would be possible to draw a "best fit" line on this chart. In this case, it would be flat, thus suggesting no relationship between the CR4 and prices.

Although this graphical approach is simple and intuitive, it is not very rigorous. For instance, it might be that the apparently positive relationship between concentration and price in Figure 14.1 is actually caused by some other factor that affects both price and concentration. If more remote areas are characterised by higher prices due to higher transport costs, but also higher concentration because they are typically smaller markets, then the apparent relationship between price and concentration in Figure 14.1 might be driven by the remoteness of the area, and not by high concentration leading to market power.

A more rigorous approach to a price concentration study is to carry out an econometric analysis (often referred to as a "reduced form" estimation). Econometric analysis allows one to take account of the factors other than concentration that also affect price. Undertaking an econometric analysis of the data in Figure 14.1 and Figure 14.2 confirms the initial conclusion drawn from the graphical analysis. In order to carry out an econometric analysis, those variables that vary between areas and which affect price in each area need to be identified. In the hypothetical example, the following relationship is postulated:

(1) *Price = f(Concentration, wages, rent, population, factors that do not change across areas)*

The reasons for choosing these variables should be clear. Concentration is included because this is the variable of primary concern. Wages and rent are included because they are costs that are likely to affect price and which are likely to vary across regions. Population is included as a measure of market size. As noted above, smaller markets might be more expensive to

608

serve. There is no need to sub-divide all those factors that do not change across regions into their component variables because by definition they are not useful. Since an understanding of why prices vary across areas is the focus of attention, variables that are constant across regions do not provide appropriate information.

The results from this regression are given in Table 14.1.[2]

**Table 14.1: Results of a price concentration study: positive    14–005 relationship[3]**

| Variable | Coefficient | t-statistic |
|---|---|---|
| Constant | 100.19 | 24.6 |
| Concentration | 0.30 | 50.9 |
| Rent | 0.54 | 2.7 |
| Wages | 0.56 | 2.4 |
| Population | −0.62 | 23.0 |
| Adj. $R^2$ | 0.98 | |
| Normality ($v^2(2)$) | 0.78 | Crit. value at 95% level: 5.99 |
| Chow test (F(5,40)) | 0.56 | Crit. value at 95% level: 2.45 |

Table 14.1 confirms the intuition of the chart in Figure 14.1. An increase in the CR4 by one percentage point increases price by 0.3. The average price in the sample is 118, so an increase of 0.3 is an increase of about 0.25 per cent on average. Thus, if the hypothetical merger were to raise the CR4 by 10 per cent in a given region, a price rise of about 2.5 per cent in the region is to be expected.

The coefficients on the other variables indicate that the other variables are all statistically significant determinants of prices. The t-statistics are all above two. It appears that the pass-through of cost differences between regions is about 0.55. This is shown by the coefficients on rent and wages of 0.54 and 0.56 respectively. This is a perfectly plausible value: prices reflect the fact that costs vary across areas, but retailers are unable to pass on all of the increases in costs, perhaps because they face competitors who do not face variation in these local costs, such as internet retailers. The coefficient on population is negative, indicating that prices fall as population rises, which is consistent with the idea that smaller markets are more expensive to serve.

---

[2]  For an explanation of econometric analysis, and how to appraise it, see the Econometric Annex to this book.

[3]  Test statistics on serial correlation or heteroscedasticity are not reported here because the data is cross-sectional, not time series. There is no discussion of the possibilities of collinearity or omitted variables to avoid cluttering the explanation. In a real case, those issues would of course be discussed in depth. Without entering into the details, there is no evidence of either problem in this data set. The issue of possible endogenous right-hand side variables is also not dealt with, but it is covered in the commentary below.

Table 14.2 contains the results of an econometric analysis of the data in the chart in Figure 14.2. Again, this confirms the intuition of the chart.

**14–006 Table 14.2: Results of a price concentration study: no relationship**

| Variable | Coefficient | t-statistic |
|---|---|---|
| Constant | 100.14 | 32.8 |
| Concentration | −0.00 | −0.02 |
| Rent | 0.56 | 3.7 |
| Wages | 0.57 | 2.3 |
| Population | −0.60 | 30.4 |
| Adj. $R^2$ | 0.95 | |
| Normality $(v^2(2))$ | 1.97 | Crit. value at 95% level: 5.99 |
| Chow test $(F(5,40))$ | 0.85 | Crit. value at 95% level: 2.45 |

The coefficient on concentration is now effectively zero. This implies that an increase in the CR4 in an area has no effect on prices.

# CASE STUDIES

## MMC Funerals[4]

**14–007** The MMC *Funerals* case in the United Kingdom provides an example of a price concentration study being used in a merger case. The issue here was whether increases in concentration in local areas (areas of radius less than three miles) as a result of the merger would lead to funeral prices rising after the merger. The parties used a price concentration study to test whether the price of funerals was positively related to market concentration.[5]

The parties estimated an equation of the following form:
(2)  *Price = f(concentration, quality, funeral costs, local wages)*
There were two measures of concentration used. One was the number of outlets within the relevant area and one was the number of different firms operating within the relevant area. Geographic market definition was in dispute and so the parties measured concentration on the basis of a number of different geographic market sizes, varying from a radius around each outlet of 0.5 miles to a radius of three miles. Quality was measured by the coffin type and by the number of "extras" bought.

The parties found that there was no relationship between local

---

[4] Monopoly and Mergers Commission (MMC) "Service Corp International and Plants-brook Group: A Report on the Merger Situation", Cm. 2880 (May 1995).
[5] Appendix 2.1 to the MMC's report contains a description of the study.

concentration and prices. They interpreted this as implying that the relevant geographic market was wider than three miles and that as a result the merger would not lead to a significant increase in market share in any relevant market. For a range of reasons of varying validity, such as concerns over the concentration variables used, the MMC chose to ignore this evidence. However, the study remains a good example of the potential uses of price concentration studies.

## UK supermarkets

There have been two recent investigations by the UK Competition Commission (CC) into the competitiveness of supermarkets in the United Kingdom. The first inquiry reported in 2000[6] whilst the second reported in 2008.[7] In both cases the CC used price concentration studies.  **14–008**

The price concentration analysis undertaken in the 2000 report took a number of forms and tried to answer a number of different questions. For our purposes, the most interesting analysis was an analysis that looked at the effect of local market share and concentration on prices. Some of the supermarket chains used national pricing and so did not vary their pricing depending on local conditions. These chains were omitted from the analysis. The pricing of those chains that did vary their prices locally was regressed on the following variables for each local area: own market share, HHI, market share of hard discounters, market share of Asda, labour costs, store size and average household income. The local areas were defined by postcode areas. The CC used prices on 200 products at each of up to 60 stores per firm.

The CC carried the analysis out separately for each of the chains that varied its prices locally. In Table 14.3 we report the results for Tesco.

**Table 14.3: Price concentration results for Tesco: CC inquiry 2000 Appendix 7.8**  **14–009**

|  | Coefficient | t-statistic |
|---|---|---|
| **Intercept** | 1.8823 | 112.04 |
| **Discounter share** | −0.0641 | 1.79 |
| **Own share** | 0.0063 | 0.47 |
| **Income** | 0.0017 | 2.83 |
| **Asda share** | −0.0494 | 2.06 |
| **Labour cost** | −0.0009 | 2.25 |

---

[6]  Competition Commission (2000) *Supermarkets: a report on the supply of groceries from multiple stores in the UK*, Cm.4842.
[7]  Competition Commission (2008) *Market investigation into the supply of groceries in the UK*.

The coefficient on "own share" indicates that Tesco's local pricing was not dependent on Tesco's local market share. Although the coefficient is positive (0.0063), it is small and not statistically significant. This result was repeated for the other chains that varied their prices locally. This suggests that single firm dominance issues did not arise. Although not shown in Table 14.3, it appears that the CC also did not find any effect of HHI on local prices. What it did find was that the presence of particular competitors, or types of competitor, could have an effect on local prices. Thus the presence of hard discounters had a negative effect on local prices. The coefficient on "discounter share" was −0.06 with a t-statistic of 1.8, which is statistically signficant at the 90 per cent level. The presence of Asda also had a negative effect on Tesco's local prices, with a coefficient on "Asda share" of −0.05 and a t-statistic of 2.1, which indicates statistical significance at the 95 per cent level.

The CC concluded that "customers tend to pay more at stores that do not face particular competitors than they would if those competitors were present in the area." (para.1.6.b) and that this practice was against the public interest when carried out by the firms with market power.

The CC was called on to investigate the supermarkets again in 2007. By this time all the major supermarkets had moved to a national pricing approach, so a price concentration study based on local pricing would not have made any sense. Instead the CC investigated how local profit margins varied with local concentration. The profit margin used was the margin over variable costs. The CC used four different measures of local concentration:

i. The number of competing supermarket firms ("fascias") operating within a ten minute drive time of the supermarket in question (i.e. the "centre store").

ii. Number of competing supermarket outlets within a ten minute drive time.

The difference between measures (i) and (ii) is that two supermarkets owned by the same firm would be counted as one under measure (i) but two under measure (ii).

iii. Combined net sales area of competitors within ten minute drive time (i.e. total competing floor space).

iv. Share of total net sales area within ten minute drive time accounted for by competitors.

In addition, the CC included variables for local costs, demographics and store characteristics (e.g. does the store include a petrol station?). The results for the four different concentration variables are given in Table 14.4.

## Table 14.4: Effect of local concentration on profit margins   14–010

| Concentration measure | Coefficient | t-statistic |
|---|---|---|
| Number of competing fascias within 10 minutes | −0.0096 | 2.74 |
| Number of competing outlets within 10 minutes | −0.0036 | 2.65 |
| Net sales area of competitors within 10 minutes | −0.0027 | 2.82 |
| Share of total net sales area within 10 minutes provided by competitors | −0.1548 | 2.75 |

*Source:* Appendix 4.4 Competition Commission 2008

The interpretation of the coefficients in Table 14.4 is as follows. The coefficient of −0.0096 on the number of competing fascias within ten minute drive time implies that each additional competitor reduces the profit margin of the centre store by almost 1 per cent. The coefficient of −0.0036 on the number of competing outlets implies that each additional outlet reduces the profit margin of the centre store by 0.36 per cent. Increasing the net sales area of competitors by 1,000 metres reduces the profit margin at the centre store by 0.27 per cent. Finally, increasing the share of net sales area accounted for by competitors by 10 per cent reduces the profit margin at the centre store by 1.5 per cent.

Since prices were invariant across local areas, the CC interpreted these results as implying that supermarkets that faced less local competition offered a lower quality service and as a result had lower costs. The CC concluded:

> "We found that, in many important respects, competition in the UK groceries industry is effective and delivers good outcomes for consumers, but not all is well. We have concerns in two principal areas. First, we found that several grocery retailers have strong positions in a number of local markets. Barriers faced by competing grocery retailers that could otherwise enter these markets mean that consumers get a poorer retail offer in terms of prices, quality and service than would otherwise be the case, while those grocery retailers with strong local market positions earn additional profits due to weak competition in those markets." (Summary, para.2)

In October 2004, Somerfield bought 115 supermarket stores from Morrisons. These stores were mainly mid-range stores in size. In its investigation of the merger, the CC based its conclusions on a geographic market of five minute drive times in urban areas and 10 minute drive times in rural areas.[8] The CC used shorter drive times than in the two supermarket

---

[8]   Competition Commission *Somerfield plc and Wm Morrison Supermarkets plc: A report on the acquisition by Somerfield plc of 115 stores from Wm Morrison Supermarkets plc* (2005).

inquiries discussed above because this merger dealt with mid-range stores and the CC believed that consumers were willing to travel less far to these stores than to large supermarkets. Somerfield argued that these drive times were too low. As part of its response to this argument, the CC carried out a margin-concentration study. This related the margin over direct costs (i.e. cost of sales, staff costs and distribution costs) to the market share of 88 Morrison stores. The results were that there was a positive but statistically insignificant relationship between margin and market share for urban stores but a positive and statistically significant relationship for rural stores. The CC concluded that:

> "in circumstances where an acquired store's local market share was higher pre-merger (i.e. where it appears to have faced less competition) its margins also tended to be higher, especially in rural areas. A corollary of this result is that the local markets for which acquired stores' market shares have been calculated by Somerfield may be relevant markets, especially in rural areas." (Appendix B, para.2)

**14–011** These three supermarket case studies illustrate the fact that price-concentration studies can be used to answer a range of different questions. In the 2000 inquiry, the relationship between prices and market share of various competitors illustrated the importance of particular competitors at a local level (i.e. the hard discounters and Asda). The margin-concentration study in the 2007 inquiry focused more on the effect of local concentration in general, rather than specific competitors, and found that less local competition was consistent with weaker competition. This provided evidence that high concentration at a local level could be to the detriment of consumers. Finally, the margin-concentration study in the Somerfield-Morrisons merger was focused on market definition and was used to validate the market definition that the CC proposed. It should be noted that although it was not the focus of the 2007 study, the results of this study (that local concentration affects profit margins) were consistent with the market definition adopted by the CC.

## UK retail banking

**14–012** In 1999–2000 the UK Treasury set up an inquiry into retail banking.[9] This was led by the ex-telecoms regulator, Don Cruickshank. One of the questions that the Cruickshank Review sought to answer was whether local retail bank concentration was related to local loan prices. The concern was that the higher the local retail bank concentration was, the higher would be loan prices in that area. In effect, Cruickshank was concerned that retail

---

[9] D. Cruickshank "Competition in UK banking: a report to the Chancellor of the Exchequer" (2000).

banking markets were local and so there was scope to exercise market power at the local level. In order to test this proposition he investigated the relationship between loan prices and concentration, measured by the HHI and by the number of firms present, within local postcode areas. Using data supplied by the banks, Cruickshank found that the coefficient on concentration was not positive, thus indicating that higher local concentration did not lead to higher loan prices. As a result Cruickshank concluded that the relevant market was national.

## Staples/Office Depot[10]

In September 1996, Staples and Office Depot, two of the three office **14–013** superstore chains in the United States, announced that they planned to merge. The FTC opposed the merger and so it went to trial. At trial both parties presented price concentration studies that were designed to predict the likely effect of the merger on prices. The outcome was that the court sided with the FTC and granted a preliminary injunction against the merger, thus effectively blocking the merger.

The parties and the FTC presented econometric evidence at trial and we discuss this briefly below. However, the FTC also presented some very simple summary statistics on the relationship between prices and concentration. Specifically, they looked at how much lower prices were in markets where Staples and Office Depot competed compared to markets where they did not compete. Table 14.5 shows how much lower prices were in markets where the parties competed compared to markets where they did not. Thus prices were on average 11.6 per cent lower in markets where Staples and Office Depot competed compared to markets where only Staples was present, and were 4.9 per cent lower in markets where all three office superstores competed compared to markets where only Staples and Office Max competed. The FTC argued that these results showed that the merger was likely to lead to price rises post-merger. If the merger could be considered as moving Staples and Office Depot-only markets to being Staples-only markets, then the implication was that prices in these markets would rise by 11.6 per cent. Similarly, in markets where all three office superstores were present pre-merger, the implication was that prices would rise by 4.9 per cent.

---

[10]   More detailed discussions of this case can be found in Dalkir and Warren-Boulton (2004) and in ABA (2005).

**14–014** **Table 14.5: Simple price comparisons in** *Staples/Office Depot*

| Benchmark market structure | Benchmark plus other merging party | Apparent price effect |
|---|---|---|
| Staples only | Staples and OD | −11.6% |
| Staples and OM | Staples, OM and OD | −4.9% |
| OD only | OD and Staples | −8.6% |
| OD and OM | OD, OM and Staples | −2.5% |

*Source:* Dalkir and Warren-Boulton (2004)

This data is potentially powerful evidence of the likely effect of the merger, although it is certainly not beyond criticism. Newmark (2006) argues that these data are likely to have been driven by market size effects, not by competitive effects (see para.14–024 for further discussion of this). However, the price analysis presented by the FTC, and by the parties, did not rely only on simple comparisons of this sort. It also included a significant amount of econometric analysis.

The data available to the parties and the FTC was panel data. This means that it covered prices at Staples and Office Depot stores across the country and over time. There were therefore two types of variation in concentration in the data: variation across locations (i.e. different levels of concentration in different areas) and across time (i.e. changes in concentration in areas where there was entry or exit of a superstore). The econometric approach taken in a price concentration study varies depending on whether you want to take advantage of the variation in concentration over time or over locations. As we discuss below (paras 14–022—14–025), there are advantages and disadvantages to both types of data. However, the FTC's analysis suggested that the results of the price concentration study did not vary significantly depending on which type of variation in concentration was focused on.[11] Since the parties much preferred to take advantage of the variation in concentration over time at each location, this was the approach taken by both sides at trial.

**14–015** The parties and the FTC disagreed over the results of the price concentration studies. The parties argued that the post-merger price rise would be of the order of 1 per cent, whilst the FTC argued that it would be of the order of 7–9 per cent. There were two main causes of this difference. One difference related to whether or not California was included in the model. Excluding California led to much lower estimates of the post-merger price rise. The other difference related to how local competition was defined. The parties based their measure of local competition on the distance between rival superstores. They categorised the closeness of rivals depending on whether they were within 5 miles, between 5 and 10 miles

[11] See fn.55 on p.362 of ABA (2005).

away or between 10 and 20 miles away. Thus a superstore within five miles was assumed to exert more price pressure than one that was more than five miles away. The FTC took a different approach. They noted that the parties pricing did not tend to vary within a metropolitan area. So whilst one superstore in a particular metropolitan area might have a competitor within five miles whilst another did not, the pricing at the two superstores would be similar. Internal documents from Staples indicated that its prices tended to be set at the level of the metropolitan area.

Table 14.6 shows how the results of the price concentration varied depending on the assumptions made about California and the correct approach to measuring local competition. If California is omitted and local concentration is measured by distance, then the predicted post-merger price rise is only 0.8 per cent. Conversely, if California is included and local concentration is measured at the level of the metropolitan area, then the predicted post-merger price rise is 8.6 per cent. It is also possible to see the effect of just the local measure of concentration. Omitting California but moving from a distance-based approach to a metropolitan area approach increases the predicted post-merger price rise from 0.8 per cent to 4.0 per cent.

**Table 14.6: Predicted post-merger prices in *Staples/Office***    14–016
***Depot***

| | | | |
|---|---|---|---|
| **California included?** | No | No | Yes |
| **Distance measure of local competition?** | Yes | No | No |
| **Predicted change** | 0.8% | 4.0% | 8.6% |

*Source:* ABA (2005) p.365.

This seems to us to be a very helpful approach to econometric evidence. The sources of the differences between the estimates of the parties and the FTC are clear and this allows an investigator to decide which assumptions are likely to be best.

There were a number of other differences in the approach used by the two sides. For instance, the parties' analysis assumed that all the Office Depot superstores would be converted to Staples stores whilst the FTC's analysis in effect assumed they would all be shut down. Also, the parties based their estimate of the likely post-merger price rise relative to prices just before the merger, whilst the FTC based it on average prices over the whole of the data period. Again, as long as these different assumptions and their effect on the final result are made clear, it is possible for an investigator to decide which assumptions they think most accord with reality.

# ANALYTICAL ISSUES

## Prices or margins?

**14–017** So far the estimation of a relationship between prices and concentration has been considered. However, economic theory states that a firm with market power will raise price relative to marginal cost. Therefore what is really of interest here is the relationship between price and concentration with marginal costs held constant. If marginal costs vary across regions and this is not taken into account, a price concentration study is likely to give misleading results.

There are two responses to this. One is to carry out a margin concentration study in which margins over variable costs, not prices, are related to concentration. The other is to carry out an econometric price concentration study in which marginal costs are included as an explanatory variable. Both approaches will avoid the danger of biased results due to omitting marginal costs from the analysis. The difference between the two is that in the former the coefficient on costs is constrained to be one whilst in the latter it can vary. In the hypothetical example above, in Tables 14.1 and 14.2, the coefficient on variable costs was about 0.55.

## Heterogeneous goods

**14–018** For a price concentration study to provide meaningful results, it is crucial that the price variable used describes the same product, or basket of products, across regions. If there is only one product under consideration and it is a homogeneous good then this is easily ensured. However, often products are heterogeneous and there is often more than one product involved. If products are very heterogeneous across regions, then "price" may reflect the differences between the products across regions rather than the effect, if any, of concentration. If this heterogeneity cannot be removed from the data, a price concentration study is not appropriate.[12]

If products are relatively homogeneous, but there are several under consideration, there are two possible responses. One is to carry out a price concentration study on each product. The other is to create a composite index of the relevant products. This was the approach used in the *Staples/*

---

[12] Another source of differences in pricing might be differences in the mix of pack sizes sold in different regions. Products are typically more expensive when bought in smaller pack sizes, so in theory a higher price in a region might just reflect the predominance of smaller pack sizes in that region. We would not expect this to be a common problem.

*Office Depot* case.[13] However, it should be noted that the creation of a price index is not entirely simple and the index used by the FTC in *Staples/Office Depot* was criticised by the parties.

## Which concentration ratio?

An important issue in any price concentration study is the choice of con-    **14–019** centration measure. There are three main candidates: the HHI, the market share of the largest firm and an n-firm concentration measure (e.g. CR3 or CR4). Other possibilities include the number of firms in the market or some measure based on capacity market shares. The answer to the question of which is the best measure to use depends on the question being asked.

Relating the market share of the leading firm to price makes sense when the competition concern is a unilateral effects concern or a single-firm dominance concern. In these cases, the issue is whether a high market share confers market power and so relating price to market share may be informative. However, it is important to confirm that any apparent correlation between prices and the market share of the leading firm is not driven by quality. It is quite possible that the leading firm in a market has the best product and so charges the highest prices.

If the concern is about coordinated effects then an n-firm concentration ratio or the HHI makes more sense. Suppose the competition authority is worried that a four to three merger will lead to coordinated effects and hence allow prices to rise. Then a price concentration study using the CR3 would allow the authority to investigate whether the market share of the three largest firms is positively related to price.[14] A price concentration study using the HHI could also be used to see if higher concentration seemed to lead to tacit collusion.

Price concentration studies are often used to help define relevant markets. In this case the question is whether a hypothetical monopolist could profitably raise prices above the current level (in a merger) or competitive level (in a non-merger case). Using either the HHI or market share of the leading firm makes sense in this situation. If a higher market share allows the leading firm to raise its price, this suggests that a hypothetical monopolist could also raise its price. If a higher HHI is associated with higher prices, then this suggests that an HHI of 10,000 (monopoly) would be associated with higher prices. However, it should be noted that a negative

---

[13]   See *Federal Trade Commission v Staples Inc* No 97–101, 1997 U.S. Dist. LEXIS 9322 at *38 (DDC June 30, 1997).

[14]   Formally, the authority should also look at whether the move from four to three firms is associated with higher prices. If the CR4 is positively related to prices, then it may be that the market is likely already to be characterised by tacit collusion and so the merger may not significantly worsen the situation. This would be important if the merger led to marginal cost efficiencies that might lead to post-merger price reductions.

result from such a test (i.e. no association between price and concentration or market share) does not necessarily imply a wide market. It could be that the strength of competition within a market is enough to keep prices at competitive levels even when it is highly concentrated, but that a hypothetical monopolist would be able to raise prices. For instance, if there is a strong competitive fringe with no capacity constraints, then we would expect to see fierce competition in the putative market even if there was little competitive constraint imposed from outside the market.

The number of firms in the market or a measure based on capacity shares are useful when there are concerns over simultaneity between price and market share. We discuss this issue briefly in para.14–026.

### Economic and statistical insignificance

**14–020** It is important in an econometric price concentration study to distinguish between *statistically* insignificant coefficients on concentration variables and *economically* insignificant coefficients. A coefficient may be statistically insignificant, but economically significant. Equally, a coefficient may be statistically significant, but economically insignificant. Suppose the following equation is estimated:

(3)  $Price_i = \alpha + \beta \; Concentration_i + \gamma \; Other \; Factors_i + \varepsilon_i$

Further, assume that the concentration and price variables are such that $\beta$ can be thought of as an elasticity. That is, a 1 per cent rise in concentration leads to a $\beta$ per cent rise in price. Now consider the interpretation of the following four possible values of $\beta$ estimated in a merger case in which concentration will rise by 20 per cent post-merger.

**14–021 Table 14.7: Economic significance and statistical significance**

|  | Value of $\beta$ | t-statistic for $\beta$ |
|---|---|---|
| **(i)** | 1.2 | 3.4 |
| **(ii)** | 0.05 | 3.4 |
| **(iii)** | 1.2 | 1.2 |
| **(iv)** | 0.05 | 1.2 |

In Case (i) the coefficient on concentration is both statistically and economically significant. This is simple to interpret. A 20 per cent increase in concentration is associated with prices that are 24 per cent higher (i.e. 1.2 * 20 = 24). Now consider Case (ii). Here $\beta$ is statistically significant but is economically insignificant. A 20 per cent rise in concentration is associated with prices that are only 1 per cent higher (i.e. 0.05 * 20 = 1). The mere fact that the coefficient is statistically significant does not mean that the result is of economic significance. Now consider Case (iii). Here the coefficient estimate is statistically insignificant, but economically significant. There is no certainty that the coefficient in this case is not zero, or even negative, in which case higher concentration would be associated with lower prices. However, the upper bound for the coefficient is about three,[15] which would imply that a 20 per cent increase in concentration was associated with prices that were 60 per cent higher. This means that we cannot rule out the possibility that increases in concentration leads to economically significant increases in prices. Where the coefficient is statistically insignificant but economically significant, the results of the price-concentration analysis are inconclusive. In Case (iv) the coefficient is arguably economically insignificant as well as statistically insignificant. The coefficient is statistically insignificant and so it could be zero. The upper bound estimate in this case is only 0.12, which would imply that an increase in concentration of 20 per cent is associated with prices that are 2.4 per cent higher. Note, however, that this upper bound is higher than the upper bound in Case (ii), which was about 0.7. This is a reflection of the fact that the coefficient of 0.05 in Case (ii) is more precisely estimated than the same coefficient in Case (iv).

The conclusion to be drawn from this discussion is that in order to show that concentration is not an important determinant of price, it is not enough to show that it is a *statistically* insignificantly determinant. Instead, it is necessary to show that there is a reasonable degree of certainty that concentration is not an *economically* significant determinant of price.

## Cross-section v time series data

Most price concentration studies are carried out using cross-sectional data, **14–022** i.e. data for a number of regions for the same time period. The advantage of data of this type is that there is often considerable variation in the level of concentration across regions and so this makes it easier to isolate the effect of concentration on price. However, cross-sectional data also has a disadvantage. Suppose that there are factors that affect price in each region, but that for each individual region these factors remain constant over time. If a price concentration study is undertaken using just one time period, the analysis may suffer from omitted variable bias. If the omitted factors are correlated with concentration, then the estimated relationship between price and concentration may actually be a relationship between price and the omitted variables. However, if the omitted factors are constant over time for each region and if data are available over several time periods for each region, this problem can be avoided. In reality the effect of changes in concentration can be looked at *within each region over time*. By assumption, the omitted

---

[15] The figure of 3 is calculated as follows. The coefficient estimate is 1.2. The standard error (i.e. the coefficient estimate divided by the t-statistic) is 1.0. We can be 95% sure that the true coefficient estimate lies within about 1.64 standard errors of the coefficient estimate. In this instance, that gives a range of between −0.4 and +2.8.

variables do not change within each region over time, so any relationship between price and concentration will be a genuine relationship. The price-concentration studies discussed in court in *Staples* were of this form.

We provide an illustration of this in Figure 14.3 and Figure 14.4. Figure 14.3 apparently shows a clear relationship between price and HHI. The "best fit" line is clearly upward sloping, showing that there appears to be a positive relationship between price and concentration.

**14–023**  **Figure 14.3: Spurious relationship in levels**

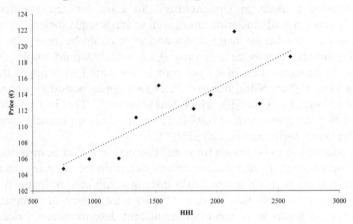

However, in this example the apparent relationship disappears when the effect of changes in concentration in each region on price in that region is considered. This is shown in Figure 14.4.

**14–024**  **Figure 14.4: No relationship in first differences**

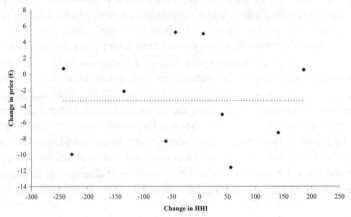

Figure 14.4 shows that changes in the HHI in a region over time do not seem to be associated with changes in price in that region. If the concern is

the potential anti-competitive effect of a merger in a particular region, the evidence in Figure 14.4 would suggest that the merger is not likely to lead to prices rising.[16]

The factor underlying the positive relationship between price and concentration in Figure 14.3 is the size of the market. We have assumed that smaller markets are more concentrated and have higher prices. Smaller markets will tend to support fewer players, particularly if fixed costs are significant, and so will tend to be more concentrated. They may also be more expensive to serve, perhaps because they are more remote. Newmark (2006) argues that the correlation between office superstore concentration and prices that the FTC found in *Staples* may have been driven by market size effects. He presents evidence that the median population of those metropolitan areas with only one office superstore was about 225,000, whilst this figure rose to more than 600,000 for two office superstore areas and to more than 1.5m for three office superstore areas.

It is important to note that carrying out a price concentration study using time series data is not without its problems. The biggest one is that there is usually not very much variation in concentration over time within each market. This makes it very hard to precisely estimate the effect of concentration on prices. Where there is entry and exit into markets concentration within a market will often vary significantly over time, but even here there are two difficulties. The first is that entry and exit do not happen randomly. Entry usually takes place in response to a perceived profit opportunity. This opportunity may be the result of relatively high prices in the market or it may be because the new entrant has a product that is of higher quality than the existing products. This new entry may well lead to the prices of existing products falling, but this is only due to a reduction in concentration in the first case. In the second it is due to the higher quality of the new product and it would be a mistake to attribute the fall in prices after entry to the reduction in concentration. Exit usually occurs because the firm in question is loss-making. This may be b~~~~~ ~~~~~ are relatively low, perhaps because there is too much capacity in the market, and the exit may lead to prices rising. But the exit may also occur because the product in question has been superceded by better products. In this case the exit is unlikely to have much effect on prices, but this does not mean that increases in concentration do not affect prices. All that it means is that the product that exits was no longer a competitively relevant product.

The other problem with using entry and exit events in a price con-   **14–025**
centration study is that these events are sometimes used as proxies for the effect of a merger. The idea is that a merger can be considered as the

---

[16]   There is an issue here to do with "out of sample" concentration changes. If we have evidence on the effect on price of changes in the HHI of up to, say, 500 we might not be convinced that this is relevant to a merger that will change the HHI by, say, 1,500. Clearly, we would prefer to have direct evidence on the effect of such large changes in concentration.

reverse of entry or as equivalent to exit. This is only true under particular circumstances. A merger in which the acquiror shut down the acquired firm would be equivalent to exit, but this is not what acquirors usually do. Equally, new entry usually leads to an increase in capacity in the market, whilst mergers do not usually lead to the removal of all of a firm's capacity. Relating this to *Staples*, it is not the case that all the Office Depots stores would have been closed.

This discussion raises the obvious question of when should an investigator prefer a cross-sectional study to a time series study? Since the aim of a price concentration study is to determine the effect of concentration on prices, it is essential that the data used includes a significant amount of variation in concentration. As noted above, time series data often has little such variation and so is often not suitable for such a study. On the other hand, studies using cross-sectional data can give misleading results when an apparent relationship between price and concentration is actually being driven by another variable, such as market size. If the other variable can be observed (e.g. market size), then this can be allowed for and a cross-sectional approach can still be used. However, if the other variable is not observable then using a cross-sectional approach is liable to misspecification.

## Simultaneity between price and concentration

**14–026**  The price concentration tests described above assume that concentration may affect price, but that price does not affect concentration, i.e. it is assumed that there is no feedback from prices to concentration. However, this may not be a good assumption. It might be expected that higher prices would encourage new entry, which would reduce concentration. In this case, econometric analysis of the type described might lead to biased coefficients on the concentration variable. This might be thought to invalidate this form of analysis. One may disagree with this for two reasons.

First, if the concern is with bias of this form, it is relatively easy to estimate a model that does not suffer from this problem. Instead of estimating a single-equation with concentration as an independent (and assumed exogenous) variable, one estimates a two-equation simultaneous equation model in which concentration is the dependent variable in the second equation. Of course, this would only be done if tests of the exogeneity of concentration to price suggested that there was simultaneity.

Secondly, the form of bias potentially entailed by the simultaneity may not be of particular concern. If high prices tend to lower concentration, then this will tend to lead to the coefficient on concentration in a single equation model being lower than the "true" effect of concentration on price. However, this in all likelihood should not be of undue concern. The concern is over whether high concentration leads to market power. If high concentration raises prices, but these raised prices then lead to new entry, reduced concentration and so reduced prices, this suggests that the short-run effect of concentration on price is larger than the long-run effect. In general, it is probably the longer run effect that is of interest. So the potential bias in the coefficient estimate from a single equation model is probably "in the right direction". Beckert and Mazzarotto (2006) argue that this may be too optimistic a view as entry may not occur quickly enough to avoid short-run consumer harm. Whilst this may be true, if entry only responds to prices with a significant lag, then the downward bias on the concentration variable will be small.

Another potential source of simultaneity are unobserved demand shocks. If there is a positive demand shock for a product (i.e. outward shift of the demand curve) then both its market share and its price are likely to rise, but it would not be the increase in market share causing price to rise. The unobserved demand shock would also lead to a correlation between market share and the error term of the equation, with the result that the coefficient estimates would be biased. Evans (1983) suggests that this simultaneity issue can be avoided by using concentration measures such as the number of players in the market or capacity market shares, as neither are effected directly by the demand shock.[17]

The general assumption behind a price concentration study is that concentration is largely exogenously determined (except for through mergers). This may well not be the case. For instance, Sutton (1991) argues that concentration can be driven by firms' decisions about the level of sunk costs to incur and this in turn can have an effect on pricing. For instance, if firms choose large advertising expenditures and as a result ensure that any successful rivals must also incur large advertising expenditures, this is likely to limit the number of firms that can survive in the market, whilst also affecting prices as prices will need to be high enough to recover the sunk advertising expenditure.

None of this, of course, alters the fact that it would be preferable to carry out a simultaneous equation estimate where appropriate and possible.

# SUMMARY

Price concentration studies are simple but potentially powerful empirical **14–027** studies. They can provide direct evidence on the question of interest: does increased concentration in a market allow prices to rise? This question is relevant to merger cases (will increased concentration lead to higher prices?), dominance cases (does the firm's high market share allow it profitably to raise prices above the competitive level?) and Article 81 cases (is this an agreement between firms with the ability profitably to raise prices

---

[17]  In the medium to long term a firm may increase its capacity in response to a positive demand shock.

above the competitive level?). This is a considerable advantage, particularly given that several of the other empirical techniques that are discussed in this book (e.g. price correlation analysis and shipment tests) do not directly answer the question of interest, but instead answer an intermediate question (i.e. market definition).

However, price concentration studies come with a health warning: unless carried out with great care, they can easily give a misleading result. This is particularly the case if there are underlying factors that drive both price and concentration or market share, such as market size or quality. So whilst price concentration studies can be very powerful tools, it is important that they are used to understand the underlying process determining concentration and price, since only then can the investigator be sure about the cause of any correlation between price and concentration.

# 15. Merger simulation

## INTRODUCTION

This chapter considers merger simulation, a quantitative technique that **15–001** has become significantly more widely used in European merger control in recent years. Although the chapter will be concerned primarily with horizontal merger simulation in unilateral effects cases, we will also discuss briefly the use of simulation models in coordinated effects cases and vertical mergers. The purpose of this chapter is not to allow readers to carry out their own merger simulation. As we explain at length in this chapter, carrying out a merger simulation that actually adds value to the decision making process is a technical exercise that requires considerable economic modelling, and ideally also econometric, expertise. Instead, the aim of this chapter is to provide readers with an understanding of when a merger simulation might be useful, and when it is unlikely to be useful, and to enable them to critically appraise a merger simulation that is presented during the course of a case. Whilst elements of carrying out a good merger simulation might be described as "rocket science", understanding whether a particular simulation is likely to be a good guide to the effect of a merger is not rocket science.

The chapter is organised as follows. Paragraphs 15–001—15–021 provide a description of the economics underlying the various different types of merger simulation model. Paragraphs 15–022—15–035 contain brief case studies of merger simulations used in actual cases in order to provide context for the discussion. Paragraphs 15–036—15–052 are then devoted to a discussion of various issues that arise in appraising a merger simulation and, importantly, of how to tell the difference between a good and a bad simulation. Finally, para.15–053 contains our conclusions on the role that merger simulations should play in merger control.

# THE ECONOMICS OF MERGER SIMULATIONS

**15–002** The basic idea behind merger simulation models is to compute directly the likely post-merger equilibrium in an unilateral effects case. Rather than first defining the market, then calculating market shares, then carrying out a competitive effects analysis and then taking a view on the likely effect of the merger, a merger simulation offers the alternative of directly calculating by how much prices will increase post-merger. In theory, this approach negates the need to engage in the exercise of defining the relevant market.

Most merger simulations start from the assumption that the industry in question can be modelled using a static Bertrand differentiated products framework.[1] By making various assumptions about key industry parameters and calibrating the model using the current competitive situation, it is then possible to estimate the post-merger equilibrium. The necessary inputs include the identities of competitors, the products they sell, marginal costs, own-price and cross-price elasticities, how these elasticities vary as prices vary, expected marginal cost efficiencies and the nature of competition post-merger.

The fact that most merger simulations are based on the assumption of Bertrand competition is a reflection of the fact that merger simulation is currently used only in unilateral effect cases. However, there are some occasions where other forms of competition are relevant in assessing unilateral effects and there are therefore merger simulation models based on Cournot models and on auction and bargaining models of competition.[2] We discuss these below, but in less detail than simulation models that assume Bertrand competition. We also discuss the possibility of using simulation models in coordinated effects cases. This is a much less well-developed field than merger simulation in unilateral effects cases and so far there are no cases that we are aware of where competition authorities have had to deal with models of this type. However, for the sake of completeness we briefly describe the current state of research on these models.

## Bertrand simulation models

**15–003** The basic idea behind Bertrand merger simulation models is very simple and entirely consistent with the logic of unilateral effects cases. The assumption is that the firms in the market sell differentiated products and compete by setting prices. Each firm has some market power in the strict economic sense of being able to price above marginal cost due to the differentiated nature of its product. The market equilibrium is assumed to be a static Nash equilibrium, which means that each firm is maximising its profits given the prices that all the other firms are setting. The model is

---

[1]  See Chapter 2 for a discussion of Bertrand competition.
[2]  We discuss Cournot competition in more detail in Chapter 2.

then recalculated assuming that two of the firms have merged and so are no longer setting their prices non-cooperatively. Once again it is assumed that the equilibrium is a static Nash equilibrium with each firm maximising its profits given the prices that the other firms are setting. The model will inevitably imply higher prices post-merger than pre-merger because the merged entity will raise its prices. Prior to the merger the firms would not have raised their prices because the loss of sales would have led to the price rise being unprofitable (by definition of the Nash equilibrium). However, some of those lost sales would have been captured pre-merger by the other merging party. Thus if Firm A had raised prices pre-merger, it would have lost sales to Firms B, C, D and so on. The same is true for Firm B: it would have lost sales to Firms A, C, D and so on. But if Firm A and Firm B merge, then post-merger any sales lost by Firm A but captured by Firm B are not sales lost to the merged entity. The same is true for sales lost by Firm B but won by Firm A. Post-merger these are not sales that are lost to the merged entity and so the merged entity will set prices higher than pre-merger.[3]

Before moving on, we should highlight the fact that the discussion above already includes important assumptions about the nature of competition, such as that it is properly described by the Bertrand model. Whilst these are not unreasonable assumptions, they are nonetheless assumptions that may not hold in reality. If they do not, then a simulation based on these assumptions is unlikely to be useful.

Another implicit assumption above is that each firm is a single product firm. The basic model can easily accommodate multi-product firms. In this case firms set the prices of their own products in a "cooperative" manner but set their prices non-cooperatively relative to other firms. The model can also incorporate the possibility that marginal costs will fall post-merger. As we discuss below, this implies that under some circumstances a merger simulation model can imply lower prices post-merger than pre-merger.

The remainder of this section discusses the basic economics of various **15–004** different approaches to merger simulations. Parts of this section will appear daunting to a non-technical reader as they include some algebraic formalisation. However, we urge such readers not to skip the rest of this section completely, but to at least read the discussion presented in each sub-section after the formalisation. This discussion highlights some of the key assumptions underlying each approach and an understanding of these assumptions is necessary to being able to appraise critically the various approaches when applied to a particular case.

---

[3]  For a more detailed discussion of the theory of unilateral effects, see Chapter 7.

## *Basic formalisation*

**15–005** Assume for now that each firm has only one brand.[4] If each firm is profit maximising, then it is choosing prices so as to maximise[5]:

(1) $(p_i - mc_i) \, Q_i \, (p_1, \ldots, p_n)$

where    $p_i$ is the price of Product i;

   $mc_i$ is the marginal cost of Product i; and

   $Q_i$ is the demand for Product i, which depends on the prices of Products 1 to n.

If a non-co-operative Nash equilibrium is assumed, then in equilibrium it must be the case that the following holds (i.e. this is the first order condition for profit maximisation):

(2)   $Q_i \, (p_i, \ldots, p_n) + (p_i - mc_i) \, \dfrac{\delta Q_i}{\delta p_i} = 0$

This gives the standard result that in equilibrium:

(3)   $\dfrac{p_i - mc_i}{p_i} = -\dfrac{1}{\varepsilon_{ii}}$

Equation (3) is the standard Lerner index result that in equilibrium a firm will set its price cost margin equal to the inverse of its own price elasticity of demand. This result is discussed in Chapter 3.

   If an estimate of the elasticity has already been obtained, the Lerner Index permits an estimate for the marginal cost of the firm to be calculated. Since our estimate for the firm's elasticity will not be precise (i.e. there will be a confidence interval around it), our estimate of the marginal cost of the firm will also not be precise. It is important at this point to confirm that the estimate of the marginal cost is not significantly at variance with reality. If it is, then either the original elasticity estimate is wrong or the industry is not in a static non-co-operative Nash equilibrium (i.e. perhaps there is some element of tacit collusion occurring). Either way, the simulation should not be continued.

**15–006**    If Brands i and j are combined as a result of the merger, then the merged entity aims to maximise:

(4)   $(p_i - mc_i) \, Q_i \, (p_1, \ldots, p_n) + (p_j - mc_j) \, Q_j \, (p_1, \ldots, p_n)$

Manipulation of the first order conditions yields:

(5)   $\dfrac{p_i - mc_i}{p_i} = -\dfrac{1}{\varepsilon_{ii}} - \dfrac{p_j - mc_j}{p_j} \dfrac{Q_j}{Q_i} \dfrac{\varepsilon_{ji}}{\varepsilon_{ii}} \dfrac{p_i}{p_j}$

If we know the marginal costs of the two products and their elasticities, then we can derive the post-merger equilibrium from Equation (5) and its equivalent for Product j.

   Equation (5) can be rewritten as:

(6)   $m_i = -\dfrac{1}{\varepsilon_{ii}} + \dfrac{m_j d_{ij} p_i}{p_j}$

---

[4]   As noted above, this is not a necessary assumption. We make it here as it keeps the algebra simpler.

[5]   We ignore fixed costs as they do not affect the profit maximisation prices of each firm.

where   $m_i$ is the price marginal cost margin for Product i; and

$d_{ij}$ is the diversion ratio from Product i to Product j (i.e. the ratio of the increase in sales of Product j relative to the reduction in sales of Product i, which is bounded at 0 and 1).

This way of rewriting Equation (5) has the implication that the higher is the diversion ratio from Product i to Product j, the greater is the post-merger mark-up over marginal cost for Product i. This implies that the greater the pre-merger diversion ratio, the greater the post-merger price rise. This is very intuitive: the greater the pre-merger diversion ratio between Product i and Product j, the greater the competitive constraint imposed on Product i by Product j, and so the greater the expected post-merger price rise due to this constraint being removed.

Furthermore, the effect on post-merger prices of any reductions in **15–007** marginal costs arising from the merger can be easily calculated. The post-merger marginal costs are just inserted in Equation (5) and the model is solved for the new value. In theory, Equation (5) could yield post-merger prices below the pre-merger prices if marginal costs fall far enough.

Whilst the underlying structure of a merger simulation assuming Bertrand competition is relatively straightforward, the details are not. In particular, the results of a Bertrand merger simulation depend heavily on the assumptions that are made about the own-price elasticities and the cross-price elasticities of the various products. There are a number of different standard approaches that are taken. The main issue is how the various elasticities vary as prices change. Whilst the elasticities at current prices can, in principle, be estimated econometrically, this is in general unlikely to be true of the way in which elasticities change as prices rise above current prices. In reality, this evolution of the elasticities will always need to be based on some assumptions about the shape of the demand curves. We briefly outline the more popular approaches to this problem below.

## *Constant elasticities and linear demand curves*

One possible assumption to make is that elasticities do not vary as prices **15–008** vary, i.e. to assume constant elasticity demand curves. Analytically this is a relatively tractable assumption to make. However, it is almost certainly wrong in practice. As prices rise, the elasticity of a product should be expected to rise as well as we usually assume that consumers become more price sensitive as prices rise. Thus using an assumption of constant elasticities runs the risk that the merger simulation will over-estimate the extent of post-merger price rises.[6] It also has the counterintuitive result that the prices of products that are not part of the merged entity do not rise post-

---

[6]   For a good example of this danger, see Froeb and Werden (1992). However, as we discuss below, it is not the case that using a constant elasticity assumption will always lead to an over-estimate of merger effects and so it cannot be used to provide an upper bound for merger effects.

merger. This is surprising because the standard expectation in unilateral effects analysis is that the post-merger price rise by the merged entity has a second order effect on the prices of all other products in the market which, as a result of the reduced competitive constraint from the products of the merged entity, also rise.

An alternative simplifying assumption to make is that demand curves are linear (i.e. straight lines). Linear demand curves exhibit sharply increasing elasticities, so they are consistent with our intuition that elasticities should rise as prices rise. However, the assumption of linear demand curves is not common in merger simulations. There are a number of reasons for this, such as that linear demand curves are not particularly analytically tractable[7] and there is no empirical evidence that demand curves typically are linear. We discuss the more commonly used alternatives below.

## *Logit demand*

**15–009**   One approach is to assume that consumer demand can be modelled using the logit model of demand. This has been advocated in particular by Werden and Froeb.[8] An advantage of the logit model is that it is based directly on utility theory (i.e. the structure of the model is consistent with how we would expect utility-maximising consumers to behave), even if at a rather basic level. The simplest logit model specifies that the utility of consumer k associated with consumption of Product i is:

$$(7) \quad u_{ik} = \alpha_i - \beta p_i + v_{ik}$$

This holds that the utility derived by the consumption of a product by consumer k is made up of three components. One is a fixed component $\alpha_i$ which varies between products but is the same for all consumers. The second component measures the effect on utility of an increase in the price of the product: as price goes up by one unit, utility falls by $\beta$. This coefficient is common to all consumers and all products. We discuss this strong assumption below. The third component of utility, $v_{ik}$, is a component that is specific to each consumer and product and is independent of the price of the product. If $v_{ik}$ is distributed according to the extreme value distribution,[9] then the choice probabilities for each product are[10]:

$$(8) \quad \pi_i = \frac{\exp(\alpha_i - \beta p_i)}{\displaystyle\sum_{j \varepsilon C} \exp(\alpha_j - \beta p_j)}$$

where   C is the set of all products.

---

[7]   i.e. they are more technically difficult to use than some other alternatives.
[8]   See Werden and Froeb (1996), Werden and Froeb (1994) and Werden, Froeb and Tardiff (1994).
[9]   The extreme value distribution is often referred to as the Gumbel distribution. It is similar to the normal distribution but has a thicker tail and so allows for a greater probability of extreme events.
[10]   See, e.g. Maddala (1983).

This version of the model includes all products[11] and so allows for the possibility that consumers choose a product outside the set of products with which the merger is concerned (i.e. choose the so-called "outside product"). A standard approach to using this model is to assume that consumers buy one of the products with which the merger is concerned (i.e. an "inside good"). The choice probabilities are then conditional on one of the inside goods being bought and so can be interpreted as volume market shares.[12] The elasticity of the market as a whole is then used to allow for the fact that as prices rise, some consumers leave the market. This approach to using the logit model is referred to as the antitrust logit model or ALM. It leads to relatively simple expressions for the own price and cross-price elasticities. The own and cross-price elasticities are:

$$(9) \quad \varepsilon_{ii} = -\frac{(\beta\rho(1 - s_i) + \varepsilon s_i)p_i}{\rho}$$

and

$$(10) \quad \varepsilon_{ij} = \frac{s_j(\beta\rho - \varepsilon)p_j}{\rho}$$

where $s_i$ is the volume market share of Product i;[13]

$\epsilon$ is the industry own-price elasticity; and

$\rho$ is the weighted average price of all the products in the market. There are only two demand parameters in this model ($\beta$ and $\epsilon$), so esti- **15–010** mation is relatively straightforward. The overall elasticity can be estimated in the standard manner (i.e. on the basis of already existing estimates, or econometrically if no such estimates exist or, at a push, through a survey) and similarly $\beta$ can be derived from a cross-elasticity estimate.[14]

The equilibrium price-marginal cost mark-up for Product i pre-merger is:

$$(11) \quad p_i - c_i = \frac{1}{\beta(1 - s_i)}$$

whilst the price-marginal cost mark-ups post-merger for Product i and Product j are[15]:

$$(12) \quad p_i - c_i = p_j - c_j = \frac{1}{\beta(1 - s_i - s_j)}$$

[11] Formally, it includes all possible purchase options.

[12] Note that this presupposes a definition of the relevant market, so this approach to merger simulation does not allow us to dispense with market definition completely.

[13] More formally, the choice probability of Product i given that an inside good as been chosen.

[14] Note that there is considerable scope to run self-consistency tests by estimating several cross-price elasticities and seeing whether they lead to a consistent estimate of $\beta$. However, an advantage of the logit model is that there is no need to carry out lots of cross-elasticity estimates. If the data to estimate these elasticities is available, then it is not clear why there should be reliance on the logit model rather than on the more standard Nash equilibrium in a differentiated products market.

[15] Although this equation appears innocuous, it actually needs to be solved iteratively due to the two unknowns $s_i$ and $s_j$. However, the solution will be unique.

There are a number of comments to be made about this model of demand when used for merger simulations. The first is that because there are only two parameters that need to be estimated, it is a very simple model to use and can therefore be implemented quickly. However, it has the considerable downside that in general the model is unlikely to be a good description of reality.

The second is that this model requires that the relevant market is defined since otherwise it is not possible to calculate market shares. This means that this approach does not, unlike some other merger simulation approaches, allow the investigator to avoid market definition.

The third is that the larger is a product's market share, the greater is the mark-up of its price over marginal cost. This can be seen from Equation (11). This is consistent with a model in which firms that offer better products are able to earn higher mark-ups and win greater market share. Whether this link between mark-ups and market share is observed can be relatively simply checked whenever the ALM is used. If that relationship does not hold empirically, then this would indicate that the ALM is an inappropriate description of actual competition (although see below for a discussion of "nests").

**15–011**  The fourth is that Equation (12) implies that the price of the merging product with the lower market share pre-merger rises more post-merger than the price of the merging product with the higher market share. This is because post-merger the price-marginal cost margins of the two products are the same but, as discussed above, pre-merger the product with the greater market share had a higher price-cost mark-up. We explain the intuition for this result below.

The fifth comment to be made about the ALM is that it exhibits what is known as the Independence of Irrelevant Alternatives (IIA). The IIA assumption implies that either adding or changing the characteristics of another alternative does not affect consumer choices as between two particular alternatives. Thus if X is twice as likely to be chosen as Y when a consumer can only choose between X or Y, then the IIA holds that X will still be twice as likely to be chosen as Y when the consumer is given further alternatives to choose from. The implication of this is that the cross-price elasticity from Product i to Product j does not depend on the identity of Product i but only on Product j. This can be seen from Equation (10) which shows that $e_{ij}$ does not depend on the identity of Product $i$. This makes the model easy (from a technical econometric perspective) to estimate and use, but at the cost of imposing the assumption that all products are equally "close" to each other. This means that when a consumer substitutes away from a product, they purchase the other products in proportions equal to their market shares. This provides the intuition behind the result that the price of the product with the lower pre-merger share rises more post-merger than the price of the product with the higher pre-merger share. Pre-merger more sales were diverted from the low market share to the high market share product than vice versa, so the merger effectively removes a greater competitive constraint from the low market share product than from the high market share product.

The IIA assumption has been heavily criticised as being unrealistic. In general, this criticism is valid. If a new product is introduced that is very similar to a product already in the market, then it is reasonable to believe that the new product will win sales primarily from the existing similar product, rather than from all the products in proportion to their market share.[16] It also rather undermines the rationale for a merger simulation, which is to move beyond a mechanical assessment of market shares. Put simply, if we assume substitutability based on market shares, then merger simulation adds very little beyond a simple assessment of market shares.

A common response to the concern about the IIA assumption implicit in **15–012** the ALM is to use a nested logit demand function. This approach allows some products to be closer to each other than to other products. It is based on the idea of a sequential decision-making process in which consumers first decide whether, e.g. they want to buy a private label or a branded product and then decide which product within the relevant class to buy. In *Lagardère/Natexis/VUP*[17] the Commission used a nested logit model to simulate a merger in the French publishing industry. This model assumed that consumers first chose what type of book they wanted to buy (e.g. science fiction, thriller, humour, etc.) and then decided which book within that class to buy.[18] The IIA then holds within each nest (i.e. all products in a nest are equally close competitors) but not across nests (i.e. products outside a nest are less close substitutes for products inside a nest than are other products within that nest). It is possible to have as many nests as you want, but the more nests you have, the more "nest parameters" you have to either estimate or assume. Thus although the nested logit is likely to be more realistic than the ALM, this advantage comes at the cost of more complexity and the need for either more data or more assumptions.[19] More data is required if the analyst is going to estimate the various cross-elasticities between products in order to assign different products to different

---

[16] A good example of why the IIA assumption is not realistic is provided by McFadden (1974). Suppose that commuters initially face a decision between two modes of transport: car and red bus. Suppose that a consumer chooses between these two options with equal probability, 0.5, so that the relative odds of choosing the two modes is 1. Now suppose a third mode, blue bus, is added. Assuming bus commuters do not care about the colour of the bus they travel in, we should expect commuters to continue to choose between bus and car with equal probability. It is natural to assume that commuters would choose car with probability 0.5, red bus with probability 0.25 and blue bus with probability 0.25. This would make the relative odds of choosing car or red bus 2 (0.5 / 0.25), not 1. But IIA implies that this would not happen. Instead, it would imply that the relative odds remain at 1 and that the probability that a commuter takes car, red bus or blue bus is one third for each mode.

[17] COMP/M.2978 *Lagardère/Natexis VUP* (January 7, 2004).

[18] For a brief description of this case, see below. For an extended description, see Ivaldi (2005).

[19] For more detail on the nested logit model, see Anderson and de Palma (1992).

nests. Alternatively, the analyst has to make assumptions about which products go in which nests. The results of the simulation exercise are sensitive to such assumptions. If these assumptions are wrong, then the results of the simulation will be biased.

## Almost Ideal Demand System

**15–013** An alternative way to model consumer demand is the Almost Ideal Demand System (AIDS) of Deaton and Muellbauer (1980).[20] This is a very general demand system of the form:

$$(13) \quad s_i = \alpha_i + \sum_{j=1}^{n} \gamma_{ij} \ln p_j + \beta_i \ln \frac{X}{P}$$

where $s_i$ is the share of Product i;

$\alpha_i$ and $\beta_i$ are product-specific constants;

$p_j$ is the price of Product j;

$\gamma_{ij}$ is a coefficient measuring the effect of a change in the price of Product j on the share of Product i; and

X/P is the total expenditure on all the products divided by a price index. In effect, it is real expenditure in the market.

This approach relates the market share of a product to its price, the price of all other products in the market and total expenditure in the market. A product's share will fall as its own price rises and rise as the price of other products rises, so $\gamma_{ii}$ is negative for all i and $\gamma_{ij}$ is positive[21] for all pairs of i and j. Whether a product's share goes up or down as total expenditure on the market increases is not a priori clear, so $\beta_i$ can be positive, negative or zero.

The AIDS is based on the idea of multi-stage budgeting whereby consumers break their purchase decisions down into a number of stages. For instance, they first decide to buy a car, then decide what type of car to buy (economy, luxury, etc.) and then decide which specific car to buy within that segment. From a technical perspective, the AIDS model has various attributes that make it a plausible approximation to consumer demand. As such, it has attractions as a model for demand underlying a merger simulation. However, unlike the logit model it requires the estimation of a large number of parameters. A full estimation requires the estimation of $N^2$ $\gamma$ coefficients (where N is the number of products) plus N $\alpha$ and $\beta$ coefficients. Even assuming that $\gamma_{ij} = \gamma_{ji}$ for all i and j still leaves $N^2/2$ $\gamma$ coefficients to be estimated. If there are ten products in the market, this gives a minimum of 70 coefficients and a maximum of 120.[22] Twenty products would imply a figure of 240 to 440. Estimating this many

---

[20] This is based on the pioneering work of Gorman (1959).

[21] Or at least, non-negative.

[22] In fact, the model implies the figures are slightly less than these because it implies other restrictions, such as that the sum of the $\alpha_i$ and $\beta_i$ coefficients must be 1 and zero respectively.

coefficients requires extremely large data sets and so is only really possible when reliable scanner data over a reasonably lengthy period is available and even then there are significant econometric difficulties with getting results that are consistent with basic economic theory (i.e. all own price elasticities negative and all cross-price elasticities non-negative).

An alternative to the AIDS model is the so-called proportionately cali- **15–014** brated-AIDS (PC-AIDS) model due to Epstein and Rubinfeld (2002).[23] The starting point for this approach is that the full AIDS model is very data intensive. However, if we make the assumption of "proportionality", then the number of unknowns in the model declines very substantially. "Proportionality" in this model is effectively the same as the IIA property in a logit model: when a firm raises its price, it loses sales to its competitors in proportion to their market share. Thus if there are three firms in a market, A, B and C, and they have market shares of 10, 30 and 60, then when A raises its price it loses twice as many sales to C as to B. The effect of imposing this assumption on the AIDS model is that the number of elasticities that need to be estimated declines to only two. All that is needed is an estimate of the industry price elasticity and the own-price elasticity for just one of the products in the market.[24] From these two figures, and the assumption of proportionality, all the other elasticities can be recovered as long as market shares are known.[25] This assumption has the obvious benefit of reducing the requirement to estimate many elasticities, but comes at the cost that it is unlikely to be a realistic description of actual competition. It is possible to include nests within the PC-AIDS model in order to allow for some products to be closer to each other and to others, in just the same way as can be done in the logit model. The assumption is then that proportionality holds within each nest, but not between nests. This is potentially more realistic, but requires assumptions or estimates to be made as to which products are in which nests and about the relative closeness of the nests. The results of the model are sensitive to these assumptions. For instance, Epstein and Rubinfeld used the model to simulate the US baby foods case in which Heinz tried to acquire Beech-Nut. This would have been a merger of the number two and three firms in

---

[23] See also Epstein and Rubinfeld (2004).

[24] Epstein and Rubinfeld go even further and suggest that you can assume that if the set of products is a relevant market as defined by the hypothetical monopolist test, then the industry elasticity must be more than 1 on the basis that a monopolist prices in the elastic portion of the demand curve. This assumption is wrong as it involves assuming that the current price in the industry is at the level that a hypothetical monopolist would set.

[25] Imposing the assumption of proportionality allows one to recover all the cross-price elasticities for a firm on the basis that $-\gamma_{ii} = \Sigma \gamma_{ij}$. The actual equations for the own price ($\varepsilon_{ii}$) and cross-price elasticities ($\varepsilon_{ij}$) are:

$$\varepsilon_{ii} = -1 + \frac{\gamma_{ii}}{s_i} + s_i(\varepsilon + 1)$$

$$\varepsilon_{ij} = \frac{\gamma_{ij}}{s_i} + s_j(\varepsilon + 1)$$

where $\varepsilon$ is the industry elasticity.

a three-firm market.[26] Epstein-Rubinfeld simulate the merger on the basis of three different assumptions about nests: one, that there are no nests; two, that Heinz and Beech-Nut are part of a nest separate from Gerber; and three, that Beech-Nut and Gerber are part of a nest separate from Heinz. Their results are shown in Table 15.1. It is clear that the expected post-merger price rises vary considerably depending on the assumption made about nests.

**15–015** ## Table 15.1: Simulated price rises in the US baby foods case

|  | No nests | Heinz Beech-Nut nest | Beech-Nut Gerber nest |
|---|---|---|---|
| **Heinz** | 6.2% | 12.3% | 3.9% |
| **Beech-Nut** | 6.8% | 13.3% | 3.4% |

*Source*: Epstein and Rubinfeld (2002) Table 7.

It is reasonable to ask what the advantage is of the PC-AIDS model over the antitrust logit model, since they appear quite similar. One advantage of the PC-AIDS model is that it does not need price data, but this is a relatively minor advantage as data on current prices is almost always available in industries where it is reasonable to use a Bertrand merger simulation approach. Another advantage is that PC-AIDS is easier to apply than the ALM. Finally, to the extent that it approximates the full AIDS model, PC-AIDS is consistent with underlying consumer theory of demand.

## Cournot models

**15–016** Cournot models are rarely used as the basis of merger simulations. There are a number of reasons for this. First, merger simulations are used in unilateral effects cases and the standard assumption employed when simulating likely unilateral effects is Bertrand price competition between differentiated products. Cournot competition, on the other hand, is usually associated with homogeneous products and hence with coordinated effects cases.[27] Secondly, most mergers do not make sense within the standard Cournot model. The post-merger equilibrium involves the merging parties reducing their output, the non-merging parties increasing their output, but total output falling and hence prices rising. In many cases the implication is that the merger is not profitable for the merging parties. Salant, Switzer and Reynolds (1983) conclude that the merger is not profitable if the merging parties have less than 80 per cent of the market. They assume a symmetric equilibrium with constant marginal costs and linear demand

[26] For a description of this case, see Chapter 7.
[27] For a detailed discussion of this issue, see Chapter 2.

curves. If these assumptions are relaxed then mergers can become profitable for the merging parties at lower market shares.[28] In particular, in a Cournot model profits and market share are directly related to cost efficiency, with the most cost efficient firms having the largest share and the highest profits. So if a merger leads to substantial cost efficiencies then this may cause it to be profitable for the merging parties. However, in the absence of capacity constraints (see below) or of substantial marginal cost savings from the merger, many Cournot mergers are not profitable for the merging parties and so it makes no sense to model a merger, which the parties presumably believe will be profitable, on the basis of Cournot competition. At a minimum, any simulation using a Cournot model must show that the simulation implies that the merger is profitable for the merging parties.

It is often argued that Cournot models can make sense when products are homogeneous and firms are capacity constrained. When non-merging firms are capacity constrained they cannot respond to any post-merger price increase by increasing their output. If the non-merging parties are unable to increase their output at all, then the merging parties effectively become a monopolist over the residual demand that the other firms cannot serve and so raise their prices to the monopoly price for the residual demand curve. This implies that the post-merger price rise will actually be larger than predicted by the standard Cournot model, at least until the other firms have been able to increase their capacity.[29] It should be noted that in this case the merger is still more profitable to non-merging firms than to the merging firms as the merging firms have to lower output in order to raise prices, whereas non-merging firms can enjoy the higher prices at their pre-merger outputs.[30]

Since the products are assumed to be homogeneous, Cournot simulations raise far fewer issues on the demand side than do Bertrand simulations with differentiated products. The only demand-side issue is the elasticity of the industry as a whole and how this varies as the industry-wide price rises. There are no issues related to how close particular firms are to other firms. The focus instead is on the cost side of the model and in particular on how marginal costs vary as output increases. As noted above, if marginal costs are constant and there are no capacity constraints, then the Cournot model usually makes no sense in a unilateral effects setting. So the use of a Cournot model needs to be motivated by homogeneous products and either substantial cost efficiencies arising out of the merger or capacity constraints. In paras 15–033—15–035 below we discuss the use of

---

[28]   See, for instance, Perry and Porter (1985) or Hennessy (2000).
[29]   Werden and Froeb (2008) state that the US DoJ's analysis in *Georgia-Pacific* was "heavily influenced" by concerns that the non-merging parties were tightly capacity constrained.
[30]   Although the same result arises in Betrand models where the profits of non-merging firms rise more than the profits of the merging firms (see Deneckere and Davidson (1985)).

Cournot models in electricity mergers, which are characterised by capacity constraints and homogeneous products.

A close relation to Cournot models are supply function equilibria (SFE) models. These are typically used in electricity mergers. They replace the pure quantity setting assumption of the Cournot model with the assumption that firms offer a "supply function" in which they specify how much capacity they will offer at any given price. The assumption is that the supply function is upward sloping: firms will offer more capacity as the price they are offered increases. Whilst the assumption that firms offer a supply function is often a better description of reality than a pure Cournot model, SFE models suffer from the significant drawback that they often lead to multiple equilibria and so do not predict a single outcome for the merger. We discuss this difficulty in more detail in the case studies section below.

## Auction and bargaining models

15–017 Both the Bertrand and Cournot models of competition assume that consumers see what prices are and then decide whether to purchase or not, and how much, on the basis of those prices. This is a reasonable description of many markets, but certainly not of all. There are many markets where prices are set as result of direct interaction between buyers and sellers. For instance, buyers often negotiate with a number of potential sellers before deciding who to buy from. An example of this would be a large international corporate deciding who to buy its telecommunications services from. The corporate would negotiate with a number of potential suppliers, discussing various prices and possible services, before finally choosing a supplier.

Modelling markets of this sort is very complex because the results of the simulation tend to be very sensitive to the exact assumptions made about how the auction or bargaining works. For instance, is the process best modelled as a second-price auction, in which the winner pays the amount of the second highest bid (as in a standard auction house auction), or as a first-price auction, in which the winner pays the amount that they bid (as in a sealed-bid auction)? However, most of the models share a similar underlying structure of valuation on the part of the bidders. There are assumed to be two parts to the valuation placed by each bidder on the product. One part is a part that is common to all bidders and that all bidders know. The other is a part that differs between bidders and is known only to the bidder. Thus the valuation of lot i by bidder j is:

(14) $v_{ij} = c_i + \eta_{ij}$

where $v_{ij}$ is the valuation of lot i by bidder j;

$c_i$ is the common part of the valuation of lot i that does not vary across bidders; and

$\eta_{ij}$ is the bidder-specific part of the valuation of lot i by bidder j.

The bidder-specific component of the valuation is assumed to vary randomly according to some specified distribution (e.g. the normal distribution or, more often, the extreme value or logistic distribution) with a mean of zero and a specified variance.[31] Bidders with a higher market share are characterised as having a higher variance as this increases the likelihood that their valuation of the product is the highest in any particular case. The intuition for this is that since only the bidder with the highest valuation wins,[32] bidders with more of their random distribution towards the extremes will win more often. Thus a higher variance will imply more wins. The variance attached to each bidder in the simulation is set so that it implies the current market shares of the various firms.

Essentially the same approach can be used when bidders are bidding to supply a product rather than to buy a product. When bidders are sellers, then they will win if they bid the lowest price to the buyer (allowing for quality differentials). We can then interpret $v_{ij}$ in Equation (14) as being the cost to bidder j of supplying product i. $c_i$ then becomes the part of the cost of supply that is common to all bidders and $\eta_{ij}$ becomes the part of the cost that is specific to bidder j. The firms with the highest market share will again be modelled as having the highest variance of $\eta_{ij}$ but this time they will win when their cost is the lowest, rather than their valuation the highest. **15–018**

The effect of a merger in this setting is that the merged entity now potentially has two valuations (costs) of the product (one for each of the merging parties) and this increases the likelihood that one of these will be the highest valuation (lowest cost). This then allows the model to account for the increase in market share as a result of the merger. However, it does not directly provide an estimate of the price effect of the merger. Mergers in bidding markets are usually considered to create competition concerns only when the two merging parties are frequently the first and second highest bidders. The intuition is clear. The competitive constraint on merging party A is only relaxed after the merger for those auctions where merging party B would previously have been the closest competitor. Thus the competitive constraint on A is only relaxed for those cases where B was previously the second highest bidder. If the closest bidder to A in an auction that A won pre-merger was C, then post-merger A faces the same competitive constraint: the need to beat C.

So estimating the price effect of the merger requires estimating how often the merging parties were the first and second highest bidders and seeing what was the third highest bid in that case. This can be done on the

---

[31]   In principle the mean of this random variable does not have to be zero. If a particular bidder systematically tends to value a product higher than other bidders, then this could be reflected in a positive mean to the random part of their valuation.

[32]   It is not quite true that bidders with the highest valuation always win, at least not in sealed-bid auctions. See below for a discussion of this.

basis of the assumptions made about the distribution of the bidder-specific components in Equation (14) above.

**15–019** This discussion about estimating the effect of the merger on prices is predicated on the assumption that the auction is a second price auction. This is usually a reasonable assumption to make. However, it should be noted that the effect of a merger in a sealed-bid auction setting is slightly different to that described above. Suppose firms are bidding to be the lowest cost supplier. In a sealed-bid auction the winner is paid what they bid. This implies that bidders will not bid their actual costs because winning at your actual costs does not increase your producer surplus. You want to win but charge more than your actual costs. This means that your bid should ideally be just slightly below the second lowest bid. However, unlike in the second price auctions discussed above, the second lowest bid will not be the actual costs of the second lowest cost bidder since they also do not want to bid their actual costs. Each firm will trade off the lower likelihood of winning with a higher bid against the greater profit earned from winning with a higher bid. Modelling this process is clearly a complex task which requires assumptions to be made about how each firm expects the other firms to bid. Vickrey (1961) showed that if bidders are symmetric, then the expected winning bid is actually the same in both types of auction discussed here. However, this result no longer holds when, as is usual, bidders are not symmetric.[33]

## Coordinated effects simulation

**15–020** All of the approaches to merger simulation discussed above relate to unilateral effects cases. To the best of our knowledge, merger simulation has not so far been used in a coordinated effects case. However Davis (2006) suggests an approach to simulating the coordinated effect of a merger in a differentiated products market.[34] He assumes that any coordination is supported by a "grim" punishment strategy, which means that if any firm cheats on the coordinated outcome, then all firms revert to the non-coordinated (competitive) outcome in all future periods. This assumption allows him to estimate relatively easily whether collusion is sustainable. First, calculate the profitability to each firm of collusion. This is done by calculating the monopoly profit for the market. Secondly, calculate for each firm whether collusion is more profitable than cheating. Cheating leads to one period of high profits where all other firms are setting the collusive price whilst the cheating firm is maximising its profits given the prices set by the other firms. Thereafter cheating yields the competitive price level in perpetuity. The competitive price level is calculated by assuming a non-cooperation equilibrium, as in unilateral effects merger

---

[33] See Maskin and Riley (2000).
[34] Sabbatini (2006) uses a similar approach.

simulation. Whether cheating is profitable for a firm will depend on how high its discount rate is. A firm will be more likely to cheat the less it values future profits relative to current profits. Only if all firms value collusion more than cheating will the collusion be sustainable.

One aspect of this approach that is very attractive is that it does not require significantly more work than a standard merger simulation. A standard merger simulation involves estimating the post-merger non-cooperative equilibrium. Estimating the monopoly outcome is not difficult. So the only extra work involved is understanding whether each firm has an incentive to cheat or not. This involves estimating the profit maximising behaviour for each firm given that all other firms are charging the monopoly price. This is not a Nash equilibrium and is relatively easy to calculate. Collusion is then sustainable if and only if for all firms:

(15)   *profit from cheating + discounted profits from future competitive outcome*
*< profit from collusion in perpetuity*

There are clearly substantial difficulties with this approach. First, the outcome is heavily dependent on the exact punishment mechanism chosen. Is a grim strategy really plausible in the long run? Secondly, in the absence of explicit collusion, how likely are firms to find the monopoly outcome? Thirdly, it abstracts from issues related to how likely cheating is to be detected. Fourthly, initial calibration of the model requires an assumption that the pre-merger situation is a Nash equilibrium. Whilst this assumption, or some equivalent, always needs to be made, it may be particularly suspect in a market in which there are concerns about post-merger coordination.

As it stands, we doubt that a merger control authority ought to place much weight on the results of such an analysis. However, this is an interesting approach to the problem of merger simulation in coordinated effects cases and we expect there to be significant further research in this area in future.

## Vertical merger simulation

Simulation techniques can be used in vertical mergers as well as horizontal **15–021** mergers. However, the theory of harm in a vertical merger tends to be different to that in a horizontal merger. In general, the direct effect of a vertical merger on prices is likely to be pro-competitive. Instead, theories of harm in vertical mergers tend to relate to foreclosure concerns. We discuss these issues in depth in Chapter 8, where we also discuss the use of "vertical arithmetic" to assess these concerns. Accordingly, we do not deal with these issues any further here.

# CASE STUDIES

**15–022**   This section contains a number of brief case studies of actual merger simulation studies that have been carried out. The purpose is to provide context to the discussion that follows regarding the appraisal of merger simulation models. The first two case studies are not formally merger simulations. However, they are early attempts at directly estimating the likely effect of a merger on prices and so are included here.

## *Staples/Office Depot* merger

**15–023**   This example is not strictly speaking a merger simulation at all but rather a form of price concentration study. However, we include it here as it is an early example of an attempt to estimate the precise price effect of a merger, rather than just arguing that prices were likely to rise but without putting any figure on the size of the likely rise.

In 1996, two US office superstores, Staples and Office Depot, announced a merger.[35] The FTC opposed the merger, the case went to court and in June 1997 the FTC was granted a preliminary injunction blocking the merger. The parties subsequently abandoned their planned merger. Econometric estimates of the extent of the likely post-merger price increases played an important role in the FTC's case.

One of the first things that appears to have concerned the FTC was internal pricing documents of the parties that implied that Staples and Office Depot both set prices on the basis of the amount of superstore competition in the vicinity of the store. Thus prices were in general higher when Staples or Office Depot did not face competition from either the other merging party or from the other office superstore, OfficeMax. The FTC carried out econometric analysis to confirm this view. In effect, they looked at how prices differed in office superstores depending on whether an office superstore faced other office superstore competition in the near vicinity.

The initial econometric analysis carried out by the FTC suggested that the merger would allow the prices of consumable office supplies to rise by more than 7 per cent in those areas where Staples and Office Depot currently competed. This figure was contested by the parties, who argued instead that prices would rise by less than 1 per cent. However, the conflict between the two sets of results was resolved. The FTC showed that the figure of 1 per cent was based on a model that suffered from two major flaws. First, it mis-measured concentration (or, more precisely, omitted a relevant concentration variable). Secondly, there was a sample selection bias caused by the omission of some observations for California, Pennsylvania and some other areas. Correcting for these two problems meant

---

[35]   This discussion of the *Staples/Office Depot* merger relies heavily on Baker (1999).

that the model now predicted price rises of between 7 per cent and 9 per cent.[36]

There are three lessons to be learnt from this case. First, econometric    15–024 analysis and merger simulation can be useful in real-world cases. Secondly, econometric analysis and merger simulation can be particularly powerful when they are used to support the implications of other evidence. In the *Staples/Office Depot* case they supported the implications of the internal pricing documents. The combination of the two types of evidence was very powerful. Thirdly, it is not the case that econometric analysis can be used to "prove" any proposition that is required. The disagreement between the FTC and the parties over econometrics in this case was resolvable. The parties' analysis was flawed: this was demonstrable and the result was a model whose predictions fitted those derived from other evidence (e.g. internal pricing documents).

## *L'Oréal/Maybelline* merger[37]

The area of concern in this merger was cosmetics (e.g. mascara). This was    15–025 where L'Oréal and Maybelline both offered products that were plausible substitutes. On a pure "market share of cosmetics" approach, the merger was potentially concerning. However, L'Oréal was a "high-end" brand which tended to compete with other "high-end" brands such as Clinique. Maybelline, on the other hand, was more a "low-end" brand that competed with brands such as Avon and Cover Girl. This was highlighted by the relatively large price differences between the two brands.

The data available in this case was rather more limited than that available in the *Staples/Office Depot* case. Although scanner data was available, this data omitted large portions of the market. For instance, it did not cover department stores or "direct to home" sales. Nonetheless it was possible to carry out some econometric analysis. The results indicated that even though both parties sold products that appeared to be in the same relevant market (i.e. "colour cosmetics"), the degree of competition between them was actually very low. This was indicated by the fact that the results implied that there would be at most only a small price rise after the merger. The results implied that the combination of the two would not lead to an economically significant loss of competition and so prices would not rise to an appreciable extent after the merger. Accordingly, the merger was not challenged by the US DoJ.

It is worth noting that in this case, as in most cases (e.g. *Staples/Office Depot*), econometric evidence was not the only empirical evidence used. For instance, it appears that the DoJ also used survey data showing that the

---

[36] For the sake of brevity and clarity, some of the complex issues raised by Baker (1999) about this case have been omitted. The interested reader is referred to that article.
[37] This section is based on Robinson (1996).

two products were not very close to each other.[38] As stated elsewhere in this book, wherever possible a range of empirical evidence should be used.

*Volvo/Scania* merger[39]

**15–026** One of the areas of concern in this merger was in heavy trucks (those over 16 tonnes) in Ireland and the Nordic countries. The post-merger shares would have been considerable in these countries.

**15–027 Table 15.2: Pre-merger and post-merger market shares in** *Volvo/Scania*

|  | Volvo | Scania | Post-merger total |
|---|---|---|---|
| Sweden | 45 | 46 | 91 |
| Finland | 34 | 31 | 65 |
| Denmark | 29 | 30 | 59 |
| Ireland | 22 | 27 | 49 |
| Norway | 38 | 32 | 70 |

*Source*: para.65 of Commission's Decision

As part of its analysis of the merger the Commission asked Professors Ivaldi and Verboven to undertake an econometric simulation of the merger on national heavy truck markets.[40] The simulation was based on a nested logit model in which the nests corresponded to rigid trucks and tractor trucks. Rigid trucks are integrated trucks from which the trailer cannot be detached whilst tractor trucks have detachable trailers. The data was list prices for 16 EEA countries in 1997 and 1998.[41] Using the results of the nested logit model, the authors then simulated the model on the assumption that the post-merger outcome would be a Nash equilibrium (i.e. they assumed no post-merger co-operative behaviour between the remaining players). They explicitly took account of the fact that if the merged entity raised its prices, this would lead to the other firms in the market also raising their prices. The results were as follows:

---

[38] Robinson (1996).
[39] Comp/M.1672 *Volvo/Scania* (March 15, 2000).
[40] The following is based on Ivaldi and Verboven (2005). The Commission's Decision itself includes very few details of the work (discussed at paras 72–75 of the Decision).
[41] The Commission's Decision states that Volvo contested the validity of the study, claiming that the analysis was seriously flawed and that the results cannot be relied on (para.75). One imagines that one of the criticisms levelled against the report was the apparent use of list prices, rather than transaction prices. The use of list prices is extremely problematic unless there is a stable relationship between list prices and actual transaction prices.

## Table 15.3: Per cent price changes after merger[42]

|  | Volvo/Scania | | Competitors | |
|---|---|---|---|---|
|  | **Rigid** | **Tractor** | **Rigid** | **Tractor** |
| **Denmark** | 11.55 | 8.17 | 0.26 | 0.19 |
| **Finland** | 10.03 | 7.83 | 0.39 | 0.24 |
| **Ireland** | 10.87 | 7.36 | 0.21 | 0.30 |
| **Norway** | 13.17 | 8.63 | 0.32 | 0.28 |
| **Sweden** | 22.34 | 12.64 | 0.47 | 0.32 |

Table 15.3 shows that in all five countries of concern the authors estimated post-merger price increases by the parties of between 10 per cent and 23 per cent for rigid trucks and between 7 per cent and 13 per cent for tractor trucks. Even when the authors allowed for cost efficiencies of 10 per cent post-merger, they still found that consumer welfare would fall in all five countries (by between 2 per cent and 14 per cent).[43]

Ultimately, the Commission chose not to rely on this study in the light of the criticisms of it made by the parties: "Given the novelty of the approach and the level of disagreement, the Commission will not base its assessment on the results of the study."[44] Instead, the merger was blocked on more conventional grounds (e.g. market shares).

### Lagardère/Natexis/VUP[45]

This case involved the publishing of French language books and included **15–029** another example of a Bertrand merger simulation based on logit demand carried out on behalf of the Commission. The authors[46] had data on 3,200 hardback and softback books and so were able to estimate elasticities econometrically.[47] They used a nested logit model in which the nests were the various different genres of book. The model predicted a post-merger price rise of 4.8 per cent. In addition, the authors provided a 95 per cent confidence interval for this figure: the correct post-merger price rise percentage lay between 3.7 per cent and 5.5 per cent with 95 per cent certainty.[48]

Unlike with the *Volvo/Scania* study, the Commission does appear to have

---

[42]  This table is based on Table 5 of Ivaldi and Verboven (2000). Although the authors report results for all 16 countries, we report those only for the five countries that the Commission was concerned about.

[43]  See Table 7 of Ivaldi and Verboven (2000).

[44]  COMP/M.1672 *Volvo/Scania* (March 15, 2000) para.75.

[45]  COMP/M.2978 *Lagardère/Natexis/VUP* (January 1, 2004).

[46]  Jérôme Foncel of the University of Lille, Marc Ivaldi of IDEI at Toulouse and Valérie Rabassa of the Chief Economists team in DG Comp.

[47]  This figure comes from Ivaldi (2005), which contains a useful description of the analysis carried out.

[48]  These figures are contained in COMP/M.2978 *Lagardère/Natexis/VUP* (January 1, 2004) para.702.

placed weight on the results of this study. Thus the Commission states that:

> "The study is particularly robust by reason of the very large number of observations, the stability of the various parameters estimated, the high degree of statistical power of the tests provided, and the simulation of a confidence interval for the calculation of a price increase."[49]

### Philip Morris/Papastratos[50]

**15–030** In 2003, Philip Morris acquired the Greek cigarette manufacturer Papastratos. The Commission allowed the merger through at Phase 1. The case included a merger simulation. What is interesting about this is that it appears to be a good example of a merger simulation not adding any value to the analysis of the case, a theme to which we return below. The decision provides no detail on the simulation model, but states only that:

> "The parties have provided the results of a merger simulation that shows that on average the market price increase post-merger would be minimal. The simulation model assumes that the merging parties' products compete in different segments, or in other words, that the degree of substitutability between their products is low. The market investigation has confirmed the market segmentation. The results of the simulation confirm that the present merger would not lead to significant price increase in the Greek cigarette market." (para.32)

It is reasonable to ask what the simulation added to the competitive analysis. The simulation was based on the assumption that the degree of substitutability between the parties' products was low, so it was hardly a surprise that it showed minimal post-merger price rises. It was not necessary to do a simulation to reach this conclusion. The assumption of low substitutability, key to the result of the simulation, had to be confirmed by the Commission's market investigation. In other words, the competitive effects analysis was first needed, which then fed into a simulation that showed what the competitive effects analysis had already shown.

### Oracle/Peoplesoft[51]

**15–031** The acquisition of Peoplesoft by Oracle in 2004 was interesting from an antitrust perspective for a number of reasons. One of these was that the Commission built a model to simulate the merger. This model is of

---

[49] COMP/M.2978 *Lagardère/Natexis/VUP* (January 1, 2004) 543.
[50] COMP/M.3191 *Philip Morris/Papastratos* (October 2, 2003).
[51] This section relies heavily on Bengtsson (2005).

particular interest because it was not a standard Bertrand model but was instead an auction model.

The product in question was enterprise application software. In the human resources (HR) and financial management systems (FMS) segments of this industry the merger was characterised, at least initially, as a three-to-two merger with only the merged entity and SAP remaining as significant players post-merger. The Commission chose to model the industry by a sealed-bid auction in which suppliers put in a bid and buyers then chose one of the bidders. This approach was preferred over an English auction approach due to the cost structure of the industry. The Commission concluded that the marginal cost of supplying a buyer was effectively zero because the development costs of the software are all sunk at the point at which firms bid. Under an English auction this would be expected to lead to prices very close to zero as firms sequentially bid down to marginal cost. But this is not what is seen in the industry, where prices are positive and significant. In a sealed-bid auction firms bid above marginal cost and trade-off the reduced likelihood of winning a bid against the increased profits if they do win a bid. This gives rise to prices above marginal cost and so is consistent with what occurs in this industry.

The model was based on the assumption that the identity of bidders was known, but what was unknown was the buyers' perception of the quality of the various suppliers' products. In effect, the unknown was how well a particular supplier's product matched the needs of the buyer. The assumption was that the Peoplesoft product would disappear post-merger.[52] The Commission looked at two possibilities for what would happen to the quality of the Oracle product. One possibility was that it would remain unchanged. The other was that it would be improved as a result of the acquisition of Peoplesoft know-how. The inclusion of this quality aspect allowed the Commission to simulate both the effect of the merger on prices and on consumer welfare, including the effect on consumer welfare of reductions in choice leading to some buyers not being able to buy products that fitted their needs as well post-merger as pre-merger.

Note that this approach means that buyers can be harmed even if the two merging parties are not close substitutes. If they are close substitutes, then the merger is likely to have a significant effect on prices. If they are not close substitutes, then whilst the merger may not affect prices significantly it may reduce available choice significantly, in a way that a merger of close substitutes would not.

The results from the simulation for HR and FMS are shown below.

---

[52] This was not a controversial assumption. Oracle publicly stated that it would support existing Peoplesoft customers but would not sell the Peoplesoft product actively after the merger.

## Table 15.4: Results from *Oracle-Peoplesoft* merger simulation

|       | Price rise | Consumer surplus decline |
|-------|-----------|--------------------------|
| **HR** | 7%–40% | 15%–39% |
| **FMS** | 14%–30% | 18%–25% |

15–032　The ranges presented in Table 15.4 are driven by a range of different assumptions. For instance, the lower figure for the loss of consumer surplus in the HR segment is based on the assumption that the Oracle product is improved post-merger by the acquisition of Peoplesoft know-how. Equally, the lowest price and consumer welfare effects in the FMS simulation are based on the assumption of a 10 per cent efficiency saving post-merger. However, it is clear that the model consistently predicted significant price increases and consumer surplus reductions.

There are a number of ways in which this simulation exercise was well designed. First, it was not an "off-the-shelf" simulation in which competitive behaviour was assumed to be adequately reflected by a particular theoretical model but a bespoke model designed for the particular market in question. Secondly, it fitted the observable data well. For instance, SAP was known as having the highest market share and the highest prices. The simulation model was consistent with this observation: higher market share is driven by higher quality and hence higher prices. The model also implied that buyers who valued the products more highly paid a higher price, which was consistent with the empirical observation that pricing in the market appeared to be linked to the willingness to pay of buyers as measured by variables such as the intensity of use or number of users of the product within the buying firm. Finally, the model dealt explicitly with the fact that the Peoplesoft product was likely to disappear as a result of the merger.

However, it should be noted that the Commission ultimately did not rely on this simulation. This was because the Commission decided that it was not correct to characterise the merger as a three-to-two merger and that there was a wider range of competitive constraints than allowed for in the model. Hence at para.196 of the decision, the Commission states that:

> "it is clear that the simulation model was based on the assumption of only three bidders being present in the market. In the light of the findings with regards to the market definition, this assumption cannot be upheld."

After a prolonged Phase 2 investigation, the Commission cleared the merger.[53]

---

[53]　There is no doubt but that the Commission clearance was heavily influenced by the fact that the DoJ had already lost its case against the merger in a federal court in San Francisco.

*Nuon/Reliant*

In 2003 Nuon, a Dutch utility firm, tried to buy Reliant, a Dutch electricity   **15–033**
generator. The transaction would have led to a significant increase in
concentration in the electricity generation market. The Dutch competition
authority, the NMa, commissioned a merger simulation.

The characteristics of the electricity market mean that Bertrand models
are not appropriate but Cournot-type models may be. Electricity is a
homogeneous product that cannot be stored, so supply has to equal
demand at all times. The way that most electricity markets work is that
generators set prices for each power station for each period (e.g. one hour
in the Netherlands) and then power stations are used, starting with the
cheapest, up to the point at which demand is satisfied. The market price is
then set by the price bid by the most expensive power station that was used
(i.e. the marginal station). An important aspect of the market is that the
elasticity of demand is very low. This is because consumers are charged an
average price and so do not respond to short-run increases in prices. The
only response to such price increases come from large industrial firms who
do face short-run fluctuations in the prices they are charged.[54] The lack of
demand side elasticity means that prices are driven almost entirely by the
cost side of the market and, in particular, by the bidding behaviour of
generators.[55] This means that Bertrand models, that concentrate on the
demand-side of the market, are not likely to provide a good description of
the competitive process.

The NMa commissioned two merger simulation models in this case.
One was a Cournot model and the other was a supply function equilibrium
model. The Cournot model assumes that generators set output only (i.e.
specify which of their plants are available at any given time), whilst the
supply function equilibrium model assumes that generators bid a supply
function. That is, a generator makes a series of bids of the following form: I
will supply power station X at €A, X+Y at €B, X+Y+Z at €C etc. where
A<B<C. This provides a good representation of what generators actually
do, whereas the Cournot model does not. Accordingly, we focus below
only on the supply function model.

As noted above, a major difficulty of supply function models is that they   **15–034**
often exhibit multiple equilibria. The NMa's response to this was to look at
the predicted effect of the merger on minimum prices, maximum prices
and median prices. The minimum prices predicted by the model did not

---

[54] This might be because they buy their electricity in the "spot" market or because they have
arrangements under which they agree to take less electricity when prices are high in return
for a discount.

[55] There is a rich academic literature on the scope for generators to bid strategically in order
to raise prices. For instance, by withholding cheaper generating plant and only bidding in
its more expensive plant, a firm may be able to raise the market price if its more expensive
plant becomes the marginal price setting plant. For an introduction to these issues, see
Harris (2006).

vary much after the merger, but the median prices rose 13 per cent and the maximum prices rose rather more.[56] This immediately raises an interesting issue. What is the correct measure to use? In some sense, the choice is arbitrary as it depends on which of the multiple equilibria that the model finds is the one that the market would actually settle on post-merger. In this case, the implication of the model was very different depending on whether the minimum price was used or alternatively the median or maximum price was used. This issue also feeds through to the question of divestments. If the model is used to estimate the effect of possible divestments on the post-merger outcome, then again this will depend on which Nash equilibrium the market settles on post-merger.

A second issue that arose was over the equilibria that the model found. It is generally not possible to determine the equilibria analytically and so the model postulates a variety of possible strategies by each firm and then sees which combination of strategies constitutes a Nash equilibrium. The model used by the NMa assumed 17 possible strategies for each firm, based on the extent to which they bid above marginal cost (i.e. between one and 15 times marginal cost). This approach leads to the model finding some Nash equilibria that are not really equilibria. Suppose one Nash equilibria is that each firm bids five times marginal cost and this is a Nash equilibria because no firm would find it more profitable to bid four times or six times marginal cost and these are the only two alternatives. It might be that in reality this is not a Nash equilibria because one firm would be better off bidding 4.9 times marginal cost, in which case the other firms would also want to bid less than five times. Certainly, the parties' economic advisors argued that the NMa's model found a number of high price equilibria that were not genuine Nash equilibria.

**15–035** Largely as a result of the simulation models, the NMa allowed the merger only after Nuon had agreed to sell a substantial amount of its post-merger capacity.[57] However, Nuon appealed the decision to the Court of Rotterdam, which held that the NMa's economic analysis was not an adequate basis on which to reach the decision it had. One of the concerns of the court was that the simulation model implied that there should have been strategic behaviour taking place before the merger (i.e. strategic withholding of capacity in order to raise prices), but the NMa presented no evidence that this was the case. This is a fair criticism of a simulation model: as we discuss in detail below, a simulation model must fit with the known facts of the current market outcome. The court was also rightly concerned over whether the simulation model was accurately finding Nash equilibria.

There are just two comments that we wish to make before ending this

---

[56] These are the prices averaged over the full year. As you would expect, the model predicted that prices rose more in the peak demand hours of winter than at other times.

[57] This was done through auctions of "virtual power plants" rather than through the selling of physical plant.

discussion. First, the NMa used simulation modelling as part of its assessment of the potential Nuon/Essent merger,[58] including commissioning a Cournot model from outside advisors. So the NMa at least believes that, notwithstanding the criticisms of the Court in Nuon/Reliant, merger simulation can be useful in electricity mergers. Secondly, a large amount of the debate around the simulation model in Nuon/Reliant centred around the identification of the correct Nash equilibrium when firms acted strategically. One important piece of information that is relevant to this question, but which we did not see discussed in this case, is how do the firms themselves set their prices? For instance, do the firms use models to help them maximise profits? If so, then analysis of those models should go a long way to answering some of the difficult questions raised by the use of SFE models.

## ISSUES IN APPRAISING MERGER SIMULATIONS

The first two sections of this chapter have provided an introduction to the **15–036** basic economics of merger simulation and a number of case studies as illustrations of the practical use of simulation models. We now turn to discuss various issues that arise when appraising whether a merger simulation presented in a case is likely to be a good guide to the post-merger competitive outcome.

### Checking the facts fit the model: current facts

A model that does not fit the current facts of the industry is unlikely to be **15–037** very good at predicting the future facts of the industry, so it is important to make sure that the simulation model is able to account for the current known facts of the industry. These facts should include at least estimates of marginal costs, elasticity estimates and current market shares. For instance, if we assume a Bertrand differentiated products equilibrium, then this implies a set of relationships between various observable variables.[59] For a single product firm we know that there is a particular relationship between marginal cost and the own-price elasticity (i.e. the price cost margin is equal to the negative of one over the own-price elasticity, the so-called Lerner index). So an investigator should confirm that prices, marginal costs and elasticities are consistent with the form of competition assumed in the model. A similar set of relationships hold in the Cournot model. Under Cournot competition firms with larger market shares should have higher margins because they have lower marginal costs and their price/

---

[58] Ultimately the parties were unable to agree terms on this merger, but the NMa still carried out a substantial amount of analysis of it.

[59] Of course, any assumed equilibrium model implies a set of relationships between the various variables.

marginal cost margin should be equal to their market share divided by the industry elasticity.

It is likely that the central estimates of the main variables will not be entirely consistent with the underlying model of competition. Elasticity estimates are often imprecise and marginal cost can be hard to measure. However, at a minimum an investigator needs to consider the possible reasons for inconsistencies before continuing with the simulation. If the marginal cost and elasticity estimates do not mesh, there are at least three possible explanations. One is that the elasticity estimate and/or the marginal cost estimate are poor estimates. The correct response to this issue is to find better estimates. The second possible explanation is that the investigator is looking at the wrong elasticity or the wrong marginal cost. Perhaps the periodicity of the elasticity estimate is wrong. This might actually convey some interesting information on the nature of competition.

The third possible explanation is that the underlying model of competition (e.g. non-collusive Bertrand differentiated products) is wrong, in which case the simulation should not be continued using that model of competition. It is worth stepping back a moment to think about what the assumption of a Nash equilibrium within a Bertrand model really means when, as in virtually all mergers where market shares suggest there may be competition concerns, there are only a few players. As a behavioural assumption, it must be wrong: sophisticated firms do not set their prices assuming that their competitors will not react. Firms in oligopoly situations are well aware that their competitors will respond to whatever they do, and so they take this into account when setting their strategy in the first place, knowing that their competitors will be responding to their strategy taking into account their response to their competitors strategy, and so on. This oligopoly interaction is entirely omitted from the Bertrand Nash equilibrium. So if the Bertrand Nash equilibrium is a good description of reality, it is a good description of where a market ends up, not of how it gets there (i.e. a static description, not a dynamic one). This is an empirical question and there is little reason to believe that in general that is where a market will end up.[60] Evidence that the facts of the market are not consistent with the assumed Bertrand Nash equilibrium assumption should not surprise us and should be taken seriously. If the facts of the market are not consistent

---

[60]   In response to this criticism of the Nash assumption, Werden argues that the assumption is reasonable because what could be more natural than that firms end up in a position where they are doing the best they can given what other firms are doing? ("Whither merger simulation" *ABA Section of Antitrust Law "Brown Bag"*, January 2004). We think this is not an adequate defence. The Nash equilibrium means firms are maximising given the current price and output decisions of other firms in a short-run sense. This is not the natural equilibrium. The natural equilibrium is that firms are maximising given what they expect other firms would do if they were to change their behaviour. This is a quite different equilibrium.

with a Bertrand Nash short-run equilibrium, then it makes little sense to model the industry as if the facts are consistent with such an equilibrium.[61]

An example of this is provided by the model commissioned by the **15–038** Commission in the *Volvo/Scania* merger. This simulation model of the heavy truck market in Europe predicted average Lerner indices ranging from 0.35 in Italy to 0.56 in Sweden. Industry experts believed that the true gross margin was 0.3. The parties evidently used this information, amongst other things, to argue that the simulation model could not be relied upon by the Commission. The authors of the study responded by noting first, that gross margins estimated from accounting data may not coincide with the economically correct gross margins and, secondly, that manufacturers may take into account future profits from after sales service when setting prices. The first of these responses clearly may be correct, but cannot just be asserted. The second response is fascinating: if it is true it tells us something very interesting about the nature of competition *that should be incorporated into the simulation model.* If firms price below the Nash equilibrium in the durable good market in the expectation of recouping the lost profits in the secondary market, then it does not make sense to use a model that assumes a simple Nash equilibrium in the durable good market and that does not take account of secondary market competition. Furthermore, the study was based on list prices as actual transaction prices were not available. Given the widespread use of discounts (usually volume-related) in the heavy truck market, one would expect that margins calculated on the basis of list prices might well be higher than actual margins. So here the relationship between the calculated margins and actual margins might actually tell us something useful about the relationship between list prices and transaction prices (always assuming the model is specified reasonably correctly in the first place).

Before leaving this issue, we note that one approach to merger simulation models is to decide upon the form of competition and then use this to allow one to derive some variables from other variables. For example, if one assumes a short-run Nash equilibrium, one can derive the own-price elasticity from a firm's price cost margin. Unless there are very good grounds for believing that the assumption about the particular assumed mode of competition is correct, we do not think this is a sensible way to proceed. It means that we elevate our assumptions about the nature of

---

[61] Nevo [2001] provides a decomposition of market power (as measured by the Lerner index) into unilateral and coordinated effects. This effectively allows one to test whether a market is in a Nash equilibrium or not. Slade [2004], using on-trade data, applies the methodology to UK brewing and finds no evidence of coordinated effects, thus suggesting that the assumption of a Nash equilibrium would actually be reasonable for this industry. Peters [2003] looks at mergers in the US airline industry in the 1980s using merger simulation models based on Nash equilibria. He finds that post-merger changes in the conduct of firms are an important determinant of post-merger pricing (i.e. the post-merger equilibria, like the pre-merger equilibria, were not pure Nash).

competition to the level of established fact, and this is virtually never a reasonable thing to do. Instead, an investigator should independently estimate the important variables and then check that these estimates are consistent with the underlying model of competition that is chosen. The facts about the market should be used to derive implications for the nature of competition in the market, rather than assumptions about the nature of competition being used to derive "facts" about the market.

### Checking the facts fit the model: past facts

**15–039**   It is generally not enough that a merger simulation is consistent with the current facts of the market for it to provide a good predictor of the likely effects of a merger. Consistency with observed facts represents a necessary, but not sufficient condition. The model should also be able to explain relevant recent past facts about the industry. For instance, have there been significant market share shifts in the recent past? If so, can these be explained within the assumptions of the model about the nature of competition? In a standard Bertrand differentiated products model significant changes in market share should be driven by changes in relative marginal costs or by shifts in demand curves. The first explanation can and should be checked. The second explanation provides rather more difficulties. Although it also can be checked, if demand curves have shifted significantly in the recent past, it is hard to be confident about our current estimates of where the demand curve is. This is for two reasons. First, it reduces the amount of historic data that we have with which to estimate the position of the current demand curve. Secondly, it raises the question of whether the demand curves could shift significantly again, particularly as a result of a merger. Simulations omit the possibility that products already in the market might be repositioned in the product space in response to a merger, or that the merger may lead to new entry if prices rise. Both of these would shift the demand curves faced by individual firms and so would mean that the post-merger elasticity matrix was different to the pre-merger one. The failure of Bertrand simulation models to take into account product re-positioning often renders this approach inadequate as a reliable predictor of the likely competitive effects of a merger.

If a simulation model is able to explain past facts, this clearly increases one's confidence in the model. For instance, if a model is able to explain past market share shifts, perhaps due to changes in marginal costs (e.g. a process innovation by one firm that reduced its marginal costs relative to its competitors), then that is strong evidence in favour of the model specification and so increases one's confidence in the results of the simulation.

**15–040**   Any model that does not fit the known facts of the industry (whether prepared by external economists or by or on behalf of the regulatory authorities) should be ignored by regulatory authorities and courts. A good example of this happening in the United States is *Concord Boat v Brunswick Corp*.[62] The plaintiff's economist argued that the behaviour of the defendant had had the effect of anti-competitively excluding the plaintiff and of increasing the market share of the defendant. The economist used a model to show this. The Court noted that the plaintiff's economic model implied the defendants would have had a 50 per cent market share in the absence of the challenged conduct. However, the defendant had had a 75 per cent market share even before it started the alleged anti-competitive behaviour. Since the economic model was at odds with known facts about the industry, the court threw out the economic evidence.

## Merger simulations are not the whole story

The standard approach to merger control in Europe is to define the rele-  **15–041** vant market, calculate market shares and then carry out a competitive effects analysis if the post-merger market shares suggest there may be a competition problem with the merger. This assessment of the likely competitive effects of a merger considers the post-merger constraints on the merged entity.[63] The principle areas of focus are usually: market structure, barriers to entry, barriers to expansion, buyer power and the increased scope for coordinated behaviour post-merger.

Merger simulations do not in general take account of these factors. The result is that in the absence of marginal cost efficiencies,[64] they always imply that prices will rise as a result of the merger. This is of course a standard theoretical result which arises in *all* horizontal mergers with differentiated products: if two firms merge in an imperfect competition setting then they will raise prices unless the cross-elasticities between them are zero. Since there has not been an efficiency defence until very recently in Europe it seems unlikely that the Commission has been permitting horizontal mergers on efficiency grounds. It also seems unlikely that they have consistently been allowing mergers that they thought would raise prices. This suggests that the Commission accepts, at least implicitly, that these other factors are important. As such, they need to be taken into account in the merger analysis.

One response to this is to argue that a merger simulation provides an upper bound on the possible post-merger price rise and that having estimated this upper bound, an investigator should then take account of other relevant factors. There is something to be said for this approach. However, this places simulation models alongside the more standard structural approaches; both approaches require a separate analysis of other factors

---

[62]  *Concord Boat v Brunswick Corp* 207 F.3d 1039, 1056 (8th Circuit. 2000).
[63]  See Chapters 7 and 8 for an extensive discussion of these issues.
[64]  See below for a discussion of marginal cost efficiencies in merger simulation models.

that play an important role in determining actual competitive outcomes. Moreover, it should be noted that a simulation based on unilateral effects may not provide an upper bound if the merger moves the market to a coordinated solution. As noted above, research into using simulation models to predict coordinated effects is still at a very early stage.

This discussion hints at another difficulty that arises with regard to the underlying model of the nature of competition. Mergers that raise competition concerns tend to be significant mergers that often represent a step change in the market. It would not be very surprising if mergers of this type often led to changes in the nature of competition post-merger. Note that this is not just to say that the merger may lead the market to become less competitive, although that is clearly one possibility. It is also possible that the merger will increase the intensity of competition post-merger, perhaps because the merger has created a significant sized number two firm with lower barriers to expansion than previously,[65] or because the merged entity has become the largest firm and this spurs the previously largest firm to respond vigorously. This requires some understanding of the strategies of the firms with respect to market share and market leadership. Simulation models typically do not capture this.

### *Retail data for mergers between manufacturers*

**15–042** Simulation models have been used most often in fast moving consumer goods markets as these markets tend to lead to copious amounts of price and quantity data, and hence relatively precise elasticity estimates. The price and quantity data that is available is almost always retail data. However, the merging parties are often manufacturers who sell to retailers. So the price that the merging parties set is the wholesale price to retailers, but the price that we observe is the retail price to consumers. Ignoring this distinction may lead to serious mistakes when carrying out merger analysis.

Retail elasticities and wholesale elasticities usually differ, although obviously the wholesale elasticity is likely to be closely related to the retail elasticity. Specifically, the wholesale elasticity of demand facing the manufacturer will be equal to the elasticity of demand at the retail level multiplied by the elasticity of the retail price with respect to the wholesale price (formally, $\varepsilon_W = \varepsilon_R\, \varepsilon_w^p$). This latter elasticity is the percentage change in the retail price engendered by a one percent change in the wholesale price. If the elasticity of the retail price with respect to the wholesale price is one ($\varepsilon_w^p = 1$), then the retail elasticity and the wholesale elasticity are equal ($\varepsilon_W = \varepsilon_R$). This would be the case, for instance, if retailers set their prices so as to

---

[65] The Commission has traditionally argued that two large firms lead to more competitive outcomes than one large firm and several smaller firms, even though concentration (e.g. HHI) is higher in the former case than the latter.

maintain a constant percentage mark-up over the wholesale price.[66] However, in general, we might expect the elasticity of the retail price with respect to the wholesale price to be less than one, in which case the wholesale elasticity will be less than the retail elasticity. For instance, if retailers seek to maintain a constant absolute margin and if the wholesale price accounts for half of the retail price, then a 1 per cent increase in the wholesale price will equate to a ½ per cent increase in the retail price (i.e. $\varepsilon_w^p = 0.5$) and so the wholesale elasticity will be half the retail elasticity.[67]

In some cases the wholesale elasticity can be larger than the retail elasticity. This would occur when a wholesale price increase led to the product being dropped by retailers. In this case, the wholesale elasticity is very high because sales fall by 100 per cent, regardless of what the retail elasticity is. This scenario is likely to be relevant when shelf-space constraints are binding on retailers and so delisting is credible.[68]

Froeb, Tschantz and Werden (2005) argue that the difficulties presented by the retail/wholesale distinction are more serious than this. They show that a simple model with a monopoly retail sector and Bertrand competition at the upstream level can lead to no pass-through or complete pass-through, depending on the exact form of contracts between manufacturers and the retailer and the exact rules of the game.[69] This means that an investigator needs to focus on the nature of the interaction between the manufacturers and the retailers when the available data is at the retail level.

There is one further difficulty that needs to be considered. Even when **15–043** copious retail data is available, there may still be significant difficulties in estimating elasticities due to "stocking up" effects. A significant amount of the variation in prices in retail scanner data is driven by short-term price promotions.[70] Some of the increase in sales from such price reductions are not genuine increases in demand for the product but rather are driven by consumers buying in advance of their need ("stocking up") at the discounted prices. Estimates of elasticities based on data that contains stocking up effects will tend to over-estimate the true elasticity of demand.[71] We discuss this issue further in Chapter 11.

---

[66] Assuming that one unit of the wholesale product translates into one unit of the retail product and there are no other variable costs of retailing the product.

[67] Stennek and Verboven (2001) survey the literature on pass-through and find that industry-wide cost changes are typically passed through to consumers fully but firm-specific cost changes are not. They cite some evidence that firm-specific pass-through might be as low as 10–20%, although they caution that the extent of pass-through will vary from case to case.

[68] For further discussion of the relationship between wholesale and retail elasticities, see Hosken (2002).

[69] They also note that with long-term contracts between retailers and manufacturers, it is even possible that fixed cost reductions could get passed-through. This is a possibility that merger control on both sides of the Atlantic does not currently allow for.

[70] Hosken and Reiffen (2004) estimate that the figure is between 20% and 50% in the United States.

[71] See, for instance, Hendel and Nevo (2006).

### The importance of non-price competition

**15–044** Merger simulation models focus on price and hence omit non-price competition issues, but are often carried out in branded goods industries where non-price competition issues, such as advertising and promotions, are important. Frequently these mergers involve manufacturers who need to deal with retailers in order to get their product to consumers. Here competition for shelf space is typically important.

The use of a merger simulation model in these types of circumstances is only reasonable if the effect of the loss of price competition between the merging parties outweighs substantially the non-price effects. It may well be that the loss in price competition between the merging parties is the most important effect of the merger, but this is an empirical question that cannot be assumed. As Scheffman argues:

> "Bertrand is a posted price model. ... You post your price. You change it if sales were not consistent with your expectations about demand. There's nothing about trying to get business away from your competitors. There's nothing about positioning your product differently, doing any of the sort of things which real world marketing is all about. I think those things are likely to be very important, but it's the empirical issue. The issue is really, does internalisation of cannibalisation—which is all that drives Bertrand simulation models—dominate all the other stuff which is really very important?"[72]

One non-price effect of a merger is that some products may be repositioned after the merger. For instance, if two products merge that are close substitutes because they are close to each other in product space, then other firms may reposition their products closer to the merging parties' products post-merger if the parties raise their prices. As noted above, a merger simulation model will not account for this possibility.[73]

### Functional form assumptions

**15–045** The results of a merger simulation depend heavily on the various own-price and cross-price elasticities between the products in question. These measure the degree of competitive interaction between products and so

---

[72] "Whither merger simulation" *American Bar Association Section of Antitrust Law "Brown Bag"*, January 29, 2004.

[73] Berry and Waldfogel (2001) highlight a different possibility. They analysed radio station mergers in the United States and concluded that stations that merged that were previously close to each other in product space tended to move apart after the merger. Berry and Waldfogel concluded that the evidence was consistent with the merged entities seeking to pre-empt post-merger entry by filling up the product space. Again, this sort of effect would not be taken into account by a merger simulation. Although note recent work by Gandhi et al (2006) which attempts to address these issues.

measure the loss in competition caused by the merging parties merging (i.e. the cross-elasticities between the products of the merging firms) and the competitive constraint imposed by the other competitors (the cross-elasticities between the products of the non-merging firms and the products of the merging firms). The greater the cross-price elasticities between the merging products, the greater the post-merger price rises, *ceteris paribus*. Equally, the greater the cross-price elasticities between the other competitors and the merging parties, the lower the increases in post-merger prices. It is therefore clear that the elasticity estimates that are used in the simulation are key to determining the results of the simulation.

There are two issues here. First, the accuracy of the elasticity estimates used matters. Secondly, the assumptions made about how these elasticities vary as prices vary matters. Walker (2005) presents evidence that the predicted post-merger price rises can vary substantially depending on the exact elasticity estimates used. He simulates a merger in a four firm oligopoly in which the second and fourth largest firm merge to create the number two player. He then allows the own-price elasticities on the merging firms to vary by 10 per cent and analyses the effect of this on the predicted post-merger outcome. Table 15.5 summarises the results.

**Table 15.5: Effect of small changes in own-price elasticities   15–046 on predicted price rises**

| | Change in elasticity | Percentage change in predicted price rise | | |
|---|---|---|---|---|
| | | Linear | AIDS | Constant elasticity |
| Firm 1 | +10% | −6 | −35 | −31 |
| Firm 2 | +10% | −9 | −24 | −23 |
| Firm 1 | −10% | 13 | 97 | 81 |
| Firm 2 | −10% | 12 | 43 | 43 |

The figures for the linear functional form seem reasonable. To a first approximation, 10 per cent changes in the relevant own price elasticity lead to changes in the predicted price change of about 10 per cent. This is not so with the AIDS specification, where the change in the predicted price change range from −35 per cent to 97 per cent. The equivalent range for the constant elasticity specification is −31 per cent to 81 per cent.[74]

It is worth putting the 10 per cent figure into context. We are usually reasonably confident that the true value of an estimated parameter is within plus or minus two standard errors of the central estimate. If a 10 per cent change in the elasticity estimate is within two standard errors, then the t-

---

[74] Walker (2005) also looks at the effect of changes in the estimated cross-price elasticities and finds similar, although smaller, effects on the post-merger equilibrium.

statistic for the parameter must be at least 20. That is a much higher level of certainty than we generally see for elasticity estimates, so the ± 10 per cent range for the own-price elasticities is a very restricted range. This means that we would usually assume that the potential range of the elasticity estimate is more than ± 10 per cent, in which case the range of the possible post-merger price rises will be even larger than suggested above.

The second issue is the extent to which post-merger predictions vary depending on the functional form chosen for the demand curve. Crooke (1999) looked at the effect on the results of a merger simulation of different assumptions about how elasticities vary as prices rise. They looked at four alternative functional forms (log-linear, linear, logit and AIDS) within a non-cooperative Bertrand model using a setting of two firms merging in an industry with between four and eight firms. They found that average post-merger price rises for the merging parties were more than three times larger for a log-linear specification than for a linear specification, with AIDS giving average price increases double the linear specification and logit giving average price increases of 50 per cent higher than linear. The hierarchy of these results is unsurprising. The log-linear specification implies that elasticities do not change as prices rise, whereas the other three specifications all have the own-price elasticities of the products rising as prices rise. The own-price elasticity rises fastest for the linear specification and so this implies the smallest post-merger price rise. This is shown in Table 15.6, which is adapted from Crooke (1999). Suppose that the competitive equilibrium (with price equal to marginal cost) in a market is a price of 4, output of 10 and industry elasticity of −2. Table 15.6 shows the monopoly price in this market, and associated industry elasticity, under the four alternative demand curves. It is clear that the less the industry elasticity rises as prices rise, the higher the monopoly price.

**15–047** **Table 15.6**

|  | Monopoly price | Elasticity at monopoly price |
|---|---|---|
| **CES** | 8.0 | −2.0 |
| **AIDS** | 6.4 | −2.7 |
| **Logit** | 5.3 | −4.1 |
| **Linear** | 5.0 | −5.0 |

The question that naturally arises is how should an investigator respond to this issue. There seem to us to be at least three responses.

First, ask what functional form has been used in a merger simulation. If the answer is that a linear demand curve has been used, then you know that the predicted post-merger equilibrium is at the lower end of what would be predicted using alternative demand curves. Equally, if the answer is that the demand curve is a constant elasticity demand curve, then this suggests that the prediction is at the top end of the possible range for a non-cooperative equilibrium.

Secondly, require that the simulation is carried out using a range of elasticity estimates and functional forms. There may be times when the model predicts such small price rises (or even negative ones) that there is no concern under any functional form and plausible set of elasticities. Equally there may be times when it predicts large price rises under any functional form and plausible set of elasticities, and then it might be argued that the model shows that the merger is a problem even under the assumptions most favourable to the merging parties.

Thirdly, focus on what marginal cost efficiencies would be necessary for the model to predict zero price rises. The advantage of this is that if prices are unchanged, then so are elasticities, so the exact shape of the demand curve is not relevant. We discuss this issue in more detail below.

## Simulations and cost efficiencies

An important potential advantage of merger simulations is that it is rela- **15–048** tively easy to take account of the effect of claimed post-merger marginal cost efficiencies on post-merger prices. If marginal cost reductions mean that prices post-merger will actually be lower than pre-merger, then the Commission will allow the merger even if it appears to lead to a significant reduction in competition between firms.[75]

There are two main approaches to accounting for marginal cost efficiencies in a merger simulation. The most obvious one is just to factor the reduction in marginal costs post-merger into the simulation. This then provides an estimate of post-merger price changes taking into account the efficiencies. If the efficiencies are large enough, the result may be that prices fall as a result of the merger. This approach suffers from the same problems outlined above with regard to the elasticity estimates and functional form assumptions. If these are wrong, then the computed post-merger price changes will also be wrong, although the sign of the price change will be correct (i.e. if prices fall under one functional form, then they fall under all the potential functional forms). However, it should be noted that the closer to zero the final results are, the less errors in the functional form will matter as the less price rises, the less the various elasticity estimates based on different functional forms diverge.

The other approach is due to Werden (1996). He suggests calculating the marginal cost efficiencies that would be needed to restore the market to

---

[75] This is not what the economic literature usually refers to as an "efficiency defence", since it focuses only on consumer welfare and not on total welfare. Traditionally, the efficiency defence referred to the argument that a merger would lead to increases in producer surplus that outweighed losses in consumer surplus, thus leading to an increase in total social welfare as a result of the merger. See, inter alia, Bork (1995) for a defence of the social welfare criterion in competition policy.

the same equilibrium post-merger as pre-merger. He refers to these as compensating marginal cost reductions or CMCRs. These can then be compared to the cost efficiency claims being made by the parties. The great advantage of this is that since the market is in the same place post-merger as pre-merger, the various elasticities should be the same post-merger as pre-merger, which avoids the need to make assumptions about the functional form of the demand curves. This approach still requires that the estimates of current elasticities are correct. Whilst this is a lesser requirement than that the functional forms are correct as well, it is still a significant requirement. Walker (2005) investigates the effect of inaccuracies in the elasticity estimates on the marginal cost required to ensure zero price rise. He shows that even small inaccuracies in the estimated elasticities of 10 per cent can have significant effects on the estimated critical marginal cost. For instance, he finds that an over-estimate of the own price elasticities of the merging firms of 10 per cent can lower the critical marginal cost estimates by up to 35 per cent. This highlights the need to calculate the critical marginal cost reductions using a range of plausible elasticity estimates.

Werden (1998) provides a formula for calculating the CMCR in the case of symmetric firms. The formula is:

$$(16) \quad CMCR = \frac{md}{(1-m)(1-d)}$$

where   m is the price-marginal cost margin; and
        d is the diversion ratio.

Whilst we do not think that formulae such as this are of practical use since mergers rarely involve symmetric firms and the formula for non-symmetric firms is significantly different,[76] it does serve to highlight that the higher the diversion ratio, or the higher the post-merger price cost margin, the higher the CMCR.

Hausman et al provides an example of the effect of marginal cost efficiencies on post-merger prices.[77] In this paper the authors estimate the own-price and cross-price elasticities of 15 beers in the United States. A selection of their own-price elasticity results are given in Table 15.7.

---

[76] For further discussion of this, see Chapter 11.
[77] Hausman, Leonard and Zona (1994).

## Table 15.7: US beer price elasticities                              15–049

|            | Elasticity | Standard Error |
|------------|------------|----------------|
| **Budweiser**   | −4.2 | 0.13 |
| **Molson**      | −5.4 | 0.15 |
| **Labatts**     | −4.6 | 0.25 |
| **Miller**      | −4.4 | 0.15 |
| **Coors**       | −4.9 | 0.21 |
| **Molson Light** | −5.8 | 0.15 |

*Source*: Hausman, Leonard and Zona (1994).

The authors then consider the predicted effect of a hypothetical merger
between Coors and Labatts. Their simulation is based on Bertrand competition with the assumption that there will be no entry or product repositioning in response to any price rise. The cross-elasticity results (not
reported here) indicate that the price of Coors is constrained more by
Budweiser and Miller than by Labatts, whilst the price of Labatts is constrained more by Molson than by Coors. This implies that one should not
expect to see prices rise much after the hypothetical merger. The authors
also investigate the effect of marginal cost synergies on prices after the
merger. Table 15.8 shows the results of their simulation.

## Table 15.8: Estimated price increases from a hypothetical   15–050
merger

|            | Marginal cost reductions | | |
|------------|------|-------|-------|
|            | 0%   | 5%    | 10%   |
| **Coors**   | 4.4% | −0.8% | −6.1% |
| **Labatts** | 3.3% | −1.9% | −7.0% |

*Source*: Hausman, Leonard and Zona (1994).

Table 15.8 shows that for even quite modest marginal cost reductions
(i.e. 5 per cent) prices after the hypothetical merger would fall.

### *A merger simulation can provide a rough first cut of the likely post-merger price rise*

It is sometimes said that simulation models can provide a useful first cut at  **15–051**
the appraisal of a potential merger. The idea is that by using a merger
simulation you can get a "quick and dirty" estimate of the likely effect of a
merger. That estimate, it is argued, can be useful at the planning stage of a
merger to give the parties an indication as to whether a potential merger
will run into competition policy concerns. We believe that this is not right.

The discussion above has illustrated that the results of merger simulation models should not be trusted except under stringent conditions, such as that the investigator has good evidence on the actual values of the necessary inputs (elasticities, marginal costs and so on), has good evidence on the actual form of competition in the market and can show that the model is able to explain recent past data as well as current data. Ensuring that these stringent conditions are met is not consistent, in our view, with a "quick and dirty" approach. For instance, estimating good elasticity estimates is usually a long and painstaking process.

The argument is sometimes buttressed with the further argument that a merger simulation model based on a log-linear specification (i.e. constant elasticities) provides an upper bound to the possible post-merger price rise, and this can be useful. In particular, if this upper bound is low, then no further investigation is needed, whilst if it is high the investigator can then undertake the competitive effects analysis. This is not an entirely unreasonable approach, but it is important to remember that this upper bound is only an upper bound on the assumption that the post-merger equilibrium is a Nash equilibrium and the estimated elasticities are correct. If the post-merger equilibrium involves an increase in co-operative behaviour, then the upper bound estimate is not a true upper bound.

### Simulations and divestment analysis

**15–052** Merger simulations can be useful in the area of divestment analysis. Suppose that we are able to put together a simulation model that is a good description of the competitive reality of the relevant market and that this model predicts that a two firm multi-product merger will lead to significant price rises even allowing for expected marginal cost efficiencies. The regulatory authorities will likely require the parties to offer remedies. By altering the post-merger ownership assumptions in the merger simulation one can see what effect the divestment of different brands might have on post-merger prices. This can be a useful way of identifying those divestments that solve the competitive problems and those divestments that do not. For instance, this was the main use that the NMa put the simulation models to in the Nuon/Reliant and Nuon/Essent merger analyses. The study carried out for the NMa in the Nuon/Essent merger used a merger simulation to estimate that up to 4,000MW of generating capacity would need to be divested post-merger to avoid prices rising significantly.[78]

---

[78] "Factors affecting geographic market definition and merger control for the Dutch electricity sector" The Brattle Group, June 2006, Final report (non-confidential version) for the NMa.

# SUMMARY

In this chapter we have outlined the underlying economics of merger **15–053**
simulation models and discussed how this changes depending on the
nature of competition in the market. This has allowed us to highlight the
various assumptions that underlie the different models. It is important that
in any merger simulation these assumptions are justified and it is shown
what effect a change in the assumption would have on the results.

There are a number of criteria that a merger simulation model must
satisfy before it can be considered useful. These include that it is consistent
with the current facts of the market, that it is consistent with the past facts
of the industry, that the authors have carried out a sensitivity analysis,
particularly relating to elasticity estimates, and that, where relevant,
wholesale/retail distinctions have been taken seriously.

Even the best merger simulation is not a basis for making a merger
control decision on its own. They omit important parts of the competitive
effects analysis, such as entry, buyer power, product repositioning and
changes in the mode of competition post-merger. This is not to say that
merger simulations are therefore not useful, but only to highlight that their
correct role is rather more limited than is often claimed. One important
role that they can play is in the assessment of the effect of post-merger
marginal cost reductions on prices.

Perhaps the most important lesson to take away from this chapter is that
a good merger simulation must be based on a good understanding of the
particular market in question. Generic simulations based on assumptions
that are not related to the facts of the market are not useful. Whilst this
might have been disputed a few years ago, we believe that this is now
uncontroversial. In this regard, we note with approval that whilst three
years ago there were numerous web-based merger simulation packages
available that required only the input of minimal data (e.g. market shares
and one elasticity), these have now virtually all disappeared.

# 16. Shipment and Transport Cost Tests

## INTRODUCTION

**16–001** In many competition investigations, a critical issue is the significance of the competitive constraint posed by firms situated in other geographic regions. This is particularly the case where a firm has a high market share in a given Member State but might be subject to competitive constraints not only from other firms located in that Member State but also from firms located in other Member States.

In principle, econometric analysis and price correlation analysis can be used to address geographic market issues.[1] In many instances, either the lack of adequate data or time implies that such tests cannot be successfully implemented. However, there are other tests available which can be used to assess the strength of competitive constraints between regions. This chapter focuses on shipment and transport cost tests. Chapter 14 assesses the information which can be deduced from the relationship between price and market structure across a number of regions (i.e. price-concentration studies).

Shipment and import penetration tests provide an intuitive test for assessing the strength of competition across regions. As such, they can provide a useful aid in helping to delineate the relevant geographic market and, in particular, in deciding whether domestic firms face significant competition from foreign suppliers. Such tests consider the extent to which sales within a given region originate from outside that region or the extent to which production in a region is exported. Shipment tests only require quantity data. They are sometimes the only type of empirical analysis which can be usefully carried out in situations where either the only data available is quantity data or the quality of other data is problematic.[2]

---

[1] But note the problems discussed in Chapter 10 associated with variable exchange rates.

[2] e.g. in some cases only data for list prices may be available. If actual transaction prices are discounted from list prices in a non-systematic fashion, then analysis using list price data will produce flawed results. In many markets list prices bear little or no resemblance to the prices at which transactions actually take place. In such circumstances, these difficulties can be avoided by recourse to shipment tests which require data only on quantities.

Transport cost tests focus on estimating from how far it is feasible to supply into a market from outside that market. This is relevant to understanding the competitive constraints faced by suppliers in a particular region. These tests can be used to show which suppliers that do not currently ship into an area could do so, either at current prices or if prices were to rise after a merger. Isochrone analysis is a similar form of analysis, but it focuses on the demand-side rather than the supply-side. Isochrone analysis seeks to define markets based on how far customers are willing to travel to a supplier, rather than on how far suppliers are able to ship product.

## SHIPMENT DATA TESTS

Shipment tests can be used to assess the extent to which firms in one region **16–002** exert a competitive constraint on firms in another region based on the notion that product flows between regions indicate the existence of a competitive constraint between the regions. The existence of substantial trade flows is often taken as providing a guide to the ease with which consumers can switch from "local" suppliers to "non-local" suppliers. Tests based on trade flows have been proposed by Elzinga and Hogarty[3] and Shrieves.[4] Both tests specify two criteria against which observed trade flows between regions are assessed.

### Elzinga-Hogarty test

The Elzinga-Hogarty test is based on the "LIFO" and "LOFI" thresholds. **16–003** LIFO stands for "little in from outside". This criterion asks whether imports into the region are small relative to total sales in that region. If imports are large relative to total sales, then the LIFO threshold will not hold and this will provide some indication that the particular region under consideration is subject to competitive constraints from outside the region. LOFI stands for "little out from inside". This asks whether exports from the region are small relative to total production in that region. If exports are large relative to the total level of production, this provides some indication that it is possible for firms to compete effectively in regions outside that in which production takes place.

In general, if observed patterns of trade fail either of these tests, this implies that the region is subject to external competitive constraints. If observed trade flows indicate that imports of a product represent a relatively large percentage of domestic consumption, this implies that outside firms are able to export to the region and so one would expect them to impose a competitive constraint on pricing in that region. If imports are a

---

[3]   Elzinga and Hogarty (1973 and 1978).
[4]   Shrieves (1978).

relatively low proportion of domestic consumption, but exports out of the region are high, this may also suggest that the relevant market is wider than just the region. The argument in this case is not so clear cut, but if exports are relatively high this implies that transport costs are not insuperable and that trade is possible. Such evidence might be expected to imply that "outside" regions impose a competitive constraint on the "inside" region, unless there are asymmetries between the two regions (such as tariff barriers to one region but not the other).[5]

## *Form of test*

**16–004**   The LIFO component of the Elzinga-Hogarty test reflects conditions on the buyers' side of the market and can be expressed as follows:

(1)   $LIFO = \dfrac{Production\ minus\ exports}{Consumption}$

where consumption is equal to production minus exports plus imports minus the change in inventory stocks. A high LIFO indicates that demand in a given region is primarily served by local production. This is consistent with the proposition that the region is a separate geographic market. If the level of inventories is assumed to be constant over time, the LIFO condition can be expressed in an alternative way. Where inventories are constant, consumption equals production minus exports plus imports. This implies that LIFO can be rewritten in the following way:

(2)   $LIFO = 1 - \dfrac{Imports}{Consumption}$

This is the more common form of the LIFO condition.

The LOFI component of the test reflects conditions on the sellers' side of the market, and can be expressed as follows.

(3)   $LOFI = \dfrac{Production\ minus\ exports}{Production}$

A high LOFI indicates that there are few exports and so the majority of local production is used to serve the local market. This is consistent with the proposition that the region is a separate relevant market. LOFI can be re-written in the following way:

(4)   $LOFI = 1 - \dfrac{Exports}{Production}$

This is the more common form of the LOFI condition.

Either condition is said to be failed if the ratio is below some threshold, usually taken to be 0.9 (or, expressed as a percentage, 90 per cent). In this case, suppliers in the region under consideration are held to be subject to

---

[5]   The extent of exports out of country also indicates the level of extra domestic output that could be put on the domestic market to defeat a domestic price rise. This is not a market definition issue, but an issue of the extent of competition within a market.

effective competitive constraints from suppliers located outside that region.[6] To identify the source of this competitive constraint, the "candidate" region should be expanded. In most cases this is done by expanding the market in a contiguous fashion.[7] The LIFO and LOFI tests are then recalculated and the process repeated until both are satisfied.

The choice of the threshold of 0.9 is somewhat arbitrary. Elzinga and Hogarty suggested either 0.9 or 0.75 as thresholds, although the 0.9 threshold is much more commonly used. However, it is true that since there is no one "correct" threshold, the level chosen will depend on a degree of judgment.

## *An example*

We provide an example below of the use of the Elzinga-Hogarty test in **16–005** assessing regional competition. It is assumed that the competitive issue of concern is the degree to which manufacturers with operations in Italy face effective competitive constraints from suppliers located in other Member States. Table 16.1 shows the level of consumption, production, exports into, imports out of and the change in inventory stocks for Italy.

## Table 16.1: Elzinga-Hogarty test data for Italy                    **16–006**

| Consumption (C) | 5,125 |
|---|---|
| Imports (M) | 735 |
| Exports (E) | 405 |
| Increase in inventories (I) | −35 |
| Production (P = C − M + E + I) | 4,760 |
| **LIFO ((P–E)/C)** | **0.85** |
| **LOFI ((P–E)/P)** | **0.91** |

These figures indicate that the LIFO criterion is not met. Imports into Italy are a significant proportion of consumption (15 per cent). This suggests that suppliers located in Italy face effective competitive constraints from suppliers located outside Italy.

To investigate the possible source of this competitive constraint, the next step is to widen the extent of the market. Suppose that France is the most likely country to impose a competitive constraint on Italy as France exports more of the product to Italy than does any other country. To examine whether France is in the same relevant market as Italy an Elzinga-Hogarty test is carried out on the combination of Italy plus France. Table 16.2 shows the relevant data for France and Italy together.

---

[6]   See paras 16–023—16–027 below for a discussion on the interpretation of the results of the Elzinga-Hogarty test.
[7]   However, as explained in below, this need not always be the case.

**16–007**  **Table 16.2: Elzinga-Hogarty test data for Italy and France**

| Consumption: | Italy | | 5,125 |
|---|---|---|---|
| | France | | 2,743 |
| | Total (C) | | 7,868 |
| **Imports:** | Italy | Total | 735 |
| | | From France | 397 |
| | France | Total | 603 |
| | | From Italy | 282 |
| | Italy plus France | | 659 |
| **Exports:** | Italy | Total | 405 |
| | | To France | 282 |
| | France | Total | 413 |
| | | To Italy | 397 |
| | Italy plus France (E) | | 139 |
| **Increases in inventories** | Italy | | −35 |
| | France | | 21 |
| | Total | | −14 |
| **Production:** | Italy | | 4,760 |
| | France | | 2,574 |
| | Total (P) | | 7,334 |
| **LIFO (P–E/C)** | | | **0.91** |
| **LOFI (P–E/P)** | | | **0.98** |

What matters now are imports into and exports out of the combination of France and Italy. Trade flows between France and Italy are no longer relevant. So the export figures are adjusted to give the total combined exports of France and Italy excluding those exports from France to Italy and those exports from Italy to France. Imports are adjusted in a similar way. Table 16.2 shows that the level of trade flows into and out of the combined region were low relative to total "local" production and consumption, implying that both LIFO and LOFI conditions are met. This suggests that the primary source of competitive constraint on suppliers in Italy is provided by suppliers located in France. On the basis of the Elzinga-Hogarty test, it can be concluded that Italy and France combined are a relevant geographic market.

### Shrieves test

**16–008**  The two criteria used in the Shrieves test are the Similarity Measure and the Significance Measure. The Similarity Measure considers whether the patterns of shipments into the two areas under consideration are similar, while the second criteria, the Significance Measure, measures the significance of the two areas for total consumption of the product concerned. As Werden notes, the test is hard to describe verbally, but it involves the degree of similarity of patterns of shipments into the two regions and the significance of the regions in terms of consumption.[8] This difficulty in verbally describing the test indicates that the Shrieves test is in some sense less intuitive than the Elzinga-Hogarty test. Partly for this reason, the Shrieves test is not widely used.[9] The remainder of this chapter focuses on the Elzinga-Hogarty test. However, for the sake of completeness we describe the Shrieves test below.

---

**BOX 16.1: SHRIEVES TEST STATISTICS**  16–009

The information required to carry out the Shrieves test is provided below.

Suppose the issue is whether Area 1 and Area 2 form part of the same geographic market. These two areas are supplied by a number of regions (including from themselves). The Similarity Measure is defined as:

$$(5) \quad \textit{Similarity measure} = \sum_{j=1}^{J} \min\left[\frac{q_{1j}}{q_1}, \frac{q_{2j}}{q_2}\right] > 0.5$$

where   $q_{ij}$ is the amount of the relevant product consumed in area i that was produced in region j;

$q_i$ is consumption in area i; and

there are J regions of production.

For each region of production, the proportion of consumption in each area of consumption that comes from that region is calculated. The lowest of these two proportions is taken. Thus if 10 per cent of consumption in Area 1 came from region j, and 7 per cent of consumption in Area 2 came from region j, then the lower number of 7 per cent (or 0.07 in proportion terms) would be used. This exercise is repeated for all regions of production and then the relevant numbers for each region (i.e. 0.07 for region j) are added together. If this summation is more than 0.5, then the Similarity Measure test is passed.

It is difficult to give a simple intuition for this measure. However, suppose that the two areas under consideration received their product from entirely separate regions. Then the minimum proportion for each region would be zero, the total summation would be zero and the test would be failed (i.e. the two areas would be presumed to lie in different geographic markets). On the other hand, suppose that the two areas under consideration received their product from the same regions in the same proportions. Then the test statistic would be 1 and the test would be passed (i.e. the two areas would potentially be in the same geographic market, depending on the result of the Significance Test). The threshold of 0.5 is rather high. Suppose that both areas

---

[8]   Werden (1981).
[9]   The authors have never seen it used in European antitrust.

consumed 80 per cent of their own production and exported the other 20 per cent to the other region. On the basis of the Elzinga-Hogarty test, and intuition, these areas are in the same market. However, the Similarity Measure would be 0.4 and so the test would suggest the two areas were in separate geographic markets.

The Significance Measure is defined as:

$$(6) \quad Significance\ measure = \sqrt{\frac{1}{N}\sum_{j=1}^{J}\frac{q_{1j}\,q_{2j}}{q_1\,q_2}} > 0.05$$

where N is the number of regions that ship product to both areas; and

$q_j$ is production in region j.

For each region of production, the proportions of production consumed in Areas 1 and 2 are calculated and these proportions are multiplied together. This is done for all regions of production. The results are then added together and divided by the number of regions that supply both areas. If the square root of this summation is greater than 0.05, then the two areas pass the Significance Measure. This test provides a measure of how important the two areas are to those regions that supply both areas. The larger the proportion of output from these regions that goes to these two areas, the more likely it is that the Significance Measure test is passed and that the two areas are considered to be in the same geographic market, subject to the results of the Similarity Measure Test.

The economic logic underlying the Shrieves test is reasonably clear. If two areas have similar patterns of trade, this implies that there are producers who could divert flows if relative prices changed between the two areas. If the two areas represent a relatively large proportion of the output of producers, then the producers are more likely to respond to a relative price change by diverting trade flows. Note, however, that failing the Shrieves test does not necessarily imply separate relevant markets. As we discuss below, an absence of trade between two regions does not necessarily imply that they are separate markets, although the presence of significant trade does imply that they are part of the same market.

## Estimating the relationship between domestic prices and imports

**16–010** Another approach to using import data is to look at the relationship between domestic prices and imports. This involves estimating the effect of changes in the domestic price on the level of imports. This is directly relevant to the question that we are interested in from a market definition perspective: would a 5–10 per cent price rise imposed by a hypothetical monopolist be defeated by an increase in imports? It is also directly relevant to the question of interest in a merger: would a post-merger price rise be defeated by imports.

The standard approach to this issue is to estimate a regression equation of the form[10]:

(7)    $M_t = \alpha + \beta \, P_t + \gamma \, GDP_t + \eta_t$

where    $M_t$ are imports at time t;

$P_t$ are prices in the importing country relative to those in the exporting country at time t;

$GDP_t$ is a measure of domestic GDP at time t;

$\alpha$, $\beta$ and $\gamma$ are regression coefficients; and

$\eta_t$ is an error term.

The price term in Equation (7) is a relative price term. This is important since what matters for a firm located in the exporting country is not just absolute prices in the importing country, but how those prices relate to domestic prices in the exporting country. The higher are prices in the importing country relative to those in the exporting country, the greater the incentive to export. If the two countries have different exchange rates, then relative prices can vary even without the domestic prices changing in either country. If the exchange rate in the importing country appreciates, for instance, then its relative price will fall and the exporting firm has less incentive to export to the importing country (although demand for imports may rise. See below for further discussion of this). In fact, even this is a simplification, since firms always look to sell in the market that will yield the highest return. Thus even if relative price rose in the importing country, if relative prices rose more in another country, then we might not see an increase in imports. Indeed, we might see a decline as product is diverted to the higher priced country.[11]

Equation (7) is based on the assumption that imports at time t respond to prices and domestic GDP at time t. This may well not be correct. First, we might expect there to be a lag between the firm seeing the price signal and being able to change the amount of product it sends to the importing country. This implies that the price variable should be lagged by a length of time that reflects how long it takes the exporting firm to respond to the price signal. Secondly, the relationship between GDP and imports might well be lagged. If increases in GDP lead to an increase in demand for the imported product, then this effect will not be reflected in imports immediately as there will be a lag whilst the exporting firm responds to the increased demand with increased exports.

---

[10]    It might also make sense to add a time trend if there is a consistent trend in imports over time that appears unrelated to prices.

[11]    This discussion is predicated on the assumption that the exporting firm has some capacity constraints which mean that it cannot supply all markets where prices are above its costs. If it does not face capacity constraints, then the firm will supply into all areas where its marginal revenue is above its marginal cost.

**16–011**   The coefficient of interest in Equation (7) is the coefficient on the price term. If the variables are in logs, then this coefficient is the elasticity of imports with respect to relative prices. This tells us how much we should expect imports to increase in response to an increase in domestic prices. If we have an estimate of the domestic demand curve, this allows us to estimate how much of any attempted price rise would be defeated by imports. Suppose that after a merger the merged entity could raise prices by 5 per cent by restricting output by, say, 1,000 units. If estimation of Equation (7) implies that this would lead to an increase in imports of only 50 units, then this implies that imports would have relatively little constraining effect. But if imports were to rise by 1,000, then they would defeat the price rise.

As it stands there is a significant technical weakness with this form of analysis. It is not clear whether Equation (7) is a demand equation or a supply equation. So far in this discussion we have been assuming that it is a supply equation, linking the incentive for a firm to export to a country to relative prices. However, it might also be thought of as a demand equation, linking the incentive for domestic consumers to buy imports as the relative price of imports changes. The result is that we would expect there to be an element of simultaneity in the determination of the level of imports and prices with prices affecting the level of imports but imports also affecting the level of prices. One possible solution to this simultaneity would be to use lagged prices, as suggested above, as we would expect lagged prices to be set independently of current imports. The other solution would be to estimate both a demand and a supply equation simultaneously and this would be the ideal approach to take. However, it is rarely possible to carry out, so in reality the lagged price approach is the most likely to be practicable.

## THE USE OF SHIPMENT TESTS IN COMPETITION POLICY DECISIONS

**16–012**   The Commission has frequently used measures of imports and exports as an aid to defining the relevant geographic market, although it has only rarely referred explicitly to the Elzinga-Hogarty test.

### Saint-Gobain/Wacker-Chemie/NOM[12]

**16–013**   In *Saint-Gobain/Wacker-Chemie/NOM*, the Commission appears to have relied heavily on shipment tests to define the relevant geographic market.[13] The Commission identified five separate product markets: silicon carbide

---

[12]   IV/M774 *Saint-Gobain/Wacker-Chemie/NOM* [1997] OJ L247/1.
[13]   op. cit. paras 99 et seq.

(SiC) for metallurgical purposes; crude crystallised SiC; processed SiC for abrasive applications; processed SiC for refractory applications; and processed SiC for other industrial applications.[14] The Commission concluded that the relevant geographic market for SiC for metallurgical purposes was a world market because imports accounted for more than 50 per cent of EEA consumption in 1995.[15] The Commission found that imports accounted for 85 per cent of crude crystallised SiC in the EEA in 1995.[16] This gave a "strong indication that the geographical scope of the relevant product market for crude crystallized SiC is wider than the EEA",[17] but the Commission left the question open because no competition concern rested on it. Imports into the EEA of processed SiC for refractory applications accounted for less than 7 per cent of consumption and accordingly the Commission concluded that the geographic market was no wider than the EEA. No competition concerns arose in the market for processed SiC for other industrial applications and so the definition of the geographic market was left open.[18]

The geographic market definition for SiC for abrasive applications was more interesting. The Commission found that imports into the EEA represented about 15 per cent of consumption (i.e. the LIFO statistic was 85 per cent).[19] However, the Commission concluded that the relevant geographic market was the EEA.[20] This conclusion is contrary to the conclusion that would be drawn on the basis of the Elzinga-Hogarty test described above. Two points arise. The first is that the Commission chose to use a different threshold to the 90 per cent threshold suggested above. As noted above, the precise threshold is somewhat arbitrary. It appears that the 80–90 per cent region may be a grey area in which the Commission may still find separate markets. The second point is that the Commission did not base its geographic market definition solely on a shipment test.[21] It looked at a range of other factors such as relative price data, comparative price evolution, customer/supplier relationships and so on. In general, a single empirical test is unlikely to be dispositive in a particular case and the piecing together of different sources of evidence is a sign of good practice.

## Mannesmann/Vallourec/Ilva[22]

In *Mannesmann/Vallourec/Ilva*, the parties used an Elzinga-Hogarty test to **16–014** define the relevant geographic market for seamless stainless steel tubes.

---

[14] op. cit. para.39.
[15] op. cit. paras 108–109.
[16] op. cit. para.110.
[17] op. cit. paras 132–135.
[18] op. cit. para.136.
[19] op. cit. para.128.
[20] op. cit. para.131.
[21] op. cit. para.130.
[22] IV/M315 *Mannesmann/Vallourec/Ilva* [1994] OJ L102/15.

The parties argued that the market was wider than Western Europe because, even though the LIFO test for imports was passed (i.e. production minus exports was more than 90 per cent of consumption) the LOFI test was failed (i.e. production minus exports was less than 90 per cent of production). The Commission rejected this argument.[23] They argued that because there were relatively few imports into Western Europe, Western Europe should be considered a separate relevant market. This is contrary to the standard Elzinga-Hogarty test as this only requires that either the LIFO or LOFI test are failed before the market should be widened.

However, it is not obvious that the Commission's view is wrong. A price rise in Western Europe will only be defeated if it is possible to import into Western Europe. While the fact that it is possible to export out of Western Europe is relevant to this question (e.g. it tells us that transport costs are not prohibitively high), it does not prove that imports provide a significant enough competitive constraint to deter price increases in the area under consideration. For instance, if there was a tariff barrier, then it might be possible to export out of an area to a non-tariff area, but not possible to import into the area due to the tariff.[24] When the LOFI test is failed but the LIFO test is passed, the correct response is to analyse why the LIFO test is passed. It may be that there is a wide market (as evidenced by exports), but there are few imports because of the prevailing price levels in the two areas (i.e. low prices in the country that has few imports). But equally it may be that there is a narrow market despite the existence of exports.

### Nestlé/Perrier[25]

**16–015**   In *Nestlé/Perrier*, the Commission "concluded that the relevant geographic market within which the power of the new entity has to be assessed is France".[26] The Commission found that "Trade flows in the Community are of minor significance".[27] Although the Commission did not formally carry out an Elzinga-Hogarty test, paras 25–27 of the decision provide the following statistics.

---

[23] op. cit. para.33.
[24] This highlights the fact that geographic market definitions may not be symmetric. Suppose that Country A is protected by a tariff, but Country B is not. If the competition concern is in Country A, the geographic market may be just Country A since imports from Country B may not be possible due to the tariff barrier. If the competition concern is in Country B, the geographic market may be both countries as exports from Country A to Country B may be possible.
[25] IV/M190 *Nestlé/Perrier* [1992] OJ L356/1.
[26] op. cit. para.21.
[27] op. cit. para.25.

## Table 16.3: Shipment statistics from the *Nestlé/Perrier* decision

| | Imports as percentage of consumption* | Exports as percentage of production |
|---|---|---|
| France | 1–2% | >10%[28] |
| Italy | < 1% | <1% |
| Spain | < 1% | <1% |
| Germany | 5% | <1% |

* 1990 figures

The imports figures imply that the LIFO test is passed for France. However, the export figure implies that the LOFI test is failed. However, as in *Mannesmann/Vallourec/Ilva* above, the Commission did not take this to mean that the market should be widened. Doubtless the lack of exports from the major contiguous countries to France played an important role in this decision.

### Ineos/Kerling[29]

The competitive concerns in this case related mainly to the production of **16–017** suspension PVC (or S PVC), which made up about 90 per cent of total EEA PVC production. Geographic market definition was a key element of the case. The Commission stated that "The issue of geographic market definition is crucial for the assessment of the case".[30] If the relevant geographic markets were national, then the parties would have had a post-merger market share of more than 60 per cent in the United Kingdom and more than 90 per cent in each of Norway and Sweden.

Kerling was the only domestic manufacturer of S PVC in Norway and Sweden and had a market share of more than 90 per cent (para.67). This indicates that the LIFO condition of the Elzinga-Hogarty test was met as it implies that imports accounted for less than 10 per cent of domestic sales. However, the Commission noted that more than 50 per cent of Kerling's production in Norway and Sweden was exported, indicating that the LOFI condition was failed. Allied to evidence that customers in Norway and Sweden consider suppliers up to 1000–1500km away as viable suppliers, this led the Commission to conclude that the geographic market was wider than just the Nordic region.

Import levels were also an important part of the analysis of the relevant geographic market for the United Kingdom. The Commission noted that

---

[28]   This figure is derived from the fact that exports to Belgium make up about 10% of French production (para.25).
[29]   COMP/M. 4734 *Ineos/Kerling* (January 30, 2008).
[30]   op. cit. para.45.

imports into the United Kingdom in 2006 accounted for between 30 per cent and 40 per cent of local consumption, in addition to some imports from the parties themselves (para.107). Table 16.4 reproduces the figures included in the decision.

**16–018** **Table 16.4 Imports into the UK in *Ineos/Kerling***

| | 2002 | 2003 | 2004 | 2005 | 2006 |
|---|---|---|---|---|---|
| **Market size (kt)** | 500–550 | 550–600 | 550–600 | 500–550 | 500–550 |
| **Competitors' imports** | 200–250 | 200–250 | 200–250 | 150–200 | 150–200 |
| **Imports (%)** | 30–40 | 30–40 | 30–40 | 30–40 | 30–40 |

The Commission concluded that imports of S PVC had been consistently high in to the United Kingdom and that this indicated that customers did consider imports as a viable alternative to domestic production. It also noted that since many customers already relied at least partly on imports, they could easily switch the rest of their demand to imports if the parties raised their prices after the merger.

## Other decisions

**16–019** In *Orkla/Volvo*,[31] the Commission found that the relevant market was beer in Norway. The Commission found there were "negligible trade flows between Norway and other countries". Imports represented only 2.6 per cent of consumption in 1994 whilst exports represented less than 1 per cent of production.

In *Shell Chemie/Elf Atochem*,[32] the Commission decided that the geographic market was EU-wide because "the intra-European exchange flows are significant and divided over the entire area".[33] The Commission concluded this despite noting that in some countries, such as France, Italy and Spain, most consumption was supplied from within the relevant country and that transport costs were "considerable".

In *DuPont/ICI*,[34] the Commission concluded that the geographic market was the Community. This conclusion appears to have been reached on the basis of an Elzinga-Hogarty test. The Commission stated that:

> "the evidence shows that the market is not wider than the Community. There are relatively low imports (less than 10 per cent), negligible

[31] IV/M582 *Orkla/Volvo* [1995] OJ L66/17.
[32] IV/M475 *Shell Chemie/Elf Atochem* [1995] OJ C35/4.
[33] op. cit. para.41.
[34] IV/M214 *DuPont/ICI* [1993] OJ L7.

exports and consequently little mutual inter-penetration between the Community and other areas".[35]

In *Mercedes-Benz/Kässbohrer*[36] the Commission found that imports of city buses into Germany were low. Imports as a percentage of consumption were only 5.6 per cent in 1994, and even this represented a considerable rise from the 1989 figure of only 2.2 per cent. Accordingly, the Commission concluded that:

> "The relevant geographic market for city buses must be confined to Germany because of the low level of imports and purchasing behaviour hitherto of the public operators of city buses."[37]

In *Cargill/Cerestar*,[38] the Commission defined the relevant geographic markets on the basis of both trade flows and transport costs. The Commission found that the geographic market for starch was Community-wide on the basis of significant cross-border trade flows. However, the Commission found that although there were significant intra-community trade flows of sweeteners, nonetheless those countries that were at a significant distance from the Benelux/northern France/Germany area (where the European production facilities were based) were likely to be separate relevant geographic markets. Transport costs were between 10 per cent and 20 per cent of total costs for long distances (e.g. northern France to Portugal) and this leads to significantly higher prices in the peripheral countries.

In *Norddeutsche Affinerie/Cumerio*,[39] the Commission explicitly noted that although there was an import duty of 4.8 per cent on semi-finished copper products imported to the Commission, this did not mean that the tariff was a barrier to entry. This was because even with the tariff barriers, there were considerable imports. The Commission noted that this was because of the high value added of the product.

## US hospital mergers

The Elzinga-Hogarty test has been used in a number of US hospital **16–020** mergers, although not in quite the same way as described above. Geographic market definition has been a significant issue in a number of these mergers. The Elzinga-Hogarty test has been applied to the origin of patients, rather than of physical product. Thus the LOFI criterion becomes "What percentage of patients treated at this hospital come from outside the

---

[35] op. cit. para.29.
[36] IV/M477 *Mercedes-Benz/Kässbohrer* [1995] OJ L211.
[37] op. cit. para.40.
[38] COMP/M2502 *Cargill/Cerestar* [2002].
[39] COMP/M.4781 *Norddeutsche Affinerie/Cumerio* (January 28, 2008).

area?" whilst the LIFO criterion becomes "What percentage of patients from within this area have used a hospital outside the area?" If either of these percentages is significant (e.g. above 10 per cent), then the geographic market is widened beyond the area initially considered.

An example is *FTC v Tenet Healthcare*.[40] The court was presented with evidence that over 20 per cent of the local residents of Poplar Bluff who received hospital care were treated outside the area. On this basis the court concluded that hospitals outside the local area were viewed by locals as substitutes for local hospitals. The court even went so far as to argue that it would be "absurd" to define the market narrowly.[41]

### Barloworld Coatings/Midas Paints

**16–021**   *Barloworld Coatings/Midas Paints* was a merger between two firms operating in the decorative paint market in South Africa.[42] Although Barloworld was a national player, Midas Paints was largely confined to the Western Cape. The question that arose was whether the geographic market was regional, in which case the merger would have led to a high post-merger market share in the Western Cape, or national. The parties presented shipment data that suggested the market was a national market. This data, summarised in Table 16.5, showed that the LIFO and LOFI conditions for separate regional markets were failed for all three regions. For the region of concern, the Western Cape, the LIFO statistic was 0.34 and the LOFI statistic was 0.69. Both of these figures are below the standard threshold of 0.9 and the lower threshold of 0.75.

**16–022**   **Table 16.5: Elzinga-Hogarty test data in *Barloworld Coatings/Midas Paints***

|  | Gauteng | KwaZulu-Natal | Western Cape |
|---|---|---|---|
| **Percentage of consumption imported from outside area** | 30% | 61% | 66% |
| **LIFO** | 0.70 | 0.39 | 0.34 |
| **Percentage of production sold outside the area** | 56% | 79% | 31% |
| **LOFI** | 0.44 | 0.21 | 0.69 |

*Source*: Econex (2006)

---

[40]   *FTC v Tenet Healthcare Corp*, 186 F. 3d 1045 (8th Cir. 1999).
[41]   Cited in Capps (2001).
[42]   See Econex (2006) for further details.

# ANALYTICAL ISSUES WITH SHIPMENT TESTS

## The relationship between the Elzinga-Hogarty test and the definition of the relevant market

The analysis of shipment data can provide useful, if not dispositive, **16–023** information on the competitive constraint that exists between suppliers located in different regions and can therefore be helpful in determining the extent of the relevant geographical market. Where it can be demonstrated that significant numbers of consumers use "non-local" suppliers, this suggests an absence of barriers to trade.

In the context of a merger inquiry, evidence of trade flows suggests that post-merger increases in the prices of "local" products would likely lead to "local" buyers switching to "non-local" suppliers whose products are now relatively cheaper. Under these circumstances, such post-merger price increases would be unprofitable if confined to the "local" market.

Evidence of substantial exports from a region may also provide evidence of the existence of effective inter-regional competitive constraints. If it is possible to export products, it is not clear why it is not also possible to import products, in which case a domestic price rise ought to lead to increased imports. However, as noted above, this is not always the case. Hence current imports are more suggestive of a wide market than current exports. If there are currently exports but no imports, the competitive assessment should seek to understand why this is the case. The reason may well be consistent with a wide market, but equally it may not be (e.g. domestic tariff barrier).

Although historic data on trade flows is informative on the question of what is the correct relevant market definition, such data does not directly answer the key market definition question: could a hypothetical monopolist within the region profitably impose a small but significant non-transitory increase in prices? In this, the Elzinga-Hogarty test suffers from the same weakness as price correlation analysis. However, this does not mean that the Elzinga-Hogarty test is not useful. It often provides a very useful indication of the relevant geographic market.

On a strict theoretical basis, the extent of the geographic market need **16–024** not include all neighbouring regions. It has been argued that differences in production costs and in transports costs can in theory lead to a relevant geographical market that does include two non-neighbouring regions. Crane and Welch (1991) argue that if a region fails the Elzinga-Hogarty test, the candidate market should be expanded on the basis of the size of trade flows between regions, not on the basis of geographic closeness. However, good reasons would need to be advanced to explain why, if two non-contiguous countries are part of the same relevant market, those countries in between are not. Thus if Italy and Belgium are in the same geographic market on the basis of an Elzinga-Hogarty test, one needs to ask why Germany is not also part of this market. Usually the answer will be that it is and so should be included. However, sometimes there will be good reasons why it is not part of the same market (e.g. tariff barriers).

## The implication of an absence of trade flows

**16–025** Although large trade flows imply wide markets, it is not the case that the converse is necessarily true. An absence of trade flows can usually be considered a necessary but not sufficient condition for finding a narrow geographic market. To understand this, consider those factors which act to limit the extent of trade between regions. There are three main factors. The first is the cost of transportation between regions. Products which have high transportation costs relative to their economic value will tend to exert an effective competitive constraint over only a relatively short distance compared to products with relatively lower transportation costs. The second factor which serves to reduce the effectiveness of competition between regions is legal obstacles. Suppliers of products that are subject to high tariffs or quotas or their equivalent are less able to pose an effective competitive constraint on suppliers located in other regions.

The two criteria contained in the Elzinga-Hogarty test neatly capture these two factors that limit the scope of the relevant market, but ignore a third. The third factor limiting trade flows relates to the degree of competition which exists in other regions. The greater the degree of competition between local suppliers, the less likely it is that suppliers located outside the region will be able to sell profitably into that region. This analysis is akin to that concerning a firm's entry into a market.[43] No firm will enter a new market unless it is profitable for it to do so and the more competitive the market currently is, the less likely it is to be profitable to enter. The Elzinga-Hogarty test ignores any notion of cross-elasticity of demand between regions. If transport costs between two regions are low, then any price rise in one region will lead to imports into that region from the other region.

Any price rise is thus likely to be defeated by imports from the other region (i.e. there would be high cross-elasticities of demand between the two regions). In this situation, producers in each region are unlikely to try and raise prices above the competitive level, with the result that there will be no incentive to trade between regions and so no trade flows. On the basis of a shipments test, the absence of trade flows would suggest that the two regions are in separate geographic markets despite the fact that they impose a competitive constraint on each other.

In these circumstances, the Elzinga-Hogarty test will be overly conservative in identifying the source of regional competitive constraints, i.e. the absence of trade flows does not necessarily imply narrow markets: they

---

[43] See Chapters 3 and 7.

may actually be due to high competition both within and between the regions. For this reason, the absence of trade between regions is not sufficient evidence to conclude that the competitive constraint between regions is ineffective. Instead, one should consider why there is no trade.

## Interpreting the results in the presence of regional price discrimination

Regional price discrimination can invalidate the results of an Elzinga-Hogarty test.[44] Assume that the LIFO and LOFI for Country A are both 0.7. This implies that according to the Elzinga-Hogarty test, Country A is not a separate geographic market. Accordingly, the market is widened. Assume that the LIFO and LOFI for countries A, B and C taken together are both 0.95. This suggests that a merger in Country A that led to a "market" share in Country A of 50 per cent but a market share in Countries A + B + C of only 10 per cent would not be of concern.

**16–026**

Now suppose that the possibility of geographic price discrimination is introduced. In particular, suppose that although Country A fails the LIFO and LOFI tests, there is an identifiable geographic grouping of consumers in Country A who can be profitably price discriminated against. Suppose further that this group of consumers is not currently discriminated against due to the force of local competition. However, suppose that, after the merger, they will be discriminated against, perhaps because the merging parties were the two main competitors in the area. This raises a competition concern that is ignored if the market is defined solely using the Elzinga-Hogarty test. The problem is that the Elzinga-Hogarty test should initially be applied to the smallest geographic area of concern for which price discrimination is not possible. In this example, this was not Country A, but a sub-section of Country A. So before applying the Elzinga-Hogarty test, the possibility of price discrimination within the initial narrowest candidate market for which shipments data are available should be considered. If it is, the Elzinga-Hogarty test is not valid.

## Imports from foreign operations of domestic suppliers

A question that sometimes arises is how should imports be treated when they come from the foreign operations of domestic suppliers. The answer depends on the question being asked. Suppose we are concerned about the possibility of unilateral effects post-merger. In this case, we are interested in the competitive effects faced by the merged entity and so imports from the foreign operations of the merged entity would not count as a competitive constraint. However, imports from the foreign operations of other

**16–027**

---

[44] See, inter alia, US Department of Justice and Federal Trade Commission Horizontal Merger Guidelines (1992).

local firms (i.e. local competitors to the merged entity) would be relevant. If instead the concern was about post-merger coordinated effects, then imports from any of the potential coordinating firms' foreign operations would have to be discounted.

If we are only interested in defining the relevant market, then the correct approach is to ignore the ownership of the firms who are importing. The market definition question is whether a hypothetical monopolist could profitably impose a SSNIP. This question is asked independently of the current ownership of the assets in question and should be answered independently of the assets in question. Failing to do this is likely to lead to analytical confusion and incorrect inferences about market power. Instead, the market should be defined without taking account of the ownership of the firms who are importing, but the assessment of market power within the market should take account of who owns the importers.

## TRANSPORT COSTS STUDIES

16–028   Analysis of the magnitude of transport costs is often used to assess the effectiveness of competitive constraints between different regions. Although at current prices a firm may not be able to profitably supply a particular region, it may be able to do so if prices in this region were to rise. Transport cost studies can therefore be used to implement the SSNIP test in merger cases by establishing how much further products could be shipped if the price in a region were to rise by 5 per cent. This test can be a useful supplement to a shipment test when the shipment test suggests relatively low levels of shipments at current prices.

In many Commission decisions, the magnitude of transport costs relative to the value of the product concerned is taken as indicative of the magnitude of the competitive constraint which exists between regions. High transport costs are taken to indicate that regional competition is at best weak. Clearly, high transport costs can explain why trade between two regions is not economically feasible and hence evidence on such costs may provide useful evidence in rebutting unsubstantiated claims that firms in one region are subject to effective competition from firms located elsewhere. But high transport costs per se do not allow one to assess what would happen if relative prices were to change. It may be the case that a relative price increase in one region changes trade between two regions from not being economically feasible to being economically feasible.

The basic aim of transport cost tests is to estimate the geographic extent of competitive constraints that a firm faces. The question posed is: given a price level X in area Y, which firms are located close enough to area Y to be able to sell product profitably in area Y.

This question is often posed in the context of geographic market definition in a merger case. Suppose prices in Area Y are €100 and there are a number of suppliers located outside Area Y who nonetheless sell into Area Y. This is illustrated in Figure 16.1. This shows that in addition to any suppliers located inside Area Y, there are six located outside Area Y who supply into Area Y. This shows that the supplier furthest from Area Y, A, is about 300km away. It can thus be assumed that at current prices, it is profitable to ship product at least 300km.

**Figure 16.1: Estimating area of supply for Area Y** 16–029

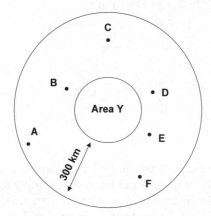

Now suppose that prices were to rise by 5 per cent inside area Y. How much further could product be profitably shipped? A reasonable answer is that it could be shipped an additional distance such that the increase in price is entirely taken up by extra transport costs. So in this example the 5 per cent increase represents an increase of €5. If it costs €0.05 per km to transport the product, then it could profitably be shipped an extra 100 km. The question then becomes whether there are any potential suppliers of the product located between 300km and 400km from Area Y and, if so, whether they are likely to supply into Area Y if prices were to rise. Figure 16.2 shows that in our example there are two such suppliers: G and H.

16–030 **Figure 16.2: Effect of a SSNIP on the area of supply for Area Y**

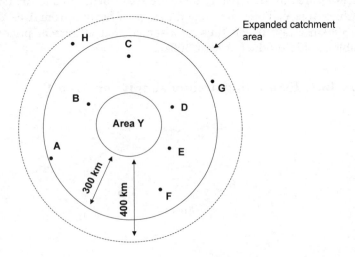

The mere fact that there are two firms located in the expanded catchment area does not mean that they would necessarily supply into Area Y if prices rose. They might, for instance, be capacity constrained, in which case any sales made in Area Y would be diverted from elsewhere. They would only wish to divert sales to Area Y if this was more profitable than the best alternative. Equally, it might be that there are sunk costs of entering Area Y that they might not be willing to incur. So having identified G and H, it is still necessary to analyse whether they are likely entrants if prices rose.

This approach to analysing the potential catchment area for suppliers able to supply Area Y is conservative. This is because we have assumed that the supplier furthest from Area Y (A in this case) is right at the edge of the catchment area. This may well not be true. Figure 16.3 shows an example in which the true catchment area is 400km, but because there are no suppliers located between 300km and 400km from Area Y, we mistakenly believe that it is 300km. This then means that when we expand the catchment area by 100km, we conclude that there are no additional suppliers capable of supplying Area Y, when in reality there are four: G, H, I and J are all located between 400km and 500km away from Area Y.

**Figure 16.3: Potential mistake in calculating the area of**   16–031
**supply for Area Y**

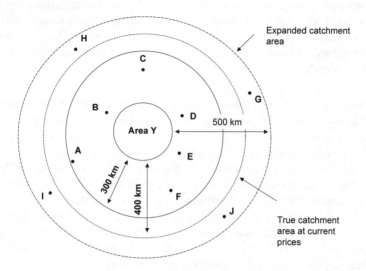

This difficulty can be avoided if it is possible to calculate directly the extent of the catchment area, rather than seeking to deduce it from where suppliers are actually located. This approach requires more data as it is necessary to have information not only on per mile transport costs, but also on all other costs, including the minimum acceptable profit margin for firms.

The Commission carried out a similar form of analysis in the *Ineos/ Kerling* merger.[45] The Commission asked the question: how much would prices in the United Kingdom have to rise post-merger in order to make is profitable for continental producers to sell in the United Kingdom rather than on the continent. The costs of transporting product to the United Kingdom were higher than for transporting the product a similar distance on the continent because of the costs of crossing the channel. In order to carry out the analysis it is necessary to know profit margins on the continent at current prices, the additional costs of selling in the United Kingdom and the current level of UK prices relative to continental prices. The Commission collected the relevant data and concluded that, depending on the particular supplier considered, it would be equally profitable for them to sell in the United Kingdom as the continent if UK prices rose by between 2 per cent and 8 per cent. The Commission concluded that this meant that the added transport costs to the United Kingdom should not be considered a barrier to entry (para.122).

The Commission has used this approach to geographic market definition

---

[45]   COMP/M. 4734 *Ineos/Kerling* (January 30, 2008).

in a number of cases. A good example is *SCA/P&G (European tissue business).*[46] One issue in this case was the extent of the geographic market for consumer tissue products. The Commission distinguished between private label and branded products. Although the Commission did not have to reach a definitive conclusion for private label products, it argued that geographic markets for private label product were of approximately 1,000km radius:

> "respondents to the market investigation in the *Kimberly-Clark/Scott* case estimated that the various tissue products could be economically transported over maximum distances of 540 to 865 km (depending on the product category). The market investigation carried out in the *SCA/Metsa* case considered that this range of distances was still valid, although there was a tendency toward the upper end of the range, with maximum distances of approximately 800 to 1000 km for full truck-loads. The market investigation in the present case has broadly confirmed these ranges and highlighted that a number of producers are nowadays active and competitive at 1000 km range from their production facilities, and sometimes even beyond.
>
> As a result, the most appropriate geographic market definition for the production and supply of private labels would appear to be 'regional', that is broader than national but narrower then EEA, and based on radii of approximately 1000 km." (paras 38–39).

**16–032** However, the Commission did not use this form of analysis for branded products. For these the Commission argued that the geographic market was national or "country clusters" (e.g. United Kingdom/Ireland, Germany/Austria) because:

> "it is largely the reflection of the situation at the retail level, where 'national' brands, languages, advertising, consumer preferences are still very strong and more than compensate for the alleged increasing 'globalisation' of producers' strategies and activities, as highlighted by the parties." (para.42)

This highlights the fact that even if it is possible to transport product economically to another market, this does not mean that it is possible to enter that market if there are barriers to entry, such as branding. Thus showing that transport costs do not make supply uneconomic is not the end of the analysis. It is still necessary to show that entry in response to a price rise is likely.

This implies that when used unthinkingly transport cost tests can be

---

[46] COMP/M.4533 *SCA/P&G (European tissue business)* (September 5, 2007).

overly inclusive and suggest that the relevant geographic market is wider than in reality it is. But they can also suggest that the geographic market is narrower than in reality it is. For instance, this can be the case when there are overlapping areas of supply which mean that even though product cannot economically flow from one region to another, competitive effects can be transmitted between regions. Consider Figure 16.4. A, B and C are production facilities. The circles around them indicate the maximum distance that it is profitable to ship product at current prices. At current prices, transport costs are too high for it to be profitable to ship product from the catchment area of A to the catchment area of C, or vice versa.

**Figure 16.4: Regional competition where catchment areas are** 16–033
**defined by "transport" costs**

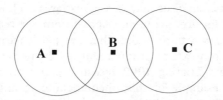

It might appear from Figure 16.4 that Plant A cannot compete with Plant C, and vice versa, and hence that they are in different markets. However, this depends on whether the overlap of both catchment areas with the catchment area of B is enough to transmit competitive effects and put them in the same geographic market. If A were to raise its prices, this would relax the competitive constraint on B in the overlap between A and B and so allow B to raise its prices. This would then relax the competitive constraint imposed by B on C in the overlap between B and C. Whether competitive constraints are communicated in this way to a large enough extent to put the three plants in the same relevant market depends on the proportion of customers in the overlap areas and on whether the firms can price discriminate between customers in overlap areas and those not in overlap areas. If B can charge a different price to customers in the overlap between A and B than it charges in the rest of its area, then even if a price rise by A engendered a price rise by B in the overlap area between A and B, this would not relax the competitive constraint on C.

The *Pilkington-Techint/SIV*[47] decision is an example of the Commission implicitly using this logic. The Commission noted that "raw float glass is a bulky, heavy product" that is "expensive to transport over great distances". This results in each float glass plant having a natural area of supply, which the Commission argued was a circle of radius 500 km

---

[47]   IV/M358 *Pilkington-Techint/SIV* [1994] OJ L158/24.

around each plant. Virtually all of a plant's output would be sold within 500 km of the plant. The implication of this is that substantial trade flows between countries should not be expected (although the Commission did not give any import or export figures). However, the Commission noted that "the various supply areas can be seen as a series of overlapping circles with their centres at the float-glass plants" (as in Figure 16.4) and concluded that:

> "given the dispersion of the individual float plants and the varying degrees of overlap for the natural supply areas, so that effects can be transmitted from one circle to another, it seems appropriate to consider that the geographic reference market is the Community as a whole".[48]

When thinking about transport costs it is also important to take account of the fact that production costs may vary across areas. Thus even if transport costs are too high for product to be shipped from one region to another, it may be that there is a third region that has particularly low production costs and hence from which product can be shipped economically. The UK Office of Fair Trading 1992 research paper on market definition provides a good example of this phenomenon: fertiliser. The costs of transporting fertiliser were high, but this did not stop exporters from countries as distant as Trinidad from exporting to the United Kingdom. The reason for this was that such producers had a significant production cost advantage over UK manufacturers and so could be competitive in the United Kingdom even after paying high transport costs. The production cost advantage arises because the major input into fertiliser, natural gas, was much cheaper (i.e. effectively free, according to the OFT) in these countries than in the United Kingdom. A simplistic transport cost approach in this market would potentially have led to a geographic market definition that was much narrower than was actually the case.

## ISOCHRONE ANALYSIS

**16–034** The discussion of transport cost tests above has focused on the ability of suppliers to ship product to their customers, i.e. it focused on the supply-side. Another approach to geographic market definition is to focus on the demand-side and ask how far consumers are willing to travel to a supplier and to identify how many competitors a particular firm faces by seeing how many competitors are within its customer catchment area.

The standard approach to defining catchment areas is to carry out a consumer survey at the relevant supplier (e.g. a supermarket) in order to find out how long it takes consumers to reach the supplier or from how far

---

[48] IV/M358 *Pilkington-Techint/SIV* [1994] OJ L158/24 para.16.

they have travelled.[49] This information enables one to estimate the time or distance that consumers are willing to travel and this information can be used to estimate the geographic market. If you have estimates of distance, then it is simple to just draw a circle around the supplier of that distance, but in general this is not the preferred approach. A better approach is to create a geographic market based on travel time using a given mode of transportation; these are known as *isochrones*.[50]

The construction of isochrones requires the use of sophisticated, but now readily available, logistics software, which uses information on road networks and average travel speeds to construct a catchment area (usually non-uniform in shape) that encompasses all geographic locations that can be reached within a given time from the point of origin.[51]

Figure 16.5 shows a hypothetical isochrone. All the points within the isochrone are no more than, say, 15 minutes drive of the supplier of interest (Firm A). The irregular shape of the isochrone is due to the road system in the area. So, for instance, the bulge in the south-west corner of the isochrone in Figure 16.5 will be caused by a fast road heading south-west from close to Firm A.

## Figure 16.5: Example of an isochrone 16–035

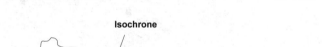

---

49  An alternative approach is to use loyalty card data when this includes the address of the customer. This is a good approach as long as we are willing to assume that customers all travel from their home. This is likely to be a strong assumption to make in many cases.

50  An exception to this would be where consumers typically travel on foot to obtain goods or services. In these cases, catchment areas based on geographic distances may better capture consumer behaviour than driving times. For an example of this, see the investigation into the acquisition by Alliance UniChem Plc by Boots Plc in 2006, where the OFT assessed local retail competition amongst pharmacies on the basis of one mile geometric radii.

51  Since different drive-time systems incorporate varying degrees of sophistication and make use of differing underlying road network and traffic speed data sets, alternative systems may not always produce the same results. However, such systems can also be customised to reflect particular competition investigations, e.g. travel can be restricted to only certain road types, or average travelling speeds can be varied to reflect different modes of transportation.

Having constructed the isochrone, the next step is to identify all the other competing suppliers within the isochrone. This is done in Figure 16.6. This shows that there are four other firms located within the isochrone (Firms B, C, D and E), of which one (Firm B) has two locations, and two firms located outside the isochrone (Firms F and G). If we were investigating a merger between Firms A and B, then Figure 16.6 indicates that there would be an increase in concentration within the relevant geographic area, whereas if the merger was between A and G then there would not be any increase in concentration.

16–036 **Figure 16.6: Isochrone showing competing firms**

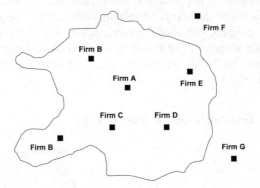

There are a number of issues that arise when using isochrones to identify geographic markets. First, what percentage of a firm's customers should be within the geographic market? Should the isochrone be derived based on the drive time for 75 per cent of the firm's customers? Or 90 per cent? In the UK Competition Commission's *Safeway*[52] inquiry the Competition Commission based isochrones on having between 75 per cent and 90 per cent of customers within the isochrones and so used 10-minute isochrones for urban areas and 15-minute ones for rural areas. However, the hypothetical monopolist test does not define any particular percentage of customers that should be within an isochrone to make that the relevant geographic market. For instance, it might be that all of a particular supermarket's customers are within a 10-minute drive time because for those consumers further away, there are closer alternatives. However, this does not mean that a 5 per cent price increase by a hypothetical monopolist of all supermarkets within 10 minutes of the supermarket of concern would be profitable. It might be that in response to such a price increase,

[52] "Safeway plc and Asda Group Ltd (owned by Wal-Mart Stores Inc); Wm Morrison Supermarkets PLC; J Sainsbury plc; and Tesco plc: A report on the mergers in contemplation" Competition Commission (September 2003).

customers within the 10-minute isochrone would be prepared to drive further. Further, we are not convinced that it makes sense to define a relevant market that excludes a significant proportion of a firm's customers. Our view is that it is better to think of isochrones as being useful for identifying a firm's closest competitors, rather than for defining a relevant market.[53]

Secondly, isochrone analysis suffers from the same issue as arises with geographic markets defined by transport costs: where alleged geographic markets overlap, competitive effects may be transmitted across a number of such markets, with the result that the correct geographic market definition is wider than the isochrone analysis might suggest for analogous reasons to those that apply to transport cost studies. Thus, firms in different isochrones might nonetheless be in the same relevant geographic market.

Thirdly, it is sometimes argued that the correct approach is not to focus the analysis on the location of the supplier but on the location of the customer. The UK Competition Commission made this argument in its *Safeway* inquiry. At para.5.197, the CC stated that:

> "Given that, for the purposes of this exercise, we are interested in the effect of each of the mergers on consumers in local areas, it could be argued that we should draw isochrones around areas of population, and carrying the point to the ultimate, around each individual household. A 10-minute isochrone drawn around a particular household would show all the grocery stores available to that household within a 10-minute drive."

The aim of such analysis would be to avoid situations in which isochrones centred on suppliers do not suggest a competitive concern but those centred on population do. Figure 16.7 illustrates the concern. Here the isochrones (conveniently drawn just as circles) around Firm A and Firm B do not include each other, thus suggesting that they are not competitors. However, the isochrones do overlap and so for consumers within the overlap area they are alternatives. As a result, a merger between Firm A and Firm B might represent a loss of competition to serve these customers.

---

[53] We note that in their draft "Merger Assessment Guidelines" (April 2009), the Competition Commission and OFT state that they will typically use a figure of more than 80% of customers to define a relevant market. Thus the Guidelines state that "the Authorities may examine the geographic catchment area within which the great majority (usually 80 per cent or more) of the retailers' custom is located" (para.4.67).

**16–037** **Figure 16.7: Example of a population-centred isochrone**

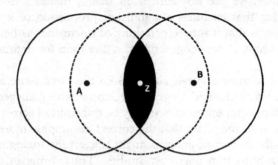

Of course, merely noting that the isochrones overlap does not mean that there is a competition concern. This will depend on issues such as what percentage of the population served by Firms A and B is in the overlap area, is there scope for the consumers in the overlap area to be price discriminated against, how many other competitors are there within the population centred isochrone, and so on. Ultimately, the Competition Commission did not use population-centred isochrones in *Safeway* due to practical difficulties. However, as discussed further below, the OFT did use them in the assessment of cinema mergers.

### Case study: Odeon/UCI

**16–038** The UK OFT used isochrone analysis in its analysis of the *Odeon/UCI* merger.[54] This was a merger between two chains of cinemas.[55] The OFT concluded, on the basis of internal documents from the parties, that a 20-minute drive time was the "core catchment area" for their customers and so used 20-minute isochrones.[56] The only exception to this was central London where the OFT considered that isochrone analysis was not appropriate due to the prevalence of public transport. The OFT decided that competition concerns were only plausible post-merger if there would be three or fewer competing cinema chains within each isochrone. Competing cinemas were defined as those with at least three screens and at least 696 seats. This latter number was derived as being three times the average number of seats per screen at the top 20 cinema chains in the United Kingdom. The basis for deciding that three or fewer competing cinemas was a concern was that the OFT found that average prices were higher in

---

[54] "Acquisition by Terra Firma Investments (GP) 2 Ltd of United Cinemas International (UK) Ltd and Cinema International Corp (UK) Ltd", OFT decision, January 7, 2005.
[55] It is worth noting that soon after *Odeon/UCI* there was another cinema merger in the UK: *Cine-UK/UGC* ("Completed acquisition by the Blackstone Group of UGC Cinemas Holdings Ltd", OFT decision of April 28, 2005). The OFT used the same analytical approach in this second merger as in the first one.
[56] Although the OFT also considered 30-minute isochrones as a sensitivity check.

areas with only three competing chains compared to those with four competing chains. The application of these criteria led to the OFT identifying ten UCI cinemas that might give rise to competition concerns. In the light of arguments from the parties about announced new entry and the competitive effect of a smaller competitor, the OFT dropped one of these ten cinemas from its list of possible concerns.

The OFT also carried out "population re-centring" analysis. This involved re-centring the isochrone on significant population centres where there was a concern that they might not be served by enough competing cinemas. The aim was to identify any areas where the merger might materially reduce competition for consumers located between the parties' cinemas but which was not identified by the isochrone analysis centred on the parties' cinemas. As a result the OFT identified four areas where the merger might give rise to competition concerns. On further analysis, the OFT concluded that two of these did not give rise to competition concerns.

As a result of the isochrone analysis, the OFT identified 10 areas, covering 12 UCI cinemas, where competition concerns might arise. The OFT also identified a concern in central London. The result was that the parties offered divestments and the merger was cleared without a referral to the Competition Commission.

# SUMMARY

Shipment tests are attractive empirical tests for two reasons. First, they are **16–039** intuitive: it is simple to understand what they imply. Secondly, they are very easy to carry out: they require only quantity data and can be quickly calculated. For these reasons, it is not surprising that shipment tests (or rather, informal versions of them) appear in many Commission decisions. The Commission tends to focus only on the level of imports and it tends to require a higher level of imports than the standard Elzinga-Hogarty test before it will define a wide geographic market.

However, shipment tests do have weaknesses:

a)   In common with price correlation analysis, they do not directly address the magnitude of competitive constraint between regions under investigation.

b)   They tend to be "one-way" tests. The presence of large trade flows tends to imply a wide market, but the absence of large trade flows does not necessarily imply a narrow market. An absence of trade flows is consistent with vigorous competition between areas. This underlines the fact that where there is no (or only a little) trade it is important to understand why there is no (or only a little) trade.

c)  In the presence of geographic price discrimination at a level below that for which trade statistics are available, the Elzinga-Hogarty test is unlikely to provide an adequate indication of the level of competition.

Transport cost tests can be used to help define the relevant geographic market and to identify potential competitive constraints from outside the particular region of interest. These tests can be used to give an indication of how much further it would be profitable to ship product if prices rose by 5–10 per cent. Analysis of transport costs can often indicate which producers who do not currently ship product to the area in question might do so after a price rise. However, such tests can imply both too wide a geographic market and too narrow a geographic market. They can imply too wide a geographic market when an investigator fails to take account of barriers to entry that might stop firms being able to sell into a region (e.g. the need to have a local brand). They can imply too narrow a geographic market when an investigator fails to take account of the fact that areas of supply overlap with each other and thus form a continuous chain along which competitive effects can be transmitted.

**16–040**  Isochrone analysis is an approach to geographic market definition that focuses on the demand-side, rather than the supply-side, and asks how far consumers are willing to travel to a supplier. This form of analysis is used frequently in the assessment of competition issues in a retail setting. Two important questions that arise are: what percentage of a firm's customers should be included within the isochrone and should the isochrone be centred on suppliers or customers? Finally, it should be noted that isochrone analysis, like transport cost analysis, can under-estimate the extent of the geographic market when isochrones overlap.

# 17. Calculating Antitrust Damages

## INTRODUCTION

Anti-competitive behaviour harms not only final consumers but also firms.[1] **17–001** For instance, cartels lead to prices being higher than they otherwise would be and this can harm both final consumers and producers who use cartelised products in their production process. Excessive pricing has the same effect. Predatory pricing, and other forms of exclusionary conduct, can harm competitors by driving them out of the market and hence stopping them from earning profits and can harm consumers by raising prices in the longer term.

This chapter address the calculation of damages arising from anti-competitive behaviour by firms; an issue that has become more prominent in Europe in recent years. In 2004, the Commission published a report that it had commissioned on antitrust damages (the "Ashursts report"[2]) and followed this up with a Green Paper on the subject in 2005.[3] It published a White Paper in April 2008.[4] A number of domestic competition authorities have also undertaken similar studies, such as the UK's Office of Fair Trading's paper on private actions in competition law.[5] We outline the broad methodology for calculating antitrust damages and then describe a number of ways in which this methodology can be implemented. Much of the discussion takes place within the context of calculating the damages arising from cartels, but the methodology and approaches described can be applied to other types of anti-competitive behaviour. Finally, we discuss a number of issues and common pitfalls that arise in calculating damages.

---

[1] In some cases, these firms are competitors (for example, in exclusionary cases) and in others customers (for example, in cartel cases).

[2] D. Waelbroeck, D. Slater, and G. Even-Shoshan "Study on the conditions of claims for damages in the case of infringement of EC competition rules" (2004).

[3] "Green Paper: Damages actions for breach of the EC antitrust rules" COM (2005) 672 (December 19, 2005).

[4] "White Paper on Damages Actions for Breach of the EC antitrust rules" COM(2008) 165 (April 2, 2008).

[5] "Private actions in competition law: effective redress for consumers and business" (2007) OFT916 resp.

## 17–001  Calculating antitrust damages

We assume throughout that the aim is to calculate compensatory damages, not punitive or restitutionary damages.[6]

# GENERAL METHODOLOGY

17–002   The key to calculating compensatory damages is to compare the position of the claimant with the anti-competitive behaviour to the position that the claimant would have been in but for the anti-competitive behaviour. We refer to this as the "counterfactual". The counterfactual is usually not observable whereas the position of the claimant with the anti-competitive behaviour usually is observable.[7] By establishing the counterfactual, the claimant's profits in the counterfactual world can be compared to the claimant's observed profits. The difference between the two is the amount of compensatory damages due to the claimant. Assuming that the anti-competitive behaviour lasted for several periods, the loss due to the claimant needs to be calculated in each period and then adjusted by a suitable interest rate to transform it in to a present day value.

### The cartel counterfactual

17–003   We start by discussing the estimation of the counterfactual in a cartel case. There are a number of reasons for focusing on the cartel counterfactual. First, antitrust damages arise most commonly in cartel cases. Secondly, the theory of harm in a cartel case is straightforward. Thirdly, the techniques available for estimating the cartel counterfactual and therefore damages are also useful for estimating the counterfactual in other types of case.[8]

There are three elements to the harm suffered by a direct purchaser in a cartel case. First, there is the "direct effect". The "direct effect" is the quantity of products purchased multiplied by the increase in price as a result of the cartel. So if a purchaser buys 100 units from the cartel at a price €10 above the non-cartelised price, that purchaser has suffered direct harm of €1,000. The second effect is the increase in the purchaser's selling price that is a likely consequence of its input prices increasing. This increase in the purchaser's selling price will lead to a reduction in the

---

[6]   Compensatory damages are damages that compensate the victim for the harm caused by the anti-competitive behaviour. Restitutionary damages are damages that are designed to remove the benefit of the anti-competitive act from the firm committing the anti-competitive act. Punitive damages are damages that are designed to punish the firm for its behaviour and so are greater than just restitutionary damages (e.g. triple damages).

[7]   The claimant's profits with the antitrust harm are not always observable. For instance, anti-competitive behaviour that does not drive a firm out of the market but does permanently damage their competitive position will have a long-run effect on the firm's profits that is not directly observable.

[8]   We discuss below other approaches that are available for estimating damages in non-cartel cases.

demand for (and hence sales of) its product. Thus, if the direct purchaser suffers a loss in demand of 10 units and its profit margin on those units was previously €10, then it has suffered an additional loss of €100. We refer to this as the "output effect". Finally, if the direct purchaser raises its selling price in response to the increase in input costs, then this reduces the harm it suffers (the "passing-on effect"). In the extreme, if a direct purchaser were able to pass on all of the input cost increase without suffering any loss in sales, it would suffer no harm.[9]

These three elements of harm are illustrated in Figure 17.1 and Figure 17.2. Figure 17.1 illustrates the position of the firm purchasing the cartelised product before the cartel begins. At this point the firm has marginal costs of $MC_0$, it sets a price of $P_0$ and sells $Q_0$ units. Its profits are shown by the shaded area in Figure 17.1, which is just sales ($Q_0$) multiplied by the per unit margin ($P_0-MC_0$).

**Figure 17.1: Profits of direct purchaser before the cartel raises prices**

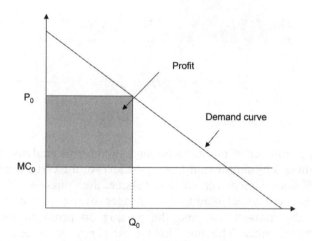

Now suppose that as a result of a cartel the firm's marginal costs rise to $MC_1$. Figure 17.2 shows the impact of this increase in costs on the purchasing firm's profits. The increase in marginal cost causes the firm to raise its price to $P_1$, which has the effect of reducing sales to $Q_1$. The new profits of the firm are shown by the solid shaded area. The "direct effect" of the cartel is shown by the area shaded with vertical lines. This is the new level of sales ($Q_1$) multiplied by the increase in marginal costs ($MC_1-MC_0$).

---

[9]   We assume that the cartel leads to an increase in the variable costs of the downstream firms. If the cartelised product is a fixed cost of the downstream firm, then the cartel should not affect downstream pricing or, therefore, output. In this case the damages are just the overcharge. However, we are not aware of any cartels that have only affected fixed costs.

The "indirect loss" is shown by the area shaded with horizontal lines. This is the pre-cartel profit margin $(P_0–MC_0)$ multiplied by the reduction in sales as a result of the firm's price rise $(Q_0–Q_1)$. However, as a result of passing on some of the cartel price increase to its customers, the purchasing firm earns additional profits on each of its remaining sales: this is represented by the solidly shaded area above $P_0$.

**17-005** **Figure 17.2: Components of loss resulting from the cartel price rise**

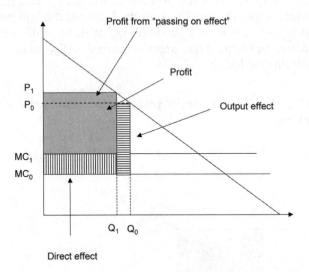

There are a number of points to be made about this analysis. First, estimating damages by simply multiplying the level of the cartel overcharge by the level of sales is incorrect. As noted above, the "direct loss" represents only one element of calculating the damages arising from cartel activity. Secondly, the indirect loss and the passing on profit to some extent counteract each other. The more that the cartel price increase is passed on, thereby increasing the per unit profit margin, the greater will be the reduction in sales and hence the greater the output effect. Thirdly, it is not, in general, possible to say whether the total harm is greater or less than the direct effect. In the situation illustrated above, the direct loss is an underestimate of the total harm because the passing-on profit is less than the indirect loss. However, if the downstream market is very competitive, then the profit margin on sales will be low and so the output effect might be small and hence less than the passing-on effect. In a perfectly competitive market with price equal to marginal cost, the output effect will be zero and so the passing-on effect will outweigh the output effect and will mean that the direct effect is an over-estimate of the harm caused to the direct purchaser.

Estimating the reduction in profits as a result of the cartel means comparing profits with the cartel to profits without the cartel, i.e. comparing observed profits with the estimated profits in the counterfactual. Estimating the profits in the counterfactual requires knowing or estimating the following:

1.  The amount of the cartel overcharge. In the context of Figure 17.1 and Figure 17.2, this means knowing the difference between $MC_1$ and $MC_0$.

2.  How much lower selling prices would have been at the lower input costs (i.e. knowing $P_0$ from Figure 17.1 and Figure 17.2).

3.  What the level of sales would have been at this lower price (i.e. knowing $Q_0$ from Figure 17.1 and Figure 17.2).

Below we discuss how these questions can be answered. It should be noted that the answers to 2 and 3 both depend on the shape of the demand curve and therefore these two issues are intertwined.


# ESTIMATING THE LEVEL OF A CARTEL OVERCHARGE

There are a number of ways in which the cartel overcharge can be estimated.[10] On the assumption that the price charged by the cartel is clear, these all relate to trying to estimate what the price would have been in the absence of the cartel.   **17–006**


## Simple comparison approaches

Perhaps the simplest reasonable approach to estimating what prices would have been in the absence of the cartel is to assume that they would have been the same as prices before and after the cartel. If we know that a cartel existed for a ten-year period and we have price data showing that prices before this period were 10 per cent lower than prices during the cartel   **17–007**

---

[10] There is a significant amount of empirical evidence on the level of overcharges that cartels are able to impose. For instance, Connor and Bolotova (2006) looked at 395 cartel episodes. They estimated that the mean overcharge was 29%, with a median overcharge of 19%. These overcharges, like those discussed below, were calculated as being the increase in the price due to the cartel divided by the price in the absence of the cartel. In an earlier paper, Connor (2005) distinguished between the level of cartel overcharges in domestic (i.e. US) cartels as opposed to international ones. He concluded that the median overcharge was 18% for domestic cartels and 32% for international ones. He also found that the overcharge was above 20% in about 60% of cases. Levenstein and Suslow (2006) looked at 35 international cartels and estimated that the mean overcharge was 25% and that it ranged between 10% and 100%.

period, and prices after the cartel were 10 per cent lower than prices during the cartel, then a reasonable assumption is that the cartel increased prices by 10 per cent. Alternatively, if prices after the cartel were, say, 5 per cent higher than prices before the cartel, then we might assume that prices would have risen steadily by 0.5 per cent per year during the ten-year cartel period in the absence of the cartel. These two possibilities are illustrated below.

**17–008  Figure 17.3: Simple "before and after" approach**

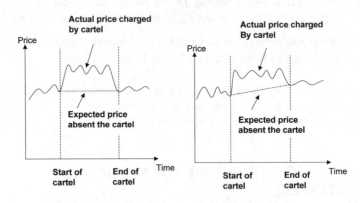

A similar approach is to consider prices during the cartel period in a different but similar market. The most obvious comparator is prices of the same product in a different geographic area. If prices of the cartelised product in a different geographic area did not increase at all during the ten-year cartel period, then we might conclude that the same would have been true in the cartelised market in the absence of the cartel.

Both of these approaches have the virtue of simplicity. However, they also have significant weaknesses.

First, they are dependent upon being able to clearly distinguish periods of cartel activity from periods of competitive behaviour and that there are sufficient data for both periods. Secondly, the simple "before and after" approach assumes that in the absence of the cartel, nothing would have changed and so prices would have remained at their pre-cartel level. However, this may be an incorrect assumption. For instance, it might be that even in the absence of the cartel prices would have risen, perhaps because of an increase in demand for the product or an increase in the costs of production (e.g. an input cost increase). Alternatively, the pre-cartel price might have been very low due to a temporary reduction in demand and that it was this that led to the creation of the cartel. Unless the reduction in demand persisted throughout the cartel period, it is not correct to assume that this low price would have persisted in the absence of the cartel. Or it may be that the cartel was set up in the expectation of a fall in demand, and hence a fall in prices, and so the pre-cartel price is higher than the price that would have prevailed absent the cartel.

Thirdly, there may not be any markets that can act as comparators. In **17–009** order for another market to be a good comparator, it must have a similar supply and demand structure to the cartelised market but cannot itself have been cartelised. Markets in other geographic areas may have significantly different structures. For instance, if the cartelised market contains only a few firms whilst the potential comparator market contains many firms, it may well not be reasonable to assume that in the absence of the cartel prices in the market with only a few players would have been the same as prices in the market with many players. It also may not be clear as to whether or not the comparator markets were themselves cartelised. However, if there is another similar market in which prices were similar to prices in the cartelised market both pre- and post-cartel, but were lower during the cartel, then this is useful evidence of the "but for" price.[11]

## Econometric approach

The preferred approach to adddress the issues that arise with simple price **17–010** comparisons is to undertake an econometric analysis, i.e. conduct a statistical assessment of the determinants of observed pricing in the industry under investigation. The econometric model might for example take into account factors such as the overall state of demand in the economy, the price of substitute products, the demand for downstream products and so on. The basic underlying idea of econometric modelling is to identify the main determinants of prices absent the cartel and then see how the predictions from this model differ from the actual prices set by the cartel. Since the model is designed to explain the level of prices in the absence of the cartel, it is necessary to have some data from a non-cartelised period, either before or after the cartel (or ideally both).

An investigator might estimate an equation along the following lines for price formation in the absence of the cartel:

---

[11] As noted above, it is sometimes argued that investigators may need to treat pre- or post-cartel data with care. Pre-cartel prices may not be a good indicator of what prices would have been absent the cartel. One reason, noted by Connor (2007), is that pre-cartel prices might be the result of an earlier cartel. Connor argues that this happened in the vitamins cartels in the period 1985–89. Another reason is that the pre-cartel price might have been below the competitive price level. Connor argues that a failure to take account of predatory pricing pre-cartel led to an over-estimate of the overcharge in the lysine cartel. A more common reason that the pre-cartel price may be too low is that cartels may be set up in periods of particularly low prices in an industry which would not have persisted in the medium term (e.g. temporary demand shock). Post-cartel prices may also not be a good indicator of the competitive price level. This might be because post-cartel the cartelists are able to use their experience of colluding explicitly to continue to collude tacitly, thus reducing the extent to which prices fall post-cartel. Harrington (2004) suggests that former cartelists may be particularly prone to continue to price high post-cartel if they think that the post-cartel price will be used as the competitive benchmark in damages claims by direct or indirect purchasers.

**17–010** Calculating antitrust damages

(1)   $Price_t = f(\text{Price of substitutes, Input costs, GDP, Capacity utilisation,}$
$\text{other factors})_t$

By collecting data for the various factors during the cartel, the investigator can then estimate the non-cartelised price. An example is shown in Figure 17.4. The effect of the cartel under this approach is then the actual price set by the cartel less the predicted cartel price.

**17–011**   **Figure 17.4: Example of using econometrics to predict the non-cartel price**

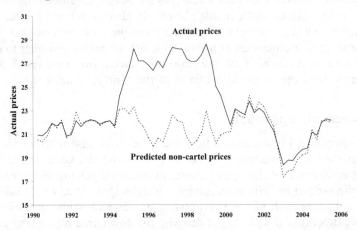

This approach is reasonable as long as the investigator has sufficient data covering non-cartel periods. However, if data is available for only a relatively few non-cartel periods, then this approach is unlikely to be useful as it will not be possible to estimate reasonably precise estimates for the coefficients on the various exogenous factors.[12] In this case, a better approach is likely to be to estimate an equation such as that above, but to do so for the whole period (i.e. including the cartel period) and to include a dummy variable for the effect of the cartel on prices. This dummy variable would take on the value of one during the cartel and zero otherwise. The coefficient on this dummy variable would be an estimate of the effect of the cartel. Thus Equation (1) would become:

(2)   $Price_t = f(\text{Price of substitutes, Input costs, GDP, Capacity utilisation,}$
$\text{dummy for whether cartel is in operation, other factors})_t$

Assuming the model is estimated in logarithms, the coefficient on the dummy variable would indicate the average proportional effect of the cartel on prices (e.g. on average the cartel raised prices by, say, 20 per cent). If it was estimated in levels, then it would indicate the fixed sum by which the cartel on average raised prices (i.e. on average by, say, €5).

---

[12]   It is also necessary to know which periods are "in" the cartel and which are "out".

We noted that econometric analysis is the preferred approach to estimating damages arising from cartel activity. However, the econometric approach is data intensive and in particular requires data on a significant number of periods during which the cartel was not operating. If a cartel was long running, then there may be no pre-cartel data available. If the cartel has only recently ended, there may be little post-cartel data. In these circumstances the econometric approach is likely to be imprecise.

However, even if insufficient data are available to enable a robust econometric analysis to be undertaken, this does not mean that no account should be taken of changes in factors that are known to affect pricing behaviour. For instance, if demand for a product has increased over time, then even if the effect of this on prices cannot be estimated directly, it should be taken into account when estimating the "true" overcharge. It would be poor analysis to know of a reason why we might expect prices to have risen even in the absence of the cartel, but to ignore this factor just because we could not quantify its effect precisely.

**17–012** It is standard practice to report the confidence intervals around any econometric estimate.[13] It is relevant information to know whether the 95 per cent confidence interval around an overcharge estimate of, say, 25 per cent, is 23–27 per cent or 0–50 per cent. It is also standard practice to check the ability of the econometric model to track periods when the cartel has broken down. If we know that the cartel broke down for a short period, thus leading to lower prices, then a good test of the robustness of our econometric model is whether the model is able to track those lower prices accurately.

## Cost-based approaches

**17–013** Another approach is to estimate the non-cartel price from the costs of the firms. The idea is that if we know the relevant costs of the firm and the margin over these costs that would be charged in the absence of the cartel, then the non-cartel price can be "re-engineered" from the costs. Whist this approach is conceptually simple and intuitive, it often requires a number of strong assumptions to be made. If there is no data available on historic price-cost margins pre-cartel, the investigator needs to make some assumption about the price-cost margin without the cartel. In effect, this implies the need to make some assumptions about the nature of competition in the absence of the cartel. Would competition have been strong enough to drive prices down to the perfectly competitive outcome of price equal to marginal cost? Or would competition amongst relatively few players mean that even in the absence of the cartel the price-cost margin would be high? Certainly, there are many occasions where a naïve

---

[13]   See the Econometric Annex for a detailed explanation of econometric analysis and the standard tests.

assumption such that absent the cartel prices would equal marginal cost will not be correct. The defendants in the lysine cartel argued that the nature of the industry was such that absent the cartel, the firms would still have been able to coordinate implicitly, thus leading to relatively higher prices.[14] On the other hand, many cartels occur in industries where there is excess capacity as a result of a decline in demand and in these circumstances we might expect prices to be competed down to close to marginal cost.[15]

One possible approach to this would be to create a theoretical model of the industry in which a particular form of competition is assumed, such as that the market is characterised by Bertrand competition.[16,17] Whilst this is an economically coherent approach, it does suffer from two very significant weaknesses. The first is that the results of such an analysis are likely to be highly sensitive to the assumed mode of competition and to the estimates of elasticities used.[18] The second is that these models assume an absence of tacit collusion. As noted above, in markets with only a few players this may be a suspect assumption as firms may be tempted to price "softly" in the expectation that this pricing will be reciprocated even without an explicit cartel being in place.

Another potential pitfall of using a cost-based approach is that costs may be higher under a cartel than they would have been absent the cartel. One of the benefits of competition is that it forces firms to be cost efficient. If firms are not competing against each other, then they may become inefficient. A cartel may also allow firms to remain in the market in circumstances where they would otherwise exit.[19] For instance, in a market with excess capacity due to a reduction in demand, we should expect to see firms exit the market. However, if the market becomes cartelised, then the cartel prices may allow firms to remain profitable even though at the competitive price level they would not be profitable.

### Sanity checking

**17–014** It is important to ensure that an estimate of the cartel overcharge is consistent with the other facts that are known about the industry.[20] If entry into the industry is very easy, then it is not plausible that a cartel could raise

---

[14] Reported in Connor, "Our customers are our enemies: the lysine cartel of 1992–95" (2001) Review of Industrial Organisation, 18, 5–21.

[15] There is also the issue of measuring marginal cost. See Chapter 6 for a discussion of these issues.

[16] This mirrors the approach of most merger simulation models.

[17] See Chapter 2 for a discussion of the Bertrand model of competition.

[18] See Chapter 15 on merger simulation models for a discussion of this.

[19] This leads to the interesting possibility that in the absence of the cartel, some firms might have exited the market and this increase in concentratoin might itself have led to higher prices.

[20] Similar comments apply to *all* empirical analyses.

prices significantly above the competitive price level.[21] Equally, if there are significant imports into the market, then again it is not plausible that a domestic cartel could successfully raise prices. If there is a significant competitive fringe that is not part of the cartel, then we should not expect the cartel to be able to raise prices unless the fringe is capacity constrained and so is unable to raise prices to defeat a price increase. A high degree of price variability is also not usually considered consistent with a cartel successfully raising prices. The success of a cartel depends on all the participants adhering to the cartel price and not trying to increase their sales by undercutting the cartel price. This implies that prices should be stable in a successful cartel.

## Estimating non-cartel downstream prices: to what extent are cost increases passed on by direct purchasers

The question of what the downstream price would have been in the **17–015** absence of the cartel is equivalent to asking how much of the input cost increase suffered by direct purchasers is passed-on in the form of higher selling prices from the direct purchasers.

The first point to note is that it is almost never correct to assume that none of the input cost increase was passed on. An increase in the per unit cost of an input has the effect of increasing a firm's marginal cost of production and this will change the profit maximising price for a firm.[22] The economic literature on pass-through indicates the following:

- In a perfectly competitive market, a general input cost increase will be passed on 100 per cent. This is because in such a market firms are only just covering their costs, and so have to raise prices in response to any input cost increase to prevent them making losses. This is true for any market where competition is strong enough to push prices close to marginal costs.

- A monopolist passes on some of any input cost increase, although generally less than 100 per cent. For instance, if the monopolist faces a linear demand curve it will pass on 50 per cent of the input cost increase.

- Changes in input costs that affect only some firms will not be passed on to the same extent. This is because competition constrains the ability to pass on the cost increase. If one firm faces a cost increase but its competitors do not, it will be unlikely to be able to pass much of this on, as it will find that its prices become

---

[21]   See Chapter 3 for more details.
[22]   This is true whether the firm in question is a monopolist or is operating in a highly competitive market. See Chapter 2 for further discussion of this.

uncompetitive compared to its rivals and therefore it will risk losing business. The more elastic its demand curve, the less a firm will be able to pass on any increases in its input costs.

- In theory, pass-through can be more than 100 per cent. For instance, if firms price on the basis of a simple "cost plus percentage" approach then pass-through will be more than 100 per cent. If prices are set at, say, 10 per cent above costs then any cost increase will be passed on 110 per cent. A monopolist facing a constant elasticity demand curve would also pass cost increases on more than 100 per cent.

Given the likelihood of some of the input cost increase being passed-on, it is necessary to estimate how much is likely to have been passed-on in each particular case. There are a number of possible approaches to doing this.

**17–016**   It may be that we can be reasonably confident about the degree of pass-through based on largely theoretical observations.[23] For instance, if we know that the direct purchasing industry is very competitive with prices driven down to costs, then we would expect pass-through to be 100 per cent. Alternatively, we might know from internal documents how firms price with respect to costs. If there is evidence of cost plus pricing, then we know that pass-through may be more than 100 per cent.

However, in general the question of the degree of pass-through is an empirical question that requires an empirical answer. The standard approach is to look at the extent of pass-through in the past using econometric analysis. This would involve estimating a price equation for the downstream market and treating the coefficient on the input cost variable as a measure of the extent of pass-through. The FTC used this approach in the *Staples/Office Depot* merger. Using monthly data for two years for 30 products in 500 stores, they concluded that only 15 per cent of firm-specific cost reductions were passed on in that industry.[24]

An alternative empirical approach is possible if there have been cost shocks in the past which can be related to price changes. For example, if there had been an exchange rate shock that led to a significant change in the domestic price of an input, then the effect of this on output prices could be looked at. Our view is that this approach is in general less good than the econometric approach suggested above as it may be difficult to disentangle the effect of the input cost shock from other factors unless those other factors are also taken account of, which requires an econometric approach. However, where the data necessary for an econometric approach is not available, this approach may be reasonable.

Before leaving this issue, there are two misperceptions that we should deal with. The first is that empirically estimating the extent of pass-through

---

[23]   For a helpful discussion of the theoretical considerations, see Ten Kate and Niels (2005).
[24]   For further details, Baker and Rubinfeld (1999).

requires that an investigator focuses only on the pass-through of the costs of the cartelised product. This is not true, unless there are particular reasons to believe that the firm treats the costs of the cartelised product differently from other costs. Unless this is the case, it is reasonable to assume that any input cost increase as a result of an upstream cartel is passed-on to the same extent as any other input cost increase.

The second misperception is the argument that if the cartelised product only accounts for a small proportion of a firm's input costs, then the cartel price rise will have only a small effect on the firm's total costs and so "will not be worth passing on". This argument shows a misunderstanding of the economics of how firms set prices. If we assume that firms aim to maximise their profits, then this implies that they set their prices with regard to their variable costs and this implies that any change in those costs will affect the price they set. They do not set their prices only with regard to their larger categories of variable cost, but with regard to the totality of their variable costs.

---

**BOX 17.1: PASS-THROUGH FORMULAE**[25]                    17–017

In the main text we argued that pass-through would be 100 per cent under perfect competition with price equal to marginal cost. However, this conclusion implicitly assumed that marginal costs did not rise as output rises. If marginal costs increase as output increases, then pass-through will be less than 100 per cent. Specifically, the proportion of the cost increase passed-through, $\tau$, will be:

$$(3) \quad \tau = \frac{1}{1 - \varepsilon w}$$

where   $\varepsilon$ is the market elasticity of demand; and
$w$ is the elasticity of supply (i.e. the proportionate rise in marginal cost when output increases by 1 per cent).

When $w = 0$, which was the assumption in the main text, then pass-through is 100 per cent. However, when $w$ is positive, meaning that marginal costs rise as output rises, then pass-through will be less than 100 per cent.

It is also possible to derive an analytic solution for Cournot competition. If the elasticity of demand rises as price rises, which is the standard assumption, then pass-through can be less under Cournot competition than under perfect competition. Specifically:

$$(4) \quad \tau = \frac{1}{1 - \varepsilon w - \frac{\eta - 1}{\varepsilon N}}$$

---

[25]   For more details on the issues dealt with in this box, see van Dijk and Verboven (2008).

> where   N is the number of firms; and
>           $\eta$ is the elasticity of $\varepsilon$ (i.e. the extent to which the price elas-
>           ticity of demand changes as price increases).
>
> If $\eta$ is zero (i.e. a constant elasticity demand curve), then the third
> term of the denominator is negative and so pass-through is greater
> than under perfect competition. If $\eta$ is one, then pass-through is the
> same as under perfect competition. If $\eta$ is greater than 1, then pass-
> through is less than under perfect competition. This would be the case
> if the demand curve was linear as in this case it can be shown that
> $\eta = 1 - \varepsilon$.

## Output effect

**17–018**   We noted above that any increase in output prices downstream will lead to
a reduction in demand for the downstream product and that this is one of
the three components of damages. We also noted that the output effect and
the passing-on effect will to some extent counteract each other. The greater
the level of pass-through, and hence the less the reduction in margin on
those sales that are still made, the greater the reduction in sales (i.e. the
greater the output effect) for any given demand curve.

The extent to which demand falls as prices rise is given by the firm's
elasticity of demand. If prices rise by 5 per cent and the elasticity of
demand is two, then sales will fall by 10 per cent. So the obvious way to
estimate the output effect is to estimate the firm's elasticity of demand and
then use this to estimate by how much higher sales would have been in the
absence of any pass-through. The elasticity can be estimated econometrically or it may be that the firm already has estimates of its elasticity.

However, this approach treats the extent of pass-through and the extent
to which sales decline as a result of a price increase as two independent
questions. In reality, as we noted above, they are necessarily intertwined.
The extent of the decline in sales depends on the firm's elasticity of
demand, but so does its profit maximising level of pass-through. This can
be illustrated with reference to the Lerner equation.[26]

$$(5) \quad \frac{Price - Marginal\ Cost}{Price} = \frac{-1}{\varepsilon}$$

The Lerner equation states that at the profit maximising equilibrium for a
single-product firm, its price-marginal cost margin is equal to the inverse of
its elasticity of demand. Equation (5) means that if we assume the firm is
profit maximising, then knowing the firm's price and marginal cost with the
cartelised input means that we also know the firm's elasticity of demand. If

---

[26]   As noted elsewhere, the Lerner equation assumes that the firm is a single-product firm and
      that the market is characterised by a Nas equilibrium. Most firms are not single product
      firms and it is quite possible that firms are not operating in a Nash equilibrium.

we also know, or are willing to make assumptions about, how the firm's elasticity varies as its price falls, then we can estimate the price without the cartelised input.

An example should make this clearer. Suppose that a direct purchaser is currently pricing at €1.5 per unit and has marginal costs of €1.2. Equation (5) implies that its elasticity is −5. Assume that we know that the firm's demand curve is a constant elasticity demand curve and that in the absence of the cartel its marginal costs would have been €1. Equation (5) implies that if marginal costs are €1 and the elasticity is −5, then price is €1.25. This represents a 17 per cent decline in price. If the elasticity is −5 then this implies an increase in output of 85 per cent.[27] We can then calculate the output effect of the cartel on the direct purchaser as we now have estimates of price and output in the absence of the cartel.[28]

# ESTIMATING DAMAGES IN ARTICLE 82 CASES

Damages can also arise as a result of a breach of Article 82. The abuse   **17–019** could be either an exploitative abuse or an exclusionary abuse. The standard exploitative abuses are excessive pricing or anti-competitive price discrimination leading to an excessive price for a particular group of customers. Estimating damages in this case is similar to estimating them in a cartel case, with the corresponding difficulty of knowing what the counterfactual price (i.e. absent the abuse) would have been. A cost based "but for" price might be reasonable for an excessive pricing case since excessive pricing is often judged against cost benchmarks. Care needs to be taken with a price discrimination case as the apparently obvious "but for" price is probably not right. The temptation is to use the non-exploitative price charged by the dominant firm as the "but for" price. But if the dominant firm was not price discriminating, then it is likely that the uniform price that it would be setting would not be the same as the lower price that it was charging when it was price discriminating. Instead it is likely to be higher.

The estimation of damages arising from an exclusionary abuse requires a different approach. In a case where a firm has been excluded completely from a market as a result of abusive conduct, it is necessary to estimate the

---

[27]   This is not quite right. To make the exposition simpler we have here assumed that the arc elasticity is −5. In fact, with a constant elasticity of −5 and a price fall of 17%, the absolute value of the arc elasticity is more than 8.

[28]   There is an important implicit assumption associated with this approach; namely, that we have a good idea of how the firm's elasticity of demand varies as prices vary. The naïve approach above assumes that the elasticity of demand does not vary as prices fall (i.e. it assumes a constant elasticity of demand). However, in general we expect that the elasticity of demand falls as prices fall. If this is so, then our naïve approach above will an overestimate the output effect. This issue is similar to the problems that arise in merger simulation work. We discuss these at length in Chapter 15 and so do not repeat that discussion here.

value of the opportunity that the firm was excluded from (e.g. what profits it would have earned absent exclusion or by how much the value of the firm would have been higher absent the exclusion). One way to do this is to estimate the stream of profits that the firm would have earned had it not been excluded from the opportunity. This is likely to be difficult. For instance, in a refusal to deal case, the investigator would need to estimate what would have been a reasonable price for the dominant firm to charge for access. In a tying or bundling case, it will be necessary to estimate the profits that the claimant would have made in the absence of the tying or bundling by the dominant firm, which is likely to be very difficult.[29]

Another approach to estimating damages in an exclusion case is to estimate the market value of the opportunity at the time of the abuse. Our view is that the second approach is preferable, although it is not always practical. We discuss both approaches below and provide an illustration of a case in which both approaches were used.

## Estimating lost profits

**17–020**  Directly estimating the profits lost by a firm as a result of being excluded from an opportunity involves putting together a detailed model of the costs and revenues that the firm would have earned, which in turn requires an understanding of both the firm and of the market that the firm was excluded from. Whilst not simple, this is a type of analysis that firms carry out on a regular basis as part of their usual business. When a firm makes a decision on an investment, it estimates the expected profitability of the investment by estimating whether the net present value of the revenues and costs of the investment is positive. Conceptually this is a simple analysis to carry out. It merely requires estimates of the revenues and costs that will be incurred in each period and then these revenues and costs are discounted according to how far in the future they will occur. We illustrate this below.

Suppose a firm had the opportunity to make an investment at time 0 of €500 and that this investment would have yielded the firm an expected profit in each period of €100 for 10 years. What is the value of this investment at time 0? At this point the expected €100 profit per year are uncertain and so should be discounted by a rate that takes account of this level of uncertainty. A common assumption to make in the absence of information to the contrary is that the firm's cost of capital, which reflects the riskiness to investors of the firm, is a reasonable estimate of the riskiness to investors of the profits from the opportunity. Suppose this is 10 per cent. Then the net present value of the opportunity was €114. This is shown in Table 17.1.

---

[29]  See Chapter 6 for a detailed discussion of these strategies.

## Table 17.1: Value of opportunity at time 0                    17–021

| Year | Profits | Profits discounted by cost of capital of 10 per cent |
|------|---------|------------------------------------------------------|
| 0 | −500 | −500 |
| 1 | 100 | 91 |
| 2 | 100 | 83 |
| 3 | 100 | 75 |
| 4 | 100 | 68 |
| 5 | 100 | 62 |
| 6 | 100 | 56 |
| 7 | 100 | 51 |
| 8 | 100 | 47 |
| 9 | 100 | 42 |
| 10 | 100 | 39 |
| **Value to firm at Year 0** | | 114 |

Now suppose that the firm was stopped from making this investment by the anti-competitive behaviour of a competitor. What are the damages arising from that conduct? It depends on the point at which the damages are being calculated. Suppose that the estimation of the damages is taking place five years after the anti-competitive behaviour occurred. What are the damages owed to the claimant?

We know that the net present value of the investment at time 0 was 114. However, if damages are being awarded in year 5 then we need to adjust this figure by an appropriate interest rate. A common mistake is to use the firm's cost of capital, but this is wrong. The firm's cost of capital includes an allowance for the riskiness of the firm's profits. But adding interest over five years to an agreed sum does not incur risk and so the firm should not be compensated for any risk. So the figure of €114 should be discounted forward by the risk-free rate of interest available to the firm. If this is 5 per cent, then the damages awarded at year 5 should be €146. If the firm's cost of capital of 10 per cent was used instead then the estimated figure would have been more than 25 per cent too high (i.e. €184).

**17–022** **Table 17.2: The importance of using the correct discount rate**

| Value at t=0 | Value at t=5 | |
|---|---|---|
| | **Correct discount rate 5 per cent** | **Incorrect discount rate 10 per cent** |
| 114 | 146 | 184 |

If the damages were awarded in year 10, then the difference between the two figures would be significantly greater. The correct answer would be €186 and the incorrect answer would be €297, which is a 59 per cent difference.

Estimating lost profits, or the net present value of an investment that would have been made some years in the past, raises a number of potentially difficult issues. First, estimating the likely costs and revenues will be hard. Secondly, there may be issues related to the allocation of joint costs across a number of investments or markets. Thirdly, there may be controversy over the correct cost of capital or discount rate to use. Fourthly, there may be opportunity cost issues to be taken into account. If a firm was excluded from Market A and so instead entered Market B, and would not have entered Market B if it had been able to enter Market A, then the lost profits are the difference between the profits that would have been expected in Market A and those that were expected in Market B. Failure to take account of the opportunity cost of not entering Market B would have led to an over-estimate of the lost profits.

### Using observable market values

**17–023** An alternative approach is to use an observable market value to infer damage. For instance, if there was a firm in existence at the time of the abuse that operated only in the market in question and was not excluded, then the market value of that firm might provide relevant information on the value of the investment.[30] Another approach would be to try and analyse the effect of the exclusionary behaviour on the market value of the firm that was excluded. Whilst this sounds simple in principle, in practice it may be very difficult to assign changes in the market value of a firm to particular exclusionary behaviour by a rival, particularly if the excluded firm operates in a number of different markets.

### An example of the two approaches: *Crehan*

**17–024** A good example of how the two approaches can give different answers is provided by the *Crehan* case. This was an Article 81 case where the

---

[30] Although if competition was less in the market because of the exclusion of a firm, then the market value of a firm that remained in the market would likely be higher than it would have been had a firm not been excluded and hence had it faced stronger competition.

damages part of it was tried in the United Kingdom. Mr Crehan ran two public houses that were "tied" to Inntrepreneur, meaning that he had to buy his beer from Inntrepreneur. He went out of business in 1993 and gave up the leases on his two pubs at this point. He argued that he was forced out of business because the price at which Inntrepreneur sold him beer was above the competitive price level. He won his case on liability and then claimed damages. At trial he was awarded damages of £1.3m. There were three components to this figure:

1. Actual losses incurred before he went out of business in 1993: £57,000.

2. Projected lost profits for the period between 1993 and 2003: £889,000.

3. Value of lease that he would have been able to sell in 2003 if he had still been in business: £361,000.

The logic underlying this award is clear. The damages were assessed in 2003 and so they included an element for past lost profits and an element for future profits. These future profits were estimated on the basis of the market value of the leases had he still held them in 2003. Using the value of the leases as an estimate of future profits is reasonable, since the value of a lease is driven by the expected profits that can be earned by owning the lease.

The plaintiffs appealed and the Court of Appeal lowered the award substantially. The Court of Appeal argued that the correct estimate of the damage suffered by Mr Crehan from being forced out of business was the losses he made up to that point plus the value of the leases at this point (i.e. 1993) if they could have been sold without the tie. Since pub leases are bought and sold on a regular basis, this figure was observable and both sides agreed that it was £74,000 in 1993 terms. The total damages awarded were therefore £131,000.

This example illustrates two important issues. First, observable market values should be used when available. The fact that the value of the leases in 1993 was £74,000 undermines entirely the suggestion that the owner of the leases could have earned profits of £889,000 over the following ten years. Secondly, it is important to confirm that calculated damages are consistent with the facts of the market. When entry into a market is easy, it is not plausible to argue that being excluded from the market leads to significant lost profits. This is because when entry is easy, prices will be driven down to the competitive level and profits will be low. The barriers to entry to becoming a publican are not high and so we would not in general expect publicans to make significant profits.

## At what point in time should damages be assessed?

**17–025**  Whilst it may be uncontroversial that the purpose of compensatory damages is to put the claimant in the same position as they would have been without the anti-competitive act, care has to be taken when considering at what point in time compensatory damages should be assessed.

Fisher and Romaine (1990)[31] provide a nice illustration of the issue. Suppose that when Janis Joplin left High School she signed the yearbook of one of her classmates. This was before she had become famous. Suppose that the signed yearbook was then stolen by another student. Ten years later, by which time Janis Joplin had become famous, it was discovered who had stolen the yearbook but the yearbook itself had been lost. Assume that at the time at which the yearbook was stolen it was worth $5 and that Janis Joplin's signature was considered worthless, but that ten years later a yearbook signed by Janis Joplin was worth $1,000. How should compensatory damages be assessed?

It is very tempting to argue that compensatory damages should be set at $1,000 since in the absence of the offence, the original owner of the yearbook would have an asset valued at $1,000. However, this would be wrong. The key to compensatory damages is that they should be assessed based on the evidence available at the time of the offence. In this case, the evidence is that the value of the yearbook was $5, not $1,000. The owner of the yearbook would have accepted $5 for it and so this is the loss that the owner has suffered. This $5 would have included the owner's valuation of the possibility that one of the signatures in the yearbook would become valuable, but obviously that was an uncertain value and discounted to very little in present value terms. So the correct answer is that compensatory damages should be set at $5, discounted forward at the risk-free rate for ten years.

**17–026**  Some people find this answer unsatisfactory, but the underlying logic is actually the same as discussed above in the section on discount rates. In that case it seemed uncontroversial that the net present value of the opportunity that the claimant was unable to pursue should be set at the expected value of the opportunity at the point at which the claimant would have invested. Since the claimant was unable to make the investment, we do not know what value the investment would actually have returned. It might have returned the expected $100 per year for ten years, but it might have returned nothing, or $200 per year, or $100 for more than ten years, or any number of other possibilities. However, for compensating the claimant for its loss it is right to use the expected value of the opportunity at the time of the offence. The example above is conceptually no different.

---

[31]   Fisher and Romaine (1990).

## Other potential damage claimants

So far in this chapter we have focused on estimating the damages of a firm   **17–027**
that was the direct recipient of the anti-competitive behaviour (i.e. the
direct purchaser in a cartel case or the firm that was directly harmed in an
Article 82 case). However, there are a number of other groups who are also
harmed by anti-competitive conduct.

### Indirect purchasers

These are purchasers who buy from the firm that was directly harmed by   **17–028**
the anti-competitive behaviour. These can either be final consumers or
other firms that buy an input from the direct purchasers. The analysis of
damages for other firms is the same as for direct purchasers and so in this
section we concentrate on final consumers. There are two elements to the
harm suffered by final consumers. First, there is the direct effect of paying
more for a product than they would have done in the absence of the cartel.
Secondly, there is the loss of consumer welfare as a result of buying less of
the product than they otherwise would have done. We refer to this as the
output effect. These two elements are illustrated in Figure 17.5.

### Figure 17.5: Harm to indirect purchasers                    17–029

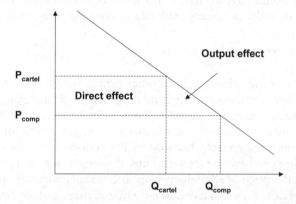

The calculation of the direct effect is conceptually the same as the calculation of the direct effect for a direct purchaser. It is just the increase in the
price due to the anti-competitive behaviour ($P_{cartel}-P_{comp}$ in Figure 17.5)
multiplied by the amount actually bought ($Q_{cartel}$ in Figure 17.5). However, the output effect is different from the output effect discussed above
for direct purchasers. The output effect for consumers is the consumer
surplus that consumers would have earned on those units that they would
have bought at $P_{comp}$ but which they do not buy at $P_{cartel}$. This is the area
under the demand curve but above $P_{comp}$ between $Q_{cartel}$ and $Q_{comp}$. Since
the demand curve maps the willingness to pay of consumers, this area is the

summation of the consumer's willingness to pay for the product less what the consumer would have had to pay. It is therefore the consumer surplus that is foregone due to the anti-competitively high price. Although this area can be estimated if the investigator knows the shape of the demand curve and the level of the over-charge (i.e. knows $P_{comp}$), it is rarely included in damages claims, which instead focus only on the direct effect. As a matter of theory, there is no justification for this.

### Non-purchasers

**17–030**   Another group who suffers harm from anti-competitive behaviour is the group of consumers who do not buy a product that they would have bought in the absence of the anti-competitive behaviour. If anti-competitive behaviour leads to the price of a product rising, there will be a group of purchasers who do not buy the product at the raised price but who would have bought it at the lower price. The harm suffered by this group is measured by the consumer surplus that this group would have generated at the lower price.

Although the logic of the harm caused to this group is clear, in practice it is extremely difficult to make such damages claims. This is because of the need to show that a potential purchaser who did not buy the product at the raised price would have bought it at the lower price. Whilst there may be occasions where the necessary evidence is available, these will be rare.

### Purchasers from other firms

**17–031**   Consumers or firms who buy from other firms can still be harmed by the anti-competitive behaviour of a firm or group of firms. Suppose that a group of firms engaged in cartel behaviour and successfully raised their prices. One effect of this is that firms that are competitors to the cartel may be able to raise their prices because of the reduction in the competitive constraint imposed by the cartel. Thus if widgets and gadgets are substitutes and the price of all widgets rises, the manufacturers of gadgets may raise their prices. This will harm those who purchase gadgets, even though the gadget manufacturers have not themselves behaved in an anti-competitive manner. A second effect is that some purchasers will switch to less good substitutes in response to the price rise. So if the price of widgets rises, some purchasers will switch to gadgets. They are harmed even if the price of gadgets does not rise because they are less well off buying gadgets than they were buying widgets at the previous lower price. This must be the case since otherwise these buyers would have already been buying gadgets.[32]

---

[32]   The only exception to this would be those consumers who were exactly indifferent between buying widgets or gadgets at the original prices.

Both of these sources of harm are conceptually clear and should in principle be quantifiable. This will particularly be the case if it is possible to show clearly that the rise in the price of a product due to anti-competitive behaviour was associated with a subsequent rise in the price of a substitute product.

### Suppliers

Firms that provide inputs to a firm that has raised its prices anti-compe- **17-032** titively will be harmed. The price rise will lower demand for the product and this will lower the demand for the inputs required to produce the product. If it is possible to estimate the reduction in demand for the downstream product due to the price rise, it should be possible to estimate the reduction in demand upstream for the input and hence to estimate damages.

## SUMMARY

The key to estimating damages from anti-competitive behaviour is to **17-033** understand what the situation would have been without the anti-competitive behaviour. In a cartel case this is the price that would have prevailed in the absence of the cartel. In an exclusionary Article 82 case this is the situation that would have prevailed without the exclusion.

Estimating cartel damages requires more than just estimating the extent of the over-charge and calculating the extra cost incurred by the downstream firm from buying its inputs at an inflated price. It is also necessary to take account of the effect of the higher input price on the downstream firm's selling price (i.e. passing on effect) and hence its downstream sales. In general a proportion of the overcharge will be passed on and there will be an effect of this on the firm's sales and profits. This effect is often incorrectly omitted from damages claims.

Damages that arise from exclusionary behaviour typically require a rather different approach to be taken as they require the estimation of the profits that a firm that was excluded would have earned if the market situation had been different. There is a danger that such estimations can become speculative and so it is important to base them on observable market values wherever possible.

Finally, it is important that any damages estimates are consistent with the known facts of the industry. Thus, if an industry is highly competitive with very low profits, it is not plausible that a firm that is excluded from the industry has suffered large damages from being denied a highly profitable opportunity. Equally, if it is very easy to enter a market and there is a high level of imports, it is not plausible to argue that a domestic cartel has successfully raised prices significantly.

# Econometric Annex: Introducing multiple regression analysis as a tool of antitrust policy

## INTRODUCTION

**AN–001** As noted in Part I and illustrated in Part II, asessing the competitiveness of an industry in the context of a competition law inquiry is a complex task. A number of factors, including, inter alia, the number of competing firms, the effectiveness of other products to act as substitutes and the ease with which new firms can enter the market, all need to be taken into consideration. In other words, there are multitudinous, interdependent factors that determine the nature of competition between firms. In undertaking the competitive assessment, a number of different empirical questions often arise, including the following: "What is the own-price elasticity of demand?", "How large a competitive constraint does Firm A impose on Firm B?", "Are prices higher when concentration is higher?", "Does new entry lead to lower prices?".

Econometric analysis consists of a set of quantitative tools employing statistical methods which are used to construct representational models of real-world competitive relationships and, most importantly, to test these alleged relationships. Therefore, in principle, it represents a powerful empirical tool to address such questions since econometric models enable one to take into account the numerous factors which are believed to affect competition (subject to data restrictions) and to estimate the economic importance of each of these factors.

Econometric analysis has been used in EC competition law investigations for many years. For instance, Hilti introduced econometric evidence on relevant market definition in *Eurofix-Bauco/Hilti* in 1987[1] whilst it played a central role in market definition in the *Procter & Gamble/VP Schickedanz*,[2] *Kimberley-Clark/Scott Paper*[3] and *Guinness/Grand Metropolitan*[4] mergers. More recently, there has been substantial econometric

---

[1]   IV/30.787 *Eurofix-Bauco/Hilti* [1989] 4 C.M.L.R. 677; [1988] OJ L65/19.
[2]   IV/M430 *Procter & Gamble/VP Schickedanz* [1994] OJ L354/32.
[3]   IV/M623 *Kimberley-Clark/Scott Paper* [1996] OJ L183/1.
[4]   IV/M938 *Guinness/Grand Metropolitan* [1997] 5 C.M.L.R. 760; [1998] OJ L288/24.

analysis carried out in *Ryanair/Aer Lingus*,[5] *GE Instrumentarium*[6] and *Oracle/Peoplesoft*.[7] It is also used in Article 81 and Article 82 inquiries. For instance, econometric analysis is routinely used in cartel cases for assessing what the price would have been absent the cartel (see Chapter 5 for further discussion of this), whilst it played an important role in market defintion in the recent *AstraZeneca*[8] Article 82 case.

The purpose of this Annex is not to give a guide to "doing econo-   **AN–002** metrics". Such a guide is beyond the scope of this book. The principal aim here is to provide an intuitive understanding of econometric analysis. We aim to provide an understanding of what is being shown by a particular set of econometric results. Moreover, we present and discuss the statistical tools that permit an initial appraisal of the quality of an econometric analysis. While there are good and bad econometric analyses, there is also a whole battery of tests that allow discrimination between good and bad econometric analyses. It is simply untrue to say, as is often claimed, that econometric analysis can be used to prove "anything".

The layout of this Annex is as follows. We introduce the basic form that econometric analysis takes in paras AN–003—AN–006. The discussion takes place at a largely intuitive level. We then provide four examples of the use of econometric analysis in past decisions in paras AN–007—AN–013. The purpose of this section is to provide context for the material in the rest of this Annex. Paragraphs AN–014—AN–039 contain advice on how to appraise the validity of an econometric model. Paragraphs AN–040—AN–043 contains a worked example of how to appraise a model. Paragraphs AN–044—AN–049 is a more advanced section dealing with some technical aspects related to estimating elasticities. A summary is given in para.AN–050.

# BASIC ECONOMETRIC ANALYSIS

This section introduces the standard econometric tool, multiple regression   **AN–003** analysis. Although this technique can be used for a variety of purposes in EC competition law, we illustrate the use of multiple regression analysis with reference to the estimation of the elasticity of demand. The own-price elasticity facing a firm is simply a way of describing the slope of the demand curve facing that firm. Estimating the elasticity facing a firm using multiple regression analysis is therefore an attempt to estimate the demand curve facing the firm. Since it is not known exactly how much of a given product is demanded at each price, an estimate based on the available observations

---

[5]   COMP/M.4439 *Ryanair/Aer Lingus* (June 27, 2007).
[6]   COMP/M/3083 *GE/Instrumentarium* (September 2, 2003).
[7]   COMP/M.3216 *Oracle/Peoplesoft* (October 26, 2004).
[8]   COMP/A. 37.507/F3 *AstraZeneca* (June 15, 2005).

of price and quantity is derived. If information on the price and sales of a
product over a number of periods or across many markets is available, a
reasonable estimate of the demand curve facing the firm can often be
derived. Figure Annex.1 shows two sets of price and quantity data and
estimates of the corresponding demand curves.

**AN–004**  **Figure Annex.1: Deriving demand curves from price and
quantity data**

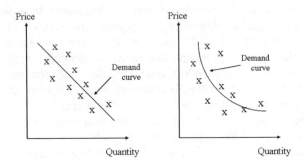

Notice that neither of the two demand curves in Figure Annex.1 pass
directly through all the observed price-quantity pairs in the data set. This
will always be the case due to unobserved factors that influence demand.
There is no reason to expect that actual demand curves will have con-
venient shapes (such as straight lines or smooth curves) and collecting data
accurately is also not easy. For instance, it is rare for there to be a single
uniform price across the whole geographic market at any particular point in
time. Different retail outlets are likely to set slightly different prices, there
will be various discounts offered and so on. In nearly all circumstances, the
issue of concern is to estimate the "best fit line" through the available data.

The principal tool of econometrics is known as multiple regression
analysis. Multiple regression analysis seeks to "explain" how one variable is
determined by a group of other variables. To use statistical terminology,
multiple regression analysis tries to determine the causal link that flows
from a number of "independent variables" to a "dependent variable". On
the basis of observed data, multiple regression analysis tries to find the
relationship between the dependent variable and the independent variables
that best "explains" the dependent variable. Figure Annex.1 shows simple,
two-dimensional relationships between quantity and price. Multiple
regression analysis enables more complicated relationships that include
more variables to be estimated. For instance, it might be believed that sales
are affected not just by price, but also by advertising, time of year, state of
the economy and so on. Multiple regression analysis in principle allows all
these factors to be taken into account.

Multiple regression analysis begins by postulating a relationship of the following form.

(1)  *Dependent variable = Some function of independent variables*

For example, the following very simple relationship might be postulated.

(2)  *Sales of Good X = f (Price of Good X, Price of Good Y)*

This says that the level of sales of X can be explained by reference to the price of X and the price of another (substitute) product, Y. Suppose that every time the price of X rises by 1 unit, sales of X fall by 5 units, but that every time the price of Y rises by 1 unit, sales of X rise by 3. This statistical relationship can be depicted in the following way.

(3)  *Sales of Good X = 1000 – (5 x Price of Good X) + (3 x Price of Good Y)*

The figure of 1,000 (in this case chosen at random) is known as a "constant". Its role is explained later. Equation (3) is a statistical relationship between the sales of X and the price of X and Y. It can be used to calculate the level of sales of X at various different prices for X and Y (see Table Annex.1).

## Table Annex.1: Potential sales of X and Y                AN–005

| Price of X | Price of Y | Sales of X |
|------------|------------|------------|
| 50         | 100        | 1050       |
| 100        | 150        | 950        |
| 100        | 100        | 800        |
| 100        | 50         | 650        |
| 200        | 200        | 600        |
| 150        | 100        | 550        |

In this example it was assumed that the effect a rise in the price of X and Y had on sales of X was known. Multiple regression analysis enables one to *estimate* such effects from a data set. If the effect of the prices of X and Y on sales of X was unknown, but data such as that in Table Annex.1 was available, then the effect could be estimated. In this case, the analysis would start from an initial equation of the following form.

(4)  *Sales of $X_t = \alpha + \beta$ Price of $X_t + \gamma$ Price of $Y_t$*

This equation states that sales of X at any given time (denoted by the subscript t) depend on a constant, on the price of X at that time and on the price of Y at that time. The Greek symbols in Equation (4) are called *coefficients* and represent the effect of the relevant variable on the dependent variable. In the example, $\beta$ was equal to −5 and $\gamma$ was equal to +3.

So far it has been assumed that the sales of X can be entirely explained by the price of X and Y. In reality, as shown in Figure Annex.1 it will not be possible to include in the analysis all of the many factors that affect a dependent variable. This means that the group of independent variables will not explain completely the dependent variable. This is noted by including an *error term* in the equation. So Equation (4) becomes:

(5)   *Sales of $X_t$ = α + β Price of $X_t$ + γ Price of $Y_t$ + $\varepsilon_t$*

where   $\varepsilon_t$ is the error term at time t.

This is illustrated in Figure Annex.2. This shows the relationship between sales of a product and its price. The Xs denote observed combinations of price and sales. In the left-hand figure, the relationship is exactly linear and the line of best fit passes directly through all eight data points. In the right-hand figure the relationship is not perfectly linear. The best fit line does not pass through all eight data points (or, indeed, any of them). The distance from each data point to the line of best fit is called a *deviation*. These deviations are represented by $\varepsilon_t$ in Equation (5).

## AN–006 Figure Annex.2: The issue of error terms and the line of best fit

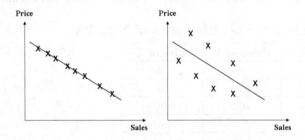

Figure Annex.2 illustrates an important intuition in multiple regression analysis. Broadly speaking, any (multiple) regression analysis is an attempt to draw a line of best fit through a data set. When there is only one independent variable, this line of best fit can be shown as above. When there are two independent variables, the best fit line would need to be shown in three dimensions. Three independent variables requires four dimensions, four requires five dimensions and so on. However, the important point is that multiple regression analysis calculates the line of best fit through multidimensional space.[9]

In summary, multiple regression analysis is a statistical technique that allows the individual effect of a number of variables (the independent variables) on the dependent variable to be estimated. It does this by calculating the line of best fit through the data. Four examples of the use of multiple regression analysis in competition cases are presented below. The aim is to motivate the following discussion.

---

[9]   Technically speaking this usually involves calculating the line that minimises the sum of the squared deviations of the data points from the estimated line of best fit, a technique called Ordinary Least Squares (OLS).

# FOUR EXAMPLES OF MULTIPLE REGRESSION ANALYSIS

In this section we present four short case studies of the use of multiple **AN–007** regression analysis in competition law cases. The first case study is an example of the use of multiple regression to estimate elasticities that are then used as part of the market definition exercise. We have included this old case (1994) in order to show that econometric analysis is not a new form of analysis, but one that has been used successfully in competition law cases over many years. The second case study is an example of using econometrics to measure the degree of competitive interaction between two firms. The third is an example of using econometrics to test whether prices are lower when there are more firms competing in a particular market. The fourth is an example of estimating elasticities as part of a regulatory proceeding.

## Procter & Gamble/VP Schickedanz[10]

In January 1994, Procter and Gamble (P&G) notified the European **AN–008** Commission (EC) of the acquisition of Vereingte Papierwerke Schickedanz (VPS). VPS was a household paper products and feminine hygiene products company. P&G was also, inter alia, a household paper products and feminine hygiene products company. Whilst P&G was active throughout Western Europe, VPS was only present to a significant extent in Germany, Spain, Italy and Austria. Prior to the agreement with P&G, VPS had been in talks with Kimberly-Clark over a possible partnership: these talks collapsed in the summer of 1993.

The focus of competitive concern was in the feminine hygiene market. VPS manufactured the *Camelia* brand of sanitary towel, as well as some secondary brands and store brands. P&G manufactured the *Always* brand of sanitary towel.

In the decision, the Commission was provided with two pieces of empirical evidence that appear to have effectively defined the product market. The first was a form of shock analysis. For more details on this technique, see Chapter 13. The second was a price elasticity study supplied by Johnson & Johnson.[11] This study was based on US scanner data. Given the absence of such data in the European Union at the time, it was identified as the best available evidence on the issue of substitution between towels and tampons. The results are shown in Table Annex.2.

---

[10]  IV/M430 *Procter & Gamble/VP Schickedanz* [1994] OJ L354/32.
[11]  The study was carried out by RLS Marketing Associates.

## AN–009 Table Annex.2: Price elasticity estimate in the Fempro market (US)

| Product | Own-price elasticity | Cross-price elasticity |
|---|---|---|
| Sanitary towels | −0.5 | 0.3 |

*Source*: para.60 of the Commision decision.

The own-price elasticity of demand for sanitary towels was estimated to be −0.5. This implies that a hypothetical monopolist of all towels within a given geographic market could profitably raise prices by more than 5–10 per cent. A 10 per cent price rise would lead to a loss of demand of only 5 per cent and hence an increase in revenue of 4.5 per cent. In addition, there would be some cost savings from the reduced production. This means that on the basis of the standard market definition test towels are a separate relevant market. The Commission concluded "that there are indeed clearly separate markets ... for pads and tampons".[12]

It could be argued that these elasticity estimates were not relevant as they refer to the US market, not the German market. However, in the absence of compelling grounds to believe that consumer switching behaviour is different in the United States to Germany, the Commission appears to have considered it strong evidence (particularly as the relative usage patterns in the United States and Germany were very similar: 40:60 tampons:towels in the United States and 39:61 in Germany).[13]

### Ryanair/Aer Lingus[14]

AN–010  In 2006, Ryanair, a low-cost airline, sought to buy Aer Lingus, the Irish flag carrier. Both parties had their main hubs at Dublin airport and competed on a significant number of routes. After extensive investigation, the Commission blocked the merger. Various forms of econometric analysis played an important role in this case. We briefly outline one of these below.

The Commission carried out a multiple regression analysis to test a number of propositions. Among these were the following questions:

1. Does the presence of Ryanair on a route reduce the price charged by Aer Lingus on that route and vice versa?

2. Does Ryanair exert a stronger competitive effect on Aer Lingus than any of the other airlines operating out of Dublin and vice versa?

3. Does the price effect of Ryanair on Aer Lingus increase as the

---

[12]  IV/M430 *Procter & Gamble/VP Schickedanz* OJ L354/32 para.60.
[13]  IV/M430 *Procter & Gamble/VP Schickedanz* OJ L354/32 para.60.
[14]  COMP/M.4439 *Ryanair/Aer Lingus* (June 27, 2007).

number of frequencies offered by Ryanair increases and vice versa?

The Commission used monthly data for five years (January 2002 to December 2006). It found that Aer Lingus' prices were on average 5–8 per cent lower on those routes where Ryanair competed with Aer Lingus compared to those where Ryanair did not compete with Aer Lingus. This provides the answer to the first question above: the presence of Ryanair on a route does reduce the price charged by Aer Lingus. As regards the price effect of Aer Lingus on Ryanair, the Commission did not find a significant effect.

Using the same data, the Commission found that Ryanair had at least double the effect of any other airline on Aer Lingus' pricing. The Commission also found that a 1 per cent increase in Ryanair frequencies had the effect of decreasing Aer Lingus' prices by 0.03 per cent.[15] Thus the Commission also answered the second and third questions above.

The Commission concluded:

> "The Commission's regression analysis confirms and complements the conclusions derived from qualitative evidence that Ryanair and Aer Lingus are close competitors. Moreover the results from the regression analysis are also in line with the majority of respondents to the Customer Survey that consider the Merging Parties to be the closest competitors when other carriers are present on the route."

An important point to note about the Commission's conclusions based on the econometric analysis is that they are consistent with the other available evidence in the case. If econometric analysis is inconsistent with other evidence, this does not necessarily mean that the econometric evidence is therefore wrong, but it does mean that the authors of the econometric analysis should explain why the conclusions from the econometric evidence differ from the conclusions from the other evidence.

## Oracle/Peoplesoft[16]

The investigation into the proposed acquisition of Peoplesoft by Oracle in **AN–011** 2004 included a substantial amount of econometric analysis. The product in question was enterprise application software. In the human resources and financial management systems segments of this industry the merger was characterised, at least initially, as a three-to-two merger with only the merged entity and SAP remaining as significant players post-merger. Sales

---

[15] In order to gauge the price effect of the frequency model the Commission simulated the effects of the merger by assuming that Ryanair would withdraw completely from overlap routes post merger. Under this assumption prices would increase by up to 13.1% on overlap routes.

[16] COMP/M.3216 *Oracle/Peoplesoft* (October 26, 2004).

in this industry are made via bidding contests whereby the potential buyers ask potential suppliers to bid for sales.

In the Statement of Objections, the Commission presented econometric analysis showing that Peoplesoft appeared to offer higher discounts (i.e. lower prices) as the number of bidders rose.[17] After the Oral Hearing, Oracle provided the Commission with additional data. The Commission also gained access to some data from the parallel US proceedings. Using these data, the Commission carried out further econometric analysis. This analysis yielded two important results. First, there was a strong positive relationship between the size of the deal and the discount offered. Secondly, once this size effect was taken into account, the apparent relationship between discounts and the number of bidders that the Commission had previously identified disappeared. The Commission wrote:

> "Once the size of the deal was taken into account in the analysis the number of final bidders no longer provided any additional explanatory element over the discount offered and no general pattern emerged regarding the presence of a particular competitor prompting particularly high discounts."[18]

This example illustrates two important aspects of multiple regression analysis. One, it is a useful technique that allows investigators to take account of the effect of multiple factors. In this case, it allowed the Commission to take into account the effect of both deal size and the number of bidders. Secondly, econometric analysis that is in some sense "mis-specified" will tend to yield misleading results. We discuss this issue, and how to avoid mis-specification, in some detail below.

## UK mobile phone call termination charges

**AN–012**  During 2001 and 2002, the UK telecoms regulator, Oftel, and then the UK Competition Commission, investigated the level of mobile phone call termination charges. These are the prices that mobile network operators charge to other telecoms operators to receive calls from those other operators. Thus if a British Telecom (BT) customer calls a Vodafone mobile phone, BT pays Vodafone a call termination charge for taking the call onto the Vodafone network and routing it to the relevant mobile phone. Mobile phone networks have very large fixed costs and costs that are common to more than one service. For instance, the physical network structure is used for making calls from mobile phones, for calls to mobile phones, for SMS messages and so on. These common costs need to be recovered from the revenues from the various services. The result was that

---

[17]  COMP/M.3216 *Oracle/Peoplesoft* (October 26, 2004) para.197.
[18]  COMP/M.3216 *Oracle/Peoplesoft* (October 26, 2004) para.201.

one of the main issues in the inquiries was whether call termination charges should be set on the basis of Ramsey prices or some other cost allocation mechanism.[19] Setting prices on the basis of Ramsey principles involves estimating the elasticities of the different products or services involved. Specifically, prices should be set so that more of the fixed and common costs are recovered on those services that are relatively inelastic compared to those services that are relatively elastic.

As part of the Oftel inquiry, BT Cellnet commissioned work to estimate the relevant elasticities so that Ramsey prices could be calculated.[20] The estimation of the elasticity of demand for fixed-to-mobile calls led to the results shown below.

### Table Annex.3: Fixed-to-mobile call elasticities          AN–013

| Daytime | −0.33 |
|---|---|
| Evening | −0.76 |
| Weekend | −0.43 |
| Weighted average | −0.43 |

*Source*: Koboldt and Maldoom (2001).

The elasticity of demand for mobile originated calls was estimated as being -0.8. Using these elasticity estimates, plus cost data and estimates for the effect on a consumer's decision to subscribe to a mobile network of subscription charges, the study provided estimates of optimal Ramsey prices. These suggested, contrary to the approach suggested by Oftel, that significantly more of the fixed and common costs of a UK mobile network should be recovered from termination charges than from either the price of mobile originated calls or subscription charges.

## APPRAISING MULTIPLE REGRESSION ANALYSIS

As stated above, the purpose of this Annex is not to provide a guide to **AN–014** undertaking econometric analysis. Rather the purpose is to provide the basic framework to allow an appraisal of any econometric evidence that might be encountered during the course of an inquiry. Multiple regression analysis is only useful when the econometric model is "meaningful". By this is meant that the model includes all the major determinants of the dependent variable and that the model makes economic sense. This section discusses issues which allow one to distinguish between a good and a bad model (i.e. one whose estimates are not good estimates of reality).

---

[19] See Chapter 6 for a discussion of Ramsey pricing in the context of optimal price discrimination.
[20] Koboldt and Maldoom (2001).

The discussion begins with an illustration of how important it is that the econometric model is a reasonable description of reality.

## A biased model

**AN–015** The following is an illustration of how a poor econometric model can lead to *biased* results. By this is meant that the coefficient estimates are not close to the true values of the coefficients. A hypothetical data set has been created as part of this illustration. This data set consists of the prices for four products: A, B, C and D. These products are all substitutes for each other to some extent. A variable for the sales of A has been constructed. Sales of A depend on the prices of A, B, C and D but also on whether it is Christmas or not. At Christmas, sales of A rise by about 40 per cent above their average level and then fall to about 30 per cent below their average level immediately after Christmas. The price of A is typically raised by about 10 per cent at Christmas. It is assumed that ten years of quarterly data are available, giving 40 data points in all.

The correct elasticities in the model are shown in Table Annex.4.

**AN–016 Table Annex.4: Correct elasticities**

| Product | Own-price elasticity | Cross-price elasticity with respect to the price of | | |
|---------|---------------------|----|----|----|
| | | **B** | **C** | **D** |
| **A** | −5.0 | 0.75 | 1.25 | 2.0 |

The own-price elasticity of Product A is −5.0. This implies that a 5 per cent increase in price would lead to a 25 per cent decline in sales and so a decline in revenue of 21 per cent.

As noted above, sales are also affected by Christmas and the period immediately after Christmas. The above results are derived from a model that included these factors. Thus the model was[21]:

(6)  *Sales of* $A_t = \alpha + \beta_1$ *Price of* $A_t + \beta_2$ *Price of* $B_t + \beta_3$ *Price of* $C_t$
$+ \beta_4$ *Price of* $D_t + \beta_5 Q4_t + \beta_6 Q1_t + \varepsilon_t$

The meaning of most of the variables in Equation (6) is straightforward,[22] but we should explain $Q1_t$ and $Q4_t$. They are both *dummy* variables. $Q4_t$ has a value of 1 in the quarter before Christmas and a value of zero at all other times. $Q1_t$ has a value of 1 in the quarter after Christmas, but is zero at all other times.

---

[21]  For technical reasons, in practice we should include a variable for total segment expenditure in this equation. We omit it here for reasons of clarity. We return to this issue at para.AN–045 below.

[22]  The model was estimated in logarithms and so the coefficients on the price variables can be simply interpreted as elasticities. See Box 1 below for further explanation.

Now suppose that the elasticities from a model that excluded the variables for Christmas and for the period immediately after Christmas were estimated. In this case the model would be:

(7)  *Sales of $A_t$ = $\alpha$ + $\beta_1$ Price of $A_t$ + $\beta_2$ Price of $B_t$ + $\beta_3$ Price of $C_t$ + $\beta_4$ Price of $D_t$ + $\varepsilon_t$*

This model produces rather different results. The results from this equation are shown in Table Annex.5.

## Table Annex.5: Incorrect elasticities AN–017

| Product | Own-price elasticity | Cross-price elasticity with respect to the price of | | |
|---|---|---|---|---|
| | | **B** | **C** | **D** |
| **A** | −1.76 | 1.59 | 2.22 | 1.34 |

The most important result from this table is that the own-price elasticity estimate is now only −1.76, rather than the correct value of −5.0 (i.e. a decline of 65 per cent). This incorrect result would have important implications for market definition. Suppose investigators were considering whether Product A should be considered as a separate relevant market. Further, suppose that they know from internal company documents that Firm A's price-cost margin is 20 per cent. If the investigators use the price-cost margin of 20 per cent and the own price elasticity estimate of −1.76 to define the relevant market, then they will find that Product A is a separate relevant market. A 5 per cent SSNIP would lead to a decline in sales of 8.8 per cent and in revenue of 4.2 per cent. But if sales decline by 8.8 per cent in response to a 5 per cent SSNIP, this will be a profitable SSNIP as long as the price-cost margin of the firm is less than 52 per cent.[23] Since the price-cost margin is actually only 20 per cent, the SSNIP would apparently be profitable. But note that the investigators reach this conclusion only because they have an incorrect elasticity estimate. If they used the correct one (−5), they would find that the 5 per cent SSNIP was not profitable. If price rises by 5 per cent and the price-cost margin is 20 per cent, then this will be unprofitable if and only if the resultant decline in sales is more than 20 per cent.[24] By assumption in this case, it will be since the own-price elasticity is −5, so a 5 per cent price increase will reduce sales by 25 per cent.

Equation (7) produces incorrect results because it has omitted two variables that are important determinants of the dependent variable (i.e. sales). The result is that the coefficient estimate of the own-price elasticity

---

[23]  For an explanation and derivation of this result, see the discussion of critical loss analysis in Chapter 11.
[24]  As above, see the discussion of critical loss analysis in Chapter 11 for an explanation of this result.

is biased. In this example, the bias was enough to lead to an incorrect market definition. In the remainder of this Annex the tools needed to be able to appraise an econometric model are discussed.

AN–018

> ## BOX ANNEX.1: FUNCTIONAL FORM
>
> The variables in a multiple regression can be transformed in a number of ways. The illustration used in Equation (3) above was in *levels*, i.e. the variables were included in the model without any transformations. An alternative *functional form* is not to include the variables in levels, but to include them in *logarithms*. This consists of converting each variable into its natural logarithm and then using these in the multiple regression equation. One of the advantages of doing this is that the coefficients on variables that have been transformed into logs are elasticities. Consider the following simple regression equation:
>
> (8)   $Sales_t = 100 - 4\ Price_t + Errorterm_t$
>
> If this equation is in levels, then when price rises by 1 unit, sales fall by 4 units. However, if the variables were in logs, the model would have a different interpretation. It would then mean that a rise in price by 1 per cent would lead to a fall in sales of 4 per cent.
>
>   For technical reasons, variables are sometimes transformed into *first differences*. This consists of calculating the change in the variable each time period. When variables are transformed into first differences, the coefficients usually have the same interpretation to when they are in levels. However, when variables are in first differences, it is not possible to know the value of the dependent variable at any point in time without knowing its past value. Thus, in the equation above, we can calculate the prediction for sales if we know the price. However, if the equation was in first differences, it would be:
>
> (9)   $Sales_t - Sales_{t-1} = 4(Price_t - Price_{t-1}) + Errorterm_t - Errorterm_{t-1}$
>
> Since the intercept (of 100) drops out in this equation, it is not possible to provide a prediction of sales at time t without knowing what sales were in an earlier period.

## Coefficients, t-statistics and t-values

AN–019 If a model is formulated and the data is available, multiple regression analysis will provide estimates of the coefficients even if the model is nonsense. For example, suppose that the variable of interest (the dependent variable) is the monthly rainfall in Germany and the independent variables are the German money supply and German inflation. This is clearly a silly model, but if multiple regression analysis is undertaken it will provide estimates of the effect of the money supply on rainfall in Germany!

So an extremely important question is how can a good model be identified and how can the coefficient estimates be evaluated. The second of these questions is considered first.

Multiple regression analysis does not only provide estimates of coefficients, it also provides estimates of how precisely the coefficients are estimated. These estimates are known as *standard errors*. Suppose that an elasticity has been estimated as being −5.0. A critical issue is how close is this estimate to the true coefficient? The standard error provides an answer. There is a 95 per cent probability that the true parameter lies within about two standard errors of the estimated coefficient. So if the standard error is 0.5 and the coefficient estimate is −5.0, then, with 95 per cent probability, the true parameter lies between about −4.0 and −6.0. With a slightly lower probability (90 per cent), the true parameter lies within about 1.64 standard errors of the estimated coefficient (i.e. between −4.18 and −5.82 in the example). The interval within which there is a given probability that the true coefficient lies is known as the *confidence interval*. In this example, the 95 per cent confidence interval is −4.0 to −6.0, whilst the 90 per cent confidence interval is between −4.18 and −5.82.[25]

A concept that is closely related to the standard error is that of the *t-statistic*. The t-statistic is the coefficient estimate divided by the standard error of the coefficient. Thus, if the coefficient estimate is −5.0 and the standard error is 0.5, then the t-statistic is −10. The t-statistic is useful for seeing how certain one can be that the true value of a particular coefficient is not zero. Suppose that the estimate of a coefficient is 1 and the standard error is 2. This implies that the 95 per cent confidence interval for the coefficient runs from −3 to +5. This means that one cannot be sure that the true coefficient is not zero (i.e. the relevant independent variable has no effect on the dependent variable) or even that it is not of the opposite sign to the estimated coefficient. Note that in this case the t-statistic is 0.5 (i.e. 1 divided by 2). On the other hand, if the standard error was 0.25, then the 95 per cent confidence interval would run from 0.5 to 1.5 and one can be almost certain that the true coefficient was greater than zero. This means that one could be almost certain that the relevant variable is a determinant of the dependent variable and that the sign of the estimated coefficient is correct. Note that the t-statistic in this case is 4 (i.e. 1 divided by 0.25).

Where the t-statistic for an estimated coefficient is greater than 2 (or less **AN–020** than −2) then one can be almost certain (95 per cent certain) that the true coefficient is not zero and that the sign of the estimated coefficient is the same as the sign of the true coefficient. Similarly, if the t-statistic is greater than 1.64 (or less than −1.64) one can be 90 per cent sure that the true coefficient is not zero and that the estimated coefficient has the same sign

---

[25] The exact number of standard errors that make up the 95% and 90% confidence intervals depends on the exact number of data points available. As the number of available data points becomes large, the relevant figures are 1.96 and 1.64. For smaller numbers of data points, the relevant figures are slightly above these numbers.

as the true coefficient. If the t-statistic is above 2 (or below −2) the coefficient estimate is said to be *statistically significant at the 5 per cent level*. Equally, if the t-statistic is above 1.64 (or below −1.64) the coefficient estimate is said to be *statistically significant at the 10 per cent level*.

Returning to the example of a nonsense regression of money supply and inflation on rainfall in Germany, it should be expected that the t-statistics for the coefficients on money supply and inflation will be less than 2, i.e. that the t-statistics will show that one cannot be certain that the true coefficients on these two variables are not zero (which is of course what one intuitively believes to be the case).

The use of standard errors and t-statistics can be illustrated by returning to the earlier example in which the own-price elasticity of Product A and three cross-price elasticities for Product A were estimated. Neither the t-statistics nor standard errors of these elasticity estimates were reported above. This omission is remedied in Table Annex.6.

**AN–021 Table Annex.6: Full details of our example regression**

| | Coefficient estimate | Standard error | t-Statistic | 95 per cent Confidence interval | |
|---|---|---|---|---|---|
| | | | | Lower | Upper |
| **Constant** | 9.81 | 0.671 | 14.62 | 8.44 | 11.17 |
| **Q1** | −0.30 | 0.005 | −57.37 | −0.31 | −0.29 |
| **Q4** | 0.40 | 0.016 | 25.69 | 0.37 | 0.43 |
| **Own Price** | −4.99 | 0.089 | −55.97 | −5.17 | −4.81 |
| **Price B** | 0.80 | 0.097 | 8.21 | 0.60 | 1.00 |
| **Price C** | 1.38 | 0.126 | 10.97 | 1.13 | 1.64 |
| **Price D** | 1.96 | 0.092 | 21.30 | 1.77 | 2.14 |

The fourth column of Table Annex.6 shows that all the coefficient estimates are statistically significant at the 5 per cent level: in none of the cases does the 95 per cent confidence interval contain 0. It is also clear that the size of the confidence intervals around the various coefficient estimates vary considerably. The confidence interval for the effect of the period after Christmas (i.e. $Q1_t$) is very small (−0.29 to −0.31) whereas that for the cross-price elasticity with respect to the price of Product C is rather larger (1.13 to 1.64). Thus, one can be pretty sure that the true coefficient for the effect of the period after Christmas is close to the estimated coefficient, whereas one cannot be so sure that the same is true for the cross-price elasticity estimate.

It is important to take note of the size of the confidence interval when dealing with coefficient estimates. However, the estimated coefficient will be the central estimate within the confidence interval and is the most likely to be correct. Thus if a coefficient estimate is 5.0, then it is more likely that the true parameter is 5.0 than that it is 4.99, or 5.01. Further, it is more likely that the true parameter is close to the estimated coefficient than that it is far away, even within the confidence interval. There is about a 70 per cent chance that the true coefficient is within one standard error of the estimate, and about a 50 per cent chance that the true parameter is within two-thirds of one standard error of the estimate.

One factor that influences the size of the confidence intervals around a coefficient estimate is the *degrees of freedom* of the model. The degrees of freedom of a model relate to the relative proportions of data periods compared to coefficients to be estimated. If you have N periods and x coefficients to estimate, then the degrees of freedom of the regression is N–x–1. Thus if you have 30 periods of data and five coefficients to be estimated, then the degrees of freedom is 24. The fewer degrees of freedom that you have, the less precise will be your estimates. This makes intuitive sense: the more coefficients you need to estimate from a given amount the data, the less precise your estimates will be as the data is having to "do more work".

## *Warning*

A word of warning about standard errors and t-statistics is appropriate. The **AN–022**
accurate calculation of standard errors (and, by definition, of t-statistics) depends on a number of assumptions about the econometric model holding. Two of the most commonly violated assumptions are the assumptions of *normality* and of *homoskedasticity*. These issues, and others, are discussed below. Suffice to say that it is not enough for a t-statistic to be above 2 (or below −2) for it to indicate statistical significance. It is also necessary for it to be an appropriately measured t-statistic. For this reason the econometric basis of the t-statistics should always be checked. A competent econometrician will always report the necessary information for this appraisal to be carried out. For more details, see paras AN–029—AN–034 below.

## *Statistical significance and economic significance*

It is important to note that statistical significance is not the same as eco-  **AN–023**
nomic significance. A coefficient can be statistically significant, but be so small as not to be of economic importance. Equally, a coefficient might be statistically insignificant but large enough to be of economic importance. Suppose that as part of a merger investigation it is of interest to establish whether increases in concentration in a particular industry are associated with raised prices. One way to investigate this might be to carry out a multiple regression analysis in which the dependent variable was price and one of the independent variables was concentration. Suppose the coefficient on concentration was 0.01 (indicating that a 100 per cent increase in concentration would raise prices by 1 per cent)[26] and this was statistically

---

[26] This assumes that the log of price is regressed against the log of concentration.

significant with a t-statistic of 2.5. This implies that it is almost certain that increases in concentration raise prices, but it also implies that they raise prices by so little that it is of little competitive concern. On the basis of the coefficient of 0.01, a merger that raised concentration by 50 per cent would still only raise prices by 0.5 per cent. Even if the true coefficient was at the top end of the confidence interval (i.e. about 0.018[27]), the merger would still only raise prices by 0.9 per cent (i.e. 50 * 0.018).

Now suppose that the coefficient on concentration was 1.0 (indicating that a 100 per cent increase in concentration would raise prices by 100 per cent), but that it was statistically insignificant with a t-statistic of 1.5. How should these results be interpreted? The best estimate for the effect of the merger on prices is now that it would raise prices by 50 per cent, but because of the relatively large standard error the effect on prices cannot be known with any degree of certainty. The possibility that prices would fall cannot be ruled out since the confidence interval for the coefficient does go negative. However, the possibility of the merger leading to a 50 per cent price increase is certainly economically significant, even though it is not statistically significant. If the true coefficient was at the top end of the confidence interval, then the merger would lead to prices rising by 117 per cent.[28] In this case, the results of the analysis are of concern, even though they are not statistically significant, in a way that the results of the earlier analysis were not of concern, even though they were statistically significant. This is not to say that an investigator should therefore believe that there is a concern, but rather that more work needs to be carried out either to confirm that there is a genuine danger of prices rising post-merger or to confirm that there is not. The mere fact of statistical insignificance in this example is not enough to dismiss the concerns.

**AN–024**  There appears to be an unwritten assumption in much of the economic literature that statistical significance equates to economic significance. McCloskey and Ziliak (1996) have noted that there is a widespread tendency in the economic literature to confuse statistical significance with economic significance. Indeed, they claim that only 30 per cent of the papers using regression analysis that were published in the American Economic Review, a major academic journal, in the 1980s made this distinction. That is, 70 per cent equated statistical significance with economic

---

[27]  If the t-stat is 2.5 and the coefficient is 0.01, then the standard error is 0.004 (i.e. 0.01/2.5) and so the upper bound of the confidence interval is 0.018 (i.e. 0.1 + (2*0.004)).

[28]  If the t-stat is 1.5 and the coefficient is 1, then the standard error is 0.67 (i.e. 1/1.5) and so the upper bound of the confidence interval is 2.34 (i.e. 1 + (2*0.67)). 50 * 2.34 is 117.

significance.[29] When McCloskey and Ziliak repeated the exercise using all the full length empirical articles from the American Economic Review in the 1990s, they found that the situation had become even worse. Of the 187 relevant articles, 79 per cent mistook statistically significant coefficients for economically significant ones and 60 per cent (compared to 53 per cent a decade earlier) relied exclusively on statistical significance as a criterion of importance.[30]

The lesson to be learnt here is that whilst the statistical significance of coefficients is of very considerable interest, it is not the sole criterion that matters. What is of far more importance is the economic significance of a coefficient.

There is a further important point to note here. Being unable to find a statistically significant relationship between two variables is not the same as proving that there is no relationship. For instance, if the available data is of very low quality (e.g infrequent data with many measurement errors) then it may well not be possible to find statistically a relationship even if in reality the relationship exists. The European Commission made this point in their *Ryanair/Aer Lingus* decision, where they wrote that:

> "However, failure to prove a statistical link is not equivalent to proving that no such link exists. Alternative explanations for an 'unsuccessful' regression include, in particular, unsuitable data sets or misspecified regression equations."[31]

In this case, the Commission argued that it was not possible to find statistically a relationship between Ryanair's prices and Aer Lingus' presence or absence on a route because of a lack of entry by Aer Lingus on Ryanair routes in the data. Conversely, there were many instances when Ryanair entered Aer Lingus routes to test whether Ryanair's presence affects Aer Lingus' prices. We do not comment on whether the Commission's views were correct in this instance, but the general sentiment is

---

[29] It is interesting to note that the authors find that this is a distinction that is apparently better understood in basic econometric textbooks than in the practice of professional economists. Wallis and Roberts (1956) state:

"It is essential not to confuse the statistical usage of 'significant' with the everyday usage. In everyday usage, 'significant' means 'of practical importance', or simply 'important'. In statistical usage, 'significant' means 'signifying a characteristic of the population from which the sample is drawn', regardless of whether the characteristic is important."

Freedman, Pisani and Purves (1978) write that:

"This chapter ... explains the limitations of significance tests. The first one is that 'significance' is a technical word. A test can only deal with the question of whether a difference is real ..., or just a chance variation. It is not designed to see whether the difference is important."

[30] Ziliak and McCloskey (2004).

[31] COMP/M.4439 *Ryanair/Aer Lingus* (June 27, 2007) para.476.

reasonable: failure to show a positive does not mean that the negative is therefore true.

## Fit

**AN–025** The idea that a multiple regression will include an error term has been discussed above (see Equation (5) and accompanying text). This error term can be thought of as the sum of all those factors that affect the dependent variable but which have not been explicitly included in the model. In general, it is hoped that all the important independent variables have been included in the model and so the error term ought to be relatively small. When regression results are reported, a measure of the *goodness of fit* of the model is usually also reported. This is an indication of how much of the variation in the dependent variable is explained by the prediction of the model (i.e. the independent variables and the functional form of the model).

The most commonly reported measure of goodness of fit is the $R^2$ statistic. This statistic lies between 0 and 1 and measures the proportion of the variation in the dependent variable that the independent variables explain. A figure of 1 means that the independent variables explain 100 per cent of the variation in the dependent variable. A figure of 0 means that the independent variables explain 0 per cent of the variation in the dependent variable.[32]

In general, it is usually assumed that the higher the $R^2$, the better is the model. There is of course a sense in which this is true: a model which explains more of the variation in the dependent variable is generally preferred to one that explains less. Looking at Figure Annex.2 above, the model in the left-hand example is preferred to that in the right-hand example. However, despite the fact that the $R^2$ is often reported, it is important not to equate the fact that a model has a high $R^2$ with it being a good model.[33] This mistake is frequently made and it is a serious misuse of econometric analysis to claim that a high $R^2$ implies a good model. It is incorrect to say that one econometric model is "better" or more reliable than another just because the $R^2$ of one model is higher than that of another model,. The $R^2$ of a model can be increased without the model being made better, and effectively similar formulations of the same model can give different $R^2$s. An illustrative example is provided below.

Figure Annex.3 shows the sales of a commodity over time. The own-price elasticity is $-4$, but the adjustment process is slow relative to the frequency of data that is available (weekly). Because of the slow adjustment

---

[32] In fact, the better measure of the goodness of fit is the *adjusted* $R^2$. This is very similar to the standard $R^2$ but for various technical reasons is a slightly better measure. In theory the adjusted $R^2$ can be negative, but in practice this is rarely seen.

[33] Or to assume that a low $R^2$ necessarily makes a bad model.

process, the level of sales at time t is a pretty good predictor of sales at time t+1.

## Figure Annex.3: Example of slow adjustment to price change AN–026

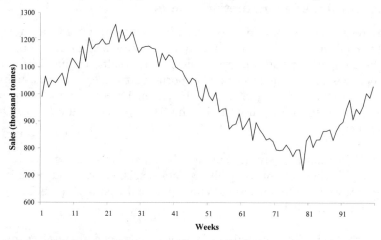

Suppose multiple regression analysis is used to investigate the (assumed unknown) relationship between price and sales. Using multiple regression analysis, it is possible to try to relate the level of sales to the level of prices. Thus:

(10)   $Sales_t = f(Price_t)$

If this is done with the data used to generate the chart in Figure Annex.3, we obtain an estimate for the coefficient on $Price_t$ (designated $\beta$) of $-4.7$ and an $R^2$ of 0.13. Suppose, however, that the model was estimated in first differences, i.e. the change in sales is related to the change in price each period. Thus:

(11)   $Sales_t - Sales_{t-1} = f(Price_t) - f(Price_{t-1})$

This is essentially the same model as in Equation (10): seeking to explain sales by reference only to price. Estimating this model with the data used to generate the chart in Figure Annex.3 produces an estimate for $\beta$ of $-5.0$ and an $R^2$ of 0.58. So the estimate of $\beta$ is now less precise (i.e. further from the true value of $-4$), even though the $R^2$ has risen from 0.13 to 0.58. Finally, suppose a lag of sales is now included in the model. Thus:

(12)   $Sales_t = f(Sales_{t-1}, Price_t)$

Estimating this model with the data used to generate the chart in Figure Annex.3 produces an estimate for $\beta$ of $-2.7$ but an $R^2$ of 0.99. The estimate of $\beta$ is even worse (i.e. now 1.3 away from the correct value), but the $R^2$ is almost 1!

   In summary, although the $R^2$ statistic is often reported, it cannot be used as a measure of how good the model is. The types of statistics that should be used to appraise a model are discussed below. The $R^2$ statistic is not one of them.

## Presentation of econometric results

**AN-027** If the results of econometric analysis, and the uses to which they are put, are to be taken seriously by a competition authority then it must be possible for the competition authority to "believe" the results. In this light, included below is a list of the three most important attributes of any elasticity or simulation study which Jonathan Baker, then Director at the Bureau of Economics at the FTC, discussed in his 1997 paper on the *Staples/Office Depot* merger[34]:

> (a) "econometric studies and simulation analysis should receive little weight when submitted without data, explanations, and other assistance we need to understand and replicate the parties' methodology in a timely manner".

Only then can the competition authority convince themselves of the validity of the analysis. The same discipline should, of course, apply to analysis carried out by a competition authority.

> (b) ". . . econometric analyses are more persuasive when key modelling choices are consistent with economic theory, informed by quantitative and qualitative information about the market, tested against plausible alternatives".

Thus in the *Staples/Office Depot* merger, the FTC was unconvinced by analysis that appeared to leave out some data without adequate economic reasons and that flew in the face of the implications of internal pricing documents. See Chapter 15 for further discussion of this case.

> (c) ". . . an econometric or simulation methodology should be treated with scepticism absent a demonstration that a reasonable alternative [does not] lead to a substantially different result, where such an analysis is possible".

Particularly in adversarial proceedings, the quantitative implications of objections to the econometric analysis of one side or another should be provided. It has been sensibly proposed that "a party objecting to an econometric model introduced by another party should demonstrate the numerical significance of his objections wherever possible".[35]

---

[34] For a similar discussion, see Werden, Froeb and Scheffman (2004).
[35] Finkelstein (1978).

# COMMON PROBLEMS

The proper way to appraise an econometric model, and thus to know **AN–028** whether the estimates that it produces are likely to be reasonable estimates, is to first confirm that the various coefficients are of a plausible sign and size and then second to carry out a number of *specification tests*. It should be stressed that it is not expected that all competition law practitioners will have to undertake econometric specification tests. Rather, it is expected that econometric analysis in this field will be presented with the results of specification tests included and it is hoped that the following explanation will allow practitioners to understand the implications of these tests. As a general rule of econometric methodology, it is hard to fault Hendry's Three Golden Rules of econometrics: test, test and test again.[36] These tests do not impose an undue burden on those carrying out econometric analysis. Most statistical packages allow users to generate these tests automatically. If a package does not allow this, it should not be used for serious econometric analysis (i.e. simple spreadsheet packages are not acceptable for this task). More importantly, in the absence of the results of these specification tests, it is not possible to appraise the model.

A few specification tests that any model ought to pass are outlined below. The results of a model that does not pass these tests should be viewed with caution.[37]

## Validity of the standard errors, the t-statistics and the confidence intervals

It was noted above that the standard errors and t-statistics that are reported **AN–029** with regression coefficients are only accurately calculated if certain assumptions hold. Whether or not the t-statistics are accurately calculated matters when making inferences about statistical significance. In general, even if the t-statistics are incorrectly calculated the regression coefficients themselves are unbiased. However, the confidence intervals around the unbiased coefficient will be incorrect if the standard errors and t-statistics are calculated incorrectly.

### Serial correlation

When the error terms of a regression are linked to each other over time by **AN–030** some relationship, this causes bias in the standard errors. This is known as

---

[36] Hendry (1995) and Doornik and Hendry (1992).
[37] The tests discussed here are relevant to standard multiple regression analysis. They are not all relevant or valid for non-standard econometric analysis such as limited dependent variable models. For further discussion of this issue and alternative tests see Greene (2007) and Maddala (1986).

*serial correlation* of the errors. A common form of serial correlation is first order autocorrelation which takes the form:

(13)  $\hat{u}_t = \rho\,\hat{u}_{t-1} + \varepsilon_t$

where  $u_t$ is the error at time $t$;

   ∧ denotes a fitted value from a regression;

   $\rho$ is a regression coefficient; and

   $\varepsilon_t$ is a white noise error term.

Autocorrelation only directly implies biased coefficient estimates if the regression equation contains a lagged dependent variable. However, it is often a sign that a relevant variable has been omitted (one that is itself serially correlated) and so should be taken seriously, i.e. it should lead an investigator to consider what variable might have been omitted.

A standard test that should be reported is the Durbin–Watson test. This tests for first order autocorrelation (i.e. for a relationship between $\hat{u}_t$ and $\hat{u}_{t-1}$). If there is no serial correlation, the Durbin–Watson (DW) statistic will be about 2. If there is positive autocorrelation, it will be close to zero and if there is negative autocorrelation, it will be close to 4.[38] Another test for autocorrelation that is often reported is a Lagrange Multiplier (LM) test. As with the DW test, if this is failed it implies that there is auto-correlation and so the estimated standard errors will be incorrect. Most standard econometric packages now also report Newey-West standard errors.[39] These are accurate even in the presence of serial correlation (or heteroscedasticity: see below).

Note that in general it only makes sense to carry out autocorrelation tests on time series data (e.g. data on sales, prices and so on over time). It does not make sense to carry them out on cross-sectional data (i.e. sales and price data across different areas at the same time).

### *Non-normality of the residuals*

**AN–031** The standard assumption is that the errors from a regression are normally distributed. This means that they are distributed according to a bell curve,

---

[38] The DW test is slightly odd in that there are no exact critical values for the test failing: the correct critical value depends on the exact set of variables in question. However, DW tables provide details of the range of possible critical values in each case. All that this oddity means in practice is that there are occasions when it is impossible to say whether the test is failed at, say, the 95% level or not.

  For instance, suppose that there are 70 observations and a constant and 5 other independent variables. Then the 5% critical value for the DW test is between 1.46 and 1.77. Thus if the DW statistic is between 1.77 and 2.23 (i.e. 4–1.77) then the null hypothesis of no first-order autocorrelation is not rejected at the 5% significance level (i.e. the test is passed). If the DW statistic is below 1.46 or above 2.54 (i.e. 4–1.46) then the null is rejected at the 5% level (i.e. the test is failed). However, if the DW statistic is between 1.46 and 1.77 or between 2.23 and 2.54, then it is not possible to say whether or not the test has been failed.

[39] Newey and West (1987).

with most of the errors close to zero and relatively few far away from zero. Non-normality of the errors does not bias the coefficient estimates, but it does make the standard t-statistics invalid. The standard test for non-normality is the Jarque-Bera $\chi^2$ test.[40] A test of this form should always be reported in any presentation of regression results.

## Heteroscedasticity

Heteroscedasticity is non-constancy of the variance of the error terms. **AN–032** What this means is that the average absolute size of the error terms varies over time.

**Figure Annex.4: Heteroscedastic error terms**                    AN–033

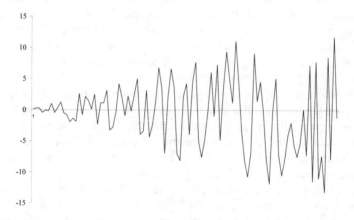

Heteroscedasticity does not bias the coefficient estimates, but it does mean that standard t-statistics cannot be used for significance testing. In general, it is recommended that investigators always use heteroscedastic consistent standard errors (most statistical packages offer these). If there is no heteroscedasticity, then these will in general be the same as the usual standard errors. If there is heteroscedasticity, they are more accurate than the usual standard errors. Note, however, that in the presence of non-normality as well as heteroscedasticity, heteroscedastic consistent standard errors are themselves biased.

A standard test for heteroscedasticity is a White test.[41] If this is failed, the residuals exhibit heteroscedasticity and so the standard errors of the coefficients are incorrect. This means that the confidence intervals around the (unbiased) coefficient estimates are incorrect.

---

[40] Jarque and Bera (1980).
[41] White (1980).

## *Stationarity*

**AN–034** If independent variables are non-stationary (meaning that their mean and variance are not constant over time), then standard significance tests will not be correct. It is therefore important to check for non-stationarity in variables (i.e. for the presence of unit roots). This is an issue that arises in price tests, such as correlation analysis, and as such we consider it in some detail in Chapter 10. For this reason, we do not consider it further here.

## Parameter constancy

**AN–035** A key property of any econometric model should be parameter constancy, i.e. the coefficient estimates should not be heavily dependent on the exact sample used. If changing the sample of data used leads to significantly (statistically or economically) different coefficient estimates, this suggests that the model is not a good one. For instance, suppose that two investigators wish to know the average age of a population of 10,000 people. In order to do this, they each choose 1,000 people, find out their age and take the average. If the two investigators come up with very different results due to their different samples, neither estimate should be believed. Conversely, if they come up with similar results, both results would be broadly believed. The same principle holds in regression analysis. If changing the sample does not change the coefficient estimates, then more confidence can be placed in the estimates than if changing the sample leads to very different coefficient estimates.

A standard test is a Chow test for within sample parameter constancy.[42] This test involves dividing the data set into two sub-samples and then testing whether the coefficients in each sub-sample are significantly different from those of the whole sample.

## Collinearity

**AN–036** If some of the independent variables are highly correlated with each other (positively or negatively), it can lead to statistical problems in a regression. The first potential problem is that high correlations between independent variables tend to lead to large standard errors and so wide confidence intervals. This is not desirable because it implies that one cannot be very precise about the likely true values of the coefficients.

The second reason for wanting to avoid highly correlated variables is that it can lead to imprecision of the coefficient estimates. The problem is that if two variables are highly correlated, inaccuracy in the estimation of one of the coefficients can lead to inaccuracy in the estimation of the other coefficient. Specifically, if there is positive (negative) correlation between

---

[42] Chow (1960).

two variables, then overshooting in the estimation of one of the coefficients will be matched by undershooting (overshooting) in the estimation of the other coefficient.

The implication of this is that investigators should always report the correlations between the various independent variables so that the likelihood of imprecise estimations and compensating biases can be evaluated.

## Omitted variables

The omission of variables that are determinants of the dependent variable **AN–037** can lead to bias in the coefficient estimates of those variables that are included in the model. More precisely, if a relevant variable is omitted, this will lead to bias of the included coefficients unless the omitted variable is uncorrelated with the included variables and the model is linear.

It is difficult to test directly for the omission of relevant variables.[43] However, there are two obvious precautions that should be taken to minimise the danger of this type of bias. The first is to graph the actual and fitted values of the dependent variable. If there are occasions where the fitted value is very different from the actual value (or, equivalently, where the residual is very large) this suggests that a relevant factor has been omitted. Suppose, for instance, that the own-price and cross-price elasticities of demand for sales of Product X were being estimated using just the prices of various substitute products and total expenditure in the relevant segment. If the actual and fitted values were plotted and it was found that several points were "outliers" (as in Figure Annex.5), then one would conclude that some relevant factor had been omitted.

[43] One test for omitted variables that can be carried out is a test of whether the lags of any of the variables included in the model should be added to the model. However, this test does not deal with the real issue: are there relevant variables omitted from our data set?

**AN–038 Figure Annex.5: An example of an omitted variable**

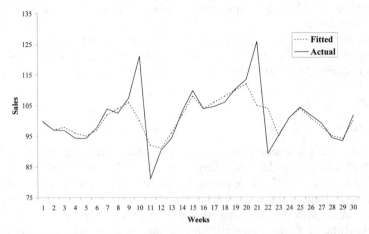

In this example, it might be concluded that some variable to do with, for instance, short-run price promotions had been omitted. The second precaution to take is to check the effect of adding variables to the model that might be expected to be relevant. It is important to show that those variables that are omitted from the model but which one might expect to be significant factors are in fact not statistically or economically significant determinants of the dependent variable.[44]

A standard test for omitted variables is the Ramsey RESET test.[45] This uses powers of the fitted values from a regression (e.g. fitted value squared and so on) and powers of the independent variables and tests whether they are significant when regressed against the dependent variable. If they are, this suggests that relevant variables have been omitted. This test is standard to most econometric packages.

## Simultaneity

**AN–039** Where one variable (X) affects another variable (Y) that in turn affects the first variable (X), the variables are said to be simultaneously determined. If one of the independent variables is simultaneously determined with the dependent variable, this is likely to lead to bias in the coefficient estimates unless particular econometric techniques are used.[46] This is a problem that often arises in macroeconomic econometric analysis: variables such as GDP, interest rates, inflation and exchange rates are all simultaneously

---

[44] To be more technical, the investigator should report the results from a series of F-tests on potential omitted variables. These are simple statistical procedures that test whether the addition of another variable to the model significantly (in a statistical sense) improves the performance of the model. If the variable does improve the performance of the model significantly, then it ought to be included in the model.

[45] Ramsey (1969).

[46] These are normally referred to as "instrumental variable" techniques.

determined. However, it can also occur in the type of microeconomic estimation that competition law inquiries are concerned with. For instance, prices and sales might be expected to be simultaneously determined in some cases. In general, we think of prices being set and then sales being determined by the price set. However, if prices vary across, say, a country and data is available on the average price across the whole country (i.e. total revenue divided by total sales), then the average price will depend to some extent on sales in each region, which in turn is determined by price in each region. Hence, the two variables (total sales and average price) are simultaneously determined.

There are a number of different tests that can be used to test for simultaneity in the determination of variables (usually referred to as exogeneity tests) and there are a number of tests available to check for bias in simultaneous equations. These are not discussed here.[47] What is important is that if there is potential simultaneity in the model, it is incumbent on the modeller to show either that in fact there is no simultaneity or to show that it does not lead to biased estimates.

## APPRAISING A MODEL IN PRACTICE

The use of these specification tests can be illustrated by returning to the **AN–040** example above in which the own-price elasticity of a product and three cross-price elasticities were estimated. The results are shown in Table Annex.7. However, Table Annex.7 now also includes the results of various statistical tests.

---

[47] Any reasonable econometric textbook will be adequate (e.g. Greene (2007)).

**AN–041**  **Table Annex.7: Tests statistics for a regression model**

|  | Coefficient estimate | Standard error | t-statistic |
|---|---|---|---|
| Constant | 9.81 | 0.671 | 14.62 |
| Q1 | −0.30 | 0.005 | −57.37 |
| Q4 | 0.40 | 0.016 | 25.69 |
| OwnPrice | −4.99 | 0.089 | −55.97 |
| PriceB | 0.80 | 0.097 | 8.21 |
| PriceC | 1.38 | 0.126 | 10.97 |
| PriceD | 1.96 | 0.092 | 21.30 |
| **Test** |  | **Test statistic** | **95 per cent threshold** |
| **Adjusted $R^2$** |  | 0.90 |  |
| **Durbin–Watson** |  | 1.94 | 1.68 |
| **Jarque–Bera normality test** |  | 1.39 | 5.99 |
| **Heteroscedasticity test (F(12,27))** |  | 1.02 | 2.13 |
| **Chow test (F(6,26))** |  | 0.73 | 2.48 |

The test statistics show that the model passes a range of statistical tests. The adjusted $R^2$ is 0.90, showing that the model explains about 90 per cent of the variation in sales over time. The Durbin–Watson test is close to 2 (1.94) and so there is no indication of serial correlation. With 40 observations and six independent variables, there would only be a suggestion of serial correlation if the Durbin–Watson statistic test was below 1.68 or above 2.32 (i.e. 4–1.68). The Jarque–Bera normality test statistic is 1.39. Only if it was above 5.99 would there be evidence of non-normality at the 95 per cent level. The heteroscedasticity test statistic is 1.02. Only if it was above 2.13 would there be evidence of heteroscedasticity at the 5 per cent level. The Chow test statistic is 0.73. Only if it was above 2.48 would there be evidence of parameter non-constancy at the 5 per cent level. So the model passes all these tests. In general, it should be simple to see this because an investigator should always report these statistics and the 5 per cent thresholds for the tests being failed.

The possibility of collinearity, omitted variable bias or of simultaneity has not yet been discussed. Collinearity arises when two or more of the independent variables are highly correlated with each other. Table Annex.8 shows that in this case the correlations are all relatively low.

**Table Annex.8: Checking the correlations between the inde-** AN–042
**pendent variables**

|  | Q4 | Q1 | Own Price | Price B | Price C | Price D |
|---|---|---|---|---|---|---|
| **Q4** | 1.00 | | | | | |
| **Q1** | −0.31 | 1.00 | | | | |
| **Own Price** | 0.18 | −0.18 | 1.00 | | | |
| **Price B** | −0.02 | 0.09 | −0.13 | 1.00 | | |
| **Price C** | 0.19 | −0.19 | 0.17 | 0.10 | 1.00 | |
| **Price D** | 0.14 | 0.05 | 0.14 | −0.05 | 0.11 | 1.00 |

The correlations are all below 0.20 (in absolute terms) except for the correlation between Q1 and Q4 (−0.31). This higher correlation is not surprising given the nature of the two variables. However, it does imply that if there is some bias in the estimation of the coefficient on Q4, there is likely to be bias in the same direction on Q1, and vice versa. As it happens, this is not a great concern in this case since the coefficients of concern are those on the price variables. However, in another model it might be very relevant (e.g. if it was Own Price and Price B that were correlated).

As noted above, there are no very reliable tests for omitted variable bias except common sense. First, are there any obvious variables that have been omitted? What about other potential substitutes beyond B, C and D? It will be assumed that in this case there were two other plausible substitutes, but that including them in the regression model did not improve the explanatory power of the model (e.g. the adjusted $R^2$ remained the same) and that the coefficients on these variables were not statistically or economically significant.[48] Secondly, does the graph of the actual and fitted dependent variable show any obvious outliers? Figure Annex.6 shows that the answer to this is "no" and that therefore there is no great concern about the possibility of omitted variable bias.

---

[48] Normally, these results should be reported in the text (or, more likely, in an Appendix). They are not reported here for reasons of brevity and clarity.

**AN–043 Figure Annex.6: Actual and fitted values for our regression example**

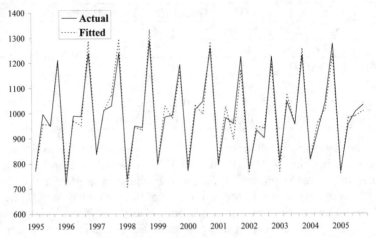

The final issue to be addressed is the possibility of simultaneity. As noted earlier, some simultaneity between sales and the own-price variable might be expected. This should be tested for using exogeneity tests and common sense. For instance, if the data is weekly data and prices are set six weeks in advance, then there is unlikely to be significant simultaneity. However, if the data is quarterly and prices are set six weeks in advance, then there may be significant simultaneity. The data graphed in Figure 6 is quarterly data, so there may be a simultaneity issue. In this case, it will be assumed that there was a simultaneity issue and so the investigator reported this and used appropriate techniques to generate the above results.[49]

## ECONOMETRIC ESTIMATION OF DEMAND SYSTEMS

**AN–044** The previous sections provided an introduction to econometric analysis. The use of econometric analysis was illustrated using an example of estimating the own-price elasticity of a product and three cross-price elasticities. However, for reasons of clarity, the example avoided a range of important issues that arise in the practical estimation of elasticities.

It should be stressed again that the following discussion of the econometric estimation of demand systems and elasticities is not an attempt to provide a "how to do it" guide. Such a task is beyond the scope of this book. Instead, the discussion of the estimation of elasticities is presented in order to provide an understanding of the relevant issues so that the quality of any elasticity estimates can be assessed. However, it should be noted that

[49]   In practice, this means using instrumental variables estimation.

this section is significantly more technical in places than the previous sections.

There are two main econometric issues that need to be faced when estimating elasticity estimates. These are:

(a)  the best demand model to use[50]; and

(b)  the best method of dealing with the problem of the simultaneous determination of prices and quantities (often referred to as the "identification" problem).

## Choice of demand model

What might be called a "standard approach" to functional form was illu-   **AN–045** strated earlier in this Annex. This related sales to various prices and other relevant factors. Thus the equation was of a similar form to the following equation.

(14)   $Sales_t = c + \gamma\ Segment\ Expenditure_t + \beta_1\ Own\ Price_t + \beta_2\ Other\ Price_t + \beta_3\ Other\ Factor + \varepsilon_t$

where the price of only one other product and only one other factor have been included (in the example above we included the prices of three other products and two other factors). This equation also contains a "segment expenditure" variable, which is a variable that captures the effect on sales of changes in overall consumer spending patterns. For instance, if one were estimating the own-price elasticity of whisky, one might include "total spending on spirits". Equally, if one were estimating the own-price elasticity of all beer, "total personal disposal income" might be included.[51] Equations of this type are estimated in logarithms so that the coefficients on each price variable can be interpreted directly as price elasticities. This type of equation has a *log-linear* functional form.

---

**BOX ANNEX.2: SYSTEMS OF EQUATIONS AND IMPOS-**   **AN–046**
**ING SLUTSKY SYMMETRY**

It is often necessary to estimate a system of log-linear equations. For example, suppose one wanted to estimate the own-price elasticity and cross-price elasticities of whisky, gin and vodka. A system such as that

---

[50]  Another way to put this would be to talk in terms of "functional form" rather than "demand model". These two phrases are used more or less interchangeably.

[51]  There are a number of technical econometric reasons for including this type of variable. However, the key point is that including a variable of this sort is necessary for ensuring that the equation is well specified. However, it should be noted that the estimated elasticities are *conditional elasticities*: they are the elasticities given that demand for the segment as a whole is unchanged.

shown below might then be estimated. This system explains the sales of each spirit in terms of consumer expenditure on all spirits and the prices of each spirit.

(15)   $Whisky\ Sales_t = \alpha_1 + \gamma_1\ Spirits\ Expenditure_t + \beta_1\ Whisky\ Price_t + \beta_2\ Gin\ Price_t + \beta_3\ Vodka\ Price_t + \delta'_1\ Other\ Factors_t + \varepsilon_{1t}$

(16)   $Gin\ Sales_t = \alpha_2 + \gamma_2\ Spirits\ Expenditure_t + \beta_4\ Whisky\ Price_t + \beta_5\ Gin\ Price_t + \beta_6\ Vodka\ Price_t + \delta'_2\ Other\ Factors_t + \varepsilon_{2t}$

(17)   $Vodka\ Sales_t = \alpha_3 + \gamma_3\ Spirits\ Expenditure_t + \beta_7\ Whisky\ Price_t + \beta_8\ Gin\ Price_t + \beta_9\ Vodka\ Price_t + \delta'_3\ Other\ Factors_t + \varepsilon_{3t}$

If one were to estimate a system of this type, there are various cross-equation restrictions that one might impose (and which can be tested). For instance, one might impose the restriction that the coefficient on "spirits expenditure" was the same across equations. Or one might wish to impose cross-equation restrictions on the error terms. However, a more justifiable restriction is to impose Slutsky symmetry on these equations. This is because one would expect there to be a relationship between the cross-price elasticity of demand for A with respect to the price of B and the cross-price elasticity of demand for B with respect to the price of A. Specifically, one should expect that:

(18)   $\varepsilon_{AB} = \varepsilon_{BA}\ \dfrac{Expenditure\ on\ B}{Expenditure\ on\ A}$

Where $\varepsilon_{AB}$ is the cross-price elasticity of demand for A with respect to the price of B. This merely states that the changes in demand consequent upon a relative price change are symmetric. In the example given above, this means that three cross-equation restrictions should be imposed. These are:

$$\beta_2 = \beta_4\ \frac{Expenditure\ on\ Gin}{Expenditure\ on\ Whisky}$$

(19)   $$\beta_3 = \beta_7\ \frac{Expenditure\ on\ Vodka}{Expenditure\ on\ Whisky}$$

$$\beta_6 = \beta_8\ \frac{Expenditure\ on\ Vodka}{Expenditure\ on\ Gin}$$

Imposing restrictions of this sort, if they are shown to be valid, makes the model more efficient. Further, this is not an arbitrary restriction that cannot be tested. It is a simple matter to test whether the data rejects these restrictions using a likelihood ratio test.[52]

[52]   For further details see Greene (2007) or Doornik and Hendry (2007).

There are two main problems with equations such as Equation (14). The **AN–047** first, and most important, is that it does not have a good grounding in economic theory. Specifically, equations of this type cannot be derived from standard economic utility theory. The second problem is a more practical problem: if there are a large number of substitute products, then equations of the above form tend to perform badly. For example, consider a differentiated products industry in which there are 20 different products (e.g. beer, cereal, cars, etc.). Estimating equations with 20 elasticities in each is likely to lead to poor coefficient estimates. This will be partly due to the difficulty of distinguishing between the different effects of each variable (i.e. collinearity problems) and partly due to having relatively little data given the number of independent variables (i.e. degrees of freedom problems).

A functional form that is used extensively in anti-trust investigations is the Nearly Ideal Demand System (NIDS) of Deaton and Muellbauer.[53] One advantage of this over a simple log-linear approach is that it can be derived from general utility theory and so can be justified on theoretical grounds. The other advantage is that this demand system is well suited to making and testing various *separability* assumptions. If there are 20 prices, not all of them need to be included in each equation. Instead, the NIDS approach allows us to estimate "segment equations" which split the products up in to narrower segments (e.g. premium, popular, diet, own label, etc.). This reduces the number of elasticities in each equation. The implied restrictions on cross-elasticities between sectors can be econometrically tested.[54]

---

### BOX ANNEX.3: THE NEARLY IDEAL DEMAND SYSTEM    AN–048

The econometric implementation of NIDS is based on the idea of *multi-stage budgeting*. This holds that consumers' purchasing decisions can be broken down into a number of stages. For instance, Hausman, Leonard and Zona use a three-stage process.[55] The European Commission used a multi-level budgeting NIDS model in Friesland Foods/Campina.[56] At the first stage the consumer decides whether or not to buy the product type (e.g. a car). At the second stage, the consumer

---

[53] Deaton and Muellbauer (1980a); Deaton (1980b).
[54] The restrictions are that the degree of substitution between products in different segments is the same for each product in the two segments. So if A and B are in segment "private label" and C and D are in segment "branded", then the degree of substitution between A and C is the same as between A and D and as between B and C and as between B and D. The testing of these restrictions is very important because it allows the analyst to reject arbitrary segmentation of the products.
[55] Hausman, Leonard and Zona (1994).
[56] COMP/M. 5046 *Friesland Foods/Campina* (December 17, 2008).

decides from which segment of the product type he wishes to purchase (e.g. small car, estate car, people carrier, luxury saloon, soft-top, etc.). At the third stage the consumer decides which specific product from within his preferred segment he wishes to choose (i.e. having decided to buy a people carrier, should it be the Espace or the Galaxy or the Zafira or the S Max?).

Corresponding to these three decision levels, there are three levels at which demand equations are estimated. The highest level equation estimates the elasticity for the market as a whole (e.g. all cars), the middle level equations estimate elasticities for segments within the market (e.g. small cars, estate cars, people carriers, etc), whilst the lower level equations estimate elasticities within each segment (e.g. Peugeot 207, VW Polo, Nissan Micra, etc).[57] The results from all three levels are then combined together to give estimates of the own-price and cross-price elasticities for each product.

The lower level equations are of the form:

$$(20) \quad s_{it} = \alpha_i + \beta_i \log \frac{y_{Gt}}{P_t} + \sum_{j=1}^{J} \gamma_{ij} \log p_{jt} + \varepsilon_{it}$$

where   $s_{it}$ is the revenue share of total segment expenditure of brand $i$ at time $t$;

    $a_i$ is a brand specific constant;

    $y_{Gt}$ is overall segment expenditure at time $t$;

    $P_t$ is a price index for segment expenditure at time $t$;

    $p_{jt}$ is the price of brand $j$ at time $t$;

    $\varepsilon_{it}$ is an error term; and

    $\beta_i$ and $\gamma_{ij}$ are regression coefficients.

This equation relates segment revenue share to segment expenditure, own price and the prices of substitutes within the segment. The segment expenditure variable allows for the absence of segment homotheticity (i.e. the possibility that expenditure shares are not constant for given prices as segment expenditure changes). It is simple to impose Slutsky symmetry by requiring $\gamma_{ij} = \gamma_{ji}$ (note that the left-hand side variable is revenue share, not quantity, so this is the correct form for Slutsky symmetry).

The middle level equations are of the form:

$$(21) \quad \log q_{mt} = \beta_m \log y_{Bt} + \sum_{k=1}^{K} \delta_{mk} \log \pi_{kt} + \alpha_m + \varepsilon_{mt}$$

where   $q_{mt}$ is the level of sales in segment $m$ at time $t$;

    $y_{Bt}$ is total expenditure on the product (i.e. across all segments);

    $\pi_{kt}$ is the price index for segment $k$ at time $t$;

---

[57] Sometimes only two levels are used: the upper and lower level.

$\alpha_m$ is a segment specific constant;

$\varepsilon_{mt}$ is an error term; and

$\beta_m$ and $\delta_{mk}$ are regression coefficients.

This equation relates sales in a segment to overall expenditure on a product and the individual price indices for each segment. The correct form of the price index (i.e. the one derived from utility theory) is rather complicated and so in practice Stone's Index is often used.[58] The $\delta_{mk}$ coefficients are segment elasticities. The overall expenditure variable can be thought of as allowing for income effects and should allow for more accurate estimates of the elasticities to be derived.

The upper level equation is of the form:

$$(22) \quad \log u_t = \beta_0 + \beta_1 \log y_t + \beta_2 \log \Pi_t + \delta Z_t + \varepsilon_t$$

where $u_t$ is overall sales of the product;

$y_t$ is deflated disposable income;

$\Pi_t$ is the deflated price index for the product;

$Z_t$ are other relevant variables;

$\varepsilon_t$ is an error term; and

$\beta_0$, $\beta_1$, $\beta_2$ and $\delta$ are regression coefficients.

This equation is a simple log linear regression to estimate the overall product elasticity.

Once all the levels of equations have been estimated, the results can be combined to produce efficient estimates of all the own-price and cross-price elasticities. As a simple check, one should expect the individual elasticities to be greater (in absolute terms) than the segment elasticities which, in turn, should be greater than the overall elasticity.

## Solving the problem of simultaneity

As it stands, one should expect there to be problems estimating these **AN-049** equations, since the equations all include endogenous variables on the right-hand side (i.e. current price variables are used to "explain" current quantity variables). As noted above, one solution to this problem is to use instrumental variables estimation.[59] However, in differentiated products

---

[58] Stone's index is the share weighted average log price of the products.

[59] Put simply, this econometric approach replaces the endogenous right-hand side variables with a set of exogenous proxy variables. For instance, if the endogenous variable was a price variable, one might "instrument" it (i.e. replace it) with a set of cost variables (where the costs are input costs to the product whose price we are concerned with).

An alternative approach is to argue that prices are set several weeks in advance and so are not simultaneously determined with quantities. The problem with this line of argument is that unless prices are uniform across the country, the reported average price will be a weighted average where the weights are determined by the volumes sold in each area, which will be dependent on the price in that area. So it is unlikely that reported prices are truly exogenous even when prices are set considerably in advance.

industries there are rarely enough instrumental variables available to allow this to be done. A solution to this problem is to make use of the fact that scanner technology means that price and quantity series are often available by region or by town.[60] Prices of a brand in one region should be expected to be good instrumental variables (i.e. proxies) for prices of the same brand in another region. So one would carry out estimations on a region by region, or town by town, basis and then average the results.

However, the assumption that prices in one region are good instrumental variables for prices in another region is not uncontroversial. It is based on the assumption that the regions face different demand shocks. The idea is that prices in a region are driven by costs plus a demand shock. Prices in another region should be driven by the same costs, and so can act as a proxy for the underlying costs that drive prices. However, if the demand shocks are correlated, then this will lead to bias in the econometric estimates. In the United States, it might be reasonable during some periods to assume that demand shocks are different across towns in different states, particularly states on different sides of the country, although clearly not during nationwide shifts in demand, such as in a nationwide recession or boom or advertising campaign. However, within European countries the reasonableness of this assumption is more questionable. This implies that traditional instrumental variable approaches, where available, may be better. It certainly implies that some thought should be given in each case to whether the assumption that the different regions face uncorrelated demand shocks is a reasonable one.

## SUMMARY

**AN–050** This Annex has introduced the basic ideas underlying multiple regression analysis and has illustrated this using a worked example of estimating various elasticities of demand. The purpose of the chapter was to provide an overview of these statistical techniques and to illustrate when these techniques might be useful. As importantly, the chapter discussed a number of specification tests which can be employed to test whether a given econometric model is well specified (i.e. when the model is such that it is worth lending weight to its results). Finally, we included a more advanced section on the estimation of demand elasticities, as this is a key, but often technically difficult, application for multiple regression analysis in antitrust.

---

[60] This solution has been suggested by Hausman, Leonard and Zona (1994).

# Bibliography

Adelman, "Economic aspects of the Bethlehem opinion" (1959) *Virginia Law Revue*

Ahlborn, Evans, D., and Padilla, J., "Competition Policy in the New Economy: Is European Competition Law Up to the Challenge?" (2001) 5 *European Competition Law Review*

Ahrel, P. (1994). "Jurisprudence relative aux practiques restrictives de concurrence en 1993" *Revue de la Concurrence et de la Consommation*, No 80

Amato, G., *Antitrust and the Bounds of Power* (Hart Publishing, 1997)

American Bar Association, *Econometrics: legal, practical and technical issues* (ABA Publishing, 2005)

Anderson, S.P. and de Palma, A., "Multiproduct firms: a related logit approach" (1992) *Journal of Industrial Economics*, p.40

Antitrust & Trade Regulation Report, various issues

Appelbaum, E., "The Estimation of the Degree of Oligopoly Power" (1982) *Journal of Econometrics* Vol.19, pp.287–299

Areeda, P.E., "Essential Facilities: An Epithet in Need of Limiting Principles" (1990) *Antitrust Law Journal* Vol.58, pp.841–853

Areeda, P.E. and Hovenkamp, H., *Antitrust Law* (Supplement, 1990) pp.740–787

Areeda, P.E. and Turner, D.F., "Predatory Pricing and Related Practices under Section 2 of the Sherman Act" (1975) *Harvard Law Review* Vol.88, pp.697–733

Areeda, P.E. and Turner, D.F. *Antitrust Law* (Boston, Little, Brown, 1978)

Areeda, P.E. and Turner, D.F., "Market Power in Antitrust Cases" (1981) *Harvard Law Review* Vol.94, pp.937–996

Ariely, D., *Predictably Irrational: The hidden forces that shape our decisions* (Harper Collins, 2008)

Armstrong, M. and Vickers, J., "The Access Pricing Problem", *Discussion Papers in Economics and Econometrics* (University of Southampton, 1995) No 9506

Armstrong, M. and Wright, J., "Mobile Call Termination" (2007) available at *http://ssrn.com/abstract=1014322* [Accessed September 18, 2009]

Bibliography

Armstrong, M., "Competition in Two-sided Markets" (2006) *Rand Journal of Economics* Vol.37, Issue 3, pp.668–691

Asch, P. and Seneca, J.J., "Characteristics of Collusive Firms" (1975) *Journal of Industrial Economics* Vol.23, pp.223–237

Azzam, A. and Pagoulatos, E., "Testing Oligopolistic and Oligopsonistic Behaviour: An Application to the US Meat Packing Industry" (1990) *Journal of Agricultural Economics* Vol.41, pp.362–370

Babusiaux, M., "Principles et modalités du contrôle du fonctionnement concurrentiel des marchés" (1996) *Revue de la Concurrence et de la Consommation*, nfa 92

Bael, I. and Bellis, J.-F., *Anti-dumping and Other Trade Protection Laws of the EEC* 2nd edn (CCH Editions Ltd, 1990)

Baer, W.J., *Report from the Bureau of Competition* Prepared Remarks of William J. Baer, Director, Bureau of Competition, Federal Trade Commission before the American Bar Association Antitrust Section

Bain, J.S., *Barriers to New Competition* (Cambridge, Harvard University Press, 1956)

Bain, J., "The Profit Rate as a Measure of Monopoly Power" (1941) *Quarterly Journal of Economics* Vol.55

Bajari, P. and Ye, L., "Deciding between Competition and Collusion" (2003) *Review of Economics and Statistics* Vol.85, pp.971–989

Baker, J., "Mavericks, Mergers and Exclusion: Proving Coordinated Effects under the Antitrust Laws" (2002) *New York University Law Review* Vol.77, pp.135–203

Baker, S. and Coscelli, A., "The Role of Market Shares in Differentiated Product Markets" (1999) 8 *European Competition Law Review* 412–419

Baker, J.B., *Contemporary Empirical Merger Analysis* (1997a) Federal Trade Commission Working Paper

Baker, J., "Econometric analysis in *FTC v Staples*" (1999) *Journal of Public Policy and Marketing*, 18:11–21

Baker, J.B., "Unilateral Competitive Effects Theories in Merger Analysis" (1997c) *Antitrust* Vol.11, pp.21–26

Baker, J.B., "The Problem with *Baker Hughes* and *Syufy*: On the Role of Entry in Merger Analysis" (1997d) *Antitrust Law Journal* Vol.65, pp.353–374

Baker, J.B. and Bresnahan, T.F., "The Gains from Merger or Collusion in Product Differentiated Industries" (1985) *Journal of Industrial Economics* Vol.33, pp.427–444

Baker, J.B. and Bresnahan, T.F., "Empirical Methods of Identifying and Measuring Market Power" (1992) *Antitrust Law Journal* Vol.61, pp.9–13

Baker, S. and Ridyard, D., "Portfolio Power: A Rum Deal?" (1999) 4 *European Competition Law Review*

Baldwin, L., Marshall, R. and Richard, J-F., "Bidder Collusion at Forest Service Timber Auctions" (1997) *Journal of Political Economy* Vol.105, pp.657–699

Banerji, A. and Meenakski, J., "Buyer Collusion and Efficiency of Government Intervention in Wheat Markets in Northern India: An asymmetric structural auctions analysis" (2004) *American Journal of Agricultural Economics* Vol.86, pp.236–253

Baumol, W.J., "Predation and the Logic of the Average Variable Cost Test" (1996) *Journal of Law and Economics* Vol.39, pp.49–72

Baumol, W.J., Panzar, J. and Willig, R., *Contestable Markets and the Theory of Industry Structure* (New York, Harcourt Brace Jovanovich, 1982)

Bavasso A., "The role of intent in Article 82" (2005) *European Competition Law Review*

Beckert, W. and Mazzarotto, N. "Price–concentration analysis in merger cases with differentiated products" (2006) *UK Competition Commission working paper*

Bellamy, C.W. and Child, G.D., *Common Market Law of Competition* 4th edn (London, Sweet & Maxwell, 1993)

Bengtsson, C., "Simulating the effect of Oracle's takeover of PeopleSoft" in P. van Bergeijk and E. Kloosterhuis (eds) *Modelling European mergers: theory, competition policy and case studies* (Cheltenham, Edward Elgar, 2005) pp.92–106. Bergstrom, T. and Varian, H., "Two Remarks on Cournot Equilibria" (1985) *Economic Letters*, Vol.19, pp.5–8

Bernheim, B.D. and Whinston, M., "Multimarket contract and collusive behavior" (1987) *Harvard Institute of Economic Research, working paper* No 1317

Bernheim, B.D. and Whinston, M., "Multimarket contract and collusive behavior" (1990) *Rand Journal of Economics* Vol.21, No.1, pp.1–26

Berry, S., "Estimation of a Model of Entry in the Airline Industry" (1992) *Econometrica* Vol.60, pp.889–917

Berry, S., Pakes, A. and Levinsohn, J., "Automobile Prices in Market Equilibrium" (1995) *Econometrica*, Vol.63, pp.841–890

Berry, S., Pakes, A. and Levinsohn, J., *Differentiated Products Demand Systems from a Combination of Micro and Macro Data: Autos Again* (Mimeo, Yale University, 1997)

Berry, S. and Waldfogel, J., "Do mergers increase product variety? Evidence from radio broadcasting" (2001) *The Quarterly Journal of Economics*, Vol.116, pp.1009–25

Bertrand, J., *Review of Recherches sur la Principes Mathematique de la Theorie des Richesses* (1883) *Journal des Savants* pp.499–508

Besanko, D. and Perry, M.K., "Exclusive Dealing in a Spatial Model of Retail Competition" (1994) *International Journal of Industrial Organisation*, Vol.12, pp.297–329

Bessler, D.A. and Brandt, J.A., "Causality Tests in Livestock Markets" (1982) *American Journal of Agricultural Economics* Vol.64, pp.140–144

Beverly, L., "Stock market event studies and Competition Commission inquiries" (2007) *Competition Commission Occasional Paper* Bishop, S.,

*Quantitative Techniques for Assessing Mergers* (unpublished handbook prepared for the Merger Task Force, EC Commission, 1984)

Bishop, S., "The European Commission's Policy Towards State Aid: A Role for Rigorous Competitive Analysis" (1997) *European Competition Law Review* Vol.18, No.2, pp.84–86

Bishop, S. and Ridyard, D., "Oscar Bronner: Legitimate Refusals to Supply" (1999) *European Economics and Law*

Bishop S., "The Elephant in the Room: A proper place for dominance in Article 82 case" (2007) unpublished mimeo

Bishop S., "Loyalty Rebates and "Merger Standards": A Roadmap for the Practical Assessment of Article 82 Investigations" (2008) in Ehlermann and Marquis (eds) "European Competition Law Annual 2007: A Reformed Approach to Article 82 EC" (Hart Publishing)

Bishop S., "Pro-competitive Exclusive Supply Agreements: How Refreshing!" *European Competition Law Review* Vol. 24, Issue 5

Bishop, B. and Bishop, S., "Reforming Competition Policy: Bundeskartellamt—Model or Muddle?" (1996a) *European Competition Law Review* Vol.17, No 4, pp.207–209

Bishop S. and Baker S., "The role of market definition in monopoly and dominance inquiries" (2001) *Economic Discussion Paper 2*, Office of Fair Trading

Bishop, B. and Bishop, S., "When Two is Enough: Competition in Bidding Markets" (1996b) *European Competition Law Review*, Vol.17, No 1, pp.3–5

Bishop, S. and Darcey, M., *A Relevant Market Is Something Worth Monopolising* (unpublished Mimeo, 1995)

Bishop and Lofaro, "Assessing Coordinated Effects: Theory and Practice of EC and US Merger Control" *Antitrust Bulletin* (2005)

Bishop S., Lofaro A., Rosati F. and Young J., "The Efficiency–Enhancing Effects of Non-Horizontal Mergers" (2005) Report for DG Enterprise, European Commission

Bishop S. and Marsden P., "The Article 82 Discussion Paper: A Missed Opportunity", (2006) *European Competition Journal* Vol.2(1)

Bishop, S., "Modernisation of the Rules Implementing Articles 81 and 82", in Ehlermann and Atanasiu (eds) *European Competition Law Annual 2000: The Modernisation of EC Antitrust Policy* (Hart Publishing, 2001)

Bishop, S. and Ridyard, D., "EC Vertical Restraints Guidelines: Effects-Based or Per Se Policy" (2002) 1 *European Competition Law Review*

Bittlingmayer, G. and Hazlett, T., "Dos *Kapital*: has antitrust action against Microsoft created value in the computer industry?" (2000) *Journal of Financial Economics*, 55, pp.329–359

Bolton, P. and Scharftstein, D., "A Theory of Predation Based on Agency Problems in Financial Contracting" (1990) *American Economic Review* Vol.80, pp.93–106

Borenstein, S. and Shepard, A., "Dynamic Pricing in Retail Gasoline Markets" (1996) *Rand Journal of Economics* Vol.27, No.3, pp.429–451

Bork, R., "The Rule of Reason and the *per se* Concept" (1966) *Yale Law Journal* Vol.75, pp.373–475

Bork, R., *The Antitrust Paradox: A Policy at War with Itself* (New York, Basic Books, 1978)

Borenstein, S., "Hubs and High Fares: Dominance and Market Power in the US Airline Industry" (1989) *Rand Journal of Economics*, Vol.20, pp.344–365

Boshoff, W., "Stationarity tests in geographic markets: an application to South African milk markets" (2007) *South African Journal of Economics* 75 Bresnahan, T.F., *Testing and Measurement in Competition Models* (Paper presented at 7th World Congress of the Econometric Society, Tokyo, 1996)

Bresnahan, T.F. and Reiss, P., "Do Entry Conditions Vary Across Markets" (1987) *Brookings Papers on Economic Activity: Microeconomics* Vol.3, pp.833–871

Bresnahan, T.F. and Reiss, P., "Entry in Monopoly Markets" (1990) *Review of Economic Studies* Vol.57, pp.531–553

Bresnahan, T.F. and Reiss, P., "Entry in Monopoly Markets" (1990) *Review of Economic Studies* Vol.57, pp.531–553

Bulletin Officiel de la Concurrence, de la Consommation et de law Répression des Fraudes 1991–97

Burns, M.R., "Predatory Pricing and the Acquisition Costs of Competitors" (1996) *Journal of Political Economy* Vol.94, pp.266–296

Carbajo, J., De Meza, D. and Seidmann, D.J., "A Strategic Motivation for Commodity Bundling" (1990) *Journal of Industrial Economics* Vol.38, pp.283–298

Carlton, D. and Klamer, M., "The Need for Co-ordination among Firms with Special Reference to Network Industries" (1983) *University of Chicago Law Review* Vol.50, p.446

Carlton, D. and Waldman M., "The Strategic Use of Tying to Preserve and Create Market Power in Evolving Industries," (2002) *RAND Journal of Economics* Vol.33(2), pp.194–220, Summer

Carlton, D. and Perloff, J., *Modern Industrial Organisation* (Harper Collins, 2004)

Cartwright, P.A., Kamerschen, D.R. and Huang, M.-Y., "Price Correlation and Granger-Causality Tests for Market Definition" (1989) *Review of Industrial Organization*, Vol.4, pp.79–98

Chamberlin, E., *The Theory of Monopolistic Competition* 6th edn (Harvard University Press, 1950)

Chérel, A., "Le principe d'interprétation stricte des textes" (1996a) *Revue de la Concurrence et de la Consommation* No 91

Chérel, A., "Responsabilités des dirigeants et délégation de pouvoir" (1996b) *Revue de la Concurrence et de la Consommation* No 94

# Bibliography

Chow, G.C., "Tests of Equality between Sets of Coefficients in Two Linear Regressions"m(1960) *Econometrica*, Vol.28, pp.591–605

Christie, W. and Schultz, P., "Why do NASDAQ Market Makers Avoid Odd-eight Quotes?" (1994) *Journal of Finance* Vol.49, pp.1813–1840

Church J., "The Impact of Vertical and Conglomerate Mergers on Competition" (2004) Report for DG Competition, European Commission

Church J., "The Church report's analysis of vertical and conglomerate mergers: a reply to Cooper, Froeb, O'brien, and Vita" (2005) *Journal of Competition Law and Economics* 1(4):797–802

Coase, R., "Durability and Monopoly" (1972) *Journal of Law and Economics* Vol.15, pp.143–149

Coate, M.B., Kleit, A.N. and Bustamante, R., "Fight, Fold or Settle? Modelling the Reaction to FTC Merger Challenges" (1995) *Economic Inquiry* Vol. 33, No 4, p.537(15)

Coe, P. and Krause, D., "An analysis of price–based tests of antitrust market delineation" (2008) *Journal of Competition Law and Economics* Vol. 4(4), pp.983–1007

Compte O., Jenny, F. and Rey, P., "Capacity Constraints, Mergers and Collusion" (2002) *European Economic Review* Vol. 46(1), pp.1–29

Connor, J., *Global Price Fixing: Our customers are the enemy* (Boston: Kluwer Academic, 2001)

Connor, J., "Price–fixing overcharges: legal and economic evidence" (2005) *Working Paper, Purdue University (Staff Paper No 04–17)*

Connor, J. and Bolotova, Y. "Cartel overcharges: survey and meta–Analysis" (2006) *International Journal of Industrial Organization*, 24(6), 1109–1137

Connor, J. and Bolotova, Y., "The impact of collusion on price behaviour: empirical results from two recent cases" (2006) *International Journal of Industrial Organization* 26, 6, pp.1290–1307

Connor, J.M., "Forensic economics: an introduction with special emphasis on price fixing" (2007) *Journal of Competition Law and Economics* 4(1), 31–59

Connor, J., "Price-fixing overcharges: legal and economic evidence" (2007) in Zerbe, R. and Kirkwood, J. (eds) *Research in Law and Economics* Vol. 22 (Emerald Group Publishing Ltd)

Conseil de la Concurrence (1987–95) *Annual Reports*

Cooper, J., Froeb L., O'Brien D. and Vita M., "Vertical Antitrust Policy as a Problem of Inference" (2005) *International Journal of Industrial Organization* 23, pp.639–664.

Cournot, A., *Researches into the Mathematical Principles of the Theory of Wealth* translated by N. Bacon (New York, Macmillan, 1838)

Cowling, K. and Mueller, D., "The Social Costs of Monopoly Power" (1978) *Economic Journal*, Vol.88, pp.727–748

Cramton, P and Palfrey, T., "Cartel Enforcement with Uncertainty About Costs" (1990) *International Economic Review* Vol.31, pp.17–41

Crane, S. and Welch, P., "The Problem of Geographic Market Definition: Geographic Proximity versus Economic Significance" (1991) *American Economic Journal* Vol.xx, pp.313–341

Cremer, J., Rey, P., and Tirole J., "Connectivity on the Commercial Internet" (2000) *Journal of Industrial Economics* Vol.48, pp.433–472

Crooke, P., Froeb, L., Tschantz, S. and Werden, G.J., "Effects of assumed demand form on simulated postmerger equilibria" (1999) *Review of Industrial Organization* 15, 205–217

Dalkir, S. and Warren–Boulton, F., "Case 2: prices, market definition and the effects of merger: Staples–Office Depot (1997)" in Kwoka, J. and White. L. *The antitrust revolution: economics, competition and policy*, 5th edn (Oxford University Press, 2004)

Dalton, J.A. and Penn, D.W., "The Concentration-profitability Relationship: Is There a Price-concentration Ratio? (1976) *Journal of Industrial Economics*, Vol.25, pp.133–142

Dansby, R. and Willig, R., "Industry Performance Gradient Indices" (1979) *American Economic Review* Vol.69, pp.249–260

Dasgupta, P. and Stiglitz, J., "Industrial Structure and Innovative Activity" (1980a) *Economic Journal* Vol.90, pp.266–293

Dasgupta, P. and Stiglitz, J., "Uncertainty, Market Structure and the Speed of R&D" (1980b) *Bell Journal of Economics* Vol.11, pp.1–28

Davidson, C. and Deneckere, R., "Excess Capacity and Collusion" (1990) *International Economic Review* Vol.31, pp.521–542

Davidson, C. and Deneckere, R., "Long-run competition in capacity, short-run competition in prices, and the Cournot model" (1986) *Rand Journal of Economics*, Vol.17, pp.404–415

Davis, P., "Coordinated effects merger simulation with linear demands" (2006) *UK Competition Commission Working Paper*

De Leyssac, L., "La réparation du dommage à l'économie" (1995) *Revue de la Concurrence et de la Consommation* No 83

Deaton, A. and Muellbauer, J., *Economics and Consumer Behaviour* (Cambridge University Press, 1980a)

Deaton, A. and Muellbauer, J., "An Almost Ideal Demand System" (1980b) *American Economic Review* Vol.70, pp.312–326

DeGroot, M.H., *Probability and Statistics* (Addison-Wesley, 1989)

Demsetz, H., "Industry Structure, Market Rivalry, and Public Policy" (1973) *Journal of Law and Economics* Vol.16, pp.1–16

Deneckere, R. and Davidson, C., "Incentives to Form Coalitions with Bertrand Competition" (1985) *Rand Journal of Economics*, Vol.16, pp.473–486

Department of Justice and Federal Trade Commission, *Horizontal Merger Guidelines* (Washington, 1992)

765

# Bibliography

Diamond, P. and Hausman, J.J., "Contingent Valuation: Is Some Number Better than No Number?" (1994) *Journal of Economic Perspective* p.45

Dick, A.R., "Are Export Cartels Efficiency Enhancing or Monopoly-Promoting?" (1992) *Research in Law and Economics* Vol.15, pp.89–127

Dick, A.R., "When Are Cartels Stable Contracts?" (1996) *Journal of Law and Economics* Vol.39, pp.241–283

Dick, A.R., *If Cartels Were Legal, Would Firms Fix Prices?* (1997) Mimeo, Economic Analysis Group, Antitrust Division, US Department of Justice

Dickey, D. A. and Fuller, W.A. "Distribution of the estimators for autoregressive time series with a unit root" (1979) *Journal of the American Statistical Association* 427–31

Dixit, A.K., "The Role of Investment in Entry Deterrence" (1980) *Economic Journal* Vol.90, pp.95–106

Dixit, A. and Pindyck, R., *Investment under Uncertainty* (Princeton Press, 1993)

Dobson, P.W. and Waterson, M., *Exclusivity Agreements between Manufacturers and Retailer* (Mimeo, University of Nottingham, 1994)

Dobson, P.W. and Waterson, M., *Vertical Restraints and Competition Policy* (1996) Office of Fair Trading Research Paper No 12

Dobson, P.W. and Waterson, M., "Countervailing Power and Consumer Prices" (1997) *Economic Journal*, Vol.107, pp.418–430

Dobson, P. and Inderst, R., "Differential Buyer Power and the Waterbed Effect: Do Strong Buyers Benefit or Harm Consumers?" (2007) *European Competition Law Review* Vol.28, Isssue 7

Dolado, J.J., Jenkinson, T. and Sosvilla-Rivero, S., "Cointegration and Unit Roots" (1990) *Journal of Economic Surveys* Vol.4, pp.249–273

Doornik, J. and Hendry, D., *Empirical econometric modelling using PcGive 12* (Timberlake Consultants Press, 2007) Vol.1

Durbin, J. and Watson, G., "Testing for Serial Correlation in Least Squares Regression—I" (1950) *Biometrika* Vol.37, pp.409–428

Durbin, J. and Watson, G., "Testing for Serial Correlation in Least Squares Regression—II" (1951) *Biometrika* Vol.38, pp.159–178

Easterbrook, F.H., "On Identifying Exclusionary Conduct" (1981) *Notre Dame Law Review* Vol.61, pp.972–980

Easterbrook, F.H., "The Limits of Antitrust" (1984) *Texas Law Review*, Vol.63, pp.1–40

Eckbo, B., "Horizontal mergers, collusion, and stockholder wealth" (1983) *Journal of Financial Economics* 11 pp.241–73

Edgeworth, F., "La Teoria Pura del Monopolio" (1897) *Giornale degli Economisti* Vol.40, pp.13–31; reprinted in English as "The Pure Theory of Monopoly" in F. Edgeworth, *Papers Relating to Political Economy*, Vol.1 (London: MacMillan & Co Ltd, 1925), pp.111–1421

Edwards, J., Kay, J. and Mayer, C., *The Economic Analysis of Accounting Profitability* (Clarendon Press, 1987)

Elhauge E., "Defining Better Monopolization Standards", (2003) 56 *Stanford Law Review* 253

Elzinga, K. and Hogarty, T., "The Problem of Geographic Market Definition in Antimerger Suits" (1973) *Antitrust Bulletin* Vol.18, p.45

Emch A. and Leonard L., "Predatory pricing after LinkLine and Wanadoo" (2009) *GCP The Online Magazine for Global Competition Policy*

Engle, R.F. and Granger, C.W.J., "Co-integration and Error Correction: Representation, Epstein, R. and Rubinfeld, D., 'Merger simulation: a simplified approach with new applications" (2002) *Antitrust Law Journal* Vol. 69, pp.883–919

Epstein, R. and Rubinfeld, D., "Effects of mergers involving differentiated products" (2004) *Technical Report for DG Competition* (European Commission)

Estimation and Testing" (1987) *Econometrica* Vol.55, pp.251–276

Esposito, F. and Esposito, L., "Excess Capacity and Market Structure" (1974) *Review of Economics and Statistics* Vol.52, pp.188–194

European Commission "Commission decision of 24 April 1996 declaring a concentration to be incompatible with the common market and the functioning of the EEA agreement (Case No.IV/M.619—Gencor/Lonrho)" (1997a) *Official Journal of the European Communities*, Vol.40, L11, pp.30–72

European Commission *Green Paper on Vertical Restraints in EC Competition Policy* (1997b) Com (96) 721; [1997] 4 C.M.L.R. 519

European Commission *Follow-up to the Green Paper on Vertical Restraints: Draft Communication on the Application of the EC Competition Rules to Vertical Restraints* (1997c) unpublished discussion document

European Commission *Notice on the Relevant Market for the Purposes of Community Competition Law* (1997d) 97/C 372/03

Evans, D. and Schmalensee, R., "Markets with Two-sided Platforms" in Wayne Dale Collins (ed.), *Issues in Competition Law and Policy* Vol.III

Evans and Schmalensee *Some Economic Aspects of Antitrust Analysis in Dynamically Competitive Industries* (2001) NBER Working Paper 8268

Evans D. and Schmalensee R., "Markets with Two-Sided Platforms" (2008) *Issues in Competition Law and Policy (ABA Section of Antitrust Law)* Vol.1, Chapter 28

Evans, W. and Kessides, I., "Localized Market Power in the US Airline Industry" (1993) *Review of Economics and Statistics* Vol.75, pp.66–75

Evans, W., Froeb, L. and Werden, G., "Endogeneity in the Concentrationprice Relationship: Causes, Consequences, and Cures" (1993) *Journal of Industrial Economics*, Vol.44, pp.431–438

Farrell, J. and Shapiro, C., "Horizontal Mergers: An Equilibrium Analysis" (1990a) *American Economic Review* Vol.80, pp.107–126

Farrell, J. and Shapiro C., "Horizontal Mergers: An Equilibrium Analysis" (1990b) *American Economic Review* Vol.80, pp.107–126

Bibliography

Farrell J. and Shapiro C., "Improving Critical Loss Analysis", (2008) *Antitrust Source*

Faull, J. and Nikpay, *The EC Law of Competition* (1999)

Fee, C. and Thomas, S., "Sources of gains in horizontal mergers: evidence from customer, supplier and rival firms" (2004) *Journal of Financial Economics* 74, pp.423–460

Fershtman, C. and Pakes, A., "A Dynamic Oligopoly with Collusive Price Wars" (2000) *Rand Journal of Economics* Vol.31, No.2, pp.207–236

Finkelstein, M., "Regression Models in Administrative Proceedings" (1978) *Quantitative Methods in Law* p.238

Fisher, "The IBM and Microsoft Cases: What's the Difference?" (2000) *American Economic Review*, 90, No 2: 180–183 6.70

Fisher, Franklin and McGowan, "On the Misuse of Accounting Rates of Return to Infer Monopoly Profits" (1983) *American Economic Review* Vol.73, 1 3.64

Fisher F., "Horizontal Mergers: Triage and Treatment" (1987) *Journal of Economic Perspectives* Vol. No.2, p.13

Forchheimer, K., "Theoretishes zum unvollständigen Monopole" (1908) 32 *Jahrbuch für Gesetzgebung, Verwaltung und Volkswirtschaft* 1

Ford, G. and Kline, A., "Event studies for merger analysis: an evaluation of the effects of non–normality on hypothesis testing" available at *http://www.ssrn.com/abstract=925953* [Accessed August 29, 2009]

Fourgoux, J.-C., "Complémentarité ou superposition des procédures de constatation et de répression des pratiques anticoncurrentielles" (1991) *Revue de Science Criminelle* p.774

Fourgoux, J.-C., "Discussion pénale et réparation du préjudice des victimes des pratiques anticoncurrentielles" (1997) *Gazette du Palais* No 43–44

Fraas, G.A. and Greer, D.F., "Market Structure and Price Collusion: An Empirical Analysis" (1977) *Journal of Industrial Economics* Vol.26, pp.21–44

Freedman, D., Pisani, R. and Purves, R., *Statistics* (New York, Norton, 1978)

Friederiszick, H.W., Röller, L-H. and Verouden, V. "European State Aid Control: an economic framework" (2006) in Buccirossi, P. (ed.), *Handbook of Antitrust Economics* (Cambridge, Mass.: MIT Press, 2008)

Froeb, L., Koyak, R., and Werden, G., "What is the effect of bid-rigging on prices?" (1993) *Economics Letters* 42, pp.419–423

Froeb, L.M. and Werden, G.J., "The Reverse *Cellophane* Fallacy in Market Delineation" (1992) *Review of Industrial Organization* p.7

Froeb, L., Tschantz, S. and Werden, G., "Pass through rates and the price effects of mergers" (2005) *International Journal of Industrial Organization* Vol.23, pp.703–15

Froot, K.A. and Klemperer, P.D., "Exchange Rate Pass-Through When Market Share Matters" (1989) *American Economic Review* Vol.79, No 4, pp.637–654

Funderburk, D., "Price Fixing in the Liquid-asphalt Industry: Economic analysis versus the 'hot document'" (1974) *Antitrust Law and Economics Review* Vol.7, pp.61–74

Galbraith, J., "Countervailing Power" (1954) *American Economic Review Papers and Proceedings* Vol.44, pp.1–6

Geithman, F.E., Marvel, H.P. and Weiss, L.W., "Concentration, Price and Critical Concentration Ratios" (1981) *Review of Economics and Statistics* Vol.63, pp.346–353

Genakos, C. and Valleti, T., "Testing the 'Waterbed' Effect in Mobile Telephony" (2008) *CEIS Working Paper No.110*, available at *http://ssrn.com/abstract=1114856* [Accessed September 18, 2009]

Geweke, J., Meese, W. and Dent, W., "Comparing Alternative Tests of Causality in Temporal Systems: Analytic Results and Experimental Evidence" (1983) *Journal of Econometrics* Vol.21, pp.161–194

Gifford, Predatory pricing analysis in the Supreme Court" (1994) *Antitrust Bulletin* 471 6.103

Gilbert, R., "Mobility Barriers and the Value of Incumbency" in R. Schmalensee and R. Willig (eds) *Handbook of Industrial Organisation* (Amsterdam, North Holland, 1989)

Gilbert, R. and Sunshine, S., "Incorporating Dynamic Efficiency Concerns in Merger Analysis: The Use of Innovation Markets" (1995) *Antitrust Law Journal* Vol.63, p.569

Goldberg, P., "Product Differentiation and Oligopoly in International Markets: The Case of the US Automobile Industry" (1995) *Econometrica* Vol.63, pp.891–951

Gorman, W., "Separable utility and aggregation" (1959) *Econometrica* Vol.27, pp.469–481

Granger, C., "Investigating Causal Relations by Econometric Models and Cross-spectral Methods" (1969) *Econometrica* Vol.37, pp.424–438

Green, E. and Porter, R., "Non-co-operative Collusion under Imperfect Price Information" (1984) *Econometrica* Vol.52, pp.87–100

Green, Edward J., "Continuum and Finite-Player Noncooperative Models of Competition," (1984) *Continuum and Finite-Player Noncooperative Models of Competition , Econometric Society* Vol. 52(4), pp.975–93, July.

Greene, W.H. *Econometric Analysis* 6th edn (Macmillan, New York, 2007)

Grout, P., and Sonderegger, S., "Predicting Cartels" (2005) *OFT Economic Discussion Paper*, OFT 773

Haag, M. and Klotz, R., "Commission Practice Concerning Excessive Pricing in Telecommunications" (1998) *Competition Policy Newsletter* No 2

Harberger, A., "Monopoly and resource allocation" (1954) *American Economic Review* 44:77–79

Harrington, J., "Post–cartel pricing during litigation" (2004) *Journal of Industrial Economics* 52, 517

# Bibliography

Harris, C., *Electricity markets: pricing, structures and economics* (2006) *Wiley Finance*

Harstad, R.M. and Phlips, L., *Informational Requirements of Collusion Detection: Simple Seasonal Markets*, (Mimeo, European University Institute, 1994)

Hart, O., "Incomplete contracts and the theory of the firm" Continuum and Finite-Player Noncooperative Models of Competition *Journal of Law, Economics and Organization* (1988) 4, 1, p.119

Hart, O. and Tirole, J., "Vertical Integration and Market Foreclosure" (1990) *Brookings Paper, Microeconomics* pp.205–286

Harvey, A.C., *The Econometric Analysis of Time Series* (Oxford, Philip Allan, 1981)

Hausman, J., Leonard, G. and Zona, J., "A Proposed Method for Analyzing Competition Among Differentiated Products" (1992) *Antitrust Law Journal* Vol.60, pp.889–900

Hausman, J., Leonard G. and Zona, J., "Competition Analysis with Differentiated Products" (1994) *Annules D'Economique et de Statistique* Vol.34, pp.159–180

Hausman, J. and Leonard, G., "Economic Analysis of Differentiated Product Mergers Using Real World Data" (1997) *George Mason Law Review* 5–3, Spring, p.321

Hawk, B. and Huser, H., *European Community Merger Control: A Practitioner's Guide* (Kluwer Law International, 1996)

Hay, D.A. and Kelly, G., "An Empirical Survey of Price Fixing Conspiracies" (1974) *Journal of Law and Economics* Vol.17, pp.13–38

Hay, D.A. and Morris, D.J., *Industrial Economics and Organisation: Theory and Evidence* (Oxford University Press, 1991)

Hemphill S., "The Role of Recoupment in Predatory Pricing Analyses (2001) *Stanford Law Review* 53, 1581

Hendry, D.F., *Dynamic Econometrics* (Oxford University Press, 1995)

Hendel, I. and Nevo, A., "Sales and consumer inventory" (2006) *Rand Journal of Economics* Vol.37, 543–61

Hennessy, D., "Cournot oligopoly conditions under which any horizontal merger is profitable" (2000) *Review of Industrial Organization* Vol.17, p.277–84

Hicks, "Annual survey of economic theory: the theory of monopoly" (1935) *Econometrica* Vol.3, p.8, 2.21

Holmstrom, B. and Hart, O., "The Theory of the Firm" in R. Schmalensee and R. Willig (eds) *Handbook of Industrial Organisation* (Amsterdam, North Holland, 1989)

Hoppman, E., "Das Konzept der optimalen Wettbewerbsintensität. Rivalität und Freiheit des Wettbewerbs: Zum Problem eines wettbewerbspolitisch adäquaten Ansatzes der Wettbewerbstheorie" (1966) *180 Jahrbuch für Nationalökonomie und Statistik 286*

Hoppman, E., "Zum Problem einer wirtschaftspolitisch praktikabelen

Definition des Wettsbewerbs" in Sneider (ed), *Grundlagen der Wettbewerbspolitick (9)* (1968)

Horowitz, I., "Market Definition in Antitrust Analysis: A Regression-based Approach" (1981) *Southern Economic Journal* Vol.48, pp.1–16

Hosken, D. and Reiffen, D., "Patterns of retail price variation" (2004) *Rand Journal of Economics* Vol.35, 128–46

Hosken, D. and Taylor, C., "Discussion of 'Using stationarity tests in antitrust market definition" (2004) *American Law and Economics Review* Vol.6, No 2, pp.465–475

Hotelling, H., "Stability in Competition" (1929) *Economic Journal* Vol.39, pp.41–57

Hovenkamp, H., *Economics and Federal Antitrust Law* (Hornbook, 1985)

Hovenkamp, H., *Federal anti-trust policy* (1994)

Hovenkamp H., "Signposts of Anticompetitive Exclusion: Restraints on Innovation and Economies of Scale" (2007) in Barry Hawk (ed.) *2006 Fordham Competition Law Institute* (Juris Publishing) Chapter 18

Howard, J. and Kaserman, D., "Proof of damages in construction industry bid-rigging cases" (1989) *The Antitrust Bulletin* 34, p.359

Howell, J., "Market Definition in Anti-trust Analysis: A Regression-based Approach: Comment" (1984) *Journal of Reprints for Antitrust Law and Economics* Vol.14, pp.1163–1170

Hsiao, C., *Analysis of Panel Data* (New York, Cambridge University Press, 1986)

Huang, M.-Y., *The Delineation of Economic Markets* (Ph.D. Dissertation, University of Georgia, Athens, Georgia, 1987.)

Inderst, R. and Valletti, T., "Buyer Power and the 'Waterbed Effect'" (2008) *CEIS Research Paper No.107*, available at *http://ssrn.com/abstract=1113318* [Accessed September 18, 2009]

Ivaldi M., Jullien B., Rey P., Seabright P. and Tirole J., "The Economics of Unilateral Effects: Interim Report for DG Competition, European Commission" (2003), available on DG Comp website

Ivaldi, M., "Mergers and the New Guidelines: lessons from Hachette–Editis" in P. van Bergeijk and E. Kloosterhuis (eds) *Modelling European mergers: theory, competition policy and case studies* (Cheltenham, Edward Elgar, 2005) pp.92–106

Ivaldi, M. and Verboven, F., "Quantifying the effects from horizontal mergers in European competition policy" (2005) *International Journal of Industrial Organisation* Vol.23, pp.669–691

Jacquemin, A., Nambu, Tsuruhiko and Dewez, I., "A Dynamic Analysis of Export Cartels: The Japanese Case" (1981) *Economic Journal,* Vol.91, pp.685–696

Jacquemin, A. and Slade, M., "Cartels, Collusion and Horizontal Merger" in R. Schmalensee and R. Willig (eds) *Handbook of Industrial Organisation* (Amsterdam, North-Holland, 1989)

Jarque, C.M. and Bera, A.K., "Efficient Tests for Normality,

Homoscedasticity and Serial Independence of Regression Residuals" (1980) *Economics Letters* Vol.6, pp.255–259

Jenny, F., "Competition and State Aid Policy in the European Community" (1994) *Fordham International Law Journal* Vol.18, pp.525–554

Jenny, F., "Les relations entre le Droit et l'Economie dans l'Ordonnance du 1er décembre 1986" (1997) *Gazette du Palais* No 43–44

Johansen, S., "Estimation and hypothesis testing of cointegrating vectors in Gaussian vector autoregressive models" (1991) *Econometrica*, 59, 1551–80

Jones, C. and González-Díaz, E., *The EEC Merger Regulation* (London, Sweet & Maxwell, 1992)

Joskow, P.L. and Klevorick, A.K., "A Framework for Analysing Predatory Pricing Policy" (1979) *Yale Law Journal* Vol.89, pp.213–270

Judd, K., "Credible Spatial Preemption" (1985) *Rand Journal of Economics* Vol.16, pp.153–166

Kamien, M. and Schwartz, N., *Market Structure and Innovation* (Cambridge University Press, 1982)

Katz, M. and Shapiro, "Systems Competition and Network Effects" (1994) *Journal of Economic Perspectives* Vol.8, No 2, Spring 6.53

Katz, M. and Shapiro, C., *Antitrust in Software Markets* Conference paper presented at Progress and Freedom Foundation conference, 1998

Katz M. and Shapiro C., "Critical Loss: Let's Tell the Whole Story", (2003) *Antitrust*, Spring

Kihlstrom, R. and Vives, X., "Collusion by Asymmetrically Informed Duopolists" (1989) *European Journal of Political Economy*, Vol.5, pp.371–402

Klein, B., Crawford R.G., and Alchian, A.A., "Vertical Integration, Appropriable Rents, and the Competitive Contracting Process" (1978) *Journal of Law and Economics* Vol.21, pp.297–326

Klein, C., Rifkin, E.J., and Uri, N.D., "A Note on Defining Geographic Markets" (1985) *Regional Science and Urban Economics* Vol.15, pp.109–119

Klein, J., "A Stepwise Approach to Antitrust Review of Horizontal Agreements" (1996) American Bar Association's Antitrust Section Semi-Annual Fall Policy Program

Klein, J., "DoJ Analysis of Radio Mergers." Address by Joel Klein, Acting Assistant Attorney General, Antitrust Division, US Department of Justice, 1997

Kleit, A.N., *An Analysis of Vertical Relationships among Railroads: Why Competitive Access Should Not Be An Antitrust Concern* (1989) Bureau of Economics, US Federal Trade Commission Working Paper No 176

Klemperer, P., "Entry Deterrence in Markets with Consumer Switching Costs" (1987a) *Economic Journal* Vol.97, pp.99–117

Klemperer, P., "Markets with Consumer Switching Costs" (1987b) *Quarterly Journal of Economics* Vol.102, pp.375–394

Klemperer, P., "The Competitiveness of Markets with Switching Costs" (1987) *Rand Journal of Economics* Vol.18, pp.138–150

Klemperer, P., "Competition policy in auctions and 'bidding markets'" in Buccirossi, P. (ed) *The Handbook of Antiturst Economics* (MIT Press, 2008)

Kobayashi B., "The Economics of Loyalty Discounts and Antitrust Law in the United States" (2005) *Competition Policy International* Vol.1, No.115, Autumn

Koboldt and Maldoom "Optimal fixed-to-mobile interconnection charges" Paper presented at the 12th European Regional ITS conference, Dublin, September 2–3, 2001 9–13

Kolasky, W., "Coordinated Effects in Merger Review: From Dead Frenchmen to Beautiful Minds and Mavericks", Speech to ABA Section of Antitrust Law Spring Meeting, 2002 (*http://www.usdoj.gov/atr/public/speeches/11050.htm* [Accessed August 29, 2009)

Korah, V., *EC Competition Law and Practice* 7th edn (London, Sweet & Maxwell, 2001)

Krattenmaker, T.G. and Salop, S.C., "Exclusion and Antitrust" (1987) *Regulation Nos 3/4*, pp.29–33

Krattenmaker, Lande and Salop, "Monopoly Power and Market Power in Antitrust Law" (1987) *The Georgetown Law Journal* Vol.76, pp.241–269 3.55

Krattenmaker, T.G. and Salop, S.C., "Anti-competitive Exclusion: Raising Rivals' Costs to Achieve Power over Price" (1986) *The Yale Law Journal* Vol.96, No 2, pp.209–293

Kreps, D., *Game Theory and Economic Modelling* (Oxford, Oxford University Press, 1991)

Kreps, D. and Scheinkman, J., "Cournot Precommitment and Bertrand Competition Yield Cournot Outcomes" (1983) *Bell Journal of Economics* Vol.14, pp.326–337

Kreps, D. and Wilson, R., "Reputation and Imperfect Information" (1982) *Journal of Economic Theory* Vol.27, pp.253–279

Kroes N. "Preliminary thoughts on policy review of Article 82", speech at the Fordham Corporate Law Institute (2005)

Kroes N., "Exclusionary abuses of dominance – the European Commission's enforcement priorities" Annual Fordham Antitrust Conference (2008)

Kühn, K., Stillman, R. and Caffara, C., "Economic Theories of Bundling and their Policy Implications in Abuse Cases: An Assessment in Light of the Microsoft Case" (2005) *European Competition Journal* Vol.1, pp.85–122

Kühn, K.-U., Seabright, P. and Smith, A., "Competition Policy Research: Where Do We Stand?" (1992) CEPR Occasional Paper No 8

Kühn, K.-U., "The Coordinated Effects of Mergers" in Buccirossi, P. (ed.), *Handbook of Antitrust Economics* (MIT Press, 2008)

# Bibliography

Kwoka, J. "The price effects of bidding conspiracies: evidence from real estate auction 'knockouts'" (1997) *The Antitrust Bulletin* 42, p.503

La Cour, L.F. and Møllgaard, P., "Meaningful and Measurable Market Domination" (2003) E.C.L.R. 363–367

Lafontaine, F. and Slade, M., "Exclusive Contracts and Vertical Restraints: Empirical evidence and public policy" in Buccirossi, P. (ed.), *Handbook of Antitrust Economics* (MIT Press, 2008)

Langenfeld J. and Li W., "Critical loss analysis in evaluating mergers" (2001) *The Antitrust Bulletin* 299–337

Leibenstein, H., "Allocative Efficiency as X-Efficiency" (1966) *American Economic Review* Vol.56, pp.392–415

Leibowitz, J., "The Good, the Bad and the Ugly: Trade associations and antitrust" (2005) *Remarks by FTC Commissioner Leibowitz to the ABA Antitrust Spring Meeting, Washington DC*

Lerner, A., "The Concept of Monopoly and the Measurement of Monopoly Power" (1934) *Review of Economic Studies* Vol.1, pp.157–175

Lesquins, J.-L., "L'existence d'un 'seuil de sensibilité' en Droit Français de la Concurrence" (1995) *Revue de la Concurrence et de la Consommation* No 94

Levenstein, M. and Suslow, V., "Cartel Bargaining and Monitoring: The role of information sharing" (2006) *Seminar to the Swedish Competition Authority*

Levenstein, M. and Suslow, V., "Private International Cartels and their Effect on Developing Countries" (2001), *Mimeo, University of Massachusetts*

Levenstein, M. and Suslow, V., "What determines cartel success?" (2006) *Journal of Economic Literature* 44(1), 43–95

Levy, N., "Kimberly-Clark/Scott and the Power of Brands" (1996) 7 E.C.L.R. 403–410

Levy, D. and Reitzes, J., "Anticompetitive Effects of Mergers in Markets with Localised Competition" (1992) *Journal of Law, Economics and Organisation*, Vol.8, p.112

Lewis, S. and Lofaro A., "GoogleDoubleClick: The Search for a Theory of Harm" (2008) *European Competition Law Review* Issue 12, pp.717–720

Lexecon, *Beyond Argument: Defining Relevant Markets* (1994) Competition Memo

Lexecon, *Boeing/McDonnell Douglas* (1997) Competition Memo

Liebeler, W.J., "Exclusion and Efficiency" (1987) *Regulation Nos 3–4*, pp.34–40

Lin, Y.J., "The Dampening-of-Competition Effect of Exclusive Dealing" (1991) *Journal of Industrial Economics* Vol.39, pp.209–223

Lind, R., Muysert, P. and Walker, M., "Innovation and Competition Policy" (2002) *Office of Fair Trading Economic Discussion Paper* 3 5.61

Littlechild, S., "Misleading calculations of the social cost of monopoly power" (1981) *Economic Journal* Vol.91, pp.348–363

London Economics, *Barriers to Entry and Exit in UK Competition Policy*, Office of Fair Trading Research Paper No 2, 1994

London Economics, *Competition in Retailing*, Office of Fair Trading Research Paper No13, 1997

London Economics for the European Commission, *The Single Market Review: Impact on Competition and Scale Effects—Competition Issues* (Office for Official Publications of the European Communities, 1997)

Lopez, R., "Measuring Oligopoly Power and Production Responses of the Canadian Food Processing Industry" (1984) *Journal of Agricultural Economics* Vol.35, pp.219–230

Lyons B. (ed.), "Cases in European Competition Policy: The Economic Analysis" (Cambridge University Press, 2009)

Maddala, G., *Limited Dependent and Qualitative Variables in Econometrics* (New York, Cambridge University Press, 1986)

Maier-Rigaud F. "Article 82 Rebates: Four Common Fallacies" (2006) *European Competition Journal, Special Supplement* pp.85–100

Majumdar, A., "Waterbed Effects and Buyer Mergers" (2005), *CCP Working Paper No.05-7*, available at *http://ssrn.com/abstract=911574* [Accessed September 18, 2009]

Mankiw, N.G. and Whinston, H.D., "Free Entry and Social Inefficiency" (1986) *Rand Journal of Economics* Vol.17, pp.48–58

Mann, H., Meehan, J. and Ramsey, G., "Market Structure and Excess Capacity: A Look at Theory and Some Evidence" (1979) *Review of Economics and Statistics* Vol.61, pp.156–160

Marion, B. and Geithman, F., "Concentration-price Relations in the Regional Fed Cattle Markets" (1995) *Review of Industrial Organization* Vol.10, pp.1–19

Marquez, J., *Life Expectancy of International Cartels: An Empirical Analysis*, Board of Governors of the Federal Reserve System, Discussion Paper No 439, 1992

Martin, S., *Advanced Industrial Economics* (Oxford and Cambridge Press, Mass, Blackwell, 1993)

Marvel, H.P., "Exclusive Dealing" (1982) *The Journal of Law and Economics* Vol.25, pp.1–25

Maskin, E. and Riley, J., "Asymmetric auctions" (2000) *Review of Economic Studies* Vol.67, pp.413–38

Mirrlees J., "The Theory of Moral Hazard and Unobservable Behaviour" (1975) mimeo Nuffield College, Oxford, subsequently published in *Review of Economic Studies*

Melamed D., "Exclusive Dealing Agreements and Other Exclusionary Conduct—Are There Unifying Principles?, (2006) *Antitrust Law Journal* Vol.73, 375

Melamed D., "Thoughts about Exclusive Dealing", (2008) in Ehlermann and Marquis (eds) "European Competition Law Annual 2007: A Reformed Approach to Article 82 EC" (Hart Publishing)

Mullin, L., Mullin, J. and Mullin, W., "The Competitive Effects of Mergers: Stock Market Evidence from the US Steel Dissolution Suit" (1995) *Rand Journal of Economics*, Vol.26, pp.314–330

Mathis, S.A., Harris, D.G. and Boehje, M., "An Approach to the Delineation of Rural Banking Markets" (1978) *American Journal of Agricultural Economics*, Vol.60, pp.601–608

McAfee, R. and Williams, M., "Can event studies detect anti–competitive mergers?" (1988) *Economic Letters 28* 199–203

McCloskey, D.N. and Ziliak, S.T., "The Standard Error of Regressions" (1996) *Journal of Economic Literature* Vol.34, pp.97–114

McFadden, D., "Conditional Logit Analysis of Qualitative Choice Behavior" in P. Zarembka (ed) *Frontiers in econometrics* (Academic Press, New York, 1974) 105–142

McGee, J., "Predatory Price Cutting: The Standard Oil (N.J.) Case" (1958) *Journal of Law and Economics* Vol.1, pp.137–169

McGee, J., "Predatory Pricing Revisited" (1980) *Journal of Law and Economics*, Vol.23, pp.289–330

Mehta, K. and Peeperkorn, L., "The Economics of Competition" in Faull, J. and Nikpay, A. (eds), *The EC Law of Competition* 2nd edn (Oxford University Press, 2007)

Milgrom, P., "Auctions and Bidding: A Primer" (1989) *Journal of Economic Perspectives* Vol.3, No 3, pp.3–22

Milgrom, P. and Roberts, J., "Predation, Reputation and Entry Deterrence" (1982) *Journal of Economic Theory* Vol.27, pp.280–312

Mncube, L., Khumalo, J., Mokolo, R. and Njisane, Y., Use of price correlation and stationarity analysis in market definition—lessons from a recent merger" (2007) *Mimeo, at http://www.web.wits.ac.za/NR/rdonlyres/37777DEF–BA14–432C–A1DD–85889BC7BBB/0/Mncube_Price-testsConferencepaper_3_.pdf* [Accessed August 29, 2009] (More detailed discussions of this case can be found in Dalkir and Warren–Boulton (2005) and in ABA (2005))

Monopoly and Mergers Commission, *Service Corporation International and Plantsbrook Group: A Report on the Merger Situation* (1995) Cm.2880

Morrison, S.A. and Winston, C., "The Dynamics of Airline Pricing and Competition" (1990) *American Economic Review Papers & Proceedings* Vol.80, pp.389–393

Motta, M., *Competition Policy: Theory and Practice* (Cambridge University Press, 2004)

Mueller, W., Khan, N. and Scharf, T., *EU and WTO Anti-dumping Law: A handbook* 2nd edn (Oxford University Press, 2009)

Murgatroyd, R., Majumdar A. and Bishop S., "Grand Theft Antitrust: Lessons from the GAME/Gamestation Transaction" (2009) *European Competition Law Review* Vol.30, issue 2 , pp.53–56

Muysert, P., Reynolds, P. and Walker, M., "The 'Waterbed Effect' in Mobile Telephony" (2006) *CRA Competition Policy Discussion Paper*

Nalebuff B., "Bundling, Tying, and Portfolio Effects," *DTI Economics Paper* No.1, (2003). Available online at *http://www.dti.gov.uk/economics*

Nalebuff B., "Bundling as an Entry Barrier" (2004) *Quarterly Journal of Economics* (2004) Vol.119, No. 1, pp.159–187

Nash, J., "Non-co-operative Games" (1951) *Annals of Mathematics* Vol.54, pp.286–295

Neven, D., Nuttall, R. and Seabright, P., *Merger in Daylight: The Economics and Politics of European Merger Control* (CEPR, 1993)

Neven, D., Papandropoulous, P. and Seabright, P., *Trawling for Minnows: European Competition Policy and Agreements between Firms* (CEPR, 1998)

Nevo, A., "Measuring Market Power in the Ready-to-eat Breakfast Cereal Industry" (2001) *Econometrica* Vol.69, pp.307–342

Nevo, A., *Mergers with Differential Products: The Case of the Ready-to-Eat Cereal Industry* (University of California, Berkeley, Mimeo, 1997) at *http://www.emlab.berkeley.edu/users/nevo* [Accessed August 29, 2009]

Newey, W. and West, K., "A simple positive semi–definite, heteroscedasticity and autocorrelation consistent covariance matrix" (1987) *Econometrica* 55, 703–708

Newmark, C., "Price concentration studies: there you go again" in Moriati, P. (ed) *Antitrust policy issues* (Nova Publishers, 2006)

Nitsche R. and Heidhues P., "Study on methods to analyse the impact of state aid on competition" European Economy, Economics Papers **244**. European Commission (2006)

O'Brien, D. and Shaffer, G., "Vertical Control with Bilateral Contracts" (1992) *Rand Journal of Economics* Vol.23, pp.299–308

O'Brien D. and Wickelgren A. "A Critical Analysis of Critical Loss Analysis" (2003) *Antitrust Law Journal* Vol. 71

Office of Fair Trading "European State Aid Control" (2005) (OFT 821)

Ordover, Janusz, Willig and Robert, "An Economic Definition of Predation: Pricing and Product Innovation" (1981) *Yale Law Revue* Vol.91: 8 6.70

Ordover, J., Saloner, G. and Salop, S., "Equilibrium Vertical Foreclosure" (1990) *American Economic Review* Vol.80, pp.127–142

Ordover, J., Sykes, A. and Willig, R., "Herfindahl Concentration, Rivalry and Mergers" (1982) *Harvard Law Review* Vol.95, p.1857

Osborne, M. and Pitchik, C., "Cartels, Profits and Excess Capacity" (1987) *International Economic Review* Vol.28, pp.413–428

Owen, B. and Wildman, S., *Video Economics* (Harvard University Press, 1992)

Oxera, "Assessing Profitability in Competition Policy Analysis" (2003) *OFT Economic Discussion Paper* 6, OFT 657

Peeperkorn, L., "EC Vertical Restraints Guidelines: Effects-Based or Per

Se Policy—A Reply" (2002) *European Competition Law Review* Vol.23, Issue 1

Perry, M. and Porter, R., "Oligopoly and the Incentive for Horizontal Merger" (1985) *American Economic Review* Vol.75, pp.219–227

Phlips, L., *Competition Policy: A Game Theoretic Perspective* (Cambridge, Cambridge University Press, 1995)

Pigou, A.C., *The Economics of Welfare* 4th edn (London: Macmillan, 1920)

Pindyck, R. and Rubinfeld, D., *Microeconomics* 7th edn (Pearson Prentice Hall, 2008)

Porter, R., "On the Incidence and Duration of Price Wars" (1985) *Journal of Industrial Economics*, Vol.23 pp.415–428

Porter, R.H. and Zona, J.D., "Detection of Bid Rigging in Procurement Auctions," (2001) *Journal of Political Economy*, pp.518–538

Posner, R., *Antitrust Law: An Economic Perspective* (Chicago, University of Chicago Press, 1976)

Quigley, C., *European State Aid: law and policy* 2nd edn (Hart Publishing, 2009)

Ramsey, F., "A contribution to the theory of taxation" (1927) *Economic Journal* 37 6.31

Ramsey, J.B., "Tests for Specification Errors in Classical Linear Least Squares Regression Analysis" (1969) *Journal of the Royal Statistical Society* Series B, Vol.31, pp.350–371

Rapp, "Predatory Pricing Analysis: A Practical Synthesis", (1990) 59 *Antitrust Law Journal* 6.87

Rapp, R., "The Misapplication of the Innovation Market Approach to Merger Analysis" (1995) *Antitrust Law Journal* Vol.64, pp.19–47

Rey P., "On the Right Test for Exclusive Dealing" (2008) in Ehlermann and Marquis (eds) "European Competition Law Annual 2007: A Reformed Approach to Article 82 EC" (Hart Publishing)

RBB Economics, "Two Sides to Every Story: Lessons from the Travelport/Worldspan EC Case" (2008) RBB Brief No. 25

Rey, P. and Tirole, J., "The Logic of Vertical Restraints" (1986) *American Economic Review* Vol.76, pp.921–939

Rey, P. and Tirole, J., *A Primer on Foreclosure* (Mimeo, 1996)

Ridyard, D., "Essential Facilities and the Obligations to Supply Competitors under UK and EC Competition Law" (1996) *European Competition Law Review* Vol.8, pp.438–452

Ridyard, D., Bishop, S. and Klass, M., *Market Definition in UK Competition Policy* Office of Fair Trading Research Paper No 1, 1992

Ridyard D., "Exclusive Contracts and Article 82 Enforcement: An Effects-Based Perspective" (2008) *European Competition Journal* Vol.4, No.2, pp.579–594

Ridyard D., "The Genzyme Case and the OFT's Margin Squeeze Muddle" (2004) *European Competition Law Review* Vol.25, Issue 1

Roberts, J., "Battles for Market Share: Incomplete Information, Aggressive

Strategic Pricing and Competitive Dynamics" in T. Bewley (ed) *Advances in Economic Theory: Invited Papers for the Fifth World Congress of the Econometric* (Cambridge, Cambridge University Press, 1987)

Roberts, K., "Cartel Behaviour and Adverse Selection" (1985) *Journal of Industrial Economics*, Vol.33, pp.401–413

Robinson, C.K., "Qualifying Unilateral Effects in Investigations and Cases" Address to George Mason Law Review Symposium, 1996

Rochet, J-C. and Tirole, J., "Competition Policy in Two-sided Markets, with a Special Emphasis on Payment Cards" in Buccirossi, P. (ed.), *The Handbook of Antitrust Economics* (MIT Press, 2008)

Röller L-H. and de la Mano M., "The Impact of the New Substantive Test in European Merger Control" (2006) *European Competition Journal* Vol.2(1)

Röller, L-H., Stennek, J. and Verboven, F., "Efficiency Gains from Mergers" in Ilzkovitz, F. and Meiklejohn, R. (eds), *European Merger Control: Do we need an efficiency defence?* (Edward Elgar, 2006)

Rosenbaum, D., "An Empirical Test of the Effects of Excess Capacity in Price Setting, Capacity-Constrained Supergames" (1989) *International Journal of Industrial Organisation* Vol.7, pp.231–241

Rotemberg and Saloner, "A supergame-theoretical model of price wars during booms" (1986) *American Economic Review* 5.18

Sabbatini, P., "How to simulate the coordinated effect of a merger" (2006) *Autorità Garante della Concorrenza e del Mercato, Temi e Problemi* 12

Salant, S., Switzer, S. and Reynolds, R., "Losses from Horizontal Merger: The Effects of an Exogenous Change in Industry Structure on Cournot-Nash Equilibrium" (1983) *Quarterly Journal of Economics* Vol.48, pp.185–199

Salop, S., "Practices that (Credibly) Facilitate Oligopoly Co-ordination" in J. Stiglitz and F. Mathewson (eds) *New Developments in the Analysis of Market Structure* (MIT Press, 1986)

Salop, S., Comments on R. Willig, "Merger Analysis, Industrial Organisation Theory and Merger Guidelines" (1995) *Brookings Papers: Microeconomics 1991* p.313

Salop, "The First Principles approach to antitrust, *Kodak*, and antitrust at the Millennium" (2000) *Antitrust Law Journal* Vol.68 (No 1), pp.187–202 3.70

Salop, S.C. and Riordan, M., "Evaluating Vertical Mergers: A Post-Chicago Approach" (1995) *Antitrust Law Journal* Vol.63, pp.513–568

Salop, S.C. and Scheffman, D.T., "Raising Rivals' Costs" (1983) *American Economic Review* Vol.73, pp.267–271

Sass, T.R. and Saurman, D.S., "Advertising Restrictions and Concentration: The Case of Malt Beverages" (1995) *Review of Economics and Statistics* pp.66–81

Scheffman, D.T., "The Application of Raising Rivals' Costs Theory to Antitrust" (1992) *Antitrust Bulletin* Spring, pp.187–206

Scheffman D. and Simons J., "The State of Critical Loss Analysis: Let's Make Sure We Understand the Whole Story" (2003) *Antitrust Source*

Scherer, F., Comment on R. Willig, "Merger Analysis, Industrial Organisation Theory and Merger Guidelines" (1991) *Brookings Papers: Microeconomics 1991*, p.314

Scherer, F., "Schumpeter and Plausible Capitalism" (1992) *Journal of Economic Literature* Vol.30, p.1416

Scherer, F.M. and Ross, D., *Industrial Market Structure and Economic Performance* (Boston, Houghton Mifflin Company, 1995)

Schina, D., *State Aids* (ESC, 1987)

Schmalensee, R., "Continuum and Finite-Player Noncooperative Models of Competition," (1981) Continuum and Finite-Player Noncooperative Models of Competition Vol.71(1), pp.242–47

Schmalensee, R., "Entry Deterrence in the Ready-to-Eat Breakfast Cereal Industry" (1978) *Bell Journal of Economics*, Vol.9, pp.305–327

Schmalensee, R., "On the Use of Economic Models in Antitrust: The ReaLemon Case" (1979) *University of Pennsylvania Law Review* Vol.127, pp.994–1050

Schmalensee, R., "Horizontal Merger Policy: Problems and Changes" (1978) *Economic Perspectives* Vol.1, pp.41–54

Schmalensee, R. and Willig, R. (eds), *Handbook of Industrial Organisation: Volume 1* (New York and Amsterdam, North Holland, 1989)

Schumpeter, J., *Capitalism, socialism and democracy* (1950)

Seidmann, D.J., "Bundling as a Facilitating Device: A Reinterpretation of Leverage theory" (1991) *Economica* Vol.58, pp.491–499

Selten, R., "A Simple Model of Imperfect Competition Where Four Are Few and Six Are Many" (1973) *International Journal of Game Theory* Vol.2, pp.141–201

Selten, R., "The chain store paradox" (1978) *Theory and Decision* 9, pp.127–159

Selten, R., "Are Cartel Laws Bad for Business" in H. Hauptmann, W. Krelle, and K.C. Mosler (eds), *Operations Research and Economic Theory* (Berlin, Springer-Verlag, 1984)

Shaffer, S., "Stable Cartels with a Cournot Fringe" (1995) *Southern Economic Journal* Vol.61, pp.74–75

Shapiro, C., Comment on R. Willig, "Merger Analysis, Industrial Organisation Theory and Merger Guidelines" (1991) *Brookings Papers: Microeconomics 1991*, p.316

Shapiro, C., "Aftermarkets and Consumer Welfare: Making Sense of Kodak" (1995) *Antitrust Law Journal* Vol.63, Issue 2, pp.483–512

Shapiro, C., "Mergers With Differentiated Products" (1996) *Antitrust* Vol.10(2), pp.23–30

Shapiro, C. and Varian, H., *Information Rules* (Harvard Business School Press, 1999)

Shrieves, R., "Geographic Market Areas and Market Structure in the Bituminous Coal Industry" (1987) *Antitrust Bulletin* Vol.23, p.589

Slade, M.E., "Exogeneity Tests of Market Boundaries Applied to Petroleum Products" (1986) *Journal of Industrial Economics* Vol.34, pp.291–303

Slade, M., "Conjectures, firm characteristics, and market structure: an analysis of Vancouver's gasoline price wars" (Mimeo, 1987)

Slade, M., "Market Power and Joint Dominance in UK Brewing" (2004) *Journal of Industrial Economics* Vol.52, pp.133–163

Sleuwagen, L., "The Relevant Antitrust Market" (1992) unpublished paper

Slovin, M., Sushka, M. and Hudson, C., "Deregulation, Contestability, and Airline Acquisitions" (1991) *Journal of Financial Economics* Vol.30, pp.231–251

Soames, T., "An Analysis of the Principles of Concerted Practice and Collective Dominance: A Distinction Without a Difference?" (1996) *European Competition Law Review* Vol.17, pp.24–39

Spence, A.M., "Entry Capacity, Investment and Oligopolistic Pricing" (1977) *Bell Journal of Economics* Vol.8, pp.534–544

Sleuwaegen, L., "On the nature and significance of collusive price leadership" (1986) *International Journal of Industrial Organization*, 4: 177–188

Stackelberg, H. von, *Marktform und Gleichgewicht Vienna: Julius Springer* (1934); reprinted in *The Theory of the Market Economy* (London: William Hodge, 1952), translated by A.T. Peacock

Stennek, J. and Verboven, F., "*Merger control and enterprise competititveness—empirical analysis and policy recommendations* (Research Institute of Industrial Economics, Stockholm, Working Paper, 2001)

Steiner, R., "How manufacturers deal with the price-cutting retailer: when are vertical restraints efficient?" (1997) *Antitrust Law Journal, 65*

Stigler, G., *The Organisation of Industry* (Homewood, Richard D. Irwin Inc, 1968)

Stigler, G., "The Theory of Oligopoly" (1964) *Journal of Political Economy*, Vol.72, pp.44–61

Stigler, G.J. and Sherwin, R.A., "The Extent of the Market" (1985) *Journal of Law and Economics* Vol.28, pp.555–585

Stillman, R., "Examining antitrust policy towards horizontal mergers" (1983) *Journal of Financial Economics* 11, pp.225–40

Stucke, M., "Behavioural Economists at the Gate: Antitrust in the twenty-first century" (2009) available at *http://www.ssrn.com/abstract=981530* [Accessed September 19, 2009]

Suslow, V.Y., *Stability in International Cartels: An Empirical Survey*, Hoover Institution Domestic Studies Program, Working Paper, No E–88-7, 1988

# Bibliography

Sutton, J., *Sunk cost and Market Structure: Price Competition, Advertising and the Evolution of Concentration* (London, MIT Press, 1991)

Telser, L., "Cutthroat Competition and the Long Purse" (1966) *Journal of Law and Economics* Vol.9, pp.259–277

Temple Lang, J., "Defining Legitimate Competition: Companies' Duties to Supply Competitors and Access to Essential Facilities" (1994) *Fordham International Law Journal* Vol.18, pp.437–524

Tirole, J., *The Theory of Industrial Organisation* (Cambridge, Mass, MIT Press, 1988)

Tirole J., "Incomplete Contracts: Where Do We Stand?" (1999) *Econometrica* Vol.67, Issue 4 (pp.741–781)

Tivig, T., "Exchange Rate Pass-through in Two-period Duopoly" (1996) *International Journal of Industrial Organization*, Vol.14, pp.631–645

Tye, W.B., "Competitive Access: A Comparative Industry Approach to the Essential Facility Doctrine" (1987) *Energy Law Journal* Vol.8, No 2, pp.337–379

US Department of Transportation, Proposed Statement of Enforcement Policy on Unfair Exclusionary Conduct by Airlines, 1998

Uri, N.D., Jowell, J. and Rifkin, E.J., "On Defining Geographic Markets" (1985) *Applied Economics* Vol.17, pp.959–977

Uri, N.D. and Rifkin, E.J., "Geographic Markets, Causality and Railroad Deregulation" (1985) *Review of Economics and Statistics* Vol.67, pp.422–428

Van Bael, I. and Bellis, J.-F., *Anti-dumping and Other Trade Protection Laws of the EEC* 2nd edn (London, CCH Editions Ltd, 1990)

Van Dijk, T. and Verboven, F., "Quantification of damages" in Wayne Dale Collins (ed) *Issues in Competition Law and Policy ABA Section of Antitrust* (2008) Vol.III

Varain, H., Microeconomic analysis (New York, WW Norton, 1984)

Varian H., "Price Discrimination and Social Welfare" (1985) *American Economic Review*, Vol. 75, No.4, pp. 870–875

Vellturo, C., "Evaluating Mergers with Differentiated Products" (1987) *Antitrust* Vol.11, pp.16–20

Vickers, J., *Competition Economics and Policy: a speech on the occasion of the launch of the new social sciences building at Oxford University* (2002)

Vickers, J., *Concepts of Competition* (Oxford, Clarendon Press, 1994)

Vickers J., "Abuse of Market Power" (2005) 115 *The Economic Journal* 244

Vickers, J. and Yarrow, G., *Privatisation: An Economic Analysis* (Cambridge, MIT Press, 1988)

Vickrey, W., "Counterspeculation, auctions and competitive sealed tenders" (1961) *Journal of Finance* Vol.16, p.8–37

Viscusi, W.K., Vernon, J.M. and Harrington, J.E., *Economics of Regulation and Antitrust* (Cambridge, MIT Press, 1995)

Vogel, L., "Pratiques anticoncurrentielles: le Conseil de la Concurrence toujours contre le seuil de sensibilité" (1995) *Contrats Concurrence Consommation, Editions du Juris-classeur* p.9

Vogel, L., "Délégation de pouvoirs et assiette de la sanction" (1997a) *Contrats Concurrence Consommation, Editions du Juris-classeur* p.7

Vogel, L., "La charge de la preuve de l'indépendance économique pèse sur l'entreprise qui argue de son autonomie" (1997b) *Contrats Concurrence Consommation, Editions du Juris-classeur,* p.37

Vogel, L., "La notoriété de l'entreprise auteur du comportement anticoncurrentiel, facteur d'évaluation du montant de l'amende" (1997c) *Contrats Concurrence Consommation, Editions de Juris-classeur* p.143

Vogel, L., "Le seuil de sensibilité de nouveau sur la sellette" (1997d) *Contrats Concurrence Consommation, Editions du Juris-classeur* p.212

Voillemot, D., "Les procédures de sanction: motivation et proportionnalité de la sanction" (1995) *Revue de la Concurrence et de la Consommation* No 86

Von Neumann, J. and Morgenstern, O., *The Theory of Games and Economic Behaviour* (New York, Wiley, 1944)

Walker, M., "The potential for significant inaccuracies in merger simulation models" (2005) *Journal of Competition Law and Economics* Vol.1, 473–496

Wallis, W.A. and Roberts, H.V., *Statistics: A New Approach* (New York, Macmillan, 1956)

Warren–Boulton, F.R. and Dalkir, S., "Staples and Office Depot: an event–probability case study" (2001) *Review of Industrial Organization* 19, pp.469–81

Weiss, L., *Concentration and Price* (Cambridge, Mass, MIT Press, 1989)

Werden, G.J., "The Use and Misuse of Shipments Data in Defining Geographic Markets" (1981) *Antitrust Bulletin* pp.719–737

Werden, G.J., "The Law and Economics of the Essential Facility Doctrine" (1987) *Saint Louis University Law Journal* Vol.32, pp.433–480

Werden, G.J., *Simulating the Effects of Differentiated Products Mergers*, Economics Analysis Group Discussion Paper, US Department of Justice, 1996

Werden, G.J., "Simulating Unilateral Competitive Effects from Differentiated Products Mergers" (1997) *Antitrust* Vol. 11, pp.27–31

Werden, G.J., "Demand Elasticities in Antitrust Analysis" (1998) *Antitrust Law Journal* Vol.66, pp.363–414

Werden, G.J. and Froeb, L.M., "Correlation, Causality and All That Jazz: The Inherent Shortcomings of Price Tests for Antitrust Market Delineation" (1993) *Review of Industrial Organization* Vol.8, pp.329–353

Werden, G.J. and Froeb, L.M., "The Effects of Mergers in Differentiated Products Industries: Logit Demand and Merger Policy" (1994a) *Journal of Law, Economics and Organization* p.10

Werden, G. and Froeb, L.M., *The Effects of Mergers in Differentiated Products Industries: Logit Demand and Structural Merger Policy* Economic Analysis Group Discussion Paper, 93–94, 1994b

Werden, G.J. and Froeb, L.M., "Simulation as an Alternative to Structural

Merger Policy in Differentiated Products Industries" in M.B. Coate and A.N. Kleit (eds) *The Economics of the Antitrust Process* (Boston, Kluwer, 1996)

Werden, G.J., Froeb, L.M. and Tardiff, T.J., "The Use of the Logit Model in Applied Industrial Organization" (1994) *International Journal of the Economics of Business* Vol.VII, p.33

Werden G., "The 'No Economic Sense' Test for Exclusionary Conduct" (2006) 31 *Journal of Corporation Law* 293

Werden, G. and Froeb, L., "Unilateral competitive effects of horizontal mergers" in Buccirossi, P. (ed) *Handbook of Antitrust Economics* (MIT Press, 2008)

Werden, G., Froeb, L. and Scheffman, D., "A *Daubert* discipline for merger simulation" (2004) *FTC Presentation* at *http://www.ftc.gov/be/daubertdiscipline.pdf* [Accessed August 29, 2009]

Whalen, G.J., "Time Series Methods in Geographic Market Definition in Banking" presented at the Atlantic Economic Association Meetings, 1990

Whinston, M.D., *Tying, Foreclosure and Exclusion*. Discussion Paper 1343, Harvard Institute of Economic Research, 1987

Whinston, M.D., "Tying, Foreclosure and Exclusion" (1990) *American Economic Review* Vol.80, pp.837–859

Whinston, M.D. and Collins, S., "Entry and Competitive Structure in Deregulated Airline Markets: An Event Study Analysis of People Express" (1992) *Rand Journal of Economics* Vol.23, pp.445–462

Whish, R. *Competition Law* 6th edn (London, Butterworths, 2009)

White, H., "A Heteroskedasticity-Consistent Covariance Matrix Estimator and a Direct Test for Heteroskedasticity", (1980) *Econometrica* Vol.48, No 4, pp.817–838

Williamson, O., *Markets and Hierarchies: Analysis and Antitrust Implications* (New York, The Free Press, 1975)

Williamson, "Transactions Cost Economics: The Governance of Contractual Relations", (1979) *Journal of Law and Economics* Vol.22, pp.233–261

Willig, R., "Merger Analysis, Industrial Organisation Theory and Merger Guidelines", (1991) *Brookings Papers: Microeconomics 1991*, pp.281–332

Yamey, B., "Predatory Price Cutting: Notes and Comments" (1972) *Journal of law and Economics* Vol.15, pp.129–142

Yule, G.U., "Why Do We Sometimes Get Nonsense Correlations between Time Series? A Study in Sampling and the Nature of Time Series" (1926) *Journal of the Royal Statistical Society* Vol.89, pp.1–64

# Index

# Index

# Index